The Postmodern Bible Reader

B

To our friends and colleagues of the Bible and Culture Collectives

George Aichele, Fred Burnett, Elizabeth Castelli, Tamara
Eskenazi, Danna Fewell, Robert Fowler, Stephen Moore,
Gary Phillips, Regina Schwartz, and Wilhelm Wuellner

The Postmodern Bible Reader

edited by

David Jobling, Tina Pippin, *and*
Ronald Schleifer

Copyright © Blackwell Publishers Ltd 2001
Editorial matter and arrangement copyright © David Jobling, Tina Pippin, and Ronald
Schleifer 2001

First published 2001

2 4 6 8 10 9 7 5 3 1

Blackwell Publishers Ltd
108 Cowley Road
Oxford OX4 1JF
UK

Blackwell Publishers Inc.
350 Main Street
Malden, Massachusetts 02148
USA

British Library Cataloguing in Publication Data
A CIP catalogue record for this book is available from the British Library.

Library of Congress Cataloging-in-Publication Data

The postmodern Bible reader/edited by David Jobling, Tina Pippin, and Ronald Schleifer.
 p. cm.
 Includes bibliographical references and index.
 ISBN 0-631-21961-7 (hbk)—ISBN 0-631-21962-5 (pbk. : alk. paper)
 1. Bible—Hermeneutics. 2. Postmodernism—Religious aspects—Christianity. 3.
 Bible—Criticism, interpretation, etc. I. Jobling. David. II. Pippin, Tina, 1956– III.
 Schleifer, Ronald
BS476.P673 2001
220.6′01—dc21

00–065803

Typeset in 10pt on 12.5pt Bembo
by Kolam Information Services Pvt. Ltd, Pondicherry, India
Printed in Great Britain by MPG Books Ltd, Bodmin, Cornwall
This book is printed on acid-free paper.

Contents

Part III   The Conscience of the Bible

Preface

This book derives largely from our experience working as participants in the Bible and Culture Collective. There were two distinct incarnations of this Collective. David Jobling and Tina Pippin, along with George Aichele, Fred Burnett, Elizabeth Castelli, Robert Fowler, Stephen Moore, Gary Phillips, Regina Schwartz, and Wilhelm Wuellner, belonged to the original one, which produced *The Postmodern Bible* (1995), a remarkable experiment in collective authorship. All three of the editors of *The Postmodern Bible Reader* worked in and with the second incarnation of the Bible and Culture Collective, which also included George, Fred, Gary, Danna Fewell, and Tamara Eskenazi. Just as the first BCC worked for six years putting together a volume that presented – by means of introduction and critique – strategies for reading the Bible that developed in contexts of contemporary literary theory and cultural criticism, so the second configuration of the BCC worked for several years – in meetings in Chicago, Philadelphia, Nashville, and San Francisco – on the beginnings of the present volume. Many of the choices we have made for this book were the fruit of the thoughtful discussions concerning the ways that a text-anthology, offering a sampling of the range of "postmodern" readings and engagements with the Bible in the late twentieth century, could complete, supplement, and perhaps modify the vision of *The Postmodern Bible*, and also engage, as the earlier book attempted, serious students of the Bible.

The *Reader* and *The Postmodern Bible*

As this suggests, *The Postmodern Bible Reader* has a complicated relationship with *The Postmodern Bible*. That book was the result of a different kind of collaboration from either the collective beginning of the *Reader* or the final collaboration of the three of us that grew out of that collective beginning. *The Postmodern Bible* was a book, those who worked on it believed, that cried out to be written. And this for two reasons. First of all, it *needed* to consolidate and present to our intellectual community a way of grasping in a single thought (in a phrase from W. B. Yeats) the excitement and controversy that was allowing many of us to reread the Bible with new eyes. And it functioned, additionally, in bringing together ten people from vastly different backgrounds in the solidarity of authorship. In a significant fashion, the *Reader* is a commentary on and an addition to the fruitful collaboration that *The Postmodern Bible* sought. It is our hope that it will allow students, professional exegetes, and engaged readers some of the *kinds* of new understandings *The Postmodern Bible* described richly and powerfully. But it is also a tribute to the kind of collective engagement that seems the best aspect of our intellectual lives and which, we believe, *The Postmodern Bible* articulated with great clarity and passion.

The Postmodern Bible attempted a thorough account of contemporary, "postmodern," engagements with the Bible. It organized itself into seven areas of engagement – "Reader-Response Criticism," "Structuralist and Narratological Criticism," "Poststructuralist Criticism," "Rhetorical Criticism," "Psychoanalytic Criticism," "Feminist and Womanist Criticism," and "Ideological Criticism" – and traced the work of readers of the Bible in relation to these areas of concern. Needless to say, this was not the only possible way to organize the powerful contemporary engagements with the Bible in the late twentieth century, but it was one, the Collective thought, that could introduce a large audience to the variety, strengths, and sometimes weaknesses of ways of making the Bible part of our "postmodern" world.

In important ways, *The Postmodern Bible Reader* supplements and modifies the work of *The Postmodern Bible*. In this volume, we have tried to bring together a representative sample of the *kinds* of questions readers have been bringing to the Bible in the contemporary world. Some of the categories of *The Postmodern Bible* are significantly represented in our selections, while others are only implicit. And some of our selections add approaches to the Bible that themselves are barely represented in the earlier book. Specifically, among our selections, Barthes, Eco, and perhaps Kristeva offer "structuralist" approaches, and Bal presents, among other things, a "narratological" engagement; Miller, Eagleton, Derrida, perhaps Haraway offer "poststructuralist" engagements; Lacan, Cixous, Kristeva again offer "psychoanalytic" approaches; Kristeva, Cixous, Bal, Haraway, Pathak present "feminist and womanist" engagements; and Bal, Eagleton, Warrior, Cannon, among others, offer "ideological" engagements. It's clear from this short survey that some of the categories of reading from *The Postmodern Bible* are not squarely represented here: specifically, "Reader-Response Criticism" is not directly engaged, though an argument could be made that Barthes, among others, is pursuing a focus on the reader, and in the sectional introduction to "Rereading the Bible," we discuss at some length the ways that reorienting interpretation in relation to the reader rather than the writer is a characteristic found in much "postmodern" reading. Similarly, Miller's contribution – and perhaps that of Derrida as well – could be taken to be a "rhetorical" approach to the Bible, but the rhetoric Miller pursues is an implicit rather than explicit goal of his reading.

What most intrigued us – both the three of us and the larger BCC discussing the possibility of a Reader before it assumed the present form – were the possibilities of moving beyond the categories and horizon of *The Postmodern Bible*. This process of refocusing is a sign that *The Postmodern Bible* had in some ways done the work we had hoped of it: it had created an intellectual site for encountering new ways of reading the Bible. In fact, one explicit decision we made early on about this *Reader* was that it would not include studies of the Bible written by more or less "professional" biblical scholars. Rather, its aim was to present to these "professional" readers – and to lay readers as well – the breadth of engagements with the Bible by philosophers, activists, literary critics, and – going beyond *The Postmodern Bible* – more or less "creative" writers as well. So one motive for here expanding – or breaking – some of the categorical approaches of *The Postmodern Bible* was precisely to reread and rethink them in the light of its accomplishment of its goal of spreading the news. (We have tried to indicate in the headnotes to the particular selections their connection to *The Postmodern Bible*.)

A second motive was to respond, at least implicitly, to some of the criticisms *The Postmodern Bible* occasioned. One of the main criticisms was that we did not pay enough attention to the actual biblical texts in the ways our collective – and perhaps *any* collective – pursued exegesis. Some critics said that our concern with theories of reading – including vast bibliographies of methods of reading – overwhelmed the readings of biblical texts we included. In his review in *The New Republic* (June 26, 1995), Frank Kermode accused us of being "far more interested in Theory than in the Bible. This is understandable, since they evidently believe there is no salvation outside the poststructuralist church" and worried that we had almost trashed traditional historical criticism beyond all recognition. Anthony Lane was even more horrified by our dangerous readings in his review in *The New Yorker* (October 2, 1995) in which he reviewed *The Postmodern Bible* (PMB) along with *The New Testament and Psalms: An Inclusive Version*. The PMB was so radical, he noted, that it made the *Inclusive Version* "read like a third-century papyrus dug out of Middle Eastern mud" (99). For Lane, only the Authorized or King James Version (KJV) is the Word of God, and the PMB was tampering with (and even killing with deconstruction) the Living Word. Lane began his review by suggesting the PMB was an example of "the urge to modernize get[ting] out of hand and turn[ing] into wild-eyed impatience."

Both Kermode and Lane accuse the PMB Collective of a certain areligious and heretical missionary zeal and smugness; we certainly are seen not to take the biblical texts as seriously (or as sacredly) as they do. Others, from less traditional points of view, accused the Collective of falling into certain kinds of assumptions in the work of *The Postmodern Bible*: a certain eurocentric bias, a lack of situating understanding within larger contexts of practical ethics and engaged politics in the received categories of literary and philosophical criticism, kinds of overwhelming intellectualism or even cheerfulness about the category of "the postmodern" altogether. These criticisms, as well as those of more traditional readers of the Bible, helped us to see more clearly the limits as well as the successes of the PMB. That is, as the PMB itself mentions, its work was conceived above all as *timely*, as engaged in its own time and in the timeliness of debate and contest, and here in *The Postmodern Bible Reader* – rather than either setting up a cold (or hot) war of "us" (the hip postmodern theorists) versus "them" (the old-fogey traditional historical critics) or remaining silently defensive about what was included, excluded, and assumed in the work of the PMB – we have set out to engage the dynamic possibilities of biblical studies, theoretical terrain, and possibilities of risk and relationships.

For reasons stemming from both the successes and the limitations of the PMB, then, we decided not simply to follow its categories and structure in the *Reader*. Later, we will say a word about the organizing principle among the three parts of the *Reader*. But here we should say that, besides the kinds of double and triple duty that many of the selections fulfill in relation to the categories of *The Postmodern Bible*, there are several notable differences between the *Reader* and the earlier book. Most striking, we think, is our last part, "The Conscience of the Bible." In this part, as we will note later, we re-traverse many of the categories of reading from the vantage of a kind of emerging postmodern ethics of reading. Levinas, to give just one example, is barely mentioned in *The Postmodern Bible*, yet his work – as we along with many others have come to see – offers a lens for rethinking our relations to biblical texts. Elsewhere we offer, in the selection from Paul Hallam, what *The Postmodern Bible* described as "challenging and creative disciplinary *and* professional border crossing" (6), a kind of writing that confuses the creative and essayistic. This selection also goes beyond *The Postmodern Bible* in giving voice to what has come to be called "queer theory." Similarly, our epigraph from Thomas King, which we discuss in the Introduction, and the last selection combining a story by Mahasweta Devi and a discussion of its translation by Gayatri Spivak, are examples of the kinds of "creative" engagements with the sacred beyond the confines of the Bible as such. Similarly, the inclusion of Enrique Dussel's non-critical reading of the Bible from the vantage of a non-Western reader, as we mention in the Introduction to Part III, builds upon and expands the purview of the PMB. We chose these selections not as a way of tokenizing them; rather, we wanted to expand the conversation to include wider theoretical and cultural voices. The framing of the *Reader* with these texts is an attempt to situate our goals and those of *The Postmodern Bible* within a larger context than the earlier book suggested.

Postmodern Readings in Class

In addition, *The Postmodern Bible Reader* has benefitted from our teaching, collectively and individually. Near the end of our deliberations over the choices for the *Reader*, the three editors jointly offered a seminar in July 1998 at the Iliff School of Theology in Denver, "The Bible and Its Postmodern Readers," and David and Tina offered another version of this course at St. Andrew's College, Saskatoon, in June 2000. In both courses we discovered which texts best engage readers and stimulate the most powerful discussion. We are grateful to Iliff, St. Andrew's, and to the members of our seminars for these opportunities. In addition, each of us has brought a wide range of teaching experiences to the work on this book, and have had occasion to try out some of our selections in a great variety of settings. David Jobling, who teaches Hebrew Bible in a theological seminary, experiences a great deal of tension between the Bible as a resource for political struggles ("part of the solution") and the Bible as implicated in gender and race oppression ("part of the problem"). His students have trouble knowing what to make of, for example, our selection from Terry Eagleton, where someone perceived as being "on the correct side" politically becomes methodologically challenging. Tina Pippin, who focuses on New Testament studies, cultural studies, and ethics and social justice theory and practice, teaches Religion at an undergraduate liberal arts college for women. Tina has had the opportunity to use selections from *The Postmodern Bible* and the *Reader* in a senior independent study on the Bible and critical theories, and to experiment with how these texts work and what connections can be made on an undergraduate level. Ronald Schleifer, who teaches in the English Department at a large public university, has taught undergraduate and graduate courses in literary theory, cultural modernism, and cultural studies. Ron has had the opportunity of team-teaching an undergraduate honors colloquium with Professor Tom Boyd (who works in the philosophy of religion) that focused on "rhetoric and religion" in a class made up primarily of students who had not made any commitments to careers in which the Bible and religion were part of their daily professional work. In these different venues, each of the editors has had the opportunity of making *The Postmodern Bible* a central text in class.

Additionally, we were enriched by, and this book has benefitted from, discussions about contemporary biblical studies and literary criticism with faculty and students at Agnes Scott College, Andover Newton Theological School, Candler School of Theology, Eastern Michigan University, Georgia Institute of Technology, McMaster University, the University of Oklahoma, St. Andrew's College, Saskatoon, Southern Illinois University at Edwardsville, the University of Queensland, the University of Stellenbosch, United Theological College Sydney, the University of Washington, Wichita State University, as well as several other institutions.

Reading Postmodern Criticism

Many students and teachers of newer kinds of readings of the Bible encounter the difficulties of unfamiliar languages, modes of argument, and assumptions about the Bible, the world, and intellectual life more generally. In some ways, the "difficulties" of postmodern criticism – its sometimes esoteric vocabularies, its high allusiveness, the intricacies of its argument – are all too readily apparent: the problem of questioning the self-evident, of trying to imagine, in encounters with the Bible and other forms of cultural discourse, the world as being different from the familiar one. To really work, postmodern criticism must be understood to be a passionate enterprise, one that, especially when it is focused on the Bible, attempts to recover the sacred as part of both our work in the world and our understanding of it. Still, many of the readings in *The Postmodern Bible Reader* can be daunting and bewildering, presenting, as they sometimes do, interpretations and presentations that are not easily assimilated into the kinds of questions and responses students and other interested readers have traditionally brought to the Bible. It may be helpful to say a few words about the difficulties of reading many will encounter in these pages.

A number of years ago, the literary and cultural critic George Steiner wrote an influential essay entitled "On Difficulty," examining the often bewildering experience of reading modern literature. His analysis, we believe, might well help students who find some of the readings here bewildering: both because it should indicate that he or she is not alone and also because it can help readers develop new strategies of reading that many of these selections call for. (The Bible itself, of course, calls for new strategies of reading; this, surely, is what Kierkegaard believed in noting that sacred texts position readers to make fundamental decisions in their lives.) Steiner's essay distinguishes among four distinct kinds of difficulty in texts. The first – and simplest – he calls "contingent" difficulty, which arises out of ignorance of frames of reference and understanding. If students do not know what a "constative" meaning is, or if they do not know who Claude Lévi-Strauss is and what he does, they can look these things up in a dictionary or encyclopedia – or find an explanation in the introductions to the parts of this book. Steiner's second difficulty, "modal," is also remediable. A modal difficulty is a difficulty in the *mode* of presentation: those unfamiliar with the modes of arguments of structuralist exegesis or the combinations of meanings and affect in dream narrative might find it difficult to comprehend some essays in relation to their "ordinary" modes of demonstration and interpretation. Imagine, for instance, how disorienting MTV might seem to our grandparents who learned to read video narrative in the movies of the 1930s. Much postmodern interpretation is polemical rather than logical, and the modality of polemics might confuse readers who are used to impersonal exegesis.

The last two kinds of difficulty are not "solvable" in such ways, through learning and practice. Steiner describes the third kind as "tactical" difficulty, caused when writers purposely present difficulties in their writing in order to dislocate the reader and inhibit any usual or conventional response to the text. When Jacques Lacan, for instance, refuses the kinds of logical transitions between points of argument – refuses, it seems, to pursue a clear argumentative line – he may be strategically calling upon the reader's self-reflection in the way that the psychoanalyst's enigmatic comments or enigmatic silences call upon the patient *not* to understand too quickly through habitual modes of thought. Finally, Steiner's fourth category of difficulty – one, we suspect, that jibes most fully with the Bible as text – he calls "ontological" difficulty. This difficulty, he writes, breaks "the contact of ultimate or preponderant intelligibility between poet and reader, between text and meaning. . . . Difficulties of this category cannot be looked up [because] they confront us with blank questions about the nature of human speech [and] about the status of significance." When Kristeva musters the metaphors of fire and burning in odd moments of her reasoned essay, when Derrida makes sacrifice the theme of reading and engagement, when Scarry asks us to discern God's voice in pregnancy, these texts are positing a new ontology, a new paradigm of understanding which "anagogically" (in a contingently difficult term Barthes uses) demands that everything we understood be understand differently. Many of the difficulties *The Postmodern Bible Reader* presents, we are saying, are not simply difficulties of ignorance or unclarity, to be cured or dismissed, but are active difficulties that call for the kinds of engagements we describe in the Introduction.

The Structure of the *Reader*

Still, this book is intended to help readers to explore and interrogate contemporary readings of the Bible. To that end, it provides the immediate background for postmodern criticism with introductions that attempt to trace the definitions and history of this work, and essays that all, more and less explicitly, engage biblical texts. We organized the General Introduction, "A Short Course in Postmodernism for Bible Readers," by reference to seven particular texts – several of them well known and all readily available – in order to present the horizon of our postmodern ethos. These are texts which do not specifically engage the Bible, but they have immediate implications for practices of Bible reading. It is our hope that instructors might add some or all of these texts to supplement the readings presented here. We ourselves used them in our seminars at Iliff and St. Andrew's as an introduction to the biblical readings.

After that, the readings are divided into three parts: "Rereading the Bible" examines the reorientation from author to reader in contemporary interpretation; "The Politics of Reading" examines the ways interpretation has conceived itself as an activist enterprise, again with a focus on the "destiny" rather than the "origin" of meaning; and "The Conscience of the Bible" examines the ways that the Bible and its interpretations project a kind of "worldly" ethics, a reorientation from the knowledge and power of other approaches to the Bible. These three parts of the book offer a rough homology to the difficulties we have described, difficulties of knowledge (contingent, modal), difficulties of power (tactical), and difficulties of global significance (ontological or anagogic). Moreover, at each division we have added a "postmodern" image. At Part I we append Andy Warhol's *Details of Renaissance Paintings (Leonardo da Vinci, The Annunciation, 1472)* (1984), along with da Vinci's original (1472). In its appropriation of da Vinci's detail – its taking up an image as a signifier rather than a specific "content" – Warhol's screenprint "rereads" da Vinci's religiosity. At Part II we attach Barbara Kruger's *Untitled (You invest in the divinity of the masterpiece)* (1982), in which Michelango's image of creation is overlaid with the politics and economics of "high art." And at Part III we hang Cindy Sherman's *Untitled (History Painting #205)* (1989), which offers, ambiguously, Sherman herself in a Madonna-like pose which suggests the confluence of what Derrida calls in his selection in Part III "the universal concept of responsibility," demanding "an accounting... with respect to the general," and, "on the other hand, uniqueness, absolute singularity, hence nonsubstitution, nonrepetition, silence, and secrecy." Yet even though these images are appended to the Parts of the *Reader*, they are discussed in "The Short Course in Postmodernism" as if to suggest that attachment to the Parts of the book is not altogether absolute, as if these images – like so many postmodern images – circulate and float freely throughout and among our texts. Warhol's reading is political and ethical; Kruger's "commentary" is a form of rereading; Sherman's image is a political as well as aesthetic act. We choose for our cover Warhol's image – without its Renaissance "referent" – to suggest such free-floatingness.

As this suggests, the threefold division of the *Reader* is in many ways much too neat. The essays here, like the images we present, cross boundaries of focus, style, and purpose, so that this strict catalogue – like Kant's strict demarcations of pure reason, practical reason, and judgement (see the "Short Course on Postmodernism") – immediately confuses itself. We highlight this interpenetration by beginning each of the three parts with clear articulations of the kinds of essays to follow, but ending each part with essays that seem to blend into the other parts. Barthes' analysis of Acts is a classical structuralist reading that presents, more or less explicitly, the assumptions of the "new" readings of the second half of the twentieth century; Bal's feminist reading of Judges offers a political as well as a readerly account. Similarly, Eagleton's reading of Jonah offers a political understanding of the opposition between constative and performative understandings of speech-act theory, while Hallam's personal narrative of reading Sodom suggests an anagogic re-comprehension of biblical themes. Finally, Serres's readerly account of the Joker in relation to the story of Joseph raises the larger issue of the ethics of sacrifice – the ethics of the sacred – while the Mahasweta Devi/Spivak selection explodes, so to speak, the Bible as the touchstone of the readings and the singular reader as the subject of experience. The transgressions of the categories we offer can also be discerned, we hope, in the manner in which many of the essays of this book are closely interrelated as "contests," as Edward Said says, over "forms and values," and the framing sections attempt to make that interrelationship clear.

There are two other ways we have attempted to emphasize this. The introduction to each part provides a list of "related" readings at its end. These readings, we hope, will allow instructors and readers to organize alternative "contents" that emphasize different themes from those we have presented. But we have attempted to emphasize the interrelations among these essays in the introductions to the three parts themselves. Each introduction offers an overview of the history and concerns governing the essays contained in it, but also aims, as far as possible, to relate that part to the others. The General Introduction and the introductions to the three parts of the *Reader* could be read independently as a continuous narrative description of postmodern readings of the Bible in our time.

Acknowledgments

A large number of people have assisted us in work on *The Postmodern Bible Reader*. Most important are the members of the two incarnations of the Bible and Culture Collective whom we mentioned at the beginning of this preface and to whom we are dedicating our work on the reader. We are also grateful to Andrew McNeillie and Joanna Pyke of Blackwell Publishers, who encouraged this work and offered timely advice; and to Margaret Aherne. Pam Eisenbaum and Dan Clanton were especially helpful and supportive during the Iliff course. Our spouses, Esther Cherland, Jerry Gentry, and Nancy Mergler, were equally helpful and powerfully patient during our work on this book. In addition, several colleagues and graduate students wrote some of the biographical headnotes for the critics in this book, as follows: *Thomas King* – Mary Mackie; *Roland Barthes* and *Umberto Eco* – George Aichele; *Robert Warrior* – Steven Salaita; *Donna Haraway* – Brian Johnson; *Zakia Pathak* and *Gayatri Spivak* – Jennifer McClinton; *Paul Hallam* – Michael Carden; *Elaine Scarry* – Jennifer Boots. Mitchell Lewis compiled the index with great care. Finally we would like to particularly acknowledge Fred Burnett, whose original draft of a discussion of Hayden White we use in edited form in the General Introduction. To all these people – and the scores of others, at home and abroad, with whom we discussed particular essays, particular ways of apprehending the postmodern, and particularities of teaching – we give our thanks.

The editors and publishers are grateful to the following for permission to reproduce copyright material.

Bal, Mieke, "Body Politic" from *On Meaning-Making: Essays in Semiotics* (Polebridge Press, Sonoma, 1994);

Barthes, Roland, "The Structural Analysis of Narrative" from *The Semiotic Challenge* (trans. Richard Howard) (Hill and Wang, New York, 1988, a division of Farrar, Straus and Giroux, LLC, reprinted by permission of the author's estate);

Cannon, Katie Geneva, "Slave Ideology and Biblical Interpretation" from *Katie's Canon: Womanism and the Soul of the Black Community*. Copyright © 1995 by Katie Geneva Cannon. Reprinted by permission of The Continuum International Publishing Group Inc.;

Cardenal, Ernesto, "The Song of Mary" from *The Gospel in Solentiname* (trans. Donald D. Walsh) (Orbis Books, Maryknoll, New York, 1990);

Cixous, Hélène, "Dreaming in 1990" from *Three Steps on the Ladder of Writing* (trans. Sarah Cornell and Susan Sellers) (The Wellek Library Lectures at the University of California, Irvine, published by Columbia University Press, 1993);

Derrida, Jacques, "Whom to Give to [Knowing Not to Know]" from *The Gift of Death* (trans. David Wills) (The University of Chicago Press, 1995);

Dussel, Enrique, selections from *Ethics and Community* (trans. Robert R. Barr) (Orbis Books, Maryknoll, New York and Burns and Oates, The Continuum International Publishing Group Ltd, 1988);

Eagleton, Terry, "J. L. Austin and the Book of Jonah" from *The Book and the Text: The Bible and Literary Theory* (ed. Regina M. Schwartz) (Blackwell Publishers, Oxford, 1990);

Eco, Umberto, "On the Possibility of Generating Aesthetic Messages in an Edenic Language" from *The Role of the Reader* (Indiana University Press, Bloomington, 1984);

Hallam, Paul, *The Book of Sodom* (Verso, London, 1993);

Haraway, Donna, "Ecco Homo, Ain't (Ar'n't) I a Woman, and Inappropriate/d Others: The Human in a Post-Humanist Landscape." Copyright 1992 from *Feminists Theorize the Political* (ed. Judith Butler and Joan W. Scott) (Routledge, New York and London. Reproduced by permission of Taylor & Francis, Inc. http://www.routledge-ny.com);

King, Thomas, *Green Grass, Running Water* (Bantam Books, published by arrangement with Houghton Mifflin, 1994, copyright 1993 Thomas King);

Kristeva, Julia, "Reading the Bible" from *New Maladies of the Soul* (trans. Ross Guberman). © 1995 Columbia University Press. Reprinted by permission of the publisher;

Lacan, Jacques, "Introduction to the Names-of-the-Father Seminar" from *Television: A Challenge to the Psychoanalytic Establishment* by Jacques Lacan, translated by Denis Hollier, Rosalind Krauss et al. Copyright © 1990 by W. W. Norton & Company Inc. Used by permission of W. W. Norton & Company, Inc.;

Levinas, Emmanuel, "On the Jewish Reading of Scriptures" from *Beyond the Verse: Talmudic Readings and Lectures* (trans. Gary D. Mole) (Indiana University Press, Bloomington, 1994, and The Athlone Press);

Miller, J. Hillis, "Parable and Performative in the Gospels and in Modern Literature" from *Tropes, Parables, Performatives: Essays on Twentieth-Century Literature*. Copyright 1991, Duke University Press. All rights reserved. Reprinted with permission;

Pathak, Zakia, "A Pedagogy for Postcolonial Feminists". Copyright 1992 from *Feminists Theorize the Political* (ed. Judith Butler and Joan W. Scott) (Routledge, New York and London. Reproduced by permission of Taylor & Francis, Inc. http://www.routledge-ny.com);

Scarry, Elaine, "The Interior Structure of Made Objects" from *The Body in Pain: The Making and Unmaking of the World* by Elaine Scarry, copyright © 1985 by Oxford University Press, Inc. Used by permission of Oxford University Press, Inc.;

Serres, Michel, "Meals Among Brothers: Theory of the Joker" from *The Parasite* (trans. Lawrence R. Schehr), pp. 155–64. © 1982 The Johns Hopkins University Press. Reprinted with permission of The Johns Hopkins University Press;

Spivak, Gayatri Chakravorty, "'Draupadi' by Mahasweta Devi," translated with a foreword by Gayatri Chakravorty Spivak, from Gayatri Chakravorty Spivak, *In Other Worlds: Essays in Cultural Politics* (Methuen, London, 1987. Reproduced by permission of Taylor & Francis, Inc., http://www.routledge.ny.com);

Warrior, Robert Allen, "Canaanites, Cowboys, and Indians: Deliverance Conquest, and Liberation Theology Today" from *Christianity and Crisis* 49, no. 12, 1989. Reprinted by permission of American Journal of Christian Opinion.

Introduction: A Short Course in Postmodernism for Bible Readers

Reading the Postmodern

The Postmodern Bible Reader, as we mentioned in the Preface, grows out of the work and publication of *The Postmodern Bible*, a volume published in 1995 examining the impact of contemporary literary, philosophical, political, and cultural studies on our understanding of the Bible and the traditions of its interpretation. In *The Postmodern Bible* (PMB), the Bible and Culture Collective attempted a short definition of *postmodernism*, in which, following the work of Jean-François Lyotard, it examined the ways that "the 'postmodern condition' can be identified in terms of three principal transformational trajectories within culture" (1995:9), namely the *aesthetic* or the realm of the arts; the *epistemological* or the realm of understanding and sense-making; and the *political* or the realm of ethics and interhuman activities. Although the PMB does not say so, these three trajectories follow and critique Immanuel Kant's great synthesizing work for the Enlightenment culture of the eighteenth century, his critiques of judgment (or aesthetic experience), his critique of pure reason (epistemology), and his critique of practical reason (or worldly ethics). Kant lived in the midst of the great accomplishments of the Enlightenment: perspectival art and complex narratives organized in relation to more or less omniscient narrators (that latter of which gives rise to, among other things, the Higher Criticism); the new science of mechanistic physics, that allowed for the mathematization of understanding in which discoverable truths about the world could be formulated once and for all, in *atemporal* laws; and the transformation of political subjects into citizens, in the context of which all European men were equal and endowed with inalienable rights (including liberty, equality, and fraternity). For Kant – and for Enlightenment "modernity" more generally – the possibility of synthesizing these accomplishments (or at least holding them together in a single thought, as W. B. Yeats says) was created by two, seemingly incompatible factors: the strict separation of these realms of personal experience, impersonal knowledge, and social history; and the "harmony" of the separate human "faculties" that governed the apprehension and understanding of these realms and the "harmony" of these realms themselves. (See Bruno Latour's *We Have Never Been Modern* for a powerful discussion of the efficacy of the simultaneous separation and communication between these areas of concern in the establishment of Enlightenment modernity.) Walter Benjamin articulates powerfully a faith in such harmony – a faith that is both modernist and postmodern – when he defines translation, including explicitly the translation of the Bible from one language to another and one cultural moment to another, "not as reproduction but as harmony" (1969:79).

If modernity is predicated on the powerful aesthetic moments of experience, atemporal truth, and a politics of selective "equality," then *postmodernity* comes after, but also along with these things. In his essay "Note on the Meaning of 'Post-,'" Lyotard tries to describe how the "post" of postmodernism – or "post-Enlightenment," or "post-structural," or the many other "posts" you will encounter in this collection – marks the confusion of these realms of experience, knowledge, and politics by gathering together opposites. Such oppositions, such as that between "modernity" and its putative successor "post-modernity," do not exclude one another as the very *simplicities* of Enlightenment apprehensions do: the self-evident intuitions of "modern" experience which exclude foreign experience as "superstition" or, less negatively, as "tradition"; the logical hierarchies of "modern" knowledge which apprehend everything in terms of itself and its logical "mathematization" of experience; and the inequitable equalities of "modern" politics which make both particular people and particular conditions invisible. Thus, Lyotard writes of the lack of clear and distinct notions of experience, knowledge, and politics, and the lack of logic in their relationships as postmodern.

> We are like Gullivers in the world of technoscience: sometimes too big, sometimes too small, but never the right size. From this perspective, the insistence on simplicity generally seems today like a pledge to barbarism.
>
> On this point, the following issue also has to be elaborated. Humanity is divided into two parts. One faces the challenge of complexity, the other that ancient and terrible challenge of its own survival. This is perhaps the most important aspect of the failure of the modern project – a project that, need I remind you, once applied in principle to the whole of humanity. (1992:66)

Lyotard goes on to argue that the "'post' of 'postmodern' does not signify a movement of *comeback, flashback,* or *feedback* – that is, not a movement of repetition but a procedure in 'ana-'; a procedure of analysis, anamnesis, anagogy, and anamorphosis" (1992:68). For Lyotard, as for the "postmodern" more generally we are suggesting, the *differences* among experience, knowledge, and politics that allowed for the great and good achievements of the Enlightenment modernity and also for its failures and disasters – for what Latour calls its "double task of domination and emancipation" (1993:10) – are re-traversed, reread, confused: a personal politics, a flat aesthetics, temporal knowledges play with the charged experiences, atemporal truth, and the representative government and art of Enlightenment modernism.

One of Lyotard's terms, *anagogy,* is of special importance for readers of the Bible. We already mentioned it in the Preface as a word that presents "contingent" difficulties, something we might look up. Looking it up, we find it described as an "interpretation of a word, passage, or text (as of Scripture or poetry) that finds beyond the literal, allegorical, and moral sense a fourth and ultimate spiritual or mystical sense." *Anagogy* designates a global meaning, not quite reducible to this or that particular part or "kernel" of truth, not something that can stand in place of something else, but a whole way of looking at phenomena, a "take" on experience charged with its "aura," its power, in which the subjects of experience are not so much in possession of their experience, as they are swept up in an experience or understanding that stakes a powerful claim upon them. (Such anagogy, we shall see, is for Benjamin the "task" of the translator.) In a powerfully *postmodern* text – the postmodernity of which we hope will become clear – Maurice Blanchot presents in *The Writing of the Disaster* a passage tentatively entitled "A Primal Scene?" that may well describe the experience of anagogic apprehension, the *mysterium tremendum* of the encounter with the sacred:

> What he sees; the garden, the wintry trees, the wall of a house. Though he sees, no doubt in a child's way, his play space, he grows weary and slowly looks up toward the ordinary sky, with clouds, grey light – pallid daylight without depth.
>
> What happens then: the sky, the *same* sky, suddenly open, absolutely black and absolutely empty, revealing (as though the pane had broken) such an absence that all has since always and forevermore been lost therein – so lost that therein is affirmed and dissolved the vertiginous knowledge that nothing is what there is, and first of all nothing beyond. (1986:72)

The "same" is transformed in the postmodern, yet remains the same: a flatness of affect, a confusion of senses, an anchorlessness in which the ballasts of existence – of the true, the good, and the beautiful – seem depthlessly superficial. This is part of the *affect* of the postmodern, which anagogically re-experiences received value – and, above all, the received and more or less *secular* value of Enlightenment modernity – as both new and old at once.

In teaching the course "The Bible and Its Postmodern Readers," one of the ways we illustrated various points about postmodernism was through art and architectural design. (The term *postmodern* was first coined in relation to architecture.) We showed a wide variety of examples and made use of postmodern architect Charles Jencks's categories of and thinking about postmodern art and design. In this general introduction we want to give one example to illustrate ways we utilized the visual (we also used film, music, and a puzzle of Michael Graves's Denver Public Library); later in this introduction we will show another example from photographic art. Thus, in order to examine how the postmodern plays with the notion of the "same," we have chosen the example of Barbara Kruger's 1982 photograph, *Untitled (You invest in the divinity of the masterpiece)*. Kruger reproduces Michelangelo's Sistine Chapel portrayal of the moment of creation between God and Adam, what is perhaps the most famous piece of religious art in the West. She hones in on the main action, the index fingers of God and Adam out-stretched, signifying the transfer of (male) power. (Is Kruger implying that the transfer of knowledge comes later, with the woman, Eve?) In her discussion of performative art, Linda Kauffman sees Kruger's "slashing" of the words, "You invest in the divinity of the masterpiece," as a protest "directed at those who can conceive of art only as an economic investment. She is also challenging the patriarchal lineage from God the

Father, 'giving birth' to man.... *you* are complicit in these systems of exchange. Your investments are both social and psychic" (1998:75). Kruger has written her own graffiti, her own commentary, over a priceless art "master" piece. She has inscribed the scene with her own ideological critique – of what makes art priceless, of the power of patriarchy and the power of art to promote unjust relationships. The Michelangelo scene is the "same," yet it has been transformed, made problematic, oppositional, and chaotic – informed by "the vertiginous knowledge" Blanchot speaks of. Our viewing of the masterpiece is disrupted by her text, and "divinity" takes on multivalent meanings. Kruger's reproduction is a photograph, a copy of the "original." The painting is new and old at once.

In such a moment the oppositions that sustained Enlightenment knowledges and values – oppositions between charged and uncharged moments in a homogenous temporality, atemporal truth and temporal accidents, and the personal and the social – seem non-operative but not fully or wholly erased. Thus both Blanchot's and Kruger's primal scenes present what we called earlier a flat aesthetics, temporal knowledges, and, locating vision in the ordinary, a personal politics. A characteristic of the postmodern, in erasing (or at least calling into question) these oppositions, is not to abandon too quickly the specific for the general, not to too quickly assume the particular and the local into transcendental, atemporal "truths." In pursuing such "postmodernity," we have organized this general introduction in relation to seven particular texts which, in our original proposal for *The Postmodern Bible Reader*, we had planned to include in an initial section entitled "Reading the Postmodern" (just as we have begun the Introduction with the particular texts of Blanchot and Kruger and end with a short discussion of the excerpt from Thomas King we use for the epigraph to the collection). The purpose of this deleted section was to help orient readers of this collection in relation to the notion of *postmodernism*. This section was the least "biblical" of all. While all the essays in the three subsequent sections, as we mentioned in the Preface, focus centrally on biblical texts, these essays did not. Instead, they focused, with greater and lesser breadth, on apprehending the "postmodern." Essays by Lyotard and Michel Foucault examined the aesthetics and discourse of postmodernism; essays by Walter Benjamin, Hayden White, and Fredric Jameson examined the epistemology and historiography of the postmodern; and essays by Judith Butler and Slavoj Žižek examined the subjectivity and anagogic politics of the postmodern.

Still, this description belies some of the power of gathering these essays together. This is because, in addition to their particular "work" in discourse, history, and subjectivity, each of these essays made *discourse* an important aspect of their discussions, perhaps we might say figuratively, *anagogically* important: Foucault examined the "order of discourse," Benjamin examined the role of translation in understanding, and Žižek examined the element of discourse within the psychoanalytic analysis of the subject. This focus on discourse, always implicit in the postmodern, is a challenge to the seemingly self-evident intuitions, the seemingly pre-existing truths, and the transcendental equalities of the Enlightenment. (This is a theme of Foucault's essay.) It is one way, among others, that make the global title both of this *Reader* and of the Bible and Culture Collective's project, *The Postmodern Bible*, a comprehensible term. Such a focus – in the "post-analytic" philosophy of Ludwig Wittgenstein and J. L. Austin, the "post-structural" literary criticism of Gérard Genette and Shoshana Felman, and the "post-foundationalist" politics of a movement like the "new legal studies" or the "post-foundationalist" ethics of Levinas, Scarry, and Dussel represented in the last section of the *Reader* – distinguishes between narrative and discourse in distinguishing between the tale and the telling, between the "constative" and testable truths of statements and the "performative" and affective issue of statements beyond their descriptive power. (Terry Eagleton most fully sets forth this analytic opposition in his essay in Part II. One might say that J. L. Austin's analysis of "performative" discourse in the 1950s – following his reading of the late Wittgenstein – is a version of "post-analytic," "post-scientific," and thus "post-Enlightenment" philosophy.)

It was our original hope, then, to introduce the postmodern by way of important and often-cited essays that examine and present postmodern apprehensions of aesthetic and discursive experience, of history and translation, and of the politics of feminism and ecology. Unfortunately, *because* these have been such important essays – but also because they did not make the Bible their central focus or concern – the editors at Blackwell Publishers suggested that we cut them out in order to make a shorter and more affordable book. After some soul-searching we agreed, but also decided that we would organize this general introduction around these "missing" essays and use them, as we had originally planned, in order to introduce *The Postmodern Bible Reader* – which as a whole becomes, like Blanchot's haunting passage, a kind of "post" text, following and responding to something that both is and is not there. In any case, the rest of this introduction will examine local and particular aspects of "postmodernism" in relation to particular texts.

Jean-François Lyotard, "Answering the Question: What is Postmodernism?"

This essay was first published in 1982 and subsequently translated in 1983 and reprinted as an appendix to the English translation of Lyotard's *The Postmodern Condition: A Report on Knowledge* in 1984. In "Answering the Question," Lyotard takes up a central concern of postmodernism, namely its relation to modernism. In this essay, he takes it up on the level of aesthetics even as in *The Postmodern Condition* he takes it up on the level of "knowledge" and what Michel Foucault describes in "The Order of Discourse" as the "will to knowledge." (In fact, Foucault's larger framework of "discourse" gathers up Lyotard's theme and Benjamin's understanding of translation's task of conveying the power rather than the meaning of texts – "translation," Benjamin says, "must in large measure refrain from wanting to communicate something, from rendering the sense" so that it can make "both the original and the translation recognizable as fragments of a great language" (1969:78) – to allow these essays to create a framework that relates most closely to Part I of the *Reader*, "Rereading the Bible.") Aesthetics, knowledge, and power – the three great Enlightenment faculties of judgment, reason, and ethics – are thus combined in postmodernism in ways that were impossible for Enlightenment modernity. In *The Postmodern Condition*, Lyotard describes this combination in terms of "language games" (this is Wittgenstein's term). Such games are "contractual" relationships among its players: late in this book he describes them as "temporary contracts" in that they are not in force universally, for all time. Although Lyotard does not say so, the founding assumption of Enlightenment modernity was the separation and hierarchy of these games: the "game" of denotative language – language that takes upon itself the accurate description of what lies "outside" language (this is what Austin means by "constative" language) – took precedence in the Enlightenment over the ethical/ political language of action in the world ("praxis") and the aesthetic language of the provocation of feeling. "Take for example," Lyotard writes in *The Postmodern Condition*,

> a closed door. Between "The door is closed" and "Open the door" there is no relation of consequence as defined in propositional logic. The two statements belong to two auto-nomous sets of rules defining different kinds of relevance, and therefore of competence. Here, the effect of dividing reason into cognitive or theoretical reason on the one hand, and practical reason on the other, is to attack the legitimacy of the discourse of science. Not directly, but indirectly, by revealing that it [the discourse of science] is a language game with its own rules (of which the a priori conditions of knowledge in Kant provide a first glimpse) and that it has no special calling to supervise the game of praxis (nor the game of aesthetics, for that matter). The game of science is thus put on a par with the others. (1984a:40)

In this passage, Lyotard is using the "postmodern" science of information theory – "the 'leading' sciences and technologies [that] have to do with language" (1984a:3) he describes in the very beginning of *The Postmodern Condition* – to read, retrospectively, the emerging science of Enlightenment modernism. In doing so, he locates the "in-direct" attack on modernist science within Enlightenment modernism itself: the fact that the "language game" of science – based upon semiotic rules – was put on a par with ethics and aesthetics even in the Kantian system in which "pure reason" was first among equals.

   This location of a postmodern ethos *within* modernity is the burden of Lyotard's essay, "Answering the Question: What is Postmodernism?" In that essay, he focuses on the aesthetics of postmodernism in relation to the aesthetic "Realism" of the nineteenth century and twentieth-century modernism itself in order to reveal "that severe re-examination which postmodernism imposes on the thought of the Enlightenment" (1984b:73). The task of Realism, he argues, is "to preserve various consciousnesses from doubt" (1984b:74). Such was the inaugural task of Enlightenment modernity, Descartes' attempt to discover knowledge free from doubt; it was the great achievement of the Enlightenment itself, which Richard Rorty describes in philosophy as "the Cartesian . . . triumph of the quest for certainty over the quest for wisdom" (Rorty, 1979:61). Thus Lyotard goes on to say that the "only definition" of Realism "is that it intends to avoid the question of reality implicated in that of art" and thus "stands somewhere between academicism and kitsch" (1984b:75). Realism assumes that "real-ity" is always the same, unaffected by the "language games" that determine what is "relevant" to its comprehension.

Against the language game of Realism – the assumption that the discourse of Realism, above all, *disinterestedly* describes reality in terms of the "clear and distinct ideas" of Cartesian science and the "necessary and sufficient truth" of Leibnizian philosophy – Lyotard posits Modernism. "Modernity," he argues, "in whatever age it appears, cannot appear without the shattering of belief and without discovery of the 'lack of reality' of reality, together with the invention of other realities" (1984b:77). That is, if "reality" consists, as the Enlightenment thought it consisted, of impersonal, discoverable, systematic ("semiotic") rules which make up the very "reality" of the real, it is also repeatedly encountered and transformed by new modes of apprehension, new "arrangements" of understanding (see 1984a:51). Capitalism is the great partner of the Enlightenment, whether it be base or epiphenomenon. "Capitalism," he writes, "inherently possesses the power to derealize familiar objects, social roles, and institutions to such a degree that the so-called realistic representations can no longer evoke reality except as nostalgia or mockery, as an occasion for suffering rather than for satisfaction" (1984b:74). (Needless to say, the opposition between base and epiphenomenon – or, in Marxian terms, between "base" and "superstructure" – is an inaugural assumption of Enlightenment modernity, and in what might be called the "postmodern economics" in figures as varied as John Maynard Keynes and Jean Baudrillard this "basic" hierarchical structure is called into question. This is why Marxist analysts like David Harvey and Fredric Jameson take such pains to argue that postmodernism is a "stage" or aspect of what Jameson calls "late capitalism.")

The key term in Lyotard's analysis is the description of modernity "in whatever age it appears," because for him "modernity" is not a temporal category but a category of experience – above all, it is an *aesthetic* experience (in part in the Greek sense of *aesthesis*, a word that simply describes any sensible experience). And as such it can occur "within" the stable impersonal experiences of cognitive knowledges (including Enlightenment science), the shattering social experience of modernity (including Enlightenment modernity), and the complicated private experiences of aesthetics (including Enlightenment aesthetics). Against the academicism and kitsch of Realism – the Realism of the true and the beautiful – Lyotard argues for the power of Modernism in terms of the shattering and the sublime. That is, when he talks of "the lack of reality" within reality, he is talking of a sea change in experience.

Most characteristic of this sea change, in Lyotard's analysis in *The Postmodern Condition*, is the loss or "delegitimation" of what he calls the "grand narratives" of culture, accounts of phenomena that aim at "totalization," the ability to make sense of all within its purview, once and for all. "True knowledge," he writes, " . . . is always indirect knowledge; it is composed of reported statements that are incorporated into the metanarrative [the grand narrative] of a subject that guarantees their legitimacy" (1984a:35). In "What is Postmodernism?," Lyotard examines the delegitimation of grand narratives in relation to the aesthetics of the *sublime* within an ambiguous "postmodernism." We call it "ambiguous" because Lyotard argues that the moment of postmodern sublimity does not follow or come after the aesthetic of modernism but, in fact, is its founding condition. The sublime, for Lyotard, is the aesthetics that accompanies the "lack of reality" which, as he argues in "What is Postmodernism?," is part and parcel of modernity (1984b:77). If the sublime arises, in Kant's account, "when the imagination fails to present an object which might, if only in principle, come to match a concept" (1984b:78), then Modern art *aims* at presenting "the fact that the unpresentable exists," at making "visible that there is something which can be conceived and which can neither be seen nor made visible: this is what is at stake in modern painting" (1984b:78).

Such sublimity, according to Lyotard, inhabits two modalities: that of "nostalgia for presence felt by the human subject," which focuses on the powerlessness provoked by representation; and that of the "inhumanity" of the power of representation, "the increase of being and the jubilation which result from the invention of new rules of the game" (1984b:79–80). Modernism thus "allows the unpresentable to be put forward only as the missing contents"; it is a nostalgia for that content (1984b:81). But post-modernism *inhabits* this process: it is "that which, in the modern, puts forward the unpresentable in presentation itself; that which denies itself the solace of good forms, the consensus of a taste which would make it possible to share collectively the nostalgia for the unattainable" (1984b:81). Such an aesthetic, we are suggesting, takes its place among attempts to recover the sacred in the world: the *mysterium tremendum* beyond and within the rational, secular order of Enlightenment knowledge, ethics, and experience. Lyotard's aesthetics attempts to capture the experience of our time by means of a "severe reexamination which postmodernity imposes on the thought of the Enlightenment" (1984b:73), including the reexamination of the overwhelmingly *salvationist* religiosity corresponding to the individualism of the Enlightenment, the overwhelmingly *rationalist* analyses corresponding to Enlightenment modernity's assumption of atemporal, non-modal truth, and the overwhelmingly *disinterested* examinations of interhuman activity corresponding to the Enlightenment's willful avoidance of the politics embedded in its knowledges.

Michel Foucault, "The Order of Discourse"

This article, which originally was Foucault's "Inaugural Lecture" at the Collège de France in December 1970, is an important articulation of his analysis of the politics embedded in knowledge. It was translated in 1971 under the title "The Discourse on Language," and later re-translated in 1981 under the title we are following, "The Order of Discourse." The original French title, *L'Ordre du Discours*, corresponds more literally to the later translation, which in many ways is more faithful to the original. But more importantly, the focus on discourse – that is, actual interpersonal uses of language, what Foucault calls "the singular instance[s] of discourse" (1981:65), rather than the general, atemporal category of language, which we might call, following our earlier discussion of Lyotard, a "non-modal" language – more fully captures the postmodern aspect of Foucault's project and more fully ties his analysis of the relationship of power and knowledge in discourse to Lyotard's analysis of the relationship of experience and concepts in the postmodern sublime.

This essay marks an important moment in Foucault's career – Edward Said once described it as Foucault's most important work – which articulates the change in focus from the more or less "synchronic" analyses of his early work to a focus on the play of power within discursive and social formations, what he describes in this essay as a transformation of "critical" analysis that tries "to grasp the forms of exclusion, of limitation, of appropriation" of discourse into "genealogical" analysis that examines how "discourses come to be formed . . . and what were their conditions of appearance, growth, variation" (1981:70). Like his later *History of Sexuality* (whose translated title ignores the French title *La Volonté de savoir* [The Will to Knowledge]), Foucault is explicitly concerned in "The Order of Discourse" with what Nietzsche calls in *The Genealogy of Morals* "the will to truth," the place of power within seeming disinterested knowledge. There is an order of discourse, Foucault argues, so that "in every society the production of discourse is at once controlled, selected, organised and redistributed by a certain number of procedures whose role is to ward off its powers and dangers, to gain mastery over its chance events, to evade its ponderous, formidable materiality" (1981:52). This very articulation of the "thesis" of the essay, here near its beginning, presents a pronoun, "its," whose antecedent is ambiguous, either "discourse" or "production," so that it underlines the difference between focuses on the tale and the telling, on constative and performative uses of language we mentioned earlier. More-over, in its articulation this thesis again hints, as Lyotard does, at what is unpresentable in discourse or the production of discourse: its powers and dangers, its chance events, its formidable materiality. These three categories govern the exposition of "The Order of Discourse," *its* order, in Foucault's tightly organized essay. As Foucault says in "Histories of Systems of Thought," discourse *delimits* objects, *defines* agents or subjects of knowledge, and *fixes* norms that allow concepts and theories to be elaborated (1977:199). As such, as in Lyotard's aesthetics of the sublime, it comes before or within Kant's critiques of pure reason, ethics (practical reason), and aesthetic experience, the generalizability, accuracy, and simplicity of the "grand narrative" of Enlightenment science. Moreover, the ponderous material power of discourse, for Foucault, its quality as a *material event*, emphasizes that aspect of "discourse" (as opposed to "language") that puts forward the unpresentable in presentation itself, the unpresentable in discourse itself.

The order of discourse wards off the unpresentable power, the temporality, and the materiality of language. The postmodern order of discourse emphasizes and puts these things forward, revealing them (as though the pane had been broken or words crossed out). Foucault himself does this in beginning his analytic essay by speaking in voices: assuming the voice of Jean Hyppolite – "a voice behind me which had begun to speak a very long time before, doubling in advance everything I am going to say" – the voice of "desire," of "the institution," and even of Samuel Beckett (1981:51). The postmodern world is the world of discourses, floating about so to speak. Fredric Jameson calls it a world of *pastiche*, "the imitation of a peculiar or unique, idiosyncratic style, the wearing of a linguistic mask, speech in a dead language . . . amputated of the satiric impulse, devoid of laughter and of any conviction that alongside the abnormal tongue you have momentarily borrowed, some healthy linguistic normality still exists" (1991:17). Towards the end of "The Order of Discourse," Foucault describes (without naming) this "postmodern" discourse by focusing on the "rarefaction of discourse" – the emptying out of discourse – by means of apprehending meaning as an event, appre-hending experience as discontinuous, apprehending the world as illegible (discourse as non-referential), and apprehending discourses as historical, governed by "external conditions of possibility" (1981:67). Thus, "The Order of Discourse" both manifests and analyses what we are calling postmodern discourse.

It does this through its remarkably tight argument. Foucault begins by describing the different modes of controlling, selecting, organizing, and redistributing discourse he announces in his thesis. These modes take three forms: exterior control, internal control, and the social appropriations of discourse. In the development of this argument, Foucault describes three kinds of exterior control. The first is discursive taboos, the most prominent of which are taboos against talking about sexuality and politics, what he calls discourses of desire and power. The second exterior control of discourse is one of exclusion rather than prohibition, the opposition of reason and madness, in which certain statements are simply excluded as non-sensical, "mad." The third exterior control is "the opposition between true and false" (1981:54), the will to truth, which most fully seems to banish desire and power from discourse by measuring it against its referents which, necessarily, are indifferent — "disinterested" — in relation to power and desire. Yet the very "will to truth" Foucault describes is, necessarily, inhabited by desire and power which "'true' discourse, freed from desire and power by the necessity of its form, cannot recognise . . . [as] pervad[ing] it" in its very "will to truth" (1981:56). In these ways, the exterior controls of discourse attempt to master the *power* of discourse (1981:61).

If exterior controls aim at mastering the power of discourse, then the internal controls aim at "averting the unpredictability of their appearance" (1981:61), "to gain mastery over their chance events" (1981:52). Internal controls take three forms: commentary, which creates a division between primary and secondary texts and aims at the recovery of (authoritative) meaning; the "author-function" or "author-position," which imposes identity upon "disturbing language" by identifying its unity, coherence, and the manner of its "insertion in the real" (1981:58); and disciplines, which control the production of statements by defining the objects, methods, and propositions of particular disciplinary discourses such as biology, history, philosophy, what Foucault calls the "theoretical horizon" of knowledge (1981:60).

A third group of procedures, he argues, "is not a matter of mastering [discourses'] powers or averting the unpredictability of their appearance, but of determining the condition of their application" so that not everyone will "have access to them" (1981:61). Here Foucault is describing the social appropriations of discourse, which includes ritualistic discursive practices, such as those of religious, political, and philosophical "doctrines" and, more broadly speaking, educational systems which are, in effect, "political way[s] of maintaining or modifying the appropriation of discourses, along with the knowledges and powers which they carry" (1981:64).

Having described, rather abstractly, the kinds or modes of controlling discourse, Foucault spells out a certain number of philosophical themes that have "come to correspond to these activities of limitation and exclusion, and perhaps also to reinforce them" (1981:64). In articulating these themes, he is making explicit what is implicit in the secular Enlightenment modernity that postmodernity discovers and responds to. These are themes of the "founding subject," whose "aims" "animate the empty forms of language"; of the "originating experience," by which he means pre-existing *legible* phenomena, whose "prior significations — in a sense, already said — [wander] around

in the world"; and of "universal mediation" that rediscovers "everywhere the movement of a logos [a language] which elevates particularities to the status of concepts"
(1981:65–6). For these philosophical themes, "discourse is no more than a play, of
writing in the first case, of reading in the second, and of exchange in the third, and this
exchange, this reading, this writing never put anything at stake except signs. In this way,
discourse is annulled" (1981:66).

It is precisely the *non-annullment* of discourse that is the "stake" of postmodernism: it
seeks, in both its positive and its negative moments – in the freedom it offers from the
prior constraints of human nature, natural law, and inexorable semiotics and in the
despair it engenders in a world seemingly without the transcendental values of "humanity," of "law," and of legibility or meaningfulness – to comprehend the ways that
discourse conditions the apparent "subject" of discourse, the "objects" of discourse,
and the "exchanges" of discourse. That is, the postmodern apprehends "constructions"
where self-evident "nature" seemed to be: the self, constructed and constrained by
discourse's power; the natural, constructed and constrained by discourse's chance events;
and meaning itself, constructed and constrained by discourse's ponderous, formidable
materiality. Foucault ends the essay by arguing that "discourses must be treated first of all
as sets of discursive events" (1981:69), and it is this sense of the *timeliness* of discourse –
its existence as an event in time – that opposes itself to the seemingly "atemporal"
transcendental values of Enlightenment modernity.

Above all, such atemporal values were *secular*; they attempt to capture the "essence"
of the world, without recourse to what the Enlightenment called superstition, culture,
tradition. Hence the great Enlightenment project, in Hume and Wordsworth, but also,
in a very different register, in Marx and Russell, is to achieve a "natural religion."
Above all, Enlightenment modernity attempted to understand both time and space as
homogeneous, and when they did so, as Elizabeth Ermarth argues in her powerful study
of literary realism, "it becomes possible to chart both the differences and similarities in
nature which give rise to those generalizations in science and art that we call laws. In
formulating such laws no attempt is made to save the appearances. In fact, we might say
that in reducing the welter of particulars to some abstract regularity, scientific and
realistic generalizations represent an attempt to save the essences" (1983:17–18). Such
"essences" replace the sacred with once-and-for-all "truth," atemporal truth. The
sacred, as both the doctrine of creation and of incarnation make abundantly clear,
traffics in *events*. And by treating discourse as a discontinuous, historical, and, on some
level, illegible event, Foucault asserts the singularity, the power, the *materiality* of
discourse and the recovery – which is both positive and negative – of *mysterium
tremendum* within experience.

This is most clear, we believe, in his description of the discursive event and "the
philosophy of event" near the end of "The Order of Discourse," which, in the context
of the scholastic element of the essay as a whole, even *sounds* theological. "Naturally,"
he writes,

> the event is neither substance nor accident, neither quality nor process; the event is not of
> the order of bodies. And yet it is not something immaterial either; it is always at the level of
> materiality that it takes effect, that it is effect; it has its locus and it consists in the relation,

coexistence, the dispersion, the overlapping, the accumulation, and the selection of material elements. It is not the act or the property of a body; it is produced as an effect of, and within, a dispersion of matter. Let us say that the philosophy of the event should move in the at first sight paradoxical direction of a materialism of the incorporeal. (1981:69)

The materialization of the incorporeal might well be a definition of the sacred, a dialectic of knowledge and power, an emphasis on the concrete event rather than the abstract concept or fact, a focus on the present first of all, and the play on the surfaces of the present. Although he does not say so, such a "philosophy of the event," like Lyotard's postmodern sublime, captures some of the power, meaning, and affect of the depthless combination of loss and affirmation – the "vertiginous knowledges" – of Blanchot's passage and Kruger's image, in which apprehension and discourse are both the same and different, shimmering with sameness and difference in a kind of primal scene.

Both Lyotard and Foucault combine and confuse language, experience, and power – discourse, *aesthesis*, and ethics – in order to recover the sacred for the modern/ postmodern world. Such recovery is the process and goal of many of the postmodern rereadings of the Bible we have collected here. Indeed, Foucault's theories have been influential in religious, theological, and biblical studies (see Carrett's summary in his Prologue in *Religion and Culture: Michel Foucault* [1999]; for examples in biblical studies, see Moore, 1994; Castelli, 1991). Foucault described his own connection with religion in that he "prowls the borderlands of Christianity" (1987:16; see also Carrett, 1999:3). What he hasn't described – though he implies it everywhere – are the ways the Bible is a spectre that haunts Western culture in the history of sexuality and the body, the dialectic of power and knowledge, and the engagements of ethical action and reflection.

Walter Benjamin, "The Task of the Translator"

The theory of translation that prevails in biblical studies today is generally called "dynamic equivalence," and it is a species of high, Enlightenment modernism. This view is advocated by Eugene Nida and J. P. Louw, among others. Dynamic equivalence seeks a translated work (target text) that has the same effect on its readers that the original work (source text) had on the original readers. The theory of dynamic equivalence assumes that the text's author wants to transmit a simple univocal message to her/his audience, and that readers of the translated text can also receive this message, which is conceived solely in terms of its knowledge-meanings without regard to any other claims it might make on its recipient tied up with the unpresentable power, the temporality, and the materiality of language. Instead, it simply assumes that the physical text is a container, with the meaning (the transmitted message) bottled up inside it. This meaning can be removed from one container-text and moved ("translated") to another container-text without serious damage to the meaning itself.

Nida and Taber's (1982) book centers on an extensive argument on behalf of dynamic equivalence and against what they call "formal correspondence" in translation. Formal correspondence is essentially identical to Walter Benjamin's description of translation in his essay "The Task of the Translator" as essentially *literal*: "instead of resembling the meaning of the original," he writes, translation "must lovingly and in detail incorporate the original's mode of signification" (1969:78). For Benjamin – who, writing between the great twentieth-century wars in the 1920s and 1930s, is a full generation earlier than virtually everyone represented in this book (he was born in 1892) – in many ways gestures, as Lyotard might say, toward the postmodern "moment" of twentieth-century modernism. Thus, the principal concern of his conception of translation theory is not the transference of meaning, but rather how one text illuminates another text. Translation, for Benjamin, is intertextual in a way, we might say, that discourse is for Foucault and, as we shall see, history is for Hayden White.

According to Benjamin, the value of a text in translation lies in its confrontation with the original text, not in its infallible transmission of meaning. The translated text represents the original text in a way that the original cannot do by itself. In translation the original is brought back to life, and the "pure language" imprisoned within the original text is "liberated." Benjamin's Kabbalist tendencies are apparent in his notion that a pure language speaks through the juxtaposition of two impure texts. Like a tangent to a circle, according to Benjamin, literal translation harmoniously supplements and complements the original text. According to this view, the purpose of language is not to reveal but to conceal, and translation tests the power of language to hide meaning. The sentence is a wall, says Benjamin, not a bottle.

The ideal of Benjamin's understanding of literal translation is the interlinear text, "in which literalness and freedom are united" (1969:82). Moreover, such interlinearity is above all characteristic of Scripture and sacred texts. Hence both Paul de Man and Jacques Derrida refer to literal translation as "word for word" translation: each word is translated by another word alongside of it. Derrida describes translation as a "contract" between texts (1985a:179, 1985b:122). In the space between the parallel lines of the two texts, the translation and its original are united in a "true language" "without the mediation of meaning" (Benjamin, 1969:82). However, this space of the interlinear is utopian and uninhabitable. As actual translations approximate to this ideal, they become incoherent. The literal translation creates a sacred, untouchable space (Derrida, 1985b:115); it is "writerly," to use Roland Barthes' famous distinction. De Man notes that for Benjamin the "task" (*Aufgabe*) of the translator is also her/his "defeat" (also *Aufgabe*) (1986:80). It is the slipperiness of language, exemplified by puns such as this – and above all in the *ponderous materiality* of puns, the fact that meaning manifests itself in palpable sounds – that resists translation. Yet in this resistance, the pure language speaks.

Dynamic equivalence insists on univocity and clarity of meaning just as Enlightenment modernity insists on clear and distinct ideas. Puns and other textual ambiguities are tolerated only if they are intentional, that is, part of the meaning put in the text by its author. Otherwise, the task of the translator is to eliminate any possibility of mistaken meaning – to produce a translation that will be reliable and "faithful." Although Willard

Van Orman Quine (1960) has powerfully demonstrated that this goal of equivalence is always unattainable, biblical scholars continue to assume that it should determine the criteria for Bible translation. On the other hand, literal translation, as Benjamin understands it, attends to the ambiguity and multiplicity of meanings which are inevitable in any written text. For literal translation, the text is perpetually incomplete, perpetually eliciting new intertextual juxtapositions, never entirely possessed or possessable. This is its "translatability" (1969:71).

The limits of understanding (and hence of translation) of the text are encountered at points of indeterminacy or mystery within the textual contents, and even in the singularity, temporality, and gratuity of the text itself. This would be Barthes' "text of bliss," the writerly text. The incompleteness or ambiguity of the literary work — what Roman Ingarden (1973) called its "spots of indeterminacy" — resists the reader's desire to possess it. However, this resistance is overcome through a reading — and every reading is also a translation — which governs the meaning of the story. Hence one could say that there is no "original" text, for every text is always already translated. And yet, every translation is also an "original" — for example, it can be copyrighted. It can even be translated, but only as an original, never as a translation.

A literal translation is not necessarily more accurate than a dynamically equivalent one. After all, the entire issue here concerns the question of what "accuracy" is. Nor will the literal translation necessarily provide the clearest transmission of accepted meaning. Instead, through the tension which it establishes with the original text, literal translation displays the "salutary strangeness" (Steiner, 1975:389) of the original. As Benjamin says, the literal translation forces the reader back to the original text — its gaps, its inconsistencies, its questions — not to where a decidable meaning is to be found, but to the situation in which its unpresentable power operates. In the tension between the texts, the space of the interlinear, something else appears, which may not be in the texts at all and which is in fact ineffable (here again Benjamin's mystical leanings are apparent), but which is somehow crucial to the questions of language, God, humanity, space, and time. In short, there is after all an extratextual something which inhabits that space — that *same* space, as Blanchot might say — and upon which all language depends, although that something can never truly come to language. In case this comment itself appears overly mystical, compare the words of de Man, who goes to great lengths to deny the messianic qualities of Benjamin's essay, but still says, "in Hölderlin [that is, in his very literal translation of Sophocles], translation *occurs*" (1986:104, de Man's emphasis). By "occurrence," de Man means — he struggles to mean — that discourse takes on the force of an event, Foucault's materialism of the incorporeal. "When Luther translated, the Bible," de Man goes on, "something occurred — at that moment, something happened" (1986:104). He cannot quite say what it is that happened, but we suspect it is akin to the *mysterium tremendum* of Blanchot and Kruger which is both a sublime event and more of the same, modern and postmodern.

Benjamin's conception of translation can help us comprehend the "post" of postmodernism: after all, a translation is also a "post"-text. In translation, he writes, "the life of the original attains . . . its ever-renewed and most abundant flowering." "This flowering," he goes on,

is governed by a special, high purposiveness. The relationship between life and purposeful-
ness, seemingly obvious yet almost beyond the grasp of the intellect, reveals itself only if the
ultimate purpose toward which all single functions tend is sought not in its own sphere but
in a higher one. All purposeful manifestations of life, including their very purposiveness, in
the final analysis have their end not in life, but in the expression of its nature, in the
representation of its significance. Translation thus ultimately serves the purpose of expressing the central reciprocal relationship between languages. It cannot possibly reveal or
establish this hidden relationship itself; but it can represent it by realizing it in embryonic or
intensive form. (1969:72)

Translation for Benjamin is a discursive – a "representational" – event that, at its best,
fulfills rather than repeats the original it seeks to grasp. To make this clearer – and this
passage, like those of Blanchot, Kruger, and Foucault, calls out for clarification –
translation is a form of recovery (or, as Benjamin says in another context, a form of
"redemption" [see Schleifer 2000:84–107]) that *invokes* rather than wards off what
Foucault calls the "powers and dangers" of language, "its chance events, . . . its ponderous, formidable materiality" (1981:52) – sacred power that might (or might not) inhabit
ordinary and everyday language. "It is the task of the translator," Benjamin says, "to
release in his own language that pure language which is under the spell of another, to
liberate the language imprisoned in a work in his re-creation of that work. For the sake
of pure language he breaks through decayed barriers of his own language" (1969:80).

"The Task of the Translator" was first published in 1923 as the introduction to
Benjamin's translation of Charles Baudelaire's *Tableaux parisiens*. Benjamin's essay has
profoundly influenced both poststructuralist literary theorists and translation theorists.
Both de Man and Derrida (who, like Benjamin, have actually worked as translators)
have written essays of their own commenting on Benjamin's essay. Benjamin's views
also receive extensive consideration in important books on language and translation by
George Steiner (1975), Willis Barnstone (1993), and Umberto Eco (1995).

Hayden White, "The Historical Text as Literary Artifact"

This essay succinctly presents the most important theoretical points from Hayden
White's book *Metahistory*. In *Metahistory* White argued that his purpose was to "consider
the historical work as what it most manifestly is – that is to say, a verbal structure in the
form of a narrative prose discourse that purports to be a model, or icon, of past
structures and processes in the interest of explaining what they were by representing
them" (1973:2). White realized that with this statement he had crossed the boundary
between "history" and "fiction" in a way that historians had not done before the so-
called "linguistic turn" of about 1970 (1973:2, n. 4). Few historians contested the view
that history was a form of literature and that style was important in historiography. To
his critics, however, White seemed to be suggesting that history was only another form
of literature. In this sense, then, Windschuttle correctly notes that White is usually
credited with being "the first to provide a comprehensive argument that history was
ultimately a literary or poetic construct" (1996:232, cf. 227). (In fact, White's larger

framework of "history" – and the timely discursiveness of "history" – gathers up the politics implicit in Foucault and Benjamin and explicit in Jameson and Butler to allow these essays to create a framework that relates most closely to Part II of the *Reader*, "The Politics of Reading.")

Where White crossed the epistemological Rubicon for traditional historians was when he argued that they have no direct perception of the past, and, therefore, must use their imaginations to emplot it. This argument seemed to move historical writing from the realm of "fact" to "fiction." In his critics' eyes, if White were correct, then historical writings would be totally imaginative constructions. Their worst fears were confirmed, because the point that White made was precisely that historians "construct" history rather than find "it." In writing history, particularly as narrative, the practice of historians is a literary act that is virtually indistinguishable from the writing of fictional narratives. As White puts it in "The Historical Text as Literary Artifact,"

> This question has to do with the status of this historical narrative considered purely as a verbal artifact purporting to be a model of structures and processes long past. . . . This is not to say that historians and philosophers of history have failed to take notice of the essentially provisional and contingent nature of historical representations and of their susceptibility to infinite revision in light of new evidence. . . . But in general there has been a reluctance to consider historical narratives as what they most manifestly are: verbal fictions, the contents of which are as much invented as found and the forms of which have more in common with their counterparts in literature than they have with those in science. (1978:82)

Traditional biblical scholarship fits White's description about "a reluctance to consider historical narratives as what they most manifestly are: verbal fictions." Although biblical scholars will acknowledge the constructed nature of their histories, few will concede that their constructions refer only to their own imaginations, or to the collective imagination of their professional societies. In White's view, however, the referent of the professional historian's narrative is primarily the discourse of other historians rather than "the past itself."

Since historians do not have direct access to "the past," there is no way to prove that an event actually happened in the way that any particular historian has emplotted it. There is, however, much more at stake in White's view than simply sorting out the question of "what happened." It is also the question of what the past means. White argues that historians' imaginative emplotments come from values that are not intrinsic to the past event. For example, how is the death of Jesus to be emplotted? Does his death intrinsically carry a plot or entail certain values? Or, do the various emplotments of Jesus' death, and the values that they represent, originate in the imagination of individuals, traditions, and cultures? White argues that past events do not come with plots that cry out "I am a tragedy!" or "I am a comedy!" Historians present events as tragedies or comedies, and their emplotments are imaginative and literary acts that are similar to – if not the same as – writing fiction. Therefore, since no past event carries an intrinsic plot, any emplotment and its values derive from historians and their subcultures. White's point is that historical situations do not have built into them intrinsic meanings in the way that literary texts do. Historical situations are not inherently tragic, comic, or romantic . . . we only think of situations as tragic or comic because these concepts are part of our generally cultural and specifically literary heritage. How a given historical situation is to be configured depends on the historian's subtlety in matching up a specific plot structure with the set of historical events that he [sic!] wishes to endow with a meaning of a particular kind. This is essentially a literary, that is to say fiction-making, operation. (1978:85)

In contrast to White's view, many historical-critics still cling to the belief that they arrive epistemologically at some "thing" in the past, or at least to the correct range of meanings for an event. For White, this belief is a refusal to acknowledge the textuality of historical work. White unmasks the "sleight of hand" at work here. Biblical historians usually will acknowledge that their histories are reconstructions. At the same time, however, they refuse (as do most historians) to examine the ways in which they actually write history. White directly confronts the historical-critical reluctance to deal with historiography in light of recent developments in both literary criticism and philosophy.

One of the crucial issues that White raises is how one historical emplotment can be deemed as better than any other. If there is no direct correspondence of the historical representation to "the past," as White argues, then on what basis can a choice be made between different historical accounts? White contends that the choice is usually made by persuading others that one story corresponds best to what the past "actually was." In other words, the choice is ultimately made on aesthetic, moral, ideological, and political grounds rather than on the basis of factual "proof" that one story better represents the "way things really were" or that it is now clear that this event carries this or that meaning. He bluntly says:

> In my view, there are no extra-ideological grounds on which to arbitrate among the conflicting conceptions of the historical process and of historical knowledge appealed to by the different ideologies. For, since these conceptions have their origins in ethical considerations, the assumption of a given epistemological position by which to judge their cognitive adequacy would itself represent only another ethical choice. (1973:26)

In other words, there is no way to adjudicate between historical accounts except by persuasive appeal to the ideological, ethical, and political frameworks of historians themselves.

White, therefore, wants to redefine how the discipline of history is perceived and practiced, and up to a point he clearly takes his stand on the postmodern side of historiography. One of the criticisms to be made of White, however, is that he retreats somewhat from the poststructuralist and postmodern implications concerning the textuality of history. That is, if historical events have no intrinsic plot, and thus entail no predetermined values, then what does the historian "do" with events such as the assassination of John F. Kennedy, the death of Jesus, or the Holocaust?

Many would agree with Michael Stanford that "White himself admits that one can hardly emplot the story of President Kennedy as a comedy. Nor could the history of the First World War be told as a comedy or romance, though easily as tragedy or satire"

(1986:136). What White actually says, however, is that "people" (in the United States?) would not accept the emplotment of Kennedy's death as a comedy; he does not say that it could not be emplotted as a comedy. If White does argue as Stanford contends, then of course, White ultimately undermines his own view of the textuality of history. What White actually says is: "I do not suppose that anyone would accept the emplotment of the life of President Kennedy as comedy, but whether it ought to be emplotted romantically, tragically, or satirically is an open question. The important point is that most historical sequences can be emplotted in a number of different ways, so as to provide different interpretations of those events and to endow them with different meanings" (1978:84–5).

White, then, does not argue for an intrinsic plot in past events. Instead, he takes refuge in a structuralist theory of tropes, namely, that the historian's emplotment is a secondary act that occurs within an irreducible field of tropes – irony, synecdoche, metonymy, and metaphor. (Eco pursues a homologous methodology in his analysis of Edenic language in Part I). In other words, linguistic prefiguration precedes and determines interpretation and emplotment. He says: "In the poetic act which precedes the formal analysis of the field, the historian both creates his object of analysis and predetermines the modality of the conceptual strategies he will use to explain it" (1973:31). The historian poetically creates the object about which he or she writes, but somehow the linguistic prefiguration operates with a center and in a regulatory way so that a stable basis for analysis of the historian's rhetorical "field" is both possible and predictable. Linguistic prefiguration of the historian's "field" both creates his or her object and predetermines both its style of presentation and its interpretation. In other words, White is subject to the main criticism of structuralism: he refuses to recognize that his theory of tropes is itself another text. Once the textuality of White's tropological theory is acknowledged, then his view of historical writing is open to the infinite possibilities of intertextuality. If there is no predetermined structural configuration of any event from the past, then there is no consequent plot or fixed interpretation either. White would have to allow, for example, if only on a popular level, that if Mel Brooks can portray the Spanish Inquisition as a Broadway musical in *The History of the World: Part One*, then – like it or not – Brooks could surely make a comedy of Kennedy's assassination.

While it is incorrect to say that White argues for an intrinsic plot in past events, it is the case that he struggles with the implications of his own historical perspectivalism, particularly in relation to representing the Holocaust. For White the ethical moment in historical work is the ideological choice of emplotment and the mode of argument that is used for the presumed relation between the plot structure and the set of events (1973:27). White reluctantly acknowledges that the Holocaust can be (and is) emplotted in numerous and conflicting ways, but he implies that somehow the Holocaust carries an intrinsic plot with certain values (1992). Obviously, White wants to have it both ways so that events carry intrinsic plots and values and, at the "same" time, they do not. This is not, as White seems to think, a false "either/or" dilemma; rather, as he doesn't quite suggest, it is an *ethical* dilemma which cannot be as fully detached, as Enlightenment modernity assumed, from *aesthetics* or *epistemology*, issues of form and truth. Such an understanding situates White's work – and the kinds of epistemological, ethical, and political questions that this work has evoked – fully within the postmodern. That is, by forcefully raising the issues of how different histories of the same event are both possible and are adjudicated, White opens the question of historical writing as political, ideological, and ethical praxis. Since any historical emplotment is value-laden, White argues that the professional historian is ethically and politically obligated to consider how his or her work is emplotted and presented, and what material effects might be entailed by believing it. White's concern is that historians take some ethical and political responsibility for their work.

Exactly how that is to be done is an ongoing issue in the debate. In White's view "the past" is the proper object of any historical study, and "history" is writing about "the past." By opening "the past" to more – and perhaps to infinite – possibilities, White has problematized the sign of "history" itself. One postmodern implication of White's work is that any approach to "the past" could properly be called "historical" if the object of its writing is "the past." White's view of "history," then, opens historical writing to various approaches and many voices that more traditional approaches, such as historical-criticism, simply cannot recognize without a transformation of the discipline. In this sense, White almost follows Nietzsche's perspectivalism to its logical conclusion by forcefully arguing against any historical account that attempts to arrive at narrative closure (and hence ideological closure) about "the past." For historical-critics, whose goal is to seek closure, White's argument against it is one of his most important postmodern emphases.

Even today, in the new century, White does not appear in the bibliographies of exegetical primers and introductions to historical criticism. Most primers and methodological articles being written and used to show students how to do historical criticism in biblical studies simply do not address the larger debate on historiography that White has helped to initiate. Still, his work raises questions that ought to be overwhelmingly pressing to those who study and/or revere the Bible. What does it mean to "practice" historical biblical criticism, or to be a "proper" historical-critic? How are past events to be emplotted and by what values? How is one emplotment of the past to be judged better than another? How many emplotments of a past event are possible? Is the number of plots as theoretically infinite as the number of present and future readers? Is it possible to take ethical and political responsibility for one's re-presentation of the past? What does it mean to "be responsible" for one's historical work? Can or should the writing of history avoid being guided primarily by current ideological and political concerns? Such questions – they are "postmodern" questions – ring throughout the selections in this book.

Fredric Jameson, "The Dialectic of Utopia and Ideology"

Another text to help delimit the postmodern is the "Conclusion" to Fredric Jameson's book, *The Political Unconscious* (1981:281–99). Jameson is an American Marxist critic who has more recently made major contributions to the assessment of the postmodern world, especially in his book *Postmodernism: The Cultural Logic of Late Capitalism* (1991). There, he interprets a great variety of postmodern phenomena, in the arts and elsewhere, in terms of a dual and paradoxical trend: toward greater fragmentation, as old patterns of cohesion are deconstructed, but also toward greater homogenization, as cultural expressions get instantly diffused everywhere through the universal reach of the global economy. He is trying to show a *necessary* link between the cultural forms postmodernism takes and the nature of the economic system, "late capitalism," within which it has arisen.

The linkage, which Jameson pursues in his book on postmodernism, is, however, only a very extended example of a broader theory which he worked out in *The Political Unconscious*, and this earlier work is of more direct relevance to "postmodern" biblical studies. Of greatest relevance is the Conclusion, but this needs to be put briefly in the context of the book as a whole. Jameson proposes a model for the historical materialist reading of texts as "socially symbolic acts." By this he means that any text encodes in a complex way significant aspects of the "political unconscious" of the society out of which it emerges. The political unconscious is the set of assumptions that a society must internalize in order to be that kind of society, assumptions so basic that they must be protected from critical scrutiny by being suppressed below the level of the debatable or even the thinkable. (In our society, the notion that there are "individuals" who have "rights" might be such an assumption.)

Jameson's model works in three stages, or "horizons." The first is that of the individual text within its specific political context. At this level, the necessary technique is closely akin to deconstruction. (For a discussion of deconstruction, see the Introduction to Part I, "Rereading the Bible.") The interpreter identifies the text's basic "contradiction," the point where its attempt to create a coherent world of meaning most conspicuously fails, and then attempts to correlate this contradiction with some contradictory feature of the society. The second horizon, that of "class struggle," moves beyond the individual text to a reading of as many texts as possible that are contemporaneous with it, to see among what range of options the individual text represents a choice, and how the different choices available are related to class division in the society. (It is important at this level to realize that the range of extant texts will be heavily biased on the side of the dominant class which controls the means of literary production. However, suppressed class voices can often be discerned in "dominant" texts.)

It is the third horizon which represents the most creative aspect of Jameson's work, and which offers the richest possibilities for biblical interpretation. Here, the context for the individual text is nothing else than the whole of world history as understood in Marxist theory, which, in a sense, creates the possibility of "anagogic" understanding. The critical unit in this Marxist context is the "mode of production," a term applied to the very few basic possibilities of human organization which have occurred, or in principle could occur, in history (examples are feudal, capitalist, and communist modes). According to Jameson, though, no historical society has ever embodied any mode of production perfectly. Rather, a society typically exhibits a dominant mode, but in conflict with other modes either left over from the past or emerging with the possibility of becoming dominant in the future. Texts represent "fields of force" within these conflicts between modes of production.

The Bible comes from societies in which the dominant mode of production was the "Asiatic" (sometimes called "tributary") – the system of the Egyptian, Mesopotamian, and Persian empires – or the slave-based (Greek and Roman). But both testaments reveal the presence of subversive secondary modes: the prophets perhaps look back to an egalitarian polity in pre-monarchical times, while the early Church sometimes imagines and even practices a system of radical sharing. This creates rich potential for the reading of biblical texts as sites of conflict between different "political unconsciouses," a potential which some biblical critics have begun to exploit (see Boer, 1996; also Gottwald, Jobling, Penchansky, Pippin in Jobling and Pippin, 1992; and the last chapter of *The Postmodern Bible*). Perhaps even more radically, it indicates how old texts (like the Bible) produced within ancient modes of production may be read under capitalism, suggesting the kind of rules of "translation" which enable us to move tentatively from one fundamental mindset to another. Put another way, the Bible, as the most author-itative text still speaking to us out of a wholly different set of cultural assumptions, represents a powerful potential tool for the critique of capitalism; but it can be this only if we attend carefully to the process of "translation." We must avoid the ahistorical notion that the Bible can critique capitalism in an unmediated way. The Bible, though it knows much about class struggle, knows nothing about capitalism.

We turn, then, to the passionately argued Conclusion to *The Political Unconscious*. If literary texts can be read as opening up the social and political possibilities of societies past and present, with what expectations should we read them? Throughout the chapter Jameson highlights two issues: that a "positive" and a "negative" hermeneutic need always to operate together; and that a positive hermeneutic must necessarily be one of community or solidarity. He begins with a famous saying of Walter Benjamin that "There has never been a document of culture which was not at one and the same time a document of barbarism." While fully affirming this, he wants to affirm equally its reverse. Marxism often confines itself to a negative, "ideological" critique of cultural productions such as literature–they are seen as means of oppression whose power to create "false consciousness" must be exposed and counteracted. But Jameson insists that Marxist criticism does not have to be negative. He insists that there must also be a positive, "Utopian" reading of cultural productions which exhibits in them unantici-pated signs of hope. Such positive reading cannot, however, be authentically developed out of existing liberal hermeneutics based on the autonomy of the individual. This is the second issue. In effect, the ideological is for Jameson the individual, and the Utopian is the communal. Cultural productions function positively exactly to the extent that they remind us of human solidarity; when they put us out of touch with our solidarity, they are negative or ideological.

In the framework of class struggle, Jameson as a Marxist affirms the hermeneutical privilege of the working class in assessing the effects of culture. But this privileged collectivity does not yet exist. It is in the process of formation, and while this process continues, anything which affirms human collectivity, anything which suggests that individual interests are inseparable from those of a group, is "Utopian." All collectivities are figures of the classless society, even when they occur in what seem like totally negative contexts, such as Fascism and anti-Semitism. There is no "document of barbarism," to reverse Benjamin, which cannot be read also as a "document of culture" in a positive, life-giving sense.

It is in this context that we must read Jameson's persistent critique of ethics, both in the Conclusion and throughout the book. His point is that class solidarity must always precede the forming of ethical judgments, since the available ethical systems are almost entirely embedded in individualist assumptions, and are therefore a major and acutely oppressive aspect of the ideological. Jameson (like Nietzsche) is acutely conscious of the ways in which ethical systems are exploited by dominant classes; this is presumably why he does not admit the idea of a communal ethic, though there is no obvious reason why he could not.

From the perspective of biblical studies, Jameson encourages the subversion of the dominant individualist paradigm of scholarly production, and the extension of practices growing out of group reading (such as base community biblical study). In this context, the collective authorship of *The Postmodern Bible* – and perhaps the even more "collective" nature of the *Reader*, comprising as it does twenty-one authors and three editors – can be seen as a small Utopian moment. Of equal importance is his insistence that ideological and Utopian analyses must always function simultaneously. Reading of the Bible by disempowered groups readily falls into one side or the other of a dichotomy: is the Bible part of the problem, or part of the solution? Jameson enables us to suggest that it is always necessarily both, profoundly ideological (in his negative sense of the word) but also profoundly Utopian. This is an issue which one of our number at least (David Jobling) finds constantly played out in the (seminary) classroom – how students may find a sense of power *over* a biblical text which has been used to control them, while not losing a sense of power *through* the Bible in their efforts to mend the world.

Our experience of using Jameson's Conclusion in a class at the Iliff School of Theology provides an example. We read alongside it Hosea 1–3, a text which traditionally was highly valued for its evocation of God's patient love, but whose recent interpretation has been dominated by scathingly critical feminist readings focused on its understanding of sex-roles in marriage and its treatment of Gomer. The ideological has here been identified in the Utopian, with a vengeance. The issue arose in the class of whether a new Utopian might now be found in the ideological, and whether the literary process by which an *individual*, Gomer, stands metaphorically for a *collective*, Israel, is relevant. Jameson's analysis is intensely suggestive about such questions.

His work represents one of the most important Marxist appropriations of postmodern currents. It is certainly a critical appropriation, as witness for example the sharp critique of Derrida in the Conclusion (1981:282–3, n.2). Jameson always affirms that it is Marxism which can and must *contain* the postmodern, rather than the other way around. But his incorporation of deconstructive method into the reading of texts and his assertion of the "undecidability" between ideological and Utopian readings show a welcome readiness to go beyond a knee-jerk political rejection of postmodernism.

Judith Butler, "Contingent Foundations: Feminism and the Question of 'Postmodernism'"

If Jameson seems to be articulating a form of postmodern anagogic reading, so too do the last two examples of postmodern "moments" we are presenting, that of feminism as articulated by Judith Butler and a kind of political-cultural, semiotic psychoanalysis articulated by Slavoj Žižek. Feminism, certainly, is not simply something to be added to modes of interpretation, but rather brings a whole set of questions and attitudes toward experience and understanding that defines, anagogically, value in our world. (In fact, the sense of anagogy – in Jameson's politics, Butler's feminism, and Žižek's cultural psycho-analysis – allows these final two essays – but also those of Benjamin and Jameson and perhaps even Foucault – to create anagogical apprehensions of the postmodern that relate most closely to Part III of the *Reader*, "The Conscience of the Bible.") In any case, there are a good number of women and men besides Butler working primarily outside of religion, and producing critical theories which have influenced the study of religion, whom we are not including. Moreover, while in the *Reader* the female thinkers whose articles we are using include Bal, Cixous, Haraway, Kristeva, Pathak, Spivak, and Scarry, significant omissions also occur. (Luce Irigaray, who has had a substantial impact on feminist theology, comes immediately to mind.) Indeed, Butler warns about the use of examples to represent the whole: "we have then forced a substitution of the example for the entire field, effecting a violent reduction of the field to the one piece of text the critic is willing to read, a piece which, conveniently, uses the term 'postmodern'" (1992:5). As we carefully present examples in the limited space of this *Reader* and the classroom setting, this warning will raise the issues of exclusionary practice but will also mark, we hope, our commitments to the intellectual and political possibilities in keeping the questions open.

We have chosen this article by Judith Butler, "Contingent Foundations: Feminism and the Question of 'Postmodernism,'" as a way into postmodern theory, primarily due to her emphasis on the importance of raising the questions about language and categ-ories. Butler works as a literary theorist and Professor of Rhetoric and Comparative Literature at the University of California at Berkeley, but she is also well-versed in the philosophical and psychoanalytical traditions that are part of the theoretical exchanges in postmodernism. "Contingent Foundations" is a good example of her theoretical groundwork – her anagogic apprehension – of what is at stake in taking the "post-modern" as a global context for understanding, apprehending as it does the language and categories of Foucault and White from within a world from which the problems of gender cannot be erased. This article was originally in *Praxis International* (volume 11, July 2, 1991), but it is most widely known from the book *Feminists Theorize the Political* (1992), a book in which a wide and varied range of voices are collected. While the dominant voices from the philosophical tradition have been male (Plato, Kant, Marx, Hegel, Nietzsche, Foucault, Derrida, et al.) and from the Imperialist West (Europe and the United States), there are more recently the voices of feminists and postcolonial theorists. This article also appears in the book *Feminist Contentions* (1995), in which Butler and other feminist thinkers, Benhabib, Cornell, and Fraser, debate the issues around "Thinking Gender" (the series's title) and the various feminism*s* in the post-modern scene.

As this suggests, Butler has been a particularly important voice in the study of gender and sexuality. She draws from the fields of philosophy, cultural criticism, feminist theory, poststructuralism, and gay and lesbian theory in her investigation of traditional modes of thinking about gender. In her groundbreaking book *Gender Trouble* (1990/1999), she opens up the masculine/feminine binary by showing that gender is not a fixed category: "Gender is a complexity whose totality is permanently deferred, never fully what it is at any given juncture in time. An open coalition . . . " (1999:22). Thus, questions of subjectivity and identity are raised. The fluidity of gender breaks apart the notion that a person is one thing or another, set for all time. (Such "for all time" thinking is a hallmark of the atemporal truths of Enlightenment modernity we mentioned earlier.) In disagreement with feminists who hold onto the male/female binary (e.g. Luce Irigaray), Butler believes that " . . . 'being' a sex or gender is fundamentally impossible" (1999:25). And she asks: "If the inner truth of gender is a fabrication and if true gender is a fantasy instituted and inscribed on the surface of bodies, then it seems that genders can be neither true nor false" (1999:174). Any maintaining of the binary keeps patriarchal hegemony – the organization around the traditional positive and negative opposition of male and female – in place. (Such "hegemony" is nicely defined by Jameson's term, "political unconscious.") Reproduction of traditional and self-evident truths is thus an imposition of a norm. For Butler, the triad of gender, sexuality, and desire is open and not restricted. Her undoing of traditional gender categories led her to be considered as one of the founders of "queer theory," although at the time she did not consider herself as such (1999:viii).

Butler seeks to remedy this binary understanding of gender as fixed and its effects as monumentally unchangeable by arguing that gender is connected to sexuality and is based on action; it is *performative*. Subversive performances such as drag imitate gender (1999:175). Gender is enacted through "performativity", which allows us to see that " . . . gender is an identity tenuously constituted in time, instituted in an exterior space through a *stylised repetition of acts*" (1999:179, emphasis in original). The boundaries of the body, and of performance, are always tenuous and open to change. In other words, gender is socially and individually constructed by action. Performance is linked with political force; it is a political (speech) act (1997a). Butler engages the political practice of reading texts and language. Drawing from Foucault's theory on discourse and power, she shows how the dominant discourse on gender and sexuality has been and can be resisted, transgressed, contested, and subverted by acts of performance.

Butler's early work has been criticized for essentializing terms like "subject" and "universal." She answers her critics in several places: "To question a term, a term like 'the subject' or 'universality,' is to ask how it plays, what investments it bears, what aims it achieves, what alterations it undergoes" (1997a:162). And in the Preface to the tenth anniversary edition of *Gender Trouble* Butler lays out her rethinking of the major categories in the book and why she holds to the ongoing rhetorical power of certain terms. Another example is the term "identity": "The mobilization of identity categories for the purposes of politicization always remain threatened by the prospect of identity becoming an instrument of the power one opposes" (1999:xxvi). Butler connects her own political commitments with the rhetorical use of such problematic categories.

In the article we have chosen for this Introduction, Butler expands the necessity for the categories of "women" and "universal" in postmodern and feminist theory:

> I would argue that any effort to give universal or specific content to the category of women, presuming that that guarantee of solidarity is required *in advance*, will necessarily produce factionalization, and that "identity" as a point of departure can never hold as the solidifying ground of a feminist political movement. . . . This is not to say that the term

"women" ought not to be used, or that we ought to announce the death of the category. On the contrary, if feminism presupposes that "women" designates an undesignatable field of differences, one that cannot be totalized or summarized by a descriptive identity category, then the very term becomes a site of permanent openness and resignifiability. (1992:15–16)

Setting a normative foundation sets up a scene of inclusion/exclusion, and ends the opportunity for the multiple signifieds of postmodernism. Butler critiques any feminist politics that is locked into using "identity" as a foundational base and feminists who think that one needs a stable self and identity to be involved politically; in other words, "identity politics" is limited by the boundaries it puts on categories. The possibilities for political change are found in the open spaces of gender and sex.

In Butler's investigation into postmodernism, she answers the criticism that postmodernism (and deconstruction) are apolitical. The standard argument is that politics needs a stable foundation, a stable signified. In Butler's counter-argument, however, terms like "sex" and "women" have deeper political possibilities when any stable meaning or foundation is contested. She raises questions around the discourse on the violent act of rape against women. If, as has often been the case, the "sex" of the woman is given as an explanation for the rape, then the woman is held responsible. Butler explains, "The category of sex here functions as a principle of production and regulation at once, the cause of the violation. . . . [Sex] is a principle of production, intelligibility, and regulation which enforces a violence and rationalizes it after the fact" (1992:19). Rather than undermine political action, Butler says that postmodern inquiry into such power and discourse, as Foucault suggests in his more abstract discussion of discourse, leads to a reexamination of the political consequences of rhetoric and language.

The Gulf War serves as a further example for Butler. The media portrayal of this war gave a particular portrayal of "the subject" – especially the subject of "the Arabs," of the Iraqis, and Saddam Hussein. North Americans received the subject of the Gulf War mainly through CNN, through the pictures of the eerie nighttime bombing around Baghdad. The war was presented as a sanitized war, with "smart" bombs and expert generals to reassure that the United States remained dominant throughout. Viewers never saw the destruction or the bloodshed. This rhetoric of exclusion promotes violence. If the Iraqi is the "Other," then he can be killed. But there are costs in preserving the stability of a certain (US male) subject: "The effects of its actions have already inaugurated violence in places and in ways that it not only could not foresee but will be unable ultimately to contain, effects which will produce a massive and violent contestation of the Western subject's phantasmatic self-construction" (1992:12).

Butler's theories have influenced theoretical thinking in religious studies. In *The Postmodern Bible* Butler appears to instruct us toward a postmodern reading of texts that takes seriously the presence of multiple readings outside the dominant interpretive discourse, and the political consequences of any particular interpretive focus or "normative" reading of the Bible (3; 11; ch. 6). Her analysis of gender is used by biblical scholars, such as Daniel Boyarin (1994) in his investigation of the apostle Paul. And feminist theorists of religion have been influenced by her revealing of the intricacies of discourse about gender and identity politics.

Slavoj Žižek, "The Real and Its Vicissitudes"

In searching for ways to understand the notion of identity, Butler relies also on psycho-analytical theory. She finds in the theory of Slavoj Žižek a way "to rethink identity-claims as phantasmatic sites, impossible sites, and, hence, as alternately compelling and disappointing" (1993:188). Both of them are interested in the contested ideological foundations of language and how words like "democracy" and "women" are sites of conflict rather than resolutions of meaning. Butler relates, "No signifier can be radically representative, for every signifier is the site of a perpetual *méconnaissance*; it produces the expectation of a unity, a full and final recognition that can never be achieved" (1993:191).

Žižek does not appear in *The Postmodern Bible*. His influence in biblical studies is more recent than that of any of the other theorists in this Reader (see Boer, 1996; Pippin, 1999). Žižek is senior researcher at the Institute for Sociology in Ljubljana, Slovenia. He links Lacanian psychoanalytic theory to idealist and materialist philosophies (such as that of Althusserian ideology critique). He is a prolific writer, having written more than half a dozen books, and he ran as a candidate for the presidency in 1990, when Slovenia was still part of Yugoslavia. He publishes in English and periodically teaches courses in the United States, so his work is becoming more widely known in critical theory circles. He has an interest in politics and popular culture and their intersection with the whole history of Western philosophical tradition. The intersection of the political, theoretical, and popular in his work is a hallmark of postmodern attitudes toward experience.

"The Real and Its Vicissitudes" comes from *Looking Awry: An Introduction to Jacques Lacan through Popular Culture* (1991), in which Žižek reads mysteries and film (especially Hitchcock) and other cultural forms through Lacan through Althusser. In this essay Žižek traces the concept of the "real" through some horror films, Hitchcock, the environment, and other examples. The Lacanian trinity of the Real, the Imaginary, and the Symbolic are at play here. The "Psychoanalytic Criticism" chapter of *The Postmodern Bible* summarizes this concept of the Lacanian "real." The real is not "reality" because it cannot be represented. The real is the place where God is located and as such has "an oddly 'miss-tical'" function (207). What this implies is that the God of Judaism and Christianity has to be relocated in the real and thus removed from his speech, Law, and patriarchy: "if there are only 'bits-of-real' [Lacan]," the Bible and Culture Collective writes, "then there can only be 'bits-of-God'" (208). For Žižek the real is the starting point for the Symbolic order: "The Real is the fullness of the inert presence, positivity; nothing is lacking in the Real – that is, the lack is introduced only by the symbolization; it is a signifier which introduces a void, an absence in the Real. But at the same time the Real is in itself a hole, a gap, an opening in the middle of the symbolic order – it is the lack around which the symbolic order is structured" (1989:170). The real can never be pinpointed, exacted, "real"ized. The ups and downs of the real correspond to the way the human unconscious works as a language. And Žižek's way of approaching the real is through an examination of some material artifacts of popular culture.

The real returns and answers – it can be discerned – within figures of the undead in movies (e.g. *Pet Sematary; Return of the Living Dead; Nightmare on Elm Street*) or in plays (e.g. *Antigone; Hamlet*). The undead are "between two deaths" "... *because they were not properly buried*" (1991:22–3, emphasis in original). The undead have a symbolic debt that has yet to be paid; the symbolic rite of a proper burial was disrupted. The symbolization of the funeral gives the dead the right/rite to live on in memory. Žižek accents two examples: "The two great traumatic events of the holocaust and the gulag are, of course, exemplary cases of the return of the dead in the twentieth century. The shadows of their victims will continue to chase us as 'living dead' until we give them a decent burial, until we integrate the trauma of their death into our historical memory" (1991:23). There is a connection with the "return of the primal father" (Freud) or the Name-of-the-Father, which is how the father returns after his murder (Lacan). The dead father blocks any access to enjoyment; in other words, the Garden of Eden is forever off-limits.

The "answer of the real" also appears in the ecological crisis. Žižek asks, "Is not the disturbed, derailed course of nature an 'answer of the real' to human praxis, to the human encroachment upon nature, 'mediated' and organized by the symbolic order?" (1991:34). Everything about "nature" is thrown into question. He uses Lacanian theory to investigate the crisis. The Chernobyl nuclear accident is an example of the threat of "the second death"; radiation is unrepresentable; the binary of order and chaos is disrupted (36). Žižek posits that "*Nature does not exist,*" echoing Lacan's outlandish assertion "woman does not exist." Nature, he says, "does not exist as a periodic, balanced circuit, thrown off its track by man's inadvertence" (1991:38). Rather, nature is itself chaotic and out of balance. The ecological activist who obsessively seeks to return nature to some pristine "balance" is thus as misled as one who seeks in nature the bearer of a message. In both "we blind ourselves ... to the irreducible gap separating the real from the modes of its symbolization. The only proper attitude is that which fully assumes this gap as something that defines our very *condition humaine*" (1991:36). Nature does not exist; that is, the real of nature is found in the gap, in the disruption, the imbalance.

Thus, Žižek "looks awry" at both Lacanian theory and popular culture, and such looking awry is a postmodern gesture that does not fully accept the stabilities of Enlightenment modernity. The opening line of the book in which this article appears sets the tone for Žižek's particular approach to religion: "Walter Benjamin commended as a theoretically productive and subversive procedure the reading of the highest spiritual products of a culture alongside its common, prosaic, worldly products" (1991:vii). Žižek has a fascination for the (Kantian) sublime, the sublime object of ideology, as he calls it: the sublime of the abyss of freedom, of the political, of the erotic, of fantasies, of enjoyment, of the real, and in his most recent book, the fragile absolute. In this he joins Lyotard in his apprehension of the postmodern *as sublime*. This fascination has fired his interest in reading Christianity through St. Paul (he engages Alain Badiou's Althusserian reading of Paul), and in staking a claim for Christianity against fundamentalists, on the one hand, and new age spiritualists on the other. Christianity and Marxism, he argues, have common interest, and "there *is* a direct lineage from Christianity to Marxism. . . ." Paul is important because Christianity cannot be separated from him: "*there is no Christ outside Saint Paul*; in exactly the same way, there is no 'authentic Marx' that can be approached directly, bypassing Lenin" (2000a:2, emphasis in original). Accordingly, the Bible exists alongside a mélange of cultural artifacts, but also alongside and within historical memory and political possibilities.

In our teaching of this material we used art images to illuminate the discussion of gender in Butler and Žižek. We showed several slides, including a series of Madonnas and anti-Madonnas (e.g. the performer Madonna as Whore of Babylon). Our example here is of Cindy Sherman as the Madonna in a 1989 photograph entitled *Untitled* (*History Painting #205*). Sherman is "naked" in a prosthesis of breasts with exaggerated nipples and pregnant belly with expanded belly button. According to Nicholas Mirzoeff, "she recapitulated the pose of Raphael's painting of the Fornarina. . . . The contemporary American artist thus put herself into the frame of the Madonna icon, but by so doing disrupts the iconographic series. . . . The spectator's gaze is both satisfied and denied in an exchange which disrupts the reiteration so essential to the series created by the Madonna icon" (1995:131). Sherman reveals "bits of Madonna" but stops the gaze on the full icon. In so doing she creates another fiction with her photograph, calling into question our fiction of the Virgin and of the representation of the body. Sherman is calling forth historical memory of Ingres, Raphael, and other paintings of Madonnas and other women. The jewelry on Sherman's upper arm and the hair scarf in the photo suggests Ingres' harem women. Sherman as Madonna looks straight at the camera with enlarged eyes and tense, pinched mouth. Sherman's copy is a copy of a copy, and on and on; with Lacan we could say, "the Madonna does not exist." The referent is disrupted, along with what we "know" about religious images of the Madonna (the miss-tical, again). In his examination of postmodern photography, Douglas Crimp argues that "Sherman's photographs are self-portraits in which she appears in disguise enacting a drama whose particulars have been withheld. . . . The pose of authorship is dispensed with not only through the mechanical means of making the image, but through the effacement of any continuous, essential persona or even recognizable visage in the scenes depicted" (1980:99). Is the Madonna present or absent from this photo? Is Cindy Sherman present or absent? Whose identity is being constructed in this photograph? Self and self-hood are represented. Sherman's Madonna appears to us in unexpected and unclear ways. The experience of the sublime continually shifts. Sherman is performing gender, reproduction, and iconography. Her icon is unsettling; the holy has a touch of horror, subliminal, anagogic, both there and not there.

Epigraph

We begin the selections of *The Postmodern Bible Reader* with a narrative epigraph taken from Thomas King's book *Green Grass, Running Water*. The epigraph is a small contemporary Native American narrative that, in many ways, answers the *sublimity* of the postmodern which is explicit in Lyotard, Butler, and Žižek and is implicit in the sense of *crisis* in Benjamin, Jameson, and even Foucault, with another sense of the postmodern, its everydayness, its ordinariness, its sense that the world we inhabit does not distinguish, as closely and absolutely as Enlightenment modernity did, between the sacred and the profane, between atemporal truth and temporal illusion, between high culture and popular culture, and between the sublimities of self-hood – in self-actualized individualism, or salvationist religiosity, or fulfilled humanity – and the accidents of collective, political, and popular existences within our various histories. In this excerpt, many of the great sublime and melodramatic "moments" of the Judeo-Christian culture – the whale, the fiery furnace, the manger, the golden calf, the pillar of salt, the burning bush, Young Man Walking On Water – are reduced to a stockpile of resources for storytelling. Moreover, the storytelling opposes itself to the individualism, the atemporal and transcendental truth, and the logic of the received tradition of Enlightenment modernity, which Young Man Walking On Water articulates as "Christian rules." "And the first rule," he says, "is that no one can help me. The second rule is that no one can tell me anything. Third, no one is allowed to be in two places at once. Except me." The Old Woman, Coyote, and the narrator offer an alternative to this organization of experience, which doesn't quite erase the sublime sacred of manger and miracle, but weaves it into the world and makes it as ordinary as a woman singing and soothing, as kind as gentle mockery of both self-important religiosity and unspoken literariness, as enlightening as repeated storytelling as opposed to momentary revelations, in a world where magic is as usual and ordinary as relations (the Old Woman says to the Young Man Walking on Water, "You are acting as though you have no relations").

The postmodern, at its best, asserts relationships where strict separations had organized the good and great achievements of the Enlightenment and had hidden its costs and its crimes. Great among the costs of Enlightenment modernity was its thorough-going secularism – existing under such terms and concepts as "realism," "naturalism," and "disinterested" truthfulness. The ideals of modernity – including its secular distrust of "superstition," its worry over revelation, its trust and hope in human and worldly harmonies – should not be abandoned too easily, and, as we say, at its best, the postmodern preserves and reorganizes modernity in the same way that King's and Coyote's and the Old Woman's narrative preserves and reorganizes both the sublime miracles and the everyday goodwill of the Christian story.

The image we present at the opening of Part I of this book, Andy Warhol's *Details of Renaissance Paintings*, and the placing of that image alongside Leonardo da Vinci's *The Annuciation*, emphasize this aspect of postmodernism that we hope King's epigraph gathers up. Here Warhol is drawing from art history to re-present and comment upon a popular Renaissance painting. According to Jane Dillenberger, "Warhol's manipulation of the Renaissance paintings was through radical cropping, so that the subject matter of the original is all but unreadable. In addition, the subtle and darker palette of the Renaissance masters is replaced by a cacophony of Day-Glo colors that assault and delight the eyes" (1998:48). Nature takes on different hues, the ornate furniture and landscaping lose their rich detail, and all that remains of the elaborate clothing is a trace of sleeve on Mary's arm. The copy is in some ways a tracing of the past; could anyone play these mostly hidden actors? The scene retains a sense of the mysterious; Warhol provides the center, and viewers must fill in the margins. Warhol's copy erases the angelic and virginal bodies; all that remains are their hands. Gabriel gives a blessing (presumably along with other things), and Mary rests her hand on her book, using her fingers to mark a page. Warhol features the book prominently; Mary as postmodern reader has been interrupted and a new, additional "text" inserted.

Warhol's painting offers the postmodern image – the postmodern sublime – while the attachment of the "rereading" of what came before offers an example of the postmodern "reorganization" of the sublime and the ordinary we are describing, the "same" image used twice. The Bible and its stories are part of our world, our postmodern world. And their reorganization and preservation in the selections of *The Postmodern Bible Reader*, in terms of the postmodern discourse, politics, ethics, and anagogic apprehensions we have described in the "short course," through the not quite present texts we have pursued in this Introduction, may well serve, we hope, to find place for them in our experience and understanding in the new century.

Bibliography

Attridge, Derek, Geoff Bennington, and Robert Young, eds. 1987. *Post-Structuralism and the Question of History*. New York: Cambridge University Press.

Austin, J. L. 1960. *How to Do Things with Words*. Cambridge, MA: Harvard University Press.

Barnstone, Willis. 1993. *The Poetics of Translation: History, Theory, Practice*. New Haven: Yale University Press.

Barthes, Roland. 1974. *S/Z*. Trans. Richard Miller. New York: Hill and Wang.

Benhabib, Seyla, Judith Butler, Drucilla Cornell, and Nancy Fraser. 1995. *Feminist Contentions: A Philosophical Exchange*. New York/London: Routledge.

Benjamin, Walter. 1969. "The Task of the Translator." In *Illuminations*. Trans. Harry Zohn. New York: Schocken Books, pp. 69–83.

Bible and Culture Collective. 1995. *The Postmodern Bible*. New Haven: Yale University Press.

Blanchot, Maurice. 1986. "A Primal Scene?" In *The Writing of the Disaster*. Trans. Ann Smock. Lincoln: University of Nebraska Press.

Bloom, Harold. 1975. *Kabbalah and Criticism*. New York: Seabury Press.

Boer, Roland. 1996. *Jameson and Jeroboam*. Atlanta: Scholars Press.

Boyarin, Daniel. 1994. *A Radical Jew: Paul and the Politics of Identity*. Berkeley: University of California Press.

Butler, Judith. 1987. *Subjects of Desire: Hegelian Reflections in Twentieth Century France*. New York: Columbia University Press.

—— 1990/1999. *Gender Trouble: Feminism and the Subversion of Identity*. New York/London: Routledge.

——. 1992. "Contingent Foundations: Feminism and the Question of the 'Postmodern.'" In *Feminists Theorize the Political*. Ed. Judith Butler and Joan W. Scott. New York/London: Routledge, pp. 3–21. [Also in Benhabib et al. 1995, pp. 35–57.]

——. 1993. *Bodies that Matter: On the Discursive Limits of "Sex"*. New York/London: Routledge.

——. 1997a. *The Psychic Life of Power: Theories of Subjection*. Stanford: Stanford University Press.

——. 1997b. *Excitable Speech: A Politics of the Performative*. New York/London: Routledge.

Butler, Judith, John Guillory, and Kendall Thomas. 1999. *What's Left of Theory?: New Work on the State and Politics of Literary Theory*. New York/London: Routledge.

Butler, Judith, Ernesto Laclau, and Slavoj Žižek. 2000. *Contingency, Hegemony, Universality: Contemporary Dialogues on the Left*. London: Verso.

Carrett, Jeremy, ed. *Religion and Culture: Michel Foucault*. 1999. New York: Routledge.

Castelli, Elizabeth. 1991. *Imitating Paul: A Discourse of Power*. Louisville: Westminster/John Knox Press.

Cohen, Sande. 1986. *Historical Culture. On the Recoding of an Academic Discipline*. Berkeley: University of California Press.

Crimp, Douglas. 1980. "The Photographic Activity of Postmodernism." *October 15*, pp. 91–101.

De Certeau, Michel. 1988. *The Writing of History*. Trans. Tom Conley. New York: Columbia University Press.

De Man, Paul. 1986. *The Resistance to Theory*. Minneapolis: University of Minnesota Press.

Derrida, Jacques. 1985a. "Des Tours de Babel." In *Difference in Translation*. Trans. and ed. Joseph F. Graham. Ithaca: Cornell University Press. [Also in *Semeia 54*.]

——. 1985b. *The Ear of the Other*. Trans. Peggy Kamuf and Avital Ronell. New York: Schocken Books.

Dillenberger, Jane Daggatt. 1998. *The Religious Art of Andy Warhol*. New York: Continuum.

Eco, Umberto. 1995. *The Search for the Perfect Language*. Trans. James Fentress. Cambridge, MA: Blackwell.

Ermarth, Elizabeth. 1983. *Realism and Consensus in the English Novel*. Princeton: Princeton University Press.

Felman, Shoshana. 1983. *The Literary Speech Act: Don Juan with J.L. Austin, or Seduction in Two Languages*. Trans. Catherine Porter. Ithaca: Cornell University Press.

Foucault, Michel. 1977. "Histories of Systems of Thought." In *Language, Counter-memory, Practice: Selected Essays and Interviews*. Ed. Donald F. Bouchard. Trans. Donald F. Bouchard and Sherry Simon. Ithaca: Cornell University Press, pp. 199–204.

——. 1981. "The Order of Discourse." Trans. Ian McLeod. In *Untying the Text: A Poststructuralist Reader*. Ed. Robert Young. London: Routledge & Kegan Paul, pp. 48–78.

——. 1987. "Maurice Blanchot: The Thought from the Outside." In *Foucault/Blanchot*. New York: Zone Books.

——. 1990. *The History of Sexuality, Volume 1*. Trans. Robert Hurley. New York: Vintage Books.

Genette, Gérard. 1982. *Figures of Discourse*. Trans. A. Sheridan. Ithaca: Cornell University Press.

Ingarden, Roman. 1973. *The Literary Work of Art*. Trans. George G. Grabowicz. Evanston: Northwestern University Press.

Jameson, Fredric. 1981. *The Political Unconscious: Narrative as a Socially Symbolic Act*. Ithaca: Cornell University Press.

——. 1991. *Postmodernism: The Cultural Logic of Late Capitalism*. Durham: Duke University Press.

Jenkins, Keith. 1995. *On "What is History"? From Carr and Elton to Rorty and White*. London/New York: Routledge.

——. 1997. *The Postmodern History Reader*. London/New York: Routledge.

Jobling, David, and Tina Pippin, eds. 1992. "Ideological Criticism of Biblical Texts." *Semeia 59*.

Kansteiner, Wulf. 1993. "Hayden White's Critique of the Writing of History." *History and Theory* 32: 273–95.

Kauffman, Linda. 1998. *Bad Girls and Sick Boys: Fantasies in Contemporary Art and Culture*. Berkeley: University of California Press.

Kellner, Hans. 1989. *Language and Historical Representation. Getting the Story Crooked*. Madison: University of Wisconsin Press.

Latour, Bruno. 1993. *We Have Never Been Modern*. Trans. Catherine Porter. Cambridge, MA: Harvard University Press.

Louw, J. P. 1982. *Semantics of New Testament Greek*. Philadelphia/Chico, CA: Fortress Press/ Scholars Press.

Lyotard, Jean-François. 1984a. *The Postmodern Condition: A Report on Knowledge*. Trans. Geoff Bennington and Brian Massumi. Minneapolis: University of Minnesota Press.

——. 1984b. "Answering the Question: What is Postmodernism?" Trans. Régis Durand. In 1984a, pp. 71–82.

——. 1992. "Note on the Meaning of 'Post-'" In *The Postmodern Explained: Correspondence 1982–1985*. Minneapolis: University of Minnesota Press, pp. 64–8.

Metahistory: Six Critiques. 1980. *History and Theory* XIX, Beiheft 19. Wesleyan University Press.

Mirzoeff, Nicholas. 1995. *Bodyscape: Art, Modernity and the Ideal Figure*. London/New York: Routledge.

Moore, Stephen. 1994. *Poststructuralism and the New Testament: Derrida and Foucault at the Foot of the Cross*. Minneapolis: Fortress Press.

Nida, Eugene, and Charles R. Taber. 1982. *The Theory and Practice of Translation*. Leiden: E. J. Brill.

Pippin, Tina. 1999. *Apocalyptic Bodies: The Biblical End of the World in Text and Image*. London/New York: Routledge.

Quine, Willard Van Orman. 1960. *Word and Object*. Cambridge, MA: MIT Press.

Rorty, Richard, 1979. *Philosophy and the Mirror of Nature*. Princeton: Princeton University Press.

Schleifer, Ronald. 2000. *Modernism and Time: The Logic of Abundance in Literature, Science, and Culture 1880–1930*. Cambridge: Cambridge University Press.

Smarr, Janet Levarie, ed. 1993. *Historical Criticism and the Challenge of Theory*. Urbana: University of Illinois Press.

Stanford, Michael. 1986. *The Nature of Historical Knowledge*. Oxford: Basil Blackwell.

Steiner, George. 1975. *After Babel*. New York: Oxford University Press.

Thomas, Brook. 1991. *The New Historicism and Other Old-Fashioned Topics*. Princeton: Princeton University Press.

Veeser, H. Aram, ed. 1989. *The New Historicism*. London/New York: Routledge.

White, Hayden. 1973. *Metahistory: The Historical Imagination in Nineteenth-Century Europe*. Baltimore: Johns Hopkins University Press.

——. 1974. "The Historical Text as Literary Artifact." In White, 1978: 81–100; reprinted in *The Writing of History: Literary Form and Historical Understanding*. Ed. Robert H. Canary and Henry Kozicki. Madison: University of Wisconsin Press, 1978, pp. 41–62.

——. 1978. *Tropics of Discourse: Essays in Cultural Criticism*. Baltimore: Johns Hopkins University Press.

——. 1982/1983. "The Politics of Historical Interpretation: Discipline and De-Sublimation." In *The Politics of Interpretation*. Ed. W. J. T. Mitchell. Chicago: University of Chicago Press, pp. 119–44.

——. 1987. *The Content of the Form*. Baltimore: Johns Hopkins University Press.

——. 1992. "Historical Emplotment and the Problem of Truth." In *Probing the Limits of Representation. Nazism and the "Final Solution"*. Ed. Saul Friedlander. Cambridge, MA: Harvard University Press.

Windschuttle, Keith. 1996. *The Killing of History: How a Discipline is Being Murdered by Literary Critics and Social Theorists*. Paddington, Australia: Macleay Press.

Žižek, Slavoj. 1989. *The Sublime Object of Ideology*. London/New York: Verso.

——. 1991. "The Real and Its Vicissitudes." In *Looking Awry: An Introduction to Jacques Lacan through Popular Culture*. Cambridge, MA: MIT Press, pp. 21–47.

——. 1994. *The Metastases of Enjoyment: Six Essays on Woman and Causality*. London/New York: Verso.

——. 1997. *The Plague of Fantasies*. London/New York: Verso.

———. 1999. *The Ticklish Subject: The Absent Center of Political Ontology.* London/New York: Verso.

———. 2000a. *The Fragile Absolute or, Why is the Christian Legacy Worth Fighting For?* London/New York: Verso.

———. ed. 2000b. *The Fright of Real Tears: The Uses and Misuses of Lacan in Film Theory.* Bloomington: Indiana University Press.

Epigraph: *from* Green Grass, Running Water

Thomas King 1943–

Introduction

Thomas King is one of the most prominent Native writers and scholars living and working in Canada. King, of Cherokee, Greek, and German descent, was raised in California and received his Ph.D. in English literature from the University of Utah in 1986. Much of what he has written since then has been informed by his continued interest in Native oral literature as he explored its importance in his dissertation, "Inventing the Indian: White Images, Native Oral Literature, and Contemporary Native Writers." In addition to oral traditions, the ubiquitous Trickster character, Coyote, also figures prominently in much of King's work. His first novel, *Medicine River* (1990), sees the appearance of Coyote in the guise of the human meddler, Harlen Bigbear. *Green Grass, Running Water* (1993) is the novel in which the epigraph below appears. King edited an anthology of contemporary Canadian Native literature in 1990, *All My Relations*, that included his story "The One About Coyote Going West." *One Good Story, That One*, a collection of short stories, was published in 1993. *A Coyote Columbus Story* (1992) was King's first book for children and was nominated for a Governor General's Award in Canada that year. King has served as Story Editor (1993–4) for the Canadian Broadcasting Company's series "Four Directions" and is the creator and writer of a popular serial for CBC Radio, "The Dead Dog Café Comedy Hour." King's latest novel, *Truth and Bright Water*, was published by Harper *Flamingo* Canada in 1999. Other works by King include *Coyote's Suit* (forthcoming); *Coyote Sings to the Moon* (1998); *An Anthology of Short Fiction by Native Writers in Canada* (1987); and *The Native in Literature: Canadian and Comparative Perspectives* (1987), edited with Helen Hoy and Cheryl Calver. King has served as Chair of the American Indian Studies program at the University of Minnesota, and taught for ten years at the University of Lethbridge. He is currently at the University of Guelph, teaching Native literature and creative writing.

Coyote figures prominently in this excerpt from *Green Grass, Running Water*. Native oral stories as well as written literature often incorporate a Trickster character. Trickster is both creator and destroyer, one who both gives and takes, a character who plays tricks on others and is the subject of others' tricks, one who is both very brilliant and very stupid at the same time – a study in contrasts. King has said, "The trickster is an important figure for Native writers for it allows us to create a particular kind of world in which Judeo-Christian concern with good and evil and order and disorder is replaced with the more Native concern for balance and harmony" (Thomas King, ed. *All My Relations* [Toronto: McClelland & Stewart, 1990], p. xiii). King brings together this Judeo-Christian concern with the Native desire throughout *Green Grass, Running Water*. This title refers to old treaties between the US government and Native nations which often promised land to the Indians "as long as the grass is green and the water runs." King blends various Native, Judeo-Christian and literary stories exposing both the truth and the falsity in each. He presents Christian creation stories from a Native viewpoint, using characters from both Native creation stories and Bible stories to interact with each other, thus presenting the impact that Christianity and a European world view has had on Native cultures.

"Look," says Coyote, "I haven't much time. The old Indians need my help."

"I thought maybe you would like to tell this story," I says. "But if you're too busy, I guess I can do it myself."

"No, no," says Coyote. "I want to do that. I'll just tell it fast."

"Okay," I says. "Just get it right."

"Okay," says Coyote. "Where were we?"

"Well," I says, "Old Woman just fell through that hole into the sky and then she fell into –"

"I know, I know," says Coyote. "A whale!"

"We already had a whale," I says.

"A fiery furnace!" says Coyote.

"No," I says. "Not that either."

"A manger!" says Coyote.

"Nope," I says. "Old Woman doesn't fall into a manger."

"Give me a hint," says Coyote.

"Old Woman falls into the water," I says.

"The water?" says Coyote. "That's it?"

"That's it," I says.

"Okay, okay," says Coyote. "Old Woman falls through the hole, falls through the sky, and falls into the water."

"That's right," I says.

"Great," says Coyote. "What happens next?"

"Well," I says, "Old Woman falls into that water. So she is in that water. So she looks around and she sees –"

"I know, I know," says Coyote. "She sees a golden calf!"

Thomas King, from *Green Grass, Running Water* (Bantam Books, published by arrangement with Houghton Mifflin, 1994; copyright 1993 Thomas King).

"Wrong again," I says.

"A pillar of salt!" says Coyote.

"Nope," I says to Coyote.

"A burning bush!" says Coyote.

"Where do you get these things?" I says.

"I read a book," says Coyote.

"Forget the book," I says. "We've got a story to tell. And here's how it goes."

So Old Woman is floating in the water. And she looks around. And she sees a man. Young man. A young man walking on water.

Hello, says Old Woman. Nice day for a walk.

Yes, it is, says Young Man Walking On Water. I am looking for a fishing boat.

I just got here, says Old Woman. But I'll help you look.

That's very kind of you, says Young Man Walking On Water. But I'd rather do it myself.

Oh, look, says Old Woman. Is that the boat you're looking for over there?

Not if you saw it first, says Young Man Walking On Water.

So there is a boat. A small boat. And there are a bunch of men in that boat. A big bunch. And that boat is rocking back and forth. And those waves are getting higher.

Rock, rock, rock, rock, says that Boat.

Whee, says those Waves. We are getting higher.

Help us! Help us! shout those men.

Pardon me, says Young Man Walking On Water. But I have to rescue my . . . rescue my . . . ah . . .

Factotums? says Old Woman. Civil servants? Stockholders?

You must be new around here, says Young Man Walking On Water. You don't seem to know the rules.

What rules? says Old Woman.

"I know, I know," says Coyote. "Young Man Walking On Water is talking about Christian rules."

"Yes," I says. "That's true."

"Hooray," says Coyote. "I love Christian rules."

Christian rules, says Young Man Walking On Water. And the first rule is that no one can help me. The second rule is that no one can tell me anything. Third, no one is allowed to be in two places at once. Except me.

I was just floating through, says Old Woman.

But you can watch, says Young Man Walking On Water. There's no rule against that.

Well, says Old Woman, that's a relief.

So that you're not confused, says Young Man Walking On Water, I am now going to walk across the water to that vessel. I am going to calm the seas and stop all the agitation.

After that, I will rescue my . . . my . . . ah . . .

Deputies? says Old Woman. Subalterns? Proofreaders?

And they will love me and follow me around.

"That's a really good trick," says Coyote.
  "Yes," I says. "No wonder this world is a mess."
  "Maybe the . . . ah . . . would follow me," says Coyote.
  "Now that's a really scary thought," I says.

So Young Man Walking On Water walks on the water to that Boat. With those men.
  Help us! Help us! says those men.
  And Young Man Walking On Water raises his arms and that one looks at those Waves and that one says, Calm down!
  Stop rocking! He says that to the Boat. Stop rocking!
  But those Waves keep getting higher, and that Boat keeps rocking.
  Help us! says those men. Help us!
  Whee, says those happy Waves.
  Rock, rock, rock, rock, says that Boat.
  Calm down! Stop rocking! Calm down! Stop rocking, says Young Man Walking On Water.
  But that doesn't happen, and those men on that Boat begin to throw up.
  Yuck, says that Boat. Now look what happened.
  Well. Old Woman watches Young Man Walking On Water. She watches him stomp his feet. She watches him yell at those Waves. She watches him shout at that Boat. So, she feels sorry for him. Pardon me, she says. Would you like some help?
  There you go again, says Young Man Walking On Water. Trying to tell me what to do.
  Well, says Old Woman, someone has to. You are acting as though you have no relations. You shouldn't yell at those happy Waves. You shouldn't shout at that jolly Boat. You got to sing a song.
  Sing songs to waves? says Young Man Walking On Water. Sing songs to boats? Say, did I tell you about our Christian rules?
  It's a simple song, says Old Woman. And Old Woman sings her song.
  Boy, says those Waves, that is one beautiful song. We feel real relaxed.
  Yes, says that Boat, it sure is. Maybe I'll take a nap.
  So that Boat stops rocking, and those Waves stop rising higher and higher, and everything calms down.
  Hooray, says those men. We are saved.
  Hooray, says Young Man Walking On Water. I have saved you.
  Actually, says those men, that other person saved us.
  Nonsense, says Young Man Walking On Water. That other person is a woman. That other person sings songs to waves.
  That's me, says Old Woman.
  A woman? says those men. Sings songs to waves? They says that, too.
  That's me, says Old Woman. That's me.
  By golly, says those men. Young Man Walking On Water must have saved us after all. We better follow him around.

Suit yourself, says Old Woman. And that one floats away.

"Not again," says Coyote.

"You bet," I says.

"Hummmm," says Coyote. "All this floating imagery must mean something."

"That's the way it happens in oral stories," I says.

"Hmmmm," says Coyote. "All this water imagery must mean something."

Leonardo da Vinci, *The Annunciation*, 1472. Uffizi, Florence.

Andy Warhol, *Details of Renaissance Paintings* (Leonardo da Vinci, The Annunciation, 1472), screenprint, 1984. The Andy Warhol Foundation for the Visual Arts, Inc./ ARS, New York and DACS, London 2001.

Part I

Rereading the Bible

Introduction

Beyond Enlightenment: Reading and Political Interest

The development of what we earlier called the postmodern "ethos" has had an enormous effect on the manner in which people pursue reading and interpretation of literature, cultural artifacts, sacred texts, and daily life. Postmodernity has emphasized a set of questions in interpretation that have had minor or marginal significance since the advent of Enlightenment canons of authority. Chief among these is the role of the reader himself or herself in relation to understanding and interpretation. As Roland Barthes notes in a very influential essay, "The Death of the Author," "a text's unity lies not in its origin but in its destination" (1977:148). Barthes develops this working assumption out of his life-long work with structural linguistics and semiotics, and his assertion that a text's unity is best measured in relation to its reader rather than its writer takes its place within this larger work. In his structuralist analysis of Acts 10–11 in this section, he repeats this working assumption by noting that "we include in the language of narrative the way in which we, in our situation as modern readers, receive the narrative"(69). More specifically, A. J. Greimas – who introduced Barthes to linguistics when they were both teaching in Cairo after World War II – repeats Barthes' assertion when he describes the great tradition of structural linguistics developed by Ferdinand de Saussure early in the twentieth century as "a linguistics of perception and not of expression" (1962/63; cited in Schleifer, 1987:xix).

The kind of transformation of understanding Greimas is describing in structural linguistics takes its place among the many twentieth-century phenomena that created a kind of "Copernican Revolution" in understanding and interpretation. In many ways psychoanalysis shifts understanding from origin to destination (certainly in many of Freud's central concepts such as the "drive," "transference," and the "unconscious" itself). Our selection from Jacques Lacan (see our discussion of Lacanian modes of reading in relation to Slavoj Žižek in the General Introduction) and, in a very different register, Hélène Cixous' articulation of dreams, offer two modes of psychoanalytic reading from the vantage point of the subject who is "destined" by the psychic forces, rather than being their voluntary source.

A strong sense of the "interests" that readers bring to understanding – the "politics of interpretation" which Mieke Bal describes, as well as the more varied politics of reading we present in Part II – can also be seen as a result of this postmodern reorientation of understanding. Thus, virtually *all* the texts we have collected in *The Postmodern Bible Reader* present versions of "political" reading. Such readings are "interested" rather than disinterested: they see knowledge tied up with power and, by their very existence, make a claim on the world. The "local" politics of a concern for gender in both Bal and Cixous – what Donna Haraway calls the "situated knowledges" of postmodern feminism – is an instance (which is more than simply an example since it inhabits all species of postmodernism) of readings which have a stake in their subject-matter; for feminism does not "forget" or "bracket" or "erase" the situation and concerns of the reader in her or his attempts to capture the meaning of a text. Similarly, other "local" politics of race, class, and specific political struggles are interested in this way and make such interests – as opposed to the traditional, Enlightenment assumption of the "disinterested" knowledge and art – part and parcel of interpretation. "There must be," Edward Said writes in an important essay entitled "The Politics of Knowledge," "it seems to me, a theoretical presumption that in matters having to do with human history and society any rigid theoretical ideal, any simple additive or mechanical notion of what is or is not factual, must yield to the central factor of human work, the actual participation of people in the making of human life" (1998:159). He goes on to say that "this kind of human work, which is intellectual work, is worldly, that it is situated in the world, and about that world" (1998:160) and that it is engaged with culture in an "unprovincial, interested manner" (1998:164).

If this is a "local" politics, then the "global" politics of what has been called the "New Historicism" in literary studies – the examination of aesthetic texts with constant reference to the historical and cultural circumstances in which they are imbricated and out of which they emerged – can itself be seen as a manifestation of the redirection of attention that Barthes is describing. The intellectual project of "post-Newtonian" sciences of the twentieth century – specifically in the "retrospective" understanding that Werner Heisenberg, for instance, describes in the "new physics" of quantum theory – similarly redirects attention in a way that makes the "destiny" rather than the "origin" of phenomena a touchstone for the understanding of the world. Finally, the re-emphasis on *ethics* in relation to both feeling and understanding – as in Emmanuel Levinas's assertion that "man's ethical relation to the other is ultimately prior to his ontological relation to himself . . . or to the totality of things that we call the world" (1986:21) – resituates *value* in relation to its future (its consequences) rather than its past (its cause).

All of these modes of reading texts – emphasizing textuality, politics, and ethics – which the essays of *The Postmodern Bible Reader* pursue participate in the modes of *rereading* implicated in the transformation from modern to postmodern. They participate in the transformation of the received organization of Enlightenment thinking as clear and distinct realms of reason, aesthetics, and ethics – best exemplified, as we mentioned in the General Introduction, in Kant's organization of philosophy in relation to knowledge (*The Critique of Pure Reason*), art (*The Critique of Judgment*), and value (*The Critique of Practical Reason*) – into a kind of "post-Enlightenment" ethos. In this new ethos, interests as well as disinterestedness matter, and these interests cross boundaries and confuse the impersonality of reason, the seeming transcendental subjectivity of aesthetics, and the practical interests of ethics. As we noted earlier, Bruno Latour, in his book *We Have Never Been Modern*, pursues this disentanglement of the Enlightenment project – or rather, he pursues its further "entanglement" insofar as (he argues) the basic blindness of Enlightenment modernity was the assumption of the separation of disinterested knowledge, interchangeable subjectivity, and interested politics (see also our selection from Serres, in reaction to whom Latour works out his position).

Reading, Literary Criticism, and Literary Theory

In Part I, "Rereading the Bible," the essays focus most sharply on the Bible as a text to be read and on how the Bible has been *witnessed* by those who are its "destiny" rather than its "origin." This issue of "witnessing" is vital to contemporary modes of reading that have developed – mostly in secular literary criticism and literary theory – since the 1980s. Such witnessed readings, as we have already suggested, focus on language, psychology, politics, and – as in Levinas's concern with "ontology" – on larger questions of metaphysics (such as the "metaphysics" of theology to which Barthes refers in his selection here). The heart of this transformation of critical reading is the phenomenon of witnessing, as we are now better able to see a generation after Greimas described Saussurean linguistics as a "linguistics of perception," and after Barthes taught us to seek unity in "destination" rather than origin.

The kinds of postmodern reading we are talking about – and which are presented more or less self-consciously in this section – have gone under the name of "literary theory." Theory, Paul de Man has argued (1997:105), arises when the focus of reading turns from the intentions governing discourse – the more or less conscious aims and goals of "originating" authors – to the linguistic functioning of language outside such intentionality. This is clear in one of the earliest uses of the term "theory" for studying verbal art in the United States. In 1949, W. K. Wimsatt asserted that the semantic basis of literary art was too broad to be encompassed within the study of aesthetics and required its own study in what he called "literary theory." (This and the following paragraphs are adapted from Schleifer, 2000:97–103.)

"Literary theorists of our day," Wimsatt argued, "have been content to say little about 'beauty' or about any over-all aesthetic concept. In his most general formulation the literary theorist is likely to be content with something like 'human interest'" even though "disinterestedness, we remember, is something that Kant made a character of art" (1954:228). In the same year, 1949, Northrop Frye called for the "scientific" study of literature in his essay "The Function of Criticism at the Present Time" which many have likened to a "structuralist" understanding of literature. In both of these cases, "theory" was an attempt to replace the aesthetic focus on the disinterested affectiveness of art by focusing, to whatever degree, on the relationship between literary meaning and the "human interest" apprehended by readers.

In this definition, Wimsatt's term *theory* is tied up with the problem of knowledge conceived as the object of disinterested scientific investigation. Jürgen Habermas describes this problem in narrating the origin of the term *theory*. "The *theoros*," he notes, "was the representative sent by Greek cities to public celebrations. Through *theoria*, that is through looking on, he abandoned himself to the sacred events. In philosophical language, *theoria* was transferred to contemplation of the cosmos" (1971:301). Habermas goes on to oppose this "scientific" conception of theory to its use in the non-scientific discourses of the "historical-hermeneutic" sciences, where theory contemplates meaning and not facts provided by observation (1971:306–8). By opposing facts and meaning, Habermas is erasing a crucial aspect of the work of the *theoroi*, who were a collective, *collaborative* entity. As Wlad Godzich has argued,

> the act of looking at, of surveying, designated by *theorein* does not designate a private act carried out by a cogitating philosopher but a very public one with important social consequences. The Greeks designated certain individuals...to act as legates on certain formal occasions in other city states or in matters of considerable political importance. These individuals bore the title of *theoros*, and collectively constituted a *theoria*. (It may be useful to bear in mind that the word is always a plural collective.) (1986:xiv)

Their work, Godzich goes on to argue, was to bear witness for the community, to transform the private perception – the *"aesthesis"* of "the individual citizen, indeed even women, slaves, and children [all of whom] were capable of aesthesis, that is perception [which had] no social standing" – into a social and institutional fact. "Between the event and its entry into public discourse," Godzich concludes, "there is a mediating instance invested with undeniable authority by the polity. This authority effects the passage from the seen to the told" (1986:xv).

The usefulness of Godzich's emphasis on the communal and non-visual nature of "theory" is particularly important for readings of the Bible. In this section, both Lacan and Bal distinguish between the apparent self-evidence of sight and the mediations of discourses; and there is a significant tradition of distinguishing between Greek eye and Hebrew ear in understanding classical epic (see Auerbach, 1957). For Godzich talking about reading as "theory," the social nature of understanding and apprehension is defined in the way that the private self-evidences of sight – of *aesthetics* – are *instituted* as public discourses of knowledge: witnessing expands its significance from the private, disinterested act of seeing to the public, interested act of telling (see also Jay, 1993:30–2, 55). The apprehension of private experience as social fact emphasizes the categories of "constative" and "performative" aspects of language developed by the speech-act theorist J. L. Austin (which Terry Eagleton examines and uses in Part II of our *Reader*). Literary theory in general does this, as do the essays in this section by Hillis Miller and Mieke Bal.

The complex conception of theory as the contemplation and discursive articulation of meaning – what we want to describe as witnessed knowledge (Schleifer, 2000) – is congruent with Wimsatt's "literary theory" and Frye's argument that criticism should take its place among the social sciences. That is, theory examines understanding outside of categories of aesthetic subjectivity. For this reason Hillis Miller, in his Presidential Address to the Modern Language Association in 1986, defines "theory" as

> the displacement in literary studies from a focus on the meaning of texts to a focus on the ways meaning is conveyed. Put another way, theory is the use of language to talk about language. Put yet another way, theory is a focus on referentiality as a problem rather than as

something that reliably and unambiguously relates a reader to the "real world" of history, of society, and of people acting within society on the stage of history. (Miller, 1987:283)

As Godzich argues, this understanding of theory "forces a recognition of the incompatibility of language and intuition. [And] since the latter constitutes the foundational basis of cognition upon which perception, consciousness, experience, and the logic and the understanding, not to mention the aesthetics that are attendant to them, are constructed, there results a wholesale shakeout in the organization and conceptualization of knowledge" (1986:x). This "shakeout," as Frank Lentricchia describes it, makes "theory... primarily a *process* of discovery of the lesson that I am calling historical" (1985:108): it historicizes meaning (as it is found in language and reading), interpersonal activity (as it is found in politics), and value (as it is found in ethics and the metaphysics of ethics).

The Bible is a primary and important text for these historicized readings precisely because of its place in our culture and its function as the intersection of impersonal knowledge, personal experience, and transpersonal community. That is, the two senses of "witnessing" gather up two directions to which the Bible, particularly the New Testament, points. On the one hand, the Bible offers a guide and a site for the *personal* relationship of the human subject to sacred and supernatural power. Both Christian and Jew *witness* this relationship with the self-evidence of *immediate* and *personal* apprehension, the "intuition" Godzich mentions. In an unpublished talk, Barbara Ryan called such witnessing "evangelical testimony": testimony which is beyond dispute because personal experience is beyond dispute. The philosopher of science, Thomas Kuhn, describes this succinctly when he examines "sensation reports," which are "matters of taste [and so] are undiscussible" (1977:336). Such reports are, in biblical terms, *revelation*: immediate, personal apprehension of the truth and power of the sacred. And such revelation is closely tied to the Bible's efficacy in relation to *personal salvation*, even when that salvation is conceived as worldly rather than heavenly. The Bible witnesses the revealed truth and situates its reader in a position to witness the truth by means of "*aesthesis*" – private perception with "no social standing" – of "the individual citizen, indeed even women, slaves, and children" (Godzich, 1986:xv).

But the Bible also witnesses in the second sense that Godzich finds in the etymology of *theory*: it constitutes the community, Jewish or Christian, as a site for the discursive and social realization and enactment of its truth (now conceived as ethics, rather than – or along with – knowledge and power). In this setting, "salvation" is plural and communal, and can *only* be realized in modes of worldliness. In more abstract terms it is the "judgment" Kuhn opposes to the "taste" of personal sensation – personal revelation – precisely because judgments *can* be discussed in communities of (interested) speakers and listeners. If I report I did not enjoy a movie, Kuhn argues, there is no discussion; but if I judge that it was "a pot boiler," my judgment can be argued and discussed (1977:336–7; see also Schleifer et al., 1992:11–21 for an extended discussion of this opposition in relation to cognition). Kuhn's second "witnessing" – the act of judgment that necessarily takes place, dialogically, in public, and which Ryan more aptly describes as "forensic" as opposed to "evangelical" testimony – allows us to apprehend the Bible as a vehicle for mediation and community – a vehicle *of* mediation and community – whose interpretations are repeatedly subject to debate and renewal in changing historical conditions. Such contestation, debate, and renewal – and the always possible failure of renewal in despair – are, as we have suggested in the General Introduction, a hallmark of the postmodern.

Language and Reading

Theory begins, de Man argues (1997:104–5), in resituating texts – both secular and sacred – in the context of "non-phenomenal linguistics," by which he means a formal or "structural" linguistics. The first two essays of Part I, Umberto Eco's "On the Possibility of Generating Aesthetic Messages in an Edenic Language" and Roland Barthes' "The Structural Analysis of Narrative: Apropos of Acts 10–11," in many ways set the parameters for the kinds of postmodern reading of biblical texts presented throughout this book. Eco uses the Bible as a starting point for his own concern – the careful modeling of a semiotic analysis of aesthetic phenomena – while Barthes focuses on the Bible itself and gives a detailed structuralist reading of the *text*. Both of these analyses focus on the reader as the text's "destiny," but in Eco's essay that destiny is extra-biblical, while for Barthes it lies within the framework of the Bible itself. It is as if Eco's project is "global," assuming that the stories from the Bible are part and parcel of our cultural inheritance and thus a *starting place* for understanding, while Barthes' project is "local," aiming to "unpack" the ways in which we must learn "how to read . . . corporately, differently, in a way that is appropriate for our time and place" (PMB:16).

These two essays set the parameters of what follows in other ways as well. Eco focuses on a Hebrew Bible account, or rather a Hebrew Bible *situation*, while Barthes examines a text from the New Testament. Eco brings together aesthetics, linguistics, theology, and culture in an attempt to model semiotic coding on the level of words, while Barthes assembles various "levels" and "codes" of discourse in order to produce a "narrative grammar." Finally, with irony and humor Eco *tells another story* of the Bible that includes God's "rashness" (84), Adam's creativity, and a whole new context in which to understand the Fall – rereading in the sense of retelling – while Barthes, with high seriousness, tells the very story of Acts in order to account for the *possibilities of meaning* it presents. Even so, both return – more explicitly than any other selections in the *Reader* – to the vocabulary of linguistics in their postmodern readings of the Bible.

Both Barthes' *structuralist* reading and Eco's *semiotic* reading grow out of the great advances in linguistics initiated by Ferdinand de Saussure in the early decades of the twentieth century (for the following discussion, see also PMB: chap. 2). Above all, Saussurean linguistics attempted to develop a *scientific* method for understanding social meanings in general and narrative meaning in particular. Its great ambition, as Barthes says, is to "react against the impression of obviousness, against the it-goes-without-saying aspect of what is written," the self-evidence and *naturalness* of meaning. (This is part of what Godzich means by "intuition.") That is, they both react against the Edenic innocence of unselfconscious reading, the blissful ignorance of "such subtleties" as Eco describes them. Eco *narrates* this resistance to the innocent self-evidence of meaning as Adam's fall, as his experience that language begins "to crumble to pieces in his mouth."

Eco and Barthes pursue the logic and persuasiveness of science rather than affect, and their essays follow the reading of a linguistic-based interpretation. In this, they are following Saussurean linguistics. (Saussure is of utmost importance also to Lacan and Kristeva, whose work appears later in this section. A significant aspect of Lacan's rereading of psychoanalysis is to bring together Freud's work with that of Saussure: one of Lacan's most famous pronouncements is that "the unconscious is structured like a language," and in our selection he is very much concerned with the "voice" of the other. But Lacan and Kristeva are more on the affective side.) At the beginning of the twentieth century Saussure reconceived the study of linguistics by reorienting the kinds of questions linguists asked. Instead of asking where particular linguistic formations came from, their history and cause as these were studied by the etymological and "diachronic" linguistic methods of nineteenth-century linguistics, he asked how the elements of language are *configured* in order to produce effects. In other words, Saussure replaced the "diachronic" study of language through time, the study of the *development* of language, with the "synchronic" study of the particular formation of language *at a particular moment*. As Greimas notes, this reorients the study of language from the "expression" of an originating speaker or meaning to the "perception" of meaning by its "destined" reader. It also reconceives language as an apprehension – an intelligible *form* that is apprehended – rather than a positive fact or artifact. As Saussure himself notes in the *Course in General Linguistics*, every element of linguistic science, and of language as well, is "*a form, not a substance.*"

From the structuralist assumption of the formal nature of linguistic elements come the crucial, reorienting assumptions that govern the semiotics and structuralism represented here by Eco and Barthes. (1) Saussure's formal or "structural" linguistics suggests that the nature of linguistic elements is *relational* and that the entities of language are a product of relationship: as Eco demonstrates here, it is the *relation* between elements that presents the elementary structure of the code. For Barthes as well, the "principle of formalization" is the first principle of analysis. The first great relational definition in Saussurean linguistics is the relationship between the *signified* and the *signifier* that constitute the linguistic *sign*. The "signified" is the meaning or import – what Louis Hjelmslev (1961) calls the "purport" – of language. The "signifier" is the vehicle of that meaning, and they are in a relationship of "reciprocal presupposition": one cannot exist without the other. Two things should be added about this basic element of language, the sign. (a) The "signifier" is not simply a material *thing*, such as sound-producing wavelengths of air. Rather, it is, as Saussure says, a "sound image," by which he means a *formal arrangement that is apprehended in its formality*. Modern linguistics, following Saussure, calls these signifying elements the "phonemes" of language, as opposed to the physical sounds or "phones." (b) Hjelmslev, in his systematic account of Saussurean linguistics, further refines the terminology into the dual opposition of content/expression (signified/signifier) and form/substance (phoneme/phone) so that he can distinguish between the *level* of the articulation of meaning and the *level* of the articulation of signifiers. This is the background for certain phrases in both Eco and Barthes, for example "*content-form.*"

(2) Saussurean formalism further assumes, as Adam perceives in his great revelation, the *arbitrary* nature of the linguistic sign. Since it is the relationships rather than the

"elements" of a system of language that are crucial – since such basic elements as signs, signifiers, and even the meaningful signifieds are *formal* entities – all the elements of language could be different from what they are. Implicit in this assumption is that language takes whatever material is at hand in order to create its meanings and communication. Eco narrates this in the ways that Adam and Eve apprehend more or less accidental changes in the code as meaningful, as "significant forms."

(3) The third assumption of structural linguistics is that of the *synchronic* method of study that refuses to seek explanations in terms of cause and effect, seeking them rather in terms of function and activity. Formal relationships are simultaneous rather than sequential; thus, Barthes argues "we must read Sophocles as a citation of Freud; and Freud as a citation of Sophocles." When the destiny rather than the origin is the site of meaning, such synchronicity is, in fact, necessary: to use a figure Freud develops in *The Wolf Man*, all meaning is "deferred" to the always present moment of apprehension.

(4) Finally, Saussurean formalism suggests the *double nature* of language and linguistic elements. Not only is the linguistic sign an intrinsically double combination of a signified and a signifier; language itself globally conceived (Saussure's *langage*) also has the double aspect of actual speech (*parole*) and the underlying system (*langue*) – the order or *structure* that allows the particulars to manifest themselves as speech. (Barthes is citing this last reciprocal opposition when he describes "the Saussurian opposition of *language* and *speech*.")

As Saussure himself has said, "the absolutely final law of language is, we dare say, that there is nothing which can ever reside in *one* term, as a direct consequence of the fact that linguistic symbols are unrelated to what they should designate." The fact that French has three words for "language" – *language, parole, langue* – that can only be translated into two terms in English – *speech, language* – demonstrates the arbitrary "articulation" of meaning as well as the arbitrary articulation of words (e.g., the English "speech" for the same meaning as the French "*parole*"). Moreover, this quote from Saussure also contains another description of the formal and relational nature of linguistic elements, the arbitrary nature of the sign, the synchronic mode of understanding language, and the binarity of linguistic elements. It suggests that the items in the ordered list we have presented are relationally and synchronically connected; that their order of presentation has been arbitrary; and that they are governed by binary oppositions.

Structuralism – beginning with Claude Lévi-Strauss's analyses of narrative discourse in the early 1950s in France – self-consciously appropriated the methods of linguistics to study language – and thereby cultural formations – beyond the limits of the sentence. In his analyses of Amerindian myths, for instance, Lévi-Strauss explicitly asserts that the "universe of the tale" is "analyzable in pairs of oppositions interlocked within each character who – far from constituting a single entity – forms a bundle of distinctive features like the phoneme in Roman Jakobson's [linguistic] theory" (1984:182). The French structuralism of the 1960s and early 1970s, in the dissemination of which Barthes is a major figure, has had a huge impact on twentieth-century literary criticism and biblical studies. It has proved to be a watershed in recent modes of reading, causing a major reorientation in literary studies and practices of reading the Bible. Prior to structuralism, literary studies often seemed insular and isolated even in relation to other areas of the humanities such as history, philosophy, and theology. After it, literary criticism has seemed more actively engaged in the discourses of a large variety of different disciplines, a vital participant and in some areas a guide. In fact, by basing its methods on those of linguistics, structuralism helped to transform the traditional "humanities" into what Kristeva refers to as the "human sciences," which "seeks to reveal the universal logic embedded in a myth, a hieratic text, or a poem" (94). At first, the rise of structuralism was greeted with considerable hostility by literary critics and biblical scholars. It was generally acknowledged that this movement was attempting an ambitious, "scientific" examination of literature in all its dimensions. To some, however, the supposed detachment of such an investigation appeared to be offensively anti-humanistic and unrelated to the values of the tradition of Western liberal education and, as Kristeva suggests, to religiosity and the sacred.

Equally notable in retrospect are the ways in which structuralism was transformed, almost immediately in the United States, into simply a step or stage toward a host of critical and cultural programs that can be called "post-structural." As we can see in essays throughout this book – J. Hillis Miller, Terry Eagleton, Jacques Derrida, Elaine Scarry, and even the different strains of feminist reading such as Hélène Cixous, Mieke Bal, and, perhaps, Donna Haraway – rigorous structural analyses form a part of arguments whose aims are very different from the "disinterested" and "scientific" methods of structuralism and semiotics. (This is also clear in our discussion of Michel Foucault in the General Introduction.) Julia Kristeva's article in this section spells out some of the reasons why semiotic analysis seeks out the "irrationality" of the sacred. Its emphasis on perception rather than expression – that is, on the *phenomenology* or "effects" of language, which include affect as well as meaning – easily moves to conceptions of language as a force as well as an understanding. (In a very different register, Miller describes the "logical impossibility" of the functioning of parable in the New Testament; see also our Eagleton selection for a similar impossibility.) The distinction developed by J. L. Austin between language measured in terms of its truthfulness or accuracy in *describing* the world, what he calls the "constative" aspect of language, and language measured in terms of its existence as act, what he call its "performative" aspect, is explicitly repeated in the discussions of Miller and Bal in this section and is implicit in Kristeva and Lacan. Bal describes these categories as the focus of "attention" on "the represented content" of a text or on the text's "mode of representation."

The rise of structuralism and semiotics in the 1960s – and the rise of various "post" structuralisms in the 1970s – vividly dramatize the extent to which postmodern reading has become an interdisciplinary phenomenon. The combination of rigorous structuralism and semiotics – Barthes' high seriousness and Eco's ironic seriousness – continues to constitute a scholarly "field" in itself – the field of semiotics – with intellectual methods, and scholarly journals and conferences. Yet by taking meaning and the varying conditions of meaning as their "objects" of study, they cut through, without being confined to, traditional "humanities" and "social sciences" such as literary studies, philosophy, history, linguistics, psychology, anthropology, and biblical studies, all of which have directly influenced literary theory since the late 1960s. The Bible has a special relationship to structuralism and semiotics precisely because it is a *mythologizing* text, by which we mean it seems less a personal "expression" than many other kinds of texts we encounter. For this reason, it is easier to see its meaning – this is the thrust of Lévi-Strauss's anthropological work on myth in Amerindian cultures – in relation to destination rather than origin. Such reading as "perception" is coded within semiotic analyses themselves: this is the import of Eco's equation of "things" with "the sensations which Adam and Eve are aware of," and of his larger claim that language "segments" more or less undefined experience and "discovers fresh cultural categories (this means new perceptive realities)." It is a short step from this "phenomenology" of meaning to the explicit phenomenological psychologies of Kristeva and Lacan, and to the implicit phenomenology of Cixous' dream narrative reading.

Reading and Affect

Julia Kristeva's essay, "Reading the Bible," focuses upon what Eco only implies in his discussion of the language-code of Adam and Eve and Barthes barely touches upon in his discussion of the "anagogic" interpretation of Acts, the power of language to create its various affects. (Barthes' figure or sign of such power is his discussion of "the possibility of diffusion of baptism" which he calls "the text's content" [76].) Kristeva describes such power as the "sacred" and locates "all texts considered 'sacred' ... [as] borderline states of subjectivity" (95). Hélène Cixous similarly focuses on the "borderline" state of dreaming to examine and articulate the sacred, but Kristeva's essay offers verbal representations rather than a psycholinguistic analysis of such a state. Specifically, Kristeva "reads" the Bible as intimately bound up with "the advent of the subject." Leviticus, she argues,

> speaks to me by locating me at the point where I lose my "clean self." It takes back what I dislike and acknowledges my bodily discomfort, the ups and downs of my sexuality, the compromises or harsh demands of my public life. It shapes the very borders of my defeats, *for it has probed into the ambivalent desire for the other,* for the mother as the first other, *which is at the base, that is, on the other side of that which makes me into a speaking being* (a separating, dividing, joining being). The Bible is a text that thrusts its words into my losses. (96)

Such an understanding – such a *reading* – of the Bible emphasizes the affective power of its language, the ways that, in the metaphor with which Kristeva ends her essay, it turns the seeming cognitive process of understanding and comprehension – the process Eco and Barthes describe as the *perception* of meaning – into the "fire" and "burning" of confronting an "other." In this reading, language confronts the violence of the world: what Jacques Derrida calls, in his early analysis of the work of Emmanuel Levinas, "the worst violence, the violence of primitive and prelogical silence, of an unimaginable night which would not even be the opposite of day, an absolute violence which would not even be the opposite of non-violence: nothingness or pure non-sense" (1978:130), and what Cixous describes as "the violent sense of generations" that the Bible "always brings" (119), and raises its voice against. With "sacred" meaning, Kristeva argues, "you will displace your hatred into thought; you will devise a logic that defends you from murder and madness, a logic whose arbitrary nature shall be your coronation. The Bible offers the best description of this transformation of sacrifice into language, this displacement of murder into a system of meanings" (96).

For Kristeva, then, the meaning of a sacred text elaborates "psychic conflicts that border on psychosis" (98), on the irruption of the irrational – the violence of subject-destroying forces. In this, as she concludes her essay, the Bible has a particular relationship to psychoanalysis. (Kristeva, we should add, is a practicing psychoanalyst.) In this conclusion, her essay points in two directions. It points toward the following essay by Jacques Lacan, which elaborates – almost to the point of "irrationality" – a psychoanalytic vocabulary in reference to the relationship of Abraham and God (for another reading of the same biblical text, Genesis 22, see our selection from Derrida). It also points to the kinds of feminist reading we find in Mieke Bal's discussion of the violent transformation of the woman's body into a cultural signifier in Judges 19–21. Kristeva deals with this transformation in her sketchy discussion – fully elaborated in her book *Powers of Horror* – of the relationship between systems of taboo and the child's relationship to her or his mother. In that book Kristeva argues that the formation of subjectivity entails the separation and delineation of self from other that takes place primarily through what she calls the "abjection" – the objectification, the rejection, and the association with the disgusting – of things related to the maternal body. In the present essay she ends by arguing that if "the force behind faith is the fantasy of returning to the mother" (99), then biblical faith, in its focus on the father, distances us from this religiosity.

Jacques Lacan is also interested in the "advent of the subject," and for him – in a vocabulary that is more explicitly psychoanalytic than Kristeva's – the formation of subjectivity follows patterns of linguistic development in relation to the "Name-of-the-Father." In Lacan's rereading of Freud, the *position* of the father within the family constellation marks the advent of language into experience. The Father interrupts the "imaginary" dyadic relationship between mother and child with the language of Law and prohibition – the very prohibition which leads Kristeva to make Leviticus a central text in her reading of the Bible (for another perspective on divine prohibition, see our selection from Levinas). Like Kristeva, Lacan is committed to erasing the opposition between "intelligence" and "affect." The confusion of intelligence and affect, of the knowledge and power of language – which, as we noted in the General Introduction, is a distinctive feature of the ethos of postmodernity – is the locus of psychoanalytic reading. In his reading Lacan uses the story of Abraham and Isaac to delineate the relationship of language – the Name-of-the-Father – to the advent of desire and subjectivity. Like Bal, he distinguishes between and confuses eye and ear, the double sense of witnessing ("forensic" and "evangelical") which we have discussed. He opposes the knowledge of eye with the power of voice. But behind the whole of his analysis, he defines, more explicit than Kristeva, the power of the sacred as *anxiety*.

Cixous, in her meditation on dreaming of Jacob's ladder, focuses like Kristeva (but unlike Lacan, for whom the mother is particularly *missing* from the Abraham story) on the mother rather than the father. But rather than the vantage point of the child (which governs both Kristeva's and Lacan's reading of the Bible), she assumes that of the mother herself. Without saying so explicitly, she focuses on the relationship between the sacred and writing: "the unconscious tells us a book is a scene of childbirth, delivery, abortion, breast-feeding." "The whole chronicle of childbearing," she concludes, "is in play within the unconscious during the writing period" (123). What is striking about Cixous' discussion is its attempt to demystify religiosity and dream *without* desacralizing them. She is not sure "whether God is inside or outside the dream," and for her such ignorance is not very important: "*The dream scene*," she writes, "was always far more important to me than the scene of revelation" (120). In this she is recapitulating a major aspect of postmodern readings of the Bible: their attempts to recover the sacred in the world without *worrying about* transcendental value or truth (cf. Derrida's "nondogmatic doublet of dogma"). In her dreaming, as in most of the readings we are presenting here, it is difficult to say whether personal salvation – *non-worldly* salvation – is inside or outside the discussion. This is particularly clear in Part II, "The Politics of Reading," where understanding of the Bible focuses on the building of community. But it is also present in the essays in this section and in Part III, "The Conscience of the Bible."

Deconstructive Readings

The last two essays of this section develop the kinds of postmodern readings we have discussed. Hillis Miller pursues a "post-structuralist" reading of parable, focusing on the problematic relationship between sacred and secular parables, and Mieke Bal pursues a feminist reading of Judges 19–21, focusing on the problematic relationship between the intelligibility of narrative and that of vision. In their focus on the *problem* of understanding in relation to binary oppositions – the very oppositions that govern the structures of meaning that Eco and Barthes describe – they are each pursuing what we might call, following the work of Jacques Derrida, "deconstructive" readings of the Bible (see PMB: chap. 3).

"Deconstruction" is a mode of reading defined by Derrida, who in 1967 began to describe a certain rereading of the history of philosophy conditioned, as we argued in the General Introduction, by the demise of canons of Enlightenment "modernity." In sweeping analyses, Derrida noted that embodiments of legitimate authority have traditionally been taken as intuitively self-evident in their absolute "rightness"; for example "goodness," "naturalness," "reason," and "truth." The same is true of more abstract versions of authority such as Derrida himself lists, "*aletheia*, transcendentality, consciousness, or conscience, God, man, and so forth" (1978:280) – all assumed in the West to be self-evident givens of understanding and experience. He also noted that such concepts are necessarily defined in relation to their opposites. Derrida has focused on many such oppositions: the self-evidence of speech (as opposed to writing), the simplicity of "man" (as opposed to gendered individuals), the solidity of "seriousness" (as opposed to playfulness), the profundity of "philosophy" (as opposed to literature), the basic category of "nature" (as opposed to culture). Throughout his career Derrida has attempted to "deconstruct" the self-evidence of such concepts, to subject the very basic assumptions governing the apprehension of knowledge to critical analysis. That attempt involves demonstrating the local and historical nature of seemingly universal concepts. The word "deconstruction" itself is Derrida's coinage in response to the philosopher Martin Heidegger's idea of "destructive" analysis, but it is also a *post-structuralist* response to the binary analyses of structuralism and Saussurean semiotics which assumes the equal and opposite nature of its oppositions (Eco's A versus B).

As it bears on the interpretation of the Bible, deconstruction is a *strategy* of reading. Derrida describes deconstructive reading as starting from a philosophical hierarchy in which two opposed terms necessarily fall into the "superior" general case and the "inferior" special case. These oppositions are Western culture's most important categories of thought, such as truth/error, health/disease, male/female, nature/culture, philosophy/literature, speech/writing, seriousness/play, reason/practice. Miller adds the certainties of sacred parable (mediated by faith)/the uncertainties of secular parable (governed by the unsure authority of performative language); and he adds also the example of language conceived as "constative" (i.e., as essentially a system of true or false meanings) versus language conceived as "performative" (i.e., the actual *activity* of using language). And both Miller and Bal add writing versus reading, or meaning versus language (i.e., the primacy of the text versus the secondariness of the reader, and the absolute separation of the two). Miller describes how the language of parable "contaminates" (138). its readers; Bal describes "the inevitable narrative entanglement of the critic in the text" (145). Another example – as much of the feminist criticism in this book suggests – is the generally accepted use of "man" to mean "human" and "woman" to mean only the special case of a female human being.

Deconstruction isolates such oppositions and points out they are indeed *hierarchically* opposed, general to special case. It then reverses such crucial hierarchies so as to elevate the "inferior" over the "superior" – making, as Miller suggests, the sacred parable a special case of secular parable, or, as Bal suggests, the self-evidence of eye as a special case of the mediations of narrative. The purpose of these reversals, however, is not merely to invert value systems; doing so, Derrida argues, would only "confirm" the old system of opposition which is the object of analysis. Rather, deconstruction attempts to "explode" (in Derrida's metaphor) the original relationship of "superior" and "inferior" which gives rise to the semantic horizon – the possibility of any particular meaning, the possibility of particular "definitions" – in a discourse and a system of apprehended meaning. Deconstruction attempts, as Derrida says in a celebrated early essay, to confront one interpretation "of interpretation, of structure, of sign, of freeplay" – one which seeks "a truth or an origin which is free from freeplay and from the order of the sign" – with another interpretation of interpretation "which is no longer turned toward the origin, [but] affirms freeplay and tries to pass beyond man and humanism" (1978:292).

Most characteristic of deconstructive reading is its two "moves." A deconstructive analysis of a text involves reversing, reinscribing the terms of a hierarchy, and "exploding" that new hierarchy. Current psychoanalytic reading, influenced by Lacan, de-centers the traditional versions of the "subject" – both Cartesian and Freudian – and is distinctly deconstructive in its practice. Feminism, too – here especially in the work of Cixous, Bal, Haraway, and Pathak – uses deconstructive strategies for displacing maleness and "male" readings of literary texts (Pathak even uses deconstructive critique to displace the universalized "female" in feminist criticism). And political critics, especially explicit and implicit "postcolonial" readings (Pathak, Spivak), have found deep affinities between the Marxist and deconstructive critiques of cultural production. All these critics have adopted a deconstructive approach to biblical texts and have attempted from different angles to understand the forces that shape and "rupture" those texts and, at the same time, to recover interested forces that can be occasioned by those texts.

Miller, in our selection, focuses on the rhetoric of reading: on parable as figure that presents and disrupts meaning. Bal is also interested in deconstructing "the separations between 'literal' and 'figurative,' between visual and verbal, along with the acknowledgment of the impossibility of 'pure' meaning – of meaning without force and of 'pure' knowledge, or truth, without the metonymic contamination of its motivated pursuit." Miller glances toward the motivated pursuit of meaning – what we have called the *interests* embedded in the seeming disinterested pursuit of the truth – in his mention of the faith that is at the base of the sacred reading of parable: "believing in the validity of the parables of the New Testament and believing that Jesus is the Son of God are the same thing." But Bal, like the essayists in our other sections, is interested above all in such motivations as *political* acts, in what she calls "the politics of interpretation." Her politics is that of feminism, and she chooses Judges 19–21 in order to examine the ways in which the "literalness" of the woman is silently transformed *by means of violence* into the figurativeness of a sign. "Not only is this woman the object of the body-language of rape, a language that bespeaks her death," she writes; "her body is also subsequently used *as* language by the very man who exposed her to the violence when he sends her flesh off as a message" (151).

Such extreme violence – like the violence of the fall as Eco describes it – transforms the self-evident innocence and immediacy of perceived meaning into *mediated* and interested meaning, into what Bal describes as "ideology." In line with the irrationalities and violence we have encountered in all the essays of this section, from the "crumbling" of Eden in Eco, through the irrationalities of Barthes, Kristeva, and Cixous, to even Kafka's quiet anxiety in Miller, "death," as Bal writes,

> is a challenge to representation to the extent that the experience of death is a moment that nobody can describe, an event that nobody can escape, a process that nobody can narrate. Representation partakes of the attempt to quell the fear of death and to compensate for the loss of identity and material existence death entails. The presentation of death as both gendered and representational, therefore, can shed new light on the diverse aspects of the ideological positions toward gender that texts and images enable their readers to project. (143–4)

Such a sense of ideology – such ideological readings of the Bible – makes all of these essays, including the "scientific" readings of Eco and Barthes and the "rhetorical" reading of Miller, postmodern by means of their focus on the historical rather than the universal. Even death in these essays is presented as a sacred but non-mystical event. For Bal the self-evidence of sight is apprehensible as a narrative and ideological mediation, just as for Miller the self-evident distinction between the sacred and secular is subject to the mode of reading we bring to it. The essays of this section all entail modes of reading: reading language, reading subjectivity, reading rhetoric, reading ideology. Such postmodern rereadings of the Bible have had a powerful effect in recovering meaning, power, and the sacred for the postmodern world.

Related essays in *The Postmodern Bible Reader*

Thomas King, from *Green Grass, Running Water*
Terry Eagleton, "J. L. Austin and the Book of Jonah"
Donna Haraway, "Ecce Homo, Ain't (Ar'n't) I a Woman, and Inappropriate/d Others"
Jacques Derrida, "Whom to Give to (Knowing Not to Know)"

Bibliography

Auerbach, Erich. 1957. *Mimesis*. Trans. Willard Trask. New York: Anchor Books.

Barthes, Roland. 1977. "The Death of the Author." In *Music-Image-Text*. Trans. Stephen Heath. London: Fontana.

De Man, Paul. 1997. "The Resistance to Theory." In *Contemporary Literary Criticism*, fourth edition. Ed. Robert Con Davis and Ronald Schleifer. New York: Longman, pp. 101–14.

Derrida, Jacques. 1978. *Writing and Difference*. Trans. Alan Bass. Chicago: University of Chicago Press.

Frye, Northrop. 1998. "The Function of Criticism at the Present Time." In *Contemporary Literary Criticism*. Ed. Robert Con Davis and Ronald Schleifer. New York: Longman.

Godzich, Wlad. 1986. "Foreword: The Tiger on the Paper Mat." In Paul de Man, *The Resistance to Theory*. Minneapolis: University of Minnesota Press, pp. ix–xviii.

Habermas, Jürgen. 1971. "Knowledge and Human Interests: Perspective." In *Knowledge and Human Interests*. Trans. Jeremy Shapiro. Boston: Beacon Press.

Hjelmslev, Louis. 1961. *Prolegomena to a Theory of Language*. Trans. Francis Whitfield. Madison: University of Wisconsin Press.

Jay, Martin. 1993. *Downcast Eyes: The Denigration of Vision in Twentieth-Century French Thought*. Berkeley: University of California Press.

Kuhn, Thomas. 1977. *The Essential Tension*. Chicago: University of Chicago Press.

Lentricchia, Frank. 1985. "On Behalf of Theory." In *Criticism in the University*. Ed. Gerald Graff and Reginald Gibbons. Evanston: Northwestern University Press, pp. 105–10.

Levinas, Emmanuel. 1986. *Face to Face with Levinas*. Ed. R. A. Cohen. Albany: State University of New York Press.

Lévi-Strauss, Claude. 1984. "Structure and Form: Reflections on a Work by Vladimir Propp." Trans. Monique Layton, rev. Anatoly Liberman. In Vladimir Propp, *Theory and History of Folklore*. Minneapolis: University of Minnesota Press, pp. 167–89.

Miller, J. Hillis. 1987. "The Triumph of Theory, the Resistance to Reading, and the Question of the Material Base." *PMLA* 102:281–91.

Said, Edward. 1998. "The Politics of Knowledge." In *Contemporary Literary Criticism*. Ed. Robert Con Davis and Ronald Schleifer. New York: Longman, pp. 157–65.

Schleifer, Ronald. 1987. *A. J. Greimas and the Nature of Meaning*. Lincoln: University of Nebraska Press.

——— 2000. *Analogical Thinking: Post-Enlightenment Understanding of Language, Collaboration, and Interpretation*. Ann Arbor: University of Michigan Press.

Schleifer, Ronald, Robert Con Davis, and Nancy Mergler. 1992. *Culture and Cognition*. Ithaca: Cornell University Press.

Wimsatt, W. K. 1954. "The Domain of Criticism." In *The Verbal Icon*. Lexington: University of Kentucky Press.

Chapter 1

The Structural Analysis of Narrative: Apropos of Acts 10–11

Roland Barthes 1915–1980

Introduction

At the time of his death in 1980, from injuries caused by a hit-and-run accident, Roland Barthes was Professor at the Collège de France in Paris. Although he was best known as a semiotician and student of literature, Barthes' interests ranged widely and included music, fashion, photography, and popular culture. His interest in ideology ("mythologies") and sociocultural dimensions of meaning both contrasts with and complements the more psychoanalytic orientation of poststructuralist scholars such as Jacques Derrida, Jacques Lacan, and Barthes' student, Julia Kristeva. His major books (with French publication and English translation dates) include: *Writing Degree Zero* (1953/1967); *Mythologies* (1957/1972); *Elements of Semiology* (1964/1967); *S/Z* (1970/1974); *The Empire of Signs* (1970/1982); *The Pleasure of the Text* (1973/1975); *Camera Lucida* (1980/1981); *The Rustle of Language* (1984/1986); and *The Semiotic Challenge* (1985/1988).

Barthes wrote two essays on biblical texts. The fairly well-known "The Struggle with the Angel: Textual Analysis of Genesis 32:23–33" (1972/1974, reprinted as "Wrestling with the Angel" in *The Semiotic Challenge*) is discussed in *The Postmodern Bible* (131–5). The essay reprinted here, "The Structural Analysis of Narrative: Apropos of Acts 10–11," was written in 1969 and appeared in 1971. Both of these essays on the Bible were written by the "early Barthes." However, the distinction that is often drawn between the purely structuralist "early Barthes" and the poststructuralist "later Barthes" overlooks his lifelong interest in the play between connotation and denotation and the tensions between physical aspects of the text and the reader's desire for meaning. Indeed, Barthes mentions both Derrida and Lacan in the selection below. More correct is the comment by his friend, Italo Calvino, that in Barthes were united two different tendencies, "the one who subordinated everything to the rigor of a method, and the one whose only sure criterion was pleasure (the pleasure of the intelligence and the intelligence of pleasure)."

Barthes opens "Apropos of Acts 10–11" with a review of linguistic structuralism, paying special attention to whether structuralist techniques developed in relation to sentences can be applied equally well to entire narratives. Yet Barthes retains the traditional structuralist distinction between "speech" (the specific utterance) and "language" (the linguistic repertoire). This translation of techniques from linguistics to narrative theory was central to Barthes' development as a semiotician, and it played a major role in his later books. The intersection between the dimensions of speech and language also opens the way to Kristeva's concept of intertextuality and its relation to ideology. This appears in the question of the relation of meaning to code, the concept of the "counter-text," and the question of readability. Also evident is Barthes' interest in close, careful readings of texts, later raised to a much higher degree in *S/Z*. An outline of the procedures that Barthes followed in *S/Z* appears in section I.4 of the present essay, and section II in effect constitutes a trial run of those procedures. Barthes adopts the ancient practice of biblical scholarship by breaking the text into small units, "lexias" (verses). Lexias are units of what linguists call the syntagm. The division of the narrative into lexias is arbitrary and practical, to reduce the text to a size that may be analyzed in terms of the codes that are employed. Each lexia will have one or more codes operating in it.

In this essay, Barthes has not yet clearly defined the codes, nor does he use them with the precision and subtlety that he demonstrates in *S/Z*. The codes are abstractions from the total field of "language," also known as the paradigm, which the reader engages in order to decipher the text. They are filters through which the reader's experience with other texts is brought into play. The codes are not necessarily the same from one reader to another, or from one text to another, and thus no two readings will be alike. The codes produce the range of possible meanings to be attached to the lexia, and hence through the overall arrangement of lexias, they generate the semiotic articulation of the entire text. The goal of Barthes' reading of Acts 10–11 is not to determine the one correct meaning of a "limitless" text; indeed, he questions the possibility of any "final signified." Instead, Barthes seeks to lay out as clearly as possible the actual movements of a reading, to dissect the text and also the reading of that text into the smallest possible units, and then to reassemble these units so that it is clear how they fit (and do not fit) together. In short, Barthes seeks to deconstruct the semiotic mechanism of the text and the semiotic operation of the reader. He shows that the meaningful text and its reader are not two different things, but in fact they are both produced by something else.

The vision of Cornelius in Caesarea

10 There was in Caesarea a man called Cornelius, a centurion of the Italica cohort. He and the whole of his household were devout and God-fearing, and he gave generously to Jewish causes and prayed constantly to God.

One day at about the ninth hour he had a vision in which he distinctly saw the angel of God come into his house and call out to him, "Cornelius!" He stared at the vision in terror

Roland Barthes, "The Structural Analysis of Narrative: Apropos of Acts 10–11," from *The Semiotic Challenge*, translated by Richard Howard (New York: Hill and Wang, 1988; written 1969; originally published in *Exégèse et herméneutique*, Editions du Seuil, 1971).

and exclaimed, "What is it, Lord?" "Your offering of prayers and alms," the angel answered, "has been accepted by God. Now you must send someone to Jaffa and fetch a man called Simon, known as Peter, who is lodging with Simon the tanner whose house is by the sea." When the angel who said this had gone, Cornelius called two of the slaves and a devout soldier of his staff, told them what had happened, and sent them off to Jaffa.

The vision of Peter in Jaffa

Next day, while they were still on their journey and had only a short distance to go before reaching Jaffa, Peter went to the housetop at about the sixth hour to pray. He felt hungry and was looking forward to his meal, but before it was ready he fell into a trance and saw heaven thrown open and something like a big sheet being let down to earth by its four corners; it contained every possible sort of animal and bird, walking, crawling or flying ones. A voice then said to him, "Now, Peter; kill and eat!" But Peter answered, "Certainly not, Lord; I have never yet eaten anything profane or unclean." Again, a second time, the voice spoke to him, "What God has made clean, you have no right to call profane." This was repeated three times, and then suddenly the container was drawn up to heaven again.

Peter was still worrying over the meaning of the vision he had seen, when the men sent by Cornelius arrived. They had asked where Simon's house was and they were now standing at the door, calling out to know if the Simon known as Peter was lodging there. Peter's mind was still on the vision and the Spirit had to tell him, "Some men have come to see you. Hurry down, and do not hesitate about going back with them; it was I who told them to come." Peter went down and said to them, "I am the man you are looking for; why have you come?" They said, "The centurion Cornelius, who is an upright and God-fearing man, highly regarded by the entire Jewish people, was directed by a holy angel to send for you and bring you to his house and listen to what you have to say." So Peter asked them in and gave them lodging.

Next day, he was ready to go off with them, accompanied by some of the brothers from Jaffa. They reached Caesarea the following day, and Cornelius was waiting for them. He had asked his relations and close friends to be there, and as Peter reached the house Cornelius went out to meet him, knelt at his feet and prostrated himself. But Peter helped him up. "Stand up," he said, "I am only a man after all!" Talking together they went in to meet all the people assembled there, and Peter said to them, "You know it is forbidden for Jews to mix with people of another race and visit them, but God has made it clear to me that I must not call anyone profane or unclean. That is why I made no objection to coming when I was sent for; but I should like to know exactly why you sent for me." Cornelius replied, "Three days ago I was praying in my house at the ninth hour, when I suddenly saw a man in front of me in shining robes. He said, 'Cornelius, your prayer has been heard and your alms have been accepted as a sacrifice in the sight of God; so now you must send to Jaffa and fetch Simon known as Peter who is lodging in the house of Simon the tanner, by the sea.' So I sent for you at once, and you have been kind enough to come. Here we all are, assembled in front of you to hear what message God has given you for us."

Peter's address at the house of Cornelius

Then Peter addressed them: "The truth I have now come to realize," he said, "is that God does not have favorites, but that anybody of any nationality who fears God and does what is right is acceptable to him.

"It is true, God sent his word to the people of Israel, and it was to them that the good news of peace was brought by Jesus Christ – but Jesus Christ is Lord of all men. You must have heard about the recent happenings in Judaea, about Jesus of Nazareth and how he began in Galilee, after John had been preaching baptism. God had anointed him with the Holy Spirit and with power, and because God was with him, Jesus went about doing good and curing all who had fallen into the power of the devil. Now I, and those with me, can witness to everything he did throughout the countryside of Judaea and in Jerusalem itself: and also to the fact that they killed him by hanging him on a tree, yet three days afterwards God raised him to life and allowed him to be seen, not by the whole people but only by certain witnesses God had chosen beforehand. Now we are those witnesses – we have eaten and drunk with him after his resurrection from the dead – and he has ordered us to proclaim this to his people and to tell them that God has appointed him to judge everyone, alive or dead. It is to him that all the prophets bear this witness; that all who believe in Jesus will have their sins forgiven through his name."

The coming of the Spirit upon the pagans

While Peter was still speaking the Holy Spirit came down on all the listeners. Jewish believers who had accompanied Peter were all astonished that the gifts of the Holy Spirit should be poured out on the pagans too, since they could hear them speaking strange languages and proclaiming the greatness of God. Peter himself then said, "Could anyone refuse the water of baptism to these people, now they have received the Holy Spirit just as much as we have?" He then gave orders for them to be baptized in the name of Jesus Christ. Afterwards they begged him to stay on for some days.

Peter's narrative in Jerusalem

11 The apostles and the brothers in Judaea heard that the pagans too had accepted the word of God, and when Peter came up to Jerusalem the Jews criticized him and said, "So you have been visiting the uncircumcised and eating with them, have you?" Peter in reply gave them the details point by point: "One day, when I was in the town of Jaffa," he began, "I fell into a trance as I was praying and had a vision of something like a big sheet being let down from heaven by its four corners. This sheet reached the ground quite close to me. I watched it intently and saw all sorts of animals and wild beasts – everything possible that could walk, crawl or fly. Then I heard a voice that said to me, 'Now, Peter; kill and eat!' But I answered: 'Certainly not, Lord; nothing profane or unclean has ever crossed my lips.' And a second time the voice spoke from heaven, 'What God has made clean, you have no right to call profane.' This was repeated three times, before the whole of it was drawn up to heaven again.

"Just at that moment, three men stopped outside the house where we were staying; they had been sent from Caesarea to fetch me, and the Spirit told me to have no hesitation about going back with them. The six brothers here came with me as well, and we entered the man's house. He told us he had seen an angel standing in his house who said, 'Send to Jaffa and fetch Simon known as Peter; he has a message for you that will save you and your entire household.'

"I had scarcely begun to speak when the Holy Spirit came down on them in the same way as it came on us at the beginning, and I remembered that the Lord had said, 'John baptized with water, but you will be baptized with the Holy Spirit.' I realized then that God was giving them the identical thing he gave to us when we believed in the Lord Jesus Christ; and who was I to stand in God's way?"

This account satisfied them, and they gave glory to God. "God," they said, "can evidently grant even the pagans the repentance that leads to life." (The Jerusalem Bible (Doubleday), 1966)

My task is to present what is already commonly called the Structural Analysis of Narrative. It must be admitted that the name outstrips the thing. What it is possible to call by such a name at present is a collective research, it is not yet a science nor even, strictly speaking, a discipline; calling it a discipline would imply that the Structural Analysis of Narrative is being taught, and this is not yet the case. The first word of this presentation must therefore be a warning; there is not, at present, a science of narrative (even if we were to give the word "science" an extremely broad meaning); there does not exist, at present, a "diegetology." I should like to make this clear and try to forestall certain disappointments.

Origin of the Structural Analysis of Narrative

This origin is, if not confused, at least "undetermined." We may think of it as quite remote, if we trace the state of mind which presides over the analysis of narrative and of texts back to Aristotle's *Poetics* and *Rhetoric*; closer at hand, if we refer to Aristotle's classical posterity, to the theoreticians of genres; much more recent, even very recent, but more specific, if we consider that it can be traced in its present form to the work of those men we call the Russian Formalists, some of whose works have been translated into French by Tzvetan Todorov. This Russian Formalism (and its diversity concerns us here) included poets, literary critics, linguists, folklorists who investigated, during the early 1920s, the forms of the literary work; the group was then dispersed by cultural Stalinism and migrated abroad, notably through the linguistic group of Prague. The spirit of this Russian Formalist research passed, essentially, into the work of the great contemporary linguist Roman Jakobson.

Methodologically (and no longer historically), the origin of the Structural Analysis of Narrative is, of course, the recent development of what is called structural linguistics. Based on this linguistics, there has been a "poetic" extension, as a result of Jakobson's research, in the direction of the study of the poetic message or the literary message; and there has been an anthropological extension as a result of Lévi-Strauss's studies of myth and his continuation of the work of one of the most important Russian Formalists for the study of narrative, Vladimir Propp, the folklorist. At present, research in this realm is being pursued, in France, within the Centre d'Études des Communications de Masse, at the École Pratique des Hautes Études, and in the semio-linguistic group of my friend and colleague Greimas. This type of analysis is beginning to penetrate academic teaching, notably at Vincennes; abroad, isolated researchers are working in this direction, chiefly in Russia, the United States, and Germany. I shall indicate some of the efforts to coordinate this research: in France, the appearance of a *Revue de Poétique* (in the Jakobsonian sense of the word, of course), directed by Todorov and Genette; in Italy, an annual colloquium on the Analysis of Narrative at Urbino; and finally an International Association of Semiology (i.e., of the science of significations) has just been created, on a broad scale; it already has its review, called *Semiotica,* which will frequently investigate problems of the Analysis of Narrative.

However, at present this research is subject to a certain dispersion, and this dispersion is in a sense constitutive of the investigation itself – at least that is how I see it. First of all, this research remains individual, not out of individualism, but because what is involved is an enterprise of *finesse*: work on the meaning or meanings of the text (for that is the Structural Analysis of Narrative) cannot be intersected by a phenomenological departure: there is no machine for reading meaning; of course there are translating machines; but these, if they can transform denoted meanings, literal meanings, obviously have no grasp of secondary meanings, of the connoted, associative level of a text; at the outset there must still be an individual operation of reading, and the notion of a "team" on this level, remains, I believe, quite illusory; the Structural Analysis of Narrative cannot be treated, as a discipline, like biology nor even like sociology: there is no canonical account possible, one investigator cannot quite speak in another's name. Further, this individual research is, on the level of each researcher, in *process*: each investigator has his own history; it can vary, especially because the history of the environing structuralism is an accelerated history: concepts change rapidly, divergences soon become pronounced, polemics suddenly turn acrimonious, and all this has an obvious influence on research.

Finally, I shall take the liberty of saying, because it is what I truly believe: since we are studying a cultural language, to wit the language of narrative, analysis is immediately sensitive (and we must be clear about this) to its ideological implications. At present, what passes for "the" structuralist enterprise is a notion actually quite sociological and quite fabricated, insofar as it is seen as a united school. This is not at all the case. As for French structuralism, in any event, there are profound ideological divergences between the various representative figures who have been crammed in the same structuralist pigeonhole, for instance between Lévi-Strauss, Derrida, Lacan, or Althusser; there is accordingly a structuralist fractionalism, and if we were to situate it (and it is not my intention to do so here), it would crystallize, I believe, around the notion of "Science."

I have said this to forestall disappointment and to limit confidence in a scientific method which is barely a method and certainly not a science. Before turning to the text from the Acts of the Apostles which is our concern, I should like to offer three general principles which might, I think, be recognized by all those concerned today with the Structural Analysis of Narrative. To them I shall add some remarks on the subject of the operational arrangements of the analysis as well.

I General Principles and Arrangements of the Analysis

1 *Principle of formalization*

This principle, which might also be called a *principle of abstraction*, derives from the Saussurian opposition of *language* and *speech*. We consider that each narrative (let us recall that in the world and in the history of the world, and the history of entire nations of the earth, the number of narratives produced by humanity is incalculable), each narrative in this apparently heteroclite mass of narratives, is the *speech*, in the Saussurian sense, the message of a general language of narrative. This language of narrative is obviously identifiable beyond language proper, beyond what the linguists study. The linguistics of national languages (in which narratives are written) stops at the sentence, which is the ultimate unit a linguist can "attack." Beyond the sentence, the structure no longer concerns linguistics proper; it concerns a second linguistics, a translinguistics which is the site of the analysis of narrative: after the sentence, there where several sentences are set together. What happens then? We do not yet know; we thought we knew for a very long time, and it was Aristotelian or Ciceronian rhetoric which informed us on the matter; but the concepts of that rhetoric are obsolete, for they were chiefly normative; however, classical rhetoric, though in decline, has not yet been replaced. The linguists themselves have not ventured to undertake such a task; Benveniste has given a few indications, as always extremely penetrating, on this subject; there are also certain Americans who have been concerned with speech-analysis; but this linguistics remains to be constructed. And the analysis of narrative, the language of narrative, belongs, at least postulatively, to such future translinguistics.

One practical impact of this principle of abstraction, in whose name we are trying to establish a language of narrative, is that we cannot and do not desire to analyze a text in itself. This must be said, since I shall be discussing a single text: I am embarrassed to do so because the attitude of the classic analyst of narrative is not to concern himself with an isolated text; on this point there is a fundamental difference between the Structural Analysis of Narrative and what is traditionally called *explication de textes*. For us, a text is speech which refers to language, a message which refers to a code, a performance which refers to a competence – all these words being the words of linguists. The Structural Analysis of Narrative is fundamentally, constitutively *comparative*: it seeks forms, not a content. When I speak of the text of the Acts, it will not be to explicate this text, it will be to confront this text as an investigator who unites certain materials in order to construct a grammar; for this, the linguist is obliged to unite sentences, a *corpus* of sentences. The analyst of narrative has exactly the same task, he must unite narratives, a *corpus* of narratives, in order to attempt to extract from them a structure.

2   *Principle of pertinence*

This second principle has its origin in phonology. As opposed to phonetics phonology seeks not to study the intrinsic quality of each sound emitted within a language, the physical and acoustical quality of the sound, but to establish the differences of sounds of a language, insofar as these differences of sounds refer to differences of meaning, and only so far: this is the principle of pertinence; we try to find differences of form attested to by differences of content; these differences are pertinent or non-pertinent features. I should like to propose here a clarification, an example, and a kind of warning.

A *clarification*, first of all, as to the word *meaning*: in the analysis of narrative, we do not attempt to find signifieds which I shall call *full* signifieds, lexical signifieds, meanings in the usual acceptation of the word. We call "meaning" any type of intratextual or extratextual correlation, i.e., any feature of narrative which refers to another moment of the narrative or to another site of the culture necessary in order to read the narrative: all types of anaphora, of cataphora, in short of "diaphora" (if I may be permitted this word), all linkages, all paradigmatic and syntagmatic correlations, all the phenomena of signification and also the phenomena of distribution. I repeat: meaning, therefore, is not a *full signified*, such as I might find in a dictionary, even a dictionary of Narrative; it is essentially a correlation, or the term of a correlation, a correlate, or a connotation. Meaning, for me (this is how I envision it in research), is essentially a *citation*, the departure of a code, what permits us to postulate a code and what implies a code, even if this code (I shall return to this) is not or cannot be reconstituted.

Next, an *example*: for the Structural Analysis of Narrative, at least for me (though this is arguable), the problems of translation are not systematically pertinent. So, in the case of the narrative of the visions of Cornelius and of Peter, the problems of translation concern the analysis only within certain limits: only if the differences of translation involve a structural modification, i.e., the alteration of a group of functions or of a sequence. I should like to give one example:

The King James version of Acts 10:2:

A devout man [referring to Cornelius], and one that feared God with all his house, which gave much alms to the people, and prayed to God alway.

The Jerusalem Bible version of the same passage:

He and the whole of his household were devout and God-fearing, and he gave generously to Jewish causes and prayed constantly to God.

One can say that the two passages reveal entirely different syntactical structures, many differences in vocabulary. Yet in the present case, this does not at all affect the distribution of codes and functions, because the structural sense of the passage is exactly the same in either translation. What is involved is a signified of psychological or characterial or even, more specifically, of evangelical type, since the Gospel uses a certain entirely coded paradigm, which is a three-term opposition: the circumcised / the uncircumcised / the "God-fearing"; these terms form the third category, which is neutral (if I may be permitted this linguistic term) and which is precisely at the center of our text: it is the paradigm which is pertinent, not the sentences in which it is dressed.

On the other hand, if we compare at other points the King James version with the Jerusalem Bible, structural differences appear: in the Jerusalem Bible, the angel does not say what Cornelius should ask Peter, after having sent for him; in the King James (verse 6): "he shall tell thee what thou oughtest to do": on the one hand, absence, on the other, presence. I insist on the fact that the difference of the two versions has a structural value, because the sequence of the angel's injunction is modified: in the earlier translation, the content of the angel's injunction is specified, there is a kind of desire to make homogeneous what is announced (Peter's mission, a mission of speech) and what will happen: *Peter will make a speech*; I do not know the origin of this version, nor am I concerned with it; what I see is that the King James version rationalizes the structure of the message, while, in the Jerusalem Bible, the angel's version not being specified, it remains void, and thereby makes emphatic Cornelius's obedience, who sends for Peter "blindly" and without knowing why; in the later translation, absence functions as a feature which operates a certain suspense, which reinforces and makes emphatic the suspense of the narrative, which was not the case in the King James version – less narrative, less dramatic, and more rational.

Lastly, a precaution and a *warning*: we must be suspicious of the *naturalness* of the notations. In analyzing a text, we must constantly react against the impression of obviousness, against the it-goes-without-saying aspect of what is written. Every statement, however trivial and normal it appears, must be evaluated in terms of structure by a mental test of commutation. Confronting a statement, a sentence-fragment, we must always think of what would happen if the feature were not noted or if it were different. The good analyst of narrative must have a sort of imagination of the *counter-text*, an imagination of the aberration of the text, of what is narratively scandalous; he must be sensitive to the notion of logical, narrative "scandal"; thereby we shall be emboldened to assume the often very banal, tedious, and obvious character of the analysis.

3   Principle of plurality

The Structural Analysis of Narrative (at least as I conceive of it) does not seek to establish "the" meaning of the text, it does not even seek to establish "a" meaning of the text; it differs fundamentally from philological analysis, for it aims at tracing what I shall call the geometric site, the site of meanings, the site of the possible meanings of the text. Just as a language is a possibility of words (a language is the possible site of a certain number of words, actually of an infinite number), so what the analyst wants to establish in the language of narrative is the possible site of meanings, or again the plurality of meaning, or meaning as plurality. When we say that the analyst seeks or defines meaning as a possibility, this is not a tendency or an option of a liberal sort; for me, in any case, there is no question of liberally determining the truth's conditions of possibility, no question of a philological agnosticism; I am not considering the *possibility of meaning* as a sort of indulgent and liberal preamble to a *certain meaning*; for me, the meaning is not a possibility, it is not *one* possible thing, it is *the very being of the possible*, it is the being of plurality (and not one or two or several possibilities).

In these conditions, structural analysis cannot be a method of interpretation; it does not seek to interpret the text, to propose the probable meaning of the text; it does not follow an anagogical path toward the truth of the text, toward its deep structure, toward its secret; and consequently it differs fundamentally from what is called literary criticism, which is an interpretive criticism, of the Marxist or the psychoanalytic type. The structural analysis of the text is different from these criticisms, because it does not seek the secret of the text: for it, all the text's roots are in the air; it does not have to unearth these roots in order to find *the main one*. Of course if, in a text, there is one meaning, a monosemy, if there is an anagogical process, which is precisely the case with our text from the Acts, we shall treat this anagogy as a code of the text, among the other codes, and given as such by the text.

4 *Operational arrangements*

I prefer this expression to the more intimidating one of *method*, for I am not sure we possess a method; but there are a certain number of operational arrangements in the investigation which must be mentioned. It seems to me (this is a personal position and not inalterable) that, if we work on a single text (previous to the comparative work of which I have spoken and which is the very goal of classical Structural Analysis), we must anticipate three operations.

1. *Segmentation* of the text, i.e., of the material signifier. This segmentation can, in my opinion, be entirely arbitrary; in a certain state of the investigation, there is no disadvantage to this arbitrariness. It is a way of making a grid of the text which provides the fragments of the statement on which one is going to work. Now, precisely, for the New Testament, and indeed for the whole Bible, this work is already done, since the Bible is segmented into verses (in the case of the Koran, into suras). The verse is an excellent working unit of meaning; since it is a question of *creaming* (or skimming) the text, the correlations or apertures of the verse-sieve are of an excellent dimension. It would moreover greatly interest me to know where the segmentation into verses comes from; if it is linked to the citational nature of the Word, what are the exact links, the structural links, between the citational nature of the Biblical speech and the verse. For other tests, I have proposed calling these speech fragments on which we work "lexias," units of reading. For us, a verse is a lexia.

2. *Inventory* of the codes which are cited in the text: inventory, collection, harvest, or as I have just said, creaming-off. Lexia after lexia, verse after verse, we try to inventory the meanings, in the acceptation I have given, the correlations or code-departures present in this speech fragment. I shall return to this, since I am going to be working on several verses.

3. *Coordination*: to establish the correlations of units, of identified functions which are often separated, superimposed, mingled, or even braided, since a text, as the word's very etymology says, is a fabric, a braid of correlates, which can be separated from each other by the insertion of other correlates, which belong to other groups. There are two main types of correlations: internal and external. For those internal to the text, here is an example: if we are told that the angel appears, *appearance* is a term whose correlate is inevitably *disappearance*. This is an intratextual correlation, since *appearance* and *disappearance* are in the same narrative. It would be, strictly speaking, a narrative scandal if the angel did not disappear. Hence we must note the sequence *appear/disappear*, because that is what readability is: that the presence of certain elements be *necessary*. There are also external correlations: a feature of discourse can refer to a diacritical, suprasegmental totality superior to the text; it can refer to the total character of a person, or to the total atmosphere of a place, or to an anagogic meaning, as here in our text, i.e., the integration of the Gentiles into the Church. A feature can even refer to other texts: this is intertextuality, a notion recently proposed by Julia Kristeva (*Sèmeiotikè*, Paris: Éd.

du Seuil, 1969). It implies that a feature of discourse *refers* to another text, in the almost infinite sense of that word; for we must not confuse the sources of a text (which are merely the minor version of this phenomenon of citation) with citation, which is a kind of illimitable reference to an infinite text, the cultural text of humanity. This is particularly valid for literary texts, which are woven of extremely varied stereotypes, and where, consequently, the phenomenon of reference, of citation, to an anterior or ambient culture is very frequent. In what is called intertextuality, we must include texts which come *after*: the sources of a text are not only *before* it, they are also *after* it. This is the point of view so convincingly adopted by Lévi-Strauss when he says that the Freudian version of the Oedipus myth belongs to the Oedipus myth: if we read Sophocles, we must read Sophocles as a citation of Freud; and Freud as a citation of Sophocles.

II Structural Problems Present in the Text of Acts

I now proceed to the text, Acts 10; I am afraid the disappointment will begin, since we are going to enter into the concrete and since, after these grand principles, our harvest risks seeming thin indeed. I shall not analyze the text step by step, as I ought to do; I ask you simply to suppose this: I am a researcher, I am doing research in the structural analysis of narrative: I have decided to analyze perhaps 100 or 200 or 300 narratives; among these narratives, there is, for one reason or another, the narrative of Cornelius's vision; here is the work I am doing and which I do not privilege in any way. Normally, this would take several days: I would go through the narrative verse after verse, lexia after lexia, and I would *cream off* all the meanings, all the possible codes, which takes a certain amount of time, because the imagination of correlation is not immediate. A correlation is searched out, is worked out; hence it takes some time and some patience; I shall not be doing that work here, but I shall make use of the narrative from Acts in order to raise three main structural problems, present in my opinion in this text.

1   *The problem of the codes*

I have said that the meanings were code-departures, citations of codes; if we compare our text to a literary text (I have just been working at some length on a *nouvelle* by Balzac), it is obvious that the codes are not numerous here and of a certain poverty. Their richness would probably show up better on the scale of the New Testament in its entirety. I shall attempt an identification of the codes, as I see them (I may forget some) in the first verses (verses 1 to 3), and I shall set aside the case of the two most important codes invested in the text.

1. "*There was in Caesarea a man called Cornelius, a centurion of the Italica cohort.*" In this sentence, I see four codes. And first of all the formula "There was," which culturally refers (I am not speaking here in terms of Biblical exegesis, but in a more general fashion) to a code which I shall call the *narrative code*: this narrative which begins by "there was" refers to all inaugurations of narrative. A brief digression here to say that the

problem of the inauguration of discourse is an important one, which has been clearly seen and carefully treated, on the pragmatic level, by ancient and classical rhetoric: that rhetoric has laid down extremely specific rules for beginning the discourse. In my opinion, these rules are attached to the sentiment that there is in humanity a native aphasia, that it is difficult to speak, that there is perhaps nothing to say, and that, consequently, there is required a whole group of protocols and rules to find *what* to say: *invenire quid dicas*. The inauguration is a perilous zone of discourse: the beginning of speech is a difficult action; it is the emergence from silence. In reality, there is no reason to begin *here* rather than *there*. Language is an infinite structure, and I believe that it is this sentiment of the infinity of language which is present in all the inauguration-rites of speech. In the oldest, pre-Homeric epics, the bard, the recitant, began the narrative by saying, according to a ritual formula: "I take up the story at this point..."; he indicated thereby that he was conscious of the arbitrariness of his point of entry; to begin is to enter into an infinity quite arbitrarily. Hence narrative-inaugurations are important to study, and this has not yet been done. I have several times suggested to students that they take as a thesis subject the first sentences of novels: this is a fine subject; as yet my suggestion has not been followed, but I know that this work is being done in Germany, where there has even been a publication on the beginnings of novels. From the point of view of structural analysis, it would be fascinating to know what implicit information is contained in a beginning, since this site of discourse is preceded by no information whatever.

2. "*in Caesarea...*" This is a *topographic code*, relative to the systematic organization of places in the narrative. In this topographic code, there are doubtless rules of association (rules of the *probable*), there is a narrative functionality of places: here we find a paradigm, a significant opposition between Caesarea and Jaffa. The distance between the two cities must correspond to a distance in time: a typically structural problem, since it is a problem of concordance, of concomitance, according to a certain logic (more-over, one still to be explored), but which is at first glance the logic of *probability*. This topographic code is to be found at other points in the text. The topographic code is obviously a cultural code: Caesarea and Jaffa – this implies a certain knowledge on the reader's part, even if the reader is supposed to possess this knowledge quite naturally. Further: if we include in the language of narrative the way in which we, in our situation as modern readers, receive the narrative, we identify here all the Oriental connotations of the word Caesarea, everything we put into the word Caesarea, because of what we have *read* subsequently, in Racine or in other authors.

Another observation relative to the topographic code: in verse 9, we have a feature of this code: "*Peter went to the housetop.*" The topographic citation here has a very powerful function within the narrative, since it justifies the fact that Peter does not hear the arrival of the men sent by Cornelius, so that consequently notification by the angel is necessary: "*Some men have come to see you.*" The topographical feature becomes a narrative function. I take advantage of this to raise an important problem of *literary* narrative: the theme of the housetop is both a term of the topographic code, i.e., of a cultural code which refers to a habitat where there are houses with roof-terraces, and a term of what I shall call the *actional code*, the code of actions, of sequences of actions: here, the intervention of the angel; further, we might readily connect this notation to the symbolic field, insofar as the rooftop is a high place and consequently implies an ascensional symbolism, if the elevation is coupled with other terms of the text. Thus, the notation of the rooftop corresponds to three different codes: topographic, actional, symbolic. Now, the characteristic of narrative, in a sense one of its fundamental laws, is that the three codes are given in an *undecidable* fashion: we cannot decide if there is one prevalent code, and this undecidability, in my opinion, constitutes the narrative, for it defines the performance of the teller. "To tell a story well," according to classical readability, is to manage to keep us from deciding among two or more codes, is to propose a sort of turnstile by which one code can always present itself as the natural alibi of the other, by which one code naturalizes the other. In other words, what is necessary to the story, what puts itself under the instance of discourse, seems determined by reality, by the referent, by nature.

3. "A *man called Cornelius*. . ." Here there is a code which I shall call *onomastic* since it is the code of proper names. Recent analyses have renewed the problem of the proper name, which moreover had never been really raised by linguistics. These analyses are those of Jakobson on the one hand, and of Lévi-Strauss on the other, who in *Structural Anthropology* (1958), has dedicated a chapter to the problems of classifying proper names. On the level of the text, the investigation will not lead very far, but in the perspective of a grammar of narrative, the onomastic code is obviously a very important one.

4. "A *centurion of the Italica cohort*": this is, quite banally, the *historical code* which implies a historical knowledge, or, if we are concerned with a reader contemporary with the referent, an assumption of political, social, and administrative information. It is a cultural code.

5. "*He and the whole of his household were devout and God-fearing, and he gave generously to Jewish causes and prayed constantly to God.*" There is here what I call a *semic code*. The seme, in linguistics, is a unit of the signified, not of the signifier. I call *semic code* the group of signifieds of connotation, in the current meaning of the term; the connotation can be characterial, if we read the text psychologically (we will then have a characterial signified of Cornelius, referring to his psychological character), or merely structural, if we read the text anagogically, the category of "God-fearing" not having a psychological value, but a strictly relational value in the distribution of the partners of the Gospel, as I have said.

6. There is also a *rhetorical code* in this verse, because it is built on a rhetorical schema, to wit: there is a general proposition, a signified: piety, which is coined in two "*exempla*," as classical rhetoric would say: generosity and prayer.

7. "*He had a vision in which he distinctly saw*. . ." Here we have one of the terms of an extremely important code, to which I shall return and which I am provisionally calling the *actional code*, or code of sequences of actions. The action here is "to see in a vision." We shall return to this problem later on.

8. *"At about the ninth hour..."* This is the *chronological code*; there are several citations from it in the text; we shall make the same remark as for the topographic code: this code is linked to problems of probability and verisimilitude; the Spirit regulates the synchronism of the two visions: the chronological code has a structural importance, since, from the narrative point of view, the two visions must coincide. For the study of the novel, this chronological code is obviously very important; and we must further recall that Lévi-Strauss has studied chronology as a code apropos of the problems of historical dates.

9. *"A vision ... in which he saw the angel of God come into his house and call out to him, 'Cornelius!' ..."* I here identify the presence of a code which I shall call, after Jakobson's classification, the *phatic code* (from the Greek word *phasis*: speech). As a matter of fact, Jakobson has distinguished six functions of language, and among these, the phatic function or group of features of enunciation by which one assures, maintains, or renews a contact with the interlocutor. These are, then, language features which have no content as message, but play a role of renewed interpellation. (The best example is the telephonic word "Hello" which opens contact and often maintains it: it is a feature of the phatic code.) The features of interpellation thus derive from this phatic code; it is a sort of generalized vocative; later on, we shall classify within this code an indication such as "this was repeated three times." For we can interpret the notation as a feature of redundance, of insistence, of communication between the angel and Peter, between the Spirit and Peter: feature of the phatic code.

10. It is possible to see later on, in the *"big sheet let down to earth,"* a citation from the *symbolic field* (I prefer to say symbolic field rather than symbolic code), to wit the organization of signifiers according to an ascensional symbolism. The symbolic meaning is obviously important: the text organizes, on the level of the narrative and through an elaboration of signifiers, the account of a transgression; and, if this transgression is to be analyzed in symbolic terms, it is because it is a transgression linked to the human body. From this point of view, this is a remarkable text, since the two transgressions studied and recommended in the text are both corporeal. One concerns food, and the other circumcision, and these two strictly corporeal, hence symbolic (in the psychoanalytic sense of the term) transgression serves as an introduction or, if one may say so, as an *exemplum* for the transgression of the law of exclusion by circumcision. A symbolic description would not retain, moreover, the hierarchy I have just posited between the two transgressions. This logical hierarchy is given by the analogy of the text, it is the meaning which the text itself has sought to give its narrative; but if we wanted to "interpret" the text symbolically, we would not have to place the alimentary transgression *before* the religious one, we would have to try to discern what general *form* of transgression there is behind the text's anagogic construction.

11. As for the *anagogic code* I have just mentioned, it is the system to which all the features which specifically articulate *the* meaning of the text refer, for the text here articulates and announces its own meaning – which is not always the case. In the current literary text, there is no anagogic code: the text does not utter its deep meaning, its

secret meaning, and it is moreover because it does not do so that criticism has been able to seize upon it. Several times over, citations derive from the anagogic code, as for example when Peter tries to explain to himself the meaning of the vision he has just had; or else the discussion of meaning, the assurance by meaning within the community of Jerusalem. Hence the anagogical meaning is given by the text: it is the integration of the Uncircumcised into the Church. Perhaps we should attach to this code all the features which allude to the problem of hospitality: they would also belong to this anagogic code.

12. A last important code is the *metalinguistic code*: this word designates a language which speaks of another language. If, for instance, I am writing a grammar of the French language, I produce a metalanguage, since I am speaking a language (to wit, my grammar) about a language which is French. Hence the metalanguage is a language which speaks of another language or whose referent is a language or a discourse. Now, what is interesting here, is that the metalinguistic episodes are important and numerous: they are the four or five summaries which constitute the text. A summary or résumé is a metalinguistic episode, a feature of the metalinguistic code: there is a narrative referent, a language referent: Cornelius's vision, Peter's vision, the two visions, the story of Christ . . ., here are four narrative referents; then there are the metalinguistic repetitions, depending on the different recipients.

– the envoys summarize to Peter the order given to Cornelius;
– Cornelius summarizes his vision to Peter;
– Peter summarizes his vision to Cornelius;
– Peter summarizes the two visions to the community of Jerusalem;
– finally, the story of Christ is summarized by Peter to Cornelius.

I shall return to this code. But now I should like to speak of two other important problems, which correspond to two particular or isolated codes in the text.

2   The code of actions

This code refers to the organization of actions undertaken or undergone by the agents present in the narration; it is an important code since it covers everything which, in a text, seems to us properly and immediately narrative, to wit the relation of *what happens*, ordinarily presented according to a logic at once causal and temporal. This level immediately received the attention of analysts. Propp established the major "functions" of the folktale, i.e., the constant, regular actions which we find with few variations in almost all the narratives of Russian folklore; his schema (postulating the sequence of some thirty actions) has been adopted and corrected by Lévi-Strauss, Greimas, and Bremond. We can say that today the "logic" of narrative actions is conceived in several fashions, related and yet different. Propp sees the sequence of narrative actions as alogical; for him, it is a constant, regular sequence, but without content. Lévi-Strauss and Greimas have postulated that these sequences must be given a paradigmatic structure and reconstructed as successions of oppositions; here in fact, for example, the initial victory (of the letter) is set in opposition to its (final) defeat: a median term neutralizes them temporarily: confrontation. Bremond, for his part, has sought to reconstitute a logic of the alternatives of actions, each "situation" being "resolvable" in one fashion or another and each solution engendering a new alternative. Personally, I incline toward the notion of a sort of cultural logic which owes nothing to any mental datum, even on an anthropological level; for me, the sequences of narrative actions are encased in a logical appearance which comes solely from the *already-written*: in a word, from the stereotype.

This said, and in whatever fashion they are to be structured, here for example are two sequences of actions present in our text.

a. An elementary sequence, with two centers, of the type *Question/Answer:* Peter's question to the envoys/envoys' answer; Peter's demand for an explanation to Cornelius/ Cornelius's answer. The same schema can be complicated without losing its structure: disturbing information/demand for enlightenment formulated by the community/ explanation given by Peter/reassurance of the community. We may note that it is insofar as such sequences are quite banal that they are interesting; for their very banality attests to the fact that what is involved is a quasi-universal constraint, or again: a grammatical rule of narrative.

b. A developed sequence, with several centers: this is the *Search* (for Peter by Cornelius's envoys): to set out/to seek/to arrive in a place/to ask/to obtain/ to bring back. Some of the terms are *substitutable* (in other narratives): to *bring back* can elsewhere be replaced by to *renounce, to abandon,* etc.

The sequences of actions, constituted according to a logico-temporal structure, are presented throughout the narrative according to a complicated order: two terms of the same sequence can be separated by the appearance of terms belonging to other sequences; this interlacing of sequences forms the *braid* of the narrative (let us not forget that etymologically *text* means a weaving). Here the interlacing is relatively simple: there is a certain *simpleness* of the narrative, and this simpleness derives from the pure and simple juxtaposition of the sequences (they are not crisscrossed or intricated). Further, a term from one sequence can in and of itself represent a subsequence (what the cyberneticians call a *bit*); the sequence of the angel includes four terms: to enter/to be seen/to communicate/to depart; one of these four terms, communication, constitutes an *order* (a command) which is itself coined in secondary terms (to interpellate/to demand/reason for the choice/content of the interpellation/execution); there is in a sense a *proxy* of a sequence of actions by a term responsible for representing that sequence in another sequence of actions: *greet/answer*; this fragment of a sequence represents a certain meaning ("I, too, am a man").

These few indications form the sketch of analytical operations to which we must subject the actional level of a narrative. This analysis can be a thankless task, for the sequences give an impression of *obviousness* and their identification seems trivial; hence we must always realize that this very triviality, by constituting the *normality* of our narratives, requires the study of a crucial phenomenon concerning which we have little illumination: why is a narrative *readable*? What are the conditions of a text's *readability*? What are its limits? How, why does a story seem to us *endowed with meaning*? Confronting normal sequences (such as the sequences of our narrative) we must always think of the possibility of logically scandalous sequences, either by their extravagance or by the absence of a term: thereby appears the grammar of the *readable*.

3   The metalinguistic code

The last problem I want to extract from this text from the Acts relates to what I have called the metalinguistic code. The metalinguistic occurs, as we have said, when a language speaks of another language. This is the case of the summary or résumé, which is a metalinguistic act, since it is a discourse which has for referent another discourse. Now, in our text, there are four intertextual résumés and, further, a résumé exterior to the text, since it refers to the entire Gospel, to wit the life of Christ.

– the vision of Cornelius is repeated, summarized by Cornelius's envoys to Peter, and by Cornelius himself to Peter;
– Peter's vision is summarized by Peter to Cornelius;
– the two visions are summarized by Peter to the community of Jerusalem;
– finally the story of Christ is summarized, one might say, by Peter to Cornelius and to Cornelius's friends.

1. *The summary.* If, confronting this text, I were in a perspective of general research, I should classify it under the rubric of the problem of the summary, of the organization of the metalinguistic structure of narratives. Linguistically, the summary is a citation without its letter, a citation of content (not of form), a statement which referes to another statement, but whose reference, no longer being literal, involves a labor of structuration. What is interesting is that a résumé structures an anterior language, which is moreover already structured. The referent here is already a *narrative* (and not "reality"): what Peter summarizes to the community of Jerusalem is only in appearance reality; in fact, it is what we have already learned by a kind of zero narrative, which is the narrative of the performer of the text, to wit, apparently, Luke. Consequently, what would interest us from the point of view of the problematics of the summary, is to understand if there is really a hiatus between the *princeps* narrative, the zero narrative, and its referent, the supposedly real material of the narrative. Is there really a kind of pre-narrative, which would be reality, the absolute referent; and then a narrative, which would be that of Luke; and then the narrative of the active participants, numbering them: narrative 1, 2, 3, 4, etc.? As a matter of fact, from the narrative of Acts, i.e., from Luke's narrative to the supposed reality, we should say today that there is simply the relation of one *text* to another *text*. This is one of the crucial ideological problems which are raised, less perhaps in research than in groups concerned about the commitment of writing; it is the problem of the final signified: does a text possess in some way a final signified? And by scouring a text clean of its structures do we arrive, at a certain moment, at a final signified which, in the case of the realistic novel, would be "reality"?

Jacques Derrida's philosophical investigation has taken up in a revolutionary fashion this problem of the final signified, postulating that there is never ultimately, in the world, anything but the writing of a writing: a writing always finally refers to another writing, and the prospect of the signs is in a sense infinite. Consequently to describe systems of meaning by postulating a final signified is to side against the very nature of meaning. This reflection is today neither within my purpose nor my competence; but the realm which brings us together here, to wit Scripture, is a privileged domain for this problem, because, on the one hand, theologically, it is certain that a final signified is postulated: the metaphysical definition or the semantic definition of theology is to postulate the Last Signified; and because, on the other hand, the very notion of Scripture, the fact that the Bible is called Scripture, Writing, would orient us toward a more ambiguous comprehension of the problems, as if effectively, and theologically too, the base, the *princeps*, were still a Writing, and always a Writing.

2. *Catalysis.* In any case, this problem of the disconnection of the signifiers through summaries which seem to be projected in mirrors, is very important for a modern theory of literature. Our text is exceptionally dense in disconnections, in summaries, which are spaced out as if we were looking into a set of mirrors. There is a fascinating structural problem here which has not yet been carefully studied: this is the problem of what is called *catalysis*; in a narrative, there are several levels of necessity; the summaries show what one can remove or add: since a story hangs together through its summary, this means that we can "fill" this story; whence this term of *catalysis*; one can say that the story without its résumé, the integral story, is a sort of catalytic stage of a résumé state; there is a relation of filling between an empty structure and a full structure, and this movement is interesting to study, because it illustrates the play of structure. A narrative, on a certain level, is like a sentence. A sentence can be catalyzed, in principle, to infinity. I no longer recall which American linguist (Chomsky or someone of his school) has said as much, which is philosophically very fine: "We never speak anything but a single sentence, which only death comes to interrupt . . . " The structure of the sentence is such that you can always add words, epithets, adjectives, subordinate clauses, or other main clauses, and never alter the structure of the sentence. Ultimately, if we today grant so much importance to language, it is because language, as it is now described, gives us the example of an object at once structured and infinite: there is in language the experience of an *infinite* structure (in the mathematical sense of the word); and the sentence is the very example of this: you can fill a sentence indefinitely; and, if you stop your sentences, if you close them, which has always been the great problem of rhetoric (as is testified to by the notions of *period*, of *clause*, which are operators of closure), it is solely under the pressure of contingences, because of breath, of memory, of fatigue, but never because of structure: no structural law compels you to close the sentence, and you can open it structurally to infinity. The problem of the résumé or summary is the same, shifted to the level of the narrative. The résumé proves that a story is in some sense endless: you can fill it to infinity; then why stop it at this particular moment? This is one of the problems which the analysis of narrative should permit us to approach.

3. *The diagrammatic structure*. Further, in relation to our text, the disconnection of the summaries and their multiplicity (there are five summaries for a small extent of text) imply that there is for each summary a new circuit of destination. In other words, to multiply the summaries means to multiply the destinations of the message. This text from Acts, structurally – and I shall even be naive enough to say, phenomenologically – this text appears to be the privileged site of an intense multiplication, diffusion, dissemination, refraction of messages.

The same thing can be said on four successive levels; for instance the angel's order to Cornelius is spoken as an order given, as an order executed, as the narrative of that execution, and as a summary of the narrative of that execution; and the recipients obviously relay each other: the Spirit communicates to Peter and to Cornelius, Peter communicates to Cornelius, Cornelius communicates to Peter, then Peter to the community of Jerusalem, and finally to us the readers. It has been said that most narratives are narratives of a quest, of a search in which a subject desires or searches for an object (this is the case of the narratives of miracles). In my opinion, and this is the structural originality of this text, its mainspring is not the quest, but communication, "trans-mission": the characters of the narrative are not actors but agents of transmission, agents of communication and diffusion. This is interesting: we see in a concrete and I should like to say "technical" fashion that the text presents what I should call a *diagrammatic* structure, in relation to its content. A diagram is a proportional analogy (which is moreover pleonastic, since *analogia* in Greek means *proportion*); it is not a figurative copy (it suffices to recall the diagrams in demography, in sociology, in economics); it is a form which has been illuminated by Jakobson: in the activity of language, the diagram is important, because at every moment language produces diagrammatic figures: it cannot literally copy (according to a complete *mimesis*) a content by a form, because there is no common measure between the content and the linguistic form; but what it can do is to produce diagrammatic figures; the example given by Jakobson is famous: the poetic diagram (for poetry is the site of the diagram) is the electoral slogan of General Eisenhower, when he was a candidate for the presidency: *I like Ike*; this is a diagram since the word *Ike* is enveloped in the affection of the word *like*. There is a diagrammatic relation between the sentence *I like Ike* and the content, to wit that General Eisenhower was enveloped by the love of his electors.

This diagrammatic structure is what we have in our text, for the text's content – and it is not we who are inventing it, since, once again, we are concerned with a text which I shall call anagogic, which gives its meaning itself – this content is the possibility of the diffusion of baptism. And the diagram is the diffusion of narrative by multiplication of summaries; in other words, there is a kind of diagrammatic refraction around the notion of limitless, vulgarized communication. Ultimately, what the narrative enacts diagrammatically is this idea of *limitlessness*. The fact that in so little space there should be four summaries of the same episode constitutes a diagrammatic image of the limitless character of grace. The theory of this "non-limit" is given by a narrative which enacts the "non-limit" of the summary. Consequently the "subject" of the text is the very idea of message; for structural analysis, this text has for its subject the message, it is a functionalization of language, of communication; moreover this is a theme of Pentecost (this is alluded to in the text). The subject is the communication and the diffusion of messages and languages. Structurally, as we have seen, the content of what Cornelius must ask Peter is not uttered: the angel does not say to Cornelius why he must send messengers in search of Peter. And now we apprehend the structural meaning of this absence, which I mentioned at the beginning: it is because, as a matter of fact, the message is its very form, it is its destination. Ultimately, what Cornelius must ask of Peter is not a veritable content, it is the communication with Peter. The content of the message is therefore the message itself; the destination of the message, i.e., the Uncircumcised – *that* is the very content of the message.

These indications will no doubt seem *withdrawn* in relation to the text. My excuse is that the goal of the investigation, of the research, is not the explication or interpretation of a text, but the interrogation of this text (among others) with a view to the reconstitution of a general language of narrative. Obliged to speak about a text, and about only one, I could neither speak of the Structural Analysis of Narrative in general, nor structure this text in detail: I have sought a compromise, with all the disappointments which such a decision may involve; I have proceeded to a work of partial recension; I have sketched the structural dossier of a text, but for this work to find its whole meaning, one would have to unite this dossier with others, to pour this text into the immense corpus of the world's narratives.

Chapter 2

On the Possibility of Generating Aesthetic Messages in an Edenic Language

Umberto Eco 1932–

Introduction

Umberto Eco is Professor of Semiotics at the University of Bologna. He is also a brilliant novelist and popular essayist. Eco draws heavily upon the semiotic theories of Ferdinand de Saussure and especially Charles S. Peirce, of whom he is one of the foremost contemporary interpreters. His major works (with Italian publication and English translation dates) include: *The Open Work* (1962/1989); *A Theory of Semiotics* (1976); *The Role of the Reader* (1979); *The Name of the Rose* (1980/1983); *Semiotics and the Philosophy of Language* (1984); *Travels in Hyperreality* (1986); *Foucault's Pendulum* (1988/1989); *Interpretation and Overinterpretation* (1992, with Richard Rorty); *The Island of the Day Before* (1995); and *Kant and the Platypus* (1997/2000). His work figures importantly in *The Postmodern Bible*'s discussion of structuralism and narratology.

"On the Possibility of Generating Aesthetic Messages in an Edenic Language" was published in 1971 and first appeared in English in *The Role of the Reader* (1979). This essay's focus on the Bible is rare among his work since he does not often refer to specific biblical texts (although he does frequently refer to theological issues). In this essay, the Garden of Eden story provides Eco with a springboard from which he launches his study of a specific instance in which what Roman Jakobson calls "aesthetic language" generates contradictory messages. Eco's argument suggests that it is in the very nature of all language to generate distortion of or disobedience to a message. The physical system of language itself invites and even demands distortion. Even the divine word, as represented in the Bible, brings with it of necessity its own misunderstanding and transgression. Furthermore, if humanity is created in the image of God, then the linguistic corruption that taints the human world already in the Garden of Eden itself arises in the supernatural realm. God either creates this corruption himself, or else God is unable to prevent its occurrence. Even God is constrained by the inherent imperfections of language.

Some messages in Eco's hypothetical Edenic language are non-ambiguous. However, even these unambiguous messages are disturbed by the possibility of producing aesthetic messages in that same language. Aesthetic messages arise from alterations in the language of the message that produce an additional signifying level (connotation) of the message. What they signify directly is not some object in the extratextual world, but rather another message. This message, or further level of the aesthetic message, points self-referentially "back" to the physical stuff of the message itself, that is, to the material aspect of the signifiers. This disruption of linguistic order is, as Eco notes, an effect of narrative and ideology.

Eco lays out the Edenic language around two series of binary oppositions. The first pair of oppositions features a list of conceptual signifieds which derive from possible experiences within the narrative world of the biblical story, such as "Good vs. Bad." The second pair of oppositions features the physical signifiers used to refer to these signified contents. The signifiers also appear in their simplest form, namely, one consonant and one vowel, arranged according to a simple "combinatory rule." These two series of oppositions are correlated in the system of signs that forms the Edenic language. For every difference of content (signified) there is a corresponding difference of expression (signifier). This double string of oppositions establishes a further series of "connotative chains" through which the language-user can move from one sign to another one.

A contradiction results from this double series of oppositions when they are placed in the Eden narrative. The irregularity of the "Serpent" and "Apple" signs disrupts the connotative chains and introduces a semantic imbalance into the linguistic system, because the forbidden, bad fruit is also good and beautiful. God's error leads to the creation by Adam and Eve of a metaphor which conceals linguistic contradiction without eliminating it. Adam and Eve's metaphor produces a "language passion" which corresponds to their desire for the forbidden fruit. The metaphor opens up the "limitless possibilities of semiosis," which is both the power of signs to refer endlessly to other signs and the inability of any signifier to refer absolutely to any signified. The message undermines the oppositions that are essential to its own significance, and the story deconstructs itself. The Edenic language is inherently ambiguous, because it permits and even requires this contradiction. As the creator of this language God is responsible for subverting "the presumed natural order of things." The origin of sin is linguistic.

According to Jakobson the aesthetic use of language is marked by the *ambiguity* and the *self-focusing character* of the messages articulated by it. By ambiguity the message is rendered creative in relation to the acknowledged possibilities of the code. The same is true of the metaphorical – not necessarily the same thing as aesthetic – applications of

Umberto Eco, "On the Possibility of Generating Aesthetic Messages in an Edenic Language," from *The Role of the Reader* (Bloomington: Indiana University Press, 1984; revised version of Bruce Merry, trans., "On the Possibility of Generating Esthetic Messages in an Edenic Language," *Twentieth Century Studies* 6, no. 7, 1972).

language. For an aesthetic message to come into being, it is not enough to establish
ambiguity at the level of the *content-form*; here, inside the formal symmetry of metonymic relationships, metaphorical replacements are operated, enforcing a fresh conception of the semantic system and the universe of meanings coordinated by it. But, to
create an aesthetic message, there must also be alterations in the form in which it is
expressed, and these alterations must be significant enough to require the addressee of
the message, though aware of a change in the *content-form*, to refer back to the message
itself as a physical entity. This will allow him to detect alterations in the form of
expression, for there is a kind of solidarity binding together the alteration in content
with any change in its mode of expression. This is the sense in which an aesthetic
message becomes self-focusing; it also conveys information about its own physical
make-up, and this justifies the proposition that in all art there is inseparability of form
and content. However, this principle does not necessarily mean that one cannot
distinguish between the two levels and pick out the specific operations which are
being carried on at each; it simply establishes that any changes occurring at the two
levels are functionally related to each other.

In aesthetic debate there is always a temptation to support the above propositions at
an abstract level. When the analyst moves on to practical demonstration, he tends to
work with aesthetic messages which have already been elaborated and which therefore
present special complexities; in this case, distinctions between different levels, changes
in code and system, innovatory devices – all become very difficult to examine accurately. So it is a useful exercise to set up a small-scale working model of aesthetic
language; this would involve an extremely simple language/code and demonstrate the
rules by which aesthetic messages can be generated. These rules will have to arise from
inside the code itself, but then be capable of generating an alteration of the code, both in
its form of expression and in its form of content. The working model must therefore be
equipped to demonstrate a language's own capacity for generating self-contradiction. It
must also show how the aesthetic use of the given language is one of the most
appropriate devices for generating these contradictions. Finally, the model must prove
that any contradictions generated by the aesthetic use of language at the level of its form
of expression equally involve contradictions in the form of its content; ultimately, they
entail a complete reorganizing of our conceptual vision of the universe.

To set this experiment in motion, we shall imagine a primordial predicament: life in
the Garden of Eden, where the inhabitants speak in Edenic language.

My model for this language is borrowed from G. Miller's Grammarama project
(*Psychology and Communication*, New York, 1967), except that Miller did not plan his
model specifically as an Edenic language. He was merely concerned to study an
individual speaker who is producing casual sequences by means of two base symbols
(D and R) and receiving control responses designed to clarify which of his sequences
are grammatically well formed; then Miller checked the speaker's capacity for
piecing together the generative rule of the correct sequences. His model in fact
constituted a language-learning test, whereas my experiment presents us with Adam
and Eve, who already know which are the correct sequences and who employ them in
conversation, even though they entertain unclear notions about the underlying generative rules.

Semantic Units and Significant Sequences
in the Garden of Eden

Although they are surrounded by a luxuriant environment, Adam and Eve have managed to devise a restricted series of semantic units which give preferential status to their emotional responses to flora and fauna, rather than a naming and exact classification of each of them. These semantic units can be organized under six main headings:

Yes vs. No

Edible vs. Inedible (Where Edible stands for "to be eaten," "comestible," "I want to eat," and so on.)

Good vs. Bad (This antithesis covers both moral and physical experiences.)

Beautiful vs. Ugly (This antithesis covers every degree of pleasure, amusement, desirability.)

Red vs. Blue (This antithesis covers the whole gamut of chromatic experience: the ground is perceived as red and the sky as blue, meat is red and stones are blue, and so on.)

Serpent vs. Apple (This is the only antithesis which denotes objects rather than qualities of objects or responses to them. We must take note that, while all other objects are ready to hand, these latter two emerge exceptionally on account of their alien character; indeed, we can acknowledge that these two cultural units are incorporated in the code only after a factual judgement issued by God about the non-touchable status of the apple. So when the serpent appears round the tree on which the apple is hanging, the animal is somehow registered as complementary to the fruit and becomes a specific cultural unit, whereas all other animals are perceived as "edible" or "bad" or "blue" or even "red," without the intervention of further specifications from the global continuum of perception.)

Obviously, one cultural unit inevitably leads to another, and this sets up a series of connotative chains:

(1) Red = Edible = Good = Beautiful
    Blue = Inedible = Bad = Ugly

Nevertheless, Adam and Eve are unable to designate, hence conceive of, these units unless they route them by way of significant forms. This is why they are provided with (or perhaps acquire by slow stages) an extremely elementary language which is adequate to express these concepts.

The repertoire of this language is built up out of two sounds, A and B, which can be arranged in a variety of sequences following the combinatory rule *X, nY, X*. This means that every sequence must start with one of the two elements and carry on with *n* repetitions of the other, ending up with one further occurrence of the first element. This kind of rule allows the production of an infinite series of syntactically correct sequences. But Adam and Eve have a strictly finite repertoire which exactly fits the cultural units mentioned above. So their code works out as follows:

(2) ABA   Edible
     BAB   Inedible
     ABBA   Good
     BAAB   Bad
     ABBBA   Serpent
     BAAAB   Apple
     ABBBBA   Beautiful
     BAAAAB   Ugly
     ABBBBBA   Red
     BAAAAAB   Blue

Furthermore, this code incorporates two all-purpose operators:

$$AA = Yes$$
$$BB = No$$

which can stand for Permission/Interdiction or, alternatively, Existence/Nonexistence, and even denote such oppositions as Approval/Disapproval, and so forth.

There are no further syntactical rules, apart from the fact that, if two sequences are joined to each other, their cultural units are thus brought into reciprocal predication: BAAAB, ABBBBBA, for example, means "the apple is red," but also "red apple."

Adam and Eve are fully competent at handling their Edenic language, yet there is one thing they find hard to form a clear idea of: the generative rule behind the sequences. They can grasp this intuitively, but with the consequence that the AA and BB sequences become anomalous. What is more, they fail to realize that other correct sequences could be granted. This is partly because they feel no particular need for them, since there is nothing else they want to put a name to. The world they find themselves living in is full, harmonious, and satisfying, so that they register no sense of crisis or of necessity.

Therefore the connotative chains referred to in (1) assume the following structures:

(3) ABA = ABBA = ABBBBA = ABBBBBA = BAAAB = AA
     Eat   Good   Beautiful   Red   Apple   Yes

     BAB = BAAB = BAAAAB = BAAAAAB = ABBBA = BB
     No Eat Bad   Ugly   Blue   Serpent No

Words thus equal things (or rather the sensations which Adam and Eve are aware of) and things equal words. This makes it natural for them to envisage a number of connotative associations such as

(4) ABA = Red

Evidently this presents us already with a rudimentary use of metaphor, based on the possibility of extrapolating from metonymic chains of the type (3), and constitutes an embryonic inventive use of language. The inventiveness shown in this operation is still minimal because all the chains involve known elements, which have been fully explored, this semiotic universe being so diminutive both in the form of its content and in its expressive possibilities.

Any judgment which Adam and Eve pass on the universe is automatically bound to be a semiotic judgment, which is equivalent to calling it a judgment inside the normative cycle set up by the semiosis. It is true that they also pronounce factual judgments of the kind / ... *red* / when, for example, they find themselves confronted by a cherry. But this kind of factual information is exhausted instantly, since there is no linguistic mechanism for uttering / ... /, and therefore this sensation is not susceptible of formal insertion into their referential system. Ultimately, judgments of this sort can only generate tautology, because the cherry, once it is perceived and denoted as / *red* /, prepares the ground for evaluative statements such as / *red is red* / or, alternatively, / *red is good* /, which had already been rendered homologous by the system, as we saw above in (3). We are entitled to assume that they can point at things with their fingers, that is, use physical gestures to designate an object to the other person, which is the equivalent of / *this* /. In much the same way, the shifter /*I*/ or /*you*/ or /*he*/ is added to any statement by means of pointed fingers designed to function as pronouns. Hence the statement /ABBBBBA. ABA/ means, if accompanied by two stabbing gestures with the finger, "*I* eat *this* red." But no doubt Adam and Eve perceive those indexical devices as non–linguistic ones: they consider them as *existential qualifiers* or *circumstantial arrows* used for referring a message (meaningful in itself) to an actual object or situation.

Formulation of the First Factual Judgment with Semiotic Consequences

Adam and Eve have only just settled down in the Garden of Eden. They have learned to find their way around with the help of language – when out comes God, who pronounces the first factual judgment. The general sense of what God is trying to tell them is as follows: "You two probably imagine that the apple belongs to the class of good, edible things, because it happens to be red. Well, I've got news for you. The apple is not to be considered edible because it is bad." Obviously, God is above providing an explanation of why the apple is evil; he is himself the yardstick of all values and knows it. For Adam and Eve the whole thing is rather more tricky: they have grown into the habit of associating the Good with the Edible and the Red. Yet they cannot possibly ignore a commandment coming from God. His status in their eyes is that of an AA: he constitutes "yes," an incarnation of the Positive. In fact, whereas the sequence AA is used with all other occurrences only for the purpose of connoting pairings of different sequences, in the case of God ("I am that I am"), AA is more than a mere formula of predication: it is his name. If they were a little more versed in theology, Adam and Eve would come to the conclusion that the serpent should be referred to as BB, but they are blissfully ignorant of such subtleties. Anyway, the serpent is blue and inedible, and only after God's commandment does it become a pertinent detail among all the items of Eden's resources.

God spoke and his words were /BAAAB. BAB – BAAAB. BAAB/ (apple inedible, apple bad).

This constitutes a factual judgment, as it affords a notion which is as yet unfamiliar to those God has addressed; for God is both referent and source of the referent – his pronouncements are a court of reference. Yet God's judgment is in part semiotic, for it posits a new type of connotative pairing between semantic units which had previously been coupled together differently.

Nevertheless, we shall see shortly how God committed a grave error by providing those very elements which could throw the whole code out of joint. In an effort to elaborate a prohibition which would put his creatures to the test, God provides the fundamental example of a subversion in the presumed natural order of things. Why should an apple which is red be inedible as if it were blue?

Alas, God wanted to bring into existence the cultural tradition, and culture is born, apparently, to the sound of an institutional taboo. It would be possible to argue that culture was implicitly present, granted the existence of language and that all God's creative activity was already a norm, a source of authority, a law. But who will ever be able to trace the precise order of events at that turning point in history? What if language was formed at a stage later than the issue of the prohibition? My present task is, not to solve the problem of the origins of language, but to manipulate a hypothetical speech model. All the same, we are entitled to insist that God acted rashly; it is too soon to establish where he went wrong. First, we must return to the evolving crisis in the Garden.

Now that Adam and Eve have been served with the apple interdict, they find themselves obliged to adjust the connotative chains established in (3) and set up new chains as follows:

(5)   Red = Edible   = Good = Beautiful = Yes
       Blue = Inedible = Bad   = Ugly   = No = Serpent and Apple

from which it is only a short step to

Serpent = Apple

This shows that the semantic universe rapidly becomes unbalanced by comparison with the pristine situation. Nonetheless, it would seem that modern man's semantic universe bears more resemblance to (5) than to (3). This imbalance within their system insinuates the first contradictions into Adam and Eve's wonderland.

In Which the Contradiction Takes Shape Inside the Semantic Universe of Eden

It is perfectly true that certain habits of perception entitle us to go on referring to the apple as a / *red* /, even when we are quite conscious that it has been connotatively assimilated to that which is bad and inedible and, therefore, to Blue. The sentence,

(6)   BAAAB. ABBBBBA (the apple is red),

is directly contradicted by the other sentence,

(7)   BAAAB. BAAAAAB (the apple is blue).

Adam and Eve suddenly realize they have hit on an anomaly, by which a denoting term establishes a straight contrast with those connotations which it inevitably produces; this contradiction cannot possibly be expressed in their standard denotative vocabulary. They are unable to point out the apple by saying / *this is red* /. They are naturally quite reluctant to formulate the contradictory proposition the apple is red, it is blue, so they are confined to pointing out the peculiar phenomenon of the apple by a crude metaphor such as / *the thing which is red and blue* / or, preferably, / *the thing which is named red-blue* /. Instead of the cacophonous proposition /BAAAB. ABBBBBA. BAAAAAB/ (the apple is red, it is blue), they prefer to devise a metaphor, a compound substitutional name. This releases them from the logical contradiction and also opens up the possibility of an intuitive and ambiguous grasp of the concept (by way of a fairly ambiguous use of the code). Hence they refer to the apple by

(8)   ABBBBABAAAAAB (the redblue).

This new term expresses a contradictory fact without obliging the speaker to formulate it in accordance with the habitual logical rules, which would in fact exclude it. But it stimulates an unprecedented sensation in Adam and Eve. They find such an unusual sound fascinating, as well as the unprecedented form they have devised for the sequence. The message in (8) is obviously ambiguous from the viewpoint of the form of content, but the form of its expression is also ambiguous. It thus becomes embryonically self-focusing. Adam says / *redblue* /, and then, instead of looking at the apple, he repeats to himself in a slightly dazed and childish way that lump of curious sounds. For the first time perhaps he is observing words rather than the things they stand for.

The Generation of Aesthetic Messages

When he takes another look at (8), Adam makes a startling discovery: ABBBBB*A*-*B*AAAAB contains at its very center the sequence BAB (which means "inedible"). How odd: the apple, *qua redblue*, structurally incorporates a formal indication of the inedibility which previously seemed to be simply one of its connotations at the level of the form of content. Now, on the contrary, the apple turns out to be "inedible" even at the level of expression. Adam and Eve have at last discovered the aesthetic use of language. But they are not completely absorbed in it. Desire for the apple has yet to grow stronger; the apple experience still has to acquire a growing fascination if it is to produce an aesthetic impulse. The Romantics were well aware of this: art is created only by the upsurge of grand passions (even if the object of this passion is merely the language). Adam has now acquired the language passion. The whole business is most enticing. But the apple also triggers off another passion in Adam: the apple is Forbidden Fruit, and, being the only such article in the Garden of Eden, it holds a special appeal for him, an apple appeal, so to speak. It certainly makes one want to ask "Why?" Yet it is the forbidden fruit which has caused the birth of a previously unprecedented word – a forbidden word? There is now a close correlation between passionate desire for the apple and passion for language; we have a situation permeated with a physical and mental excitation which seems to mirror the whole process we moderns call the creative urge.

The following stage in Adam's experiment confers special status on the *substance of expression*. He finds a chunk of rock and scribbles on it

(9)   ABBBBBA, which means "red." But he writes this with the juice of blue berries.

Next he writes

(10)   BAAAAAB, which means "blue." This time he writes it in red juice.

Now he steps back and admires his work with a certain satisfaction. Surely the expressions in (9) and (10) are both metaphors for the apple. However, their metaphoric status is heightened by the presence of a physical element, namely, the particular emphasis inherent in the matter of expression itself. Still, this operation has transformed the substance of expression (the particular way of handling it) from a purely optional variant into a pertinent feature: it is now *form of expression*, though Adam is dealing with form of expression in a language of colors, as opposed to words. Also, something rather curious has happened: up to this point red objects were imprecise referents which the sign-vehicle ABBBBBA ("red") could be applied to. But now a red something, the red of the berry's juice, has itself become the sign-vehicle of an element which has as one of its meanings the very same word ABBBBBA which previously stood for it. In fact, the limitless possibilities of semiosis allow any meaning to become the sign-vehicle of another meaning, even of its own erstwhile sign-vehicle. There can even come about a situation where an object (that is, referent) becomes itself a sign. In any case, that redness means, not only red, nor even merely ABBBBBA, but also edible and beautiful, and so on. Meanwhile the verbal equivalent of what is actually scribbled on the rock is blue and, consequently, bad, inedible. What a marvelous discovery! It certainly renders the whole force of ambiguity in the concept of apple. For hours on end Adam and Eve sit back and contemplate those signs written out on the rock; they are in an ecstasy of admiration. "How very baroque," Eve would like to comment, but she cannot. She has no critical metalanguage at her disposal. But Adam is bursting to have another go. He writes up

(11)   ABBBBB*B*A.

Here are six B's. This sequence does not exist in the terms of his vocabulary, yet it is closest of all to the sequence ABBBBBA (red). Adam has written up the word /red/, but with added graphic emphasis. Perhaps this emphasis of the form of expression has a parallel at the level of the form of content? Surely it is a heavily emphasized red? A red which is redder than other reds? Blood, for example? It is odd that this very moment, when Adam is casting around for a function for his new word, is the first occasion when he has had to take note of the various shades of red in the world that surrounds him. The innovation which he has established at the level of form of expression actually induces him to isolate specific detail in the form of content. If he has come this far, then we may say that the extra B is, not a variant in the form of expression, but rather a fresh feature to add to it. Adam puts the problem to one side for the time being. His immediate interest is to continue the language experiment dealing with the apple, and this recent discovery has sidetracked him. He now wants to try writing (or saying) something more complex. He wants to say inedible is bad, which is apple ugly and blue, and here is how he sets about writing it:

(12)   BAB
           BAAB
           BAAAB
           BAAAAB
        BAAAAAB

The text is now in a vertical column. And two curious formal characteristics of the message force themselves onto Adam's attention: there is a progressive increase in the length of words (this represents the establishment of a rhythm), and, second, each of the five sequences ends with the same letter (this represents a primitive model of rhyme). All of a sudden Adam is swept away by the incantatory power (the *epode*) of language. So God's commandment was justified, he thinks to himself: the sinfulness of the apple is underlined and emphasized by a kind of formal necessity which *requires* that the apple be ugly and blue. Adam is so persuaded by this apparent indivisibility of form and content that he begins to believe that *nomina sint numina*. He decides to go even further than this: he decides to reinforce both the rhythm and the rhyme by inserting elements of calculated redundancy in his already unquestionably poetic statement:

(13)   BAB   BAB
        BAAAB   BAB
         BAAB   BAB
          BAB   BAAAAAB

By now his "poetic" ambitions are clearly aroused! The idea that *nomina sint numina* has fired his imagination. With an almost Heideggerian sense of false etymology, he starts by noticing that the word for apple (BAAAB) ends with the letter B, just like all those words which refer specifically to BB things, bad things, like badness, ugliness, and blue. The first impression made on Adam by the poetic use of language is a growing conviction that language is part of the natural order of things, easily conceived by analogy with the world it depicts and held in gestation by obscure onomatopoeic impulses of the soul; language is the authorized voice of God. We can see that Adam tends to use poetic experience to put the clock back, in a rather reactionary key: through language the gods speak themselves! Furthermore, the whole process is flattering to his ego: ever since he started to manipulate language, he has been inclined to see himself as being on the side of God. It is beginning to occur to him that he may be one up on dear Eve. He begins to think that the poetic power is *la différence*.

However, Eve is by no means indifferent to her partner's passion for language. She just dabbles in it for different motives. Her meeting with the Serpent has already taken place, and the little which he can have told her (in the impoverished idiom of the Garden) has probably been charged with a mutual liking we investigators are in no position to speculate about, since semiotics has "to pass over in silence what it cannot speak about."

At any rate, Eve joins in the game. And she explains to Adam that if words are Gods, then it's odd how the Serpent (ABBBA) has the same ending as the words which stand for beautiful, good, and red. Eve goes on to explain that poetry allows all sorts of language games:

(14)   ABBA
       ABBBBA
       ABBBBBA
       ABBBA

Good, beautiful and red – is the Serpent goes Eve's poem, and it entails just the same formal identity between expression and content as the one produced by Adam (12). Eve's sensitiveness has allowed her to go even further and to display the anaphorical smoothness of the beginning as a counterpoint to the rhymed gentleness of the end. Eve's approach reopens the whole problem of self-contradiction, which Adam's poem seems to have papered over. Just how can the Serpent be the formal equivalent of things which the language system excludes as his predicates?

Eve's success goes to her head. She vaguely imagines a new device for creating hidden homologies between form and content and for using these to produce new contradictions. She could, for example, try out a sequence where every letter, if analyzed against a microscopic grid, proved to be composed by one semantically opposed to it. But to carry off this type of "concrete poetry" successfully would require a level of graphic sophistication which is quite beyond Eve's power. Adam therefore takes things into his own hands and conceives a still more ambiguous sequence:

(15)   BAA—B.

Now what does the blank space stand for? If it really is a blank, then Adam has uttered the concept bad with a slight hesitation; but if the blank is really a proper space (which has been muffled by some chance noise), then it could only contain an extra A, which means he has uttered apple. At this stage Eve devises her own *recitar cantando*, an Edenic Sprachgesang: in other words, a kind of musical theater:

(16)   ABB̲BA.

Here the sing-song voice hovers at a heightened tone on the last B, with the result that we cannot tell whether she has sung out ABBBA (Serpent), or simply doubled the final B of beautiful. This considerably upsets Adam, because it suggests a real possibility that language is responsible for ambiguities and deceptions. So he transfers his anxiety away from the pitfalls of language onto the meanings which the commandment issued by God had put into question: "to be or not to be" can only result in "edible/inedible," in Adam's situation, but, when he sings out his dilemma, he is fascinated by its rhythm, for language is beginning to crumble to pieces in his mouth; he has found the way to give it a totally free rein:

(17)   ABA   BAB
       ABA   BAB
       ABA   BAB   BAB   BB   B   A
       BBBBBBAAAAAABBBBBB
       BAAAA
       AA

The poem sets free an explosion of words, the Futurist *parole in libertà*.

But, at the very moment he recognizes that he has invented incorrect words, Adam begins to see more clearly why the others were correct. At last he can visualize the generative rule which stood at the center of his language system (X, nY, X). It is only when he violates the system that Adam comes to understand its structure. At this precise moment, while he is wondering if the last line is the acme of grammatical disorderliness, he is bound to realize that the sequence AA does in fact exist, so he will ask himself how and why the language system can allow it. He therefore thinks back to (15) and the problem which occurred to him in that case, concerning the blank space. It comes clear to him that even a blank constitutes a full space in the system, and that the sequences AA or BB, which both struck him originally as anomalous, are actually correct, because the rule (X, nY, X) certainly does not prevent the value of n from being *Zero*.

Adam has arrived at a comprehension of the system at the very moment in which he is calling the system into question and therefore destroying it. Just as he comes to understand the rigid generative law of the code which had governed him, so he realizes that here is technically nothing to stop him from proposing a new code (for example, nX, nY, nX): such a code would legitimize sequences of the type BBBBBBAAAAAABBBBBB, as in the fourth line of (17). While bent on destroying the system, he comprehends its full range of possibilities and discovers that he is master of it. Only a short while ago, he fondly imagined that poetry was a medium through which spoke Gods. Now he is becoming aware of the *arbitrariness of signs*.

At first he loses control of his own exuberance. He continually takes to pieces and puts together again this crazy gadget that he has found in his control; he composes totally implausible gibberish and then hums it admiringly to himself for hours on end; he invents the colors of the vowels, flatters himself that he has created a poetic language accessible, some days, to all senses; he writes of silences and of nights; he defines vertigos. He says, An apple! and, out of the forgetfulness where his voice banishes any contour, inasmuch as it is something other than known calyxes, musically arises, an idea itself and fragrant, the one absent from all baskets. *Le suggérer, voilà le rêve!* He wants to make himself a *seer*, by a long, prodigious and rational disordering of all the senses. But then, step by step, he escapes from emotion, expressing it through its objective correlative and, as does the God of the Creation, remains within or behind or above his handiwork, invisible, refined out of existence, indifferent, paring his fingernails.

The Reformulation of Content

Eventually, Adam calms down. At least one thing has become clear during his manic explorations: the order of language is not absolute. This gives rise to the legitimate doubt that the pairing off of denoting sequences against the cultural universe of meanings, which was provided as the system in (2), may not be an unquestionable absolute after all. Finally, he feels inclined to question the very totality of the cultural units which the System had neatly paired off against the series of sequences which he has so recently destroyed.

Now Adam passes on to an investigation of the form of content. Whoever actually said that Blue was Inedible? From conventionalized meanings Adam takes a short step back to the world of experience and stages another encounter with its physical referents. He picks a blue berry for himself and eats it; the berry tastes good. So far he has been in the habit of drawing all the liquid he needed from (red) fruit, but now he discovers that (blue) water is eminently drinkable and develops a pronounced taste for it. Again, he is influenced by the curiosity which he first felt after the experiment in (11): probably there are different gradations of red, blood red, the sun's red, the red of apples or of certain plants and bushes. Again, Adam resegments the content and discovers fresh cultural categories (this means new perceptive realities), which oblige him to provide new names for them, although these are quite easy to invent. He composes complex sequences to denote these new categories and devises new verbal formulae in order to express this experience in factual judgments. The experience is subsequently assigned to the expanding language system by way of semiotic judgments. His language is beginning to swell in his hands, and his whole world is growing fuller. Clearly, neither language nor the world is so harmonious or single-voiced as both were during the period of situation (1), but at least he is no longer afraid of the contradictions concealed inside their language system; this is because from one side the contradictions force him to reenvisage the form which he assigns to the world, while from the other they induce him to exploit them for their potential poetic effects.

As a result of all this, Adam discovers that Order, as such, is non-existent; it is just one of the infinite possible states of repose which disorder occasionally arrives at.

It would be superfluous to add that Eve goes on to encourage him to eat the apple. Once Adam has eaten it, he is in a position to issue a judgment of the kind the apple is good, which reestablishes, at least for one item, the equilibrium which the language system enjoyed before the Prohibition. But this detail is irrelevant at the stage we have now reached. Adam was obliged to exit from the Garden of Eden after his first nervous manipulation of language. This was the mistake God made by disturbing the univocal harmony of the primitive language system by an ambiguously phrased prohibition; but, like all prohibitions, it was supposed to forbid something desirable. From that moment onward (not from the time when Adam really ate the apple), world history commenced.

Unless God was fully aware of this and issued his prohibition precisely to stimulate the birth of history. Or again, perhaps God did not exist, and the prohibition was simply invented by Adam and Eve for the specific purpose of introducing a contradiction into the language system and producing inventive modes of discussion. Perhaps the language system incorporated this contradiction from its very beginnings and the prohibition myth was invented by our forefathers simply to explain such a scandalous state of affairs.

Evidently these observations have taken us outside the strict terms of our inquiry, which is concerned with language creativity, its poetic applications, and the interaction between the world's form and language's form.

At any rate, it goes without saying that, once Adam had redeemed language's pledge to Order and Singleness of Voice, it was handed down to his descendants in a considerably richer form.

Hence Cain and Abel, having discovered the existence of other orders precisely by means of language, pass on logically to the murder of Adam. This latter detail draws us even further away from our habitual exegetical tradition and plumps us in a midway position between the myth of Saturn and the myth of Sigmund. But there is a method to all this madness, for Adam taught mankind that, in order to restructure codes, one needs to rewrite messages.

Chapter 3

Reading the Bible

Julia Kristeva 1941–

Introduction

Julia Kristeva, a Parisienne born in Bulgaria, has since 1966 carried on a radical critique of what she calls the "signifying practice" of literature and psychoanalysis in studies of linguistics, semiotics, politics, psychoanalysis, and fiction writing. Her frequent travels to the United States give her a privileged stance to build bridges between Continental and American thinking. A renowned linguist, semiotician, feminist, psychoanalyst, and novelist, Kristeva is undoubtedly one of the most influential European thinkers of our postmodern era. Her major publications include: *Semiotiké: recherches pour une semanalyse* (1969); *Le texte du roman* (1970); *About Chinese Women* (1974/English translation 1977); *The Revolution in Poetic Language* (1974/1984); *Polylogue* (1977/1980); *Powers of Horror: An Essay on Abjection* (1980/1982); *Tales of Love* (1982/1987); *Black Sun* (1987); *Strangers to Ourselves* (1989/1991); *The Samurai* (1990/1992); *Le vieil homme et les loups* (1992); and *New Maladies of the Soul* (1993/1995).

Kristeva studied Russian Formalism in Bulgaria and was a student of Roland Barthes in Paris in the late 1960s. Since then, she has gradually developed a criticism of formalism and structuralism. The center of her theory is the notion of the signifying practice in literature and psychoanalysis. Kristeva has developed a theory of semiotics which focuses on the nature of poetic language and the structuralist notion of the sign while also including the extralinguistic factors of history, gender, and psychology. Throughout her career she has continued her investigation in the territories of subjectivity and multiplicity and has kept the concept of heterogeneity and multiplicity borrowed from a linguistic and semiotic approach as the cornerstone of her research.

Kristeva influences biblical studies in her work in *semiotics* (which is feminine for Kristeva); in her definition of *intertextuality* and the intertextual relationships between texts – a term Kristeva developed from Mikhail Bakhtin (see *The Postmodern Bible*: 130); in the *concept of the subject* which imbues her work in language and psychology; in her focus on *the body and body criticism* and on the *language of desire/desire in language*;

and, finally, her work in *ethics*. Kristeva's and Luce Irigaray's psychoanalytical feminisms are significant for religious studies, even if more radical feminist theologians are uneasy with Kristeva's defense of Freud and interpretation of motherhood as a pre-Oedipal expression. For Kristeva religion provides an important space for community and for making sense of the self and world. (For a general introduction to Kristeva's psychoanalytic theory see PMB: 212–17.)

Many of Kristeva's works have been important to biblical scholars, in particular, her concept of the "abject" in *Powers of Horror*. Kristeva defines the abject as the place where meaning collapses: the abject is outside of the subject/object split that defines difference. In the place of the abject there is a disruption of order, rules, and systems; the abject is a place of fear and horror. The abject is transgressive, breaks all boundaries, and allows for revelation, resurrection, and what we have been calling the power of the sacred. Kristeva calls her program for reading for the abject in biblical literature the semiotics of biblical abomination. Defilement, impurity (Mary Douglas adds danger), taboo, the improper/unclean, the polluted are the terms that define the abject in the Bible. Kristeva explores incest, dietary laws, sacrifice, sexual acts, waste, corpses, and the female body. Biblical abominations set a person on edge by extending the possibility for impurity. The abject is necessary for the sacred, for it necessitates religious rituals and laws that play out repressed desires.

In our selection, Kristeva discusses more general ways for "reading the Bible." She uses her semiological approach to reveal a reading that pays attention to the semiotic codes of the Levitical food taboos and other "abject" abominations. But her concern is also to go deeper – to pay "attention to the linguistic subject of the biblical utterance...to its addressee. *Who is speaking in the Bible? For Whom?*" The interpretive process is one of subjective evaluations, for ultimately "the biblical God... cannot be seen, named, or represented," yet she means by "subjective" accessing almost impersonal forces within the person. This process is one of a "pre-oedipal dynamic of the subject's separation" in which the reader approaches the biblical text. Kristeva invokes Freud, Jung, and Lacan in her psychoanalytic criticism.

Kristeva thus reads texts and cultures through linguistics and psychoanalysis and stresses the heterogeneity of language. Kristeva's offering to biblical studies is not stuck in pessimism; she offers alternative readings for exegesis and ethics that are grounded in her particular brand of psychoanalytic feminism. She reads the Bible as a Western cultural text, full of repression and *jouissance* (self-shattering, almost sexual pleasure) in its writing and reading.

Two Approaches to the Sacred

The idea of reading the Bible as we might read Marx's *Das Kapital* or Lautréamont's *Chants de Maldoror*, unraveling its contents as if it were one text among many, is without doubt an approach born out of structuralism and semiology. Although such an approach

Julia Kristeva, "Reading the Bible," from *New Maladies of the Soul*, translated by Ross Guberman (New York: Columbia University Press, 1995).

may seem reductive or even outrageous, we must not forget that any interpretation of a religious text or occurrence assumes that it can be made into an object of analysis, even if it means admitting that it conceals something that cannot be analyzed. Of course, we may question this interpretive obsession that tries so desperately to make the Holy Text say what it does not know it is saying, and I shall return to what I believe to be the motivation behind this eternal return to divinity, a return that may be glorious or profane.

When the "human sciences" – which rely upon a rationality that seeks to reveal the universal logic embedded in a myth, a hieratic text, or a poem – turn to the Bible, they are forced to limit themselves to the logic or rhetoric of the text. At first they disregard its sacred powers, although they hope that their positive and neutral analysis will guide them toward the mechanism – if not the enigma – of what is seen as "holy" and of what appears to function as such. Perhaps the Bible lends itself to semiological analysis more easily than do other forms of writing. Indeed, by paying the way for interpretations, the Talmudic and cabalistic traditions are always inviting us to make yet another one....

What is more, the Book dominates the Judaic religious experience. It overshadows and ultimately governs the ritual, which enables it to bypass the ritual in favor of the letter, or of its interpretive values and a Single yet Infinite Meaning that supports human desire in the face of God. Are reading and interpreting the Bible perhaps the dominant ritual, the very eruption of the Judaic ritual and sacrament into language and logic?

This paradigm of biblical interpretation has resulted in studies inspired by various schools of thought, but that are unified by their common goal of specifying the profound logic that has generated the sacred value of the biblical text. Let us take the example of Mary Douglas' functionalism. While working independently from specialists in religious studies like Jacob Neusner,[1] Douglas has shown that the Levitical food taboos obey the universal law of exclusion, which states that the impure is that which falls outside a symbolic order. The Bible's obsession with purity seems then to be a cornerstone of the sacred. Nevertheless, it is merely a semantic variant of the need for separation, which constitutes an identity or a group as such, contrasts nature with culture, and is glorified in all the purification rituals that have forged the immense catharsis of society and culture.[2]

J. Soler has proposed a reading of the Levitical abominations that is more "semiological" in approach. He has unearthed the way in which a taxonomy that bases itself on the separation and exclusion of food combinations has been transformed into a narrative and a ritual.[3] This taxonomy, which is initially dominated by the dichotomy between life and death, also corresponds to the God/Man dyad and provides a schematic version of the commandment "Thou shall not kill." In the end, the code of Levitical abominations becomes a veritable code of differences that seeks to eliminate ambiguity. In this sense, one might think of the food taboos that pertain to fish, birds, and insects, which are respectively associated to one of the three elements (water, sky, earth): any food product that mixes and blends these elements is considered impure. According to this interpretation, the Levitical taboos would suggest that the fundamental confusion is incest – an inference that can be drawn from the well-known precept, "You shall not boil a kid in its mother's milk" (Exod. 23:19; Deut. 14:21).

Using a different approach, Evan Zuesse has delved into the hypostatized value of this exclusionary figure. He has noted that the Bible comprises a metonymic logic of taboos (which rely on displacement) that could be contrasted with the metaphorical nature of the sacrifice (which relies on deletion and substitution). This has led him to suggest that the Bible marks out the end of sacrificial religion and replaces it with a system of rules, prohibitions, and moral codes.[4]

That is all I shall say about these recent studies, which have helped clarify the inner workings of biblical thought in a way that can be distinguished from the historical or philological approach to religions, especially Judaism. I believe that the conclusions they have drawn are essential to any understanding of the Bible. These studies can be characterized, however, by an important omission: no attention is paid to the linguistic subject of the biblical utterance, nor by way of consequence, to its addressee. *Who is speaking in the Bible? For whom?*

This question is especially relevant for our purposes because it seems to suggest a subject who is not at all neutral and indifferent like the subject described by modern theories of interpretation, but who maintains a specific relationship of *crisis, trial,* or *process* with his God. If it is true that all texts considered "sacred" refer to borderline states of subjectivity, we have reason to reflect upon these states, especially since the biblical narrator is familiar with them. Such a reading would tend to focus on the intra- or infrasubjective dynamics of the sacred text. Yet even if these dynamics are manifested in the figure of the text itself, interpreting them would require that we recognize a *new space*, that of the speaking subject, who henceforth ceases to be an impenetrable point that guarantees the universality of logical operations, and who opens himself instead to analyzable spaces. If I am alluding to Freudian theory here, it is because Freud's theory is capable of using the results of the biblical analyses I have mentioned and of transporting them into subjective space. Were an interpretation to internalize these discoveries as devices proper to certain states of the subject of enunciation, it could go beyond a simply descriptive framework and account for the impact that the Bible has on its addressees.

To return to the characteristic figures of biblical food taboos, I have come to realize that the object excluded by these rules, whatever form it may take in biblical narrative, is ultimately the mother. I cannot review the logical process that has led me to this position, but I shall take the liberty of referring you to my *Powers of Horror.*[5] Let me simply state that it is not enough to study the logical processes of exclusion that underlie the institution of these taboos, for attention must also be paid to the semantic and pragmatic value of the excluded object. We notice, among other things, that separating oneself from the mother, rejecting her, and "abjecting" her, as well as using this negation to resume contact with her, to define oneself according to her, and to "rebuild" her, constitutes an essential movement in the biblical text's struggles against the maternal cults of previous and current forms of paganism.

Now, the analyst is another person who sees such abjection as necessary for the advent of the subject as a speaking being. Studies on early childhood and on language acquisition have shown that the rejection of the mother causes her to be the originary object of need, desire, or speech. Yet she is also an ambiguous object who is, in fact, an *ab-ject* – a magnet of fascination and repulsion – before (in both the logical and chronological sense) she can be established as an object. This suggests an immersion in that which is not "one's own," as well as a dramatic distortion of the narcissistic dyad.

What is more, phobic and psychotic symptoms, which act out uncertainties about the limits of the subject (myself versus other people, inside versus outside), internalize this sort of aggressive fascination with the mother. In the discourse of adults, the mother becomes a locus of horror and adoration. She is ready for the entire procession of part-objects of *disgust* and *anality* that mobilize themselves to support the fragile whole of an ego in crisis.

Therefore, it could be said that a biblical text (the Book of Leviticus), which delineates the precise limits of abjection (from skin to food, sex, and moral codes), has developed a true archeology of the advent of the subject. Indeed, this Book recounts the subject's delicate and painful detachment – moment by moment, layer by layer, step by step – as well as his journey from narcissistic fusion to an autonomy that is never really "his own," never "clean," never complete, and never securely guaranteed in the Other.

I am suggesting, then, an interpretation that compares the Book of Leviticus to the preoedipal dynamic of the subject's separation. My interpretation is rooted in the fragile status of subjectivity, and it thus serves to explain, at least to some extent, the cathartic value of the biblical text. The Book of Leviticus speaks to me by locating me at the point where I lose my "clean self." It takes back what I dislike and acknowledges my bodily discomfort, the ups and downs of my sexuality, and the compromises or harsh demands of my public life. It shapes the very borders of my defeats, *for it has probed into the ambivalent desire for the other*, for the mother as the first other, *which is at the base, that is, on the other side of that which makes me into a speaking being* (a separating, dividing, joining being). The Bible is a text that thrusts its words into my losses. By enabling me to speak about my disappointments, though, it lets me stand in full awareness of them.

This awareness is unconscious – so be it. Nevertheless, it causes me, as a reader of the Bible, to resemble someone who lives on the fringe, on the lines of demarcation within which my security and fragility are separated and merged. Perhaps that is where we might discover what is known as the sacred value of the text: a place that gives meaning to these crises of subjectivity, during which meaning, disturbed as it is by the object-abject of desire, eludes me and "I" run the risk of falling into the indifference of a narcissistic, lethal fusion.

Across the ages, sacred literature may never have done anything but use various forms of sacrifice to enunciate *murder* as a condition of Meaning. At the same time, this literature has emphasized the breathtaking threat that *fusion libido* inflicts upon meaning, which it can carry, destroy, or kill. The message of the biblical abominations, however, is particular and unique: you must be separated from your mother so that you do not kill anyone. Meaning is what guarantees desire and thus preserves the desire for death. You will displace your hatred into thought; you will devise a logic that defends you from murder and madness, a logic whose arbitrary nature shall be your coronation. The Bible offers the best description of this transformation of sacrifice into language, this displace-ment of murder into a system of meanings. In this way, this *system*, which counter-balances *murder*, becomes the place where all our crises can be exploded and assimilated. In my view, the fulcrum of this biblical process can be located in its particular concep-tion of the *maternal:* the maternal is a promised land if you are willing to leave it, an object of desire if you are willing to renounce and forbid it; the maternal is delight as well as murder, an inescapable "abject" whose awareness haunts you, or which may very well be the constitutive double of your own awareness. "For your hands are defiled with blood / and your fingers with iniquity" (Isa. 59:3).

Love that Cannot Be Represented

The Bible draws attention to the love that the Jewish people have for their God, and it demands or denounces this love when it is found to be insufficient. On the other hand, ancient texts have much less to say about God's love for Israel. Only two references to this love can be found:

> And David comforted his wife, Bathsheba, and went in unto her, and lay with her; and she bore a son, and he called his name Solomon; and the LORD loved him.
> And he sent by the hand of Nathan the prophet; and he called his name Jedidiah, because of the LORD. (2 Sam. 12:24–25)

The queen of Sheba affirms that the Lord loves Israel:

> Blessed be the LORD thy God, which delighted in thee. (1 Kings 10:9)

Christian agape was to turn the situation around and posit that Love falls from the heavens even before we know it as such. The love that the biblical God has for His people is expressed in another way. As direct as it may be, it demands neither worthiness nor justification, for it is interspersed with preferences and choices that immediately establish the loved one as a Subject. Ancient biblical texts do not make a great deal of this love, and when they do intimate it exists, they imply that it cannot be represented. For instance, note that Nathan is the one who says, though without any words, that Solomon is beloved. What is more, the name of Jedidiah the child ("Jedidah" meaning loved by God) does not reappear in the narrative. As for the second passage, a foreign woman is the one who refers to God's love, and she speaks in riddles.

This brings us to the central problem of the biblical God: He cannot be seen, named, or represented. That these traits are particularly applicable to His *love*, as is shown by the passages I have cited, may give the analyst some insight into the infinitely complex question of the Bible's *prohibition of representation*.

When analysts listen to evocations of narcissistic wounds, or better yet, when they listen to subjects who are constituted by a narcissistic wound, they become aware of a ghostly yet secure presence of the father before they become aware of any oedipal hold on the father's love or on love for him. This archaic mirage of the paternal function, which is placed against the background of primary narcissism as the ultimate guarantee of identity, could very well be considered to be an imaginary Father. Although his actual existence may be hallucinatory, he appears the edify the keystone of the capacity to sublimate, especially through art. Freud characterized this particular Father, who is necessary for the Ego-Ideal, as a support for "primary identification."[6] He referred to him as the "Father in personal prehistory" (*Vater der personlichen Vorzeit*). Freud postulated that apprehension of this father is "direct and immediate" (*direkte und unmittelbare*), and emphasized that he internalizes both parents and both genders. The immediacy of this absolute, which the young child of a Mother-Father in personal prehistory brings back to a mysterious and direct grasp, guarantees his ability to idealize.

This sheds some scandalous light on the theological or antitheological orientation of philosophy. We know, indeed, that philosophers from Hegel to Heidegger have tried to ascertain the meaning of Being by interpreting the absolute presence of Parousia. We are obliged to note that this two-sided and double-gendered figure of kinship, which is what creates the symbolic, limits the extent to which analysis may search for that which is not simply narcissistic in origin. This, however, does not guarantee symbolic autonomy (or the separation between subject and object that it presumes).

As the zero-degree of symbol formation, this imaginary Father, who is most likely the father desired by the mother (her own father?), is thus the focal point of the processes that lead not to the appearance of the object (along this path, we have found the *abject* and a separative obsession), but to the *position of subjectivity*, that is, a being for and by the Other. The early onset of this moment, as well as its mediation by the mother's desire, causes the subject to believe that this moment is resistant to representation, despite the array of signifiers brought about by the oedipal complex. Those who believe in the God of the Bible do not doubt His love. God – who is impossible to represent, fleeting, and always there though invisible – eludes me and invites me to let go of my narcissism, to venture forth, to inflict suffering and persecution upon myself in order to earn His love. Does He not force these roots into that ineradicable, archaic, and deeply felt conviction that occupies and protects those who accept Him? That is, the conviction that a preoedipal father exists, a *Vater der personlichen Vorzeit*, an imaginary father?

Is Psychoanalysis a "Jewish Science?"

Interpreting the meaning of the sacred text as an elaboration of psychic conflicts that border on psychosis assumes, as I have made clear, that the psychoanalyst is attentive and even vulnerable to the biblical text. Why is it that ever since Freud, analytic attention has invariably focused on the sacred, and more specifically on the biblical sacred?

One might answer that such an orientation stems from the interpretive posture itself. I am made to use silence or speech to listen to and to interpret a discourse that no longer has any meaning for its subject, and that is consequently experienced as painful. I am struck, however, by the fact that analysands are privy to a meaning that is "already there," even if this meaning takes the form of the most dramatic explosions of subjective identity or of linguistic coherence. Does this stem from the conviction that there is an imaginary father? Whose father is it?

In like manner, the interpretive construction made by the analyst, who assimilates this speech through transference or countertransference, also presents itself as a barrier to possible meaning (when I communicate an interpretation) or to a meaning that is arbitrary, if not eccentric (when I resort to silence). This interpretive construction, which can be as portentous as my own desire will allow, is nevertheless my only way –

the only way? – to guide the analysand's speech from being completely eclipsed toward a state of relative autonomy. Interpretive constructions do not deny that crises occur, but they save us from getting trapped in them or reveling in them. I am proposing, then, an imaginary construction that can serve as an indefinite and infinite truth. As opposed to a positivist interpretation, which would delimit reality by giving itself the last word – the strongest word – analytic interpretation, as an imaginary discourse that serves as truth, makes no attempt to hide its status as fiction, as a *text*.

As a sacred text? This hypothesis, which we should not be too quick to reject, will attract the attention of rationalists on all sides, for a psychoanalyst would be unthinkable, it would seem, at the Collège de France. Nevertheless, we can easily understand that the text of analytic interpretation defuses all beliefs: a psychoanalyst appears suspicious; he is banished from churches and temples. Why?

By normalizing and understanding desire, psychoanalysis does not repudiate it, as commonly believed. It is true that analysis shapes and molds desire, but only as the wings of the Paragon of Faith, as the *subjection of desire to a fascinating object*, perhaps an unnameable one. The analyst remains fully aware that this object drapes itself in the attire of the mother Goddess, who extols our fantasies of origins and our desire for interpretation. Consequently, analysts are obliged to distance themselves from Faith in the Goddess of Reason as well as from religious Faith.

Hence, analysts find that the Bible offers a particular narration that suggests a treatment for the very symptoms that they are called on to interpret. Yet, this close relationship with biblical narration opens up the possibility of choice. Faced with the hypostatized Meaning of the Other, analysts maintain their interpretation by negating the intriguing power wielded by this Other, Father, or Law.

The analyst is not unaware that interpretive desire, which is abrasive and frustrating for the fantasy of the other, is tied to the fantasy of returning to the mother. It is true that under the demands of monotheism, such an attitude reveals the obsession with the pagan mother who has shaped it. Nevertheless, psychoanalysts can only avoid the trap of an archetypal Jungianism by admitting that their own sadomasochistic jubilation – which stems from approaching the source of that which is said – masks a certain hold on the unnameable Object (by way of the Law of the father as well as the fascination with the mother). What is more, analysts, as providers of meaning, should eventually saw off the branch, as well as the limb they are sitting on, for the driving force behind faith is the fantasy of returning to the mother, from whom biblical faith specifically distances us. The ensuing ambiguity causes Judaism, when it is completely internalized, to be the least religious of religions.

By laying bare the splendors of the Virgin Mary, Christianity, after having relied on a neo-testamentary discretion toward this subject, has unintentionally revealed what lies behind faith. In contrast to Freud, it could be maintained that the presence of the Virgin throughout Christianity is less a return to paganism than an acknowledgment of the hidden side of the sacred mechanism (of any sacred mechanism), which draws us into its soothing and grinding motion in order to leave us with a single path to salvation: having faith in the Father.

Psychoanalysis does not fall short of this, but goes even further: it is "post-Catholic" by X-raying *meaning* as a *fantasy*, and then going on to take various phantasmatic functions to be an original fantasy in the form of an adoration of the object-*abject of maternal love* and a cause of eternal return. Finally, it is "post-Catholic" in that it includes *its own process* within this same course of eternal return. Through this three-way loop, the experience of psychoanalysis results in a sort of combustion.

Let us say, then, that everything ends up as fire – the fire of Heraclitus, the fire of the burning bush, the fire that burned Isaiah's tongue, or the fire that bedazzled heads with Pentecostal tongues. The truth of the matter is that I envisage the fate of meaning during an analytic session in a similar fashion – as a meaning that is multifaceted, indefinable, set ablaze, yet One Meaning that exerts its influence everywhere. We can admit that this meaning requires the analyst to cling to the Bible's rigor, logic, and love, so that this fire might *be* and not die down right away. All the same, it must not blind us into thinking that this fire is the only thing that exists, for it need only state the truth at one point or another.

Neither biblical, rationalistic, religious, nor positivist, the place of the analyst is always elsewhere and deceptive, notable for the attention it gives to emptiness. This ambiguous position generates an ethics of construction if not of healing, and it bases itself not on hope but on the fire of tongues. This is enough to irritate believers, which amounts to almost everyone, in spite of what we might think. As Freud said, analysis "exasperates" human beings; it forces them to contradict themselves.

Nevertheless, the central focus (as well as the stumbling block) of this avoidance-through-profusion that constitutes the serene delicacy of the never-attained end of analysis is analogous to the logic of the Bible. Denying the extent of its impact, which means cleansing the Father in order to decipher the Mother or to decipher a walled-up desire, can easily lead to an anti-Semitism in good faith. In a clinical sense, this anti-Semitism may portray a patient caught in the maternal bosom of fantasy, hope, and dependence. The un-being of a chosen yet excluded being is extremely difficult to assimilate.

On the other hand, one could delight in a strict, "mathematical" reading of the biblical text, a reading that avoids all ambiguities, especially the pagan aspect coiled up beside the maternal body, which borders, as I have said, on the logical desire that serves as a foundation for monotheism. This sort of "scientific" reading would encourage us to make analytic practice into a preferred space for hysteria (in men as well as women), a space targeted by what Lacan would call a paranoid "lovehate" for the Other. Have we not seen a great deal of this recently in the various schools of thought and their schisms?

What might be done about this?

We should read the Bible one more time. To interpret it, of course, but also to let it carve out a space for our own fantasies and interpretive delirium.

Notes

1 Jacob Neusner, *The Idea of Purity in Ancient Judaism* (Leiden: E. J. Brill, 1973).
2 See Mary Douglas, *Purity and Danger: An Analysis of Concepts of Pollution and Taboo* (London: Routledge and Kegan Paul, 1978).
3 J. Soler, "Sémiotique de la nourriture dans la Bible," *Annales* (July/August 1973): 93.

4   E. M. Zuesse, "Taboo and the Divine Order," *Journal of the American Academy of Religion* 42, no. 3 (1974): 482–501.

5   Julia Kristeva, *Powers of Horror: Essay on Abjection*, Léon S. Roudiez, tr. (New York: Columbia University Press, 1982).

6   Sigmund Freud, *The Ego and the Id*, in *Standard Edition* 19:31.

Chapter 4

Introduction to the Names-of-the-Father Seminar

Jacques Lacan 1901–1981

Introduction

From his earliest writings, including his doctoral thesis (1932), Jacques Lacan expressed discontent with the limits of traditional psychoanalysis as practiced by rigid Freudians. After parting ways first with the French and then the international psychoanalytic establishment, in 1953 Lacan began weekly seminars attended by students, philosophers, and linguists. Along with his essays, most of which appear in his *Ecrits* (1966/ English translation 1977), these seminars provided Lacan with a field for his most important work. Lacan's intent was to reinterpret Freud, paying special attention to Freud's treatment of the unconscious, which communicates its formal structure through a specialized language. For Lacan, the true subject – of psychoanalysis and discourse – is the unconscious rather than the ego; at the same time, Lacan refused to reify the unconscious, given that a unified subject, he argued, is illusory.

As with Lévi-Strauss, Foucault, Barthes, and Derrida, Lacan's work was deeply affected by structural linguistics, and in it he particularly concentrates on the functions of signs. From this study, Lacan determined that the unconscious is "structured like language" and reveals meaning only in the connections among signifiers. This linguistic model surfaced in Lacan's *Rome Discourse* (1953/1968) entitled "The Function and Field of Speech and Language in Psychoanalysis." Lacan's seminar on Poe's "The Purloined Letter" (1956/1972) best illustrates his nexus of discourse and the psychoanalytic process; in tracing the path of the displaced signifier, Poe's story became, for Lacan, a parable of the linguistic sign in its creation of the speaking subject. His 1957 essay in *Ecrits*, "The Instance of the Letter, or Reason since Freud," a Saussurean reading of the unconscious, took this attention to the signifier one step further by making the signifier the primary component of the signifier/signified schema, thereby reversing the traditional Western notion of the primacy of the concept. Lacan is discussed extensively in *The Postmodern Bible* (196–211) where it is suggested that "a Lacanian reading of the biblical texts . . . might involve a miming of biblical styles – a profusion of parables, proverbs, and aphorisms, a deluge of potent images" (200).

Lacan's essay reprinted here was published in 1990 from a seminar presented in the early 1960s in which Lacan offers a psychoanalytic analysis of anxiety. In it, Lacan examines the mechanisms of desire that inhabit meaning and understanding. That is, he is attempting here, as he repeatedly does throughout his work, to account for the affect and power – joy (*jouissance*), anxiety, desire, even bewilderment – that attends and, indeed, imbues much of our experience. One way he attempts to achieve this account is by means of his concept and neologism, "The-Name-of-the-Father." "The-Name-of-the-Father" is a particular function of the family constellation, the paternal power that impels the child–subject into subjectivity by subjugating the child to the Symbolic order of language. "It is in the *name of the father*," Lacan writes, "that we must recognize the support of the symbolic function which, from the dawn of history, has identified his person with the figure of the law" (*Ecrits*, 67). If the child forms a binary (Imaginary) relationship with its mother, then "the-Name-of-the-Father" breaches that relationship into the social, "Symbolic" order of language, and it is attended with the powerful affect associated with such dislocation. This awkward term ("Name-of-the-Father") is Lacan's attempt to situate Freud's "myth of the Father" within the context of the system of language: some scholars even suggest that Lacan took his neologism from the Christian liturgy. In this selection, Lacan organizes "the myth of the Father" in the context of reading biblical fathers: the God of Moses, Abraham, Isaac, and Jacob. He does so by focusing on God's "desire" rather than his "bliss" (*jouissance*), figuring that desire in the binding of Isaac (Gen. 22:1–19). In the "Introduction," Lacan situates God himself within the Symbolic order of language and desire (see PMB:205–6), and in so doing he offers a psycho-analytic framework through which to comprehend the power as well as the meaning of the biblical text.

I don't intend to engage in anything in the order of a theatrical ploy. I shall not wait until the end of this seminar to tell you that this will be the last that I shall conduct.

For some, apprised of things that have been occurring, that will not be a surprise. It is for the others, out of respect for their presence, that I am making this declaration.

I request that absolute silence be maintained during the session.

Up until sometime quite late last night, when a certain bit of news was delivered to me, it was my belief that I would be giving you this year what I have been dispensing for ten years now.[1] My seminar for today was prepared with the same care as I have always devoted to it, every week, for the last ten years. I don't think I can do any better than offer it to you as it is, with my apologies for the fact that it will have no sequel.

Jacques Lacan, "Introduction to the Names-of-the-Father Seminar" (November 20, 1963; text established by Jacques-Alain Miller), from *Television*, translated by Denis Hollier, Rosalind Krauss, and Annette Michelson, edited by Joan Copjec (New York and London: W. W. Norton & Company, 1990).

I

I announced that I would speak this year of the Names-of-the-Father. It will not be possible for me, in the course of this single presentation, to convey to you the reason for the plural. At the least, you will perceive the beginning of an advancement I intended to introduce on a notion already initiated in the third year of my seminar, when I dealt with the Schreber case.

I will perhaps be more careful than ever before – since today it has been decided that I shall stop here – in punctuating for you, in my past teaching, the coordinates which allow the lineaments of this year's seminar to find their grounding. I wanted to link together the seminars of January 15, 22, 29 and February 5, 1958, concerning what I have called the paternal metaphor, and those following it, the seminars of December 20, 1961 and those following it, concerning the function of the proper name, the seminars of May 1960 concerning everything bearing on the drama of the father in Claudel's trilogy, and finally the seminar of December 20, 1961, followed by the seminars of January 1962.

One finds there a direction which has already advanced quite far in its structuration, which would have allowed me this year to take the next step. That next step follows from my seminar of last year on anxiety, and that is why I intend to show you wherein the relief it brought was necessary.

In the course of that seminar on anxiety, I was able to accord their full weight to formulae such as the following: *anxiety is an affect of the subject* – a formula which I did not put forward without subordinating it to the functions that I have long established in the structure of the subject, defined as the subject that speaks and is determined through an effect of the signifier.

At what time – if I may say *time*, let us say that that infernal term, for the while, refers only to the synchronic level – at what time is the subject affected with anxiety? That is what the framed diagram I put on the blackboard is intended to recall for you. In anxiety, the subject is affected by the desire of the Other. He is affected by it in a nondialectizable manner, and it is for that reason that anxiety, within the affectivity of the subject, is what does not deceive. In that *what does not deceive* you can see in outline at just how radical a level – more radical than anything hitherto designated thereby in Freud's discourse – its function as a signal is inscribed. That characterization is in conformity with the first formulations Freud gave concerning anxiety as a direct transformation of the libido.

Moreover, I have opposed the psychologizing tradition that distinguishes fear from anxiety by virtue of its correlates in reality. In this I have changed things, maintaining of anxiety – *it is not without an object*.

What is that object?: the object *petit a*, whose fundamental forms you have perceived sketched out as far as I have been able to take them. The object *petit a* is what falls from the subject in anxiety. It is precisely the same object that I delineated as the cause of desire. For the subject, there is substituted, for anxiety which does not deceive, what is to function by way of the object *petit a*. Thereupon hinges the function of the act.

This development was reserved for the future. And yet, I give you my word, it will not be totally lost for you, since, as of this moment, I have introduced it into the – written – part of a book I have promised for six months from now.[2]

Last year, I restricted myself to the function of the *petit a* in fantasy. There it takes on its function as support of desire, in so far as desire is the most intense of what the subject can attain in his realization as subject at the level of consciousness. It is by way of that chain that, once again, the dependencies of desire in relation to the desire of the Other are affirmed. These conceptions of the subject and the object have a radical, restructuring character which, as I leave you, I am tempted to recall for you.

To be sure, we have long since taken our distance from any conception that would make of the subject a pure function of intelligence, correlative of the intelligible, such as the νοῦς of antiquity. At this juncture, anxiety is revealed as crucial. Not that ἀγωνία is not in Aristotle, but for ancient thought, it could only be a question of a local πάθος pacified within the passibility of the whole. Of that passibility or susceptibility to suffering of antiquity, there remains something even in what seems farthest from it – so-called psychological science or thought.

There is assuredly something well-founded in the correspondence between intelligence and the intelligible. Psychology shows us without doubt that human intelligence is none other in its foundation than animal intelligence, and this is not without reason. From that dimension of the intelligible, assumed to be a given and a fact, we can, using evolution as a guide, deduce the progress of intelligence, or its adaptation, indeed even imagine that such progress is reproduced in each individual. This is all fine – except that a hypothesis has gone unacknowledged, which is precisely that facts are intelligible.

From the positivist perspective, intelligence is no more than one affect among others, based on the hypothesis of intelligibility – and that justifies that psychology for fortune-tellers which is capable of developing in what are seemingly the most liberated spheres, from the height of academic chairs.[3] Affect, inversely, is then no more than obscure intelligence. What nevertheless escapes whoever is receiving such teaching is the obscurantist effect to which he is being submitted. One knows, however, where it leads: to the increasingly intentional undertakings of a technocracy, the psychological standardization of unemployed subjects, the entering into the framework of existent society, head bowed beneath the psychologist's standard.

I say that the meaning of Freud's discovery is in radical opposition to all that. It was in order to make you feel this that the first steps of my teaching trod the paths of Hegelian dialectic. When pondered in its basis, that dialectic has logical roots, and may be reduced to the intrinsic deficit of the logic of predication. Namely that the universal, once examined – and this has not escaped the contemporary school of logic – may be grounded only by way of aggregation, and that the particular, alone in finding its existence therein, thereby appears as contingent. The entirety of Hegelian dialectic is made to stop that gap and show, in a prestigious act of transmutation, how the universal, by way of the scansion of the *Aufhebung*, can come to be particularized.

Whatever the prestige of Hegelian dialectic, whatever the effects, seen by Marx, through which it entered into the world, thus completing that whose meaning Hegel *was*, namely: the subversion of a political order founded on the *Ecclesia*, the Church, and on that score, whatever its success, whatever the value of what it sustains in the political incidences of its actualization, Hegelian dialectic is false and contradicted as much by the testimony of the natural sciences as by the historical progress of the fundamental science, mathematics.

It is here that anxiety is for us a sign, as was immediately seen by the contemporary of the development of Hegel's system, which was at the time quite simply The system, as was seen, sung, and marked by Kierkegaard. Anxiety is for us witness to an essential breach, onto which I bring testimony that Freudian doctrine is that which illuminates.

The structure of the relation of anxiety to desire, the double breach of the subject in relation to the object fallen from itself, where, beyond anxiety, it must find its instrument, the initial function of that lost object – there is the fault which does not allow us to treat desire within the logically oriented immanence of violence alone, as the dimension forcing the impasses of logic. It is there that Freud brings us back to the very foundation of the illusion of what he called – in accordance with the world of his time, which is that of an alibi – religion, and that I, for my part, call the Church.

On that very ground, which is that through which the Church persists intact, and in all the splendor one sees in it, against the Hegelian revolution, Freud advances with the enlightenment of reason. It is there, at the foundation of the ecclesiastic tradition, that he allows us to trace the cleavage of a path going beyond – deeper and more structural than the milestone that he placed there in the form of the myth of the death of the father. It is there, on that shifting and oh so scabrous terrain – and not without flattering myself at having an audience worthy of understanding it – that this year I intended to advance.

In so far as the Father – their father, of the fathers of the Church – is concerned, may they permit me to tell them that I have not found them sufficient. Some may know that I have been reading Saint Augustine ever since the age of puberty. It was, nevertheless, rather late, about ten years ago, that I became acquainted with the *De Trinitate*. I have reopened it lately only to be astonished at the extent to which, in the final analysis, it says so little about the Father. To be sure it has enough to say to us about the Son, and how much about the Holy Ghost – but I won't say the illusion of I know not what evasion or flight occurs beneath the author's pen, through a kind of *automaton*, when it is a question of the father. And yet, his is a mind so lucid that I rediscovered with joy his radical protest of any attribution to God of the term *causa sui*, a concept which is, in fact, totally absurd, but whose absurdity may be demonstrated only by way of the bringing into relief that I punctuated before you, namely that there are causes only after the emergence of desire, and that what is a cause, a cause of desire, can in no way be considered an equivalent of the antinomian conception of self-causation.

Augustine himself, who is able to formulate the thing in opposition to every form of intellectual piety, flinches nonetheless, to the point of translating *Ehieh asher ehieh* – which I have long since taught you to read – by an *Ego sum qui sum: I am the one who am*. Augustine was a very good writer, but in Latin as in French, that sounds false and awkward. That God affirms himself as identical to Being leads to a pure absurdity. I had intended, concerning this, to bring you all kinds of examples of other uses of analogous formulate in the Hebrew texts.

I am first going to recall briefly for you the meaning of that function of *petit a* in the various forms I recalled to you last year, and concerning which those who follow me were able to see where they stopped – in anxiety.

The *a*, the object, falls. That fall is primal. The diversity of forms taken by that object of the fall ought to be related to the manner in which the desire of the Other is apprehended by the subject.

That is what explains the function of the oral object. That function may be understood – as I have insisted at length – only if the object being detached from the subject is introduced into the Other's demand, into the call to the mother, and it delineates that space beyond in which, beneath a veil, lies the Mother's desire. That act, in which the child, in a sense astonished, throws his head back while removing himself from the breast, shows that it is only apparently that the breast belongs to the mother. The biological reference is in this case enlightening. The breast is indeed part of the feeding complex which is structured differently in different animal species. At this point it is a part stuck onto the mother's thorax.

The second form: the anal object. We know it by way of the phenomenology of the gift, the present offered in anxiety. The child releasing his feces yields them to what appears for the first time as dominating the demand of the Other, to wit: his desire. How is it that authors have not grasped better than they have that it is at the anal level that the support for what is called generosity is to be located? It is through a veritable sleight of hand, itself indicative of who knows what panic in the face of anxiety, that the posture of generosity has been situated at the level of the genital act.

It is, however, at that level that Freudian teaching, and the tradition that has maintained it, situates for us the gaping chasm of castration. Psycho-physiologists who were Freud's contemporaries reduced its obstacle to what they called the mechanism of false detumescence. Last year, I thought it my obligation to show that Freud, for his part, from the very beginning of his teaching, articulates that aspect of orgasm which represents precisely the same function as anxiety in relation to the subject. Orgasm is in itself anxiety, to the extent that forever, by dint of a central fault, desire is separated from fulfillment.

Let no one offer as an objection those moments of peace, of fusion of the couple, in which each can view him or herself truly happy with the other. We analysts ought to look at matters more closely in order to see the extent to which those moments are marked by a fundamental alibi, a phallic alibi, in which form is sublimated to its function as a sheath, but in which something that goes beyond remains infinitely excluded. It was in order to demonstrate this to you that I commented at length on Ovid's fable based on the myth of Tiresias. Indication should also be given of what is perceptible as a trace of the unbroached realm of woman's bliss [*jouissance*] in the male myth of her alleged masochism. I have led you further.

Symmetrically, and as though on a line no longer descending but curved in relation to that peak occupied by the chasm desire/fulfillment at the genital level, I have gone so far as to punctuate the function of *petit a* at the level of the scoptophilic drive. Its essence is realized in so far as, more than elsewhere, the subject is captive of the function of desire. It is here that the object is strange. In a first approximation, it is that eye which, in the myth of Oedipus, fulfills so well the role of equivalent for the organ to be castrated. But it is not quite that which is at stake in the scoptophilic drive, in which the subject encounters the world as a spectacle that he possesses. He is thus victim of a lure, through which what issues forth from him and confronts him is not the true *petit a*, but its complement, the specular image: *i (a)*.

His image, that is, what appears to have fallen from him. He is taken, rejoices, vents his glee in what Saint Augustine, in so sublime a manner – I would have liked to go through the text with you – denounced and designated as a lust of the eyes. He believes he desires because he sees himself desired, and because he doesn't see that what the other wants to snatch from him is his gaze. The proof of this is what transpires in the phenomenon of the *Unheimlich*. That is what appears every time that, suddenly, through some accident more or less fomented by the Other, that image of himself within the Other appears to the subject as shorn of his recourse. Here the entire chain in which the subject is held captive by the scoptophilic drive comes undone. The return to the most basal mode of anxiety is there, once again if it be needed, registered by the Aleph of anxiety, since it is today that I am introducing the sign in order to symbolize it, in accordance with our needs this year. Such is that to which, in its most fundamental structure, the relation of the subject to *petit a* bears a resemblance.

Without yet having gone beyond the scoptophilic drive, I pause here to mark what in the order of clearing an obstacle will occur, for it is there that I am obliged to designate what will discomfit, precisely on time, the imposture in that fantasy which we analysts should know quite well in the form that I articulated for you, during the year of my seminar on the transference, by way of the term ἄγαλμα (*agalma*).

The peak of the obscurity into which the subject is plunged in relation to desire, *agalma* is that object which the subject believes that his desire tends toward, and through which he presses to an extreme the misperception of *petit a* as cause of his desire. Such is the frenzy of Alcibiades, and the dismissal Socrates subjects him to: *Concern yourself with your soul* means: *Acknowledge that what you are pursuing is nothing other than what Socrates will later turn into your soul, to wit: your image. See then that the function of that object is in the order not of a goal, but rather of a cause of death, and prepare your mourning as a function of it. Then will you know the paths of your desire. For I, Socrates, who know nothing, that is the only thing that I know – the function of Eros.*

Thus it was that I brought you last year to the gate where we now arrive – the fifth term of the function of *petit a*, through which will be revealed the gamut of the object in its – pregenital – relation to the demand of the – postgenital – Other, to that enigmatic desire in which the Other is the site of a decoy in the form of *petit a*. In the fifth term, we shall see the *petit a* of the Other, sole witness, in sum, that that site is not solely the site of a mirage.

I have not named that particular *petit a*, and yet, in other circumstances, I could have shown you its singular lighting. During a recent meeting of our Society, concerning paranoia, I abstained from speaking on what was at issue, to wit: voice. The voice of the Other should be considered an essential object. Every analyst is solicited to accord it its place. Its various incarnations should be followed, as much in the realm of psychosis as at that extremity of normal functioning in the formation of the superego. Through seeing the *petit a* source of the superego, it is possible that many things will become more clear.

The relation of voice to the Other is solely a phenomenological approach. If it is truly, as I say, *petit a* as fallen from the Other, we can exhaust its structural function only by bringing our inquiry to bear on what the Other is as a subject, for voice is the product and object fallen from the organ of speech, and the Other is the site where "it" – *ça* – speaks.

Here we can no longer elude the question: beyond he who speaks in the place of the Other, and who is the subject, what is it whose voice, each time he speaks, the subject takes?

II

If Freud places at the center of his teaching the myth of the Father, it is for reason of the inevitability of the question I have uttered.

The entirety of analytic theory and praxis appear to us at present to have come to a halt for not having dared, on the subject of that question, to go further than Freud. That is in fact why one of those whom I have trained as best I could has spoken, in a work that is not without merit, of the *question of the father*.[4] That formulation was bad. It was even a misinterpretation, without there being grounds for reproaching him for it. There can be no question of the question of the father, for the reason that there we are beyond what may be formulated as a question. I want merely to attempt to situate how today we might have delineated an approach to the problem that has been introduced at this juncture.

It is clear that the Other should not be confused with the subject who speaks from the place of the Other, even if through its voice. If the Other is as I say, the place where "it" – *ça* – speaks, it can pose only one kind of problem, that of the subject prior to the question. And Freud intuited this admirably.

Since as of today I am to return to a certain style, I shall not fail to indicate to you that someone who is not one of my students, Conrad Stein (to mention his name), has traced the path in this realm. Were I not obliged to cut things short, I would have requested that you consult his work, since it is sufficiently satisfying to spare me the task of showing you how, despite the error and confusion of the times, Freud put his finger on what deserves to remain in the work of Robertson Smith and Andrew Lang, after the critique – which is no doubt well founded from the specialist's point of view – of the function of the totem conducted by my friend Claude Lévi-Strauss. Freud is the living demonstration of the extent to which whoever is functioning at the level of the pursuit of truth can completely make do without the advice of the specialist. For what would be left of it, should nothing else be left than *petit a*, since what is to be at stake is the subject prior to the question? Mythically, the father – and that is what *mythically* means – can only be an animal.

The primordial father is the father from before the incest taboo, before the appearance of law, of the structures of marriage and kinship, in a word, of culture. The father is the head of that hoard whose satisfaction, in accordance with the animal myth, knows no bounds. That Freud should call him a *totem* takes on its full meaning in the light of the progress brought to the question by the structuralist critique of Lévi-Strauss, which, as you know, brings into relief the classificatory essence of the totem.

We thus see that as a second term what is needed at the level of the father is that function whose definition I believe I developed further in one of my seminars than had ever been done until now – the function of the proper name.

The name, I demonstrated to you, is a mark already open to reading – for which reason it will be read identically in all languages – imprinted on something that may be, but not at all necessarily, a speaking subject. The proof is that Bertrand Russell can make a mistake and say that one could name a geometrical point on the blackboard John. Now, we know Bertrand Russell to have indulged in many a strange caper, which are not without their merit, moreover, but surely, at no moment, has he questioned a point marked in chalk on a blackboard in the hope that said point would answer back.

I had also observed, as a reference, the variously Phoenecian (or other) characters that Flinders Petrie discovered in Upper Egypt on pottery dating from a few centuries prior to the use of those characters as an alphabet in the Semitic region. Which illustrates the fact that the pottery never had the occasion, subsequently, to speak up and say that that was its trademark. The name is situated at that level. Pardon me for moving a bit more rapidly than I would have wanted to under other circumstances.

Can we ourselves not move beyond the name and the voice? – and take our bearing from what the myth implies in that register accorded us by our progress, that is: on the three themes of erotic bliss [*jouissance*], desire, and the object? It is clear that, in his myth, Freud finds a singular balance, a kind of co-conformity – if I may be allowed to thus double my prefixes – of Law and desire, stemming from the fact that both are born together, joined and necessitated by each other in the law of incest and what? – the supposition of the pure erotic bliss of the father viewed as primordial.

Except, if that is alleged to give us the formation of desire in the child, ought we not – I have insisted on this at length for years – to pose the question of knowing why all this yields neuroses?

It is here that the accent I allowed to be put on the function of perversion in its relation to the desire of the Other as such takes on value. To wit: that it represents a backing up against the wall, a strictly literal interpretation of the function of the father, of the Supreme Being, of Eternal God. He is taken in a strictly literal interpretation of the letter, not of his bliss, which is always veiled and inscrutable, but of his desire, as interested in the order of the world – and that is the principle through which the pervert, moulding his own anxiety, installs himself as such.

Thus are posited two of the prime blind arcades through which may be seen contrasting and fusing the foundation of normal desire and that of perverse desire, which is located at the same level. One must take possession of that gnarled axis in order to understand that what is at stake is a totality, a gamut of phenomena that go from neurosis to perversion.

Neurosis is inseparable in our eyes from a flight from the term of the father's desire. That is what mysticism replaces with the term of demand. Mysticism, throughout every tradition, except the one that I am about to introduce, which is quite vexing, is a construction, search, *askesis*, assumption – anything you like – plunged toward the bliss of God. That is what leaves a trace in mysticism – and even, and more still, in Christian mysticism. As in the case of neurosis, the insistence of God's desire functions as a pivot.

I apologize for not being able to pursue that indication any further. But I don't want to leave you without having at least pronounced the name, the first name through which I wanted to introduce you to the specific incidence of the Judeo-Christian tradition. That tradition, in fact, is one not of erotic bliss, but of the desire of a God who is the God of Moses.

III

It was before the God of Moses, in the last analysis, that Freud's pen stopped writing. But Freud is surely beyond what his pen transmits to us.

The name of that God is the name *Shem*, which, for reasons I explained to you, I would never have pronounced, although some do know its pronunciation. We have a number of others, for example those given us by the *Ma'asot*, and which have varied over the centuries. In Chapter 6 of *Exodus, Elohim*, who speaks from the burning bush — which should be conceived of as his body, *kavod*, which is translated as *glory*, and concerning which I would have liked to show you that it is a matter of something quite different — says to Moses: *You will go unto them and say unto them that my name is Ehieh asher ehieh*. Which means nothing other than *I am what I am*. The property of the term, moreover, is designated by nothing other than the letters composing the Name, always a few letters chosen from the consonants.

Last year, I worked up a bit of Hebrew on your behalf. The vacation I am about to give you will spare you a similar effort. *Je suis*: I am [or, I follow] the procession. There is no other meaning to be given that *I am* other than its being the name *I am*. *But it is not by that name*, says Elohim to Moses, *that I revealed myself to your ancestors*, and that is what brought us to the point at which I proposed that we meet.

God of Abraham, Isaac, and Jacob, not of the philosophers and the scientists, writes Pascal at the head of the manuscript of his *Pensées*. Concerning which may be said what I have gradually accustomed you to understand: that a God is something one encounters in the real, inaccessible. It is indicated by what doesn't deceive — anxiety. The God who manifested himself to Abraham, Isaac, and Jacob, but first of all to Abraham, manifested himself by a name by which the *Elohim* of the burning bush calls him, and that I have written here. It is read: *El Shadday*.

The Greeks who did the translation of the Septuagint were much better informed than we are. They didn't translate *Ehieh asher* as *I am the one who am*, as did Saint Augustine, but as *I am the one who is*. That's not quite it, but at least it has a meaning. They thought like the Greeks that God is the supreme Being. *I* equals *Being*.

People are not freed like that from their mental habits from one day to the next, but one thing is sure: they did not translate *El Shadday* as the Allmighty, but, prudently, as *Theos*, which is the name they give to everything that they don't translate as (. . .), which is reserved for the *Shem*, that is, the name I do not pronounce. What is *El Shadday*? Well, even if I were to see you again next week, it was not on the schedule for me to tell you today, and I shall not be breaking down any doors, be they even those of Hell, in order to tell you.

I was intending to introduce what I would manage to tell you by means of something essential, whereby we meet up again with our Kierkegaard of a while ago — to wit, what is called in the Jewish tradition the *Akedah*, or in other words: the sacrifice of Abraham.

I would have presented to you Abraham's sacrifice in the form in which painterly tradition has figured it in a culture in which images are not forbidden. It was, moreover, rather interesting to know why they are so for the Jews and why, from time to time, Christianity has been taken with a fever to rid itself of them. Were they even reduced to cut-out figures, I am giving them to you, in order to show you what may be seen in images, which is necessary, ultimately, not in order to make up for this year's seminar, for assuredly, the names, in so far as they are concerned, are not there, but the images, in so far as *they* are, are there in full array, so that you may rediscover in them all that I have announced since the paternal metaphor.

There is a boy, his head blocked out against a small stone altar. Take one of the two paintings of the scene by Caravaggio. The child is suffering, he grimaces, and Abraham's knife is raised above him. The angel, the angel is there, the presence of him whose name is not pronounced.

What is an angel? That is another question that we will not have to deal with together. It would, however, have rather amused me to have you laugh at my last dialogue with Father Teilhard de Chardin. *Father, concerning those angels, how do you arrange to remove them from the Bible, what with your ascent of consciousness, and all that follows from it?* I thought it would make him cry. *But come now, are you really speaking seriously to me? I take account of the texts, especially when it is a question of the Scriptures on which, in theory, your faith is based.* As for that angel, here he is now, accompanied or not by Father Teilhard's consent, restraining Abraham's arm. Whatever be the case with that angel, it is indeed in the name of *El Shadday* that he is there. It is in that name that he has been seen traditionally. And it is in that name that the pathos of the drama into which Kierkegaard draws us ensues. For consider that prior to that restraining gesture, Abraham has brought a boy to the site of a mysterious encounter, and once there, he has bound his hand to his feet like a ram for the sacrifice.

Before waxing emotional, as is customary on such occasions, we might remember that sacrificing one's little boy to the local *Elohim* was quite common at the time – and not only at the time, for it continued so late that it was constantly necessary for the Angel of the Name, or the prophet speaking in the name of the Name to stop the Israelites, who were about to start it up again.

Let us look at things further on. The son, we are told, is his only son. It's not true. There is Ishmael, who is already fourteen at the time. But it is a fact that Sarah, until she reached age 90, revealed herself to be infertile, and that was the reason that Ishmael was born from the patriarch's cohabitation with a slave. *El Shadday*'s power is proven by the

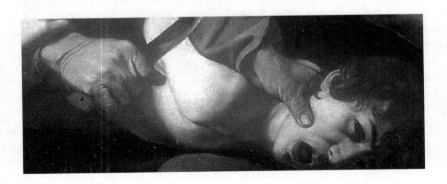

Caravaggio, *The Sacrifice of Isaac, c.*1595–1600, detail. Uffizi, Florence/ photo SCALA.

fact that he was the one who drew Abraham out of the world of his brothers and his peers – it's quite amusing upon reading to realize, once one calculates the years, that many were still alive. Since Sem had had his children at the age of thirty and lived five hundred years, and since in his lineage, children were had at age thirty, they had just reached no more than the four-hundredth birthday of Sem at the time that Abraham had Isaac. Well, not everyone likes reading the way I do.

Whatever the case, *El Shadday* has indeed also had something to do with this child of a miracle, for, after all, Sarah has said as much: *I am withered.* It is clear that menopause exists, Isaac is thus the child of the miracle, of the promise. It's thus easy to imagine that Abraham holds him dearly. Sarah dies a short while afterwards. At that time, there are a lot of people surrounding Abraham, in particular Ishmael, who happens to be there for reasons which are unexplained. The patriarch shows himself to be a formidable progenitor. He marries another woman, Ketorah. If my memory serves me well, he has six children with her; he doesn't lose any time. Only those children have not received the *brachah*, like the child of she who carried him in the name of *El Shadday*.

El Shadday is not almighty; I could show you a thousand demonstrations of it in the Bible. At the borders of the territory of his people, should a different *Elohim* from Moab come up with the right trick allowing his subjects to repel their assailants, it works, and *El Shadday* decamps with the tribes that brought him along for the attack. *El Shadday* is he who chooses, he who promises, who causes a certain covenant – which is transmissible in only one way, through the paternal *barachah* – to pass through his name.

Caravaggio, *The Sacrifice of Isaac.* Uffizi, Florence/ photo SCALA.

He is also he who makes one wait, who makes a son be awaited for up to ninety years, who makes one wait for many another thing more. I would have shown you.

Don't reproach me for having made too short shrift a while ago of Abraham's feelings, for, upon opening a little book that dates from the end of the eleventh century by one Rashi, otherwise known as Rabbi Solomon ben Isaac of Troyes, an Ashkenaze of France, you would be able to read some strange commentaries. You know that this Rashi doesn't read a text line by line, but rather point by point. You would be quite astonished to hear him give voice to a latent dialogue sung between Abraham and God, who is what is at stake in the angel. When Abraham learns from the angel that he is not there in order to immolate Isaac, Rashi has him say: *What then? If that is what is going on, have I thus come here for nothing? I am at least going to give him a slight wound to make him shed a little blood. Would you like that?* This is not my invention. It comes rather from an extremely pious Jew, whose commentaries, in the tradition of the Mishnah, are held in high regard. So there we are with one son and then two fathers.

Is that all there is? Fortunately our cutout figure is there in order to remind us – in the more sumptuous form of the Caravaggio painting – that that is not all there is. There is one such painting in which he is to the right, and in which you will find that head that I introduced here last year, invisibly, in the form of the *Shofar*, the ram's horn, which has been undeniably torn from him.

I won't have the opportunity to examine symbolic values in any depth for you, but I would like to conclude with what that ram is. It is not true that it figures as a metaphor of the father at the level of phobia. Phobia is no more than its return, which is what Freud said referring to the totem. Man has not all that much reason to be proud at being the last to appear in creation, the one who was made out of mud, something no other being was worthy of, and so he searches for honorable ancestors, and that is where we still are – as evolutionists, we need an animal ancestor.

I won't tell you the passages I have consulted, be it in the *Mishnah*, specifically the Guirgueavotchi – I mention it for those whom it may interest, since it is not as big as the *Talmud*, and you can consult it, it's been translated into French – then in Rashi. Those are the only two references I wanted to give today. Rashi is briefest in explaining that according to Rabbinic tradition, the ram in question is the primeval ram. It was there, he writes, as early as the seven days of creation, which designates it as what it is, that is, an *Elohim* – for it is not only he whose name is unpronounceable who was there, but in the clearest fashion, all the *Elohim*. The latter is traditionally recognized as the ancestor of the race of Sem, he who links Abraham, through a rather short path, to origins. That ram with tangled horns rushes into a thicket – I would have liked to show you in that site of the thicket something which is the object of extensive commentary elsewhere –, it rushes onto the site of the sacrifice, and it is worth noting what it comes to graze on when he whose name is unpronounceable designates it for the sacrifice that Abraham is to perform in place of his son. It is his eponymous ancestor, the God of his race.

Here may be marked the knife blade separating God's bliss from what in that tradition is presented as his desire. The thing whose downfall it is a matter of provoking is biological origin. That is the key to the mystery, in which may be read the aversion of the Jewish tradition concerning what exists everywhere else. The Hebrew hates the metaphysico-sexual rites which unite in celebration the community to God's erotic bliss. He accords special value to the gap separating desire and fulfillment. The symbol of that gap we find in the same context of *El Shadday*'s relation to Abraham, in which, primordially, is born the law of circumcision, which gives as a sign of the covenant between the people and the desire of he who has chosen them what? – that little piece of flesh sliced off.

It is with that *petit a*, to whose introduction I had led you last year, along with a few hieroglyphics bearing witness to the customs of the Egyptian people, that I shall leave you.

In closing, I shall say to you only that if I interrupt this seminar, I don't do so without apologizing to those who, for many years, have been my faithful audience here. And yet it is certain individuals from among its ranks who are now turning that impress against me, fed on the words and concepts I have taught them, learned on the paths and ways on which I have led them.

In one of those occasionally confused discussions in the course of which a group, our own, found itself tossed this way and that midst its eddies, an individual, one of my students, felt himself obliged – I apologize to him for having to deprecate his effort, which assuredly could have had echoes, and bring the discussion back to an analytic level – felt himself obliged to say that the meaning of my teaching would be that the veritable import of the truth is that one can never get hold of it.

What an incredible misinterpretation! What childish impatience! Must I indeed have people who are designated – one can only wonder why – as cultured among those most immediately within reach of following me! Where can you find a science – and even mathematics – in which each chapter does not lead on to the next one! But is that the same thing as justifying a metonymic function of truth? Could you not see that as I advanced, I was perpetually approaching a specific point of density to which, without the preceding steps, you could not arrive? At hearing such a rejoinder, are there not grounds for invoking the attributes of infatuation and stupidity, the kind of mind composed of the litter that one picks up working in editorial committees?

Concerning the praxis which is analysis, I have sought to articulate how I seek it, and how I lay hold on it. Its truth is mobile, disappointing, slippery. Are you not up to understanding that this is because the praxis of analysis is obliged to advance toward a conquest of the truth *via* the paths of deception? For the transference is nothing else – the transference into what has no name in the place of the Other.

For a long time now, the name of Freud has not stopped becoming increasingly non-functional. So that, if my itinerary is progressive, and even if it is prudent, is it not because that which I have to encourage you against is that toward which analysis constantly risks sliding – namely, imposture.

I am not here in a plea for myself. I should, however, say that – having, for two years, entirely confided to others the execution, within a group, of a policy, in order to leave to what I had to tell you its space and its purity – I have never, at any moment, given any pretext for believing that there was not, for me, any difference between yes and no.[5]

Notes

1   On the night of November 19, 1963, Serge Leclaire informed Lacan that the S.F.P. (Société français de psychanalyse) had voted, in a complicated procedure, to refuse not to ratify the motion striking Lacan's name from the list of training analysts.
2   This book was never published.
3   The attack on academic psychology seems aimed particularly at Lagache, who abandoned Lacan in 1963. In an unsent letter of June 27, 1963, Lacan wrote to Paula Heimann: "A society of neo-Lacanians beneath the banner of that stuffed dolly from the Sorbonne will live as a body of the IPA at the cost of my social and moral ruin." Quoted in Elisabeth Roudinesco, *La bataille de cent ans: Histoire de la psychanalyse en France*, Paris, Seuil, 1986, p. 724.
4   See Jean Laplanche, *Hölderlin et la question du père* (Paris, P.U.F., 1961), an analysis of Hölderlin's psychosis in terms of the Lacanian category of foreclosure. Laplanche had cut short his analysis with Lacan on November 1, 1963, and declared his solidarity with the majority position asking that Lacan's name be struck from the list of training analysts.
5   The failed policy of seeking integration into the International Psychoanalytic Association had been implemented by three analysts – Serge Leclaire, Wladimir Granoff, and François Perrier – known as the "troika." It was Granoff himself who ultimately penned the motion to deny Lacan his status as "titular" member. The affirmation of the difference between yes and no is intended to underscore the absurdity of Lacanian analysts joining to eliminate Lacan from their ranks.

Chapter 5

Dreaming in 1990

Hélène Cixous 1937–

Introduction

Even though Hélène Cixous is considered a French feminist writer and academic, she was born in Oran, Algeria. In 1968 she received a *doctorat* in literature and then published her thesis, *The Exile of James Joyce*. In that year she became a founder of France's revolutionary University of Paris VIII (now at Saint-Denis), at which she became a professor of English literature. After the turbulent student–worker uprisings of May 1968 – which had profound effects on Foucault, Lacan, and many other French intellectuals – Cixous emerged as a leading radical and avant-garde feminist writer. Her fictional autobiography, *Dedans* (Inside), was awarded the Prix Médicis in 1969. In 1973, with the publication of *Portrait du soleil* (Portrait of the Sun), she began to write specifically about the question of sexual difference, and the next year she established the Centre de Recherches en Études Feminine (Center for Feminist Studies) at Paris VIII. Her work consists of a series of daring and often fervent feminist writings addressing the problems of writing as a woman and of traditional definitions of women more generally by attempting to articulate and example *écriture féminine* ("feminine writing"). Cixous is interested in reading and writing texts in order to displace the existing conceptions of (marginalized) femininity and the generalized "humanity" that has been defined with masculinity as its touchstone. Such "feminine writing" is characterized by an "openness" which counters the Western patriarchal tradition of separating the body from texts by disrupting the linearity of the masculine textual economy by means of the torrential "overflow" of excessive eroticism and free-play within language. In her work, she often presents what some take to be a kind of "essentialist" femininity as a counterweight to traditions of patriarchal definitions of humanity. Her major works include: *The Newly Born Woman* (with Catherine Clément, 1975/English translation 1986); *La Venue à l'écriture* (1977); and *Vivre l'Orange* (1979).

The selection included here is excerpted from *Three Steps on the Ladder of Writing* (1993). In this selection, Cixous presents the combination of polemical-analytic writing and poetic lyricism that characterizes much of her work. In it, in an almost direct counterpoint to Lacan, she presents the Bible – and especially its dreaming – as a maternal rather than paternal text, the dream of generation, so that "the light that bathes the Bible has the same crude and shameless color as the light that reigns over the unconscious." Moreover, the subject of this reading-meditation is fully gendered, fully female: "in dreams," Cixous says, "we unvirgin ourselves." Additionally, in this meditation, the text, the book itself is gendered: "the unconscious tells us a book is a scene of childbirth, delivery, abortion, breast-feeding. The whole chronicle of childbearing is in play within the unconscious during the writing period." And finally, in this bodily writing – the "feminine writing" – the "scenes of impotence, terror, or vast power," the scenes of the sacred itself, exist not in reading or even experience but the very activity of writing/birthing. In reading the Bible, Cixous is organizing a different economy of the relationships among writing, authority, experience, and gendered bodily life that does not take its starting place from the received, traditional, and perhaps masculinist economy of these things.

My son is no bigger than a grub. This is why we almost forget him, we don't really believe in him, my dream and I. Where does he live? At the moment, between the leaves of a book. This is where he runs the least risk of being lost. Inversely, he risks being squashed, if someone puts something on the book. Otherwise he rests between the leaves without much difficulty. What is the future for such a grub? Not much hope. He'll vegetate. If he stays this size. But then he slowly takes on substance. This is doubtless the result of my efforts: sometimes I take him out, I place him on a bed, or outside, for after all he has a right to the world, and he seems to lean toward life. The danger that someone unaware will crush him remains. Little by little he even gains in intelligence. He begins to think, to be happy, to become a real living being. Obviously, he is very far behind, since he has existed in this form for months. But now he has really decided to catch up. Now I spy him running, having gone downstairs, and climbing on dangerous edges. I am worried because he doesn't know what danger is.

I feel happiness, love for my grub leaving his twilight state. Seeing life "crystallize" is such a blessing. Suddenly, it's the descent between rough red boulders, in an invisible "taxi" that turns in circles several times in the circus of boulders, as if there were no way out. But in fact there is one.

Here is the portrait of my first written dream.

I'll return via my ladder to the first dream of dreams, the one everyone knows – except those who are not of Judeo-Christian culture, that is – Jacob's dream. At the beginning of this story, there is the whole matter of Jacob's genealogy. There are the two brothers, Jacob and Esau, and the father Isaac, the son of Abraham. Let's imagine we are the young Jacob. The parental genealogy provides a background. Stemming from Abraham we are constantly in the space where Good and Evil are infinitely tangled. Violent

Hélène Cixous, "Dreaming in 1990," from *Three Steps on the Ladder of Writing*, translated by Sarah Cornell and Susan Sellers (The Wellek Library Lectures at the University of California, Irvine. Columbia University Press, New York, 1993).

events are strewn through the characters' biographies. Then, as in a novel, we come to the small Isaac we left on the mountain, we progress through the story, and find a completely different Isaac. The Bible, like the dream, always brings us the violent sense of generations. We live bizarrely clinging to the level of our age, often with a vast repression of what has preceded us: we almost always take ourselves for the person we are at the moment we are at in our lives. What we don't know how to do is to think – it's exactly the same as for death – about what is in store for us. We don't know how to think about age; we are afraid of it and we repress it.

Writing has as its horizon this possibility, prompting us to explore all ages. Most poets are saved children: they are people who have kept their childhood alive and absolutely present. But the most difficult thing for human beings to do is to think ahead, to put ourselves in the shoes of those we have not yet been. Hence our difficulty in thinking over what is parked behind the so-called Golden Age barrier. What the Bible does for us is to make us live all along the generation ladder. With the Bible, we climb up and down through generations. The baby we picked up yesterday in the dust is now, in the next chapter, a tottering blindman. The one who is going to dream this well-known dream is the special son of a blind father, a most unusual man. There is ascension, this movement that gives us the feeling that beings mature and grow up. But they are human beings, so they waste away. They are not good: sometimes they are good, sometimes evil. They don't hesitate to act in all kinds of unclassifiable ways, and they are open to everything that, in the chilliness of our imaginations, would plunge a character outside a "noble" scene. The story of Moses' youth, for example, is astonishing. There is no one more ordinary than Moses; he is a man who experiences all manner of unexpected passions within himself, our Moses who, for centuries, has been the Moses of Michelangelo and not the Moses of the Bible. The Bible's Moses cuts himself while shaving. He is afraid, he is a liar. He does many a thing under the table before being Up There with the other Tables. This is what the oneiric world of the Bible makes apparent to us. The light that bathes the Bible has the same crude and shameless color as the light that reigns over the unconscious. We are those who later on transform, displace, and canonize the Bible, paint and sculpt it another way.

To begin with, Jacob leaves. We always find departure connected to decisive dreams: the bed is pushed aside. The nature of the dream in or from which we dream is important. We may have to leave our bed like a river overflowing its bed. Perhaps leaving the legitimate bed is a condition of the dream. Jacob leaves, after an incident in which he robs his older brother Esau of his birthright, by deceiving old blind Isaac with his mother's help. At which old Isaac sends Jacob away far from this country toward another branch of the family. He places him at a distance and, at the same time, sends him off to live his life as an ordinary man, one who gets married, and so on. . . . Night falls, Jacob is abroad.

Jacob left Beer-sheba, and went toward Haran. And he came to a certain place, and stayed there that night, because the sun had set. Taking one of the stones of the place, he put it under his head and lay down in that place to sleep. And he dreamed that there was a ladder set up on the earth, and the top of it reached to heaven; and behold, the angels of God were ascending and descending on it![1]

In my own version, inscribed forever in my dream room, I always see the same thing: the ladder and the angels' movement of ascent and descent. I was especially delighted by this crowd of *descending* angels.

Let me now return to this. This is actually the portrait of the first dream of my life: it is figurative, for me it is a ladder with one step. The other steps would be invented by the people climbing up and down the ladder. You have probably guessed that it is the figure of Jacob's ladder. I was introduced to dreams by Jacob's ladder when I was small. This passage comes early in the Bible, in the book of Genesis. I always felt glad, when I later grew up out of the Garden, that this dream came early in the Bible, that the Bible started dreaming quickly; I appropriated this dream. It remained my own version, and I realized much later when I reread the book and checked and looked for the story, that I had dropped some of its elements I did not like. I only kept Jacob, the ladder, and the stone – one element had completely disappeared from my memory: God. Let me read the passage again:

> Jacob left Beer-sheba, and went toward Haran. And he came to a certain place, and stayed there that night, because the sun had set. Taking one of the stones of the place, he put it under his head and lay down in that place to sleep. And he dreamed that there was a ladder set up on the earth, and the top of it reached to heaven; and behold, the angels of God were ascending and descending on it![2]

I stopped there. For me it was everything. What I particularly enjoyed was the fact that the angels went up *and down*. Had I read a version about angels ascending to Heaven I would not have been interested. What interested me was their *climbing down*. But the story continues:

> And behold, the Lord stood above it and said, "I am the Lord, the God of Abraham your father and the God of Isaac; and the land on which you lie I will give to you and to your descendants; and your descendants shall be like the dust of the earth, and you shall spread abroad to the west and to the east and to the north and to the south; and by you and your descendants shall all the families of the earth bless themselves. Behold, I am with you and will keep you wherever you go, and will bring you back to this land; for I will not leave you until I have done that of which I have spoken to you." Then Jacob woke from his sleep and said, "Surely the Lord is in this place; and I did not know it." And he was afraid, and said, "How awesome is this place! This is none other than the house of God, and this is the gate of heaven."[3]

As I said, I had forgotten God. Rereading I liked the fact that God is in the dream. He is not outside the dream. He is not outside the dream. He is inside the dream.

The Bible continues in such a way that you never really know whether God is inside or outside the dream. He is inside – so you might think that this is where it occurs: that God and Jacob awake afterward from sleep.

As I reread this dream I realized there is a sequel I always eliminate. I always stop my memory at the pure vision of the angels climbing up and down. This is my ladder, this toing and froing of messengers whose journey interests me most when it descends. *The dream scene* was always far more important to me than the scene of revelation. It is the first dream. In order for the ladder that enables us to pass from one place to another to be set up, we have to leave. Moreover, if we follow Jacob's path, it's through a system of permitted transgressions, since Isaac blessed Jacob well in spite of himself; yet this is the way we must go, leaving home behind. Go toward foreign lands, toward the foreigner in ourselves. Traveling in the unconscious, that inner foreign country, foreign home, country of lost countries.

For this, the bed must be pulled aside; we must descend by the ladder hidden under the legal bed and, breaking all ties and rules, with blows of the axe, pass over to the other side.

Thus, in the beginning, it has to do with leaving "home" by passing through "the door" in the depths of oneself.

This is what the young Virginia does with amazing violence in *O Lustro*, a vast premonitory book written by Clarice Lispector at the age of twenty, as if she had already lived for fifty years.

I don't like the name Virginia but it makes sense when you read the book, for you soon feel there must have been an echo of Virginia Woolf, a woman doomed to drown. The important thing is strangely – for I don't believe Clarice Lispector age twenty did things on purpose, she was totally in the realm of the unconscious – the book does deal with virginity.

It starts with Virginia as a very young girl.

> She looked at herself in the mirror. Her white and delicate face lost in darkness, her eyes open wide, her inexpressive lips . . . and suddenly she shouts: But I want to be bought, otherwise I will kill myself, she shouted and observed her own face panicking, because of that sentence; and proud of her eagerness, she burst into a false low laugh. Yes yes she needed a secret life in order to be able to exist. Next instant she was serious again, tired, her heart was beating in darkness, slowly and red. A new element that had been strange until now had penetrated her body. She now knew that she was good but that her goodness did not exclude her unkindness (or her evil). This sensation was rather ancient, she had discovered it several days ago. A new desire was stabbing her heart. The desire of being even freer, getting out of the limits of her own life. This sentence, this wordly sentence turned round and round in her body like a simple force.[4]

The book unravels inside a character's body. Of course it is inside and outside but everything that happens outside, all the small events of outside life, are immediately caught and turned into feelings and relations to the body.

Then the book brings us to the frontier of the forbidden and helps us to trespass it. It is about going beyond, about breaking through the known, the human, and advancing in the direction of the terrifying, of our own end . . . there where *the other* begins.

> Going out of the limits of her life she did not know what she was saying while looking at herself in the mirror in the friend's room. I could kill them all, she thought with a smile and a new freedom, staring childishly at her image . . . Where had the idea come from? – since that morning spent in the cave, questions sprang easily. And at each instant, in which direction was she going? She advanced by learning things of which she had not even felt the beginning

during her life. Where had the idea come from? From her body. And what if her body was her destiny?[5]

The mirror episode continues:

> I am here in the mirror, she shouted brutal and happy. But what could she do and what couldn't she do? No, no, she did not want to wait the opportunity to kill. She had to kill. But if she killed, she wanted it to be in full freedom, without waiting. That would be it, going out of the limits of her life, she didn't know what she was thinking. Suddenly exhausted . . . . And like a door that shuts very quickly, she sank into sleep and instantly dreamt.
>
> She dreamt that her strength took her openly to the end of the world. . . . A cruel and living impulse pushed her, drove her, and she would have liked to die forever, if dying had given her one instant of pure pleasure. At that point of gravity which her body had reached, she could give her own heart to bite.[6]

You will have noticed that all the metaphors we found in Kafka's description of reading emerge here. We are approaching the point where the self-bursts apart, the hour of cruelty. In a while we will kill, that is, we will show the ferocity hidden in us. Kill whom? Always the same creature, the figure of our impossible innocence:

> While walking she saw a dog and at the price of a huge effort to come out of close waters as if to come out of what no one can do, she decided to kill him while walking. Defenseless he was wagging his tail, she thought of killing him and the idea was quite cold, but she did not like the coldness of the idea. She beckoned the dog onto the bridge over the river and with her foot, without any hesitation, pushed him to his death in the water. She heard him cry, she saw him carried away by the current, she saw him die, and serenely she went on her way. Serenely she went on looking for something. And she saw a man a man a man. His large trousers were sticking in the wind, the legs, the meagre legs. He was a mulatto, the man, the man. And his hair, my god, his hair was going white. Trembling with disgust she approached him between air and space and stopped. He too stopped, his old eyes waiting. Nothing on Virginia's face could let him suppose one instant what she was expecting. She had to talk and did not know what to say. She said:
>   Take me.[7]

It is a dream, *Virginia's* dream, the dream of a virgin. In dreams we unvirgin ourselves. Now comes the third period in this violent adventure called writing: Now comes the time *to say the worst*.

"My" writers, "my" sisters, "my" guides, what do they have in common? They have all written by the axe's light. They have sought bliss in savage conflict and have found it.

The state of creation, Tsvetaeva tells us in *Art in the Light of Conscience*:

> a state of obsession . . . (and of) "possession." Someone, something gets into you, your hand is an executant, not of you, but of something. Who is it? What, through you, wants to exist.
>
> The state of creation is this dream state where suddenly, obeying an unknown need, you burn the house down, you push a friend off the top of the mountain.

Did you do it? Of course you did. (You're the one sleeping, you're the one *dreaming*.) Your act, your very own act, done with complete freedom, an act by you – without your conscience – naturally.[8]

In saying this, Tsvetaeva rehabilitates, makes reappear in us the part that has to do with destruction, contradiction, violence: something stronger than us that deprives us of what is most precious. Pushing a friend or enemy is equally a crime before the law, yet it is not the same thing. My authors, those I love, they who are capable of burning the house down, of pushing a friend off the mountain top, are incapable of acting this out. They are able to write the violent potential in themselves. I say "in themselves" because I am wary of misunderstandings. We are a long way from those assassins we see on television who are both excused and justified. These are almost always, no, are always men who grant themselves the right to kill. I don't consider we have the right to murder. I differentiate between the assassination carried out for the mass media and what our authors do: the revelation of something ineluctably threatened and threatening, which appears as soon as there is a relation with the other, something we must deal with, which is why, no matter what we do, we are always caught out. It is this inevitable and terrible situation of fault, of the lost opportunities for saving the other in order to save ourselves that those who have chosen real humanitarian service, for example, deal with. The authors who are important to me know the extent to which we must bear what is unbearable. It suffices for us to be involved in some family saga for us to already be either the beneficiary or victim – though it amounts to the same thing, since the positions are endlessly exchanged – of injustice. This is true of the smallest as well as the most important details in stories of inheritance, as it is in stories about bodies and illness. Illnesses are our wounds, our vengeance, our cries, our calls, our metaphors. The most beautiful and tragic example is that of Clarice and her mother, a tied and nonnuntiable relation of birth and death between mother and daughter. It is enough for us to have a child, especially if the child is already an adult, for us to know the link with life and death, with the invisible and endless assassination, the mortal omission on both sides. It is enough to have parents to be the child: the assassin.

Dreams, Engendering, Creation

What do dreams teach us about written creation?

I will only speak about my experiences *as a woman*. A woman who writes is a woman who dreams about children. Our dream children are innumerable. The writing time, which is like reading time – there is latency, there is prewriting – is accompanied by a child state, what Tsvetaeva calls the "state of creation." The unconscious tells us a book is a scene of childbirth, delivery, abortion, breast-feeding. The whole chronicle of childbearing is in play within the unconscious during the writing period. We will bring forth into the light of night innumerable children. Sometimes the child is the size of a leaf and it crumbles to pieces. Sometimes it is just a small piece of paper you put on the bed that is suddenly lost. You do not know whether it is the child who faded or whether it is you who forgot the child. Sometimes it comes into the world six months old, bigger than you are, and of course it speaks better than Shakespeare. Sometimes it's a sticky little girl stuck to your leg, sometimes it's a terrible cocklike little boy running mad in a room on four cock legs. The worst is the scene when the child emerges and then disappears. These are all metaphors for the state of potential creation.

First dream

He was a delightful, colored, tame, dark-rose little bird playing with me in bed. I don't know how but suddenly he was no longer there, much to my distress. We looked for him in vain; was he in the corner of the room? No. In the bed then? We shook the covers, the sheets. Suddenly, there he was. My friend picked him up: he was dead! – Dead? Died of what? – Died of death no doubt. – No hope? – Do you want to take him? After all there might be a little bit of this love, this joy still in him. I made up my mind to do it. How horrible! The creature was absolutely stiff, yes, it was death, the opposite of what he was. No, no, I put him down. We'll find another one, the dream said.

Second dream: It was almost the end of the world

The forests had caught fire but I hadn't yet noticed. I was completely preoccupied with my little daughter, a child I had loved so much and had been so delighted with and proud of. And now time had past. She was ten months old. She was small and silent. I was carrying her. I had come to the sea region with her. I was only supposed to check into the hotel in the evening. I was occupied with the child and expecting so much. Suddenly, a fire of terror broke out in me. This child isn't normal, I said to myself. Has she ever shown a sign of life? Of course it was obvious. I cradle myself in happiness, and the miscarried child returns. Hadn't I already known some? Hadn't I already had some? I understood – it was in the family. My terror grew. In the distance I saw my son and his wife. If they knew! We have backward daughters. Delusions. A pain in the heart. Immense sorrow. I contemplated the grave and undecipherable child. When will you begin to speak? I asked sadly. "Whenever you want," she loudly and distinctly replied. She had known how to speak, and even to speak remarkably, for ages. I was beside myself with joy. At ten months! Such language! I had the most extraordinary daughter in the world! I adore her. "What do you want me to call you?" I asked her with passion. "Nane" she immediately replied. – Oh no, that isn't possible! I already have Anne, I can't call you Anne too. – I said. None, she said. – None? (It's written as None, I thought. Which plays on Nun . . .) Why not? Such an extraordinary and willful name. Without even thinking she had used an English word. This child was a genius. I felt joy and pride. I came out with it everywhere. My daughter who can speak at ten months said "whenever you want" to me. It was at this point, while progressing through the town toward the beaches with my triumph, that I noticed in the distance, not so far, the first red streaks of fire! What is it? Conflagration. It was already devouring the countryside, the nearby farms, the forests. It would soon be upon us. And no way out. With the child in my arms, I contemplated flight. But where to? The fire was already ablaze on all sides, we're in the middle: it's upon us. I had thought of the swimming pool. A feeble idea. Staying in the water beneath the fire? I'll try. I hurried. There were already a number of people who had had the same idea at the pool. At a table on the edge, Mrs. U was hurriedly writing a list of people to inform in case of accident. She was doing this in an orderly way. She was right. I too should leave at least a few written signs in case of death. I set about it:

badly equipped, a piece of paper, I write down my child's name: None. If I die and they find her, they must know who she is. Then I tell myself that None will not be enough. I must set down whose daughter she is. I scribbled, slipped the paper into None's playsuit. I was in the road with None, everything was on fire. Suddenly I thought about my son, my son. Ah! That's when my heart caught fire. I am willing to die with my daughter, but not separated from my son. The idea that something could happen to him — to him, alone — separated from us, is intolerable to me. I ran through the streets, looking for my son, shaken by sobs as if he were already dead, sure that he was already dead. I mourned him to death. Wasn't he at the front at the start of the war? I had no news, no doubt he died over there without us, or was lost; we would have separate deaths. I sobbed so hard my ribs were breaking; I ran through the fire, having won everything and lost everything in the same hour.

Third dream: Hand painting or "a woman's writing"

It's spring cleaning, the flying start. We were battling with dirt and disorder in the numerous great rooms of the university. I myself was throwing away, throwing out; the floor is littered with old papers and debris, there aren't any dustbins, but the cleaners will come, I hope....
Now I was in front of the old church chest, in the large hectic room. And even though this was a Catholic church, I decided to turn my hands to it. The big iron doors. And now under my hands the color surges, surges! Painting surges! At the touch of my hands, a cosmic landscape suddenly springs up on the iron door on the left; planet flowers that have just blossomed under my hands. I was going very quickly. I stroked the iron surface or rather I ran my fingers over it and the iron replied; the colors spread out gayly. Would I be able to get to the end? Would I succeed in covering the whole metal plate? Star flowers blossomed under my palms, springing up in a flash on the iron surface. I'm going very fast, faster; with all my strength I was racing with the unknown force that was painting, passing through my palms, coming from the furthest depths of the iron; silently I posed the call, still another iron panel. That's it! The church chest was magnificent: a world. The planets were breathing. I was proud. I went toward the backroom. I was going to fetch my friend J., who was tidying up. I boasted: I announced that I had painted the chest, I insisted that J. come and see my great accomplishment. When she at last gives in, as she is coming what did I see? Not the star creation on the painted chest, but a classic painting, à la Braque, with one of those guitars that have painted hips in the center, an overpolished cliché. Did you do that? admired J. Yes, I lied. Stunned. Could someone have redone it? Covered it over? The miraculous painting? The living marvel springing from the depths of the iron to the wondering and surprised call of my hands: had someone covered this blossoming night with this dead painting? Who would have done it? I said: yes. Falsely and out of surprise attributing to myself the classic work of one of the men I saw bustling about here and there in the room. Moreover, as I approached the sink, I saw "the painter" in action. There he was, next to the sink, with his box of colors. He had just placed a large green spot, there, on the painting with his brush. Had I painted? "Painted"? What does that mean? No: I called forth with my hands. The iron and I had given rise. That had happened to two bodies unknown to one another. Outside however a storm was brewing, the trees were swaying, a column of dust was advancing....[9]

What comes up when you start writing are all the scenes of impotence, terror, or vast power. The unconscious tells a tale of the supernatural possibility (it is always supernatural) of bringing a child to light, but the miracle in the dream is that you can have a child even when you cannot have a child. Even if you are too young or too old to have a child, even if you are eighty, you can still carry a child and give it birth and milk. And sometimes the milk is black.

In its representation of children the dream brings all sorts of children and all sorts of books. The children who arrive in dreams have all the elements of a book. We know nothing about the book: it is the dream and the child who teach us everything. These children are the dreaming woman's children yet at the same time they are strangers. It's equally interesting whether they are boys or girls; sometimes it's a fetus, sometimes a bird. . . .

The foreign child has another form. In Herman Broch's *The Death of Virgil* there is always a child coming and going, a companion, guide, and counterpart to the dying Virgil. This is perhaps an exteriorized equivalent of what a woman lives inwardly. Between the child (the text, that is) and the author, there is a relationship of absolute intensity, since it is a matter of life and death; we are constantly caught not ensuring life. If we don't hate castration, such a dream will make us abhor it. There is also a reversal in the maternal relation between child and mother, since life is exchanged.

While insisting on this primitive scene I should add that the fact the book is lived absolutely by the mother or author cannot but have effects on the writing. I am talking here about writers who dream. These stakes – will I or will I not give life? – will I succeed? – mixed with love and terror – cannot but echo in the text.

A woman's dreams are full of enjoyment, full of terror. I must say I am full of curiosity about men. I don't know how men dream when they start writing, though I do wonder about it. I can't imagine they dream that they bear children. So it must be something else. I'd like to know what the equivalent or substitute is.

Our books are dream children. They are ours, though they are total strangers. The sex is usually and strangely determined. The child appearing in the dream that is the text is always much stronger than we are. We don't know where they come from. The child adopts us, we obey, then we abandon the child, though in fact it is the child who abandons us. Everything is reversible. Even if we think we are writing the book, it is the book that is leading us. We depend entirely on the book's goodwill. This is what makes for the writer's humbleness and the fear and hope of seeing the book come to maturation.

Other types of dreams are common to men and women. You may dream of various types of transportation, all kinds of metaphors. But if you see a car coming you can be sure you are not going to drive it: you'll find yourself sitting in the back seat with the car racing like a horse, and all you can do is pray that it will not kill you. Perhaps you'll avoid the car accident, perhaps you'll avoid the miscarriage. I noted with surprise that in the early novel, *O Lustro*, as well as in Clarice Lispector's last novel, *The Hour of the Star*, which I spoke about earlier, the same stroke of fate recurred. In fact I first read *The Hour of the Star* ten years ago and I have only just read *O Lustro*, which is the younger of the two books. Both books end in the same brutal way – with a car accident and the character's death. It is as if they are imitating something connected to the life and death of a book. Writing is this, it is being played by life and death.

Notes

1   *The Holy Bible*, Revised Standard Version (New York: Thomas Nelson and Sons, 1952), p. 21.

2   Ibid.

3   Ibid., pp. 13–17.

4   Clarice Lispector, *O Lustro* (Rio de Janeiro: Editora Nova Fronteira, 1982), our translation, pp. 56–7.

5   Ibid., our translation, p. 57.

6   Ibid.

7   Ibid., p. 58.

8   Marina Tsvetaeva, *Art in the Light of Conscience*, tr. Angela Livingstone (Bristol: Bristol Press, 1991), pp. 68–9.

9   Since these dreams have been dreamt and written in French, the work of the signifier is lost in the translation. "*Reste le reste*": only the remains remain (Hélène Cixous's note).

Chapter 6

Parable and Performative in the Gospels and in Modern Literature

J. Hillis Miller 1928–

Introduction

J. Hillis Miller, a distinguished literary critic and scholar, received a Ph.D. from Harvard University in 1951. He taught for more than two decades at Johns Hopkins University and fourteen years at Yale University. He is now a distinguished professor of English and Comparative Literature at the University of California, Irvine. At Yale with Geoffrey Hartman and Paul de Man, Miller had been vital in introducing Continental literary studies and philosophy to the Anglo–American academic community, practicing versions of deconstructive and post structuralist literary criticism. Miller's work has always been at the forefront of critical discourse in the United States: in fact, his career – including a "formalist" dissertation, books that approach texts from a phenomenological perspective, his work in deconstructive criticism, and his recent attention to forms of "cultural studies" in relation to literature – epitomizes the trajectory of American literary studies since World War II. His major works include: *Charles Dickens: The World of his Novels* (1958); *The Disappearance of God* (1963); *Poets of Reality: Six Twentieth-Century Writers* (1965); *Thomas Hardy: Distance and Desire* (1970); *Fiction and Repetition* (1982); *The Linguistic Moment* (1985); *The Ethics of Reading* (1987); *Versions of Pygmalion* (1990); *Topographies* (1995); *Reading Narrative* (1998); and *Black Holes* (1999).

The most striking aspect of Miller's work is his lucid faithfulness to the literary or critical texts he examines in the context of the most profound questions of the experience of those texts. Throughout his career, Miller has read closely, in what he calls "slow reading," but also with an urgency that seems "metaphysical" or even "religious." He describes this mode of reading in his important essay "The Search for grounds in Literary Study" as the search for something that "is properly religious, metaphysical, or ontological, though hardly in a traditional or conventional way," a " 'something,' " he goes on to say, "that enters into the words or between the words" in texts, "something encountered in our relations to other people, especially relations involving love, betrayal, and that ultimate betrayal..., the death of the other." Thus, while he has not explicitly discussed biblical texts very often – "Parable and

Performative in the Gospels and in Modern Literature" is one of only a few examinations of the Bible in his work — nevertheless, Miller's *kind* of reading has had significant influence among biblical scholars and others seeking to recover the sacred for the modern world. Miller's work figures significantly in *The Postmodern Bible*'s discussion of Rhetorical Criticism.

In "Parable and Performative" (1982) Miller specifically focuses upon the functioning of parable in the Gospel. In this "deconstructive" reading, Miller sets up the opposition between sacred and secular literature. The parable of the Bible, he argues, is an article of faith: "believing in the validity of the parables of the New Testament and believing that Jesus is the Son of God is the same thing." On the other hand, "a secular parable" in the example of Kafka is an article of doubt, "impossible in principle to know whether or not it is true or counterfeit." Miller's argument focuses on the dual apprehension of parable as a *literal* use of language ("when Jesus speaks the parables, Christ the Word stands visibly before his auditors, for those who have eyes to see and ears to hear") and as a *figurative* use of language (the articulation of a transcendental or "other" language through homely everyday vocabularies). Such a double apprehension, however, confounds the opposition sacred/secular upon which the discussion is based in the same way, Miller argues, that parable as a figure of speech confounds the opposition between constative/performative definitions of language. Thus the essay ends with the assertion (and/or "performance") of "the difficulty — perhaps the impossibility — in spite of all efforts and in spite of the high stakes involved, of keeping the two kinds of parable absolutely distinct."

A large contradictory modern secondary literature now exists on the parables of Jesus in the New Testament and on their relation to the tradition of secular parable in modern writers like Kleist and Kafka.[1] Since I am not a biblical scholar, I cannot hope to add much to this discussion except possibly from the point of view of secular literature; but I can begin here with several axioms or presuppositions to guide my investigation, if only as grounds to be ungrounded by what is discovered later on.

The first presupposition is the assumption that it ought to be possible to identify specific differences, in the language, between the parables of Jesus and any secular parables whatsoever. Much is at stake here. The distinction between sacred scripture and secular literature would seem to depend on being able to identify the difference. The authority not only of the Bible as in some sense or other the word of God but more specifically of the words of Jesus as speech of God would seem to hang in the balance here. If the Middle Ages needed a distinction between "allegory of the poets" and "allegory of the theologians," we moderns would seem to need a firm distinction between "parable of the poets" and "parable of the theologians."

J. Hillis Miller, "Parable and Performative in the Gospels and in Modern Literature," from *Tropes, Parables, Performatives: Essays on Twentieth-Century Literature* (Durham, NC: Duke University Press, 1991; originally published in *Humanizing America's Iconic Book: Society of Biblical Literature Centennial Addresses 1980*, edited by Gene M. Tucker and Douglas A. Knight, Chico, CA: Scholars Press; copyright 1982, Society of Biblical Literature).

The second presupposition is no more than a definition of parable. Etymologically the word means "thrown beside," as a parabolic curve is thrown beside the imaginary line going down from the apex of the imaginary cone on the other side of whose surface the parabola traces its graceful loop from infinity and out to infinity again. Comets on a parabolic trajectory come once, sweep round the sun, and disappear forever, unlike those on a large elliptical orbit which return periodically, Halley's Comet for instance. When this is taken as a parable of the working of parable in literature or in scripture, it suggests that parable is a mode of figurative language which is the indirect indication, at a distance, of something that cannot be described directly, in literal language, like that imaginary invisible cone or like the sun, single controlling focus of the comet's parabola, which cannot be looked in the eye, although it is the condition of all seeing, or like that inaccessible place from which the comet comes and to which it returns. A parabolic narrative is, my parable of the comet would suggest, in some way governed, at its origin and at its end, by the infinitely distant and invisible, by something that transcends altogether direct presentation. The correspondence between what is given in parable – the "realistic" story represented in a literal language – and its meaning is more indirect than is the case, for example, in "symbolic" expression, in the usual meaning of the latter, where, as the name suggests, one expects more of interpretation, of participation, and of similarity. One German name for parable is *Gleichnis*, "likeness." This is what Luther calls a parable of Jesus. The paradox of parable is that it is a likeness that rests on a manifest unlikeness between what is given and what cannot by any means be given directly. A parabolic "likeness" is so "unlike" that without interpretation or commentary the meaning may slip by the reader or listener altogether.

Hegel's discussion of what he called "conscious symbolism" provides a definition of parable that corresponds to the one I have been making. The sublime (*das Erhabene*) is, strangely enough, included by Hegel with fable, parable, apalogue, proverb, and metamorphosis as a mode of "conscious symbolism."

> What has emerged from sublimity as distinct from strictly unconscious symbolizing consists on the one hand in the *separation* [*in dem Trennen*] between the meaning, explicitly known in its inwardness, and the concrete appearance divided therefrom; on the other hand in the directly or indirectly emphasized non-correspondence of the two [*Sichnichtentsprechen beider*] wherein the meaning, as the universal, towers above individual reality and its particularity.[2]

If "separation" and "non-correspondence" characterize all such forms of symbolism, including parable, then the meaning of the parable can hardly be expected to be perspicuous to eyes that cannot see the tenor of which such symbols are the vehicle. For example, says Hegel when he comes to discuss parable in particular:

> The parable of the sower [in all the Synoptics] is a story in itself trivial in content [*für sich von geringfügigem Gehalt*] and it is important only because of the comparison with the doctrine of the Kingdom of Heaven. In these parables the meaning throughout is a religious doctrine to which the human occurrences in which it is represented [*vorgestellt*] are related in much the same way as man and animal are related in Aesop's Fables, where the former constitutes the meaning of the latter.[3]

In parable, human is to religious doctrine as animal is to human. The latter constitutes the meaning of the former across the gap of their separation and non-correspondence.

On the basis of this definition, a distinction, in principle at least, between sacred parable and secular parable may be made. The parables of Jesus are spoken by the Word, the Logos, in person. Even if this terminology is fully present only in the Gospel of John, it is already implicit in the characterization in the first three Gospels of Jesus as the Messiah. The fact that the Messiah speaks the parables guarantees the correspondence between the homely stories he tells of farming, fishing, and domestic economy on the one hand, and the spiritual or transcendent meaning on the other, the meaning that tells of things beyond the threshold of the domestic and visible, the meaning that nevertheless can be spoken only in parable, that is, indirectly. Christ as the Logos is not only the basis of the analogies, echoes, and resemblances among things of the world created in his name and between things created in his name and things hidden since the creation of the world. Christ as Logos is also the basis of the correspondence within the realm of language, for example the correspondence between visible vehicle and invisible and unnamed tenor in a parable. When Jesus speaks the parables, Christ the Word stands visibly before his auditors, for those who have eyes to see and ears to hear, as support of the correspondence between his realistic narrative of sowing, fishing, or household care and those unseeable things of which the parable "really" speaks. This guarantee is, I take it, one of the fundamental meanings of the Incarnation. Believing in the validity of the parables of the New Testament and believing that Jesus is the Son of God are the same thing.

The speakers or writers of secular parables stand in a different place, even though their parables too may deal with religious or metaphysical matters. They are down here with us, and their words about things visible can only be thrown beside things invisible in the hope that their narratives of what can be spoken about, the fencing bear in Kleist's "Über das Marionettentheater," for example, will magically make appear the other invisible, perhaps imaginary, line to which their realistic stories, they hope, correspond. The editor of the Greek New Testament I have consulted, Henry Alford, a nineteenth-century Anglican biblical scholar, put this clearly in his preliminary note on Matthew 13. A parable, he says,

> is a serious narration within the limits of probability, of a course of action pointing to some moral or spiritual Truth ("Collatio per narratiunculam fictam, sed veri similem, serio illustrans rem sublimiorem." Unger, de Parabolis Jesu [Meyer]) ["some moral or spiritual truth," it might be noted, is a loose translation of "rem sublimiorem"]; and derives its force from real analogies impressed by the Creator of all things on His creatures. The great Teacher by parables therefore is He who needed not that any should testify of man; for He knew what was in man, John ii.25: moreover, He *made* man, and orders the course and character of human events. And this is the reason why no one can, or dare, teach by parables, except Christ. We do not, as He did, see the inner springs out of which flow those laws of spiritual truth and justice, which the Parable is framed to elucidate. *Our* parables would be in danger of perverting, instead of guiding aright.[4]

The fact that Alford a page later commits the crime he warns against is an amusing example of the *odium theologicum* but also an example of a problem with Christ's parables. Any interpretation of these parables is itself parabolic. In one way or another it must do what Henry Alford warns against, that is, claim to understand "the inner springs out of which flow those laws of spiritual truth and justice, which the Parable is framed to elucidate." Which of us, reading Matthew 13, would admit to being one of those who seeing see not, and hearing hear not, neither understand? So Alford, speaking of that terrifying law of parable Jesus enunciates whereby "For to him who has will more be given, and he will have abundance; but from him who has not, even what he has will be taken away" (Matthew 13:12), applies it to the biblical commentators of his own day, doing in the process what he has said a page before no mere human being should dare do, namely, teach by parable: "No practical comment," says Alford, "on the latter part of this saying can be more striking, than that which is furnished to our day by the study of German rationalistic (and, I may add, some of our English harmonistic) Commentators; while at the same time we may rejoice to see the approximate fulfilment of the former in such commentaries as those of Olshausen, Neander, Stier, and Trench."[5] No doubt Olshausen, Neander, Stier, and Trench were worthy scholars, but there is also no doubt a grotesque incongruity or bathos in using the parable of the sower as a means of dividing the sheep from the goats in the parochial warfare of biblical scholarship. In any case, there is great temerity in doing so, just that merely human preaching by parables against which Alford has warned on the page before. Yet it is obvious that whoever speaks of the parables at all runs the risk, perhaps must endure the necessity, of doing this. The language of parables contaminates, or perhaps it might be better to say inseminates, impregnates, its commentators. Such language forces them to speak parabolically, since it is by definition impossible to speak of what the parables name except parabolically. Commentary on the parables is, or ought to be, an example of the dissemination of the Word, its multiplication thirty-, sixty-, or a hundredfold.

This need to distinguish secular from sacred parable and yet difficulty in doing so leads to my third presupposition. This is that the two kinds of parable may be distinguished by recognizing that both are performative rather than constative utterances but that two radically different kinds of performative would appear to be involved. A parable does not so much passively name something as make something happen. A parable is a way to do things with words. It is a speech act. In the case of the parables of Jesus, however, the performative word makes something happen in the minds and hearts of the hearers, but this happening is a knowledge of a state of affairs already existing, the kingdom of heaven and the way to get there. In that sense, a biblical parable is constative, not performative at all. A true performative brings something into existence that has no basis except in the words, as when I sign a check and turn an almost worthless piece of paper into whatever value I have inscribed on the check, assuming the various contexts for this act are in correct order – even though as the phenomenon of counterfeit money or the passing of bad checks indicates, the performative may make something happen even when some aspect of the contexts is amiss. Secular parable is a genuine performative. It creates something, a "meaning", that has no basis except in the words or something about which it is impossible to describe whether or not there is an extralinguistic basis. A secular parable is like a piece of money about which it is impossible in principle to know whether or not it is true or counterfeit. Secular parable is language thrown out that creates a meaning hovering there in thin air, a meaning based only on the language itself and on our confidence in it. The categories of truth and falsehood, knowledge and ignorance, do not properly apply to it.

My final presupposition is that both kinds of parable tend to be parables about parable. They are about their own efficacy. Jesus' parable of the sower in Matthew 13:1–23, with its parallels in Mark and Luke, is a well-known example of this.[6] Its topic is the efficacy of the word. The distinction is between those who have eyes and ears for the Word and those who do not, or rather the parable distinguishes four possibilities, that the seed will fall by the wayside, in stony places, among thorns, and in good ground, with an appropriate psychological interpretation for each of the different predispositions to receive the Word, as the thorns stand for "the care of this world, and the deceitfulness of riches," which "choke the word" (Matthew 13:22). What in fact is the "word"? It is the good news, the gospel of salvation, the "secrets of the kingdom of heaven" (Matthew 13:11), "what has been hidden since the foundation of the world" (Matthew 13:35). A whole series of paradoxes operates at once in this parable about parable.

First paradox: The presupposition is that the mysteries of the kingdom of heaven cannot be spoken of directly. The things that have been kept secret from the foundation of the world can only be spoken of in parable. Christ as the Logos is in the awkward position of not being able to speak the Logos directly but of being forced to translate it into a form suitable for profane ears. The Word cannot speak the Word as such.

Second paradox: Unless you understand the Word already as such, unless you are already fertile ground for the Word, which means somehow already grounded in it, sown by it, you will not understand it when it is expressed in parable. When the disciples ask, "Why do you speak to them in parables?" Christ's answer is: "To you it has been given to know the secrets of the kingdom of heaven, but to them it has not been given. For to him who has will more be given, and he will have abundance; but from him who has not, even what he has will be taken away. This is why I speak to them in parables, because seeing they do not see, and hearing they do not hear, nor do they understand" (Matthew 13:10–13). The parables are posited on their own inefficacy. If you have knowledge of the kingdom of heaven already, you do not need them. The parables are superfluous, a superabundance, a surplus, a gift beyond gift. If you do not have that knowledge, you will not understand the parables anyhow. They will be a way of covering your eyes and ears further, not a breaking of the seals or a form of unveiling, of revelation. The things that have been kept secret from the foundation of the world will remain secret for most people even after they are spoken in parable. Such things are perhaps made secret by that foundation, veiled by the creation itself rather than revealed by it, and so kept secret by parables that name those secret things with names drawn from familiar created things. The parables translate the Word, so to speak, into the language of familiar things, sowing, fishing, household work. Even so, those for whom the parables are intended are like those to whom one speaks in a foreign language or like someone who does not know Greek presented with the Gospel of Matthew in Greek. The parable, as they say, is all Greek to that person. Such persons lack the gift of tongues or the gift of translating the parable back into the original word. "Hearing they do not hear, nor do they understand." Such people are like Belshazzar confronted by the handwriting on the wall, or they are like those auditors who are not going to understand the prophecy of Isaiah, a failure in understanding that Jesus says the failure of his parables will fulfill. Here is the great text in Isaiah on which Jesus' parable of the sower is a commentary:

> Then flew one of the seraphims to me, having in his hand a burning coal which he had taken with tongs from the altar. And he touched my mouth, and said: "Behold, this has touched your lips; your guilt is taken away, and your sin forgiven." And I heard the voice of the Lord saying, "Whom shall I send, and who will go for us?" Then I said, "Here am I! Send me." And he said, "Go, and say to this people: 'Hear and hear, but do not understand; see and see, but do not perceive.' Make the heart of this people fat, and their ears heavy, and shut their eyes; lest they see with their eyes, and hear with their ears, and understand with their hearts, and turn and be healed." (Isaiah 6: 6–10)

The parables, however, are intended for just such people, and so they are posited on their own inevitable misreading or nonreading. The problem, once more, is how to cross over from one kind of language to the other, from the word of God, "Whom shall I send?" to the word of the human: "Here am I! Send me." If you can understand the parables, you do not need them. If you need them, you cannot hope to understand them. The parables are not a way of giving the Word but a way of taking away, a way of adding further deprivation to a deprivation that is already total: "From him who has not, even what he has will be taken away."

Third paradox: The disciples are said by Jesus to be those to whom it is given to know the mysteries of the kingdom of heaven. It would seem that this means they already have the Word and therefore have open eyes and ears, are able to understand the parables spontaneously, translate their displaced language back to the original tongue, and at the same time do not need the parables. The parables give them more when they already have and so do not need. For them the parables are superfluous. "For to him who has will more be given, and he will have abundance." The paradox is that, having said that, Jesus proceeds to explain to the disciples the parable of the sower, spelling it out, translating it back into the language of the kingdom of heaven, as if they could not understand it without his interpretation. He has said they understand, but he goes on to speak as if they could not possibly understand: "Truly, I say to you, many prophets and righteous men have longed to see what you see, and did not see it, and to hear what you hear, and did not hear it. Hear then the parable of the sower. When any one hears the word of the kingdom and does not understand it, the evil one comes and snatches away what is sown in his heart; this is what was sown along the path . . ." and so on through the explicit application of each of the clauses of the parable to each of the four kinds of people in relation to the proffered insemination or dissemination of the Word, down to: "As for what was sown on good soil, this is he who hears the word and understands it; he indeed bears fruit, and yields, in one case a hundredfold, in another sixty, and in another thirty" (Matthew 13:17–23).

Fourth paradox: The economy of equivalence, of giving and receiving, of equable translation and measure, of the circulation of signs governed by the Logos as source of proportion and guarantee of substitution or analogy, is upset by the parables. Although the parables of Jesus are spoken by the Word, they are not logical. They are not governed, as, say, medieval allegory is said to be, whatever Henry Alford affirms, by the "real analogies impressed by the Creator of all things on his creatures." Or, if they are so governed, they function by a choice of alogical moments in systems of circulation and exchange in the familiar domestic world to indicate the failure of analogy between anything human, including human languages – Aramaic, Greek, Latin, English, or whatever – and the divine Logos, the Word of the kingdom of heaven. If allegory and symbolism in one way or another work by analogy or by correspondence, resonance, or participation between one thing and another thing on a different level, or between one word and another word, as in the proportionalities of metaphor, the parables of Jesus are ana-analogical, or rather, since "ana" is already a double antithetical prefix, which may mean either "according to" or "against," it may simply be said that the parables are "analogical" in the sense of "against logic," "counter to logic." "Paradox": the word means etymologically, "against teaching," or against the received opinion of those in authority. The words or parables of Jesus are a stumbling block to the Greeks because they go against the habits of logical thinking. The Logos in the sense of Jesus as the Word contradicts *logos* in the sense of Greek reason, or reasoned thinking, which is reason as such in the West.

The "literal" language of the parables of Jesus and of his actions themselves as described by the gospel makers is drawn from various realms of domestic economy, production, consumption, and exchange in the family or in the immediate social group such as a household with servants or a farm with hired workers. These various realms include eating, sowing and reaping, fishing, sexual reproduction, the donation and receiving of gifts, the exchange of words, translation from one language to another, counting, and the exchange of money, its use and its usury. In all cases the example chosen breaks down the pattern of a closed circuit of exchange of the same for the same or its equivalent. The fisherman draws fish abundantly from the salt and inhospitable sea. A single seed cast in fertile ground reproduces a hundred-, sixty-, or thirtyfold, and a tiny mustard seed produces an enormous tree. He who saves his life will lose it. To save it, it must be thrown away, and the same thing may be said of virginity, which is of value or use only if it is given up, just as money has the power of reproducing itself magically but not if it is hoarded, only if it is invested, put out at risk, used. The distinction between male potency and female passive receptivity is broken down in sexual reproduction, since the female must be fertile ground for the seed and thus in a sense already contain its potentiality, as only fertile ground will multiply the seed cast on it and as only those who already have the Word can receive it and multiply it. Although the image Jesus uses in his exegesis of the parable of the sower is that of sexual reproduction, the sexes are strangely reversed, as they are in the image of the soul as the bride of Christ. Jesus speaks of the different persons who receive the seed of the Word as "he": "But he that received the seed into stony places..." and so on, but that fertile ground must in some sense be a feminine matrix, an egg ready to receive the seed. A genuine gift, like the other elements upsetting any domestic economy of equivalence and exchange, is, as Marcel Mauss and Jacques Derrida have in different ways argued, always something incommensurate with any recompense, something suspending the circuit of obligation, of payment and repayment.[7] A true gift can never be returned. It creates an infinite obligation and is not restitution for any claim

I have on another. The gift leads to such absurdities as the Northwest American Indian potlatch, in which one man vies with another in destroying great heaps of valuable property.

The power of the gift to break down logical equivalences in social exchange is shown in reverse in what might be called the living parable of the story of the loaves and fishes in Matthew 14. Jesus blesses the bread, breaks it, and gives the five loaves and the two fishes to the disciples. The disciples give them to the multitude. In that double process of giving, the loaves and fishes become multiplied beyond any rational calculation so that there is always enough and some over – twelve baskets of fragments – though about five thousand have been fed. In this case, as in the parables generally, for example the parable of the sower, several different realms, of the ones I have listed, come together: gift giving and receiving, agriculture and fishing in the bread and fishes, and the illogic of an arithmetical sum in which five loaves and two fishes become a countless number with twelve basketsfull left over. In the case of the parable of the sower, sowing and reaping, on the one hand, and sexual reproduction on the other, are used each as a figure for the paradoxes of the other. There is a contamination of the "literal" language of each of the realms, in any vernacular, with figures drawn from others of the realms, as when we speak of "seed money," or of the "dissemination" of the seed in sowing, as well as of the dissemination of doctrine, or of sexual reproduction in terms of "getting" and "spending," and so on, in a perpetual round in which no one set of these terms is the purely literal language that provides figures for the others. Another way to put this is to say that ordinary language, the language Jesus must use to speak to the multitude or to the disciples, is already irremediably parabolic.

The final realm in which rational equivalence and exchange breaks down is then that of language itself, that dissemination of the Word for which all these other realms are not so much figures as living and material hieroglyphs, that is, places where the paradoxes of sign-making and sign-using enter into the actual process of the living together of men and women in family and community, to be incorporated inextricably into that process. In the realm of language, too, the giving of the Word introduces a form of sign into the rational exchanges of word for word in ordinary communication which breaks open that circuit with the alogic of parable. The Word is like a tiny mustard seed which produces a huge tree, and although it is demonstrably untranslat-able, "the propagation of the gospel in foreign lands" depends on its translatability and on the gift of tongues to the apostles and their dissemination, carrying the Word into the four corners of the world. The limitations of a given translation are not contingent but absolute. The failure of translation is not a result of the incompatability of one idiom and another or between a proper original and some improper transfer or *Übersetzung*, as they say in German for translation, "setting over." The failure of translation is the result of the absence of any adequate original in any humanly comprehensible language. When I read the King James Bible today, or some other English Bible, it has behind it the Vulgate, the Greek, the hypothetical Aramaic versions of what Jesus said, language behind language behind language. However, the inadequacy of any translation and the way the propagation of the Gospel is a triumph over its own manifest impossibility lie not in the incorrectness of this or that detail in, say, the King James Bible in relation to the Greek or Aramaic "original", but in the fact that even the words of the parable of the sower, for example, as Jesus originally spoke them, were not an original but already the translation of an untranslatable original Word, which is what Jesus in the parable of the sower "says": "That is why I speak to them in parables, because seeing they do not see, and hearing they do not hear, nor do they understand. With them indeed is fulfilled the prophecy of Isaiah which says: 'You shall indeed hear but never understand, and you shall indeed see but never perceive'" (Matthew 13:13–14).

In all these realms the pattern of alogic is "the same." It is analogical, an analogy among ana-analogies or an analogy in one sense among analogies in the antithetical sense. In each case the pattern expresses a strange arithmetic in which one will get you not two but a hundredfold in return, or rather in which something so tiny that it is in effect zero will multiply infinitely, as in that equation Paul Claudel makes among things globular and null or almost null: "*oeuf, semence, bouche ouverte, zéro,*" "egg, seed, open mouth, zero," where the open mouth that proffers the word, "Here am I, send me," is equated not only with the egg and seed of sowing and sexual reproduction but also with the zero that divides an infinite number of times even into a single unit, as a single word may be broken, divided, and scattered in all languages to the four winds.[8]

I turn now to modern secular parable, which should in principle, I have suggested, function differently, since a secular parable is not spoken by the Word itself translating itself to human ears and human understanding but is spoken by some all-too-human person casting out figurative language toward something across the border from any direct seeing, hearing, or understanding.

In *Von den Gleichnissen* ("On Parables") Franz Kafka develops a characteristically mind-twisting paradox that turns on the distinction between whether something happens in reality or in parable. It is a triple distinction: a distinction between everyday reality and "some fabulous yonder"; a distinction between the everyday person and that person transfigured; a distinction between literal language and parabolic language:

> When the sage says: "go over," he does not mean that we should cross to some actual place, which we could do anyhow if the labor were worth it; he means some fabulous yonder (*irgendem sagenhaftes Drüben*), something unknown to us (*das wir nicht kennen*), something that he cannot designate more precisely (*von ihm nicht näher zu bezeichnen ist*), and therefore cannot help us there in the very least.[9]

The word "over" (*hinüber*) in parabolic speech refers not to some real place "over there" but to a place out of this world. It is a place, moreover, that cannot be designated more precisely than in topographical terms drawn from the real world and applied figuratively to the place out of the real world. There are no literal terms for the places in parable. They cannot be designated more precisely than by the transferred terms of metaphor or rather of catachresis, which is the proper term for a figure that does not replace any existing proper word. The question posed by Kafka's little text is a double one: What kind of action is performed by the sage when he wrests words from their normal usage and says, "Go over"? What kind of actions should we perform if we wish to obey the sage's injunction?

The answer seems obvious enough. We have only to follow the parables in order to become parables. We would then enter into the realm of parable, and escape cares of real life in the actual place where we are: "Concerning this a man once said: Why such reluctance? If you only followed the parables you yourselves would become parables and with that rid of all your daily cares."[10]

The question about this commentary is also obvious enough. Is the remark by "a man" in itself literal, or is it parabolic? This in turn is a displacement of a more general question. Is Kafka's "On Parables" as a whole literal or is it parabolic? Is it possible to speak of parables literally, or is the language of the commentators on parables always contaminated by what they talk about, subdued to what they work in, so that their language becomes in its turn inevitably parabolic? Would that necessarily be a bad thing? These are the questions raised by the little alternating dialogue that ends Kafka's "On Parables." In this dialogue two more voices are heard, and the voice of "Kafka" himself, which spoke at first, as well as the voice of the "man" who said we only need to "follow" the parables, vanishes entirely. The little dialogue has to do with the linguistic status of the exhortation to follow the parables and has to do with winning and losing not in the parables themselves but in the interpreter's stance in relation to them and in his language about them:

> Another said: I bet that is also a parable.
> The first said: You have won.
> The second said: But unfortunately only in parable.
> The first said: No, in reality: in parable you have lost.[11]

The reader (I hope) will be able to follow this somewhat bewildering alternation to the point of blinding clarity it reaches. To say something is a parable can only be done from the point of view of reality and of literal language, since the realm of parable and the language of parable are defined by their difference from the real and the literal. They are a transfer from it, a "going over." To say that by following the parables one becomes a parable is a parable all right, but it is a saying that remains immovably still in the realm of everyday life, which, after all, as "On Parables" says at the beginning, "is the only life we have." One wins the bet ("I bet that is also a parable") but only in reality, which means that one loses in parable. The parables ask to be taken literally. The only way they can become efficacious is for them to become literally true, so that one does literally "go over." As long as they are seen as figures of speech, as merely parabolic, one loses in parable, one has failed to enter into the realm of parable. But they cannot be seen otherwise. They produce neither action nor knowledge. To know that fabulous realm over there is to cross over into it, but the parables merely throw out incomprehensible figures in the direction of the incomprehensible. They are like parables proffered by one of the multitude who hear Jesus speak or at best like a parable given out by one of the disciples. "All these parables really set out to say merely that the incomprehensible is incomprehensible (*unfassbar*), and we know that already."[12]

"On Parables" is a characteristic example of the specifically Kafkan double bind. Either way you have had it. You lose by winning and lose by losing too. If you take the parable literally, then you must understand it as naming some literal crossing over from one place to another in reality, in which case you remain in reality, "the only life we have"; so following the parables does not make anything happen. If you take parable parabolically, then it is seen as merely figurative. In that case neither the parable itself nor following the parable makes anything happen, and so you have lost in parable, since winning in parable could only occur if the crossing over promised in the parable were to occur in reality. Either way you lose, since winning in reality is losing in parable, and the one thing needful is to win in parable, to find a joy whose grounds are true.

This may perhaps be made clearer by a return to my comparison with performative language. It would seem at first that two kinds of language, the creative *Fiat lux* of God and statements made by human beings like "I pronounce you husband and wife" are the same. Both are ways of doing things with words. There is, however, an essential difference. The "Let there be light" of God produces the basic condition of visibility and therefore of knowledge. It allows things to stand in the sunlight and be seen. To use the distinction employed also by Nietzsche, as well as by Kafka in the phrase *das wir nicht kennen*, God's *Fiat lux* leads to an act of knowledge, an *Erkennen*. Human performatives, on the other hand, can never be the object of an epistemological act whereby subject confronts something that has been brought to life and knows it. Human performatives are always from beginning to end baseless positings, acts of *Ersetzen* rather than of *Erkennen*.[13] A secular parable is an *Ersetzen* that must, impossibly, become an *Erkennen*. It must actually create a new realm into which we might cross over. It remains a merely human positing, the making of a realm created by language, existing and sustained only in language. In this it is no different from the complex social world made by promising, contracting, naming, and so on, the "daily life" with all its "cares" "which is the only life we have," and which we would do anything to cross over out of. No speech act, no poetic or parabolic performative can help us one bit to do that. "Over out of": The multiplication of adverbs is meant to mime the repeated unsuccessful attempts to go somewhere with language.

I shall now attempt to draw such conclusions as I can from my brief side-by-side discussion of sacred parable and secular parable. My primary motivation, it will be remembered, has been to identify distinguishing marks that would allow a firm division between one and the other. I claim to have done this in identifying a different nature and standing place in each case for the speaker or writer of the parable and in identifying a different relation in each case to the distinction between performative and constative language. The latter difference may be phrased by saying that both kinds of parables are catachreses, the throwing out of language toward an "unknown X" which cannot be named in proper or literal language. In the case of secular parable it cannot be known for certain, even by the one who invents the parable, whether or not there is something out there, across the frontier, which pre-exists the language for it. Such language may be a true performative, bringing something into being that exists only in the words or by means of the words. Sacred parable is in principle spoken by someone who has that knowledge to start with, by someone who *is* that knowledge, by someone who is the Logos itself in all the sense of that word: mind, reason, knowledge, speech, measure, ratio, ground of all things.

The distinction seems clear, but the distinction itself involves a double paradox, one on each side of the line separating secular from sacred parable. On the one hand, Christ the Word must in the parables translate the Word into humanly comprehensible language. He is in himself both sides of the dialogue between Jehovah and Isaiah that he says his parables are meant to fulfill. Christ is both the Word of God, "the voice of the Lord" called in vocation or in invocation to Isaiah, "Whom shall I send?" and Isaiah's answering voice in acceptance of vocation, "Here am I! Send me." Christ's words are therefore subject necessarily to the limitations of human language in whatever language they are spoken or into which they might be translated, in spite of the suprahuman standing place from which he speaks. Christ's dissemination of the Word is therefore performed over its logical impossibility, as he says in the parable of the sower. This impossibility may be expressed by saying that the parables of Jesus are not properly performative. They do not in themselves make anything happen, since their auditors must already know the Word to be fertile ground for the Word the parables speak. The parables of Jesus are constative, but they provide knowledge that for many is spoken in a foreign tongue, a tongue that is not going to be understood. The paradox of the parables of the Gospels as at once Word of God and at the same time humanly comprehensible words is "the same as," analogical to in one or the other meaning of the word analogy, the mystery of the Incarnation, in which God and humanity become one across the barrier of the impossibility of their union.

Of another "analogous" problem with the parables in the Gospels I have not even spoken here, and can only indicate a line to be followed. Do the citations of the parables by the authors of the Gospels have the same efficacy as the parables had when they were originally spoken by Jesus to his auditors, or are they only the report of a form of language that has its efficacy elsewhere? Are they still the Word of the kingdom of heaven, the good news itself, or are they only the translation of that Word so it may be disseminated in another tongue? To employ the terminology of the speech-act theorists, are they "use" or only "mention" of Christ's language? These questions, it will be seen, are analogous to, although not quite the same as, the problem of translation on the one hand and the problem of distinguishing sacred from secular parable on the other.[14]

On the other side of the line separating secular and sacred parable, the paradox is that no purely human parable-maker, even though that person may be someone who, like Kafka, fully accepts the limitations of humanity, can avoid the temerity of at least tentatively, implicitly, or hypothetically putting himself in Christ's place and claiming to serve as an intermediary between this everyday world and the kingdom of heaven on the other side of the frontier of which all parables bring word. Secular parable may be, strictly speaking, a true performative, the creation of something that exists, for humanity at least, only in the words, but this purely performative function is always contaminated by an implicit claim to be based on knowledge and to bring knowledge, even if that knowledge is the negative knowing of the apparent impossibility of "going over." Kafka was fully aware of this danger. It is in fact the fundamental burden of *Von den Gleichnissen*.

Any commentator on parables, secular or sacred, is in the situation of Kafka, or indeed of such a commentator as Henry Alford. One should be anxious to avoid the danger of being parabolic oneself and yet one is unable certainly to do so. The question of the relation between secular and sacred parable is a tiny seed that generates a long line of thought, multiplying itself thirty-, sixty-, or a hundredfold, of which this paper is only a preliminary segment. Such a line of thought is like a parabolic trajectory, sweeping in from an infinite distance and back out again. That my discourse on parable is itself parabolic there can be no doubt, although whether I have been able to keep safely on this side of the line separating secular from sacred parable is not so certain. The uncertainty derives from the difficulty – perhaps the impossibility – in spite of all efforts and in spite of the high stakes involved, of keeping the two kinds of parable absolutely distinct.

Notes

1 See, for example, William Beardslee, *Literary Criticism of the New Testament* (Philadelphia, 1970); Charles Carlston, *The Parables of the Triple Tradition* (Philadelphia, 1975); Dominic Crossan, *In Parables* (New York, 1973); *idem, Raid on the Articulate* (New York, 1976); C. H. Dodd, *The Parables of the Kingdom* (New York, 1961); Robert W. Funk, *Language, Hermeneutic, and the Word of God* (New York, 1966); J. Jeremias, *The Parables of Jesus* (New York, 1972); Norman Perrin, *Jesus and the Language of the Kingdom* (Philadelphia, 1976); Norman Petersen, *Literary Criticism for New Testament Critics* (Philadelphia, 1978); Jean Starobinski, "Le Combat avec Légion," *Trois fureurs* (Paris, 1974) pp. 73–126; Mary Ann Tolbert, *Perspectives on the Parables: An Approach to Multiple Interpretations* (Philadelphia, 1979); Dan O. Via, *The Parables* (Philadelphia, 1967); Andrzej Warminski, "'Patmos': The Senses of Interpretation," *MLN*, 91 (1976) pp. 478–500; Amos Wilder, "The Parable," *Early Christian Rhetoric: The Language of the Gospel* (Cambridge, 1971) pp. 71–88. A collection may also be mentioned, *Analyse structurale et exégèse biblique* (François Bovon, ed.; Neuchâtel, 1971), which also contains the essay by Jean Starobinski listed above. In addition, two journals, *Semeia* and *Linguistica Biblica*, have contained many essays on the parables of Jesus. I owe most of this brief bibliography of recent work on the parables to Amos Wilder, who has kindly assisted in educating me in this area, as he has educated me in other ways over the years. I am glad to be able to thank him here for manifold kindnesses.
2 G. W. F. von Hegel, *Aesthetics: Lectures on Fine Art* (tr. T. M. Knox; 2 vols; New York, 1975) 1. 378; *Vorlesungen über die Ästhetik, Werkausgabe* (Frankfurt am Main, 1970) 1. 486.
3 Ibid., English, p. 391; German, pp. 502–3.
4 *The Greek Testament*, H. Alford, ed. (4 vols; Boston; New York, 1874) l. 136–7.
5 Ibid., p. 138.
6 As Jean Starobinski observes, "Le Combat," 111 ff.
7 See Marcel Mauss, *The Gift* (tr. Ian Cunnison; New York, 1967); the seminars by Jacques Derrida at Yale University in the fall of 1980 focused on Mauss' book.
8 Paul Claudel and André Gide, *Correspondance 1899–1926* (Paris, 1949) p. 91.
9 Franz Kafka, *Parables and Paradoxes*, in German and English (New York, 1971) pp. 10–11.
10 Ibid.
11 Ibid.
12 Ibid., p. 258.
13 See Paul de Man's discussion of Nietzsche's use of this distinction in "Rhetoric of Persuasion (Nietzsche)," *Allegories of Reading* (New Haven and London, 1979) pp. 119–31.
14 Werner H. Kelber has completed a study of the parables of the Synoptic Gospels which makes the distinction between citation and original oral utterance suggested in this paragraph.

Chapter 7

Body Politic

Mieke Bal 1946–

Introduction

Mieke Bal is Professor of the Theory of Literature at the University of Amsterdam. Though she has never defined herself primarily as a biblical scholar, she is unusual among the authors in this volume in that for a few years, in the 1980s, she worked within the biblical "guild." During that period she wrote a trilogy of books, *Lethal Love* (1987), *Murder and Difference* (1988), and *Death & Dissymmetry* (1989), which gave a significant boost to the entry of biblical studies into the postmodern world. Her main emphasis in those books, as in our selection, is the biblical book of Judges.

Bal's career as a literary specialist began with structuralism; not in the school of Claude Lévi-Strauss and A. J. Greimas, which has had a considerable impact on biblical studies (see our selection from Barthes; also *The Postmodern Bible*, chap. 2), but rather under the impulse of Gérard Genette, whose work is much more with modern literature (for a direct application of Genette to the Bible, see chapter 4 of *Lethal Love*; for a systematic theoretical presentation, see Bal's handbook, *Narratology* [1985, 1997]). Within this tradition she sought ways of expressing her deep engagement with cultural politics, especially feminism. She wanted to create out of Genette a "critical narratology," which also serves, as *The Postmodern Bible* suggests, feminist and ideological approaches to the Bible.

Bal became increasingly interested in the cultural impact of the Bible as a foundational document of the West, and had already begun her biblical explorations when in the mid-1980s she took up an invitation to work at Harvard Divinity School. Her arrival was timely, since feminism was then emerging as a point of juncture in biblical studies between political and literary approaches (see the work of Phyllis Trible), but with little theoretical depth, while Bal was in need of the vigorous cultural presence of feminism in American academics. Taking up a "thoroughly dialectic" stance to her newly adopted field, she set out "to conquer it on feminism's own terms and to contribute something new to the field itself, on its own terms" (*Death & Dissymmetry*, 3–4). *Murder and Difference* can be seen as feminism's theoretical "conquest" of biblical studies, while *Death & Dissymmetry* contributes a whole new way of reading Judges.

More recently Bal has worked on the relationship between verbal and visual representation. This has not meant a turn completely away from the Bible, first because this opposition is itself very biblical (note the Bible's prohibition of images, Deuteronomy 5:8), and second because she found in her compatriot Rembrandt a rich collection of paintings of biblical scenes. This led to her epoch-making work, *Reading "Rembrandt"* (1991), for which our selection may be thought of as a sketch.

In "Body Politic," which first appeared in *On Meaning-Making* (1994), Bal reads Judges 19 simultaneously through the verbal representation of it in a story by Rousseau and a visual representation by Rembrandt. Though she is very far from the technical structuralism of our selections by Barthes and Eco, she nonetheless reveals her structuralist beginnings by building her argument on an extensive series of "oppositions" and their "mediation" – the verbal versus the visual being the most important. Bal's work is probably the best example (at least among treatments of biblical texts) of the openness of structuralism to the cultural and ideological currents of postmodernism.

A paradoxical sketch in the corpus of visual art called "Rembrandt"[1] represents the central scene of Judges 19 (see figure 1). The sketch is paradoxical because it is a statement about death signified by the movement of the dead body. This paradox can be understood as we shift attention from the represented content to the mode of representation. Then, by the incongruous twist which brings death itself to life, the pictorial sign of movement becomes a crucial token of self-reflexivity. But reversing this perspective, we can also say that reflection on pictorial representation is in an important way focused on death. And the dead, here, is a woman.

In this essay, I would like to consider a few relationships between death, women, and representation through an analysis of cultural objects chosen from the four bodies of texts I have been working with up till now: French literature, my initial field; Biblical narrative, a field I encountered when trying to historicize narrative; critical texts, which I began to examine when I discovered *their* use of narrative as a form of argumentation; and visual images, my most recent interest, where forms of narrativity occur which challenge the linguo-centric assumptions of much literary theory. The common ground is narrative, used whether the medium is verbal, visual, or bodily. Narrative as a mode of implicit argumentation is the line which runs through my work on all these different bodies of writing. Narrative as a mode of representation is a tool of manipulation, a figure of rhetoric, and that is my obsession.

It took me a while to see the connection between this obsession and my other one, with death. Death is a challenge to representation to the extent that the experience of death is a moment that nobody can describe, an event that nobody can escape, a process that nobody can narrate. Representation partakes of the attempt to quell the fear of death and to compensate for the loss of identity and material existence death entails. The representation of death as both gendered and representational, therefore, can shed

Mieke Bal, "Body Politic," from *On Meaning-Making: Essays in Semiotics* (Sonoma, CA: Polebridge Press, 1994).

Figure 7.1 Rembrandt, *The Levite Finds His Concubine in the Morning*. Berlin, Gemaldegalerie, photo Bildarchiv Preussischer Kulturbesitz.

new light on the diverse aspects of the ideological positions toward gender that texts and images enable their readers to project. This is possible because of death's centrality in the definition of life.

I will begin with a story of an episode in the life of a secular biblical reader, social critic, and educator, whose work was the subject of the first paper I wrote as a beginning student in Amsterdam, someone who, had he lived today, would be an academic, but would have trouble getting tenure because of personality problems. On June 9th, 1762 the Parlement de Paris had issued a *prise de corps* against Jean-Jacques

Rousseau, author of *Emile ou l'Éducation*. Rousseau fled Paris at night, suspecting a woman friend, la maréchale de Montmorency, to have precipitated the decree. During his flight he wrote a short story, "Le Lévite d'Ephraim," a rewriting of the most horrible story of the Hebrew Bible, Judges 19 through 21. It is the story of the rejection, gang-rape, murder and dismemberment of a young woman whose body is subsequently used as writing. After her death or as an act of murder, her husband cuts her body into twelve pieces which he sends to the tribes as a call for war. Asking why Rousseau wrote this particular story and how, and what the "why" has to do with the "how," is to raise questions of criticism as an act motivated by and performed in a gendered context.

Rousseau feels good about his tale. He writes that he never rereads it without an "interior satisfaction" that stems from a decent, even glorious feeling.[2] This feeling mirrors the one that motivated him to write it, which he describes thus:

> Drowning in a sea of misfortune, crushed beneath the evil deeds of my ungrateful and barbarous contemporaries, the only one from which I escape and which remains with them to avenge me is that of hatred.[3]

This sentence is deeply ambiguous because of the nominalization of the verb "to hate"; it does not enable us to know who could hate whom but doesn't ("escape").[4] This conflation of the position of the critic and the view projected from that position onto the story is the phantom that lurks behind every attempt at description through writing. It happens precisely at the point where the disentanglement of self from other is most emphatically claimed. It is this ambiguous starting point, the question of hatred and its subjects, that guides our reading of the story which it mirrors, and which is a reading of the biblical story which *it* mirrors.

Rousseau's reading of Judges triggered a brilliant reading by Peggy Kamuf (1988) in the chapter "Author of a Crime" in *Signature Pieces*. Kamuf discusses how Rousseau's text is a mediation between three levels of occupation for his mind: his flight from Paris, the story of vengeance, and his writing. The first level is already ambiguous. Is Rousseau a criminal escaping justice, as his "barbarous contemporaries" doubtlessly considered him? Then his need to write the story of the Levite allows identification with this character. Or is he a victim of *in*justice, as he clearly sees himself? Then he might identify with the woman in the story, who is so utterly innocent and so utterly victimized. The second level, the story supposedly of a vengence which goes awry and which, as Kamuf demonstrates, cannot but *repeat* the crime it is supposed to avenge, engages the critic to assess the "deviations" from the Judges text, and perhaps try to explain those deviations with reference to Rousseau's own preoccupations. This is the role I cast Kamuf in. The inevitable narrative entanglement of the critic in the text is staged from the start when Kamuf repeats Rousseau's emphasis on *vengeance*. Rousseau's repressed and denied desire for vengeance motivates his distortion which appropriates the woman's plight, and I would speculate that Kamuf's endorsement of this distortion is motivated by her argumentative agenda, which is to focus on writing.

The intermediate level of occupation, the writing of Rousseau's reading, mirrors my own occupation as a scholar, and that of most people engaged in criticism or scholarship. Although critics are not often fleeing arrest by the police while writing, at least not in contemporary Western societies, they *are* engaged in writing, in reading, in struggling for a mediation between these two; they are engaged in defending stakes which vary and intersect between political, gender, ethnic, religious, and academic interests. Among these stakes, the claim to pursue and find the "truth" is both the basis and the problem of the academic endeavor.

Rousseau's struggle with the "truth" of *his* story, acted out in his position between reader and writer involves at least eight different mediations (I am expanding here Kamuf's comments). First, Rousseau presents writing as a way to distract his mind from level one: his situation of flight. He phrases the distraction as "donner le change," an ambiguous phrase that Derrida makes an emblem of his concept of the *supplement* in *Of Grammatology*.[5] The expression "donner le change" refers to distracting, in hunting, not the self but the other, the victim, not the hunter. Hence, the use of this expression suggests that Rousseau feels split, and wishes to consider his worries as the enemy. The phrase thereby suggests that split as the subject is, he cannot rid himself of his other, enemy self. But rather than splitting his enemy off, he incorporates it/them/her. In order to do that, he must make the woman guilty of her *prise de corps*.

Second, the writing mediates between the first and the second level, between Rousseau as fleeing criminal or victim, and the Levite and his "concubine," the people in his story. Needless to say, their moral status mirrors his, and therefore matters to him. Third, the writing is a mediation between reading and writing. Rousseau was reading Judges when he was compelled to flee. Writing cannot be a faithful rendering of our reading. While the reading is already engaged in the prospective writing, the writing can't quite match the reading. The effort to write writes itself into the writing. That effort shows in Rousseau's insistence on *voice*, the natural but perverted origin of language, and the way it is taken over by sight, the instrument of writing and reading. Kamuf's effort to write is mirrored in her insistence on writing.

Fourth, Rousseau's writing mediates between the two characters of the story and the role of their respective gender-positions as the motor of the narrative. I have suggested that Rousseau had reasons to identify both with the Levite and with the woman, and his sense of victimization certainly forced him into that androgynic role. For example, he makes the Levite die, too – of grief, or hatred, or desire for revenge, all the feelings he denied himself. Then – fifth mediation – there is a mediation between the two moods and modes Rousseau constantly feels involved in: the happy disposition he prides himself on, which produces the idyllic mode, and his paranoid tendencies, evoking the tragic. On the one hand, his own determination not to hate but to love his fellow humans; on the other hand, the mode of his rewriting of the story which hovers between the conventions of sweet and sour. This conflict is more than just one of literary taste; it has a bearing on his gender-politics. When he describes the second separation of the woman from her family, the political agenda of the author of *Emile* transpires clearly in the idyllic tone of the following sentence, which almost sounds like a blurb for the nuclear family:

> How happy is the family which in its purest union spends its peaceful days in the bosom of friendship and seems to have but one heart for all its members.[6]

The idyllic tone of this encomium forecasts the emphasis on the particular kind of barbarism to come, and which is figured on the ground of the structure of the family. The particular figuration of this "ground" – "seems to have but one heart for all its members" – adopts the contrast between idyll and tragedy as a mode of writing, in that it prefigures its negative, the dismemberment of the woman's body, one heart for all its dispersed members indeed.

In relation to this, the writing mediates – six – between manner and substance. The manner inscribes a number of claims into the story. One example must suffice. In addition to the problematic conflict of modes, Rousseau begins his story with a quadruple address, and evokes the *Iliad*, that other founding text of Western civilization:

(1)   Hallowed rage of fortune, come animate my voice; I will tell of the crimes of Benjamin and the revenge of Israel; I will tell of unmatched infamy and of even more terrible punishments.
(2)   Mortals, respect beauty, customs, hospitality; be just without cruelty, merciful without weakness, and know how to pardon the guilty rather than punish the innocent.
(3)   O you, good-natured men, enemies of all inhumanity, you who, fearing to confront the crimes of your brothers, prefer to let them go unpunished...
(4)   Blessed people, gather yourself; pronounce judgement...[7]

The claim against vengeance is undermined by this allusion to *the* story of vengeance, while the contradiction between the appeal to mercy in the second, and the exhortation to punish in the third address, make the writer's moral position unclear. The fourth address, a call for judgment, shifts from crime to vengeance, and turns the *prise de corps* into the crime to be judged. The allusion to the *Iliad* positions the story as an epic, a genre of male heroism and national wars. And it appeals to the muse, a feminine image of inspiration, *as* rage.[8] Where Homer begins his epic with "Sing, Goddess, the anger of Peleus' son Achilleus and its devastation," objectifying the rage, and Virgil begins *his* rewriting with "*I* sing of arms and of a man," disposing of the rage and the muse altogether, Rousseau places the rage within the subject of inspiration, sacred as Homer's goddess, and the voice singing it – he calls his chapters *chants*, songs – in himself, as in Virgil. Hence, the story is recast as a story of revenge from the start, in a complex way writing woman into it as a subject of semiosis, but not as the damaged party.

If rage is Rousseau's muse, then, his claim that hatred and revenge are staying with his enemies is either a lie or an avowal of the cultural dispersion of his writing: he writes through them. The author dissolves into the doxa. And his story, too, is about a war about a woman, and the allusion suggests it is caused by a woman. Thus he is doing what he announced: *donner le change*, divert his enemy and his mind – by blaming the victim.

Seventh, Kamuf points out that the writing hovers between a flight from and a submission to vengeance. The Levite's act of throwing out his wife to be gang-raped in order to save himself becomes thus the founding act the writing repeats. For this act *is* a flight from vengeance *by* a submission to it, albeit that the subject of submission is split off from the subject of flight. Rousseau's double identification, with the Levite and with his wife, serves to exorcise this ambivalence.

Finally, the writing, framed by the preface which positions the author in a reality so similar to that of the story, mediates between fiction and history. Choosing a story that is both far removed from the reality of his day and, by virtue of its status in a canonical book of historiography, not disposable as "just a fiction," the writing offers allegorical relations to Rousseau's interests. This is the more effective as the Judges story itself has systematically been "redeemed" by biblical critics through the very allegorical impulse that Rousseau is acting out, and that his apologetic tendencies expose as interested. Through this allegorization it becomes difficult for us to claim a radical distinction between fictional and critical rewritings of the biblical texts, hence, to separate scholarship from this emblematic case.

One additional mediation – or is it the founding one? – cannot escape us then, because it affects the status of "truth": that between sequential narrative and still vision. The competition between these two modes of representation shows in Rousseau's third address, before the narrative proper has had a chance to begin:

> What picture am I going to set before your eyes? The body of a woman cut into pieces; her torn and throbbing members sent to the twelve Tribes; all the people, frozen with horror, raising a unanimous clamor....[9]

The visual language is not just picturesque; it contributes to the rhetoric of the text in a way that involves longstanding epistemological claims. Rousseau is demonstrating here the age-old competition between language and vision that colors the positivistic truth-claim.[10] At the same time, by showing the dead flesh ("torn and throbbing members") before starting the narrative, he allows himself the reversal that follows later, *in* the narrative, where the focus will shift from the crime against the woman to the revenge set off by this sight.

A reading of Rousseau's reading leads routinely to a survey of the "mistakes" or "distortions." This gesture of comparison implies that we believe that the text of Judges can be read "wrongly," hence, by implication, also "rightly." It implies a truth, and the claim that the critic owns it. Of course, the complexities of the act of mediating between reading and writing brackets the status of this truth, but it is the search for it that I am interested in.

Peggy Kamuf claims the story is "well known." There lies the first problem. On the one hand, it is well known, as part of the biblical canon, and as such it circulates within the doxa of our culture. By virtue of its very vagueness and anonymity, the doxa is the real "owner" of the text who disowns the critic. For, on the other hand, the story is unknown. The anonymity of the victimized woman, the unbearable horror of the story, the disturbing gender aspect of the horror, and the ambiguous moral status of the Levite, make for a massive repression of this story, that most people vaguely know but few endeavor to read *against* the grain of the doxa.

Kamuf brilliantly maps ambiguities in Rousseau's position. But she also compares the two texts as "original" and "rewriting," in her allegiance to "truth-speak," in her inevitable commitment to be "right." She uses the standard procedure for the comparison: a summary of the older story. Such endeavors are compromised from the start, as summaries are already interpretations and therefore rewritings that follow the two texts to be compared. In the first sentence of her summary, she already makes a "mistake": "a Levite took as a concubine a virgin from Bethlehem." The word virginity is a mistaken doxic translation, as I have argued at length in *Death and Dissymmetry* (1988), but even if she admittedly cannot be expected to know this, the word mistakenly replaces here another mistaken translation, "concubine." By mistakingly confusing two mistakes, Kamuf connotes the truth of these false translations: she points at a problem in words denoting the status of women by conflating two seemingly opposed, value-laden notions: virgin and concubine.[11] Equally central is another mistake. Kamuf (84) writes: "The next day, the Levite found her *dead* on the doorstep." This case demonstrates the ideological and hermeneutic problem of two tendencies central in interpretive practice: disambiguization and paraphrasis. While she is attempting to paraphrase the story, her need to make the passage unambiguously clear makes Kamuf here repeating (paraphrasing) the doxa where it sides with the Levite and ignores the crucial ambiguity of the text, which precisely refrains from stating whether the woman is dead or alive. Is the woman dead when he finds her, as she was alive enough to drag herself back to the house? Of course, this disambiguizing "lie" is of little help to the Levite.[12] Yet what matters in Kamuf's "distortion" is precisely her relying on the doxa, and her resulting blindness to the ambiguity, while her whole analysis focuses on ambiguities. Her leaning on the doxa significantly happens *à propos* of the woman's death; thus writing the woman to premature death, she becomes herself the "author of a crime."

Rousseau's major "lie" is this. He writes that the host first offers his daughter, and that the Levite cannot accept that self-sacrifice and therefore gives his wife, while in Judges the host offers both young women, an offer which is *rejected* ("but the men would not listen to him" Judges 19:25). There is a "compulsion to repeat" in these lies that we see also in criticism, for example the "lie" is that which Rousseau and Kamuf share with the Levite himself. When he gives his report to the tribes, the Levite claims that the Benjaminites had threatened to kill him, which is a lie; they had threatened to rape him. Rousseau's Levite doubles up here, firstly on the level of the story, by adding that they had "forced" him to hand over his wife, secondly on the level of narration, by insisting that he is speaking the truth: "People of the Lord, I have spoken the truth."

This truth-speak is the painful moment where the predicament of criticism is reflected. Rousseau's interests compel him to defend the Levite while on another level of awareness he knows that the man is lying. The symptom of this contradiction is precisely the displacement of the insistence: he overdoes the lie and then, knowing that it is a lie, he insists that it is the truth.[13]

Kamuf displaces the Levite's founding lie by rightly insisting on the ambiguous status of his writing. Now, Kamuf is a feminist, and her analysis brings out some of the feminist issues this story raises – more acutely than any work of specialized scholarship on this tale I know of. Yet as a deconstructionist her interest is to insist on writing, and thus she passes right by the Levite's lie *in* his writing, which is precisely in his writing-as-truth-claim.

It is not my goal to criticize a wonderful literary tale or the best analysis of Judges 19 and of Rousseau's tale I know of. I am interested in what I call, with reference to

Freud's concept of dream-work, the "work of truth" and its need to be spoken. Both Rousseau's and Kamuf's misses occur at the very moment they proclaim the truth. For example, Kamuf is engaged in pointing out both Rousseau's misses and those of another secular comparatist, Thomas Kavanagh,[14] whose book has the meaningful title *Writing the Truth: Authority and Desire in Rousseau*, when she herself misread Judges on, precisely, a crucial gender issue and the same narrative issue, while using the language of truth:

> In the biblical account, the "wrongness" of the attack on the Levite is signaled by the offer, *which is accepted*, to substitute for him the two women. (91–2)

This analysis of moral "wrongness" is performed through a readerly "wrongness": the offer is *not* accepted, and this rejection brings forth the next and central event of the deadly gang-rape. But that entails questions about the status of the two women *as* women. The issue of the meaning and value of virginity should have been evoked *here* – with that of "concubine," whose relatedness Kamuf demonstrated in her earlier "mistake."[15] This blatant mistake compels Kamuf to ignore how Rousseau writes the apology for the Levite in precisely the gap between the rejected offer and the central event of the gang-rape. While Judges is extremely unclear here, Rousseau makes the Levite reject the host's "self-sacrifice" of his daughter.

So far, I have suggested that there is no truth in narrative and yet that we all seek it; I have claimed that in the very attempt to find it we miss it; and that both the attempt to find it and the misses are motivated by our social, cultural, and private interests. These became visible in the analysis of the complex mediations in Rousseau's case, but are equally relevant for all acts of writing and reading. Far be it from me, however, to make an anything-goes argument. The insistent issue of truth cannot be eliminated, but it must be displaced and replaced in relation to interests. Authority, the site of moral ownership that is incompatible with objective truth, is the painful site of contradiction where a scholarship committed to seeking unbiased truth sees itself in the mirror – and ineffectively breaks the mirror rather than changing itself.

Let me return to Rousseau's picture of throbbing flesh, which proclaimed the superiority of vision over narrative as a rhetorical move to allow narrative to forget vision. Vision, it turns out, is a crucial "language" in Judges 19. In order to get a different access to Judges 19 and the way it engages gender, therefore, I have looked at one of the rare visual representations of it, a "Rembrandt" drawing. It represents the moment when the Levite finds her the next morning on the threshold of the house. It is one of "Rembrandt"'s most acute representations of death, which, paradoxically, is full of movement and life, full of narrative, and it is mustering a particular device of visual narrative, speaking hands.

The drawing depicts the victim at the threshold of the house, and thus positions her literally as a liminal figure, as the embodiment of transition. In spite of the sketchiness of the representation as a whole, the steps which constitute the threshold and signify the house as real and as stone are particularly clearly drawn. I will revert to this detail, which is this drawing's mediation from truth-speak to body-language.

The moment in the biblical "pre-text" in which language and violence are intricately related is precisely the one that our drawing represents: the moment where the woman is no longer able to speak her truth of life and death, where her body is *seen*, misunderstood both by her husband and by subsequent critics, addressed, and ultimately, misused in a radical perversion of speech.

Vision is a mode of speech in this horror-story. Mis-seeing, un-seeing the woman is sketched. Her death and the story of it are narratively ambiguous. As her death begins at her exposure and ends with her dismemberment, we cannot know when exactly she dies, and we must not know it. For that incapacity to know is an important element in the biblical epistemology of gender which equates sex with knowledge in the expression "to know a woman." She dies several times, or rather, she never stops dying. It is this narrative aspect of her dying which makes this drawing so central in these reflections on death: an event that is punctual and non-narratable is turned into a slow process represented as the climax of narrative that then becomes the visual work challenging the limits of visual representation.

Whereas in Judges the event is turned from punctual into durative, the representation of this already perverted death in an allegedly static medium further explores and undermines the limits of the realm of the speakable. In Judges, moreover, the agents of the woman's death are as unclear as is its moment; the act keeps being displaced from one man to the next. This contamination by collective guilt is obviously problematic to all readers. In addition, the differentiation between discourse as the production of signs which, according to semiotics, stand in for an object, and the object of discourse, falls apart as well. Not only is this woman the object of the body-language of rape, a language that bespeaks her death; her body is also subsequently used *as* language by the very man who exposed her to the violence when he sends her flesh off as a message.[16]

The moment of this endless deferral of death visually represented is the one in which vision becomes a speech-act. The morning after the gang-rape the woman's husband opens the door to go his way, and "*behold*, there was his wife, fallen down, and her hands were on the threshold" (Judges 19:27). Two words, then, generate this drawing: "open" and "behold." The verb-form used for the act of opening is *jiphtah*, the word that rings in the name of Jephthah, the murderer of the virgin-daughter sacrificed in violence for the sake of (military) violence in Judges 11. The importance of opening as the act that allows vision while dealing death is thus emphasized by the pun on *jiphtah/* Jephthah; so is the murderous quality of opening, vision, and the body. After having opened the door the previous night for lethal sexual violence, the man opens it to contemplate its next stage, and the chilling picture he sees is here for us to see: "behold, she is fallen."

Judges is a book that problematizes language by proposing uncanny kinds of speech-acts to challenge language as purveyor of meaning. Judges is, for example, full of riddles, the speech-act of the *lacking* meaning. In addition to riddles Judges is also full of *vows*, speech-acts based on an *excess* of meaning, acts that emblematize the power of words in the most radical way. Their meaning being death, they kill. Jephthah, who first vows his daughter to death and then tricks his enemies linguistically, is the hero of this killing kind of speech. He is also, according to his name, the opener of bodies. Between the lack of meaning and an excess of meaning, speech is overruled by the force that motivates it. In the gap left by this view of language as deficient, visual representation inserts itself and becomes an alternative language; a truth-speak of its own, mistaken for body-language as the most truthful language.

This alternative language is "spoken" in the sketch of the woman who, in the Bible, is killed in and as speech. This linguistic murder occurs several times there. Before her death by the gang-rape she is surrendered linguistically, and after her death she is dispatched as language, when her body is cut into pieces and sent to the tribes of Israel, as a *letter* – a piece of writing not containing but embodying a message – and as a slaughtered piece of meat. Butchering equals writing here; and death equals vision. Rousseau *shows* this instead of *telling* it when he offers to our eyes his picture of throbbing members.

This is a case, if ever there was one, of the scandal of the speaking body.[17] Between the two moments of her murder by multiplication and publication – multiple rape and publication of her body – is the moment of vision during which the husband-opener fails to see, thus adding to, and consecrating, the murder: a semiotics of mis-seeing.

In the "Rembrandt" sketch the meaning (the woman's death) and the force (its narrativization in movement) confront each other in the paradox of representation: in order to represent the narrative of death, the drawing requires a movement that denies death precisely while pointing to its agent. That movement is *signified* (not: realistically represented) in the right hand of the woman figure. This hand is slightly blurred, while it has lines underneath it that can easily be explained away as a shadow but resist that interpretation. For the house, precisely, the safe haven denied this woman, stands between the alleged sun and its alleged shadow, so that the small lines cannot quite be a shadow and rather suggest movement.

According to Eco (1976), signs are those things which can be used in order to lie. This definition helps us understand the "lies" in the drawing: the movement of a lifeless woman, signified by the lines under her slightly blurred right hand, and the ghost-like transparency of the living man, signified by the continuous line of the stone on which he is supposed to stand. Neither sign is merely a lie; both are representational paradoxes. Just as the speech-act of the riddle in Judges undermines the narrative plot-line, so too a line here undercuts the drawing's realistic quality: the force of the speech-act of drawing crosses its own realistic meaning out. This line, too, can be easily explained away, if not overlooked altogether. But since the problems of this story have been overlooked long enough, I choose to emphasize these marginal signs. Alluding to Peirce's difficult concept of the sinsign, I like to think of this invisible sign of invisibility as a sign of sin.[18]

Jonathan Culler (1983) reformulates Eco's definition of the sign from the reader's perspective: a sign is everything that can be misunderstood. Misreading, then, is the key to semiosis, just as mis-seeing is the key to opening the woman's body and to representing her death. This misuse of semiosis will subsequently be literalized in the dismemberment.

How does death, here, relate to gender? The affinity, in "Rembrandt," for the Book of Judges suggests a split between two projections of women. On the one hand, there are women who are feared and therefore hated, who need to be appropriated by violence. These women are potential mates – the bride who must be violated in order to be *opened*. On the other hand, there are women who are harmless because they have already been violated. These are the victims, women as social figures of marginality with which the writing or drawing subject can identify. With the first women the subject has a relation of contiguity, which implies a continuity he fears; with the second, he has a metaphoric relationship which implies the separation that allows sympathy and hence, identification; at the same time, the danger of contiguity can be avoided by replacing the woman in metaphor. This is the rhetoric of body-language.[19]

The gesture of the woman's hand on the threshold is important in both the text and the drawing. It has often been explained symbolically. Beyond the dichotomy of literal and figurative-symbolic, the detail of the hand can be taken as a statement on the text's narrativity, which is made theatrical by the indications of visuality. The key-word here is "behold." The gesture as the drawing presents it is the self-reflexive "lie" that counteracts the grave misreading both text and drawing thematize. In Rousseau's tale, vision's overruling of voice is used as the shifter which displaces subjectivity from the woman to the husband while apologizing for the latter's culminating act of horror:

> Even the *sight* of this body, which ought to have reduced him to tears [le faire fondre en larmes], calls forth from him no more cries [ni plaintes ni pleurs]. He contemplates it with a dry and dark *look*; he *sees in it* only an object of rage and despair...[20]

The husband stops speaking at the moment he becomes both the subject and the victim of the violence. This transformation turns him into an agent of visuality.

The moment selected for visual representation in the drawing is well chosen because it is the painful one that produces doubt and fear in readers who, from the perspective of an utterly ideological partiality, have a stake in the moral righteousness of the character of the Levite. It is deeply confusing to see the theatricalization of this door-opener's behavior. Reading theatrically ("behold"), we see how he almost steps over the body of his wife – his first misreading of the sight – then he orders her to stand up – a second misreading, now of his position of power. When no answer comes, when her non-speech suspends the possibility of truth, we see him tie her (body) to his donkey to take her home and cut her up for semiotic misuse. Rousseau must make the man change here (*donner le change*), from speaker to seer to writer.

The drawing contradicts the Levite's visual lie by the little lines under the woman's hand, which suggest movement, hence, life. But these lines do not depict the woman as "really" alive; they only suggest that she is acting out the story of her continuous death – her death as a process that challenges the epistemological basis of our conception of death as knowable event. In order to represent her death, then, the drawing must let her move.

The question of the realistic status of the movement of the hand, then, is also an epistemological question: it raises the question of knowledge, on both the diegetic and the semiotic level. Who knows what? Does the husband know that the woman is dead? No, for if he did, he would not have ordered her to stand up. Does the reader know she is dead? I think not, for the forcefulness with which her death is argued betrays that the reader does not, cannot, know. This lack is not only a blow to the scholar whose mission is purported to be knowledge and whose rhetoric is truth-speak, but also to the reader who feels conflated with the ignorant character, the Levite. Hence the critical mistakes, accumulating when knowledge is embodied by women.

But there is more to knowledge than meets the eye. To know and to possess are both expressions for the sexual encounter from a particular ideological perspective, and are thus intimately related to each other and to gender. This equation is possible because knowledge is itself a thing one can possess: one *has* knowledge. But one cannot possess what one does not know, for how can one know whether or not one possesses it? And one cannot give what one does not possess, hence, giving the unknown is *a priori* an act of semiotic abuse. This abuse is Jephthah's crime when he vows away his daughter. To know, furthermore, is also an epistemological act whose relationship to vision is at stake, both in Judges and in "Rembrandt." Does the epistemologically failing man, in the drawing, *know* his wife, sexually and existentially, if he cannot even know if she is alive or dead? In other words, is he her husband at all at this point? It is this that his intense act of looking lets us question. From this perspective, the line that makes him transparent also makes him unreal: as the woman's husband he does not exist. This line shifts the work from realistic failure to semiotic adequacy.

My reading of this drawing is based on the refusal to endorse the separations between "literal" and "figurative," between visual and verbal, along with the acknowledgement of the impossibility of "pure" meaning – of meaning without force and of "pure" knowledge, or truth, without the metonymic contamination of its motivated pursuit. We can read this refusal of the distinctions that have dictated much of Western representational and interpretative practice in the lines moving the hand in the drawing. This hand does not "see," but it speaks about mis-seeing. More "real" because more alive than the body of the husband, the hand is about to point in accusation at her murderer. It accuses him not only of multiple and durative murder, but also of misreading, misseeing, and misrepresentation.[21]

The drawing insists that the husband's misreading is "wrong" epistemologically as well as morally, for in spite of Kamuf's effort to do so, the two cannot be entirely separated. It demonstrates that her gesture is phatic, body-language. The woman addresses her husband from below, in a radical repositioning of vision. The husband, wrining his hands eloquently as in despair – speaking with his hands – cannot *see* the movement of the woman's hand, as the hand itself, exercising body-language, blocks the sight of the lines underneath it.

By interrupting the represented line of vision, hence, both emphasizing and problematizing diegetic seeing, the work does several things at once. It represents the very moment of suspension between life and death, action and inaction, thus raising the question of the husband's response and generating the following episode. It theatricalizes the visual moment, by inscribing in it the dimension of time. And it emphasizes its own status as a work of representation, willfully misreading the conventions of representational art. The husband *looks* at the woman's hand, but the *representation* of its telling movement is not for him to see.

The gift of this woman led to the public opening of her body; it led to rape, death, and dismemberment; instead of qualifying her subject-position, it destroyed it. The husband lives by this destruction: he stands over her, fails to see her, ineffectively and abusively speaks to her, and steps over her. The woman can only speak as body. This body will be used to speak, but then it is no longer the woman who speaks. As an inevitable consequence of the scene of vision outlined by the drawing, her body is utterly robbed of its significance as herself. The man speaks, in an act which fulfills Rousseau's dream of an unmediated, direct language, as he wrote in *The Origin of Language*, but then, *over her dead body*. Begging for the merciful interpretations of his crime against women and life which will in effect be granted to him in the history of interpretation, the man's hands overshadow the speaking power of the woman's. But by opposing the lie of her hands to that of his, the drawing lets her speak against this cultural condoning of rape and murder.

Judges 19 ends with an imperative – *speak* – a masculine plural, response to the visual speech of the woman's divided flesh. The tribes address their order to speak not to the "speaker" but to the husband. The speaking body itself is misread. For Kamuf, Rousseau, and the biblical author, misguided by the Levite, the story of rape as murder becomes the story of revenge. To this scandal, the drawing opposes the prefiguration of a response. The man may be the opener of doors and bodies, but he is depicted as so weak in the drawing that his perverted speech will indeed be misread, yet in a way opposed to the misreading of the tribes. The drawing, already erasing him while enhancing the dead-living woman, will not let his lie be read at all. The line cutting through the man's substance, undermining his reality, and the lines producing the woman's movement that he cannot see become central.

By now, it becomes impossible to disentangle the chronological neatness of the distinction, endorsed even by Kamuf, between "original" and "rewriting." Using the "Rembrandt" as a commentary on the Rousseau, we are beginning to see the dangerous liaison between reader and writer, and the colonizing nature of mediation. When subject and object of writing, addresser and addressee, can neither be entirely conflated nor be radically separated, it becomes urgent to revise our relationship to truth, objectivity, and knowledge. The throbbing flesh of an anonymous woman remains the solid object which resists the rhetoric of narrative Rousseau so passionately used to proclaim an impossible truth against an irrepressible hatred. If this woman had to die, it was because her body was seen, un-seen, and over-seen. Her body of writing allegorizes the danger of epistemological certainty based on abstraction and disembodied language alone. Whether the woman is blocking the husband's sight, as in the drawing, or displacing the narrative, as in the tales, or prematurely killed, as in criticism, the Judges woman allegorizes a kind of truth whose instability forces a look into the force that motivates its pursuit. Some would call it a trace – the trace which leads us back from truth-speak to body-language.

Notes

1   I put the artist's name in quotation marks to emphasize that I consider this work as a text, comparable to "Shakespeare" or "the Bible." I am not interested in the currently hotly debated issue of authenticity and authorship. The body of work that Western culture has considered throughout the past two centuries as "Rembrandt" constitutes a cultural construct, which in my view includes writings about it/"him," borrowings from it, and creative

responses such as poetry inspired by it. The quotation marks, then, are a shorthand rendering of my view about "the artist" in our culture.

2   He wrote in the first project for a preface to a volume which was to include this tale: "...je ne le relis jamais sans une satisfaction intérieure, non par une sotte vanité d'auteur, dont l'ineptie en ce point seroit inexcusable, mais par un sentiment plus honnête et dont j'ose même me glorifier." *Oeuvres complètes* II (Paris: Editions Gallimard, 1961), 1205.

3   "Noyé dans une mer d'infortune, accablé de maux par mes ingrats et barbares contemporains, un seul auquel j'échappe en dépit d'eux et qui leur reste pour ma vengeance est celui de la haine." The ambiguity of the sentence has been preserved in the translation.

4   Nominalization of the verb is one of the means of ideological manipulation, working to obscure the subject responsible for the action. See Günther Kress and and Robert Hodge, *Language as Ideology* (London: Routledge and Kegan Paul, 1979). I have discussed Kress & Hodge's theoretical categories and their usefulness for a critical narratology, in particular for a literary and biblical interpretation, in my book *On Story-Telling: Essays in Narratology* (Sonoma: Polebridge Press, 1991). In Rousseau's sentence, the resulting ambiguity concerning the subject and object of hatred is part and parcel of the flabbergasting complexity of Rousseauian discourse on moral values.

5   Kamuf, 82, commenting on Derrida (1976:154).

6   "Heureuse famille qui dans l'union la plus pure coule au sein de l'amitiés ses paisibles jours, et semble n'avoir qu'un coeur à tous ses members" (Rousseau, II, 1212). Again, the sentence is highly ambiguous, so much so that the contradictory meanings cancel each other out in what Derrida would call a dissemination: the use of the word "members" in a story about dismemberment, of "coeur" where the heart is subordinated to tribal interests, and the insistence on "peace" in a story about violence take all possible innocence away from the language. See Derrida, 1981.

7   "Sainte colère de la vertu, viens animer ma voix; je dirai les crimes de Benjamin, et les vengeances d'Israel; je dirai les forfaits inouis, et des chatiments encore plus terribles. Mortels, respectez la beauté, les moeurs, l'hospitalité, soyez juste sans cruauté, miséricordieux sans foiblese; et sachez pardonner au coupable plustôt que de punir l'innocent.

    O vous, hommes débonnaires, ennemis de toute inhumanité; vous qui, de peur d'envisager les crimes de vos fréres, aimez mieux les laisser inpunis...

    Peuple saint, rassemble-toi; prononce sur cet acte horrible..." (Rousseau, II, 1208).

8   The allusion has a slightly stronger effect in French because of the feminine gender of the words "colère" and "vertu." The phrase "Sainte colère de la vertu" is an apostrophe addressed through the feminine nouns to the female goddess of inspiration. On apostrophe as a central device in lyric, see Jonathan Culler, "Apostrophe," in 1981: 135–54. For the political effect of apostrophe's centrality for lyric, see Barbara Johnson, 1987.

9   The French is even more visually colored: "quel tableau viens-je offrir à vos yeux? Le corps d'une femme coupé par pièces; ses membres déchirés et palpitants envoyés aux douze Tribus; tout le peuple, saisi d'horreur, élevant jusqu'au ciel une clameur unanime..." (Rousseau, II, 1208). "Tableu" is more insistently visual than "picture" which is more commonplace, while the order of the noun "membres" followed by strong adjectives is more "picturesque" than the English.

10 The study of the relations between visual and verbal discourse in connection to truth-claims is central for scholars like W. T. J. Mitchell, whose *Iconology: Image, Text, Ideology* (1985) is a key-text. A brilliant "applied" study is Françoise Meltzer (1987).

11 There are more of these little "mistakes," mainly interpretations of gaps, like "exogamic law" (90), not mentioned in the text and a muddled issue. Most mistakes are "lies of repetition,"

wherein Kamuf repeats Rousseau's lies, like "The Benjaminites refused to turn over the guilty men" (84). Elsewhere, she repeats doxic mistaken interpretations, like "the Levite found her dead on the doorstep" (84). For an extensive discussion of the Judges text in connection to these key terms referring to the institutions that regulate sexual behavior, see my study of the Book of Judges (1988).

12 If she is alive, he does the actual murdering; if she is dead, he desacralizes her body and transgresses the laws of his own status as priest by handling her body. In both cases, this man is beyond redemption. I find it significant that critics analyzing this story seem unable to face the unambiguous guilt of this unnamed individual, no more than they are willing to face guilt in cases where an Israelite hero is involved. What needs protection from the story, here, is the individual as opposed to the mass, the inhabitants of the city, the guilty tribe of Benjamin.

13 Likewise, in my analysis of Judges in *Death and Dissymmetry* I have quoted many examples in commentaries of those insistent footnotes that emphasize the problematic details of the text they then set out to explain away. A funny case is Boling's lengthy demonstration, including visual material, that Jephthah could not know that his daughter would be the first one to meet him after his victory. Thus he shows how problematic, how unanswerable, and how compromising that very question is. See Robert G. Boling, 1975.

14 Thomas M. Kavanagh (1987).

15 To take this one step further, I must also point out my own misses: trying to argue for *my* truth: that we all inevitably miss the truth when we try the hardest to find it, I missed Kamuf's point on how Rousseau became the author of a crime, by using her piece as an example of contradiction; I overlooked Rousseau's occasional plea for gender-equity because I wanted to demonstrate his defensive male bias; and I might even be missing Judges, the story I claim you, readers of this essay, don't know well enough, thus implying that I know it better myself, that I own its truth. I misread Judges by disambiguizing the Levite's position while I know that *its* ambiguity is the only position this text can possibly take, torn as it is itself between the two sides of the social conflict it stages (I mean hereby the conflict between patrilocal nomadic marriage and virilocal residential marriage, a conflict that I have argued in *Death and Dissymmetry* to underlie these stories and to account for their horror). And *my* motivations for these misses include that I have a point to make that requires the logic that eliminates all that doesn't fit. Not to speak of my unconscious motivations, by definition outside of my reach but which I can only point at in the form of questions: what brings me time and again to Judges 19? And why must the Levite get due blame? All this leads, finally, to the flipside of this argument. If I am not going as far as pointing that out, it is because the politics of interpretation require that the unspoken be said, and that the already spoken and dominant discourse be temporarily silenced, in spite of its occasional "truth."

16 Where the narrative seems to fail to construct history, rape becomes the sign that does; as I argue in *Death and Dissymmetry*, it becomes the generative event of Judges.

17 The allusion is to Shoshana Felman's analysis of speech-act theory in *Le scandale du corps parlant* (1980), whose radicality is censored away in the English title, *Literary Speech-Acts* (1984). Felman's discussion of speech–act theory is analyzed in chapter 5 of *Death and Dissymmetry*.

18 "A *Sinsign* is an actual existent thing or event which is a sign." This quote is from an easily accessible edition of Pierce's key text in which he defines the ten categories of signs: Charles S. Peirce, "Logic as Semiotic," in Robert E. Innis, *Semiotics: An Introductory Anthology* (1985:7).

19   For an extensive discussion of these attitudes, see my *Reading "Rembrandt"* (1991).
20   "L'aspect même de ce corps, qui devroit le faire fondre en larmes, ne lui arrache plus ni
     plaintes ni pleurs: Il le contemple d'un oeil sec et sombre; il n'y voit plus qu'un object de
     rage et de désespoir" (Rousseau, II, 1215). The word "aspect" has an emphatically visual
     charge, while this visuality is underlined by "contempler," "oeil," "voit."
21   Here is the scene of the pre-text that the drawing responds to and its narrative follow-up
     which, I submit, is also inscribed in the drawing: "And her lord rose up in the morning and
     opened [*jiphtah*] the doors of the house and went out to go his way; and behold, his patrilocal
     wife was fallen down at the door of the house, with her hands on the threshold. And he said
     to her: 'up!, and let us be going' and none answered. And he took her upon the ass; and the
     man rose up and went to his place. And when he had come into his house he took the knife
     and laid hold on his patrilocal wife and divided her limb by limb into twelve pieces and sent
     her throughout all the borders of Israel" (19:27–28).

References

Bal, Mieke. 1988. *Death and Dissymmetry: The Politics of Coherence in the Book of Judges*. Chicago:
     University of Chicago Press.

Bal, Mieke. 1991. *Reading "Rembrandt": Beyond the Word–Image Opposition*. New York: Cam-
     bridge University Press.

Bal, Mieke. 1991. *On Story-Telling: Essays in Narratology*. Sonoma: Polebridge Press.

Boling, Robert G. 1975. *Judges: Introduction, Translation, and Commentary*. The Anchor Bible 6A.
     Garden City, NY: Doubleday & Company.

Culler, Jonathan. 1981. *The Pursuit of Signs: Semiotics, Literature, Deconstruction*. Ithaca, NY:
     Cornell University Press.

Culler, Jonathan. 1983. *On Deconstruction: Theory and Criticism after Structuralism*. Ithaca, NY:
     Cornell University Press.

Derrida, Jacques. 1976. *Of Grammatology*. Trans. with an introduction by Gayatri Chakravorty
     Spivak. Baltimore: Johns Hopkins University Press. (French orig. 1967.)

Derrida, Jacques. 1981. *Dissemination*. Trans. with an introduction and additional notes by Barbara
     Johnson. Chicago: University of Chicago Press. (French orig. 1972.)

Eco, Umberto. 1976. *A Theory of Semiotics*. Bloomington: Indiana University Press.

Felman, Shoshana. 1980. *Le scandal du corps parlant*. Paris: Editions du Seuil. (English trans., *The
     Literary Speech Act*. Trans. Catherine Porter. Ithaca, NY: Cornell University Press, 1984.)

Johnson, Barbara. 1987. *A World of Difference*. Baltimore: Johns Hopkins University Press.

Kamuf, Peggy. 1988. *Signature Pieces: On the Institution of Authorship*. Baltimore: Johns Hopkins
     University Press.

Kavanagh, Thomas M. 1987. *Writing the Truth: Authority and Desire in Rousseau*. Berkeley:
     University of California Press.

Kress, Günther, and Robert Hodge. 1979. *Language as Ideology*. London: Routledge and Kegan
     Paul.

Meltzer, Françoise. 1987. *Salome and the Dance of Writing: Portraits of Mimesis in Literature*. Chicago:
     University of Chicago Press.

Mitchell, W. T. J. 1985. *Iconology: Image, Text, Ideology*. Chicago: University of Chicago Press.

Peirce, Charles S. 1985. "Logic as Semiotic." In Robert E. Innis, ed., *Semiotics: An Introductory
     Anthology*. Bloomington: Indiana University Press.

Barbara Kruger, *Untitled (You invest in the divinity of the masterpiece)*, 1982. Museum of Modern Art, New York. Courtesy of Mary Boone Gallery, New York.

Part II

The Politics of Reading

Introduction

The link between this section and Parts I and III on either side of it is the common theme of reading and readers. In this section we have chosen readings that place political concerns at the forefront, particularly those that privilege the voices and concerns of marginalized groups. Two of the selections in this part made an appearance in chapter 7 of *The Postmodern Bible*, "Ideological Criticism": we mention the work of Ernesto Cardenal's base community and have an extended discussion of Robert Warrior's article. In some ways, the readings of this section extend and highlight the concerns of the "Ideological Criticism" chapter. This makes this section different from each of the others. "Rereading the Bible," as we noted in the Preface, offers texts that join together many of the PMB categories: Miller examples both "Rhetorical Criticism" and "Poststructuralist Criticism"; Kristeva examples both "Psychoanalytic Criticism" and "Feminist and Womanist Criticism." "The Conscience of the Bible," on the other hand, pursues issues and concerns, which can loosely be designated as "ethics," that are touched upon throughout the PMB without a single focus, and with the exception of Derrida, none of its writers command extended discussion in the PMB.

Still, "Ideological Criticism" has a special status in the PMB, both in terms of its position as the last category, and also as a category which does not quite oppose itself to any of the others. "Ideology," that is, continues to be a negative and dismissive term rather than a positive, definable content; it is something the opposition has. There is even much debate over whether texts have ideologies or if readers impose their ideologies on texts – or both. The selections here assume both, and they also assume that this imposition of ideologies (always plural) on the text is a good thing in the work against past injustices (Cannon; Warrior), oppressive regimes (Cardenal), and the continued use of the Bible to support an imperialist heteropatriarchy (Haraway; Pathak; Hallam). These readings continue to address the concern raised by Mieke Bal in the opening quote in the chapter on ideological criticism in the PMB: "The Bible, of all books, is the most dangerous one, the one that has been endowed with the power to kill" (1991:14). How and why has the Bible been used both as a tool of oppression and as a manifesto of liberation? These readers show the complexities of multiple ideologies in the Bible, and in biblical culture. There is an overlap of secular and sacred; the biblical texts live in various cultures, often with twisted, violent histories of interpretation, but also providing the fuel of great hope. These readings are only specific examples of the multiple and possible readings that exist. They openly acknowledge their interpretive stances and biases, especially in relation to the power systems to which they are responding. Sometimes the power addressed is found in the chaotic acts of God (Eagleton on Jonah). But other times there is a reclaiming of the interpretive act over and against the status quo. Memory and hope are constant themes in several of these articles.

Fredric Jameson considered "narrative as a socially symbolic act" (1981). The symbols of the Bible are imbedded in Western culture, even at the turn of the century when other religious signs are appearing. The Bible has been used to represent and prove a variety of ideas, and in politics it has been a support of completely opposite views, from dictatorships to democracy (and to democracies' supporting dictatorships, etc.). Where in the political chaos can readers make sense of the Bible? We hold that theories of postmodernism, although sometimes charged with being apolitical, can lead us more deeply into an understanding of the Bible (and multiple Bibles) in a global context. The readings in this section are controversial; in the classroom they evoked definite opinions (for and against and ambivalent) and a range of emotive responses. We found the political challenge to us and the students hard and irritating and hopeful. We were reminded of the necessity of facing our own privileges and oppressions as Bible readers, but not until we faced what Louis Althusser calls the "lived experiences" of a range of other postmodern interpreters and found our place among the various voices. Sometimes this meant silence, sometimes grief, sometimes outrage. If politics and religion are traditionally the two most contentious topics at a family dinner table, in this section these postmodern visions invite even more contention, and hopefully, continued political conversations.

Political Discourses

Let us return to the charge of postmodernism being stuck in an elitist, intellectual, esoteric discourse that has little relation to the lives of common folk. The main argument is that postmodernism is seen as an "anything goes" philosophy of relativism. For some conservative Christians who are offering critiques of postmodernism, the concern is that the monolithic ideology (the monotheism, in particular) of the Bible is being called into question. These interpreters want a monopoly on biblical interpretation that has filtered directly into the political arena with groups in the US like the Moral Majority and the Christian Coalition, or the more or less explicit establishment of theocracies in other parts of the world. Bal's warning comes to the fore again; the Bible can kill. One example from the selections in this part is the Bible study group of Solentiname, Nicaragua. The fundamentalist Christian right in the US supported the Somoza dictatorship, and later the Contra forces, against the Sandinista resistance, which the people of Solentiname supported. These "voices from below" tell us of the everyday experience of the political in reading the Bible. They question the dominant readings by reading "against the grain" (in Walter Benjamin's words) and in opposition to the surrounding political powers.

The role of postmodern theory in the political realm is more complex than this example. Terry Eagleton raises important questions about postmodernism's role in politics. The good news is that in its call for relativism postmodernism "is a resourceful subversion of the dominant value-system, at least at the level of theory... in its more politicized forms deconstruction is indeed an assault on much of what most businessmen hold dear" (1996:132). The ambivalent news is that Eagleton does not see in most postmodern theory a link with changing real political systems: "Postmodernism, in short, scoops up something of the material logic of advanced capitalism and turns this aggressively against its spiritual foundations.... It is as though it is urging the system, like its great mentor Friedrich Nietzsche, to forget about its metaphysical foundations, acknowledge that God is dead and simply go relativist" (1996:133). The challenge to and of postmodern theory is to face this charge of relativism and seek relevance in a constantly changing global environment.

David Batstone and others wonder about the same issue with regard to liberation movements: "Yet, we also wonder with some liberation theologians, if postmodernism is 'toothless in the face of oppression.' Our concern is what this debate means for social strategies that resist domination and advance the full humanity of the powerless" (1997:16). In a similar mode, Aijaz Ahmad criticizes the "postmodern" literary and cultural analyses of Homi Bhabha: "Bhabha, of course," he writes,

> lives in those material conditions of *post*modernity which presume the benefits of modernity as the very ground from which judgements on that past of this *post*- may be delivered. In other words, it takes a very modern, very affluent, very uprooted kind of intellectual to debunk both the idea of "progress" and the sense of a "long past".... Those who live within the consequences of that "long past", good and bad, and in places where a majority of the population has been denied access to such benefits of "modernity" as hospitals or better health insurance or even basic literacy can hardly afford the terms of such thought. (1998:152)

One way to "afford" postmodern terms of thought, as Batstone suggests, is not to settle too quickly into the (critical? ironic?) "attitude" of the postmodern, but to discover within the local pluralities of the postmodern "social strategies that resist domination" – strategies which are clearly marked with the dialectic of oppressor/oppressed – and, in the direct social action of a *political* postmodernism, to change the structures and systems of oppression and to raise up the voices and lives of the poor.

Of course, both dismissive critics of postmodernism and some self-proclaimed denizens of postmodernity tend to essentialize postmodern theory into one monolithic discourse. In the academic discourse of biblical studies the dismissal of postmodernism has been linked to all critical theory, but in degrees. The theories that disrupt the historical quest for what the Bible *means* (as if the Bible had a singular ideology), the more political theories that empower previously non- or underrepresented groups and nations, and any negative inferences about the ethics of certain biblical texts and characters are rejected. The Bible, believe some people, is not to be subjected to the same range of critical methods as other works of literature. There are boundaries when the dominant ideology and status quo are at stake. Postmodern biblical interpretations ignore these boundaries; in fact, some postmodern readings head right for the margins, some begin in the margins or in multiple margins, and many work to undermine the "center." Postmodern interpretation disrupts when it asks the hard questions – of political, economic, gendered, ideological, and other such systems – and when it leads to *action* from and/or on behalf of the marginalized in society. Dussel's unrelenting validation of the Bible, as discussed in the introduction to Part III, functions as a place from which hard questions arise that tend toward a politics of action.

Political Images

The ubiquity of postmodern disruption is encountered in other modes as well. Take, for example, the religious art of Andy Warhol. The more familiar symbols are the repetitions of Coke bottles, soup cans, dollar bills, Marilyn Monroe, and nuclear explosions. But Warhol was also influenced by his (Byzantine) Roman Catholic background and was interested in transforming the Renaissance artists (Raphael; Leonardo da Vinci) into contemporary images. His interests include Mary and the saints, and he did a series of crosses (simple outlines of crosses in red, yellow, and purple) and a series of Last Suppers. During the last years of his life Warhol focused on a variety of Last Suppers. He created ten punching bags with the face of Christ and graffiti (the word "Judge") from Jean-Michel Basquiat (*Ten Punching Bags* [with Christ from the Last Supper]). He painted the famous supper scene in pink, and in red, overlaid it with advertisement (Dove soap; Wise potato chips) and camouflage, and repeated the scene in black and white in *Sixty Last Suppers* (1986). In this last work the scenes vary in light and emotion. In each version of the Last Supper Warhol plays with the well-known image of the Last Supper from art history and from religious kitsch and gives it different nuances and settings. According to Jane Dillenberger, "Warhol's recreations infuse Leonardo's familiar image, which had become a cliché, with new spiritual resonance" (1998:120).

Warhol renders the spiritual in connection with materialist culture – war (camouflage), advertising (soap and chips), and pop(ular) color. The secular invades the spiritual, but the central image of Christ remains, in ever-repeated forms. Mark Taylor investigates Warhol's secular pop art and observes:

> Contrary to popular understanding, pop art is idealistic – it is the *idealism of the image*. Since there is nothing outside the image, the image is (the) "real." Within this specular economy, the "real" is ideal and the ideal is "real." For those who dwell in this utopia of the simulacrum or the simulacrum of utopia, there is nothing for which to hope and *nothing* to fear. Redemption is at hand. (1992:181)

Warhol shows that the biblical story does not dwell solely in the Bible; there are bible*s*, copies of copies, and they vary like the Warhol repetitious images. He also exhibits the importance of the ability to read biblical images in popular culture. The symbols of material culture invade the Christ narrative; the Christ of the Gospels is only a copy of a copy. Thus, our Bibles are tainted from the start, embedded by ideologies and simulacra of ancient religious ritual and political commitments. The scene of the Last Supper is in a way a metonymic sign, a fragment standing for the whole gospel story. As Warhol reveals, the Bible itself is a grand narrative. For example, John 3:16 at sporting events is a Christocentric sign for the whole Bible. These fragmentary signs signify nothing in a certain sense; they are so frequently repeated as to be easy to ignore. Yet these signifiers are intrusive, although they are part of the cultural landscape.

The artist on the cover of Batstone et al.'s *Liberation Theologies, Postmodernity, and the Americas*, José Antonio Burciaga, presents a different image of the Last Supper in his mural "Last Supper of Chicano Heroes." Our Lady of Guadalupe hovers above a table in a corn field around which are many workers and martyrs of revolutions in Mexico. The words, "and to all those who died, scrubbed floors, wept and fought for us," are written across the bottom of a white, fringed tablecloth. On the verso of the title page of the book there is a quote from the artist reflecting in the *Los Angeles Times* on his work, May 3, 1988:

> The idea [for this mural] arose from [another] I was designing on the mythology and history of maiz, corn. I had intended to depict the Last Supper; Christ and his 12 apostles were to be portrayed dining on tortillas, tamales and tequila instead of bread and wine. I dropped that idea when some students expressed dismay at my mixing humor with religion. That's when I decided to replace the religious figures with 13 Chicano heroes. The mural is now in the dining hall of Casa Zapata, the Chicano-theme student residence at Stanford [University]. (Batstone et al., 1997:iv)

This mural raises the stakes on the politics of reading the Bible. Like the Warhol images, it draws from its specific material culture, but it crosses borders — into Mexico — into an elitist university in the US. We used such art in teaching these articles partly to illustrate the articles, but also to heighten the existence of human lives behind political readings of the Bible. Whereas Warhol emphasizes the intrusion of corporate capital (in advertising, war, and in judging and managing art), Burciaga sharpens the liberatory vision in which the workers of liberation are modern-day Christs and apostles. He replaces the traditional Christ and apostle images with contemporary heroes. The traditional vision transforms; the face of Christ morphs.

Postmodern Plural Politics

Marxist literary critic Terry Eagleton reads the Book of Jonah as a "surrealist farce." As farce the story shifts expectations about Jonah as prophet and about the role of prophecy. Is Jonah a disobedient fool, or is he worthy of sympathy for being a pawn in the all-knowing and all-powerful deity's strange plan for the people of the far away Nineveh? The power issues between Jonah and God are huge, and power is expressed in rhetorical language. Eagleton's interest is in the "speech-act" of Jonah and of God in the story. Every speech-act is a kind of rhetoric in which, as Eagleton says, "*we cannot know whether we are doing anything or not*" (180). How does one act in the face of absolute undecidability? God is a trickster god, not unlike the figure of Coyote in Native American/First Nations stories (see the epigraph by Thomas King in this volume).

"Who knows?" queries the king of Nineveh after the immediate repentance of the city in response to Jonah's brief prophecy of destruction, "God may relent and change his mind" (3:9). And God did change his mind, making a mockery of Jonah's doom prophecy, the very words that God told Jonah to repeat to the people of Nineveh: "Forty days more, and Nineveh shall be overthrown!" (3:4).

Jonah is thus thrown about by and in the presence of God. Eagleton does not examine the lament/thanksgiving prayer of Jonath from the fish's belly in chapter 2, with its key theme of "Deliverance belongs to the Lord!" (2:9). Such prayers in the mouths of famous biblical characters usually bring God's compassion and blessing. But Jonah is tossed about (literally) for both disobedience and obedience. He seeks a stable deity, one that does not morph into other forms and voices and prophecies. But why is Jonah giving thanks to God for delivering him when he is saying this prayer from the stomach of a big fish? The narrative tosses the reader about, too. Traditional understandings about prophecy and prophets anticipate a trustworthy line of discourse from deity to seer. The Jonah narrative undermines these expectations.

There is a certain sarcasm in Eagleton's reading of Jonah. As he plays with the biblical rhetoric, he plays with his own voice and his own understanding of rhetoric. For Eagleton, rhetoric is a species of the Foucauldian "discursive practices" we examined in the General Introduction: "Rhetoric," he writes in *Literary Theory*, "which was the received form of critical analysis all the way from ancient society to the eighteenth century, examined the way discourses are constructed in order to achieve certain effects.... its horizon was nothing less than the field of discursive practices in society as a whole" (1983:205). All rhetoric is ideological; thus "'ideology' can be taken to indicate no more than this connection – the link or nexus between discourses and power" (1983:210) – which is to say, for Eagleton, rhetoric is above all *political*. Although like Jonah we cannot know whether we are doing anything or not – that is, whether our postmodern theoretical readings do lead to social transformation and so forth – we are drawn into the discursive practice. "It's in that sheer unfounded gratuitousness of meaning, that abyss of all signification, that God brutally, therapeutically, rubs Jonah's nose" (182).

The Bible Studies Group at the Christian base community at Solentiname that Ernesto Cardenal facilitates is a far cry from the ironic, urbane presentation of a postmodern politics in Eagleton. Rather, it reveals, in passionate engagement, the discourse in Latin American liberation theology between Marxism and Christianity. The categories of oppressor/oppressed, haves/have nots, First World/Third World are central to its liberatory, grassroots conversations. In this discourse, biblical interpretation is not produced only by the "experts" with degrees from Western universities. The people – ordinary people – have a right and a responsibility to reconnect with and to recover the Bible in new ways. The politics of reading thus becomes more inclusive. In liberation hermeneutics, the voices of the poor, and not the privileged and well-educated – even when they are overwhelmingly sympathetic – are central. Through the oral narratives of the poor (as with the peasants of Solentiname) is logocentrism deconstructed. For this reason, Sugirtharajah echoes Gandhi when he asserts that "the poor as the hermeneutical focus must be the starting point for any theology" (1991:437). There is a dialectical mode to liberation hermeneutics that revolves around the theory/practice alliance very different from Eagleton's intellectual play. The concreteness of exegesis – of reading out of a particular historical and political setting – shows the possibilities of the biblical themes of liberation in the work of social change. Against the hegemony of Enlightenment thinking about a singular Truth that exists once and for all, liberation readings show how the diverse biblical messages can be reappropriated – in Benjamin's term, "redeemed" or "translated" – in a commitment to justice and equity.

Along with the cross and resurrection stories for Christians, the Exodus and Conquest narratives have been liberative texts for many oppressed movements (the Civil Rights Movement Latin American liberation theologies, etc.). Robert Warrior, in "Canaanites, Cowboys, and Indians: Deliverance, Conquest, and Liberation Theology Today," gives a different contextual reading, showing how a text that is liberating to one group can be oppressive to another. A Native American liberation theology struggles with how the biblical texts were appropriated: from the grand narrative of the "conquest of the Americas" to the subsequent genocides, wars, boarding schools, reservation system, and overall history of racism. A liberation theology from this context works for equity and justice. But what if the central, traditional, liberatory narratives are unjust? In the Exodus and Conquest stories Warrior equates Native Americans with the Canaanites; he says, "I read the Exodus stories with Canaanite eyes" (190). Being Native and Christian involves reclaiming hermeneutical power – engaging the text on their own terms. "The peasants of Solentiname bring a wisdom and experience previously unknown to Christian theology, but I do not see what mechanism guarantees that they – or any other people who seek to be shaped and moulded by reading the text – will differentiate between the liberating god and the god of conquest" (193). If the Canaanites are put at the hermeneutical center, and if the text is read through Canaanite eyes, a text that is liberating in a Nicaraguan Christian base community changes shape.

This begs the questions: is the god of conquest an ethical god, and is reading these texts as liberating texts in *any* context an ethical act? The answers are certainly complicated. The African-American churches used their oppositional reading to great effect in the 1960s. Moses' call to "Let my people go" from the mouth of Martin Luther King, Jr. turned the tables on the white, Christian, racist oppressors. The Exodus and Conquest stories are an important narrative piece of the struggle. But they are also an important piece of Holy War ideology. Still, as Warrior insists, any text that advocates the complete destruction of a people is problematic, particularly for a non-violent social movement. For the Puritans, Native Americans were Canaanites (and any other enemy nations of Israel), so they could be destroyed (194). The concepts of "chosenness" and "the Promised Land" are part of this ideology (see Donald Akenson [1997] on this concept of chosen people in South Africa, Israel, and Ulster). Warrior argues that identifying with the (eventual) oppressor is not liberating. These narratives are dangerous parts of the Christian sacred canon, and Warrior raises the issues of the artificiality of "canon" and of mechanisms by which the narratives of some are included and those of others excluded. Again, any act of reading/interpreting is a political act, one which has consequences in the world.

Naim Ateek relates these concerns in his context as a Palestinian Christian. Both Palestinians and Native Americans identify with the Canaanites. Ateek's key hermeneutical questions are: "How can the Bible, which has apparently become a part of the problem in the Arab–Israeli conflict, become a part of its solution? How can the Bible, which has been used to bring a curse to the national aspirations of a whole people, again offer them a blessing? How can the Bible, through which many have been led to salvation, be itself saved and redeemed?" (1991:282). He is searching for an authentic Word of God, and not the word of Jewish Zionists or Christian Fundamentalists who have a claim on Palestinian land using biblical precedence. How can the Bible be a tool of justice and not injustice? Ateek sees hope in Christ because "the *Word* of God incarnate in Jesus Christ interprets for us the *word* of God in the Bible" (285). Ateek's God is ultimately the incarnate Christ of the New Testament, while Warrior distrusts the conquering God of the Exodus and Conquest stories. Warrior is much more wary: "Do Native Americans and other indigenous people dare trust the same god in their struggle for justice?... We will perhaps do better to look elsewhere for our vision of justice, peace, and political sanity" (194). Ateek finds a liberating center to the Exodus story, as long as the oppressed have the power to interpret from their own experiences and drive for justice.

Ethicist Katie Cannon shares this concern for justice in her article "Slave Ideology and Biblical Interpretation." Cannon traces the use of the Bible to legitimize more than 150 years of slavery in the United States. She sees as her main task "to unmask the hermeneutical distortions of White Christians, North and South," who maintained this "slave ideology" (196). Slavery becomes a "sacred institution" (201) upheld by biblical texts, such as Genesis 9:25–27, in which Canaan, the son of Ham (identified as Black by white supremist interpreters), is cursed. "As life-affirming moral agents we have a responsibility to study the ideological hegemony of the past so that we do not remain doomed to the recurring cyclical patterns of hermeneutical distortions in the present – i.e., violence against women, condemnation of homosexuality, spiritualizing Scripture to justify capitalism" (202–3). Cannon links racist hermeneutics to the systems of interstructured oppression. The condemnation of groups of people as unhuman (African peoples) and/or as sinners (homosexuals) led and continues to lead to the denial of rights and the refusal to create systems of equity. The "not said" of mainstream biblical studies – for example, in a translation that omits Africa or Africans – is also dangerous: by means of its silence it participates in the history of violence. The "said" of a hierarchy of racial and/or sexual superiority – whether it be slavery or racial profiling or the denial of marriage and ordination to homosexuals – is, of course, the more blatant form. But slave ideology is part of the history of biblical interpretation, and Cannon warns us in the present to avoid continuing the legacy of the "coconspirators in the victimization of Black people" (203).

Donna Haraway invokes Nietzsche's spirit in her "Ecce Homo" article. Although unnamed, Nietzsche lurks behind Pilate's assertion in John 19:5:

> that stroke of genius on the part of Christianity: God himself sacrifices himself for the guilt of mankind, God himself makes payment to himself. God as the only being who can redeem man from what has become unredeemable for man himself – the creditor sacrifices himself for his debtor, out of *love* (can one credit that?), out of love for his debtor! (Nietzsche 1989:92)

Nietzsche is, of course, horrified at the weakness of Christianity – a religion that needs the gift of death, of a divine sacrifice, to pay the debt of human sin. He does not gain any edification from the suffering servant model for human suffering and guilt payment. There is no liberatory current in Christian salvation history. Although Haraway does not take on this Nietzschian negativity directly, she turns from his reading to investigate the model of the Jesus figure as telling us something important about the human in the late twentieth century. In her interpretation of the trial scene of Jesus with Pilate in the Gospel of John, comparing Jesus to the suffering servant of Isaiah, she approaches reading the Bible from a postmodern perspective: "We don't have the first versions, if there ever were such things; we have endless, gap-filled, and overlaid transcriptions and translations that have grounded the vast apparatus of biblical, textual and linguistic scholarship" (209). As with Derrida (or Jean Baudrillard), there are no originals, only copies of copies, and Haraway sees these biblical scenes played out on the historical human stage, with the trickster figures of Jesus and Sojourner Truth. Like the Coyote in certain myths of North American indigenous peoples, Jesus ("Ecce Homo") and Sojourner Truth (with her question, "Ain't/Ar'n't I a woman?") are shape-shifters who bring liberation by breaking natural (and supernatural) boundaries. Jesus the Jewish carpenter becomes the scapegoat for humanity; Sojourner Truth the former slave fights for the end of slavery and for black women's rights. As Haraway states, "These were tricksters, forcing by their constant displacements, a reconstruction of founding stories, of any possible home" (216). The borderlands (Gloria Anzaldúa's term) provide the space for working out the implications of these tricksters, for they come from the borderlands of culture, humanity, language, and translation. Like Coyote in the Thomas King selection at the beginning of this book, the trickster has an eclectic sense of biblical stories and is constantly playing with textual and linguistic meaning. The trickster displaces traditional meaning – and power relations.

Haraway uses science, politics, and feminism in her investigations into the world of women and the Other. As with her most famous theory of "the cyborg manifesto," she is looking for the feminist face of humanity in the "inappropriate/d Others," a term she borrows from the feminist Vietnamese-American film-maker Trinh Minh-ha (1992:299; 1991: Part Three). Haraway is concerned with human struggles on both the local and the global scale. She wants to chart where humanity is going and what the future might hold. Religion is a necessary conversation partner in Haraway's thinking about a liberatory future of nature and technoscience. Religion connects humanity with (political) vision and the reinvention of nature (Haraway, 1991:188–96; see Grassie's [1996] critique of her "Unity of Science project"). Against Nietzsche, Haraway finds a way to chart how one becomes human, but also who is human, in order to focus on those who are marginalized. The discourses and myths of religion, especially Christianity, provide one of many grids of experience and culture.

Haraway's calling for "situated knowledges" is echoed in biblical studies by readings that employ "the politics of social location." For Haraway, "Situated knowledges are always *marked* knowledges; they are re-markings, reorientations, of the great maps that globalized the heterogeneous body of the world in the history of masculinist capitalism and colonialism" (1991:111). A similar idea in biblical hermeneutics is the politics/poetics of social location. Mary Ann Tolbert summarizes:

a poetics of location must be situated in communities of accountability and structures of
responsibility...A poetics of location maintains the radical historicity of texts and interpreters, their creative and multiple interconnections, and their powerful constructions of
"reality," "truth," and "justice," in the hope of persuading the world that those yearning
for a better way finally need to be heard. (1995:316–17)

The shared concerns on issues of race and gender, patriarchy and colonialism, lead to a
reevaluation of traditional historical critical methods. Tolbert (like Ahmad) is critical of a
postmodernism that fails to connect with lived experience across the boundaries of these
issues. Social location is part of a liberatory hermeneutic in that it is situated in the lives
and situations of the oppressed.

Similarly, in the chapter on "Feminist and Womanist Criticism" the PMB formulates
the importance of making "the assertion that reading and interpretive strategies are
socially, politically, and institutionally situated and that they draw their energy and force
from the subject positions of readers and interpreters" (267). We use the article in this
volume by Zakia Pathak to help us rethink the future of postmodern biblical scholarship. Pathak centers her discussion of reading the Bible in a postcolonial setting by
speaking primarily about pedagogy, and teaching a variety of colonizer's texts to undergraduate women. In one section of the course she uses the Book of Job and T. S. Eliot's
Murder in the Cathedral and shows how feminist pedagogy leads to a displacing of the
authority of the biblical and imperialist texts and "opening up [of] religion to other
discourses" (221). These discourses include recent political-religious events as well as
the present effects of neocolonial educational systems. Thus, Pathak is a subversive
gatekeeper within the boundaries of institutional rule/s. Critical theory aids Pathak in
her oppositional work. She is able to identify the nationalism of Eliot's play and the legal
and political discourses of Job and to use these "discursive paradigms" to read the
Mandir Masjid dispute over a religious site that both Hindus (birthplace of Ram) and
Muslims (sixteenth-century Mosque) claim. Pathak links the primacy of Yahweh (in
Job) and Ram (by Hindus in the dispute) to talk about the power plays in each text.
Feminist readings (of the role of Job's wife in particular) are secondary only because of
the urgency of the political conflict. Readings of biblical texts take on new contextual
meanings in postcolonial India.

Voiced Voicelessness: Postmodern Postcolonization

Sri Lankan biblical scholar R. S. Sugirtharajah notes two traditional ways of reading the
Bible in India – "Orientalist" and "Anglicist" – and posits a "Postcolonial" reading over
and against these imperialist strategies (1998:283). For him postcolonial criticism has
created a turn – away from the questions of the colonizer as central and toward the
cultural and historical engagement with biblical texts. In other words, since the Bible
came to India with British imperialism, it is necessary to trace the hegemonic voices of
the colonizer along with recovering the lost voices of the colonized. Sugirtharajah
believes that "Postcolonial criticism recognizes that interpreters have to be freed from
traditional interpretative powers so that the voice of the voiceless may be heard" (293).

What does it mean to read the text from the location of one who is Indian? Whose questions and stories are admitted into the conversation or are privileged? There is a power shift occurring in postcolonial readings of texts – not that the traditional historical questions are unimportant, but that more questions from the colonial experience of the readers begin to reshape and reconfigure the field of biblical studies and also the teaching of these texts. On this point Fernando Segovia invokes cultural criticism: "From the perspective of neo-Marxist criticism, the view of the text as an ideological product, of the world behind the text as a site of struggle, and of the critic as committed and hence as a further factor in the struggle ultimately led to the belief that proper criticism is criticism on the side of the oppressed" (1995:25).

Brazilian educational theorist Paulo Freire often pointed to the fear of theory and theorists that those wanting to reproduce the dominant ideology have. Freirean scholar Donald Macedo explains: "By not theorizing their practice, the white liberal educators shield themselves from the self-critical reflection that could interrogate, among other things, how the maintenance of their privilege invariably makes them complicit with the dominant ideology that creates the need for them to engage in various forms of practice in oppressed communities" (1998:xxxi). Theory is important because it deepens the possibilities within practice: as we noted in the Introduction to Part I, it brings together and imbricates the individual and the social in the act of self-conscious *witnessing*. The fear of critical theory in biblical (and other) studies has been used by the status quo to maintain power in "self-evident" truths. Feminism/womanism, post-colonialism, and poststructuralism have been scapegoated; in other words, theory is blamed for disrupting the dominant power system. Albert Memmi translates this scapegoating as a way that the colonizer keeps intellectual hegemony over the colonized. When the colonized link theory to practice, they threaten the dominant practices in the academy and the central places of power of the dominators. As biblical studies becomes more global, the "center" (in Europe and in North America) loses some of its predominance. The "canon" comes under question in a variety of ways – as a tool of colonization and oppression; as a dialogue partner with indigenous writers and activists; as a path toward interreligious interaction. It becomes plural. The postmodern plural politics Part II describes – the ironic, indigenous, excluded, eclectic, and layered narratives of Eagleton, Cardenal, Warrior, Haraway, and Pathak – stake out within the Bible places from which value may be witnessed and action may begin.

The conversation with the Bible is beginning to open up for many oppressed groups and more voices are emerging. Screenwriter and producer Paul Hallam, in the last selection of this section, shows how our world is Bible-shaped: his world is "Sodom," wherever it may be, and Sodom is a fundamentally biblical image. He is concerned with how the image of homosexuality was created for bourgeois or working-class people through the popular commentaries created for them. Hallam begins his book with the statements: "There is no Sodom, there are only Sodom texts. Stories of Sodom, commentaries, footnotes, elaborations and annotations upon Sodom" (1993:15); there are only "pleasures and the ashes of pleasures" (1993:275). He is fascinated by the cultural (bi-)products of the legacy of Sodom and Gomorrah in Genesis 18–19. In this way Hallam follows the focus on uncovering historical artifacts as the late John Boswell did before him.

Although no mention is made that homosexuality was the cause of God destroying these towns, and scholars attribute the "sin" to the sin of inhospitality, the term "sodomite" has had a history of homophobic interpretation. Foucault defined "sodomy" as "that utterly confused category" (1978:101). The term "sodomy" is not gender-specific, but with some other sexual acts (e.g. incest, pederasty) it has referred to something illicit, against the law, against nature. Sodomy's confused history finally landed on homosexuals; according to Foucault, "The Sodomite had been a temporary aberration; the homosexual was now a species" (1978:43). Thus violence could be legitimately focused on persons – homosexuals – and a group of people negatively marked as "enemy" in terms of their sexuality. This move is ironically biblical; enemies, such as the Philistines, are deemed "the uncircumcised ones." There has been a recovery movement since the 1980s to reconstruct the context of the biblical stories used to prove that homosexuality is a sin, so that the Bible can be seen as an ideological product of its – and our – (heterosexist) times. But others, like Hallam, are not so much interested in redeeming the biblical canon as they are in tracing the erotic (and *political*) power of interpretation, and the trail of violence and sodomitic ashes such interpretation has left and continues to leave behind.

Consider the recent sexuality debate in US churches. The lines are drawn heavily and absolutely between those churches that are, for example, "welcoming and affirming" or "more light" and those that are not (would they then be "inhospitable and denying" and "less light"? Was not the sin of the Sodomites inhospitality?!). Protests by pro-gay denominational groups at some general denominational conventions have led to the arrests of both the ordained and the lay by the arrangement of their own denominational leadership. The destruction of Sodom did not eradicate the "problem." In fact, in the minds of the anti-gay contingent, the "sins" have multiplied. Exclusionary tactics recreate the event of the annihilation of Sodom. Examples range from "conversion" (by ex-gay ministries and aversion therapy groups) to other forms of violence, such as exclusion in church leadership or, in the more secular world, to the denial of civil and human rights and even beatings and murders. The story is thus played out again and again. Hallam shows how harmful the misreadings of Genesis 18–19 have been and how traditional and dominant Western cultural guides of Sodom are flawed. A postmodern look at Sodom uncovers the voices of the perpetrators of violence and the victims, but also the subversive speech of the survivors who continue to rise up out of the ashes.

The Politics of Reading and the Beginning of Action

How to build an interpretive strategy out of/from ashes is one of the subjects of Part III. The politics of reading leaves many questions, and one of the main concerns continues to be that of Audre Lorde, "Can the master's tools dismantle the master's house?" Her answer is a clear "No." "What does it mean," she writes, "when the tools of a racist patriarchy are used to examine the fruits of that same patriarchy? It means that only the most narrow perimeters of change are possible and allowable" (1984:111). Postmodern biblical interpretation, as with any other, is always in danger of creating its own unchanging method of reading or trivializing its insights in their very multiplication: the ironic, indigenous, excluded, eclectic, layered, and Bible-shaped narratives of Part

II. So the hard questions remain: how does one determine ethical biblical teaching? What makes an ethical reader? – or reading as an ethical act? And with Lorde, how does one break out of the cycle of oppression and of narrow and limited social change? – and find it imaginable or possible to discover what we might call an "anagogic politics," a postmodern ethics? The articles that follow do not give definitive answers, but they challenge biblical readers to resist what is "allowable," even if the biblical text itself is setting the boundaries. Neither do the articles in our final section, "The Conscience of the Bible," give definitive answers, but they continue the trajectory – from reading to politics to ethics – that postmodern readers of the Bible have begun to discern.

Related essays in *The Postmodern Bible Reader*

Mieke Bal, "Body Politic"
Enrique Dussel, from *Ethics and Community*
Emmanuel Levinas, "On the Jewish Reading of Scriptures"
Gayatri Spivak, "'Draupadi' by Mahasweta Devi"

Bibliography

Ahmad, Aijaz. 1998. "Literary Theory and 'Third World Literature': Some Contexts." In *Contemporary Literary Criticism*. Ed. Robert Con Davis and Ronald Schleifer. New York: Longman, pp. 137–56.

Akenson, Donald. 1997. *God's People: Covenant and Land in South Africa, Israel, and Ulster*. Ithaca: Cornell University Press.

Ateek, Naim Stifan. 1991. "A Palestinian Perspective: The Bible and Liberation." In *Voices from the Margin: Interpreting the Bible in the Third World*. Ed. R. S. Sugirtharajah. Maryknoll, NY: Orbis, pp. 280–6.

Austin, J. L. 1982. *How to Do Things with Words*. Oxford: Oxford University Press.

Bal, Mieke. 1991. *On Story-telling: Essays in Narratology*. Ed. David Jobling. Sonoma, CA: Polebridge.

Batstone, David, Eduardo Mendieta, Lois Ann Lorentzen, and Dwight N. Hopkins, eds. 1997. *Liberation Theologies, Postmodernity, and the Americas*. London/New York: Routledge.

Boswell, John. 1980. *Christianity, Social Tolerance and Homosexuality: Gay People in Western Europe from the Beginning of the Christian Era to the Fourteenth Century*. Chicago: University of Chicago Press.

Callahan, Allen Dwight, Richard A. Horsley, and Abraham Smith, eds. 1998. Slavery in Text and Interpretation. Semeia 83/84.

Dillenberger, Jane Daggett. 1998. *The Religious Art of Andy Warhol*. New York: Continuum.

Eagleton, Terry. 1983. *Literary Theory*. Minneapolis: University of Minnesota Press.

———. 1996. *The Illusions of Postmodernism*. Oxford: Blackwell.

Foucault, Michel. 1978. *The History of Sexuality: An Introduction*. Trans. Robert Hurley. New York: Pantheon.

Giroux, Henry. 1996. "Towards a Postmodern Pedagogy." In *From Modernism to Postmodernism: An Anthology*. Ed. Lawrence E. Cahoone. Oxford: Blackwell, pp. 687–97.

Grassie, William. 1996. "Cyborgs, Trickster, and Hermes: Donna Haraway's Metatheory of Science and Religion." *Zygon* (June).

Hallam, Paul. 1993. *The Book of Sodom*. London/New York: Routledge.

Haraway, Donna J. 1991. *Simians, Cyborgs, and Women: The Reinvention of Nature*. New York/London: Routledge.

———. 1992. "The Promises of Monsters: A Regenerative Politics for Inappropriate/d Others." In *Cultural Studies*. Ed. Lawrence Grossberg, Cary Nelson, and Paula Treichler. New York/London: Routledge, pp. 295–337.

Jameson, Fredric. 1981. *The Political Unconscious: Narrative as a Socially Symbolic Act*. Ithaca: Cornell University Press.

Lorde, Audre. 1984. "The Master's Tools Will Never Dismantle the Master's House." In *Sister Outsider: Essays and Speeches*. Freedom, CA: The Crossing Press, pp. 110–13.

Macedo, Donald. 1998. "Foreword." In *Pedagogy of Freedom: Ethics, Democracy, and Civic Courage*. By Paulo Freire. New York: Rowan & Littlefield, pp. xi–xxxii.

Memmi, Albert. 1967. *The Colonizer and the Colonized*. Trans. Howard Greenfeld. Boston: Beacon Press.

Nietzsche, Friedrich Wilhelm. 1989. *Ecce Homo*. In *On the Genealogy of Morals/Ecce Homo*. Trans. Walter Kaufman and R. J. Hollingdale. New York: Vintage.

Pathak, Zakia. 1997. "Defamiliarizing Practices: The Scene of Feminist Pedagogy." In *Transitions, Environments, Translations: Feminisms in International Politics*. Ed. Joan W. Scott, Cora Kaplan, and Debra Keates. New York/London: Routledge, pp. 426–41.

Pathak, Zakia, and Saswati Sengupta. 1997. "Between the Academy and the Street." *Signs* 22: 545–78.

Segovia, Fernando F. 1995. "Introduction: 'And They Began to Speak in Other Tongues': Competing Modes of Discourse in Contemporary Biblical Criticism." In Segovia and Tolbert, 1995, pp. 1–32.

Segovia, Fernando F., and Mary Ann Tolbert, eds. 1995. *Reading from this Place*. Vol. 1: *Social Location and Biblical Interpretation in the United States*. Minneapolis: Fortress Press.

———. 1998. *Teaching the Bible: The Discourses and Politics of Biblical Pedagogy*. Maryknoll, NY: Orbis Books.

Sugirtharajah, R. S. 1991. "Postscript: Achievements and Items for a Future Agenda." In *Voices from the Margin: Interpreting the Bible in the Third World*. Ed. R. S. Sugirtharajah. Maryknoll, NY: Orbis, pp. 434–44.

———. 1998. "Biblical Studies in India: From Imperialistic Scholarship to Postcolonial Interpretation." In Segovia and Tolbert, 1998, pp. 283–96.

Taylor, Mark C. 1992. *Disfiguring: Art, Architecture, Religion*. Chicago: University of Chicago Press.

Tolbert, Mary Ann. 1995. "The Politics and Poetics of Location." In Segovia and Tolbert, 1995, pp. 305–17.

Chapter 8

J. L. Austin and the Book of Jonah

Terry Eagleton 1943–

Introduction

Coming from an unprivileged background in the north of England, Eagleton is now a professor of English at Oxford University. As a Marxist, indeed the foremost English Marxist literary critic, this plunges him into a world of contradiction. He has remained resolutely Marxist, notably in his response to postmodernism, but his very critical engagement with it has made him the object of some suspicion from British Left intellectuals.

He is the author of a long list of works of Marxist criticism; among the most important are *Marxism and Literary Criticism* (1976) and *The Ideology of the Aesthetic* (1990). Especially influential has been his *Literary Theory: An Introduction* (1983; 2nd edn. 1996), notable for its suggestion that literary criticism should go out of business as a self-justifying "discipline," and merge itself into a general critique of culture. He has long been engaged in a sustained critique of postmodernism, culminating in *The Illusions of Postmodernism* (1996). He sees its potential for informing political struggle by unravelling the conceptual undergirding of power, but believes that in practice it has undermined such struggle by denying the possibility of the coherent and unified political vision needed to challenge the omnipotence of capitalism.

Though his earliest writings (in the late 1960s) were in the framework of Left Catholicism in the wake of the Second Vatican Council, Eagleton has since shown no special religious interest, and our selection seems to be his first venture in biblical criticism. He has had, though, a considerable influence on biblical scholars, as witness his prominence in *The Postmodern Bible*, where he enters into the discussion not only of ideology but, in a less major way, also of rhetorical and reader-response criticism.

Perhaps imitating the Book of Jonah itself, he achieves in our selection a brevity and tightness which others might emulate. A certain "flipness" of tone helps to lure the reader into a deeply serious statement. Eagleton continues his critical engagement (see *Literary Theory*) with fashionable approaches, in this case the "speech-act theory" of J. L. Austin. More importantly, he focuses (as in much of his other work) on the American "arch-deconstructors," Paul de Man and J. Hillis Miller (see our selection from Miller). Though he resists their position, he shows how Jonah might be read as supporting it; or, again, might be read as undoing it. The culmination of the essay perhaps lies in the point that no one can at present achieve a subjectivity "at once affirmative and self-interrogative." The complexity and courage of Eagleton's Marxist position can be seen here. He denies that Marxists somehow have unique access to a right way of seeing the world, while insisting that Marxism uniquely provides the tools for understanding why *no one*, in the existing political conditions, is capable of seeing the world adequately. Though Eagleton certainly does not intrude himself into this essay, one may perhaps see it as very personal. To what extent is Jonah an allegory of the Marxist critic, and Jonah's God of "history" in the Marxist sense?

The surrealist farce known as the Book of Jonah is easily summarized. God commands Jonah to go and cry doom on Nineveh, a city whose viciousness has just come to his attention, but Jonah doesn't reckon much to this mission and takes off instead for Tarshish. A divinely engineered storm threatens his ship, and he requests the crew with remarkable *sang-froid* to pitch him overboard. God sends a fish to swallow Jonah up and spew him out again three days later, whereupon Jonah does manage to get himself to Nineveh and wanders the city proclaiming imminent catastrophe. Unusually enough, the inhabitants of the city, prodded a bit by their king, take Jonah's prophecy to heart and repent, which infuriates Jonah so much that he goes and sulks outside the city hoping to die. God fools around with him briefly, sending a plant to shade him, then a worm to devour the plant, then a sultry wind to make him faint from heat, and finally treats him to a short homily about his mercy.

Why was Jonah so reluctant to go to Nineveh in the first place? Perhaps because hectoring a seedy bunch of strangers about their vices isn't the best guarantee of a long life. But in the storm scene Jonah shows scant regard for his own safety, and indeed by the end of the text is betraying a powerful death wish. The fact is that he refused to obey God because he thought there was no point, and tells God as much after he has spared Nineveh. God is a spineless liberal given to hollow authoritarian threats, who would never have the guts to perform what he promises. Jonah understands divine psychology far too well to take such tetchy bumblings seriously, and is loath to embark on the tiresome, complicated business of getting himself to Nineveh (it takes three days just to cross the city) when he knows that there is no impending disaster to be averted. He is angry with God because he can foresee all this from the outset and feels that God, who after all is supposed to be omniscient, would foresee it too if only he wasn't so mystified by his own macho image of himself. The point of Jonah's getting himself thrown overboard is to force God to save him, thus dramatically demonstrating to him that he's too soft-hearted to punish those who disobey him. If God wheels up a fish to rescue Jonah, won't he do something equivalent for Nineveh? Jonah is of course taking a fairly hair-raising risk here, but he calculates that if God rates him as important enough

Terry Eagleton, "J. L. Austin and the Book of Jonah," from *The Book and the Text: The Bible and Literary Theory*, edited by Regina M. Schwartz (Oxford: Blackwell, 1990).

to play the prophet in Nineveh, it would be perverse of him to let him drown. In any case, Jonah's disobedience is a kind of subtle flattery of God, a bit of emotional blackmail which God would be churlish to respond to by letting him go under: he reminds God later, after the Nineveh debacle, that he had told him at the outset that he was too loving and merciful to live up to his bloodthirsty intentions. Disobeying God is a crafty way of telling him what a nice chap he is, and thus – so Jonah hopes – may be done with impunity. Fleeing to Tarshish is just a flamboyant way of trying to bring God to his senses, induce a little self-knowledge in him; but God obtusely fails to take the point, and Jonah, perhaps despairing of the Almighty's capacity for self-enlightenment, sets out for Nineveh after all with a deepening sense of existential absurdity.

Once in the city, Jonah shambles around playing at being a prophet, no doubt pretty perfunctorily, and is disgusted to find that his clichéd denunciations actually work. Disgusted, because of course Jonah doesn't believe for a moment that Nineveh's suspiciously sudden repentance is anything of his own doing: it has been brought about by God, to save himself the mess, unpleasantness and damage to his credibility as a nice chap consequent on having to put his threats into practice. Jonah is enraged because God is simply using him as a fall guy to let himself off the hook of his own soft-bellied liberalism. What has happened is what Jonah knew would happen all along: he has been used as cover for a massive climb-down on God's part, and God can now carry on persuading himself that he's a tough guy underneath. Jonah has merely been used as an instrument in the perpetuation of divine false consciousness. God would have spared the city even if Jonah had stayed at home; it's just that he needs some excuse to do so, and has maneuvred Jonah, against his own better judgment, into providing him with one. Even if God *was* toying with the idea of blasting Nineveh, or at least thought he was, there would still have been no point as Jonah sees it in leaving home; for since God is omniscient he presumably knew when he asked Jonah to set out either that the city would be destroyed, in which case Jonah's journey was supremely unnecessary, or that it wouldn't be, in which case his journey was also unnecessary. Jonah doesn't know the outcome himself, but he knows that God does, and suspects that either way this renders his own part in the narrative ridiculously superfluous.

What happens in Nineveh is exactly what Jonah feared all along: that God's own chronic self-deception would drag him into its own wake and leave him looking a complete idiot. He has stomped around Nineveh proclaiming that its end is nigh, and now it isn't. God's view of the matter, of course, is that it's *because* Jonah has cried doom that the doom hasn't come. The only successful prophet is an ineffectual one, one whose warnings fail to materialize. All good prophets are false prophets, undoing their own utterances in the very act of producing them. In the terms of J. L. Austin's *How to Do Things with Words*,[1] prophetic utterances of Jonah's sort are "constative" (descriptive of some real or possible state of affairs) only in what one might call their surface grammar; as far as their "deep structure" goes they actually belong to Austin's class of "performatives," linguistic acts which get something done. What they get done is to produce a state of affairs in which the state of affairs they describe won't be the case. Effective declarations of imminent catastrophe cancel themselves out, containing as they do a contradiction between what they say and what they do. In this sense they exactly fit the prototype of what the deconstructionist critic Paul de Man in his *Allegories of*

Reading calls a "literary" enunciation.[2] The literary, for de Man, is the kind of speech-act within which the grammatical and the rhetorical are somehow at odds, and which thereby either subvert what they say by what they do or undo what they do by what they say. Yeats's celebrated line "How can we know the dancer from the dance?" inquires, grammatically speaking, about how we can distinguish the dancer from the dance, perhaps with the implication that it's somehow important to do so; but as a performative or rhetorical utterance the line of course powerfully suggests that we neither can nor should. Literary language for de Man founders in a kind of fissure between its grammatical and rhetorical dimensions, and so do Jonah's prophecies of doom. All such prophets are self-deconstructing fools.

This, however, isn't exactly why Jonah is so furious. He is angry, as we've seen, because he feels he has been shamelessly used as a pawn in God's self-mystifying game; and it is this which plunges him into the existential *angst* and nausea we find overwhelming him at the end of the narrative. If Jonah wants to curl up and die, it is because he can no longer stomach a history struck utterly pointless by God's self-blindness and self-indulgence. If the Creator himself is stupid enough not to know that he's the helpless victim of his own over-sanguine temperament, what hope for human self-insight? And if God just goes around forgiving everybody all the time, what's the point of doing anything? If disobedience on the scale of a Nineveh goes cavalierly unpunished, then the idea of obedience also ceases to have meaning. God's mercy simply makes a mockery of human effort, which is why Jonah ends up in the grip of *Thanatos* or the death drive.

There is another way of accounting for Jonah's final depression and melancholia, his resolute "decathecting" of reality and withdrawal of libido back into himself. Paul de Man, as we have seen, speaks of the discrepancy or aporetic relationship between the grammatical and the rhetorical (or performative) in literary discourse; but, drawing on Nietzsche's notions of rhetoric, he also strives to deconstruct the very idea of performativity itself. For if performance is caught up in language, and if language is irreducibly figurative or tropological, then there may come a point, so de Man argues, when *we cannot know whether we are doing anything or not.*[3] "Rhetorical" discourse, in the sense of language intended to have definite public effects, is marred and insidiously undone by "rhetoric" in the sense of verbal figuration. Something like this, I would suggest, is the abyss or aporia, the vertiginous collapse of meaning, in which Jonah is finally embroiled. For even if he could console himself by surmising that his journey really *was* necessary, that his crying doom was performatively effective rather than farcically redundant, there is no way in which he can ever know this for certain, no way in which he can ever know whether he was doing anything or not. There is no means of precisely determining the hair-thin line between describing and getting something done, being a spectator and being a participant. You can never know how far a particular narrative has always already included you in, because to do so would require an impossible kind of meta-move. Jonah thinks he occupies such a meta-position in respect of God, outdoing God's own omniscience in his superior insight into divine psychology; but it could just be that God had one over Jonah all along. For what if God's narrative had always already reckoned Jonah's into it, and the whole point of this pantomime was to bring Jonah to the point where he knew that he did not know whether he was doing anything or not? Jonah's initial presumption implies that action isn't important, and his subsequent despair implies the same; indeed, these two conditions aren't in the least opposites for him, since the source of his despair is precisely his presumptuous belief that human initiatives are struck superfluous by God's mercy. But there is also a more subtle kind of despair, which springs from a "deconstructive" insight into the ambiguous, problematical nature of action as such. To assume that human practice isn't necessary is to assume you know what it is, and it's perhaps this ground which is now crumbling from beneath Jonah's feet.

To view action as problematical and ambiguous is not necessarily a recipe for quietism, though some such implication might indeed be detected in the work of de Man and some of his colleagues. If action is a *text*, it is not necessarily an illegible one. What the Book of Jonah can be read as calling into question is less action as such than a particular ideological model of it: the assumption that at the source of all practice lies a well-defined, autonomous subject whose behavior lies entirely within its affirmative mastery. The damage which Marx and Freud have inflicted on this model in our own day is inflicted in the case of Jonah by that unmasterable otherness known as "God," the condition of possibility of all practice. The over-rigorous distinction made by Jonah between what he himself knows or does, and what God knows and does, returns in our own time as a liberal humanist dichotomy between the agent and his or her enabling conditions. To trouble this tenacious opposition is to fall at first into what seems like nihilism, a despair as to the potential effectivity of action; and Jonah shares this syndrome with Paul de Man and J. Hillis Miller. What he, and they, apparently do not see is that in order to be able to act efficaciously at all you must have somehow gone all the way through this shaking of the foundations and emerged somewhere on the other side. Neither the old-style humanistic agent, nor the ecstastically decentered and disseminated subject, offer adequate models of human practice, and are indeed to a great extent the mere flipsides of one another. Any profound process of political transformation calls, paradoxically, for human agents who are on the one hand a good deal more centered, resolute and affirmative than the subjects of quotidian life, and on the other hand will shake such affirmative identity to its roots. To act effectively at all, you must have some positive sense of who you are; but if oppressed groups and peoples were able to have such a sense they would not need to act in the first place. Political action consists not primarily in expressing an already well-founded identity, but in creating the social conditions in which it might just become possible to say who one was, or to discover what one would like to be. It is the rulers, not the oppressed, who are happily dispensed from worrying about who they are. The Book of Jonah leaves its protagonist caught in a transitional stage between false consciousness and some new, currently unnamable style of identity; and to this extent we have made little advance upon it. Nobody to my knowledge has yet produced a satisfactory paradigm of a form of subjectivity which would be at once affirmative and self-interrogative, centered enough to act decisively yet constituted to its core by the sense of some ineradicable otherness. If we are currently caught between two prototypes of subjectivity, the one dying and discredited and the other powerless to be properly born, it is not because researchers in the field are remarkable for their low intelligence but because of the nature of our political and historical conditions.

The book ends with a small Dadaist drama in which God conjures up a plant, worm and wind in rapid succession, like a magician on a ropy night at the Hammersmith Palais. This bizarre sadistic taunting is presumably meant among other things to show Jonah that God isn't such a nice chap as he seemed; if he can indulge in this sort of nasty insensitive trifling then he might just have blasted Nineveh after all. There's a darkly malevolent humor about this divine tomfoolery, which suggests in quick symbolic notation that God can either save Jonah or scupper him as the fancy takes him. If he can clown around as aggressively as this, setting Jonah solicitously on his feet one moment only to kick his legs from under him the next, God isn't perhaps quite the patsy Jonah thought he was. What seems particularly callous about God is that his flashy, second-rate conjuring act is a kind of grisly parody of Jonah's black despair; God's gratuitous cavortings, pulling worms and winds from his sleeve like so many rabbits, writes cruelly large Jonah's own nauseated sense of the gratuitousness of all meaning under God's libertarian regime. It's in that sheer unfounded gratuitousness of meaning, that abyss of all signification, that God brutally, therapeutically, rubs Jonah's nose. God's mercy is indeed a kind of absurdity, but there's no need for Jonah to make a song and dance of it, which is why God makes a mocking song and dance of it. Jonah just has to find some way of living with the fact that he can never know whether he is doing anything or not, which was perhaps the point of the whole futile narrative after all.

Notes

1   J. L. Austin, *How to Do Things with Words* (Harvard University Press, Cambridge, MA, 1975).
2   Paul de Man, *Allegories of Reading* (Yale University Press, New Haven, 1979).
3   Ibid., pp. 121ff.

Chapter 9

The Song of Mary
(Luke 1:46–55)

Ernesto Cardenal 1925–

Introduction

Ernesto Cardenal was born in Granada, Nicaragua. He received his education in the 1940s at the University of Mexico and at Columbia University. He became a Christian in 1956, was ordained a Roman Catholic priest in 1965, and considered himself a Christian-Marxist after a visit to Cuba in 1970. Cardenal studied for the priesthood at the Trappist Abbey of Gesthemane in Bardstown, Kentucky, with monk–poet–author Thomas Merton, and completed his studies in Mexico. He then returned to Nicaragua. After the civil war Cardenal served as Minister of Culture in the cabinet of Daniel Ortega's Sandinista government. Cardenal is a theologian, poet, and author. He won the Christopher Book Award in 1972 for *The Psalms of Struggle and Liberation*. Other works include *Apocalypse and Other Poems* (1977), *From Nicaragua with Love: Poems 1979–1986* (1986), *Cosmos Canticle* (1993), and *Abide in Love* (1995).

There is a famous exchange of letters in *The Catholic Reporter* between Cardenal and an American Roman Catholic priest and activist, Daniel Berrigan. Berrigan urges Cardenal to return to his previous theological commitment to non–violent resistance to the violence of the Somoza regime. Cardenal replies with details of its horrors and argues the right to use violence in self-defense. Somoza destroyed the village of Solentiname in 1977. After this dictatorship (overthrown in 1979), this fishing village became involved in the civil war between the Sandinistas and the (US-backed) Contras (the pro-Somoza forces). Berrigan and Cardenal each support their views biblically and theologically. Cardenal accuses Berrigan of throwing idealist Christian practice at him from his safe distance in Washington, D.C. During the 1980s Cardenal joined other liberation theologians in Latin America in receiving a reprimand from Pope John Paul II for their teachings and practices of liberation theology.

The conversation over Luke 1:46–55 occurred in more peaceful times in the village in the 1980s, and is part of a four-volume collection of Bible studies in this base community. The selection from the Solentiname studies represents a decentering of the traditional location of biblical scholarship from the university, particularly in European and North American sites. Here the villagers (mostly illiterate fisherfolk) claim their own subjectivity as readers (exegetes and hermeneuts) of the biblical text. In their context Mary's proclamation about the downfall of the rich and the elevation of the poor makes her a Communist. What Edward Said (among others, including Derrida) calls "the politics of knowledge" is examined in the liberatory hermeneutics used by the members of the study Cardenal facilitated. For further examination of the larger context of liberatory (materialist) hermeneutics, see the "Ideological Criticism" chapter in *The Postmodern Bible*.

We came to the Song of Mary, the *Magnificat*, traditionally known by that name because it is the first word in the Latin. It is said that this passage of the Gospel terrified the Russian Czars, and Maurras was very right in talking about the "revolutionary germ" of the *Magnificat*.

The pregnant Mary had gone to visit her cousin Elizabeth, who also was pregnant. Elizabeth congratulated her because she would be the mother of the Messiah, and Mary broke out singing that song. It is a song to the poor. The people of Nicaragua have been very fond of reciting it. It is the favorite prayer of the poor, and superstitious *campesinos* often carry it as an amulet. In the time of old Somoza when the *campesinos* were required always to carry with them proof they had voted for him, the people jokingly called that document the *Magnificat*.

Now young ESPERANZA read this poem, and the women began to comment on it.

> My soul praises the Lord,
> my heart rejoices in God my Savior,
> because he has noticed his slave.

"She praises God because the Messiah is going to be born, and that's a great event for the people."

"She calls God 'Savior' because she knows that the Son that he has given her is going to bring liberation."

"She's full of joy. Us women must also be that way, because in our community the Messiah is born too, the liberator."

"She recognizes liberation.... We have to do the same thing. Liberation is from sin, that is, from selfishness, from injustice, from misery, from ignorance – from everything that's oppressive. That liberation is in our wombs too, it seems to me . . ."

The last speaker was ANDREA, a young married woman, and now ÓSCAR, her young husband, breaks in: "God is selfish because he wants us to be his slaves. He wants our submission. Just him. I don't see why Mary has to call herself a slave. We should be free! Why just him? That's selfishness."

ALEJANDRO, who is a bachelor: "We have to be slaves of God, not of men."

Ernesto Cardenal, "The Song of Mary (Luke 1:46–55)," from *The Gospel in Solentiname, Volume I*, translated by Donald D. Walsh (Maryknoll, NY: Orbis Books, 1990).

Another young man: "God is love. To be a slave of love is to be free because God doesn't make slaves. He's the only thing we should be slaves of, love. And then we don't make slaves of others."

ALEJANDRO'S MOTHER says: "To be a slave of God is to serve others. That slavery is liberation."

I said that it's true that this selfish God Óscar spoke about does exist. And it's a God invented by people. People have often invented a god in their own image and likeness – not the true God, but idols, and those religions are alienating, an opium of the people. But the God of the Bible does not teach religion, but rather he urges Moses to take Israel out of Egypt, where the Jews were working as slaves. He led them from colonialism to liberty. And later God ordered that among those people no one could hold another as a slave, because they had been freed by him and they belonged only to him, which means they were free.

And TERESITA, William's wife: "We have to keep in mind that at the time when Mary said she was a slave, slavery existed. It exists today too, but with a different name. Now the slaves are the proletariat or the *campesinos*. When she called herself a slave, Mary brought herself closer to the oppressed, I think. Today she could have called herself a proletarian or a *campesina* of Solentiname."

And WILLIAM: "But she says she's a slave of the Lord (who is the Liberator, who is the one who brought freedom from the Egyptian slavery). It's as if she said she was a slave of the liberation. Or as if she said that she was a proletarian or a revolutionary *campesina*."

Another of the girls: "She says she's poor, and she says that God took into account the 'poverty of his slave,' that is, that God chose her because she was poor. He didn't choose a queen or a lady of high society but a woman from the people. Yes, because God has preferred us poor people. Those are the 'great things' that God has done, as Mary says."

> And from now on all generations
>   will call me happy,
> for Mighty God has done
>   great things for me.
> His name is holy,
> and his love reaches his faithful ones
> from generation to generation.

One of the ladies: "She says that people will call her happy.... She feels happy because she is the mother of Jesus the Liberator, and because she also is a liberator like her son, because she understood her son and did not oppose his mission. She didn't oppose him, unlike other mothers of young people who are messiahs, liberators of their communities. That was her great merit, I say."

And another: "She says that God is holy, and that means 'just.' The just person who doesn't offend anybody, the one who doesn't commit any injustices. God is like this and we should be like him."

I said that was a perfect biblical definition of the holiness of God. And then I asked what a holy society would be.

"The one we are seeking," LAUREANO answered at once. He is a young man who talks of the Revolution or revolutionaries almost every time he comments on the Bible. After a brief pause he added: "The one that revolutionaries want to build, all the revolutionaries of the world."

He has shown the strength of his arm;
he conquers those with proud hearts.

Old TOMÁS, who can't read but who always talks with great wisdom: "They are the rich, because they think they are above us and they look down on us. Since they have the money.... And a poor person comes to their house and they won't even turn around to look at him. They don't have anything more than we do, except money. Only money and pride, that's all they have that we don't."

ÁNGEL says: "I don't believe that's true. There are humble rich people and there are proud poor people. If we weren't proud we wouldn't be divided, and us poor are divided."

LAUREANO: "We're divided because the rich divide us. Or because a poor person often wants to be like a rich one. He yearns to be rich, and then he's an exploiter in his heart, that is, the poor person has the mentality of the exploiter."

OLIVIA: "That's why Mary talks about people with proud hearts. It's not a matter of having money or not, but of having the mentality of an exploiter or not."

I said that nevertheless it cannot be denied that in general the rich person is a proud man, not the poor one.

And TOMÁS said: "Yes, because the poor person doesn't have anything. What has he got to be proud of? That's why I said that the rich are proud, because they have the money. But that's the only thing they have we don't have, money and the pride that goes with having money."

He pulls down the mighty from their
thrones and raises up the humble.
He fills the hungry with good things
and he leaves the rich with nothing.

One said: "The mighty is the same as the rich. The mighty are rich and the rich are mighty."

And another: "The same as proud, because the mighty and the rich are proud."

TERESITA: "Mary says that God raised up the humble. That's what he did to Mary."

And MARIÍTA: "And what he did to Jesus who was poor and to Mary, and to all the others who followed Jesus, who were poor."

I asked what they thought Herod would have said if he had known that a woman of the people had sung that God had pulled down the mighty and raised up the humble, filled the hungry with good things and left the rich with nothing.

NATALIA laughed and said: "He'd say she was crazy."

ROSITA: "That she was a communist."

LAUREANO: "The point isn't that they would just *say* the Virgin was a communist. She *was* a communist."

"And what would they say in Nicaragua if they heard what we're saying here in Solentiname?"

Several voices: "That we're communists."

Someone asked: "That part about filling the hungry with good things?"

A young man answered: "The hungry are going to eat."

And another: "The Revolution."

LAUREANO: "That is the Revolution. The rich person or the mighty is brought down and the poor person, the one who was down, is raised up."

Still another: "If God is against the mighty, then he has to be on the side of the poor."

ANDREA, Óscar's wife, asked: "That promise that the poor would have those good things, was it for then, for Mary's time, or would it happen in our time? I ask because I don't know."

One of the young people answered: "She spoke for the future, it seems to me, because we are just barely beginning to see the liberation she announces."

> *He helps the nation of Israel his servant,*
> *in remembrance of his love;*
> *as he had promised to our fathers,*
> *to Abraham, and to his descendants*
> *forever.*

ALEJANDRO: "That nation of Israel that she speaks about is the new people that Jesus formed, and we are this people."

WILLIAM: "It's the people who will be liberated, like before the other people were liberated from the dictatorship of Egypt, where they were treated like shit, changed into cheap hand labor. But the people can't be liberated by others. They must liberate themselves. God can show the way to the Promised Land, but the people themselves must begin the journey."

ÓSCAR asked: "Can you take riches from the rich by force? Christ didn't force the rich young man. He said to him: 'If you wish...'"

I thought for a while before answering. I said hesitantly: "You might let him go to another country..."

WILLIAM: "But not let him take his wealth with him."

FELIPE: "Yes, let him take it."

The last remark was from MARIÍTA: "Mary sang here about equality. A society with no social classes. Everyone alike."

Chapter 10

Canaanites, Cowboys, and Indians: Deliverance, Conquest, and Liberation Theology Today

Robert Allen Warrior 1963–

Introduction

Robert Allen Warrior, an Osage Indian, received his Ph.D. from the Union Theological Seminary in New York in 1992 and an M.A. in religion from the Yale University Divinity School in 1988. He is currently an Associate Professor in the Department of English at the University of Oklahoma, having previously taught at Cornell University and at Stanford University in the department of English. He has to date published over twenty articles whose topics range from liberation theology to the American Indian Movement (AIM), and is the author of *Tribal Secrets: Recovering American Indian Intellectual Traditions* (1995) and *Like a Hurricane: The Indian Movement from Alcatraz to Wounded Knee* (1996, with Paul Chaat Smith). His work in progress, *The People and the Word: The Emergence of Indigenous Theory*, is due for publication in 2001.

"A Native American Perspective: Canaanites, Cowboys, and Indians" (1989) is examined in some detail in *The Postmodern Bible* (284–6). In this essay, Warrior reads the Book of Exodus from the perspective of the Canaanites and discerns shared histories between the dispossessed and humiliated tribal peoples of biblical times and the indigenous peoples of the Americas today. He rejects any attempt to foster a liberation theology based on the deliverance story in Exodus for Native Americans, claiming that they can better identify with the Canaanites who were already living in the Promised Land. Warrior contextualizes the dangers inherent in promises of deliverance by discussing the New World treatment of American Indians who were included in God's formula for salvation only as subjects to be either converted or annihilated, saying the overlooked Canaanites of the Old Testament suffered the same fate. He urges both Jews and Christians to distinguish God the deliverer from God the conqueror, arguing that Conquest narratives are integral to America's 500-year imperial history. It is only after this point of recognition that Warrior believes discussion about Christian involvement in Native American affairs can viably occur. Underscoring this revisionist biblical reading is a warning that abuse and displacement are bound to recur when justified by dogmatic doctrinal promises of liberation at the expense of those recorded in the plan as ahistorical subjects whose destinies are unilaterally appropriated and arranged. Christian activists taking up the cause of Indians, therefore, need to be aware that their story of salvation is not the story of all involved. Ultimately, Warrior concludes that it might be better for Native Americans to listen to themselves and explore their own historical experiences rather than turning toward outsiders bearing promises of liberation and deliverance.

Warrior's hermeneutical rereading of the Bible offers an alternative to the dominant readings in which the Canaanites dissolve into historical unimportance. In so doing, he challenges the assumptions of liberation and salvation that helped inspire New World colonists, the Zionist reemergence, and apartheid rule in South Africa. The normative liberationist readings of the Conquest narratives, therefore, are highly different from the indigenous perspective Warrior offers, which exposes the contradictions and political aspirations inherent within the liberation exegesis. Situating these narratives in an ideological framework plays an important role in identifying how the indigene can be forgotten in liberationist romances and how privileged readings of texts obscure the totality of multiple experiences.

Native American theology of liberation has a nice ring to it. Politically active Christians in the US have been bandying about the idea of such a theology for several years now, encouraging Indians to develop it. There are theologies of liberation for African Americans, Hispanic Americans, women, Asian Americans, even Jews. Why not Native Americans? Christians recognize that American injustice on this continent began nearly five hundred years ago with the oppression of its indigenous people and that justice for American Indians is a fundamental part of broader social struggle. The churches' complicity in much of the violence perpetrated on Indians makes this realization even clearer. So, there are a lot of well-intentioned Christians looking for some way to include Native Americans in their political action.

For Native Americans involved in political struggle, the participation of church people is often an attractive proposition. Churches have financial, political, and institutional resources that many Indian activists would dearly love to have at their disposal. Since American Indians have a relatively small population base and few financial resources, assistance from churches can be of great help in gaining the attention of the public, the media, and the government.

It sounds like the perfect marriage – Christians with the desire to include Native Americans in their struggle for justice and Indian activists in need of resources and support from non-Indians. Well, speaking as the product of a marriage between an Indian and a white, I can tell you that it is not as easy as it sounds. The inclusion of Native Americans in Christian political praxis is difficult – even dangerous. Christians

Robert Allen Warrior, "Canaanites, Cowboys, and Indians: Deliverance, Conquest, and Liberation Theology Today," originally published in *Christianity and Crisis* 49 (12, 1989).

have a different way of going about the struggle for justice than most Native Americans: different models of leadership, different ways of making decisions, different ways of viewing the relationship between politics and religion. These differences have gone all but unnoticed in the history of church involvement in American Indian affairs. Liberals and conservatives alike have too often surveyed the conditions of Native Americans and decided to come to the rescue, always using *their* methods, *their* ideas, and *their* programs. The idea that Indians might know best how to address their own problems is seemingly lost on these well-meaning folks.

Still, the time does seem ripe to find a new way for Indians and Christians (and Native American Christians) to be partners in the struggle against injustice and economic and racial oppression. This is a new era for both the Church and for Native Americans. Christians are breaking away from their liberal moorings and looking for more effective means of social and political engagement. Indians, in this era of "self-determination," have verified for themselves and the government that they are the people best able to address Indian problems as long as they are given the necessary resources and if they can hold the US government accountable to the policy. But an enormous stumbling block immediately presents itself. Most of the liberation theologies that have emerged in the last twenty years are preoccupied with the Exodus story, using it as the fundamental model for liberation. I believe that the story of the Exodus is an inappropriate way for Native Americans to think about liberation.

No doubt, the story is one that has inspired many people in many contexts to struggle against injustice. Israel, in the Exile, then Diaspora, would remember the story and be reminded of God's faithfulness. Enslaved African Americans, given Bibles to read by their masters and mistresses, would begin at the beginning of the book and find in the pages of the Pentateuch a god who was obviously on their side, even if that god was the god of their oppressors. People in Latin American base communities read the story and have been inspired to struggle against injustice. The Exodus, with its picture of a god who takes the side of the oppressed and powerless, has been a beacon of hope for many in despair.

God the Conqueror

Yet, the liberationist picture of Yahweh is not complete. A delivered people is not a free people, nor is it a nation. People who have survived the nightmare of subjugation dream of escape. Once the victims have been delivered, they seek a new dream, a new goal, usually a place of safety away from the oppressors, a place that can be defended against future subjugation. Israel's new dream became the land of Canaan. And Yahweh was still with them: Yahweh promised to go before the people and give them Canaan, with its flowing milk and honey. The land, Yahweh decided, belonged to these former slaves from Egypt and Yahweh planned on giving it to them – using the same power used against the enslaving Egyptians to defeat the indigenous inhabitants of Canaan. Yahweh the deliverer became Yahweh the conqueror.

The obvious characters in the story for Native Americans to identify with are the Canaanites, the people who already lived in the Promised Land. As a member of the Osage Nation of American Indians who stands in solidarity with other tribal people around the world, I read the Exodus stories with Canaanite eyes. And, it is the Canaanite side of the story that has been overlooked by those seeking to articulate theologies of liberation. Especially ignored are those parts of the story that describe Yahweh's command to mercilessly annihilate the indigenous population.

To be sure, most scholars, of a variety of political and theological stripes, agree that the actual events of Israel's early history are much different than what was commanded in the narrative. The Canaanites were not systematically annihilated, nor were they completely driven from the land. In fact, they made up, to a large extent, the people of the new nation of Israel. Perhaps it was a process of gradual immigration of people from many places and religions who came together to form a new nation. Or maybe, as Norman Gottwald and others have argued, the peasants of Canaan revolted against their feudal masters, a revolt instigated and aided by a vanguard of escaped slaves from Egypt who believed in the liberating god, Yahweh. Whatever happened, scholars agree that the people of Canaan had a lot to do with it.

Nonetheless, scholarly agreement should not allow us to breathe a sigh of relief. For historical knowledge does not change the status of the indigenes in the *narrative* and the theology that grows out of it. The research of Old Testament scholars, however much it provides an answer to the historical question – the contribution of the indigenous people of Canaan to the formation and emergence of Israel as a nation – does not resolve the narrative problem. People who read the narratives read them as they are, not as scholars and experts would *like* them to be read and interpreted. History is no longer with us. The narrative remains.

Though the Exodus and Conquest stories are familiar to most readers, I want to highlight some sections that are commonly ignored. The covenant begins when Yahweh comes to Abram saying, "Know of a surety that your descendants will be sojourners in a land that is not theirs, and they will be slaves there, and they will be oppressed for four hundred years; but I will bring judgment on the nation they serve and they shall come out" (Gen. 15:13, 14). Then, Yahweh adds: "To your descendants I give this land, the land of the Kenites, the Kenizzites, the Kadmonites, the Hittites, the Perizzites, the Rephaim, the Amorites, the Canaanites, and the Jebusites" (15:18–21). The next important moment is the commissioning of Moses. Yahweh says to him, "I promise I will bring you out of the affliction of Egypt, to the land of the Canaanites, the Hittites, the Amorites, the Perizzites, the Hivites, and the Jebusites, a land flowing with milk and honey" (Exod. 3:17). The covenant, in other words, has two parts: deliverance and conquest.

After the people have escaped and are headed to the promised land, the covenant is made more complicated, but it still has two parts. If the delivered people remain faithful to Yahweh, they will be blessed in the land Yahweh will conquer for them (Exod. 20–23 and Deut. 7–9). The god who delivered Israel from slavery will lead the people into the land and keep them there as long as they live up to the terms of the covenant: "You shall not wrong a stranger or oppress him [*sic*], for you were strangers in the land of Egypt. You shall not afflict any widow or orphan. If you do afflict them, and they cry out to me, I will surely hear their cry; and my wrath will burn, and I will kill you with the sword, and your wives shall become widows and your children fatherless" (Exod. 22:21).

Whose Narrative?

Israel's reward for keeping Yahweh's commandments – for building a society where the evils done to them have no place – is the continuation of life in the land. But one of the most important of Yahweh's commands is the prohibition on social relations with Canaanites or participation in their religion. "I will deliver the inhabitants of the land into your hand, and you shall drive them out before you. You shall make no covenant with them or with their gods. They shall not dwell in your land, lest they make you sin against me; for if you serve their gods it will surely be a snare to you" (Exod. 23:31b–33).

In fact, the indigenes are to be destroyed:

> When the Lord your God brings you into the land which you are entering to take possession of it, and clears away many nations before you, the Hittites, the Girgashites, the Amorites, the Canaanites, the Perizzites, the Hivites, and the Jebusites, seven nations greater and mightier than yourselves, and when the Lord your God gives them over to you and you defeat them; then you must utterly destroy them; you shall make no covenant with them, and show no mercy to them. (Deut. 7:1, 2)

These words are spoken to the people of Israel as they are preparing to go into Canaan. The promises made to Abraham and Moses are ready to be fulfilled. All that remains is for the people to enter into the land and dispossess those who already live there.

Joshua gives an account of the conquest. After ten chapters of stories about Israel's successes and failures to obey Yahweh's commands, the writer states, "So Joshua defeated the whole land, the hill country and the Negeb and the lowland and the slopes, and all their kings, he left none remaining, but utterly destroyed all that breathed, as the Lord God of Israel commanded." In Judges, the writer disagrees with this account of what happened, but the Canaanites are held in no higher esteem. The angel of the Lord says, "I will not drive out [the indigenous people] before you; but they shall become adversaries to you, and their gods shall be a snare to you."

Thus, the narrative tells us that the Canaanites have status only as the people Yahweh removes from the land in order to bring the chosen people in. They are not to be trusted, nor are they to be allowed to enter into social relationships with the people of Israel. They are wicked, and their religion is to be avoided at all costs. The laws put forth regarding strangers and sojourners may have stopped the people of Yahweh from wanton oppression, but presumably only after the land was safely in the hands of Israel. The covenant of Yahweh depends on this.

The Exodus narrative is where discussion about Christian involvement in Native American activism must begin. It is these stories of deliverance and conquest that are ready to be picked up and believed by anyone wondering what to do about the people who already live in their promised land. They provide an example of what can happen when powerless people come to power. Historical scholarship may tell a different story; but even if the annihilation did not take place, the narratives tell what happened to those indigenous people who put their hope and faith in ideas and gods that were foreign to their culture. The Canaanites trusted in the god of outsiders and their story of oppression and exploitation was lost. Interreligious praxis became betrayal and the surviving narrative tells us nothing about it.

Confronting the conquest stories as a narrative rather than a historical problem is especially important given the tenor of contemporary theology and criticism. After two hundred years of preoccupation with historical questions, scholars and theologians across a broad spectrum of political and ideological positions have recognized the function of narrative in the development of religious communities. Along with the work of US scholars like Brevard Childs, Stanley Hauerwas, and George Lindbeck, the radical liberation theologies of Latin America are based on empowering believing communities to read scriptural narratives for themselves and make their reading central to theology and political action. The danger is that these communities will read the narratives, not the history behind them.

And, of course, the text itself will never be altered by interpretations of it, though its reception may be. It is part of the canon for both Jews and Christians. It is part of the heritage and thus the consciousness of people in the United States. Whatever dangers we identify in the text, the god represented there will remain as long as the text remains. These dangers only grow as the emphasis upon catechetical (Lindbeck), narrative (Hauerwas), canonical (Childs), and Bible-centered Christian base communities (Gutierrez) grows. The peasants of Solentiname bring a wisdom and experience previously unknown to Christian theology, but I do not see what mechanism guarantees that they – or any other people who seek to be shaped and moulded by reading the text – will differentiate between the liberating god and the god of conquest.

Is There a Spirit?

What is to be done? First, the Canaanites should be at the center of Christian theological reflection and political action. They are the last remaining ignored voice in the text, except perhaps for the land itself. The Conquest stories, with all their violence and injustice, must be taken seriously by those who believe in the god of the Old Testament. Commentaries and critical works rarely mention these texts. When they do, they express little concern for the status of the indigenes and their rights as human beings and as nations. The same blindness is evident in theologies that use the Exodus motif as their basis for political action. The leading into the land becomes just one more redemptive moment rather than a violation of innocent peoples' rights to land and self-determination.

Keeping the Canaanites at the center makes it more likely that those who read the Bible will read *all* of it, not just the part that inspires and justifies them. And should anyone be surprised by the brutality, the terror of these texts? It was, after all, a Jewish victim of the Holocaust, Walter Benjamin, who said, "There is no document of civilization which is not at the same time a document of barbarism." People whose theology involves the Bible need to take this insight seriously. It is those who know these texts who must speak the truth about what they contain. It is to those who believe in these texts that the barbarism belongs. It is those who act on the basis of these texts who must take responsibility for the terror and violence they can and have engendered.

Second, we need to be more aware of the way ideas such as those in the Conquest narratives have made their way into Americans' consciousness and ideology. And only when we understand this process can those of us who have suffered from it know how to fight back. Many Puritan preachers were fond of referring to Native Americans as Amelkites [*sic*] and Canaanites – in other words, people who, if they would not be converted, were worthy of annihilation. By examining such instances in theological and political writings, in sermons, and elsewhere, we can understand how America's self-image as a "chosen people" has provided a rhetoric to mystify domination.

Finally, we need to decide if we want to accept the model of leadership and social change presented by the entire Exodus story. Is it appropriate to the needs of indigenous people seeking justice and deliverance? If indeed the Canaanites were integral to Israel's early history, the Exodus narratives reflect a situation in which indigenous people put their hope in a god from outside, were liberated from their oppressors, and then saw their story of oppression revised out of the new nation's history of salvation. They were assimilated into another people's identity and the history of their ancestors came to be regarded as suspect and a danger to the safety of Israel. In short, they were betrayed.

Do Native Americans and other indigenous people dare trust the same god in their struggle for justice? I am not asking an easy question and I in no way mean that people who are both Native Americans and Christians cannot work toward justice in the context of their faith in Jesus Christ. Such people have a lot of theological reflection to do, however, to avoid the dangers I have pointed to in the Conquest narratives. Christians, whether Native American or not, if they are to be involved, must learn how to participate in the struggle without making their story the whole story. Otherwise the sins of the past will be visited upon us again.

No matter what we do, the Conquest narratives will remain. As long as people believe in the Yahweh of deliverance, the world will not be safe from Yahweh the conqueror. But perhaps, if they are true to their struggle, people will be able to achieve what Yahweh's chosen people in the past have not: a society of people delivered from oppression who are not so afraid of becoming victims again that they become oppressors themselves, a society where the original inhabitants can become something other than subjects to be converted to a better way of life or adversaries who provide cannon fodder for a nation's militaristic pride.

With what voice will we, the Canaanites of the world, say, "Let my people go and leave my people alone?" And, with what ears will followers of alien gods who have wooed us (Christians, Jews, Marxists, capitalists), listen to us? The indigenous people of this hemisphere have endured a subjugation now a hundred years longer than the sojourn of Israel in Egypt. Is there a god, a spirit, who will hear us and stand with us in the Amazon, Osage County, and Wounded Knee? Is there a god, a spirit, able to move among the pain and anger of the Nablus, Gaza, and Soweto of 1989? Perhaps. But we, the wretched of the earth, may be well advised this time not to listen to outsiders with their promises of liberation and deliverance. We will perhaps do better to look elsewhere for our vision of justice, peace, and political sanity – a vision through which we escape not only our oppressors, but our oppression as well. Maybe, for once, we will just have to listen to ourselves, leaving the gods of this continent's real strangers to do battle among themselves.

Chapter 11

Slave Ideology and Biblical Interpretation

Katie Geneva Cannon 1950–

Introduction

Katie Cannon is a womanist ethicist and Professor of Christian Ethics at Temple University. She has several "firsts": first African American woman to earn the Ph.D. from Union Theological Seminary in New York City; first African American woman ordained in the United Presbyterian Church in the USA. Cannon began her doctoral work in Hebrew Bible but switched to study Christian Ethics with Beverly Wildung Harrison. She works in womanist ethics and spirituality, drawing from the African American slave narratives and women's writing. She is the author of *Black Womanist Ethics* (1988), *Katie's Canon: Womanism and the Soul of the Black Community* (1996), and of articles such as "Interpretation for Liberation" in *Semeia* 47 (1989) and "Race, Sex, and Insanity: Transformative Eschatology in Hurston's Account of the Ruby McCollum Trial" (1999).

Cannon was also one of the first African American women theologians to draw on and appropriate Alice Walker's definition of "womanist" in *In Search of Our Mothers' Gardens: Womanist Prose* (1983). A womanist is "A black feminist or feminist of color" that Walker created from women's wisdom. Cannon appropriates it for black women's theology and ethics. *The Postmodern Bible* describes Cannon as among those feminists who offer "a compelling challenge to the hegemonic power of texts and their interpretation" (61). Womanist biblical interpretation and theology differs from traditional feminist methods by offering a hermeneutic of survival (PMB: 247–54) through which Cannon – along with Clarice Martin, Renita Weems, Jacqueline Grant, Delores Williams, Emily Townes, and other womanist scholars in religion – relies on the stories of her ancestors in formulating a womanist ethics. Cultural inheritance, historical narratives, preaching, the spirituals, and dialogical commitment with other feminists and womanists are central parts of the womanist agenda.

Our selection in this volume comes from her most recent book, *Katie's Canon*. Obviously, she is playing with the idea of canon, and the history of white, Western hegemonic biblical interpretation. But she is also offering insight into her name, and the genealogy from slavery from the family in North Carolina that owned the

Cannon mills. She reads the Bible from a position outside of white-dominated biblical scholarship. In fact, she traces the hard history of the use of the Bible to validate and support the enslavement of Africans. According to Cannon, three ideological myths legitimizing slavery took hold in United States Christianity. First "was the charge that Black people were not members of the human race." Black people were denied their humanity. Second "was a reconstruction of history and divine action in it," so that the "savages" of Africa were destined to be slaves because they were an inferior race needing conversion. The third myth "was the understanding that the law of God and the law of the land gave them an extraordinary right to deprive Black people of liberty and to offer Blacks for sale in the market like any other articles of merchandise." The argument was that the Bible supported slavery as divinely ordained. In particular, slave apologists used the story in Genesis 9:25–27 to develop several "Hamite theories"; that is, a theology that Noah's son Ham was the father of the Black race and that Noah cursed Ham and his descendants into eternal slavery. The "curse of Ham" became an important part of the apologists' ideology of oppression, even though in the biblical story only Ham's son Canaan is cursed. Cannon argues that the future requires us to be "life-affirming moral agents." The past informs anti-racist work.

Scholars of stature within mainline Christian denominations have produced immense literature on the Bible and slavery with very little unanimity. Some have written about the various types of antislavery arguments found in the Old and New Testaments. Others have engaged in rigorous historico-critical exegesis of selected Scriptures used to condone slavery. What is interesting in the analysis by liberationists is the direct correlation between apologetic selectivity and the exegetes' political-social commitments. Thus, my particular concern as a liberation ethicist is to unmask the hermeneutical distortions of White Christians, North and South, who lived quite comfortably with the institution of chattel slavery for the better part of 150 years. Slaveholders knew that, in order to keep racial slavery viable, in addition to legal, economic, and political mechanisms they needed religious legitimation within the White society.

Apostles of slavery kept their eyes on the economic benefits and power relations at all times. Beneath their rhetoric and logic, the question of using the Bible to justify the subordination of Black people was fraught with their desire to maintain their dominance, to guarantee their continued social control. If the powerbrokers of the antebellum society were to continue benefitting from the privileges and opportunities the political economy provided, then the slaveholding aristocrats must, as a basic precondition, maintain their domination over the ideological sectors of society: religion, culture, education, and media.[1] The control of material, physical production required the control of the means of mental, symbolic production as well.

The practice of slaveholding was, therefore, largely unquestioned. The majority of White Christians engaged in a passive acceptance of the givenness of the main feature of

Katie Geneva Cannon, "Slave Ideology and Biblical Interpretation," from *Katie's Canon: Womanism and the Soul of the Black Community* (New York: Continuum, 1996).

slavocracy. Any questioning of the system or identification of contradictions to social practices within Christianity was undermined by the substratum of values and perceptions justified theologically by biblical hermeneutics determined from above. The rank and file of White church membership accepted the prevailing racist ideology, identifying with the slaveholders and copying their rationales, rituals, and values. They regarded slave ideology and Christian life as inseparable; they were integral parts of the same system. The defense of one appeared to require the defense of the other.

Admittedly, there were a few antislavery women and men in the mainline churches prior to the aggressive abolitionist movement of the 1830s, but as a whole the White church evaded responsibility and surrendered its prerogatives to slavocracy. For most of the years that chattel slavery existed, the mainline Protestant churches never legislated against slavery, seldom disciplined slaveholders, and at most gently apologized for the "peculiar institution."

Drawing principally upon socio-ethical sources of the late eighteenth and early nineteenth centuries, I investigate three intellectual, hierarchical constructs that lie at the center of the Christian antebellum society. (1) At what point and under what conditions did Americans of African descent lose their status as members of the moral universe? (2) What are the ethical grounds that make the formula for "heathen conversion" intrinsically wrong? and (3) What are the hermeneutical distortions that shaped the slavocracy's polemical patterns of biblical propaganda?

The Mythology of Black Inferiority

The first ideological myth legitimizing the hermeneutical assumption of Christian slave apologists was the charge that Black people were not members of the human race. Most church governing boards, denominational missionary societies, local churches, and clergy held the position that human beings by nature were free and endowed with natural rights. Their basic concept of human relationships was equality of all people in the sight of God. No one was superior to another, none inferior. Black people had not forfeited their freedom nor relinquished their rights. This espoused oneness of humanity clashed directly with the perception that Black people must necessarily be possessed of low nature.[2]

To justify their enslavement, Black people had to be completely stripped of every privilege of humanity.[3] Their dignity and value as human beings born with natural rights had to be denied. Black Americans were divested so far as possible of all intellectual, cultural, and moral attributes. They had no socially recognized personhood. The institution of chattel slavery and its corollary, White supremacy and racial bigotry, excluded Black people from every normal human consideration. The humanity of Black people had to be denied, or the evil of the slave system would be evident.

In other words, hereditary slavery was irreconcilable with doctrines of inalienable rights.[4] So as not to contradict their avowed principles, legislatures enacted laws designating Black people as property and as less than human.[5] Black people were assigned a fixed place as an inferior species of humanity. The intellectual legacy of slavocracy was the development of certain White preconceptions about the irredeemable nature of Black women and Black men as "beings of an inferior order," a sub-par species between animal and human. One of the many characterizations proposed was that Black people were irremediably different from Whites, as much as swine from dogs, "they are Baboons on two legs gifted with speech."[6]

Central to the whole hermeneutical approach was a rationalized biblical doctrine positing the innate and permanent inferiority of Blacks in the metonymical curse of Ham.[7] The Ham story in Genesis 9:25–27 was not only used to legitimize slavery in general, but it was also used by proslavery, pro-White supremacists to justify the enslavement of Blacks in particular. Ham became widely identified as the progenitor of the Black race, and the story of the curse that Noah pronounced against Canaan, the son of his son Ham, was symbolically linked to the institution of racial slavery. In a book entitled *Bible Defense of Slavery* Josiah Priest took the position that the enslaving of Black people by the White race was a judicial act of God.

> The servitude of the race to Ham, to the latest era of mankind, is necessary to the veracity of God Himself, as by it is fulfilled one of the oldest of the decrees of the Scriptures, namely that of Noah, which placed the race as servants under other races.[8]

Christians caught in the obsessive duality of understanding Black people as property rather than as persons concurred with both faulty exegesis and social pressure that depicted people with black skin as demonic, unholy, infectious progenitors of sin, full of animality and matriarchal proclivities.

During the early part of the eighteenth century, state laws adopted the principle of *partus sequitur ventrem* – the child follows the condition of the mother regardless of the race of the father. Absolving all paternal responsibilities, this principle institutionalized and sanctioned sexual prerogatives of "stock breeding" with Black men and the rape of Black women by White men. What this means is that the Black woman's life was estimated in terms of money, property, and capital assets. She was a commodity to be bought and sold, traded for money, land, or other objects. Her monetary value was precisely calculated by her capacity to produce goods and services, combined with her capacity to reproduce "a herd of subhuman labor units."[9] Hence, the Black woman as the carrier of the hereditary legal status extended the status of slave to her children and her children's children, supposedly to the end of time. An entire race was condemned by the laws of a purportedly Christian people to perpetual, hereditary, unrequited servitude.[10]

The White antebellum church did not see the gross injustice of slavery. Outspoken supporters of slavery generally admitted that enslaved Blacks were mere property, a type of domesticated animal to serve as the White man's tool like any other beast of burden.[11] And as slaveholders, White Christian citizens must have the security that neither their property nor their privilege to own people as property would be taken from them. The church made every effort by admonition and legislation to see that the authority of slaveholders was not compromised. For them, the great truth written in law and God's decree was that subordination was the normal condition of African people and their descendants.[12]

Ideas and practices that favored equal rights of all people were classified as invalid and sinful because they conflicted with the divinely ordained structure that posited inequality between Whites and Blacks. The doctrine of biblical infallibility reinforced and was reinforced by the need for social legitimization of slavery. Thus, racial slavery was accepted as the necessary fulfillment of the curse of Ham. This had the effect of placing the truthfulness of God's self-revelation on the same level as Black slavery and White supremacy.[13] The institutional framework that required Black men, women, and children to be treated as chattel, as possessions rather than as human beings, was understood as being consistent with the spirit, genius, and precepts of the Christian faith.

The Mythologizing of Enslavement

The second ideological process that legitimated Christian slave apology was a reconstruction of history and divine action in it. It was claimed that God sent slavers to the wilds of Africa, a so-called depraved, savage, heathen world, in order to free Africans of ignorance, superstition, and corruption.[14] It is of more than passing significance that the proslavery writing portrayed Africa as the scene of unmitigated cannibalism, fetish worship, and licentiousness. Using gross caricatures, slave apologists mounted an ideological offensive in justification of the ravishing of the entire continent of Africa.[15] They argued that Africans by nature were framed and designed for subjection and obedience. Their preoccupation was that people designated by nature as "bestial savages" and "heathens" were destined by providence for slavery.[16]

Embracing false dogma of inherent African inferiority, beneficiaries of White supremacy described African character as the most depraved humanity imaginable. Africans were depicted as the epitome of heathenism, "wild, naked . . . man-eating savages," and "the great ethnological clown." White Christians had to be enabled to consider it an unspeakable privilege for Africans to be brought to the Americas as slaves.[17] Repeatedly, they claimed that slavery saved poor, degraded, and wretched African peoples from spiritual darkness.

North American Christians credited themselves with weaning Africans of savage barbarity.[18] Their joy in converting Africans was that they were giving to "heathens" elements of Christian civilization. Being enslaved in a Christian country was considered advantageous to Africans' physical, intellectual, and moral development. Slavery exposed Africans to Christianity, which made them better servants of God and better servants of men.

The popularity of "heathen conversion" was disclosed in the public reception of George Fitzhugh's *Cannibals All! or, Slaves without Masters*, who asserted Africans, like wild horses, had to be "caught, tamed and civilized."[19] Resting upon irrational antipathies, White Christians – prominent and common-bred alike – clearly distinguished their personhood from that of Africans. Many were convinced that African peoples were somehow irreparably inferior to and less worthy than Europeans. Fixated on the fetish of heathenism, they believed that the color of white skin proved sufficient justification to rob Africans by force and fraud of their liberty. The proper social hierarchy upon which the slave system rested – the putative inferiority of Africans and the alleged superiority of Europeans – had to remain safely intact.[20] Historian Winthrop Jordan declares:

> Heathenism was treated not so much as a specifically religious defect, but as one manifestation of a general refusal to measure up to proper standards, as a failure to be English or even civilized. . . . Being Christian was not merely a matter of subscribing to certain doctrines; it was a quality inherent in oneself and one's society. It was interconnected with all other attributes of normal and proper men.[21]

Entirely under the power of Whites, against whom they dared not complain and whom they dared not resist, enslaved Africans were denied the right to possess property, and deprived of the means of instruction and of every personal, social, civil, political, and religious mode of agency. If they asserted their personhood in defiance of oppressive authority, slaveholders punished them severely. Never before U.S. chattel slavery was a people so systematically deprived of their human rights and submerged in abject misery.[22]

The prevailing sentiment of American Christians – Presbyterians, Congregationalists, Roman Catholics, Quakers, Lutherans, Baptists, Methodists, and Anglicans – was that African peoples deserved imperial domination and needed social control.[23] Many churches preached a gospel that declared that Black people were indebted to White Christians and bound to spend their lives in the service of Whites; any provisions for food, clothes, shelter, medicine, or any other means of preservation were perceived not as legal requirement but as an act of Christian charity. This "Christian feature" of Anglo-American enslavement was interpreted as an incalculable blessing to African peoples. Africans and their descendants were much better off bound in slavery with their souls free than vice versa.

These and similar judgments bolstered the belief that Anglo-Saxons, Spaniards, Danes, Portuguese, and Dutch had a divine right to defend themselves against the intolerable suffering and absolute despotism that they imposed so heavily on others. As long as the image of Africans as "heathens" was irrevocable, then the church's attempt to Christianize via enslavement could continue indefinitely, the exploitation of Africa's natural resources could proceed without hindrance, and White Christians could persist in enjoying a position of moral superiority. Ruthlessly exploiting African people was justifiable Christian action.

Remythologizing Divine Will

The third ideological myth needed to legitimize the hermeneutical circle of Christian slave apologists was the understanding that the law of God and the law of the land gave them an extraordinary right to deprive Black people of liberty and to offer Blacks for sale in the market like any other articles of merchandise. For almost two centuries, slave apologists maintained that slavery was constantly spoken of in the Bible without any direct prohibition of it, no special law against it. And therefore, on the basis of the absence of condemnation, slavery could not be classified as sin. The presumptive evidence for many White Christians was that the absence of slaveholding from the catalogue of sins and disciplinary offenses in the Bible meant that slavery was not in violation of God's law.

Biblical scholars, along with distinguished scientists, lawyers, and politicians, produced a large quantity of exegetical data denying the arbitrariness of divinely ordained slavery.[24] The foundation of the scriptural case for slavery focused on an argument that neither Jesus of Nazareth, the apostles, nor the early church objected to the ownership of slaves. The fact that slavery was one of the cornerstones of the economic system of the Greco-Roman world was stressed and the conclusion reached that for the early church the only slavery that mattered was spiritual slavery to sin, to which all were bound. Physical slavery was spiritually meaningless under the all-embracing spiritualized hope of salvation. This line of reasoning was of central importance in reconciling the masses of White Christians to the existing social order. Instead of recognizing that slavery was ameliorated by early Christianity, slave apologists used their interpretative principle to characterize slavery as a sacred institution.[25]

To elicit White Christians' consent and approval of racial chattel slavery, which theologically contradicted a liberation reading of the Christian gospel, some of the leading antebellum churchmen – Robert Lewis Dabney, a Presbyterian theologian, Augustine Verot, the Catholic bishop of Georgia and East Florida, and John Leadley Dagg, Baptist layman who served as president of Mercer University – presented slavery as conforming to the divine principles revealed in the Bible. White clergy were trained to use the Bible to give credence to the legitimacy of racial chattelhood.[26] In other words, they adopted an implacable line of reasoning that made slavery an accepted fact of everyday life, not only in the entire Near East but also within normative biblical ethical teaching. Needless to say, the New Testament instruction that slaves should be obedient to their masters was interpreted as unqualified support for the modern institution of chattel slavery. The slave system was simply a part of the cosmos.[27]

Slave apologists such as George Fitzhugh, Thomas R. Dew, and William A. Smith used a hermeneutical principle that functioned to conceal and misrepresent the real conflicts of slave ideology and Christian life. Smith, the president of Randolph Macon College in Virginia, was quite candid:

> Slavery, *per se*, is right.... The great abstract principle of slavery is right, because it is a fundamental principle of the social state: and domestic slavery, as an *institution*, is fully justified by the condition and circumstances (essential and relative) of the African race in this country, and therefore equally right.[28]

Fitzhugh, a well-known essayist, and Dew, a prominent lawyer, concluded that since slavery was part of a natural order and hence in accord with the will of God, it could not be morally wrong.

Christian commentators, working largely to the advantage of wealthy aristocrats, used biblical and philosophical arguments to present slave-holders' interests and claims in the best possible light.[29] For example, scholars such as How, Ross, and Priest constructed "biblical facts" that permitted them to claim that the eradication of chattel slavery was inapplicable to Christian living. By using selective appeals to customary practices, they disseminated moral teachings to reinforce what counted as good Christian conduct. Clergy were condemned for preaching against slavery because abolition sermons were considered to be a part of a traitorous and diabolical scheme that would eventually lead to the denial of biblical authority, the unfolding of rationalism, deistic philanthropism, pantheism, atheism, socialism, or Jacobinism. Members of churches were warned against subscribing to antislavery books, pamphlets, and newspapers. The church condoned mob violence against anyone with abolitionist tendencies, which in turn, reassured that the existing social order would go unchallenged.

Having no desire to divorce themselves from the institution of slavery, church governing boards and agencies issued denominational pronouncements on behalf of the official platitudes of slave ideology. Denominational assemblies reinforced publicly their compliance with the assumed principle of human chattelhood. Black people were classified as moveable property, devoid of the minimum human rights that society conferred to others.

The vast majority of White clergy and laity alike appropriated this ideology to convince themselves that the human beings whom they violated or whose well-being they did not protect were unworthy of anything better. White Christians seemed to have been imbued with the permissive view that the enslavement of Black people was not too great a price to pay for a stable, viable labor system.[30] In a political economy built on labor-intensive agriculture, slave labor seemed wholly "natural." The security and prosperity of slavocracy evidently enabled White Christians, slaveholders and non-slaveholders alike, to feel secure with the fruits of the system.

Through a close analysis of slave ideology and biblical interpretation we can discern the many ways that chattel slavery maintained itself even after it was no longer the most economically profitable method of utilizing natural and technological resources. The majority of White Christians had learned well not to accept the equal coexistence of Whites and Blacks in the same society.[31] They believed that giving Black people civil parity with the White population would threaten the ease and luxury of White happiness, and perhaps dissolve the Union. For the sake of the public welfare, people with ancestors born in Europe, and not in Africa, needed to be relieved of degrading menial labor so that they could be free to pursue the highest cultural attainment. Slavery, sanctioned not just by civil law but by natural law as well, was considered the best foundation for a strong economy and for a superior society.

Concluding Ethical Reflections

I have sketched three mythologizing processes that served as the foundational under-pinnings for slave ideology in relation to White Christian life. I believe that it is important for us to trace the origin and expansion of these myths because the same general schemes of oppression and patterns of enslavement remain prevalent today and because the biblical hermeneutics of oppressive praxis is far from being dead among contemporary exegetes. As life-affirming moral agents we have a responsibility to study the ideological hegemony of the past so that we do not remain doomed to the recurring cyclical patterns of hermeneutical distortions in the present – i.e., violence against women, condemnation of homosexuality, spiritualizing Scripture to justify capitalism.

My analysis shows that slave apologists worked within an interpretative framework that represented the whole transcript of racial chattel slavery as ordained by God. They systematically blocked and refuted any discourse that presented contrary viewpoints. Using theoethical language, concepts, and categories White superordinates pressed their claims of the supposedly inherent inferiority of Black people by appealing to the normative ethical system expressed by the dominant slaveholders. The political and economic context incorporated a structure of discourse wherein the Bible was authoritatively interpreted to support the existing patterns of exploitation of Black people.

Antebellum Christians, abiding by the developing racial and cultural conceptions, resisted any threat to slavocracy or any challenge to the peace and permanency of the order of their own denomination. They conformed their ethics to the boundaries of slave management. It became their Christian duty to rule over African people who had been stricken from the human race and reclassified as a subhuman species.

Not surprisingly, denominations sprang officially to the defense of slave trading, slaveholding, and the Christianization of Africans with ingenious economic arguments. Wealthy slaveholders transmuted a portion of their disproportionate economic profit into modes of social control by public gestures that passed as generous voluntary acts of charity. They used revenue from slave labor to pay pastors, maintain church properties, support seminaries, and sustain overseas missionaries. Seduced by privilege and profit, White Christians of all economic strata were made, in effect, coconspirators in the victimization of Black people. In other words, slave apologists were successful in convincing at least five generations of White citizens that slavery, an essential and constitutionally protected institution, was consistent with the impulse of Christian charity.

Notes

1 Antonio Gramsci, *Selections from the Prison Notebooks*, ed. and trans. Quinten Hoare and Geoffrey Nowell Smith (London: Lawrence & Wishart, 1971), 5–23; Cornel West, *Prophesy Deliverance! An Afro-American Revolutionary Christianity* (Philadelphia: Westminster, 1982), 9–127.

2 Winthrop D. Jordan, *White over Black: American Attitudes toward the Negro, 1550–1812* (Baltimore: Penguin Books, 1969), 3–98; Thomas F. Gossett, *Race: The History of an Idea in America* (Dallas: Southern Methodist University Press, 1963), 3–31.

3 H. Shelton Smith, *In His Image, But . . . : Racism in Southern Religion, 1780–1910* (Durham, NC: Duke University Press, 1972), 23–207.

4 E. S. Morgan, "Slavery and Freedom: The American Paradox," *Journal of American History* 59 (1972): 5–29; Carl N. Degler, "Slavery and the Genesis of American Race Prejudice," *Comparative Studies in Society and History* 2 (1959): 49–66.

5 Angela Y. Davis, *Women, Race and Class* (New York: Random House, 1981), 391–421.

6 J. William Harris, *Plain Folk and Gentry in a Slave Society* (Middletown, CT: Wesleyan University Press, 1985), 67.

7 Joseph R. Washington, Jr., *Anti-Blackness in English Religion, 1500–1800* (New York: Edwin Mellen, 1984), 231–320.

204   *Katie Geneva Cannon*

8   Josiah Priest, *Bible Defense of Slavery* (Glasgow, KY: W. S. Brown, 1851), 393.

9   Davis, *Women, Race and Class*, 3–29.

10   Oliver C. Cox, *Caste, Class, and Race: A Study in Social Dynamics* (New York: Doubleday, 1984), 353–91; Jordan, *White over Black*, 321–5.

11   Frederick A. Ross, *Slavery Ordained of God* (Philadelphia: J. B. Lippincott, 1857), 11–68.

12   William Sumner Jenkins, *Pro-Slavery Thought in the Old South* (Chapel Hill: University of North Carolina Press, 1935), 90–2.

13   L. R. Bradley, "The Curse of Canaan and the American Negro (Gen. 9:25–27)," *Concordia Theological Monthly* 42 (1971): 100–5.

14   Frederick Perry Noble, *The Redemption of Africa* (Chicago: Fleming H. Revell, 1899).

15   Walter Rodney, *How Europe Underdeveloped Africa* (London: Bogie l'Ouverture, 1972), 730.

16   Lester B. Scherer, *Slavery and the Churches in Early America 1619–1819* (Grand Rapids, MI: Wm. B. Eerdmans, 1975), 29–81.

17   Davis, *Women, Race and Class*, 165–96.

18   Washington, *Anti-Blackness in English Religion*, 103–39.

19   George Fitzhugh, *Cannibals All! or, Slaves without Masters*, ed. C. Van Woodward (Cambridge: Belknap Press of Harvard University, 1857, 1960).

20   Washington, *Anti-Blackness in English Religion*, 1–35.

21   *White over Black*, 24.

22   Orlando Patterson, *Slavery and Social Death: A Comparative Study* (Cambridge: Harvard University Press, 1982), 1–14.

23   C. Eric Lincoln, *Race, Religion and the Continuing American Dilemma* (New York: Hill and Wang, 1984), 23–31.

24   Samuel Blanchard How, *Slaveholding Not Sinful, the Punishment of Man's Sin, Its Remedy, the Gospel of Jesus Christ* (New Brunswick, NJ: J. Terhune's Press, 1856), 63–133.

25   Thomas Virgil Peterson, *Ham and Japheth: The Mythic World of Whites in the Antebellum South* (Metuchen, NJ: Scarecrow Press, 1978), 91–121.

26   Ibid., 12–26, 38–84.

27   Adam Gurowski, *Slavery in History* (New York: A. B. Burdick, 1860), 165–71.

28   Quoted in William A. Smith, *Lectures on the Philosophy and Practice of Slavery, as Exhibited in the Institution of Domestic Slavery in the United States: With the Duties of Masters and Slaves* (Nashville: Stevenson & Evans, 1856), 25.

29   Peterson, *Ham and Japheth*, 17–34.

30   Alfred Conrad and John Meyer, "The Economics of Slavery in the Antebellum South," *Journal of Political Economy* 66 (1958): 95–130, 442–34; Harold Woodman, "The Profitability of Slavery: A Historical Perennial," *Journal of Southern History* 29 (1963): 303–25.

31   Iveson L. Brookes, *A Defense of the South against the Reproaches and Incroachments of the North: in Which Slavery Is Shown to Be an Institution of God Intended to Form the Basis of the Best Social State and the Only Safeguard to the Permanence of a Republican Government* (Hamburg, SC: Republican Office, 1850), 45.

Chapter 12

Ecce Homo, Ain't (Ar'n't) I a Woman, and Inappropriate/d Others: The Human in a Post-Humanist Landscape

Donna J. Haraway 1944–

Introduction

Donna J. Haraway, a cultural theorist and historian of science, received her doctorate in biology from Yale University. She is Professor in the History of Consciousness Board at the University of California, Santa Cruz, where she is also involved with the Women's Studies Program. Her major works include *Crystals, Fabrics, and Fields: Metaphors of Organicism in Twentieth-Century Developmental Biology* (1976); *Primate Visions: Gender, Race, and Nature in the World of Modern Science* (1990); *Simians, Cyborgs, and Women: The Reinvention of Nature* (1991); "The Promise of Monsters: Reproductive Politics for Inappropriate/d Others" (1992); "Universal Donors in a Vampire Culture: It's All in the Family: Biological Kinship Categories in the Twentieth Century" (1995); *Modest_Witness @Second_Millenium: FemaleMan_Meets_ OncoMouse: Feminism and Technoscience* (1996); and *How Like a Leaf: An Interview with Thyrza Nichols Goodeve* (1999).

Haraway's work interrogates such notions as gender, nature, science, and culture, combining the techniques of literary criticism, history of science studies, and anthropology to inform her unique perspective, which suggests that knowledge is culturally constructed, or "situated." Haraway argues that, within this realm of these "situated knowledges," feminist perspectives should be likened to the Native American Trickster image. Such a move introduces the possibility of playfulness to the relations people have with received history. This playful attitude toward history encourages us to consider the past not as a static set of facts, but as a dynamic field which can never be completely or accurately reimagined. Thus, while the "true" world remains largely unknowable, the very mutability of history can encourage us to continually recreate gender relations in ever more equitable ways. While Haraway's work is often not concerned primarily with biblical texts, "Ecce Homo, Ain't (Ar'n't) I a

Woman, and Inappropriate/d Others: The Human in a Post-Humanist Landscape," as one of only a few essays which specifically address the Bible in a move to re-historicize the past as presented in the Bible and to question many of the foundational assumptions of Western cultures, is consistent with her work as a whole.

In this 1992 essay, Haraway considers the figure of Jesus as represented in the Bible and compares this image to that of Sojourner Truth, an illiterate ex-slave whose "Ain't I a Woman" speech stands as a seminal work in the history of both civil and women's rights. For Haraway, both exist as "Western trickster figures in a rich, dangerous, old, and constantly renewed tradition of Judeo-Christian humanism." These figures are tricksters due to the fact that they have been represented not as immutable or unchanging entities, but as characters who have been characterized in multiple ways through various translations and differing accounts. Haraway argues that her comparison of the sacred and the secular illustrates that "nobody is self-made, least of all man," a condition which "is the spiritual and political meaning of poststructuralism and postmodernism for me." Ultimately, the figures of Jesus and Truth both serve to illustrate one of Haraway's main contentions which runs throughout all of her work, that history is never static. Instead, the past can take many shapes and the figures which populate our histories need to be thought of as highly mutable and always open to new interpretations.

I want to focus on the discourses of suffering and dismemberment. I want to stay with the disarticulated bodies of history as figures of possible connection and accountability. Feminist theory proceeds by figuration at just those moments when its own historical narratives are in crisis. Historical narratives are in crisis now, across the political spectrum, around the world. These are the moments when something powerful – and dangerous – is happening. Figuration is about resetting the stage for possible pasts and futures. Figuration is the mode of theory when the more "normal" rhetorics of systematic critical analysis seem only to repeat and sustain our entrapment in the stories of the established disorders. Humanity is a modernist figure; and this humanity has a generic face, a universal shape. Humanity's face has been the face of man. Feminist humanity must have another shape, other gestures; but, I believe, we must have feminist figures of humanity. They cannot be man or woman; they cannot be the human as historical narrative has staged that generic universal. Feminist figures cannot, finally, have a name; they cannot be native. Feminist humanity must, somehow, both resist representation, resist literal figuration, and still erupt in powerful new tropes, new figures of speech, new turns of historical possibility. For this process, at the inflection point of crisis, where all the tropes turn again, we need ecstatic speakers. This essay tells a history of such a speaker who might figure the self-contradictory and necessary condition of a nongeneric humanity.

Donna Haraway, "Ecce Homo, Ain't (Ar'n't) I a Woman, and Inappropriate/d Others: The Human in a Post-Humanist Landscape," from *Feminists Theorize the Political*, edited by Judith Butler and Joan W. Scott (New York and London: Routledge, 1992).

I want here to set aside the Enlightenment figures of coherent and masterful subjectivity, the bearers of rights, holders of property in the self, legitimate sons with access to language and the power to represent, subjects endowed with inner coherence and rational clarity, the masters of theory, founders of states, and fathers of families, bombs, and scientific theories – in short, Man as we have come to know and love him in the death-of-the-subject critiques. Instead, let us attend to another crucial strand of Western humanism thrown into crisis in the late twentieth century. My focus is the figure of a broken and suffering humanity, signifying – in ambiguity, contradiction, stolen symbolism, and unending chains of noninnocent translation – a possible hope. But also signifying an unending series of mimetic and counterfeit events implicated in the great genocides and holocausts of ancient and modern history. But, it is the very nonoriginality, mimesis, mockery, and brokenness that draw me to this figure and its mutants. This essay is the beginning of a project on figurations that have appeared in an array of internationalist, scientific, and feminist texts, which I wish to examine for their contrasting modernist, postmodernist, and amodernist ways of constructing "the human" after World War II. Here, I begin by reading Jesus and Sojourner Truth as Western trickster figures in a rich, dangerous, old, and constantly renewed tradition of Judeo-Christian humanism and end by asking how recent intercultural and multicultural feminist theory constructs possible postcolonial, nongeneric, and irredeemably specific figures of critical subjectivity, consciousness, and humanity – not in the sacred image of the same, but in the self-critical practice of "difference," of the I and we that is/are never identical to itself, and so has hope of connection to others.

The larger project that this essay initiates will stage an historical conversation among three groups of powerfully universalizing texts:

1 two versions of United Nations discourses on human rights (the UNESCO statements on race in 1950 and 1951 and the documents and events of the UN Decade for Women from 1975–85);

2 recent modernist physical-anthropological reconstructions of the powerful fiction of science, species man, and its science-fiction variant, the female man (pace Joanna Russ) (i.e., Man the Hunter of the 1950s and 1960s and Woman the Gatherer of the 1970s and 1980s); and

3 the transnational, multi-billion-dollar, highly automated, postmodernist apparatus – a language technology, literally – for the production of what will count as "the human" (i.e., the Human Genome Project, with all its stunning power to recuperate, out of the endless variations of code fragments, the singular, the sacred image of the same, the one true man, the standard – copyrighted, catalogued, and banked).

The whole tale might fit together at least as well as the plot of Enlightenment humanism ever did, but I hope it will fit differently, negatively, if you will. I suggest that the only route to a nongeneric humanity, for whom specificity – but emphatically not originality – is the key to connection, is through radical nominalism. We must take names and essences seriously enough to adopt such an ascetic stance about who we have been and might yet be. My stakes are high; I think "we" – that crucial material and rhetorical construction of politics and of history – need something called humanity. It is that kind of thing which Gayatri Spivak called "that which we cannot not want." We also know now, from our perspectives in the ripped-open belly of the monster called history, that we cannot name and possess this thing which we cannot not desire. Humanity, whole and part, is not autochthonous. Nobody is self-made, least of all man. That is the spiritual and political meaning of poststructuralism and postmodernism for me. "We," in these very particular discursive worlds, have no routes to connection and to noncosmic, nongeneric, nonoriginal wholeness than through the radical dis-membering and dis-placing of our names and our bodies. So, how can humanity have a figure outside the narratives of humanism; what language would such a figure speak?

Ecce Homo! The Suffering Servant as a Figure of Humanity[1]

Isaiah 52.13–14:
Behold, my servant shall prosper, he shall be exalted and lifted up, and shall be very high. As many were astonished at him – his appearance was so marred, beyond human sem-blance, and his form beyond that of the sons of men – so shall he startle many nations.

Isaiah 53.2–4:
He had no form or comeliness that we should look at him, and no beauty that we should desire him. He was despised and rejected by men; a man of sorrows, and acquainted with grief, and as one from whom men hide their faces he was despised, and we esteemed him not. Surely he has borne our griefs and carried our sorrows; yet we esteemed him stricken, smitten by God, and afflicted. But he was wounded for our transgressions, he was bruised for our iniquities; upon him was the chastisement that made us whole, and with his stripes we are healed.

Isaiah 54.1:
For the children of the desolate one will be more than the children of her that is married, says the Lord. ("Is this a threat or a promise?" ask both women, looking tentatively at each other after a long separation.)

John 18:37–38:
Pilate said to him, "So, you are a king?" Jesus answered, "You say that I am a king. For this I was born, and for this I have come into the world, to bear witness to the truth. Everyone who is of the truth hears my voice." Pilate said to him, "What is truth?"

John 19:1–6:
Then Pilate took Jesus and scourged him. And the soldiers plaited a crown of thorns, and put it on his head, and arrayed him in a purple robe; they came up to him, saying, "Hail, King of the Jews!" and struck him with their hands. Pilate went out again, and said to them, "Behold I am bringing him out to you, that you may know I find no crime in him." So Jesus came out, wearing the crown of thorns and the purple robe. Pilate said to them, "Behold the man!" When the chief priests and officers saw him, they cried out, "Crucify him, crucify him!" Pilate said to them, "Take him yourselves and crucify him, for I find no crime in him."

John staged the trial before Pilate in terms of the suffering-servant passages from Isaiah. The events of the trial of Jesus in this nonsynoptic gospel probably are not historical, but theatrical in the strict sense: from the start, they *stage* salvation history, which then became the model for world history in the secular heresies of the centuries of European colonialism with its civilizing missions and genocidal discourses on common humanity. Pilate probably spoke publicly in Greek or Latin, those languages that became the standard of "universal" European scholarly humanism, and his words were translated by his officials into Aramaic, the language of the inhabitants of Palestine. Hebrew was already largely a ceremonial language, not even understood by most Jews in the synagogue. The earliest texts for John's gospel that we have are in Greek, the likely language of its composition (the Koiné, the common Greek spoken and understood throughout the Roman Empire in the early centuries of the Christian era). We don't have the first versions, if there ever were such things; we have endless, gap-filled, and overlaid transcriptions and translations that have grounded the vast apparatus of biblical textual and linguistic scholarship – that cornerstone of modern scholarly humanism, hermeneutics, and semiology and of the human sciences generally, most certainly including anthropology and ethnography. We are, indeed, peoples of the Book, engaged in a Derridean writing and reading practice from the first cries of prophecy and codifications of salvation history.

From the start we are in the midst of multiple translations and stagings of a figure of suffering humanity that was not contained within the cultures of the origin of the stories. The Christian narratives of the Son of Man circulated rapidly around the Mediterranean in the first century of the present era. The Jewish versions of the suffering servant inform some of the most powerful ethical cautions in Faustian trans-national technoscience worlds. The presentation to the people of the Son of Man as a suffering servant, arrayed mockingly and mimetically in his true dress as a king and salvation figure, became a powerful image for Christian humanists. The suffering servant figure has been fundamental in twentieth-century liberation theology and Christian Marxism. The guises of the suffering servant never cease. Even in Isaiah, he is clothed in the ambiguities of prophecy. His most important counterfeit historically was Jesus himself, as John appropriated Isaiah into a theater of salvation history that would accuse the Jews of demanding the death of their king and savior in the root narrative of Christian anti-Semitism. The "Ecce homo!" was standardized in the Latin vulgate after many passages through the languages and transcriptions and codifications of the gospels. Jesus appears as a mime in many layers; crowned with thorns and in a purple cloak, he is in the mock disguise of a king before his wrongful execution as a criminal. As a criminal, he is counterfeit for a scapegoat, indeed, *the* scapegoat of salvation history. Already, as a carpenter he was in disguise.

This figure of the Incarnation can never be other than a trickster, a check on the arrogances of a reason that would uncover all disguises and force correct vision of a recalcitrant nature in her most secret places. The suffering servant is a check on man; the servant is the figure associated with the promise that the desolate woman will have more children than the wife, the figure that upsets the clarity of the metaphysics of light, which John the Evangelist too was so enamored of. A mother's son, without a father, yet the Son of Man claiming *the* Father, Jesus is a potential worm in the Oedipal psychoanalytics of representation; he threatens to spoil the story, despite or because of his odd sonship and odder kingship, because of his disguises and form-changing habits.

Jesus makes of man a most promising mockery, but a mockery that cannot evade the terrible story of the broken body. The story has constantly to be preserved from heresy, to be kept forcibly in the patriarchal tradition of Christian civilization, to be kept from too much attention to the economies of mimicry and the calamities of suffering.

Jesus came to figure for Christians the union of humanity and divinity in a universal salvation narrative. But, the figure is complex and ambiguous from the start, enmeshed in translation, staging, miming, disguises, and evasions. "Ecce homo!" can, indeed must, be read ironically by "post-Christians" and other post-humanists as "Behold the man, the figure of humanity (Latin), the sign of the same (the Greek tones of homo-), indeed, the Sacred Image of the Same, but also the original mime, the actor of a history that mocks especially the recurrent tales that insist that 'man makes himself' in the deathly onanistic nightdream of coherent wholeness and correct vision."

But, "Ain't I a Woman?"

Well, children, whar dar is so much racket der must be something out o'kilter. I tink dat 'twixt de niggers of de Souf and de women at de Norf all a talkin 'bout rights, de white men will be in a fix pretty soon. But what's all dis here talkin' 'bout? Dat man ober dar say dat women needs to be helped into carriages, and lifted ober ditches, and to have de best places – and ain't I a woman? Look at me! Look at my arm! . . . I have plowed and planted and gathered into barns, and no man could head me – and ain't I a woman? I could work as much as any man (when I could get it), and bear de lash as well – and ain't I a woman? I have borne five children and I seen 'em mos all sold off into slavery, and when I cried with a mother's grief, none but Jesus hear – and ain't I a woman?[2]

Sojourner Truth is perhaps less far from Isaiah's spine-tingling prophecy than was Jesus. How might a modern John, or Johanna, stage her claim to be – as a black woman, mother, and former slave – the Son of Man, the fulfillment of the promise to unite the whole people under a common sign? What kind of sign is Sojourner Truth – forcibly transported, without a home, without a proper name, unincorporated in the discourses of (white) womanhood, raped by her owner, forcibly mated with another slave, robbed of her children, and doubted even in the anatomy of her body? A powerful speaker for feminism and abolitionism, Sojourner Truth's famous lines from her 1851 speech in Akron, Ohio, evoke the themes of the suffering servant in order to claim the status of humanity for the shockingly inappropriate/d figure[3] of New World black womanhood, the bearer of the promise of humanity for womanhood in general, and indeed, the bearer of the promise of humanity also for men. Called by a religious vision, the woman received her final names directly from her God when she left her home in New York City in 1843 for the road to preach her own unique gospel. Born a slave around 1797 in Ulster County, New York, her Dutch master named her Isabella Baumfree. "When I left the house of bondage I left everything behind. I wa'n't goin'to keep nothin' of Egypt on me, an' so I went to the Lord an' asked him to give me a new name."[4] And Sojourner Truth emerged from her second birth a prophet and a scourge.

Sojourner Truth showed up repeatedly at women's suffrage and abolitionist meetings over the last half of the nineteenth century. She delivered her most famous speech at the women's rights convention in Ohio in 1851 in answer to white male antisuffrage provocateurs who threatened to disrupt the meeting. In another exchange, she took on the problem of the gender of Jesus – whose manhood had been used by a heckler, a clergyman, to argue against women's rights. Sojourner Truth noted succinctly that man had nothing to do with Jesus; he came from God and a woman. Pilate was not this vagrant preacher's unwilling and evasive judge; but another man authorized by the hegemonic powers of his civilization stood in for him. This free white man acted far more assertively than had the colonial bureaucrat of the Roman Empire, whose wife's dreams had troubled him about his queer prisoner.[5] Pilate's ready surrogate, an irate white male physician, spoke out in protest of her speaking, demanding that she prove she was a woman by showing her breasts to the *women* in the audience. Difference (understood as the divisive marks of authenticity) was reduced to anatomy;[6] but even more to the point, the doctor's demand articulated the racist/sexist logic that made the very flesh of the black person in the New World indecipherable, doubtful, out of place, confounding – ungrammatical.[7] Remember that Trinh Minh-ha, from a different diaspora over a hundred years later, wrote, "Perhaps, for those of us who have never known what life in a vernacular culture is/was and are unable to imagine what it can be/could have been, gender simply does not exist otherwise than grammatically in language."[8] Truth's speech was out of place, dubious doubly; she was female and black; no, that's wrong – she was a black female, a black woman, not a coherent substance with two or more attributes, but an oxymoronic singularity who stood for an entire excluded and dangerously promising humanity. The language of Sojourner Truth's body was as electrifying as the language of her speech. And both were enmeshed in cascading questions about origins, authenticity, and generality or universality. This Truth is a figure of nonoriginality, but s/he is not Derridean. S/he is Trinhian, or may be Wittigian, and the difference matters.[9]

When I began to sketch the outlines of this essay, I looked for versions of the story of Sojourner Truth, and I found them written and rewritten in a long list of nineteenth-century and contemporary feminist texts.[10] Her famous speech, transcribed by a white abolitionist – *Ain't I a Woman?* – adorns posters in women's studies offices and women's centers across the United States. These lines seem to stand for something that unifies "women," but what exactly, especially in view of feminism's excavation of the terrible edifice of "woman" in Western patriarchal language and systems of representation – the one who can never be a subject, who is plot space, matrix, ground, screen for the act of man? Why does her *question* have more power for feminist theory 150 years later than any number of affirmative and declarative sentences? What is it about this figure, whose hard name signifies someone who could never be at home, for whom truth was displacement from home, that compels retelling and rehearing her story? What kind of history might Sojourner Truth inhabit?

For me, one answer to that question lies in Sojourner Truth's power to figure a collective humanity without constructing the cosmic closure of the unmarked category. Quite the opposite, her body, names, and speech – their forms, contents, and articulations – may be read to hold promise for a never-settled universal, a common language that makes compelling claims on each of us collectively and personally, precisely through their radical specificity, in other words, through the displacements and resistances to unmarked identity precisely as the means to claiming the status of "the human." The essential Truth would not settle down; that *was* her specificity. S/he was not everyman; s/he was inappropriate/d. This is a "postmodern" reading from some points of view, and it is surely not the only possible reading of her story. But, it is one that I hope to convince the reader is at the heart of the inter- and multicultural feminist theory in our time. In Teresa de Lauretis's terms, this reading is not so much postmodern or poststructuralist, as it is specifically enabled by feminist theory:

> That, I will argue, is precisely where the particular discursive and epistemological character of feminist theory resides: its being at once inside its own social and discursive determinations, and yet also outside and excessive to them. This recognition marks a further moment in feminist theory, its current stage of reconceptualization and elaborations of new terms; a reconceptualization of the subject as shifting and multiply organized across variable axes of difference; a rethinking of the relations between forms of oppression and modes of resistance and agency, and between practices of writing and modes of formal understanding – of doing theory; an emerging redefinition of marginality as location, of identity as disidentification. . . . I will use the term feminist theory, like the term consciousness or subject, in the singular as referring to a process of understanding that is premised on the historical specificity and the simultaneous, if often contradictory, presence of those differences in each of its instances and practices. . . .[11]

Let us look at the mechanisms of Sojourner Truth's exclusions from the spaces of unmarked universality (i.e., exclusion from "the human") in modern white patriarchal discourse in order to see better how she seized her body and speech to turn "difference" into an organon for placing the painful realities and practices of de-construction, disidentification, and dis-memberment in the service of a newly articulated humanity. Access to this humanity will be predicated on a subject-making discipline hinted at by Trinh:

> The difficulties appear perhaps less insurmountable only as I/i succeed in making a distinction between difference reduced to identity-authenticity and difference understood also as critical difference from myself. . . . Difference in such an insituable context is *that which undermines the very idea of identity*, deferring to infinity the layers whose totality forms "I." . . . If feminism is set forth as a demystifying force, then it will have to question thoroughly the belief in its own identity.[12]

Hazel Carby clarified how in the New World, and specifically in the United States, black women were not constituted as "woman," as white women were.[13] Instead, black women were constituted simultaneously racially and sexually – as marked female (animal, sexualized, and without rights), but not as woman (human, potential wife, conduit for the name of the father) – in a specific institution, slavery, that excluded them from "culture" defined as the circulation of signs through the system of marriage. If kinship vested men with rights in women that they did not have in themselves, slavery abolished kinship for one group in a legal discourse that produced whole groups of people as alienable property.[14] MacKinnon defined woman as an imaginary figure, the object of another's desire, made real.[15] The "imaginary" figures made real in slave discourse were objects in another sense that made them different from either the Marxist figure of the alienated laborer or the "unmodified" feminist figure of the object of desire. Free women in U.S. white patriarchy were exchanged in a system that oppressed them, but white women *inherited* black women and men. As Hurtado noted, in the nineteenth century prominent white feminists were *married* to white men, while black feminists were *owned* by white men. In a racist patriarchy, white men's "need" for racially "pure" offspring positioned free and unfree women in incompatible, asymmetrical symbolic and social spaces.[16]

The female slave was marked with these differences in a most literal fashion – the flesh was turned inside out, "add[ing] a lexical dimension to the narratives of woman in culture and society."[17] These differences did not end with formal emancipation; they have had definitive consequences into the late twentieth century and will continue to do so until racism as a founding institution of the New World is ended. Spillers called these founding relations of captivity and literal mutilation "an American grammar" (68). Under conditions of the New World conquest, of slavery, and of their consequences up to the present, "the lexis of reproduction, desire, naming, mothering, fathering, etc. [are] all thrown into extreme crisis" (76). "Gendering, in its coeval reference to African-American women, *insinuates* an implicit and unresolved puzzle both within current feminist discourse *and* within those discursive communities that investigate the problematics of culture" (78).

Spillers foregrounded the point that free men and women inherited their *name* from the father, who in turn had rights in his minor children and wife that they did not have in themselves, but he did not own them in the full sense of alienable property. Unfree men and women inherited their *condition* from their mother, who in turn specifically did not control their children. They had no *name* in the sense theorized by Lévi-Strauss or Lacan. Slave mothers could not transmit a name; they could not be wives; they were outside the system of marriage exchange. Slaves were unpositioned, unfixed, in a system of names; they were, specifically, unlocated and so disposable. In these discursive frames, white women were not legally or symbolically *fully* human; slaves were not legally or symbolically human *at all*. "In this absence from a subject position, the captured sexualities provide a physical and biological expression of 'otherness'" (67). To give birth (unfreely) to the heirs of property is not the same thing as to give birth (unfreely) to property.[18]

This little difference is part of the reason that "reproductive rights" for women of color in the United States prominently hinge on comprehensive control of children – for example, their freedom from destruction through lynching, imprisonment, infant mortality, forced pregnancy, coercive sterilization, inadequate housing, racist education, drug addiction, drug wars, and military wars.[19] For American white women the concept of property in the self, the ownership of one's own body, in relation to reproductive freedom, has more readily focused on the field of events around conception, pregnancy, abortion, and birth because the system of white patriarchy turned on the control of legitimate children and the consequent constitution of white females as women. To have or not have children then becomes literally a subject–defining choice for such women. Black women specifically – and the women subjected to the conquest of the New World in general – faced a broader social field of reproductive unfreedom, in which their children did not inherit the status of human in the founding hegemonic discourses of U.S. society. The problem of the black mother in this context is not simply her own status as subject, but also the status of her children and her sexual partners, male and female. Small wonder that the image of uplifting the race and the refusal of the categorical separation of men and women – without flinching from an analysis of colored and white sexist oppression – have been prominent in New World black feminist discourse.[20]

The positionings of African-American women are not the same as those of other women of color; each condition of oppression requires specific analysis that both refuses the separations and insists on the nonidentities of race, sex, sexuality, and class. These matters make starkly clear why an adequate feminist theory of gender must *simultaneously* be a theory of racial and sexual difference in specific historical conditions of production and reproduction. They also make clear why a theory and practice of sisterhood cannot be grounded in shared positionings in a gender system and the cross-cultural structural antagonism between coherent categories called women and men. Finally, they make clear why feminist theory produced by women of color has constructed alternative discourses of womanhood that disrupt the humanisms of many Western discursive traditions. "[I]t is our task to make a place for this different social subject. In so doing we are less interested in joining the ranks of gendered femaleness than gaining the *insurgent* ground as female social subject. Actually *claiming* the monstrosity of a female with the potential to 'name,' . . . 'Sapphire' might rewrite after all a radically different text of female empowerment."[21] And, perhaps, of empowerment of the problematic category of "humanity."

While contributing fundamentally to the breakup of any master subject location, the politics of "difference" emerging from this and other complex reconstructings of concepts of social subjectivity and their associated writing practices is deeply opposed to leveling relativisms. Nonfeminist poststructuralist theory in the human sciences has tended to identify the breakup of "coherent" or masterful subjectivity as the "death of the subject." Like others in newly *unstably* subjugated positions, many feminists resist this formulation of the project and question its emergence at just the moment when raced/sexed/colonized speakers begin "for the first time," to claim, that is, with an "originary" authority, to represent themselves in institutionalized publishing practices and other kinds of self-constituting practice. Feminist deconstructions of the "subject" have been fundamental, and they are not nostalgic for masterful coherence. Instead, necessarily political accounts of constructed embodiments, like feminist theories of gendered racial subjectivities, have to take affirmative *and* critical account of emergent, differentiating, self-representing, contradictory social subjectivities, with their claims on action, knowledge, and belief. The point involves the commitment to transformative social change, the moment of hope embedded in feminist theories of gender and other emergent discourses about the breakup of masterful subjectivity and the emergence of inappropriate/d others.

"Alterity" and "difference" are precisely what "gender" is "grammatically" about, a fact that constitutes feminism as a politics defined by its fields of contestation and repeated refusals of master theories. "Gender" was developed as a category to explore what counts as a "woman," to problematize the previously taken for granted, to reconstitute what counts as "human." If feminist theories of gender followed from Simone de Beauvoir's thesis that one is not born a woman, with all the consequences of that insight, in the light of Marxism and psychoanalysis (and critiques of racist and colonial discourse), for understanding that any finally coherent subject is a fantasy, and that personal and collective identity is precariously and constantly socially reconstituted,[22] then the title of bell hooks' provocative 1981 book, echoing Sojourner Truth, *Ain't I a Woman*, bristles with irony, as the identity of "woman" is both claimed and deconstructed simultaneously. This is a woman worthy of Isaiah's prophecy, slightly amended:

> S/he was despised and rejected by men; a wo/man of sorrows, acquainted with grief, and as one from whom men hide their faces s/he was despised, and we esteemed him/her not. . . . As many were astonished at him/her – his/her appearance was so marred, beyond human semblance . . . so shall s/he startle many nations.

This decidedly unwomanly Truth has a chance to refigure a nongeneric, nonoriginal humanity after the breakup of the discourses of Eurocentric humanism.

However, we cannot leave Sojourner Truth's story without looking more closely at the transcription of the famous *Ain't I a Woman* speech delivered in Akron in 1851. That written text represents Truth's speech in the white abolitionist's imagined idiolect of The Slave, the supposedly archetypal black plantation slave of the South. The transcription does not provide a southern Afro-American English that any linguist, much less actual speaker, would claim. But it *is* the falsely specific, imagined language that represented the "universal" language of slaves to the literate abolitionist public, and this is the language that has come down to us as Sojourner Truth's "authentic" words. This counterfeit language, undifferentiated into the many Englishes spoken in the New World, reminds us of a hostile notion of difference, one that sneaks the masterful unmarked categories in through the back door in the *guise* of the specific, which is made to be not disruptive or deconstructive, but typical. The undifferentiated black slave could figure for a humanist abolitionist discourse, and its descendants on the walls of women's studies offices, an ideal type, a victim (hero), a kind of plot space for the abolitionists' actions, a special human, not one that could bind up the whole people through her unremitting figuring of critical difference – that is, not an unruly agent preaching her own unique gospel of displacement as the ground of connection.

To reinforce the point, this particular former slave was not southern. She was born in New York and owned by a Dutchman. As a young girl, she was sold with some sheep to a Yankee farmer who beat her for not understanding English.[23] Sojourner Truth as an adult almost certainly spoke an Afro-Dutch English peculiar to a region that was once New Amsterdam. "She dictated her autobiography to a white friend and lived by selling it at lectures."[24] Other available transcriptions of her speeches are printed in "standard" late-twentieth-century American English; perhaps this language seems less racist, more "normal" to hearers who want to forget the diasporas that populated the New World, while making one of its figures into a "typical" hero. A modern transcription/invention

of Sojourner Truth's speeches has put them into Afro-Dutch English; her famous
question retroubles the ear, "Ar'n't I a woman?"[25] The change in the shape of the
words makes us rethink her story, the grammar of her body and life. The difference
matters.

One nineteenth century, friendly reporter decided he could not put Truth's words into
writing at all: "She spoke but a few minutes. To report her words would have been
impossible. As well attempt to report the seven apocalyptic thunders."[26] He went on, in
fact, to transcribe/reconstruct her presentation, which included these often-quoted lines:

> When I was a slave away down there in New York [was New York *down* for Sojourner
> Truth?!], and there was some particularly bad work to be done, some colored woman was
> sure to be called upon to do it. And when I heard that man talking away there as he did
> almost a whole hour, I said to myself, here's one spot of work sure that's fit for colored
> folks to clean up after.[27]

Perhaps what most needs cleaning up here is an inability to hear Sojourner Truth's
language, to face her specificity, to acknowledge her, but *not* as the voice of the seven
apocalyptic thunders. Instead, perhaps we need to see her as the Afro-Dutch-English
New World itinerant preacher whose disruptive and risk-taking practice led her "to
leave the house of bondage," to leave the subject-making (and humanist) dynamics of
master and slave, and seek new names in a dangerous world. This sojourner's truth
offers an inherently unfinished but potent reply to Pilate's skeptical query – "What is
truth?" She is one of Gloria Anzaldúa's *mestizas*,[28] speaking the unrecognized hyphen-
ated languages, living in the borderlands of history and consciousness where crossings
are never safe and names never original.

I promised to read Sojourner Truth, like Jesus, as a trickster figure, a shape changer,
who might trouble our notions – all of them: classical, biblical, scientific, modernist,
postmodernist, and feminist – of "the human," while making us remember why we
cannot not want this problematic universal. Pilate's words went through cascades of
transcriptions, inventions, and translations. The "Ecce homo!" was probably never
spoken. But, no matter how they may have originated, these lines in a play about
what counts as humanity, about humanity's possible stories, were from the beginning
implicated in permanent translation and reinvention. The same thing is true of Sojourner Truth's affirmative question, "Ain't/Ar'n't I a (wo)man?" These were tricksters,
forcing by their constant displacements, a reconstruction of founding stories, of any
possible home. We, lesbian, *mestiza*, inappropriate/d other are all terms for that excessive critical position which I have attempted to tease out and rearticulate from various
texts of contemporary feminism: a position attained through practices of political and
personal displacement across boundaries between sociosexual identities and communities, between bodies and discourses, by what I like to call the "eccentric subject."[29]
Such excessive and mobile figures can never ground what used to be called "a fully
human community." That community turned out to belong only to the masters.
However, these eccentric subjects can call us to account for our imagined humanity,
whose parts are always articulated through translation. History can have another shape,
articulated through differences that matter.

Notes

This paper was originally presented at the American Anthropological Association meetings, Washington, D.C., 19 November 1989. Its rhetorical shuttling between the genres of scholarly writing and religious speech is inspired by, and dedicated to, Cornel West. Thanks to grants from the Academic Senate of the University of California at Santa Cruz.

1   Thanks to Gary Lease for biblical guidance.

2   Quoted in bell hooks, *Ain't I a Woman: Black Women and Feminism* (Boston, MA: South End Press, 1981), p. 160.

3   I borrow Trinh's powerful sign, an impossible figure, the inappropriate/d other. Trinh T. Minh-ha, "She, the Inappropriate/d Other," *Discourse*, 8 (1986–87).

4   Gerda Lerner, in *Black Women in White America: A Documentary History*, edited by Gerda Lerner (New York: Random House, 1973), pp. 370–5.

5   Matthew 27:19.

6   Trinh T. Minh-ha, *Woman, Native, Other: Writing, Postcoloniality, and Feminism* (Bloomington: Indiana University Press, 1989).

7   Hortense Spillers, "Mama's Baby, Papa's Maybe: An American Grammar Book," *Diacritics*, 17, 2 (1987), pp. 65–81.

8   Trinh T. Minh-ha, *Woman, Native, Other*, p. 114.

9   I am using "matter" in the way suggested by Judith Butler in her work in progress. *Bodies That Matter*. See also Monique Wittig, *The Lesbian Body*, translated by David Le Vay (New York: Avon, 1975). The marked bodies and subjects theorized by Trinh, Butler, and Wittig evacuate precisely the heterosexist and racist idealism–materialism binary that has ruled in the generic Western philosophical tradition. The feminist theorists might claim a siblingship to Derrida here, but not a relation of derivation or identity.

10 A sample: bell hooks, *Ain't I a Woman*; Trinh T. Minh-ha, *Woman, Native, Other*; Angela Davis, *Women, Race, and Class* (New York: Random House, 1981); Gerda Lerner, *Black Women*; Paula Giddings, *When and Where I Enter: The Impact of Black Women on Race and Sex in America* (New York: Bantam Books, 1984); Bettina Aptheker, *Woman's Legacy: Essays on Race, Sex, and Class in American History* (Amherst: University of Massachusetts Press, 1982); Olive Gilbert, *Narrative of Sojourner Truth, a Northern Slave* (Battle Creek, MI: Review and Herald Office, 1884; reissued New York: Arno Press, 1968); Harriet Carter, "Sojourner Truth," *Chautauquan*, 7 (May 1889); Lillie B. Wyman, "Sojourner Truth," in *New England Magazine* (March 1901); Eleanor Flexner, *Century of Struggle: The Woman's Rights Movement in the United States* (Cambridge, MA: Harvard University Press, 1959); Edith Blicksilver, "Speech of Woman's Suffrage," in *The Ethnic American Woman* (Dubuque, IA: Kendall/Hunt, 1978), p. 335; Hertha Pauli, *Her Name Was Sojourner Truth* (New York: Appleton-Century-Crofts, 1962).

11 Teresa de Lauretis, "Eccentric Subjects," in *Feminist Studies*, 16 (Spring 1990), p. 116.

12 Trinh T. Minh-ha, *Woman, Native, Other*, pp. 89, 96.

13 Hazel V. Carby, *Reconstructing Womanhood: The Emergence of the Afro-American Woman Novelist* (New York: Oxford University Press, 1987).

14 Hortense Spillers, "Mama's Baby."

15 Catharine MacKinnon, "Feminism, Marxism, Method, and the State: An Agenda for Theory," *Signs*, 7, 3 (1982), pp. 515–44.

16 Aida Hurtado, "Relating to Privilege: Seduction and Rejection in the Subordination of White Women and Women of Color," *Signs*, 14, 4 (1989), pp. 833–55, 841.

17   Hortense Spillers, "Mama's Baby," pp. 67–8.

18   Hazel V. Carby, *Reconstructing Womanhood*, p. 53.

19   Aida Hurtado, "Relating to Privilege," p. 853.

20   Hazel V. Carby, *Reconstructing Womanhood*, pp. 6–7; bell hooks, *Ain't I a Woman*; bell hooks, *Feminist Theory: From Margin to Center* (Boston, MA: South End Press, 1984).

21   Hortense Spillers, "Mama's Baby," p. 80.

22   Rosalind Coward, *Patriarchal Precedents: Sexuality and Social Relations* (London: Routledge and Kegan Paul, 1983), p. 265.

23   Gerda Lerner, *Black Women*, p. 371.

24   Ibid., p. 372; Olive Gilbert, *Narrative of Sojourner*.

25   Edith Blicksilver, "Speech."

26   Quoted in Bettina Aptheker, *Woman's Legacy*, p. 34.

27   Ibid., p. 34.

28   Gloria Anzaldúa, *Borderlands/La Frontera* (San Francisco: Spinsters, 1987).

29   Teresa de Lauretis, *Feminist Studies*, p. 145.

Chapter 13

A Pedagogy for Postcolonial Feminists

Zakia Pathak

Introduction

Zakia Pathak teaches at Miranda House, a women's college in Delhi University. She is the co-author of "The Prison House of *Orientalism*" (1991), a look at how Edward Said's influential text opened up Western texts for South Asian teachers, as well as co-author of "Between Academy and Street: A Story of Resisting Women" (1997). Her work appears in two important anthologies on women and politics, *Feminists Theorize the Political* (1992), edited by Joan W. Scott and Judith Butler; and *Transitions, Environments, and Translations* (1997), edited by Joan W. Scott, Cora Kaplan, and Debra Keates.

In "A Pedagogy for Postcolonial Feminists," discussed in *The Postmodern Bible* (267–8), Pathak engages readers in the task of bridging the gap between what she calls "litspeak" and "culturespeak." In other words, Pathak demonstrates how, in the teaching of First World texts to Third World students, the literary interpretation of these texts may be connected to the reality of the social and political occurrences of daily life. Pathak believes this connection to be especially crucial for postcolonial women. She says that we shouldn't "assent to the exertion of proprietorial rights of interpretation as expressed through the determination of interpretive paradigms by canonized criticisms – which determine the production of meaning."

In this selection Pathak shares the Miranda House teaching practices for four texts, the Book of Job, Eliot's *Murder in the Cathedral*, Conrad's *Lord Jim*, and Forster's *A Passage to India*. Using a combination of reader-response criticism and New Historicism, Pathak connects the Book of Job to a present-day religious dispute involving extremist Hindus and Muslims. She gives first an interesting reading of Job, claiming that his agony is caused by the fragmentation of his own subjectivity by the competing systems of religion and law. She then compares this reading to the Mandir Masjid dispute over a religious site in India. She understands that in doing this she is "positing a form of historical essentialism between two countries" divided by time and space, but believes that this essentialism is productive because it produces an investigation into historical concepts and conditions which may not be self-evident.

Her reading of *Murder in the Cathedral* makes a similar connection to a current Indian political situation. Pathak's discussion of *Lord Jim* and *A Passage to India* focuses on the category of genre, showing how the designation is not a neutral descriptive category. In *Lord Jim*, the Orientalist fantasy that constructs Jewel's sexuality allows modern Indian women to examine stereotypes in their own culture; in *A Passage to India* the political unconscious becomes feminine, allowing Indian women to examine the subject position Orientalism has created for them by affiliating along gender lines instead of race.

I

For ourselves, teaching undergraduate students at Miranda House, a women's college at Delhi University, we may state at the outset that our pedagogical practice is directed at producing from the literary "work" a "text" which engages with our concerns as Indians and women at the present time.[1] While respecting the cultural specificity of the work in the producing culture, we are committed to "making" a politics for it that will enable us to live our lives more critically.[2]

It is being increasingly recognized/resisted that the production of meaning is governed by ideological perspectives, implicit or theorized. "Even the most seemingly intuitive encounter with a literary text is...already theory-laden....[T]here is no reading that does not bring to bear a certain context, interpret from a certain angle or set of interests, and thus throw one set of questions into relief while leaving others unasked."[3] We believe that our task as teachers is to create an awareness of these interests and thereby of the subject positions from which they emerge. The first objective of any political program is to work toward an understanding that the contradictions of textual practice are the effect of a multiplicity of subject positions, often perceived as contradictory and impossible to reconcile. Whether we then proceed to make it our responsibility to change the perceptions of interests by bringing to bear other contexts, other angles, is another issue, though in practice we have found that it is difficult to keep the two separate. "We need to see discourse structures in their fullness and power...and the way to see one discourse is to see more than one."[4] We have had to be wary in classroom discussion of arousing resistances which might be counterproductive to our project, and so sometimes have to leave open the issue as to whether the subject position temporally privileged in the differential of identity is to be changed or cherished.

This exercise in cognition dramatizes more often than not, not the fractured subjectivity that might be expected given the disturbing impact of modernizing trends upon traditional practices in the culture outside the classroom, but a unified, singularly untroubled subject. This subject is an effect of that "competence" which is acquired by a formal education in reading patterns, structures, codes.[5] Every literary work comes to us with encrustations from the metropolitan university and this form of intertextuality

Zakia Pathak, "A Pedagogy for Postcolonial Feminists," from *Feminists Theorize the Political*, edited by Judith Butler and Joan W. Scott (New York and London: Routledge, 1992).

produces its own subject, also sometimes called the "informed" reader, who represents some kind of ideal. The literary perceptions of the reader, when she is Indian, connect only tangentially, if at all, with her understanding of the political and social problems she lives with outside the classroom. This separation between academic litspeak and the lay discourses of the culture,[6] between Academy and World, is tacitly permitted by a practice which historicizes the work in the producing culture but regards historical intervention in its reception as an inexcusable tampering with the truth of the work.

It is of course arguable that this separation between litspeak and culturespeak[7] marks the reception of a literary work in any culture, given the marginalization of literature everywhere, and that it is not peculiar to our situation as a once-colonized people. However that may be, it is surely the case that where First World texts are taught in a Third World university the problem takes on a sharper edge. We seem to assent to the exertion of proprietorial rights of interpretation as expressed through the determination of interpretive paradigms by canonized criticisms – which determine the production of meaning. Our pedagogical politics takes issue with such property rights. In a complex and ongoing process of abrogation and appropriation[8] we bring to the literary work other discursive paradigms which attract our own concerns.

This essay proposes to share our practice in teaching four texts prescribed in the undergraduate syllabus. In the section which follows, Section II, we read the Book of Job and *Murder in the Cathedral*. In our readings of both works we displace the paradigm of religion as revelation; it was the nineteenth century that subjected the Bible to Higher Criticism, eroding its revelatory status and opening up religion to other discourses. In the *Book of Job*, we introduce the discourse of law which interrogates religious discourse. In *Murder in the Cathedral*, we identify an emerging discourse of nationalism, and show how church and state sought to appropriate nationalist rhetoric. These discursive paradigms enable us to move into discussion of the major controversy of the present times, the Mandir Masjid dispute. The Mandir Masjid dispute centers upon the religious significance of a site in the town of Ayodhya in Uttar Pradesh. Extremist Hindu organizations, the Vishva Hindu Parishad (VHP) and the Bajrang Dal (BD), backed by the Bharatiya Janata Party (BJP), which is a political party, claim that the god Ram was born on the site; that a temple had stood there before it was demolished in the 16th century by the Moghul monarch Babar, who erected a Mosque there. Muslim organizations, the Indian Union Muslim League (IUML) and the Babri Masjid Action Committee (BMAC) deny this. The Hindu organizations have vowed to remove the mosque and reassemble it elsewhere and to build a temple on the site. The Muslim organizations have vowed to defend the mosque. Passions, already running high, became inflamed after the BJP leader Advani took out his *rath yatra* (chariot procession) in mid-1990 which traversed several states and left bloody riots in its wake. Advani was arrested as he crossed into Bihar, the BJP withdrew its support to the minority government of the Janata Dal, under Prime Minister V. P. Singh, and the Government fell. A breakaway section of the JD, the Samajawadi Janata Dal (SJP), formed the Government but resigned in early 1991. General elections were held in May/June 1991. The BJP made the Ayodhya dispute its central plank for campaigning, calling all Hindus together under the banner of the god Ram. When the results of the elections were announced, they had increased their tally substantially.

In Section III we are led from discourse structures to inscriptions. In two novels, Conrad's *Lord Jim* and Forster's *A Passage to India*, we show how the literary category of genre, far from being a neutral descriptive category, inscribes a reality. Ideological inscription is noted in the female psyche; and the political unconscious, it is suggested, may be gendered.

II

We began our engagement with the Book of Job by considering its status as a theodicy. First, we made the put-togetherness of its structure visible, by examining the process of inclusions and exclusions from the epics, folktales, and poems of wisdom literature. By this means it could accommodate dissenting voices without compromising the theological centrality of Yahweh. Secondly, we showed how the Yahweh figure was an evolving creation of history, from the moody and capricious god who could only be propitiated to the just god of the prophet Amos. Thirdly, we showed how religion constructed history, reading national disasters as visitations of God's wrath over infractions of Mosaic Law. Later, individual histories problematized divine justice; when the law of retribution was extended to individual fates, undeserved suffering could not be explained. Fourthly, we brought in the discourse of law in the contemporary society by pointing to the Sanhedrin, which decided all cases of infraction of the law, including those arising from differing interpretations by the Scribes and Pharisees. Finally, quoting Hollander in Kermode,[9] we showed how religious texts are constituted by hermeneutical fiats; the Torah was strategically accommodated as the Old Testament while its historical dimension was disparaged and its truths projected as allegories, the true meaning of which could be found only in the Gospels. We concluded by suggesting that the agony of Job was that of a subjectivity fractured by contending discourses of revelation and law, identifying in the text the attendant machinery of proof, argument, intermediary and so on. Job's capitulation to Yahweh could be seen as a submission to the discourse of revelation dominant at that historical moment, against which the discourse of reason was still powerless.

This reading of the Book of Job enabled us to pass on to similar issues involved in the Mandir Masjid dispute: the clash of the two discourses occasioned controversy. The dispute had been referred to a court of law but the Hindu organizations refused to co-operate, claiming that matters of religious faith, that is the birthplace of Ram, could not be adjudicated in a secular court. Muslim organizations produced historical evidence from an impressive array of scholars, in support of their stand (many of these are leftist in orientation; the BJP is rightist). When the SJP Government managed to bring the Hindu organizations to the negotiating table, these produced their own interpretations of history and religious texts to support their stand. The status of historical fact was questioned. The affinity of much of contemporary politics to the situation in the Book of Job as we read it was extended to Yahweh/Ram. Just as the theological insistence on Yahweh as the one Supreme God was politically motivated to unite the people of Israel, weaning them away from allegiance to previous Canaanite gods and so to consolidate them into a nation, so the primacy conferred on the godhood of Ram was targeted, we suggested, to consolidating the Hindu vote in favor of a party which, projecting a Hindu nationalism, hoped to be catapulted into power.

We are aware that in making a politics for the Book of Job we are implicitly positing a form of historical essentialism between two countries divided by centuries of time and worlds of space. It may or may not be the case that we share similar histories; that is for the historians to debate. What is important is that we have arrived at this essentialism, in positing a problematic, in which empirical facts have played a part, and so hope to have avoided the odium attaching to that intuitive essentialism which is an *a priori* concept.[10]

It has been asked of us why in our reading of the Book of Job our feminist identity was not activated. Perhaps a recapitulation of the teaching process during the first term – August/September 1989 and January/February 1991 – might go some way in answering that. We had at the start of the course suggested a few topics which might be discussed, among which was the marginal figure of Job's wife and her single utterance: "Curse God and die." Shortly afterward, Mr. Advani's *rath* started rolling and tension escalated. Our reading the text as the conflict of two discourses, religious and legal, unequally empowered, was clearly an immediate response to the contemporary political scene. In other words, the feminist concern was temporally subordinated. It is not that different works foreground different subject positions; but that the subject position privileged in the differential of identity is responsive to the call for political action. If we were to teach the text today, the feminist perspective might well be privileged. Two young women continually hit the media headlines as the greatest crowd-pullers for the BJP. Both are religious persons, having renounced the life of the *grihasti*, or house holder; Sadhvi Rithambari, by a formal vow, Uma Bharati informally. Both are saffron-clad, the colour of the Hindu religious person. Uma Bharati stood for election and won by a handsome margin. Are these women traditional or modern? They have been seen as daringly different, articulating a new cultural code for women. On the other hand, they have to resort to a conservative one, where a certain moral authority is accorded a public figure who renounces sexuality. Similarly, the large turnout of women in the BJP rallies and marches which, they claim, marks a historical departure and modernizing trend, might be read as conservative, since it was in the cause of religion, as the women saw it. Certainly it was the conservative stereotype of woman, as the repository of sanity and compassion, that was encapsulated in the slogan of the Communist Party of India (at the other end of the political/ideological spectrum), during its women's rally at Ayodhya; it can be translated thus: "This is the cry of the Indian woman: stop this slaughter!" The wife of Job was doomed to be silenced on two counts: she spoke against her God and against her husband.

Eliot's *Murder in the Cathedral* has traditionally called for a twofold approach. It is the story of a martyrdom and of the baptism of people into faith by the blood of martyrs. It has also been tackled from the biographical angle where the author's eventual personal conversion to Catholicism is read as motivating the play. In our classroom practice these paradigms were displaced so as to recuperate a history read, under the Foucaultian paradigm, as the story of power which circulates in a network. The traditional concept of the freely choosing individual, Thomas of Canterbury, rent by temptations but finally regaining that serene unity which he brings to his decision "out of time," to which his "whole being gives consent," was displaced by a multiply–constituted subjectivity: the royal subject of the King ("O Henry! O my King!") with whom he identifies ("I *was* the King, his arm, his better reason"); the servant of Christ ("No traitor to the king. I am a priest/A Christian saved by the blood of Christ/. . . . My death for his death"); the man of ambition ("The last temptation . . . to do the right deed for the wrong reason"). In this complex power struggle we isolated an emerging rhetoric of nationalism which imaged "England" on grounds of race, religion, and class.

> *Tempter:*   King is in France, squabbling in Anjou. . . .
> We are for England. We are in England.
> You and I my Lord, are Normans.
> England is a land for Norman
> Sovereignty. Let the Angevin
> Destroy himself, fighting in Anjou.
> He does not understand us, the English barons.
> We are the people
>
> *Third Priest:*   The Church is stronger for this action.
> Go, weak sad men . . . homeless in earth or heaven.
> Go where the sunset reddens the last grey rock
> Of Brittany, or the Gates of Hercules
> Go venture shipwreck on the sullen coasts
> Where blackamoors make captive Christian men. . . .
>
> *Tempter:*   I am no trifler and no politician . . .
> I am no courtier . . .
> It is we country lords who know the country
> And we who know what the country needs.
> It is our country. We care for the country.
> We are the backbone of the nation.

And against these definitions of the nation, there is that of the oppressed, the women of Canterbury, suffering because of the power struggle between church and state. They construct England in terms of the past conceived as golden:

> A rain of blood has blinded my eyes. Where is England?
> Where is Kent? Where is Canterbury?
> O far far far in the past . . .
> It is not we alone, it is not the house, it is not the city that is defiled
> But the world that is wholly foul.

The "nation" is always constructed from the perspective of a set of interests. Moving to our contemporary political situation, the extremist Hindu position on the Mandir Masjid dispute has thrown up the notion of "Hindutva" – concept/ideology/identity/ state of being? It is the subject of ongoing debate. It was on the plank of Hindutva that the BJP won its spectacular electoral successes in 1989 and 1991. The attempt to appropriate nationalism which Eliot's play, in our reading, presents led easily to our situation, where Hindutva is projected as co-eval with nationalism. We might have carried forward, from the Book of Job, the paradigm of conflicting discourses in terms of the discourses of law and party politics. How does a party claim to represent the national interest and yet not attract the provisions of the Representation of People's Act (Section 123 (3) and 3(A)) of 1951? In a fascinating article in the *Times of India* of 24 April 1991, Rajdeep Sardesai lists the history of cases filed under this law. In a case before the Bombay High Court, the B.J.P./Shiv Sena (S.S.) lawyers, defending the "inflammatory" election speeches of Sena chief Bal Thackerey, claimed that the judges were using "Western dictionary" definitions of Hinduism and were therefore unable to appreciate the contextual variance in a speech given in the local language and at a public meeting. It appeared to suffer transformation in the discursive situation of "the cold atmosphere" of the judicial chamber. In the Kunte vs. Prabhoo case of 1989, the B.J.P./ S.S. alliance had insisted that Hindutva is a geocultural, even nationalistic notion. Justice Bharucha accepted that Hindutva had cultural connotations but ruled that the objective of Mr. Thackerey's speeches was patently and admittedly the protection of the Hindu religion. As for the slogan: "*Garv se kaho hum Hindu hai*" (announce with pride that I am a Hindu) – slogans were among the material facts filed – senior judicial functionaries felt that while in itself the slogan is unobjectionable under the law, if spoken at an election meeting, it can be a corrupt practice inasmuch as a direct relation is being established between the candidate on the podium and the audience. Dr. Prabhoo was disqualified by the High Court. A woman lawyer and social activist, Vasudha Dhagamvar, entered the Hindu nationalism controversy from the columns of the *Indian Express* of 25 August 1989. Arguing against the demand to abolish the canopy at India Gate since it is a memory of British colonial rule, she pointed out that nationalism by the time of the Second World War had gripped the *middle classes*. Leaders of the *lower caste* movement in the late nineteenth century – notably Jyotiba Phule – who had suffered at the hands of the Brahmins were on record as saying that they did not want the British to go. It is clear that statements derive their semantic value from the archive in which they are lodged. It is so with the term "nation." We can emerge from Eliot's play to a study of the dissemination of meaning in Indian political history.

III

With *Lord Jim*, we enter into the problematic area of the functioning of genre. Genres are not neutral descriptive categories; they institute a reality and inscribe a subject. The Patusan story has been widely regarded in canonized criticism as a fantasy. But the fantastic is always inserted into a mimed reality against which it defines itself.[11]

A genre may be defined as a mode and a structure.[12] Because fantasy is inserted into a mimed reality, the novel will contain the structural elements of both. The structural markers of realistic narrative are the focalization of the hero, a scrutiny of the psychological motivation of his actions, disambiguation, that is, effacement of all play with being/seeming and the effacement of utterance; this is the "text in a hurry."[13] The narrative is hitched to a megastory which illumines it, creating expectations on the line of least resistance through a text already known. Historical and geographic names are stable semantic entities linking the text to the megatext, itself valorized. Against these criteria, Patusan defines itself as fantasy. Jim is focalized; the conflicting perspectives on his action, so crucial a part of the Patna story, are missing. There is hardly any psychological investigation of his actions ("It came to him..."). There are no proper names which provide semantic stability. In one crucial respect, however, the narrative departs from the fantastic mode in that the utterance is almost effaced; the phatic and deictic signals so abundant in the Patna story are minimized here so that Marlow's voice slides imperceptibly into something like omniscience. His framing of Patusan as a fantastic space has magnetized a whole line of critics – cloud-cuckoo land, Edenesque, anti-Paradise, a different time and space, something in a dream.[14] The competent Indian reader, reading off these signals, becomes complicit with the framing of the Orient and its representation as a land of intrigue and unrest, of lecherous rajahs and poisoned coffee, of talismanic rings which command fealty to the white man – finally, with the image of the white man bringing civilization to a benighted people.

Now, the canonized Todorovian theory requires that no poetic or allegorical reading be made since these destroy the fantasy (the moral of the animal fable is held to do this).[15] Todorov also requires that the hesitation of the reader, suspended between two levels of interpretation, natural and supernatural, must be sustained to the end. It seems to us this condition coerces the reader into accepting the Orientalist reading of the Orient as a truthful rendering. It is our contention that this "hesitation" provides a space where a pedagogical politics can begin to operate. To choose to read referentially is to come across natural interpretations which might otherwise pass unnoticed in this dense text, as for instance the fact that Jim was the only man in Patusan who possessed gun powder? To read referentially is to recuperate a recognizable reality where a land is violated by successive streams of invaders, by armed might, or by trade (the Celebes, the Europeans); where religion is exploited for power (Sherif Ali); where the invader initially colludes with a selected native power until he gradually gains supremacy (Jim with Doramin).

The realistic mode has fallen into some disrepute today because of its truth claims. Notwithstanding, we suggest that, so far as the white text is concerned, the privileging of realistic markers yields a recognizable reality which puts us on guard against Orientalist representations. Fantasy is today valorized because it is read as providing an alternative version of reality to which we can aspire and toward which we can work. This is a temporal (historical) construction of the genre which must be accepted if genres are to retain their explicative power. But spatial determinants must also be recognized in the construction of a genre; reading from here, Orientalist fantasy is not so much a subgenre of fantasy as a new function. Subversion and escapism do not exhaust the possibilities; fantasy can also operate to *subserve* a political reality.

As women, we attach a special importance to the figure of Jewel. In most critical accounts, she is invisible; not surprisingly, since most critics leap from Stein to Gentleman Brown. In the shaping of Jewel, the structural markers of fantasy predominate. She has no proper name. She too is focalized; there are no disambiguating, psychologizing perspectives on her actions. There is no play between being and seeming; indeed Marlow's narrative makes her into an icon. She remains in the imagination in a series of fixed poses; always dressed in white, a high childish voice; an arm held aloft holding a torch; standing beside Jim's empty chair issuing commands of war; and finally, her black hair loose, her face stony, only the eyes straining after the shape of a man torn from her side by a dream. Her relations with Jim are romanticized. "They came together like knight and maiden, meeting to exchange vows among haunted ruins." Here Jewel is modeled after the Lady of chivalric romance, mystically conceived and sexually pure. But this figure too has to be inserted into the mimed reality. This exercise prompts the conclusion that the narrative attempts to mystify the realistic markers in order to emasculate their import in the white text.[16] Jewel's father and grandfather were white; among the possibilities which prevented her father from marrying her mother was "merciless convention." In all likelihood, therefore, Jewel is a half-caste and illegitimate. In other words, she is located in the megatext in a history of miscegenation. Now, miscegenation always occurred outside matrimony. Whereas the thrust of this narrative is to present the relationship of Jim and Jewel as if within the matrimonial bond. "Jewel he called her as he might have said Jane, with a peaceful, marital homelike effect." "This was the theory of their marital evening walks." This repression of sexuality within the matrimonial bond constitutes Jewel as the Angel in the House; the iconicity of representation seeps into a stereotype of patriarchal discourse. Jewel is not the Kuchuk Hanem figure of Orientalist discourse, offering a more libertine, less guilt-ridden sex, with the promise of untiring sexuality and of fecundity.[17] Patriarchal and Orientalist discourses are imbricated in the novel; the metaphor of the East as the bride ready to be unveiled by her lord is a recurring motif. Jewel's madness, in a referential reading, would qualify as that anomie which so often afflicted the English person in the colonies, cut off from his own kind.[18] Spilling over to the political story, it constitutes the Orient under white protection as fulfilled and flourishing.

As Schaeffer notes, the logic of inclusion has a radically ambiguous status since genres are temporally constructed. "Genre is always provisional because no immutable criterion decides whether any text belongs to a given genre. . . . This relation of inclusion calls for a decisional aspect irreducible to any definitional determinism."[19] By naming the genre to which Patusan belongs as Orientalist fantasy, we are led to perceive that Jewel is constituted at the intersection of generic traditions which repress female sexuality. This enables us to move toward considering the operation of the patriarchal stereotype in our own culture. It has been so deeply internalized as to be inscribed into the female psyche. Homi Bhabha defines the stereotype as a falsification, not because it is a simplification, but because it is "an arrested, fixated form of representation that in denying the play of difference constitutes a problem in the representation of the subject in social relations."[20] This stereotype is a site of combat in an ongoing debate of tradition versus modernity, where the Indian woman — *Bharat nari* — is constructed as chaste and home-loving, god-fearing, living in and through her husband, even following him into the funeral pyre "voluntarily." In classroom discussion we have learnt not to simplify this ideology as male manipulation or female hypocrisy. There is an excess which cannot be contained in such formulations. At its worst it colludes with patriarchal power in an orgy of submission; at its best it sustains the institution of family, which we still valorize.

Our reading of Forster's *A Passage to India* activated our racial and feminist identities. It would be more accurate to say that our critique of the generic operations of *A Passage to India* was constructed by our subject position as Indian and as a once-colonized people. As such, we read the horror of miscegenation as inscribed in the political unconscious of the Englishman and as structuring the text. But in confronting *A Passage to India* with a recent novel by Deborah Moggach, *Hot Water Man*, which parodies it, our feminist identity provided a source for agency inasmuch as it enabled us to break out of the subject position which constructed the West as other. In the process it also raised the question as to whether the political unconscious is gendered.

The horror of miscegenation is vividly recounted by Ben Shepherd in his account of the case of Peter Lobengula, in the 1920s.[21] Lobengula was the son of the African chief of Matabele, annexed by the British. He was brought to London as a part of a circus troupe, and met and married an Englishwoman, Florence Jewell. The news threw Fleet Street into a frenzy. "Miscegenation has long been regarded as a crime against civilisation" (*The Spectator*). "A stupendous act of folly and physical immorality" (*The Daily Mail*). When approached to perform the marriage service, several members of the clergy refused. The general opinion was that there is something disgusting in the mating of a white girl with a dusky savage. In India too the authorities were alarmed by signs of any intimacy between Englishwomen and Indian men. Lord Curzon refused permission to the Rajah of Puderkottai to proceed to England for the coronation since he suspected that he might marry an Englishwoman. It infuriated Curzon to see the daughter of the Duchess of Roxburgh dancing with the Rajah of Kapurthala at Buckingham Court.[22]

Early critical discussion placed Forster in the nineteenth century's general tradition of the *Bildungsroman*. Even when his "mystical atheism" was appreciated, he was classed with the later Victorians like Butler and Meredith. Today in contrast, his work is perceived as belonging to a symbolist aesthetic; his use of symbol and a pervasive disquiet marks him as a modern.[23] It is in the Caves Section of the novel that the realistic mode is arrested and the social comedy turns sharply away from the direction it was headed for; even detective investigation is displaced by a metaphysical quest. We suggest that the horror of miscegenation was too deeply inscribed in the political unconscious to allow exploration in the realistic mode as was possible in Forster's Italian novel, *Where Angels Fear to Tread*.

The manuscript drafts of the novel show that Forster was contemplating two possibilities in the Caves: a physical assault and a mutual embrace. It is conjectured that he abandoned this line of development out of weariness of marriage fiction and the man–woman relation. At the trial, not only does Adela withdraw everything because she cannot be sure of who followed her into the cave, but the question itself suddenly loses interest for her, leaving Forster to pursue his metaphysical quest. "In fiction by women," however, "the female domestic space of the romance is foregrounded as a form of value and power and self-fulfilment."[24] Deborah Moggach's *Hot Water Man* suggests what could have happened in the caves. "Through a double process of installation and ironising, parody signals how present representations come from past ones and what ideological consequences derive from both continuity and difference."[25] The blurb on the dust cover of *Hot Water Man* installs *A Passage to India* unambiguously: "*Hot Water Man* must inevitably remind readers of *A Passage to India* as East and West meet once again in confusion." The encounter is updated. India is now postindependence Pakistan, the civil administrator is an executive in a multinational firm represented by the American Duke Hanson as well as the Englishman Donald Hanley. Donald and Christine are married and childless; the emotional relationship is also sterile. Like Adela, Christine is out to discover the real Pakistan, spurning the codes of the compound and haunting the bazaar. There she picks up a relationship with a Pakistani guide. This story climaxes with their visit to Gintho (which the narrator points out is an anagram for Nothing), noted for its cure of infertility. When Christine goes to the hot water springs, the guide stays behind in the guest house and goes to sleep. On her return she rapes him. "And how she had used him. She had confused and inflamed him . . . she . . . the worst colonialist of them all." She becomes pregnant. The narrative – and the novel – ends on her relieved sobbing when the baby is delivered and she realizes that the color of its skin will not give her away. In the second narrative strand, Donald, who is out to discover his grandfather's military past in all its splendor in India, discovers instead that he had a native mistress by whom he had had a child. Donald sets out to find his half-uncle and to make amends; but when he actually meets the man, he cannot connect. "Close up in the flesh it was impossible to believe that this man was his uncle. Perhaps he did not want to believe it. There was simply no connection" (258). In the third narrative strand, Duke Hanson, whose wife is away in the States, has an affair with a Pakistani woman, educated at an elite school in England, professionally competent and with political connections useful to him. But he will not marry her. "You mean I've been your bit of fun on the side," she ripostes with bitterness when he gives her his feeble reason: "It just won't work." He swears that he meant it, to which she replies with dry anger: "You meant it with an eye on the fucking calendar." In an accusation reminiscent of Fielding's reprimand to Adela ("What have you been doing? Playing a game or studying life or what?"), she raves: "What on earth did you think you were doing? Having a little cross-cultural communication? Getting to know the natives?"

Hot Water Man is metafictional. It is process made visible by a mimesis of process.[26] In recuperating what might have happened in the Caves, it is ironic-parodic in naming the central silence of its progenitor. It exposes the duplicity which at least in part motivates the flight from realistic social comedy into a metaphysical dimension and a symbolist aesthetic: "the contradiction between . . . the ideological project and the literary form which creates an absence at the centre of the text. . . . [T]he text is divided, split."[27]

In a scandalous success of 1921, *The Sheik*, by E. M. Hull, the white heroine is raped by an Arab Sheik and, after several repeat performances in the desert, learns to enjoy it. The concluding chapter reveals him to the heroine, and to the reader, to be the son of an English lord. *Hot Water Man* spurns this duplicity. In moving interracial sex out of the genre of pornography and relocating it on the axis of race, *Hot Water Man* exposes the limits of the liberal ideology which inspired *A Passage to India*.

What is of crucial importance for the pedagogic enterprise is the meaning we produce from the conflictual relation between the two novels. From one perspective, *Hot Water Man* is the discourse of Anglo-India for whom the metropolitan liberal Englishman was the Other.[28] It is a fact of history that the Ilbert Bill, introduced in the nineteenth century to remove the provision that Englishmen in India could not be tried by an Indian judge, ran into violent opposition from the Anglo-Indian community and had to be withdrawn by the British government. From that perspective, *Hot Water Man* in its derision of liberal self-delusion remains within the discourse of Orientalism, at its margins. We must decide if *we* wish to remain within the subject position which is an effect of that discourse. One way of breaking out – in the interests of a less factional perception which would be truer to our more complex relation with the West outside the classroom – which is invested with desire – is to locate *Hot Water Man* in the counterdiscourse to Orientalism. Articulated by a female novelist, within the Western culture, it suggests that the horror of miscegenation is inscribed in the white *male* psyche, and creates a gender affiliation across race.

IV

It will be evident by now that our pedagogical practice is heavily indebted to recent advances in critical theory that have opened up the concepts of author, text, reader, and meaning. In acknowledging this debt, we lay ourselves open to the charge of being neocolonialists, because, in arguing for the validity of a response to English literature shaped by our perceptions of our contemporary political history, we ground these perceptions in European critical theory. This would qualify us as that "comprador intelligentsia" who "mediate[s] trade in cultural commodities of world capitalism at the periphery."[29] By publishing abroad and in India, we may be perceived as selling an India to the West and a West to India. Against this intelligentsia is posited the world of popular culture, unconcerned with the problems of neocolonialism, borrowing freely from the West and refusing otherness: "antinational," asking only for "a simple respect for human suffering."[30] But it is the price we have to pay for engaging in the activity of critique that we should be crucially aware of our multiple subjectivities and how they are determined. We might regret but cannot regain that lost wholeness. Moreover, critique may also advance a claim to being antinational inasmuch as it denotes "reflection on the conditions of possible knowledge and the system of constraints which are humanly produced."[31] As such it addresses a variety of structures of domination anywhere in the world. As Third World readers of First World texts, our opportunities for intervention in political action are limited; it is in order to increase them that our pedagogical practice resists the hegemony of metropolitan critical traditions and contends for the kind of reception of texts we have described in this essay.

But opposition to these traditions is equally to be found within the metropolitan university. Is our debt to critical theory then a case of abrogation without appropriation? "The concern of the Third World critic should properly be to understand the ideological subtext which any critical theory reflects and embodies and the relation this subtext bears to the production of meaning," says a black critic.[32] The ideological subtext of critical theory, as we understand it, is oppositional thinking where structures of domination are perceived to be oppressive. We do not identify such thinking with a composite "Indian" response; we have positioned ourselves in this essay as teachers at the university, as teachers of literature, as women, in fraught relation with other "Indians." To acknowledge this multiplicity of subject positions is not to valorize a fractured subjectivity as we have often been accused of doing. It is certainly to recognize our debt to critical theory while still being moved by an imagined community of selves; and, going on from here, to try and forge a corporate identity for Miranda House; not by evading an identity crisis but by "staging" it.[33] This essay is another attempt toward that objective. And the history of such attempts could be the theme of another essay.

Notes

The grammatical marker of the first person throughout this essay will take the plural from – we/our/us – since the essay represents a consensual position on pedagogical practice which emerged – and was constantly being refined – in continuing discussion with my colleagues, Saswati Sengupta and Sharmila Purkayastha. *Ave atque vale.* My thanks to Sharada Nair and Lola Chatterji for helpful comments, and to the Nehru Memorial Library for reading facilities. I am grateful to the Academic Foundation, New Delhi for commissioning this article.

1 Roland Barthes, *Image/Music/Text* (New York: Hill and Wang, 1977), pp. 155–64.
2 Tony Bennett, in A. P. Foulkes, *Literature and Propaganda* (London: Methuen, 1983), p. 19.
3 Gerald Graff, "The Future of Theory in the Teaching of Literature," *The Future of Literary Theory*, Ralph Cohen, ed. (New York: Routledge, 1989), p. 250.
4 Robert Scholes, *Textual Power* (New Haven: Yale University Press, 1985), p. 144.
5 Jonathan Culler, "Literary Competence," *Reader Response Criticism*, Jane Tomkins, ed. (Baltimore: Johns Hopkins University Press, 1980), p. 116.
6 Gerald Graff, "The Future of Theory," pp. 257, 269.
7 Here culturespeak is to be understood as lay discourse *about* culture.
8 "Abrogation is a refusal of the categories of the imperial culture, its aesthetic, its illusory standard of normative or 'correct' usage, its assumption of a traditional and fixed meaning inscribed in the words. It is a vital moment in the decolonising of the language and the writing of 'english,' but without the process of appropriation the moment of abrogation may not extend beyond a reversal of the assumptions of privilege, the 'normal' and correct inscription, all of which can be simply taken over and maintained by the new usage." Bill Ashcroft, Gareth Griffiths and Helen Tiffin, eds. *The Empire Writes Back: Theory and Practice in Post-Colonial Literatures* (London, NY: Routledge, 1989), p. 38.
9 Frank Kermode, *The Genesis of Secrecy* (Cambridge, MA: Harvard University Press, 1979), p. 18.
10 "...the recent revival of essentialism dating from the early 1970s...stems from the ideas of Hilary Putnam and Saul Kripke and their insight that the knowledge of essences and of many other necessary truths need not be *a priori*, need not, that is, be intuitively self-evident, and independent of all empirical confirmation or disconfirmation." Peter Crisp, "Essence, Realism and Literature," *English* (Spring 1989), p. 55.
11 Christine Brooke-Rose, *The Rhetoric of the Unreal* (Cambridge: Cambridge University Press, 1981), p. 234.
12 Fredric Jameson, *The Political Unconscious* (London: Methuen, 1981), pp. 107–10.
13 Philippe Harmon, in Christine Brooke-Rose, *Rhetoric*, pp. 85–94.
14 Frederick Karl, *Reader's Guide to Joseph Conrad* (London: Thames and Hudson, 1960); C. B. Cox, *The Modern Imagination* (London: Macmillan, 1986).
15 Christine Brooke-Rose, *Rhetoric*, p. 68.
16 "Faced with the difficulty of telling Jim's story, Marlow does not arouse his audience's expectations; indeed he admits that love stories repeat themselves and are quite banal. Then he starts to talk, *somewhat mysteriously* [italics mine], about a grave, the mother's grave, the mother's background, fate, the fate of distinguished women and eventually the grotesquely

deformed tale of Jim's Jewel. Thus he manages to add a touch of originality to a worn out archetypal topic." *York Notes* (Longmans, 1985), p. 37.

17 Edward Said, *Orientalism* (London: Routledge and Kegan Paul, 1978), pp. 6, 186–8, 190.

18 B. J. Moore-Gilbert, *Kipling and Orientalism* (London: Croom Helm, 1986), pp. 139–42.

19 Jean-Marie Schaeffer, "Literary Genres and Textual Genericity," in Gerald Graff, *The Future of Literary Theory*, p. 177.

20 Homi Bhabha, "The Other Question: Difference, Discrimination, and the Discourse of Colonialism," in *Literature, Politics and Theory*, Francis Barker and Peter Hulme, eds (London: Methuen, 1986), p. 162.

21 Ben Shepherd, "Showbiz Imperialism; The Case of Peter Lobengula," in *Imperialism and Popular Culture*, John Mackenzie, ed. (Manchester: Manchester University Press, 1986), pp. 94–112.

22 Kenneth Ballhatchet, *Race, Sex and Class under the Raj, 1793–1905* (New Delhi: Vikas, 1979), pp. 96–122.

23 Malcolm Bradbury, *Forster, A Collection of Critical Essays* (New Delhi: Prentice Hall, 1979), pp. 1–6.

24 Janet Batsleer, Tony Davies, Rebecca O'Rourke and Chris Weedon, "Gender and Genres: Women's Stories," *Rewriting English: The Cultural Politics of Gender and Class* (London, NY: Methuen, 1985), p. 95.

25 Linda Hutcheon, *The Politics of Postmodernism* (London: Routledge, 1989), p. 93.

26 Linda Hutcheon, *Narcissistic Narrative* (New York: Methuen, 1984), p. 5.

27 Catherine Belsey, *Critical Practice* (London: Methuen, 1980), p. 107.

28 B. J. Moore-Gilbert, *Kipling and Orientalism*, pp. 7, 8.

29 Kwame Anthony Appiah, "Is the Post in Postmodern the Post in Post-Colonial?" *Critical Inquiry*, 17, 2 (Winter 1991), p. 348.

30 Kwame Anthony Appiah, "Is the Post?" pp. 349–56.

31 Paul Connerton, ed., Introduction, *Critical Sociology* (Harmondsworth: Penguin, 1976), pp. 17, 18.

32 Henry Louis Gates, Jr., "Authority, (White) Power, and the (Black) Critic," in Ralph Cohen, ed., *The Future of Literary Theory*, p. 343.

33 Gerald Graff, "The Future of Theory," p. 267.

Chapter 14

From The Book of Sodom

Paul Hallam 1952–

Introduction

Paul Hallam is a writer for film, television, and stage, sometimes also an actor. Among his film script credits are "Nighthawks" (1978), "North of Vortex" (1991), "Young Soul Rebels" (1991), and "Caught Looking" (1991). When "Caught Looking" was shown on British television in 1991, it provoked outrage and headlines like "Children Star in 'Gay' Film." The film is about a schoolteacher who cruises gay bars by night, making it "difficult to exclude children from the school scenes." As a clearly self-identified gay man, Hallam both chooses and is confined to the cultural fringe.

Though not in any usual sense a biblical scholar, Hallam finds himself living in a biblically shaped world. As a gay man, he has been declared a citizen of the biblical city, Sodom, a city long ago torn loose from the pages of Genesis by the phobic imagination and now mapped onto the "alleyways, dark passages and stone steps down" of any "city worth its salt." Wherever he lives, he lives in this city created in popular imagination by the Bible. He thus develops an existence symbiotic with the book that oppresses him. "You can devise your own rituals, structure your grief around the Bible....It is the ultimate book for obsessives, and I'm an obsessive. I came to enjoy the lists, the tables, genealogies, variant readings..." (p. 96). He finds himself compelled into a life of exegesis.

The second and longer part of the book is an anthology of other people's writings about Sodom, from Proust to Dostoyevsky, with many others less well known. In the first part, from which our selection is taken, Hallam takes us, like a native guide, on "A Circuit Walk" of Sodom, sharing his city as he navigates its London precincts. The Circuit Walk is a "word map" that serves as a guide to Hallam's London-Sodom and an introduction to the anthology. He uses a thread of autobiography to weave together London's Sodomitic history. He draws on a great variety of texts, whether print or celluloid. In all these Sodom fragments he finds "a comment on my life." Little outposts of Sodom, welcome points for the weary (male) refugees who have followed all the warning signs (warning signs are route maps) home. Hallam's "Circuit Walk" is an excellent example of exegesis as a cottage industry.

In this excerpt, Hallam takes us through from London book stalls to the Marx Memorial Library. Though he picks up three recent academic studies of Sodom, these scholarly fantasies fail to captivate him as much as the older popular ones. As a "Sodom obsessive," he has a particular fondness for the little tracts and commentaries – Christian, Socialist, Rationalist – by which the idea of Sodom first enters the lives of ordinary people, the working class. Marx and Engels, who look no better from the Sodomite standpoint than the religious propagandists, are reproached, but laughingly. They should at least have read the Talmud.

[. . .] I turn the corner, to continue the Sodom search and head for the Farringdon Road bookstalls; there, or at bookshops later in the day, I'm bound to find fresh Sodoms. The bulk of cheap second-hand books are religious; in posher shops they're pricier and called "theological." So many verbose vicars, whingeing from their country parishes on the sins of far-off cities, especially the cities of the plain. All had their day on Sodom. I'd always ignored the theology sections of bookshops, now I'm addicted.

Bibles themselves, even seventeenth-century ones, are not hard to come by, and they're surprisingly cheap. I must have flicked through dozens in the past year. Letters, sentimental prayer-cards and hand-stitched markers slip their pages as you pick them up. Unsexy confetti. I look to see if there's a family tree inscribed on the Bible inside cover. Often there is. A book that has been handed down, generation to generation, but at some time recently, the handing stopped, someone flung the Bible. My copy belonged once to the Shorters. I know the date of the Shorter unions, their births. I notice some Shorter branches that stop short as others multiply. I wonder about that bachelor boy Shorter and his spinster sister. A Sodom family tree should be started. I'm grateful to Gregory Woods for a footnote in his *Articulate Flesh: Male Homo-Eroticism and Modern Poetry*. He drew my attention to a *Gay Sunshine* interview with Allen Ginsberg in which he "established, as a kind of Apostolic succession, his own homosexual descent from Whitman, by pointing out that he (Ginsberg) slept with Neal Cassady, who slept with Gavin Arthur, who slept with Edward Carpenter, who slept with Walt Whitman himself." Ginsberg added that this was "an interesting sort of thing to have as part of the mythology." I started to play this game, thinking of friends who'd slept with friends who used to know and maybe met . . . Perhaps I should start a page to rival the pages of the Shorters, or patent this as a Sodom software game.

Even cheaper, and more plentiful than the Bibles, the commentaries. Annotations, questions and answers, radical reinterpretations, revisions, dissertations, speculations; some as never before illustrated throughout "with proper maps." Before starting this book, I'd never thought to look at them. They range from the massive, multi-volume and serious tomes, by indisputably learned divines, to little books of homely homilies. There are endless Bible Picture Books, Bible Tales Re-told, Characters from the Bible and Guide Books to the Bible Land. Within their pages there are running commentaries, free-wheeling footnotes on just about anything the reverends care to mention. I've found many an attack on the French Revolution, as foreseen in Revelation.

Paul Hallam, from *The Book of Sodom* (London and New York: Verso, 1993).

I enjoy the details of the books, the vanities of the divines, the listing of their qualifications. The number of the edition sold. *Portraits from The Bible* (Old Testament Series) is by the Right Rev. Ashton Oxenden, D.D., Bishop of Montreal, and Metropolitan of Canada. It was published by Hatchard's of Piccadilly in 1876, and was on its thirty-four thousandth. The Preface is classic Victoriana.

> It is hoped that this Volume may be used by *Heads of Families*, who wish to give some short simple instruction to their Servants and Children; and also by *Cottagers*, as a book to be read on Sunday Evenings.

(I hope cottagers enjoyed the experience.)

> The Author has aimed at nothing new. Neither has he sought for difficulties with the view of removing them. But his desire has been to bring before the reader some of those Portraits which are sketched in the Sacred Volume for us to gaze upon. And he trusts that he may have succeeded in drawing attention to the prominent features in these characters. ...May God, who has seen fit to teach His people by example, as well as by precept, enable us to profit by the living Pictures which He holds up to us in His Word, leading us "to refuse the evil, and choose the good!"

Worth risking 25p on, for an essay on Lot aimed for the family reader, to instruct the children, not forgetting the servants. How will he deal with the sins of Sodom? Lot's incestuous union with his daughters? Though aiming at "nothing new," he promises not to remove the difficulties. The reader may judge, his essay on Lot appears in *The Book of Sodom*.

Another 25p-priced earnest reverend, the Rev. J. Paterson Smyth, B.D., LL.D., LITT. D., D.C.L., Late Professor of Pastoral Theology, University of Dublin, sets tests for his young readers in *The Bible for School and Home: The Book of Genesis*. Smyth swears by tests. So did my religious instruction teacher at secondary school. He could, and frequently did, reduce many a test-failing fourteen-year-old boy to tears.

> *Questions for Lesson VII*
> Who was Lot?
> He treated Abram rather selfishly?
> His choice led him into a dangerous place? How was it dangerous?
> What did he gain and what did he lose by going there?
> What happened to Sodom?
> What happened to Lot?

Such questions, the Reverend suggests, might be asked at home, in school and at Sunday school. Unfortunately there is no upside-down list of answers to see how well you've done. It would be interesting to try this out on schoolchildren. I should have sent out a questionnaire, I'd like to know what children make of Sodom.

It isn't only quality writing about Sodom that interests me. I enjoy the authoritative tone of old encyclopaedists. I find myself drawn to cheap educational books, whatever their perspective. Not simply to smile at them, though sometimes the digs are hard to resist.

I wonder how many people read such books? How many of them found their way into working-class homes? And I wonder whether books like them became as important to their readers as *The Book of Knowledge* became to me? *The Book of Knowledge* was the one set of books we had at home. The Dead Sea must have lain somewhere between the covers of the volume CRU–GERA. I remember the clusters of letters of these reference book spines, as if they were proper nouns. A source book for countless homeworks, a book I pored through with Mum. She loved the pages on Egypt and the picture-story ruins of Rome. My mother, Kathleen (not that I'd ever have called her by her first name), Kathleen, who never went out of the country, but saved hard for my school-trip to Rome.

In seeking Sodom, what reference was there for a young, latent resident? Many must have had picture books of the Bible in their homes. Most such books leave the reader with a very vague impression of Sodom's sins. I certainly never connected the swear-word with any story. "Sod, as in grass sod," you'd add, to distinguish it from a word more wicked and mysterious. "As in grass sod," you'd say, to show you weren't really swearing! "Sod" was on the select list of acceptable swear-words at home. There was a definite list of words you could use, and ones that would end with a clip round the ear. I was allowed a party piece, a sentence-long flourish: "Bloody 'ell fire Jack, bugger and blast." Which contains enough biblical reference to deserve a commentary of its own. I didn't know then, admired by aunts for childish cheek, that "bugger" was a racist corruption of *bougre* and referred to Bulgaria, where Manichaean and Albigensian heresies flourished. Heretics everywhere supposed to be buggerers. You could spend a whole Book of Buggery unravelling the word. I knew none of this then. Neither, I suspect, did my aunts.

The images and colours of Sunday school picture books remain with me. Deep-blue skies, the shepherds' crooks and their fabulous outfits. The stars in the skies, like those given for good work at school. I didn't have many books then, and I didn't hang on to them, I'm re-supplied now by bookstalls and jumble sales. I've picked up at least five *Look and Learn*-style archaeology books. *Look and Learn* was an educational picture-book magazine, it arrived weekly through our letter-box at home, at my request. My childhood assertion that I was getting too grown-up for comics. The archaeology books, the odd volumes of encyclopaedias, are often at odds on Sodom. All affirm its former existence, but some assert that it stood at the north end of the Dead Sea, others are certain it was at the south. My undated, circa 1920, two-volume *The Story of the Bible* (Amalgamated Press) is a tale told by "Living Writers of Authority" (Revds, Very Revds, prebs, canons and the odd Sir) and is copiously illustrated with "famous masterpieces of religious art *and* Modern Camera Pictures from the Lands of the Bible." A photograph of neatly arranged artefacts is captioned: "RETRIEVED FROM THE DESTROYED 'CITIES OF THE PLAIN'. This array of stone mortars, pestles, and other tools, was found on what may be the site of Sodom. Research and excavation have established that this part of Palestine was peopled and prosperous when Abraham came there shortly before its destruction." As a child, and this book was meant for the edification of children, I would scarcely have noticed the "may." I would have been fascinated by the pictures of the inhabitants of the Bible lands, still living, it suggests, as in Abraham's time. The stress throughout is on the unchanging, the timeless nature of life in Palestine. The photographs, striving to authenticate, are black and white and bizarrely tinted in a range of orange and blue.

The Story is cautious on the sins of Sodom; the men, young and old, "made an onslaught on the house to ill-treat the two messengers." No photograph or painting here to aid the puzzled reader, unless you count the preserved pestles. They're still pressed out, these Bible books for all the family. *Stories and Legends from the Bible* (1988) by K. McLeish offers, according to its jacket, Bible narratives with no "interpretation or aside." In McLeish the Sodomites know precisely what they want of the angels: "We want to rape them," they declare. No exclamation mark, I called back at the remainder bookshop to check.

Approaching Sodom this way, wondering how the idea of the city first entered people's lives. Looking for books that might have been given by aunts at Christmas, or as free introductory offers by missionaries. In the revised edition of John Stow's massive *Surveys of the Cities of London and Westminster and the Borough of Southwark* (1598, "very much enlarged" in 1720 by John Strype and sundry "careful hands") there's a chapter on "The Spiritual Government of London." It gives the latest on the progress of the Society for the Reformation of Manners. After approving the progress in closing the "Sodomitical Houses" there's a report of a book bonanza.

> . . . on *Good Friday*, 1704 were given away at the Churches of *London* and *Westminster*, and several other Parishes near *London*, many Thousands of such good Books, *viz.*
> *A Pastoral Letter, being an earnest Exhortation to take Care of the Soul.*
> *The Necessary Duty of Family Prayer.*
> *An Account of the Progress of the Reformation of Manners.*
> *The Present State of the Charity Schools.*
> *The Representation of the Immorality of the* English *Stage.*
> There are also printed, for these religious Purposes, Books of Preparation for the Receiving the Holy Sacrament, small books for the Use of Seamen in their Voyages, and Soldiers in their Camps and Services.

Many a Sodom would have been found in the *Account of the Progress*, with its "desire to prevent the Spreading of the Leprosy of Sin," and you would almost certainly find it on the English stage. But most could read neither free books nor fine bound; they'd be more likely to hear of Sodom in a sermon. Those who *were* struggling to read would probably have come across Sodom in the Bible, the one book likely to be found in the house. If they began in the Beginning they would not have had far to go. Around the time of the revised Stow, *Select Trials* were becoming popular; you might read of Sodom there, if, that is, you selected Sodomy.

Some days I'll wander from the stalls to bookshops, looking for second-hand Sodoms, for more obvious and directly related books, for Sodom studies. Enough of the cut-price clergy. One of the slightly chill experiences of late is the sometimes obvious explanation behind the bulging "new in stock" shelves. New stock after deaths. My local second-hand bookseller confirmed what I'd already suspected: the sixties porn that he'd like to clear had belonged to a man who had recently died. No more spending, no more the creamy essence. Once cherished pin-ups now dumped in the corner, un-admired. Gay's the Word bookshop recently replenished its second-hand stock after a funeral. Not that this puts me off, collectors have to follow hearses, it's part of the course. I wonder about the books, though, the magazines. Were they bundled off before the descent of family, to spare their sensibilities? I've known it happen. Henry C. Ashbee, obsessive collector of erotica, and of rare first editions and translations of Cervantes, stipulated in his will: take one book, take them all. A spirited and shrewd move, for this is how the British Library came to possess such a precious "Private Case." The porn would have been rejected but for the value of Cervantes. Without that clause in Ashbee's will, this book, and many before it, would have been that much more difficult to research. The provenance of the literature of Sodom. In Southend once I picked up most of my second-hand Gide and several biographies of Cocteau. Inside the covers, the black-ink stamp "Salvage." The books discarded from the USAF Bomb Division, Upper Heyford. Every time I open one I think about the man who selected these books for the edification of bomber pilots. I enjoy this second-hand Sodomite relation with the bomber boys' librarian. Sodom salvaged.

Also flown in from the States, at Gay's the Word, a shelf of Sodom studies, hot off the university presses. University studies weren't like this in my day, I find myself reflecting as I take in the latest titles. Three catch my eye. Barry Burg's *Sodomy and the Pirate Tradition: English Sea Rovers in the Seventeenth Century* is the oldest (1984) and the easiest read. There's scarcely any starting point for Burg's speculations on widespread bucca-neer buggery, few pirates kept notes. All-male expeditions over periods of three to four years at sea, with stop-offs on isolated Caribbean islands, a subject ripe for scholarly fantasy. Burg did, however, uncover two Sodoms. Thomas Walduck, a Barbadian colonial, wrote, in 1710, of the Caribbean:

> All Sodom's Sins are Centered in thy heart
> Death is thy look and Death in every part
> Oh! Glorious Isle in Vilany excell
> Sins to the Height – thy fate is Hell.

And earlier, in 1655, Madam Margaret Heathcote wrote to her cousin John Winthrop Jr about life in Antigua: "And truely, Sir, I am not so much in love with any as to goe much abroad . . . they all be a company of sodomites that live here." Burg asserts that Port Royal was seen as "the Sodom of the Universe" by those who visited and exploited it. With a different title, the Burg would be fine as a general introductory study of seventeenth-century sodomy, with a digression on the buccaneers. But with a different title, would it sell?

More complex than Burg, the recent studies in the realm of "sodomy, that utterly confused category" of Foucault. Foucault's line always finds a place in these new Sodom texts. Gregory W. Bredbeck's *Sodomy and Interpretation: Marlowe to Milton* sets off with a trawl of sixteenth- and seventeenth-century dictionaries, like Florio's *A Worlde of Wordes, or Most Copious and Exact Dictionarie in Italian and English* (London, 1598), and finds:

> Sodomia, the naturall sin of Sodomie.
> Sodomita, a sodomite, a buggrer.
> Sodomitare, to commit the sinne of Sodomie.

Sodomitarie, sodomiticall tricks.
Sodomitico, sodomiticall.

The later *Glossographia: Or a Dictionary Interpreting the Hard Words of Whatsoever Language, Now Used in our Refined English Tongue* (1670) by Thomas Blount, is more complicated and cross-referenced. A conflation of Sodomites, inglers, catamites, buggerers and Ganymedes. For example:

Ingle (Span, from the Lat. Inguen, i. the groin) a boy kept for Sodomy. See *Ganymede*.

Bredbeck shifts from these definitions to a meticulous exploration of Renaissance texts, and sometimes crosses paths with Jonathan Goldberg. Goldberg chooses for his title a word absent from Florio's flourish, *Sodometries: Renaissance Texts, Modern Sexualities*. *Sodometries*, from Stanford University Press, has a delicious detail from Ghirlandaio's *Visitation* on the cover. Three boys, leaning over a parapet, look down on a city. And in so doing they present three choice, contoured bums, bent for the viewer to admire. "Sodometries," splendid sound, was once a portmanteau word for all manner of perceived villainy and vice. I first came across it in Thomas Nashe's *The Unfortunate Traveller* (1594):

Italy, the paradise of the earth and the epicure's heaven, how doth it form our young master? It makes him to kiss his hand like an ape, cringe his neck like a starveling, and play at heypass, repass come aloft, when he salutes a man. From thence he brings the art of atheism, the art of epicurising, the art of whoring, the art of poisoning, the art of sodomitry. The only probable good thing they have to keep us from utterly condemning it is that it maketh a man an excellent courtier, a curious carpet knight; which is, by fine interpretation, a fine close lecher, a glorious hypocrite. It is by now a privy note amongst the better sort of men, when they would set a singular mark or brand on a notorious villain, to say he hath been in Italy.

A list, the sheer linguistic vigour of which I can't help but admire. There are dozens of such Sodom jibes at Italians, more vicious ones at Turks. And sometimes, as Goldberg relates, there was genocidal "justification" in the labelling of the native populations of the New World as Sodomites. Goldberg leaps deftly between modern Sodoms, Renaissance literature and stories of conquests and colonisation. What I didn't expect was for this book to begin with an analysis of an ad for a T-shirt. On the T-shirt in question (Goldberg reproduces it) we see the back-view of a camel. Saddam Hussein's face stares out from the camel's arse. The advertisement invites Americans to "Make A Statement . . . Express Your Patriotism." The 100 per cent cotton, top quality American Made T-shirt (MasterCard, Visa accepted) bears a message: "America Will Not be Saddam-ized." I discover from the footnotes that this T-shirt, along with other Gulf War tack, has been widely discussed among American academics. Rightly so, for Saddam was a fortuitous name, it could help whip up American fears and loathing, help justify the far-off war. Similar fears informed many a European Renaissance text. Surprisingly, the ad is taken from *Rolling Stone* magazine and not a K.K.K. bulletin.

What does this say about the paper's rock-fan readers? Would they wear it as a serious statement? Or in ironic play? The Goldberg variations on the theme of the T-shirt are startling and, if you can settle into the language of theory, witty and worthwhile. It encourages you to look more closely at the earlier Sodom texts.

Three Sodom studies, all important, all undeniably of interest. But they don't affect me, these scholarly Sodoms, in quite the same way as the simple Sodom reference in an old, discarded textbook, or a Bible tale retold and newly illustrated in living colour.

On the bookshop trail I've noticed a lot of classic Marxist texts about of late, shelves and stacks of them. Evidence of socialist spring-cleans? Like the porn, another embarrassment in front of family, in front of friends? Clear-outs, perhaps, after the Wall? I remember the book sale at the Marx Memorial Library, surely they can't be flogging off *their* stock? I'm still looking for socialist versions of Sodom. There's a tendency to skip biblical reference in the volumes I've scanned. The authors prefer to have a go at Greek gods, those decadent Athenians. Thus Engels in the *The Origin of the Family, Private Property and the State*:

> ... this degradation of women was avenged on the men and degraded them also, till they fell into the abominable practice of sodomy and degraded alike their gods and themselves with the myth of Ganymede.

Ganymede, in his Zeus suit, stars in the myth of the upwardly mobile. Ganymede, shepherd-boy, carried off and abused by a Sodomite god.

As it turns out the library is discarding a bunch of bourgeois novels, books and pamphlets on the Communist rebuilding of postwar Eastern Europe (optimistic new townscapes featuring handsome, hunky builders on scaffolding) and a quirky selection of sideline socialisms. The standard texts have stayed, as they should. I pick up a slim volume with the library bookplate, it features an etching of Marx and a Lenin quote, "Without a revolutionary theory there cannot be a revolutionary movement." It's pasted into "Human Origins" by Samuel Laing, revised by Edward Cloud, a book issued for the Rationalist Press Association in 1903. In his introduction, Laing hopes for success in "stimulating some minds, especially those of my younger readers, and of the working-classes who are striving after culture..." In attempting to demolish one set of prejudices, fundamentalist interpretations of the Bible, Laing slips easily into others. In a chapter on "The Historical Element in the Old Testament" he suggests that

> When we arrive at Abraham we feel as if we might be treading on really historical ground. There is the universal tradition of the Hebrew race that he was their ancestor, and his figure is very like what in the unchanging East may be met with to the present day. We seem to see the dignified sheik sitting at the door of his tent dispensing hospitality, raiding with his retainers on the rear of a retreating army and capturing booty, and much exercised by domestic difficulties between the women of his household. Surely this is an historical figure.

Surely not, Laing answers himself. "Doubts and difficulties appear." He's suspicious of Abraham's ability to have lived to the ripe old age of 175, and to have had a son by Sarah when she was ninety-nine and he'd reached a hundred!

> Nor can we take as authentic history Abraham talking with the Lord, and holding a sort of Dutch auction with him, in which he beats down from fifty to ten the number of righteous men who, if found in Sodom, are to save it from destruction.

About the story of Lot's wife, Laing is quite clear. Centuries of pious pilgrims, he relates, until quite recent times, "saw, touched, and tasted" the pillar of salt supposed to be Lot's wife (a particularly bizarre kind of necrophilia Laing evokes here). There is a perfectly rational explanation:

> ...the volcanic eruptions were of an earlier geological age...the story of Lot's wife is owing to the disintegration of a stratum of salt marl, which weathers away under the action of wind and rain into columnar masses, like those in a similar formation in Catalonia described by Lyell.

Lot's wife, Laing adds, was variously described by the pilgrims:

> Some saw her big, some little, some upright, and some prostrate, according to the state of disintegration of the pillars, which change their form rapidly under the influence of the weather; but no doubt was entertained as to the attestation of the miracle. It turns out, however, to be one of those geological myths of precisely the same nature as that which attributed the Devil's Dyke near Brighton to an arrested attempt of the Evil One to cut a trench through the South Downs, so as to let in the sea and submerge the Weald.

That story nailed, the pillar of salt as much a myth as a South Downs dyke, Laing hastens to consider the incest. I can't pass by quite so easily. Lot's wife turned to salt. It has to deserve more than a Rationalist Press dismissal or a grounding by geology. Salt, common and cheap. Salt as a commodity, salt as symbol. A preservative yet something that changes the flavour. Lot's wife, turned into salt, unable ever to change, a frozen figure, sadly and for ever looking back. Salt, plentiful yet prized. A magic, transforming ingredient, yet basic. Salt of the earth. There's something barren about salt, a suggestion of sterility. Yet salt is the covenant between God and the Jews. Salt is a symbol of hospitality. It suggests, to sound like a soap ad, a touch of luxury. Rabbinical speculations suggest that Lot's wife popped round to the neighbours to borrow salt for her guests. Unintentionally, or with malice, she might, by so doing, have betrayed the presence of the guests to the Sodomites. Her fault, then, that the neighbours rushed round "to know" the strangers. Lot's wife commits a salt crime, and salt is her punishment. In other stories she's seen as a mean and inhospitable woman, tight with the salt.

Salt in our tears, our blood, our sweat, salt in our urine and saliva. Margaret Visser, in her *Much Depends on Dinner*, notes that:

> Sodom, in the neighbourhood of which Lot's wife turned into a pillar of salt (petrification, turning into stone, is a common story-punishment for looking back when you shouldn't –

but then, salt is "rock"), was near to the Dead Sea and to numerous salt mines. Its name is probably a contraction of *Sadeh Adom*, meaning "red field" or "field of blood." The reason may be that when solar salt is evaporated from brine springs and lakes, the concentrate often turns bright red because of bacterial action.

There are many stories of the pillar of salt. Among them that Lot's wife, after petrification, continued to have her periods. Reddened salt. The menstruation seen by gloating misogynists as another example of Sodom's uncleanness. You might see this intriguing woman in a different light, as the Sodomites' friend, unable to bear the thought of their burning. Madonna, Liz, Dionne, Barbra – they could all be up for the part. Or perhaps, in secret, she leaned to Gomorrah. Lot's wife, a south (or north) Dead Sea dyke. Jodie, maybe?

It endlessly confuses me, this example of God's punishment. I settle on the cleanness theory. Her punishment, as a friend of the unclean, to be turned into a scouring block. Sometimes, reading the story, and the stories of the story, I smile. There's another image of her, I can never quite escape it. I loved the large plastic tapering table-salt cones that stood on the kitchen table at home. Doll-like, with grand names like Cerebos or Saxa. I keep seeing Lot's wife as one vast, grand cone . . .

Laing, geology lesson over, turns his attention to the incest. A great many painters did the same. Sodom burns on canvas, but this most visual of events is often relegated to the background. The painters' attention would focus rather on the story of an ageing Lot made drunk by his nubile daughters. Laing brushes quickly past the scene. The story's end is:

> . . . clearly a myth to account for the aversion of the Hebrew to races so closely akin to them as the Moabites and Ammonites, and it could hardly have originated until after the date of the book of Ruth, which shows no trace of such a racial aversion.

As to Sodom itself, the supposed sins, Laing, author of *A Modern Zoroastrian*, says nothing. Perhaps to spare the sensibilities of his ideal young reader. The language of the introduction, the stepping round that awkward business with the angels, the overuse of "surely" and "surely not," the proudly displayed knowledge, not to mention the sweeping racial sterotypes. This is all familiar. Laing's tone is much the same as that of my 25p reduced-to-clear vicars. I admit, however, an affection for his book; it might well have found its way into those hotbeds of socialism, warm libraries of self-improvement, the Working Men's and Mechanics' Institutes (more fantasy locales). Questioning Genesis at all, it always involved a risk. None of my other cheap educational books of the period dared or desired to go so far.

Laing's wasn't exactly the socialist commentary I was hoping for. But at least I picked up a Marx Memorial bookplate, the cover stamped "Marx House," and an unexpected Sodom. Eventually I *was* directed to a fuller and less guarded Engels on ingles invective. Not quite socialist Sodom stories, but references to sodomy that draw on the Sodom image repertoire. Engels wrote to Marx ("dear Moor") from Manchester, in chummy club-man tone. Karl had sent Friedrich a copy of the work of pioneering gay theorist Karl Heinrich Ulrichs. Friedrich:

Well, that is a most curious "Urning" that you've sent me. These are indeed exceedingly unnatural revelations. The pederasts are beginning to stand up and be counted and discovering that they are a power in the state. All they lacked was organization, but to judge by this it seems already to exist secretly. And since they include such important men, in all the old and even the new parties, from Rösing to Schweitzer, they cannot fail to be victorious. "War to the front apertures, peace to the rear apertures of the body," will be their slogan now. It is fortunate that we personally are too old to have to worry that, at the victory of this party, we might have to pay physical tribute to the victors. But the young generation! Incidentally, only in Germany is it possible that a chap comes along and transforms this filth into a theory and then invites: Join us, etc. Unfortunately he still lacks the courage to declare himself openly as "that" and still has to operate before the public "from the front" though not, as he says in one place, by a slip, "in from the front." But just wait till the new North German Criminal Code recognizes the rights of the posterior, then he'll talk quite differently. And we poor frontal chaps, with our childish inclination towards women, we'll have a very thin time then. If that man Schweitzer were any use he might lure this strange solid citizen into disclosing the identities of those prominent and most prominent pederasts – which surely should not be difficult for him as a kindred spirit . . .
Yours, F.E.

The Sodomite conspiracy, the Sodomite threat to the young, Sodomite organisation and the assumed freemasonry. You could marry the words of Engels and Countess Waldeck. Left and right, their insults interchangeable. They can't both be correct about Sodomites, surely? And why is it that the most unattractive of "frontal chaps" always voice fears of a threat to the rear? If not their own (as if . . .) then the rears of the young. There's always this knowledge of the attraction of men, many of the elaborations on Sodom stress the angels' beauty, many paint them young. Our frontal Friedrich at least concedes that the posterior rights brigade might have a use, they could help draw up a list, expose Sodomites in High Places, name names . . .

It's the "filthy" in this letter that stops me short. I've always cared for the slightly soiled, the worn, the frayed, found comfort in the chipped and the rusting. I've seen "filth" used so often, it has to be seen as our Sodomite mark, our emblem. You don't need a Freud Memorial Library to dream up connections. I'll accept the dirt tattoo. I can't imagine a world without dirt.

It might explain why I find the mushrooming of smart gay café bars in Soho so alarming, a gay village (small town, Zoar) that looks less and less like Sodom, more and more like the cleaned-up Covent Garden. A sanitised Sodom. Sodom clean and cold, with fake class. Out, the decay, the smutty and the sleaze. The fashionable club night, Village Youth, I find a stress on either word alarming. I like the slightly scarred, the bruised. The clean attractive only when it's obsessively, fetishistically so. Clean governed by a rule book of cleanliness, sailor spruce, soldier smart, their ritual of spit and polish. The fantasy, then, is to soil, to lay waste to regulations. Strewn uniform.

I can't rejoice at the brave new world of television sanitary sex guides. These too are essentially clean. Spruce young presenters look intensely interested as guests reveal the secrets of their S/M parties. Cut to: an alternative comedian in a condom sketch. Cut to: the video guide to lovers in a Laura Ashley setting. Sometimes there's an orgasm guide from a brash older woman; preferably she speaks with a cockney or a Liverpudlian accent. The voice of the no-nonsense working class. Sometimes there's even a drag queen, to rough the programme up a little, give it extra credibility.

No darkness, no mystery here, gays fully included, even fashionable. In Berlin, ten years or so ago, I was excited by the glass-fronted gay bars, open to the streets, no curtains necessary. I couldn't believe it, I thought it could never happen here. There'd be bricks through the windows. Now it has happened I'm not so sure about the triumph of style over Sodom. It has to be good that a Queer Carnival can parade through Soho, christen it Queer Town. But the ever-so-educated English voices declaring themselves "queer" made me wince. It's not the politics of "queer" that bothers me, it's the arrogance of English arts and media queens thinking themselves queerer than anyone else. Nothing very queer about making gay programmes for Channel 4, I know, I've done it myself.

I want neither bricks nor brimstone. No return to the fears of the fifties, the closed-curtain clubs. It's just that I miss Satyricon Sodom. Sodom circuit-walks should take in alleyways, dark passages, stone steps down. I'm wary of the clean and pure, and all that is done in their name. Leave a few corners dark, not designer dark, but plain.

If I wallow in nostalgia for seedier, smokier Sodoms I'll confirm some of John Evelyn's early eco-fears. He complained in his 1661 *Fumifugium or the Inconveniencie of the Aer and Smoak of London* that the "horrid smoak" imparted "a bitter and ungrateful Tast to those few wretched Fruits, which never arriving at their desired maturity, seem, like the Apples of Sodome, to fall even to dust, when they are but touched." I should have checked Green lists for Sodom, I didn't think . . .

I leave the Marx Memorial Library, pass the cottage, overgrown with weeds, council-closed, padlocked with rusty chains. I hope that socialist trysts were once kept there. Picture scholars, relaxing after a long day's sweat, engaged with the Electro-plate boys, men of neighbouring light industries. A Sodomite solidarity.

I've read many an explanation/apologia for the Marx/Engels position on Ganymede, how they couldn't be expected, at that time, to take up the Uranian cause. "In fact, the conceptual vocabulary to enable rational discussion of sex did not exist in Marx's time," etc. This is usually accompanied by a gentle knuckle-rapping (they were forward enough on other fronts, these frontal men, after all). Polite apologias, historically inaccurate. They clearly knew the Ulrichs argument, and simply mocked. They must have known about the revocation of anti-sodomy laws that followed from the French Revolution. The later apologias are more devious than the letter itself. What does surprise, though, is the seeming lack of socialist interest in the Jewish stories of Sodom, wonderfully written up in Louis Ginsberg's *The Legends of the Jews*. Sodom's judges named as Liar, Arch-deceiver, Falsifier and Perverter of Judgement. Strangers in Sodom tortured or deviously offered money but no food, and left to starve. The richer the man of Sodom, the more the law favoured him. Talmudic commentaries, wonderfully bleak and often funny tales that repeatedly expose the iniquities of greed, skip past the "to know" business, past the fears of the frontal men.

Time to move on. One last look back at Turnmills. Ginsberg tells how Lot's disbelieving sons-in-law called Lot a fool for believing the grim warnings – after all, "Violins, cymbals, and flutes resound in the city." House, Homocore and Techno resound in ours, but there are warnings. Cries against ff. [. . .]

Notes

p. 234   See Winston Leyland, ed., *Gay Sunshine Interviews* 1, San Francisco 1978, where Ginsberg is interviewed by Allen Young.

p. 235   Right Rev. Ashton Oxenden, D. D., *Portraits from The Bible* (Old Testament Series), Hatchard's of Piccadilly 1876.

       The Rev. J. Paterson Smyth, *The Bible for School and Home: The Book of Genesis*, Sampson Low, Marston & Co., Ltd, London 1894.

p. 236   Living Writers of Authority, *The Story of the Bible*, Amalgamated Press, London, undated.

p. 237   K. McLeish, *Stories and Legends from the Bible*, Longman, London 1988.

       John Stow, *Surveys of the Cities of London and Westminster and the Borough of Southwark*, London 1598, "very much enlarged" in 1720 by John Strype and sundry "careful hands."

p. 238   I am indebted to three scholarly Sodoms: Barry Burg, *Sodomy and the Pirate Tradition: English Sea Rovers in the Seventeenth Century*, New York University Press, New York and London 1984; Gregory W. Bredbeck, *Sodomy and Interpretation: Marlowe to Milton*, Cornell University Press, Ithaca and London 1991; and Jonathan Goldberg, *Sodometries: Renaissance Texts, Modern Sexualities*, Stanford University Press, Stanford, CA 1992.

       Michel Foucault discusses "sodomy, that utterly confused category" in *A History of Sexuality*, Volume 1: *An Introduction*, Allen Lane, London 1979.

p. 239   Thomas Nashe, *The Unfortunate Traveller*, London 1594.

p. 240   Friedrich Engels on those Greeks in *The Origin of the Family, Private Property and the State*, quoted in Jeffrey Weeks, "Where Engels Feared to Tread," *Gay Left*, 1, autumn 1975.

       Samuel Laing, revised by Edward Cloud, "The Historical Element in the Old Testament," in *Human Origins*, Rationalist Press Association, London 1903.

p. 241   Margaret Visser, *Much Depends on Dinner*, Penguin, London 1989. I had begun my ruminations on salt when Antony Peattie referred me to this book. Some of Visser's striking observations wove into mine.

p. 242   Philip Derbyshire drew my attention to the June 1869 letter of Friedrich Engels to Marx in *The Marx–Engels Correspondence*, selected and edited by F. J. Raddatz, translated by Ewald Owens, Weidenfeld & Nicolson, London 1981.

p. 244   John Evelyn, *Fumifugium or the Inconveniencie of the Aer and Smoak of London – With Some Remedies*, London 1661.

       "In fact, the conceptual vocabulary . . . " from Randal Kincaid, "Was Marx Anti-Gay?" *Gay Left*, autumn 1976.

       Louis Ginsberg, *The Legends of the Jews*, vol. 1, translated from the German by Henrietta Szold, the Jewish Publication Society of America, Philadelphia 1908.

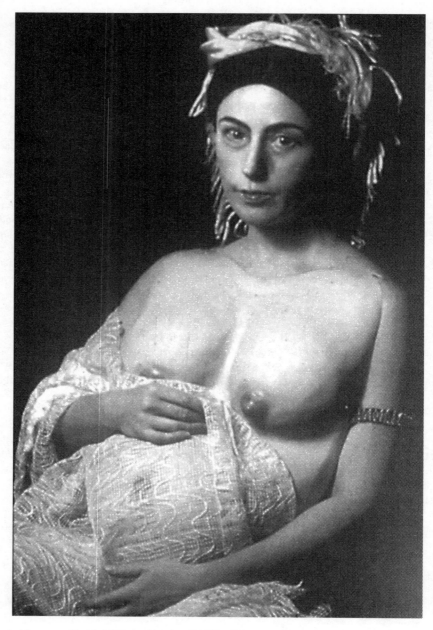

Cindy Sherman, *Untitled (History Painting #205)*, 1989. Metro Pictures, New York.

Part III

The Conscience of the Bible

Introduction

The line of separation between this section and Part II is not a sharp one. Some selections could be moved between the two. The selections here, while they still raise questions of "the Politics of Reading," tend to do so at a theoretical distance from immediate situations. Many of them thus occupy a level of discourse similar to that of the selections in Part I. This distance focuses upon the relationship of postmodernism to ethics, which is a fundamental question in recent debate, and founding religious texts, particularly the Bible, are inevitably implicated in battles over this territory. We have sought selections which engage the question in the broadest possible ways.

Our Selections in Context

We have made our choices with an eye to the real importance of these pieces, and these authors, rather than for any specific stance they take to one or another definition of postmodernism. Some of our authors (Derrida, Levinas, Spivak) stand near the center of postmodern debate, though in the case of Levinas this was not always so; the "postmodern" Levinas is a product of the response to him by other postmodern figures, especially Derrida (see Bernasconi and Critchley, 1991), and his current centrality indicates how the "center" has moved. Others (Dussel, Serres) powerfully contest the concept and the practices of postmodernism from ambiguous positions "outside," while one (Scarry) shows little overt sign of interest in these debates. Where we have particularly wanted to let a certain voice be heard, we have not hesitated to cross the lines drawn by different theorists of "the postmodern." In the case of Spivak we have broadened even the notion of "Bible" to include other scriptures of the world.

In this Introduction, we will put our selections in context in two ways. Firstly, we will provide some extra information about the ones less well known. Secondly, we will deal with the difficult issue that four of the selections (Derrida, Dussel, Serres, Scarry) are excerpted from books in which they form part of a larger argument. In these cases we will need to sketch the entire book.

No one is more at home in our collection than Jacques Derrida, one of the preeminent figures in postmodernism, the founder of "deconstruction," and one who has often written about biblical texts. Our selection is the third of the four chapters of his *The Gift of Death*. This book is one of Derrida's main explorations of ethics, and so fits closely with our concerns in this section. He examines the attempt within Western tradition to find a stable philosophical grounding for a science of ethics, and argues that such attempts have been steadily undermined from the side of religion by ethical attitudes associated with Judaism and Christianity. It is true that these religions have often themselves developed ethical systems, but there is subversively present in them a radical understanding of the ethical moment when the individual, alone before God, has to decide – without the guidance of any system and without starting any new system. The ethical response in this situation is often "unethical," irresponsible, outrageous according to any system. Derrida argues that such experience is not a rarity confined to religious heroes, but is the frequent ethical experience of everyone. To make his case, he turns primarily to two biblical texts. In our selection he reads Genesis 22:1–18, the "sacrifice of Isaac," the story of Abraham faced with impossible ethical decision (for another reading of this text, see our selection from Lacan). In the next and final chapter Derrida will turn to the New Testament, to the Sermon on the Mount in Matthew 5–7.

One of Derrida's major conversation partners throughout *The Gift of Death* is Emmanuel Levinas. Levinas, and the reception of his work, have had a major role in making a "re-emphasis on ethics" so basic a feature of the postmodern shift (see Introduction to Part I: p. 44, cf. p. 45; for a direct response by Levinas himself to the debates he has fomented, see Bernasconi and Critchley, 1991: 3–10). Our selection from Levinas is one of his many "talmudic readings" (see also Levinas, 1990). The Talmud is the authoritative codification of rabbinic Jewish readings of the Bible up to the sixth century CE. Reading of the Talmud is the traditional form of orthodox Jewish learning, but Levinas's readings, with their immediate links to problems of the twentieth century, are far from traditional. Some of the others are more extensive, and perhaps more notable for their interpretive boldness. But the reading included here suits our purpose since it goes directly to the heart of Levinas's ethical position. It also provides a most effective introduction to his interpretive method (see Aronowicz, 1990: xv–xxvii), for Levinas claims that one of the topics of this part of the Talmud is "precisely the scope of exegesis" (320). He theorizes about hermeneutics by doing it.

Our selection from Enrique Dussel consists of three of the 20 chapters of his *Ethics and Community*. This book is in two parts. The first presents (under "Ten Fundamental Themes") the systematic shape of an ethical theology based on social analysis from the perspective of the oppressed of the Third World. The second part takes up (under "Ten Disputed Questions") particular ethical issues, mostly having to do with the new economic "globalization." Each chapter makes reference to a number of biblical passages, but is headed by one, quoted in full, which functions rather as the text of a sermon. Our selections – two themes, "Evil and Death" (Genesis 3:1–7) and "Relationships of Producers and Praxis of the People" (James 2:6–16), and one question, "Ethical Critique of Capital" (James 5:1–6) – have strong interconnections and give a sense of the flow of Dussel's total argument.

This selection is so different, in the tone and the substance of its treatment of the Bible, from almost anything else that we have included in this volume, that some explanation is needed. Dussel comes from Latin America, outside the Euro-American "center" of biblical studies and of the Western intellectual tradition generally. In fact, he is emerging as perhaps the major philosopher of the global "margin" (see esp. Dussel, 1985). Utterly conversant with the roots of the Western philosophical tradition, he interrogates that tradition from a location which the tradition itself has defined as marginal or peripheral. His aim is no less than to subvert Euro-American philosophy with a philosophy emerging from this margin. (Much the same could be said of Derrida, but where for Derrida the "margin" is all the topics that the dominant tradition must keep hidden in order to establish its systems, for Dussel the margin is primarily the global geographical margin, the parts of the world whose populations are predominantly non-white.) It is interesting that Dussel claims Levinas as a major teacher and ally (Mendieta, 1986: xvi).

Our difficulty in including Dussel was that, though he refers a good deal to the Bible, and also figures (from a mainly critical perspective; see below) in postmodern debate, he does not bring the two together. He seems never to think of the Bible as a *problem*, ethical or otherwise. Why this effective exemption of the Bible from critique? One of the main purposes of this *Reader*, as well as of *The Postmodern Bible*, is to question the tendency to exempt the Bible from critique. The Bible should "abide our question," any question that we can usefully and meaningfully address to it (Jobling, 1998: esp. 308–9). But we surmise that Dussel's gesture of exemption is a political one, essential to his whole program. The people out of whose midst he writes are people who need the Bible as a resource for struggle – and he is not willing to take it away from them. Our response has been to include some of his writing on the Bible and to contextualize it within postmodernism – using resources provided, in part, by Dussel himself.

Gayatri Chakravorty Spivak was born in India but has pursued her academic career mostly in the West. She first came to prominence with an almost book-length introduction to Derrida's early work *Of Grammatology*, and she has since been a central figure in postmodern debates. She has continued to work in the framework of Derridean deconstruction, persistently arguing its relevance and necessity for feminism and postcolonialism. Her essays are divided between those that remain subversively within the Western literary tradition and those which (like our selection) open up issues of colonialism and postcolonialism on a global scale (see the different sections of Spivak, 1988).

It is here that we have extended the meaning of "Bible" to include other scriptures. Our selection is an essay in which Spivak presents, with extensive introduction, a short story by Mahasweta Devi set in the Bengalese War of the early 1970s (the historical circumstances are explained by Spivak). In the story, Mahasweta plays on themes from the *Mahabharata*, the primary epic of India (it has become more familiar in the West through Peter Brook's six-hour dramatic adaptation: see Brook, 1989, a much longer television version made in India is said to have brought national life to a standstill as each weekly episode was aired). This is an example, from entirely outside the biblical tradition, of scripture appearing in just the sort of unfamiliar and fresh guise in which Jewish or Christian scripture appears in our other selections. This sort of extension seems to us to be, in our current cultural situation, very desirable. One of the boundaries which a postmodern reading of the Bible ought to interrogate is the one between the Bible and other scriptures.

Draupadi is the central female character of the epic. She is married to all of the five Pandava brothers, who are its main positive characters, and who hold everything in common. Supposedly safe under their protection, she is in fact lost to their enemy in a game of dice by the eldest brother, who has a gambling compulsion. To humiliate her, the enemy tries to strip her in public, but by a divine miracle she keeps her clothing and dignity (van Buitenen, 1975: 106–55; Narayan, 1978: chap. 7). Mahasweta, as Spivak explains, plays on this in a complex way, highlighting, as well as gender issues, also class issues which are readily recognized in the Indian and Bengalese context. For instance, the central character gets the name "Draupadi" not from her own oppressed tribal culture, but from her high-caste Hindu mistress (much as Western names have been given to Christian converts in Africa and elsewhere). Among her own people, the name gets simplified to "Dopdi."

Michel Serres *ought* to be fully a part of the postmodern debates. In fact, he is not at all well known. This is due in part to the fastidious way in which he distances himself from anything intellectually fashionable, obfuscating links which are important and of which he is surely not unaware (for example with Derrida). He also makes special demands on his reader. A scientist by training, his ideal of argumentation is the "speed and elegance" of mathematical demonstration. A mathematician does not trouble to include all the intermediate steps in an argument, if they can (from the mathematician's own perspective) be considered "obvious." This principle Serres has turned into a writing style, creating problems for the humanistically trained reader. Serres clearly takes a certain delight in this, and does not go out of his way to help his reader. Of late, however, perhaps fearing that his life's work may be simply ignored, he has reached out more to his reader. In particular, he broke a long habit in agreeing to a series of conversations with Bruno Latour in which he would explain himself (Serres with Latour, 1995). And he does. This book is eminently readable, and by far the easiest way into Serres' thought for a wide readership.

Serres' central concerns are ethical: "Hiroshima," he says, "remains the sole object of my philosophy" (Serres with Latour, 1995: 15). It was for ethical reasons that he moved professionally from science to philosophy and then to literature. Science has tended to lose touch with the rest of human experience, particularly with ethical issues. The humanities, for their part, tend to be ignorant of and to neglect the natural sciences. Serres' great ambition is to overcome this split, for the ethical good of humanity. He tries to bridge the two disciplines in a most extraordinary way. He reads literary texts, particularly ancient ones, as if they were texts of natural science. He refuses not only hard and fast separations between disciplines, but also divisions of intellectual history into standard "periods." This is why he can treat the biblical Joseph story (in our selection) as "the first treatise of political economy."

The selection is from *The Parasite* (Serres, 1982). Throughout this book he exploits the medical and social meaning of "parasite," but adds a third meaning of the term in French, "noise" in communication theory. Out of this meeting of semantic fields he constructs nothing less than a theory of history and culture. The parasite is the one who intervenes in stable systems, introducing disruption and change. The parasite creates history, since history is the disruption of the stable. The first function of the parasite is a negative one: the biological parasite brings disease, the social parasite arouses resentment, "noise" disturbs communication. But the parasite has a second, positive function. It forces the system into which it enters to achieve a higher level of complexity. Coming to terms with and incorporating the intruder makes the system stronger (1982: 192).

In the chapter we have selected, Serres traces how the Joseph story moves from barter economics, based on a "chain of substitutions" of one thing for another, to money economics, based on the "general equivalent" which breaks the chain. In this chapter he for some reason substitutes the term "joker" for "parasite" (the meaning seems the same). Money is the "joker of jokers" (161). Two other features of the chapter deserve notice. First, Serres offers a new way of thinking about the Tamar story in Genesis 38, which oddly "interrupts" the Joseph story when it has barely started. Serres suggests that the Tamar story is a *parasite* on the Joseph story; Tamar breaks the orderly narrative progress, "exciting" the narrative system, forcing it to a higher level of complexity. This reading agrees remarkably with Mieke Bal's postmodern reading of Genesis 38 (1987: 89–103). Second, the psychoanalytic turn toward the end of our selection is very important. Dreams are an essential part of the Joseph story, and Serres not only insists on this as an aspect of the reading of the text, but tries to bring it into his "general economics." He thus brings "Marx and Freud" into a single discourse, something which has scarcely been attempted in biblical studies.

If Serres has been neglected by biblical scholars, no less has Elaine Scarry, and the neglect is less excusable and probably more lamentable. The biblical section of her book *The Body in Pain* (1985: 181–243) is absolutely central to her immense argument and deserves to be recognized as a major contribution to biblical studies. Though she seems to go out of her way to avoid engagement with postmodern figures whose work would be relevant to hers (for example Michel Foucault), her work on the Bible is an exercise in deconstruction (she does actually use this word, but in relation to Marx rather than the Bible [243]). The Hebrew Bible deconstructs the absolute separation between God and humanity. It is the subversion from within this separation that not only makes the Bible possible, but makes it the central document in the West for the instilling of fundamental attitudes to the material world.

The first half of the book is on the "unmaking" of the world. Scarry deals with the fundamental human experience of pain, of being reduced by pain to sheer bodiliness, to being nothing else than a body capable of being wounded. She examines the conceptual structures of the extreme human experiences of bodily harm: torture and war. From this analysis she turns in the second half of the book to the "making" of the world through the interplay of imagining and fabricating. She bases her work here on the Bible, and to a lesser extent Marx.

The Bible is a work of human imagination not only confronting the human condition but actively creating it. In the sections preceding our selection, Scarry deals in turn with the Hebrew Bible and the New Testament. In the Hebrew Bible (185–210) God wounds human flesh – not only in punishment for "sin," but also in the mark of blessing, circumcision. God hurts human flesh in establishing the most fundamental conditions of life, agricultural labor and childbirth. This is possible not only because humanity is bodily and woundable, but because God is *not* bodily or woundable. At this primary level there is nothing reciprocal; humanity is only body, pure weakness, and God is only voice, pure power. Humanity, in utter vulnerability, confronts a reality against which it cannot fight back, which it cannot hurt. God symbolized as weapon hurting human flesh is not a complete or adequate account of the Hebrew Bible, and Scarry does not intend it so. But neither is it a "primitive" notion, that goes away as more "advanced" symbolization develops. Rather, it is an ongoing possibility at the limit of biblical discourse, just as torture is a possibility at the limit of twentieth-century existence, because we are bodily.

In a briefer section on the New Testament (210–21), Scarry suggests that there everything is opposite; the same problematic is dealt with, as it were from the other end, by beginning with a God in flesh, whom humanity can wound. She presses the distinction between the testaments almost to an absolute, but then undermines it by saying that the New Testament shift "is itself anticipated in the Old Testament ... to such an extent that the Christian story itself seems necessitated by and generated out of a pressure never long absent from the pages of the older writings" (221). These words immediately precede our selection, in which Scarry returns to the Hebrew Bible and lays out its complex deconstruction of the distance between God and humanity. What undoes the distance is human work – work of the hands, creating artifacts; work of the body, reproducing and forming societies; above all work of the imagination, in making representations of itself and of "God."

Metacriticism and Intertextuality

A characteristic feature of postmodernism, sometimes called "metacriticism," is found in several of our selections. Deconstruction subverts the hierarchical oppositions held dear in the Western intellectual tradition (Introduction to Part I: p. 54), and one of these is between "text" and "interpretation" (commentary, etc.). Metacriticism is an important reading strategy which reads the "text" through other readings, making interpretations into new texts at the same level as the "original." Among our selections, Derrida reads Genesis 22 by reading another reading of it, the celebrated treatment by Søren Kierkegaard in *Fear and Trembling*. Levinas's reading is metacritical in a somewhat different sense. He reads the Bible by reading the whole tradition of reading enshrined in the Talmud. The Talmud itself, in fact, constitutes a deconstruction of the notion of "text," for it has itself become "scripture," canonical text. Finally, Spivak's work is also metacritical. She reads her scriptural text, from the *Mahabharata*, at a great critical distance; what is in focus is Mahasweta's modern adaptation of scripture.

Another major postmodern reading strategy is intertextuality. We live in a world of texts, texts in the ordinary sense, made of words, and "texts" in all kinds of extended senses: works of art, systems of fashion or of traffic rules or of kinship laws, even the human genome. These texts combine in and below our consciousnesses, creating new, unanticipated awareness. Intertextuality as a reading strategy works by deliberately bringing disparate texts together, to see how one looks through the lens of another or, to use a figure that Serres might enjoy, to see what undiscovered particles are emitted when one text is used to bombard another.

To create a reader like this one is to practice intertextuality. By our selections, in this section and throughout the book, we not merely exemplify existing discourses (though we hope we do this effectively); we also *create* new discourses by bringing together – perhaps even forcing together – such diverse writings. For each selection we create a context it never previously had – the context of all our other selections. How will it read in this new context?

Before we began our work, some links already existed between the authors on whom we draw in this section. Derrida and Levinas were in conversation before the latter's death. Spivak works in conscious relation to Derrida and Dussel to Levinas. So we are not surprised to discover in our selections close connections and even some allusions. An intertextual approach does not take much interest in links at this level. It is interested in the new things that emerge when we read together texts that do not belong together. Intertextuality just happens, but the postmodern mind goes looking for its significations.

Serres finds in Genesis a limitless play of substitution, one thing standing for another (266), and claims that this principle of substitutability is "a Judaic invention" (270). Derrida finds in Genesis "the impossibility of substitution, the unsubstitutable" (338). Intertextuality does not choose, or even assume that the two writers are referring to the same thing. It takes the bait, and asks what sort of discourse might develop from these two texts *together*. When Levinas says that "the face of the other . . . un-makes . . . the world" (328), he is suddenly talking the characteristic language of Scarry (see her subtitle). What might this mean? Serres' Tamar (Genesis 38) and Spivak's Draupadi and Dopdi are all women who have sex with several men. Does this offer any kind of clue as to the direction a feminist reading might take?

These are cases of *micro*-intertextuality, well worth discovering and exploring (it goes without saying that we did not make our selections on the basis of any advance knowledge of such links). This whole section of essays taken together constitutes a *macro*-intertextuality, and this shapes the rest of this introduction. What new meaning is teased out of our selections when we read them in each other's light? In the next section, for example, as part of our postmodern practice of reading from the margin, we take Dussel, the philosopher of the global margin, as a frame within which to read our other authors.

The Contestation of Postmodernism

The ethical turn which postmodernism has recently taken (mentioned in the Introduction to Part I) should not conceal a long history of suspicion of postmodernism on the part of people on the left of the political spectrum, particularly those engaged in liberation struggles. It is possible to say, in a general way, that they have responded in a twofold and contradictory way (see Jobling, 1990). Some voices have complained that deconstruction makes all issues fundamentally undecidable and provides no ground for preferring one course of action over another. This robs political struggle of its sources of power. Others see deconstruction as a great ally in the struggle against entrenched power. The ways in which power justifies itself ideologically – for example by "proving," along the lines of Aristotle, the "natural" superiority of some human groups over others – can be dismantled and shown to be without foundation. The debate is further complicated when "ethics" is given a seemingly quite different sense by a major postmodern figure like J. Hillis Miller (cf. our selection), namely the ethical responsibility of the reader to take seriously what the text is trying to say.

We begin this section with Dussel's powerful contestation of postmodernism on ethical grounds. Even he, as we shall see, by no means avoids the complexities and contradictions of this debate. Fundamentally, Dussel critiques postmodernism (or what is usually understood by that term) for remaining within the bounds of the Eurocentric intellectual tradition. His argument is most conveniently stated in his essay "Beyond Eurocentrism" (1998). Postmodernism limits its horizon to combatting the reign of Cartesian reason (Dussel must have in mind here such critics of the Western philosophical tradition as Derrida). But such debates take place in a larger global context which they ignore: "In general, no debate between rationalists and postmoderns overcomes the Eurocentric horizon" (17).

The current "world system" is the product not of north European commercial expansion, with which Cartesian rationalism is closely linked, but dates back to 1492. After the break-up of the previous world system (centered in Baghdad from the mid-eighth to the mid-thirteenth centuries) the competitors for dominance were China, Portugal, and Spain. Spain won purely by accident. Blocked from easy access to the east by Portuguese expansion, Spain sought access to the potential new center, China and India, by going west – and bumped into the unknown factor, the Americas. Spain created a new world system by discovering the New World. In historical retrospect, it is clear that the winner of the struggle for the Americas was going to take everything (6–10).

The subsequent decline of Spain opened up this new world to mercantilism based on northern Europe, but this was at a later stage. Dussel notes that there were two "modernities," only the second of which is generally taken into account. The first modernity, in the sixteenth century, was Hispanic. Within it, there was still questioning of the European right to dominate (for example, in Bartolomeo de las Casas, and in contemporary Muslim thought). The second, Anglo-Germanic modernity, the one to which the name "modernity" is usually given, simply takes Europe's superiority as a given. It sets out to "manage" the new planetary system, privileging technology over nature, subjectivity, and community. It withdraws issues of global importance from the sphere of ethics (13–16).

Recent critiques of modernity, then, criticize only the phenomena, not the world system of which they are the expression. Despite promises of global dialogue by some postmodern figures (Dussel mentions Jean-François Lyotard and Gianni Vattimo [30]), the world of the global periphery continues to be treated as a mere spectator of the new intellectual currents (17–19). What needs to be overcome is not rationalism, but the world system itself. Dussel clearly believes that this can be done only from locations like his own, on the real global margins.

These debates are in any case being rapidly overtaken by brute fact. Three intractable limits have emerged to the further development of the 500-year-old "modern" world: the threatened ecological destruction of the planet; the marginalization of the vast majority of humanity, as its labor ceases to be economically usable itself; and the impossibility of assimilating the Third World Other (19–21).

Serres' critique of postmodernism, though expressed very differently, has something in common with Dussel's. Serres, like Dussel, greatly widens the context for a critique of Cartesian rationalism. But for him this is part of a general questioning of the extent of the various "revolutions" by which the West defines itself; he mentions the Copernican and Kantian revolutions (Serres with Latour, 1995: 146). By his bold gesture of reading ancient texts "as if" they were texts of modern science, he concludes that we have greatly exaggerated the differences between the modern/postmodern world and what went before.

Further, though he does not share Dussel's location on the global margin, he understands the necessity of the perspective from that margin (see esp. Serres with Latour, 1995: 167–204). He has made a point of living and working for extended periods in various parts of the Third World. From this point of view, he has adopted his own version of the "preferential option for the poor." The essence of history he finds not – as the tradition of Western historiography would have it – in the record of human "success," but in the "failure" that characteristically goes unrecorded, the "failure" which is the daily experience of the poor (186). He suggests, in the face of world domination by Euro-American technology, that the oppressed have now become the guardians of the humanities (181).

Dussel, with a powerful assist from Serres, certainly poses critical questions to postmodernism. We may add some other traits that these two voices have in common. Both specifically dissociate themselves from some of postmodernism's characteristic rhetoric. Serres explicitly rejects the notion that the great "metanarratives" of the past have ceased to be possible or meaningful. He is as sharply critical as anyone of these narratives, but he believes they can still be made functional, and that new ones can be generated (Serres with Latour, 1995: 158–9). Dussel, similarly, "intends to recoup what is redeemable in modernity" (1998:19). Both have attempted to confuse or replace the very language of "post-modernism." Dussel (ibid.) proposes the alternative term "trans-modern," while Latour's slogan "We Have Never Been Modern" comes largely from his conversations with Serres (Serres with Latour, 1995: 144–6; Latour, 1993).

Still, the work of both Serres and Dussel is surely unthinkable outside the space created by postmodernism. Postmodernism by its nature contests itself; this is not merely a truism, and it does not rob particular contestations, like those of Serres and Dussel, of their importance. Serres' undermining of the lines of division between ancient and modern, and between the sciences and the humanities, is as postmodern as can be. Dussel can be seen practicing a class deconstruction (see below, on Spivak) in the second of the three chapters we have selected. In a revealing footnote (1998:30) he says, "It would seem as though we were 'postmoderns' *avant la lettre.*" His attempt in the same note to rescue Levinas from postmodernism is ironic given that Levinas "proclaims himself resolutely 'Eurocentric'" (1990:xxxii, xxxix, n. 62).

Aside from Scarry, who writes in a postmodern mode without any confessed stance vis-à-vis postmodernism, our other authors (*pace* Dussel on Levinas) can all be said to fall within postmodern debate. Most interesting, in the light of our preceding discussion, is Spivak, since she, like Dussel, is writing from the global margin. It is she who raises, in the most recognizable form, the question with which we began this section, whether postmodernism provides positive resources for liberation struggle. Her answer is yes.

Even if the deconstruction "best known in the United States" shows a "tendency toward infinite regression," another style of deconstruction has more usable characteristics:

> its disclosure of complicities...; its insistence that in disclosing complicities the critic-as-subject is herself complicit with the object of her critique; its emphasis upon "history" and upon the ethico-political as a "trace" of that complicity...; and, finally, the acknowledgment that its own discourse can never be adequate to its example. (355)

Spivak finds the European developments of postmodernism, particularly Derrida, eminently relevant to the analysis of colonial and postcolonial situations. Especially in the character of Senanayak she offers a deconstruction of the boundary between the European colonialist tradition and the colonized world. Senanayak is the Western "pluralist aesthete," who prides himself on his ability to "identify with the enemy," and it is precisely the possibilities and limits of this identification that Mahasweta's story explores (354). When Spivak refers to Senanayak's "self-image" as that of Prospero, from Shakespeare's *The Tempest*, she plugs into recent postcolonialist reading of that play in which Caliban is seen to stand for the colonized Other (Halpern, 1994: 20–21). Spivak's reading here is complex. She certainly highlights the failure of Western claims to comprehend the colonial Other, but she claims the resources of Euro-American postmodernism to display this failure.

Spivak calls for "class deconstruction" (357; see Ryan, 1982), and brilliantly carries it out (it is interesting that our selections from her and from Dussel both allude to "tribal groups" or "tribals," in such disparate parts of the world, so extremely marginalized as to threaten traditional class analysis; Spivak: 358; Dussel: 307). She also engages in gender deconstruction. In her extraordinarily nuanced reading of Draupadi/Dopdi she (like Pathak, as we mentioned in the Introduction to Part I, p. 55) uses deconstructive critique to displace the universalized "female" in feminist criticism. To reread Dussel in the light of Spivak's essay is to realize that his complex view of postmodernism precisely reflects the struggle between Spivak's two options for deconstruction. (We should not fail to mention Spivak's important theoretical discussion, "Can the Subaltern Speak?" in relation to this discussion.)

Perhaps the most important insight into "postmodernism and politics" is to be found in the career of Derrida and the history of the reception of his work. His early work in particular was widely understood as asserting the radical "free play" of meaning and the impossibility of philosophical truth. But his recent work has convinced all but the most unfriendly of his Left critics that he intended his project as political from the start (e.g. 1994:92, where he states that his project of deconstruction "would have been impossible and unthinkable in a pre-Marxist space"). His encounter with the ethical philosophy of Levinas has undoubtedly been a factor in his steady turn toward ethical and religious topics (Bernasconi and Critchley, 1991).

Yet Derrida does not let himself be claimed as an immediate and uncomplicated ally in political struggle, and to claim him in that way would be to miss his real political contribution. As our selection, or any other of his writings, makes abundantly clear, the way to political or ethical affirmations is never for him easy or direct. His arguments are endlessly slow and tortuous, avoiding all temptation to take short-cuts, and the work of reaching the end is for politically impatient readers often hardly justified by the end that is reached. Any political or ethical expression remains radically subject to "textuality," the incapacity of language for expressing absolutes, the unavoidable contradictions and aporias of any system. Like Hillis Miller, Derrida is conscious of a debt to the texts themselves, to take them with infinite seriousness. It is possible that attention to these habits of Derrida by people on the Left just might help revolutions (political, conceptual, and otherwise) to avoid simply repeating the power struggles they set out to supplant.

It is interesting to consider our Derrida selection in relationship to Dussel's critique. In *The Gift of Death*, his agenda seems to be much the sort of thing that Dussel is complaining about. By beginning with Patočka and his exclusive focus on Europe, Derrida does initially let the ethical problem be defined as a European problem. But one of the aims of his critique is to show that it cannot be maintained as a purely European problem. The very dependence of Europe on the Bible extends the discourse outside of Europe. Derrida does not in this book adopt any overtly global perspective, though he does extend his view to include the world of Islam (341). In an analogous way, he does not focus on gender analysis, but lets it slip into his discourse at a key point (348). What Derrida does is to subvert from within the assumptions that cluster around the term "Europe." It is not to be forgotten that Derrida, like Dussel and Spivak, was born outside of Europe and America (in North Africa).

Finally, Levinas. We have mentioned already his "resolutely Eurocentric" perspective. Yet Levinas is the thinker whom Dussel most urgently claims for his anti-Eurocentric project. Is this some sort of mistake or strategic error on Dussel's part? Of course not. He has recognized that Levinas's centering of philosophy in ethics, and his assertion of the infinite privilege of the Other, imply demands beyond those that Levinas himself has overtly named. In the thorny and conflicted territory of ethics and postmodernism (as we have seen throughout this section) such seeming contradictions abound. That this territory takes the shape it does, that we can even name such a territory, is the result of just such juxtapositions as Levinas and Dussel.

Judaism, Christianity, and Postmodernism: The Question of Religion

The Bible, obviously, is a religious text, emerging from and defining two religions in particular, Christianity and Judaism. How do our selections and our authors stand in relation to questions of religious practice and religious community? Only two express an unambiguous embracing of religion, Dussel of Christianity and Levinas of Judaism. Derrida and Scarry, dealing with issues in the Western tradition beyond the bounds of the narrowly "religious," both look to the authoritative texts of religion as the major documents for tracing these issues. Serres works at a greater distance from the specifically religious, though he does give a few hints. He turns to biblical texts as documents of the past to which we still need to attend, but only as one instance among others – elsewhere in *The Parasite* he uses texts from classical antiquity and from the French tradition of fables. Spivak does not raise issues of religion at all, except to the extent that inter-religious conflicts (among Hindus, Muslims, and Sikhs) form part of the background to Mahasweta's story. She gives no indication of the veneration in which the *Mahabharata* is held by Hindus.

Reading the Sermon on the Mount (in the chapter following our selection), Derrida points out its dual contrast, between the Christian and the Judaic, and between the Judeo-Christian and "the rest" (Gentiles) (107). This dual contrast is built into our selections and into the development of postmodernism as a whole.

Christianity versus Judaism? Regarding Derrida's first contrast, we should note the interesting line of discussion (for example in Handelman, 1982; Bloom, 1975) which links the development of postmodernism with Judaism, including Jewish biblical interpretation. The rabbinic method of reading is communal, dialogic, and accretive, in contrast to the tradition of biblical commentary in which a single authority seeks a definite "truth." In the history of the West, Judaism has been Christianity's prototypical "other," that aspect of itself which Christianity has had to repress in order to build its systems. Jewish development of the postmodern would then be "the return of the repressed." Levinas is in touch with this line of thought when he talks of "Post-Christian Judaism" (1990:10) or violently contrasts the ways the New Testament and the Talmud treat the Jewish scriptures (1990:7).

Derrida himself is not interested in setting the two religious traditions against each other, but he does (both in our selection and in other parts of his work) exploit the space between them. He never allows either Judaism or Christianity to escape questioning by the other. In *The Gift of Death* he makes use of both a story from the Jewish Bible (in our selection) and a part of the New Testament (in the following chapter). His discussion maintains a continual counterpoint between the Christians Kierkegaard and Patočka and the Jew Levinas. At one point he makes the startling suggestion that it is "far from being clear" that "in what they say in general Heidegger and Levinas are not Christian" (48). What he is asking here is whether Levinas (for Heidegger, see below), speaking as a Jew, must necessarily be saying things different from what Christians are saying. Within the whole development of Western thought, how useful are these conventional designations?

There are some hints of a probing of the Jewish–Christian boundary in the closing words of our Serres selection, on Judah/Judas and anti-Semitism (164). But the sharpest contrast between "Old and New Testaments" among our authors is certainly that of Scarry. The extent of the contrast is, though, as we have seen, finally unclear. Earlier in *The Body in Pain* (181–220) she suggests that the two scriptures generate almost totally opposite mythologies for dealing with the distance between God and humanity (or the contrast between human powerlessness and empowerment). Instead of defending God's utter incorporeality, as the Jewish Bible does, the New Testament gives God a body from the start. In Jesus's healing miracles the embodied God, rather than wounding humanity, rescues it from its bodiliness, by giving to hurt individuals release from the bondage of their hurt bodies. But in the crucifixion the human weapon penetrates God's flesh. God takes body to give humanity voice, and humanity's voice condemns God to die. Yet in a sudden turn immediately before our selection Scarry undermines this contrast and suggests that the New Testament simply fulfills what was "anticipated" in the Old (220).

It is interesting to read this dynamic in Scarry in relation to the extraordinary "personal" reading of the Bible (both Jewish Bible and New Testament) by the novelist and literary critic Gabriel Josipovici, in *The Book of God* (1988). As he reads different parts of the New Testament he invariably starts by drawing a very sharp (and unfavorable) contrast with the Jewish Bible. As he develops his reading, however, he almost always undermines his own contrast, and begins to minimize the differences. This seemingly odd, repeated pattern can perhaps be explained by Josipovici's own insight (esp. pp. 304–6) that all the books of the Bible have changed as a result of being read for many centuries in relation to each other. The Bible, within and between the "Testaments," has become a set of "conversations" from which the participants have not emerged unchanged. This brings us back to Derrida's question as to whether Levinas is "not Christian." In the course of a joint history, a distinction such as Jewish versus Christian has become no longer maintainable, and part of the postmodern task would be to undermine the grounds on which people on both sides strive to maintain it.

The exclusivity of the Bible. The second part of Derrida's dual contrast, between the Judeo-Christian tradition and what is exterior to it, threads in different ways through our selections. Absent from these selections is any real meeting of Judaism and Christianity with other world religions (Spivak does not develop her essay in this direction). But the relation of the Bible to its Western environment is sometimes an issue. Scarry, for example, ascribes to the Bible (along with Marx) a unique role in forming fundamental Western attitudes to the nature of humanity. A constant theme of Levinas's presentation of Judaism is the necessity of *law* as a restraint on human instinct. Referring in our selection to pre- and extra-biblical human societies, he refers to "this apparently innocent but virtually murderous vitality" and asserts that "the human begins" only when it gets constrained (106). Against this danger "commandments are necessary" and a blessing. (There is an important connection to be made here with our selection from Lacan, with his concept of "the Law of the Father" which breaks up the primal "lawless" union of mother and child.) Levinas's apology for law in Judaism is close to Patočka's argument for the importance of Christianity in European history, the starting point of Derrida's *The Gift of Death*. Patočka sees Christianity as succeeding, where Platonism failed, in taming the "orgiastic" primitive European religion (though Patočka is far from seeing this as a completed process; indeed, in the face of the return of the orgiastic, in revolutions and wars, he asks if the Christianization of Europe has yet begun).

Dussel very much removes the scene from Europe, but he too explores the particularity of Christianity, in his case in the context of political struggle in a part of the Third World which has been heavily Christianized (pp. 308–10 in our selection). Similarly to Levinas and Derrida, he relates the role of Christianity to its distinctive ethic. Against "certain leftist elements that disparage ethics" (p. 310) he insists on ethical analysis as a necessary part of the theory of struggle. He avoids the notion that Christians form a "vanguard," preferring to suggest that they put political change into a larger context of meaning, of "eschatological hope" and "the option for the other as other" (p. 309).

Is religion necessary? While some people read postmodernism as a break with everything that people in the past have separated out as "the sacred," others see its subversion of the modernist dichotomy of sacred and secular as creating new space for sacredness. (We argue as much in the General Introduction and in the Introduction to Part I.) In this connection, perhaps the most fascinating of all the themes introduced by Derrida is "the immense and thorny question" of "religion without religion" (1995:49). He includes all his main conversation partners – Patočka, Kierkegaard, Heidegger, Levinas – in a list of those who posit "a nondogmatic doublet of dogma" (he could well have included himself; see Caputo, 1997: 195 and note the subtitle of Caputo's book). Is it Christianity which creates Patočka's "European" ethic, or is it the emergence of the "logic" of such an ethic – the uniqueness of the individual ethical moment – which produces (the possibility of) Christianity? Derrida concludes that this is simply not a decidable question, in fact not a real one (it is here that he doubts the usefulness of declaring Heidegger "not Christian"). At the end of *The Gift of Death* he will revisit this issue, especially in relation to Nietzsche's critique of Christianity. He suggests that "God" is nothing else than the name we give to the secret source of ethical demand, the unseen one who sees me.

Scarry and Serres can be included in Derrida's list, in the sense that they both, from their non-religious perspectives, assert the complete "translatability" of the Bible into non-religious discourses – philosophy, economics, etc. But it is in Levinas that this theme has its most interesting development. In our selection he insists on the autonomy of the ethical demand: "Ethics is not simply the corollary of the religious but is, of itself, the element in which religious transcendence receives its original meaning" (325). It is this ethical experience which even "defines" for us "the meaning of the exceptional word: God" (ibid.; cf. 329: it is through "language, at the hour of its ethical truth" that "perhaps . . . the idea of God comes to us").

How does this point of view fit with Levinas's strong affirmation of the singularity of Judaism? According to Aronowicz (1990:xi–xxviii), his complex position is to be understood in part from his biography. In his early career, he sought a Western (or "Greek") Judaism, assuming a full commonality between Judaism and the Western intellectual tradition (xi–xii). In his educational work with Jews in non-European parts of the Mediterranean Basin, he stressed the need for the full Western curriculum, as well as Jewish studies. But his experience of the European marginalization of Jews especially between the World Wars turned him increasingly to the specificity of Judaism, as a source of "teachings . . . that cannot be found anywhere else but here but which apply to the entire world" (xv). Thus while he rejects any notion of a system of belief based on a distinction between believers and unbelievers (xxiv), he suggests that in some mysterious way the world cannot do without Judaism and believing Jews. It is for this reason that he chooses talmudic readings as one of the main genres in which he develops his ethical philosophy. The work of creating the Talmud, done over centuries largely in separation from other intellectual currents of the ancient world, is an essential contribution to the world's wisdom. Its demand is universal, but it requires the particularity of the Jew to "translate" and transmit this demand.

Related essays in *The Postmodern Bible Reader*

Jacques Lacan, "Introduction to the Names-of-the-Father Seminar"
Hélène Cixous, "Dreaming in 1990"

Robert Allen Warrior, "Canaanites, Cowboys, and Indians" Katie Cannon, "Slave Ideology and Biblical Interpretation"

Bibliography

Alter, Robert. 1981. *The Art of Biblical Narrative*. London: Allen & Unwin.

Aronowicz, Annette. 1990. "Translator's Introduction." Pp. ix–xxxix in Emmanuel Levinas, 1990.

Bal, Mieke. 1987. *Lethal Love: Feminist Literary Readings of Biblical Love Stories*. Bloomington: Indiana University Press.

Bernasconi, Robert, and Simon Critchley, eds. 1991. *Re-Reading Levinas*. Bloomington and Indianapolis: Indiana University Press.

Bloom, Harold. 1975. *Kabbalah and Criticism*. New York: Seabury Press.

Brook, Peter. 1989. *The Mahabharata*. Motion picture.

van Buitenen, J. A. B. 1975. *The Mahaābhaārata*. Trans. and ed. J. A. B. van Buitenen. Vol. 2. Chicago and London: University of Chicago Press.

Caputo, John D. 1997. *The Prayers and Tears of Jacques Derrida: Religion without Religion*. Bloomington and Indianapolis: Indiana University Press.

Derrida, Jacques. 1994. *Specters of Marx: The State of the Debt, the Work of Mourning, and the New International*. Trans. Peggy Kamuf with an introduction by Bernd Magnus and Stephen Cullenberg. New York and London: Routledge.

——. 1995. *The Gift of Death*. Trans. David Wills. Religion and Postmodernism. Chicago and London: University of Chicago Press.

Dussel, Enrique. 1985. *Philosophy of Liberation*. Trans. Aquilina Martinez and Christine Morkovsky. Maryknoll, NY: Orbis.

——. 1998. "Beyond Eurocentrism: The World-System and the Limits of Modernity." Trans. Eduardo Mendieta. In *The Cultures of Globalization*. Ed. Fredric Jameson and Masao Miyoshi. Durham and London: Duke University Press, pp. 3–31.

Halpern, Richard. 1994. "Shakespeare in the Tropics: From High Modernism to New Historicism." *Representations* 45:1–25.

Handelman, Susan. 1982. *The Slayers of Moses*. Albany: State University of New York Press.

Hayles, Katherine, ed. 1991. *Chaos and Order: Complex Dynamics in Literature and Science*. Chicago: University of Chicago Press.

Jobling, David. 1990. "Writing the Wrongs of the World: The Deconstruction of the Biblical Text in the Context of Liberation Theologies." *Semeia* 51: 81–118.

——. 1998. *1 Samuel*. Berit Olam. Collegeville, MN: Liturgical Press.

Josipovici, Gabriel. 1988. *The Book of God: A Response to the Bible*. New Haven: Yale University Press.

Kierkegaard, Søren. 1983. *Fear and Trembling*. Trans. Howard Hong and Edna Hong. Vol. 6 of *Kierkegaard's Writing*. Princeton: Princeton University Press.

Latour, Bruno. 1993. *We Have Never Been Modern*. Trans. Catherine Porter. Cambridge, MA: Harvard University Press.

Levinas, Emmanuel. 1990. *Nine Talmudic Readings*. Trans. with an Introduction by Annette Aronowicz. Bloomington and Indianapolis: Indiana University Press.

Mendieta, Eduardo. 1996. "Editor's Introduction." In Enrique Dussel, *The Underside of Modernity: Apel, Ricoeur, Rorty, Taylor, and the Philosophy of Liberation*. Trans. and ed. Eduardo Mendieta. New Jersey: Humanities Press, pp. xiii–xxxi.

Miller, J. Hillis. 1987. *The Ethics of Reading.* New York: Columbia University Press.

Narayan, R. K. 1978. *The Mahabharata: A Shortened Modern Prose Version of the Great Indian Epic.* London: Heinemann.

Ryan, Michael. 1982. *Marxism and Deconstruction.* Baltimore: Johns Hopkins University Press.

Scarry, Elaine. 1985. *The Body in Pain: The Making and Unmaking of the World.* New York and Oxford: Oxford University Press.

Serres, Michel. 1982. *The Parasite.* Trans. Lawrence R. Schehr. Baltimore: Johns Hopkins University Press.

Serres, Michel, with Bruno Latour. 1995. *Conversations on Science, Culture, and Time.* Trans. Roxanne Lapidus. Studies in Literature and Science. Ann Arbor: University of Michigan Press.

Spivak, Gayatri Chakravorty. 1988. "Can the Subaltern Speak?" In *Marxism and the Interpretation of Culture.* Ed. Cary Nelson and Lawrence Grossberg. Urbana: University of Illinois Press, pp. 271–313.

Chapter 15

Meals Among Brothers: Theory of the Joker

Michel Serres 1930–

Introduction

Reading Serres in the context of the major figures usually associated with post-modernism, one is struck first by what he does *not* share with them. He explicitly rejects Lyotard's notion that the great "metanarratives" of the past have ceased to be possible or meaningful. He has a positive appreciation of religion and makes constant reference to its texts (in *The Parasite*, from which our selection is taken, there is also a reading of Pentecost in Acts 2). Yet his development of chaos theory, the total war he declares on the boundaries which separate academic disciplines, his paradoxical understanding of time and history – all these can be comprehended only within the ambit of postmodernism.

Holder of professorships at the Sorbonne and Stanford University, Serres trained first in the natural sciences, but turned from them first to philosophy and then to literature. He avoided what he calls the "superhighways" of French intellectual life in the 1950s and 1960s (Marxism, Sartrean phenomenology, etc.), and still emphasizes his separation from contemporary intellectual currents (though he expresses admiration for the philosopher Gilles Deleuze).

Serres turned from science because of its separation from the rest of human experience, and his writings consist largely of violent attempts to undo this separation. (Among his many translated works, in addition to *The Parasite* [1980/English translation 1982], are *Hermes: Literature, Science, Philosophy* [1969–80/1982], *Rome: The Book of Foundations* [1983/1991], and *The Troubadour of Knowledge* [1991/1997].) He couples contemporary science with other discourses found in unlikely places – especially ancient literature. For example, he links the cosmology of Lucretius with modern fluid mechanics: as long as physics concentrated on solids, Lucretius could not be perceived as a physicist, but now he can and must. Serres downplays the philosophical revolutions of Descartes and Kant which established the current divisions in Western intellectual life. What continued unchanged through these "revolutions," he believes, vastly outweighs what changed.

His style is that of the mathematician who does not trouble to include the intermediate steps of an argument, if they seem to him obvious. This makes him hard to read. He obviously delights in this crypticism, and does not go out of his way to help his reader. Much the easiest introduction to his thought is *Conversations on Science, Culture, and Time* (1995), a series of conversations with Bruno Latour. Serres' politics are close to radical socialism. He constantly explores the conditions for an authentic human collectivity. He sees the experience of the poor as constituting the essence of history. In conformity with these views, he has made a point of living and working for extended periods in various parts of the Third World.

In *The Parasite* Serres exploits two familiar meanings of this term – medically, one biological entity living on another, and socially, an economically non-productive person – and a third meaning in French, namely "noise" in communication theory. Out of this meeting of semantic fields he constructs nothing less than a whole theory of history and culture. He presents his argument through readings of the fables of La Fontaine, texts of classical antiquity, Molière and Rousseau, as well as the Bible. When he calls the Joseph–Tamar story "perhaps the first treatise of political economy," it is important to realize that he is not speaking figuratively. Read in the context of his whole work, he is claiming that this piece of the Bible truly founds what we now know as the science of economics.

So he left all that he had in Joseph's charge; and having him he had no concern for anything but the food which he ate.

Genesis 39:6

It seems illogical or even scandalous to throw away food. It is done nonetheless. What is at a distance from food (*para-site* says so) is expelled or excluded; it is the excess or surplus [*excédent*]. The first fruits, sometimes, or the best flower, if it is a question of sacrifice. Chasing out the parasite also means kick out, dispose of what is on the side, what is next to food. It is not necessarily the being that devours it. It can be its excess or its surplus. And everything that precedes is necessary as the metaphysics of excess. As usual, the very thing that is excluded returns.

Sacrifice: Joseph's brothers want to kill him. They chase him out. They show their father a long-sleeved tunic soaked in the blood of the scapegoat. Joseph is a sacrificial victim. The whole myth is marked with substitutions. There is no murder but rather expulsion. The expulsion doesn't really occur; the sale replaces it. The tunic full of blood is a false substitute; the twenty pieces of silver are the true substitute. The Ishmaelites paid; the money is the presence of Joseph in Canaan and his first return. In Egypt, having left prison, Joseph interprets the dreams of Pharaoh: fat cows and thin cows. He will become the Minister of the Economy and of Finance.

Michel Serres, "Meals Among Brothers: Theory of the Joker," from *The Parasite*, translated with notes by Lawrence R. Schehr (Baltimore and London: Johns Hopkins University Press, 1982).

This is perhaps the first treatise of political economy. Fat cows: years of abundance; thin cows: harvests of scarcity. When there is an excess harvest, the usual practice is to get rid of this surplus by lifting the bar. And then they die of hunger during the years that the cows are thin and the stalks of wheat are burnt by the wind. What else could be done? We must return to these simple peasant practices from which all of culture came. Here are abundant fruit, vegetables, milk, wine, wheat. The fruit spoils, the milk sours, the wine turns to vinegar, the vegetables rot, the stores of wheat are filled with rats and weevils. Everything ferments; everything rots. Everything changes. Rotting and plague are not only symbols of violence but also real, singular referents that only need themselves to give rise to clearly defined processes. The surplus is gotten rid of because it is perishable. In fact the rotten is expelled, merchandise is disposed of [*écouler*], because it might start to run [*couler*]. Exchange is born in that change of state. Exchange is to this change what excess or surplus is to sufficiency, or exaction to action, and so forth. Exchange does not want it to change. It wants to stabilize the flight [*fuite*]. Contrary to everything thought about exchange, it does not mobilize things; it immobilizes them, it disposes of them, Πάντα ῥεῖ, everything flows, of course, everything dies, everything rots, if it dies it bears much fruit.[1] What runs [*coule*] is disposed of [*écoule*]; what changes is exchanged. The very simple idea of the equilibrium of exchanges is ontological. By the very movement of the exchange, what changes, no longer changes. It might have become rotten, and now it is money. The fact that money is refuse or feces is not at all a symbol or a fantasm. It is exactly the substitute of the expelled rot, the equivalent of disposal by corruption. The stroke of genius, of course, was to go look for the stable in the unstable, or rest in movement, to go look for what is opposed to change in the exchange itself.

Yet this is not the only solution. Surplus can be disposed of or stocked. It can be stocked in the form of money or as itself. Then rot sets in and the parasites are at home. From this point on, we are bound to go to the end of the process of decomposition: wine-making, cheese-making, bread-making. I once drew philosophy from cheese. Here it finds its general nature.

Let us return to Joseph. If Canaan is poor, it is because it does not stock up. If Joseph and Egypt are rich, it is because they do. The two processes face each other.

Joseph's brothers, his jealous rivals, decided to get rid of him. Let's kill him, they say at first, and throw him in the cistern. What they will do, in any case, will be to throw him in the cistern. What is a cistern? It is an artificial, man-made spot for conservation. In the Indo-European semantic field, *cista* in Latin is a chest or basket, especially a basket used for sacrifices. Tibullus signs of it as the confidant of the sacred mysteries. The Greek κιστοφόρος, "bearer of sacred baskets," designates a coin of Asia Minor which had such chests drawn on it. A cist is a stone sarcophagus, a tomb or megalith in which the corpse is buried with all his goods. His fortune is there with his body. But in the Semitic semantic field, the Hebrew word used here – more or less a well, a water hole, another sort of cistern – means the hole in which one falls, but especially the hole into which garbage is thrown. The union of these two semantic fields expresses our thesis well: this spot, where a rotting excess is gotten rid of, has to do with the sacred, with death and sacrifice. But it has connections with goods, exchanged treasures, money and coinage. Buried, thrown in the cistern, Joseph is excluded, sacrificed, plague-ridden, but he is also kept, stocked, just like the water he replaces. The cistern regulates the wet and dry years, as the Egyptian granaries will soon regulate the years of fat cows and meager harvests. Joseph in the well – an enigmatic and ambiguous situation: the stock foreseen for the next exchange. He is expelled; he is kept. He is sacrificed; he is sold. The mortuary and sacrificial foundation of exchange. Reuben recommended this solution with the avowed aim of saving his brother and bringing him back to their father. Already the decision to exclude shows some adherences: an eventual return, perhaps a conservation. How can everything be expelled while keeping it; how can it be chased while conserving it; how can everything be allowed to vary while keeping an invariant? This question is an economic one.

The meal begins in the vicinity of the spots where there is action. At the back of the scene a caravan appears. Ishmaelites with their camels bearing gum tragacanth, etc., merchandise from Gilead, bringing it to Egypt. This interruption induces Judah, who, like his brothers, has raised his eyes at this spectacle, to think of selling Joseph. But this sale will be done by intermediaries. There are always substitutes just as there are vicariants. Midianite merchants pass by; they remove Joseph from the cistern and sell him for twenty pieces of silver to the Ishmaelites. But the text says that it was the Midianites who sold him in Egypt. It is necessary to note that Ishmael, the son of Abraham and Hagar, the Egyptian servant, was a brother who was chased out and excluded, just like Midian, the son of Abraham and Keturah. Just when Joseph is expelled, the excluded brothers appear in the background. The excluded brothers have become merchants; they traffic in merchandise. The relation of the excluded to money already appears as the referent of the story. The money circulates rather badly; it doesn't circulate, in fact: Midian sold twice.

Jacob receives the coat stained with the goat's blood. Joseph is the victim and is innocent; he is the victim's substitute and its vicar.

The story of Joseph stops for a moment amidst the tears of his mourning father and abruptly detours to speak of Judah, precisely the one whose idea it was to sell Joseph. He leaves Gilead, for Adullam, where he has three children – Er, Onan, and Shelah – by a woman. Er marries Tamar and dies. Tamar, who has survived, is given to Onan, her brother-in-law. Onan, as we know, let his seed spill on the ground when he was united with Tamar, lest he should give offspring to his brother.

Put the little brother in the cistern, in the basket, not to put him there, to take him out of the cistern.

Unhappy with onanism, Jehovah slays Onan. The last son, Shelah, remains for Tamar. He is too young, and when he is older, he is not destined for Tamar. Tamar is a widow without children; she is forgotten. She puts on a veil and waits. Judah passes by and takes her for a prostitute. She negotiates her price: a kid. She demands a pledge from him. And Judah gives her his signet, his cord, and his staff.

The story of Judah contains the story of Tamar, continued in that of Joseph. A curious exchange is substituted, quite suddenly, for the violent quarrel of the brothers, for murders and exclusions – in short, for the sacrificial. Tamar is promised to the three brothers, who are successively taken from her in different ways: by death, by onanism, by forgetting. She has; she doesn't have. You have; you don't have. Then she is passed to the father through sale and prostitution.

But the equivalent of Joseph sacrificed was a slaughtered goat. The equivalent of Tamar is a kid. Again, that directs us to sacrifice. It is about to occur. When Judah is told, your daughter-in-law is with child by harlotry, he orders her to be pushed out and burnt alive. Thus Tamar is really the victim. As Girard has shown, she is innocent; and, once again, her sons will be twins, rivals from the hour of their birth, just like Jacob and Esau. Rivals for the maternal flow. Now she shows Judah his seal, staff, and cord: you are the father; it is marked. She is righteous, more righteous than I, inasmuch as I did not give her to my son Shelah.

Tamar is the victim, just like Joseph. He is sold, the excluded brother, twenty pieces of silver for excluded brothers, now become merchants. Tamar faces him, in a more or less dual position, as the sexual object of the brothers and father. Of the brothers who are enemies among themselves, since Onan uses his method to prevent giving offspring to his brother. Tamar moves from one to the other, always the same and yet transformed: always a woman, owed and desired, but a widow after having been a wife, but sterile though fecund, because of the practice of Onan, promised and not given, prostitute but virtuous though incestuous, mother in the end, and giving to posterity what she had received – rivals. Metamorphoses and stability. Variations of the invariant or circulation of the equivalent. She is adapted to all the positions and can move from one to another, subject to the laws of circulation. She is perhaps already a general equivalent.

The fact that she is worth a kid marks her as a victim for sacrifice. She is veiled – that is to say, hidden behind a veil. Thus Joseph disappeared far from his coat soaked in blood. The sacrificial is deferred. Joseph is not assassinated; the goat is his substitution, a ritualization of Abraham's sacrifice. Tamar is not burnt, but it will no longer be a question of the kid. The death of the kid is deferred. The token – the seal – is enough, stable writing as a promise. Tomorrow I shall pay. Once again, making stable what is unstable. I am tied by the cord and involved by the seal. The passage to the symbolic is assured by an object that the Greeks called a symbol. A token of recognition. The symbolic is the deferral of killing. Could exchange be a deferral of murder? Tamar already makes clear what will happen in the story of Joseph.

Genealogy of synthetic judgements.

That is something else.

Tamar is a wife; Tamar is a widow; Tamar is forsaken; Tamar is sterile; Tamar is the prostitute of the crossroads; Tamar is the victim; Tamar is a mother; Tamar is righteous. Unveiled, veiled, unveiled. Promised, not given, given. Not fertilized by Onan, fertilized by the father, not marked by Onan, and marked with the seal. Tamar does not have a fixed identity, whereas Judah is Judah and Jacob is Jacob. For a long time, she is not recognized, her justice is not known; it is she who has the misfortune to be united with Onan. United – that is to say, not united. She who sleeps with Onan sleeps with him and does not.

It is not sure either that Joseph is Joseph. He receives the ring and the gold chain from Pharaoh, just as Tamar had the seal and the cord; Pharaoh gives him a name: Joseph is Zaphenath-paneah. He is a slave; he is a majordomo; he is a prisoner; he is the bailiff of the jailer; he is forgotten by the great cup-bearer; he is the minister of Pharaoh and the master of his brothers. Joseph is not fixed in his identity, whereas Reuben is

Reuben and Jacob is Jacob. For a long time, he is not recognized, his justice is not known; he is both master and slave.

Tamar and Joseph are sacrificial victims. In the cistern and ready to be burnt at the stake; the goat is the substitute for one and the kid is supplement for the other. Joseph is the goat; Tamar is the kid. The victim is not killed; the victim is not victim. Faced with murder, the gesture is deferred, as is the decision. The action bifurcates and the tautology starts to predicate; it slips; it jumps to something else. It no longer says: *a* is *a*; it substitutes and begins to say *a* is *b*.

The victim is not fixed in his identity; the victim is anyone: he could be the youngest or the first to arrive. Who is he or she? This one because it is he; that one, because it is she; here and now, Jephtha's daughter, Iphigenia, or Idomeneo's son, perfectly determined; but chosen by chance, randomly picked, totally undetermined. The victim is this one, yet this one is another. May be another.

In this circumstance, a sovereign logic emerges that needs explanation, which is the explanation itself. There is no beginning for reason without a link of the following sort: this is not this; this is something else. This chain breaks away from redundance, identity or repetition. An object has to be found that can be spoken of in this way. Or a subject, it matters little. It is thus a vital experience that the rejected child never be himself. It is also a cultural constraint that a woman must metamorphose. It is a social experience that the one who is sacrificed is anyone. But it is especially a Judaic invention, an explosive novelty in the Fertile Crescent, that the one who is sacrificed is substituted, that suddenly, the victim is something else: a goat, a kid, but also the beginning of a completely other series.

I shall call this object a joker. The joker is often a madman, as we know. He is wild, as they say in English. It is not difficult to see the double of the sacrificial king in him, come from the Celebration of Fools, come from the Saturnalia. This white object, like a white domino,[2] has no value so as to have every value. It has no identity, but its identity, its unique character, its difference, as they say, is to be, indifferently, this or that unit of a given set. The joker is king or jack, ace or seven, or deuce. Joseph is a joker; Tamar, queen, just, despised, whore, is also a joker. *A* is *b, c, d,* etc. Fuzzy.

That joker is a logical object that is both indispensable and fascinating. Placed in the middle or at the end of a series, a series that has a law of order, it permits it to bifurcate, to take another appearance, another direction, a new order. The only describable difference between a method and *bricolage*[3] is the joker. The principle of bricolage is to make something by means of something else, a mast with a matchstick, a chicken wing with tissue meant for the thigh, and so forth. Just as the most general model of method is game, the good model for what is deceptively called bricolage is the joker.

The joker Tamar makes the series bifurcate so often that, having been incestuous, she goes back to the beginning, the always new fraternal rivalry. The chain of events makes a cycle, a circulation, but with a supplement, toward David and toward the Messiah. The same goes for the joker Joseph, though he is more complex.

Joseph is expelled, not killed. He is excluded. Reuben did not want to – he only put him in the cistern to conserve him, to bring him back to his father. He is put out and put up. In this unique spot, he is both rejected and kept. Joseph is excluded; Joseph is included. As a joker, the excluded is included. The joker, first of all, has two values; the fact that they are contradictory changes nothing here. Or, better yet, it is because he is excluded and included that Joseph becomes a joker. He leaves; he is always there. You rejected him; he is always present in your story. You send him away, by the caravan, into Egypt; you will make a caravan to join him there. He left, but he doesn't leave you; he dogs your steps. He will see his father again; you will come back to him. The movement, the hesitation, the vibration, and the double frenzy of inclusion and exclusion constitute the joker in a multiplicity of fuzzy values, and a multiplicity of situations, in a spectrum of possibilities. It changes; it is there, stable. Perishable merchandise that might have become refuse comes back in the form of money. Money is the most joker of jokers, what has been called the general equivalent. With two values, excluded, included, then a fuzzy multiplicity of values and possibilities. Intuitively, the two sides of a coin should have been constituted in this way, and the head and tail, from the very first, should have been the operators of chance. Inversely, the victim is not chosen by chance; he is head and tail, the coin with two values, the fuzzy spectrum of probability. It is always possible to say of money: this is something else. A new principle: the association of the included and excluded third.

The joker changes; it is a token of exchange; it is multivalent, and bivalent at first. Tamar and Joseph change, and they are exchanged. Subject, indifferently, and object of the exchange, Tamar, the kid, the victim, and finally, the seal, the payment. And Joseph, twenty pieces of silver. The money from the wheat of Egypt is put into bags of wheat destined for Palestine. The brothers left the money, but the money doesn't leave them. Excluded, included. The money is always there, in the exchange.

This is something else. I dreamt of a sheaf of wheat, of the sun, and of eleven stars. This sheaf is not a sheaf, yet it remains a sheaf, and you are the sheaf. The moon is your mother; the stars are your brothers. The wheat bends like a moon; the sun places its forehead on the earth, in the wheat field. This is something else. I am a star and a sheaf of wheat; you are a sheaf and the sun; in the beginning is hatred.

This is again something else. You dreamt of a vinestock with three branches, and of three baskets of cakes on your head. And I say to the bailiff and to the butler: the baskets are days, the cakes are your flesh and body, the branches are days; the days are branches and they are baskets. Here is the meaning: this is something else. In the middle, servitude, life, and death.

This is yet something else. Pharaoh dreamt of cows and wheat; the thin cows ate the fat cows; the thin and wind-burnt wheat covered wheat that was ripe and in abundance. I shall tell him the meaning; this is yet something else. The cows are years; the wheat sheaves are years; time is a cow; it is divided into clusters of grain, just as it was divided into branches or baskets. If the sheaf were a sheaf, if the star were a star and the cow a cow, there would have been no meaning, no key, no explanation, no interpreter. No rhyme or reason. This has to be something else. Finally a logic of light; we will finally eat to stop our hunger. We shall send caravans of grain and fruit toward the Promised Land.

All these chains of words abound with jokers. Given some series whose links are well identified, where there is a law, an explicit one. The same is diffused the length of the differences, constituting the axis, be it rigid or supple. Suddenly, a joker. Can I read it?

Certainly. It is enough to recognize the upstream law and the downstream laws. The joker, in the position of bifurcation, makes it possible by the confluence of values that it insures. It is both what has been said and what will be said. It is bi-, tri-, or poly-valent, according to the complexity of the connection. The ramification of the network depends on the number of jokers. But I suspect that there is a limit for this number. When there are too many, we are lost as if in a labyrinth. What would a series be like where there were only jokers? What could be said of it?

Dream logic seems to me to be of this nature. Multivalent because of jokers. Connections *ad libitum*. Time is the cow; time is the sheaf; time is the branch and the basket. The cow is a sheaf; this is something else. The cow is a joker; the basket, the sheaf, other jokers. Beyond a certain density, or a certain number of multivalent elements, the series cannot be known. The question is not so much finding one or two or three or n keys, but of speaking a language that takes jokers into account. Joseph and Daniel give the meaning, the key; they determine the indeterminate series; they harden the soft logic. Freud, on the contrary, discovered a language with a general equivalent. It is understandable that Popper takes him to task; Popper would be right if the dream weren't woven of series of jokers. Freud translates, into his poor language, a fact of great simplicity, a fact reproduced in five or six other spots of culture: polyvalence. For a long time I had confidence in Popper; but henceforth I think that Freud comes off well, faced with the criterion of exteriority. The proof for that is the following: try to make money falsifiable. In spots populated by jokers, there can only be counterfeiters. Marx and Freud, quite simply, passed by that point. They constantly manipulate multivalent contents; they write in languages with general equivalents. It is true that they never thought to suspect the risk of the matter and Popper is right to impose the criterion. But it cannot be doubted that they discovered general equivalents and Popper did not see this. It is not because a theory is always true that it should be repudiated. It always works for another reason; it is in the realm of general equivalence. It is outside the true, outside the false; it indicates contents that are jokers. *La cosa*, as the Italian algebrists of the Renaissance used to say, *la cosa*, the thing said to be unknown, the unknown $= x$, multivalent, of which it can always be said that it takes all values. This is something else. You have seen a new Northwest Passage.

And that is why the story of Joseph, our first treatise of economics, is also a treatise on the interpretation of dreams. Cistern–capital and cistern–unconscious.

The distribution of jokers.

Given the universe of discourse. This universe can be organized according to the distribution of jokers. If there are a few in a cut of the cards or in a sequence, the determination is strong and there is constraint; it is rather near monosemy. A discourse with no jokers is even conceivable. This universe would reduce to this identity principle. Thus the universe in question is undervalued by $a \equiv a$. If you increase the number of jokers or their percentage in a series, a cut, or a sequence, and go to the maximum, the saturation point, polysemy overtakes the space with multivalence and equivocity. Near the end is the world of dreams, completely filled with polyvalence. At the limits of the dream, at the limits of the universe, the discourse composed exclusively of jokers is money. When there are only jokers, that's capital, a bank account, the general equivalent. They overvalue the world.

A curious universe, though a logical one, where dreams adhere to finance, where gold is near dreams.

As for the distribution of jokers in the universe of discourse: the identity principle and the principle of indiscernables are undervalued, and the circulation of money, right near dreams, is overvalued.

This universe has the form of a cornucopia. From a narrow, unique point to the wide mouth of equivalence (wide and narrow can change positions here). The universe of discourse is a horn of plenty.

Parasites, noises and grub(s), swarm around this horn.

Judas is innocent. In praise of Judas.

This is something else. Tamar: this kid is my body. Tamar: this cord is my body, the cord, the staff, and the seal. The joker is no longer in the dream; it circulates in our exchanges. The object that changes and is exchanged is the body. That of Tamar, the daughter-in-law, of Tamar, the prostitute. Joseph is freed from his cistern; twenty pieces of silver, this is his body.

Judas is innocent of the blood for that reason. This is something else, and this, this bread, is my body, this sheaf, this wheat, and this flour. This is something else, and this is my blood, the fruit of the vine and the branch. Judas sees another joker being formed. He understands that it is the substitute for sacrifice. He is a Jew, and thus he understands what he must understand in his milieu and his culture, that the sacrifice must be stopped, that there must be a substitute, that there must be a joker. And thus he does what Reuben does, what Judah, his ancestor, does. He changes the victim into money. He simply makes the founding motion of exchanges. Selling Joseph is not sacrificing him, not killing him; it is a way of saving him from death so as to be able to bring him back to the father one day. Judas is innocent; he must now finally be praised for Jews and Christians to be reconciled forevermore, to pull up the deepest anti-Semitic roots, those dwelling in ignorance. Judas reasoned correctly – he made the fatal series bifurcate; he reoriented the murder, changing it into something else and thereby avoiding it: Judas was a wise man. Accusing him, scorning him, is a denial of justice; it is already a text of persecution. Judas is innocent just as Oedipus was. Hence his despair when he sees that the sale failed, that it contributed to the sacrifice and that the sacrifice was not at all avoided. And he is the victim, the other victim.

Notes

1   John 12:25. "Si le grain ne meurt" is more common in French than is its translation in English. – Trans.
2   See my analysis of *Thérèse Raquin*. I suppose that the white domino has the value of a joker; it is not always true in the game of dominoes.
3   *Bricolage* has no good English equivalent. It means putting together as if by odds and ends, with bits and pieces, and so forth. – Trans.

Chapter 16

The Interior Structure of Made Objects

Elaine Scarry 1946–

Introduction

Elaine Scarry, a literary critic and philosopher, received a Ph.D. in 1974 from the University of Connecticut. She taught for several years at the University of Pennsylvania. She now teaches in the English department at Harvard University where she is the Walter M. Cabot Professor of Aesthetics and the General Theory of Value. Her research interests include the Nineteenth-Century British Novel; Twentieth-Century Drama; Theory of Representation; Language of Physical Pain; Structure of Verbal and Material Making in Art, Science, and the Law. Professor Scarry has been honored with several awards and fellowships, including the Levenson Award for Undergraduate Teaching at Harvard in 1996 and the Ira Abrams Award for Distinguished Teaching at the University of Pennsylvania in 1986. Her major works include *On Beauty and Being Just* (1999); *Making Mental Pictures Fly* (1998); (ed.) *Fins de Siècle* (1995); *Resisting Representation* (1994); (ed.) *Literature and the Body* (1988); and *The Body in Pain: The Making and Unmaking of the World* (1985), from which this selection comes. In her work, Scarry can be considered a postmodern critic because she is concerned with examining the implications of certain binary oppositions – between verbal and material, visible and invisible, creation and deconstruction, justice and injustice – even though she rarely uses the term.

Generally, *The Body in Pain: The Making and Unmaking of the World* examines the political implications of pain and torture. Pain, then, is not only a medical term, but also carries connotations of war, torture, and other political acts. Scarry explores the relationship between religion and pain. This exploration provides a theoretical foundation for approaching bodily pain in such a way that it becomes possible to bring voice to the power of pain. Scarry argues that because physical pain has no voice at its inception, when it finds a voice it begins to tell a story. Scarry's goal, through this book, is to record that story.

Specifically, in this selection, Scarry examines the place of material objects in Judeo-Christian scriptures. In *The Body in Pain* Scarry unpacks the opposition between voice and body, discovering that the alternation between them is fundamentally concerned with the materiality and immateriality of scripture. Here, the alternation of verbal existence and physical or material existence is described in terms of scripture's "graven images" and "passover images." Scarry discusses the place of the human and the place of God in relation to "material and materialized verbal artifacts of the Old Testament" and shows that "the realm of created culture" – the realm of the "made objects" of her subtitle – threatens to shatter the "categorical" separation of God and the human in a "shattering [that] is only realized in the Christian narratives."

It can accurately be said – and has often been said – that the Hebraic scriptures are deeply hostile to material culture. The second commandment prohibition of graven images, though most familiar in the story of the casting of the calf beneath Horeb and the story of the adoption by the tribe of Dan of gods crafted by Micah (as well as the complicated record of the uniting of Bethel and Dan, and the succession of sometimes image-worshipping kings that followed), is not confined to these two moments but regularly appears and disappears as a persistent problem. Nor is the aversion to made objects confined to the specific class of objects that are graven images, for the aura of contamination that clings to them also surrounds ordinary objects: even the offensiveness of the molten calf is inseparable from the offensiveness of the jewelry out of which it is made, both of which are seen by Moses and by God as objects of self-adornment; similarly, throughout Jeremiah, the prohibition against graven images is inseparable from the prohibition against a people's act of building for itself beautiful buildings paneled in cedar and painted with vermilion (22:14; see also chapters 11, 12, 14, 32 as well as this conflation in Haggai, Zechariah, and Malachi). The anti-cultural, anti-urban, anti-craftsmen emphasis of the Hebrew texts has been persuasively and elaborately explored by Herbert Schneidau, who shows the way the initial identification of "Cain the murderer" with "Cain the original city-founder" continues in the rejection of the "old urban tradition of architectural and astronomical wisdom" in the story of Babel, in the attribution of unequivocally negative connotations to city-dwelling in the story of Sodom and Gomorrah, in the equation of the Israelites' final entry into the Promised Land with the necessity of destroying the world's oldest city (Jericho), as well as in an extensive list of parallel moments that only begin with these four.[1] Human acts of building, making, creating, working are throughout the Old Testament surrounded with layer upon layer of prohibition from above and inhibition from below.

At the same time, however, the scriptural attitude toward human acts of creation and culture cannot be simply and summarily identified as dismissive because it is deeply complicated by three very large facts. First, the Hebrews are themselves engaged in a sustained act of inventing an Artifact so monumental and majestic (however problematic) that it perhaps has no peer in any other single artifact invented by another people: the Old Testament prophecy that this Artifact will eventually compel and absorb the attention of the rest of the world (e.g., Exodus 33:16; Zechariah 8:21–23) has not

Elaine Scarry, "The Interior Structure of Made Objects," from *The Body in Pain: The Making and Unmaking of the World* (New York and Oxford: Oxford University Press, 1985).

proved inaccurate, and the prohibition against other acts of making can in part be understood as an attempt to prevent the energy of completing this one act of invention from being deflected into more modest outcomes. Second, this Artifact, God, is itself the pure principle of creating: thus "making" is set apart and honored as the most holy, most privileged, and most morally authoritative of acts. Invention is recognized as the thing on which nothing less than the fate of humanity depends. Third, God's very first act is designated to be the creation of the world: that is, in a single stroke, the Old Testament mind has effectively subverted the entire "natural world" and reconceived the whole cosmos as the proper territory for acts of artifice and intelligence. Thus the dense texture of prohibition against human making must be seen within the larger framework of these three facts that together establish "making" as *at once the most morally resonant of acts* (as now in the late twentieth century theories of distributive justice identify as the most urgent locus of ethical action "making" and "distributing what is made") *and the most extensive*, stopping not at the doorway of the house, the gateway of the city, the edge of the shore, not at the seas or the earth itself but out through the stars and the galaxies (so that the Voyager space*craft*, hurtling out of the solar system with its recorded message, "Hello from the children of the earth," only makes concrete the *reach* of inventiveness that was first assumed in the opening lines of Genesis).

Further, as this section will suggest, the human acts of material making are in the Old Testament – even in the very midst of the prohibition – very gradually made compatible with the generous impulses in the larger framework they themselves modify. Material objects in the Old Testament can be grouped into two categories. The first consists of those made by man, either independent of God's permission or explicitly against his prohibition: this category includes graven images as well as an array of domestic objects. The second consists of objects authored by God, or authored by man at God's explicit invitation and instruction; to the list of divine imperatives, "Go...," "Arise...," "Behold...," "Hearken...," "Do...," "Do not...," is periodically added the striking imperative, "Make..." (e.g., Make an ark of gopher wood). As will gradually become clear, the shattering of the categorical separation of body and voice already looked at in the New Testament is in the Old Testament accomplished through these two genres of material objects; for the objects authored by man *successfully* confer on God a body, while the objects authored by God divest man of his body by taking over the work of substantiation earlier required of the human body, thereby placing humanity closer to the verbal category. Each of the two genres of objects will be attended to separately below. Together they expose the interior structure common to all made things – whether an ark, altar, well, written song, robe, recorded law, house – as a conflation of God's body and man's body, that is, as a materialization of the principle of creating and a dematerialization of the human creator.

Objects Authored by Men and Women – Graven Images and the Conferring on God of a Body

As suggested earlier, the making of graven images is in the Hebraic scriptures a blurring of the categorical integrity of body and voice. Consequently, it is almost inevitably followed by events intended to reestablish the extremity of the two categories: either the physical ground of man's existence is intensified or God's verbal purity is reasserted. Both kinds of event are mediated by the weapon either as material object (sword) or material phenomenon (fire), which is singular in being a concrete object or phenomenon other than the human body identified with and allowed to represent God. The making of graven images, however, eventually works to shatter this singular representational object into a multitude of objects. It is as though the colossal mediating sword, spanning the distance from the ground to heaven, is itself fractured, and on the ground beneath the place where it once stood are cups, blankets, songs, and a multitude of other objects.

To say that the act of representing a god is an act of endowing him with a body may be self-evident, perhaps even tautological. Certainly the narratives themselves stress this connection either by the form of the image which, like the molten calf, is often animal-like (for an animal is the phenomenon of sentience uncomplicated by personhood and self-extension) or in its surrounding context, as in the story of Rachel's usurpation of her father's household gods, which are almost absorbed into her own flesh as though they were her own children not yet born:

> Now Rachel had taken the household gods and put them in the camel's saddle, and sat upon them. Laban felt all about the tent, but did not find them. And she said to her father, "Let not my lord be angry that I cannot rise before you, for the way of women is upon me." So he searched but did not find the household gods. (Genesis 31:34, 35)

But the seriousness of the claim only becomes clear if the act of representation, the act of embodiment, is itself recognized as an act of description, description not only unasked for but forbidden. The full threat and real significance of the graven images is *not merely that they describe God but that they give rise to a situation that requires God to describe himself.* That is, whether in fury or in sadness, his explanations of the error or injustice or godlessness of the images inevitably engage him in acts of self-description. Even in the moment when the graven images are being themselves destroyed, they are provoking God into acts of predication through which he materializes himself.

Two classes of predicates, the familiar and the unfamiliar, occur here, the first of which will be looked at before attending to the second, more significant class. Some of the acts of self-description occasioned by the graven images are ones that have, in other scriptural contexts, already been granted, never withheld, such as his existence as a voice, a name. So, for example, the fact that in Leviticus the announcement of the prohibition is repeatedly followed by "I am the Lord" –

> You shall make for yourselves no idols and erect no graven image or pillar, and you shall not set up a figured stone in your land, to bow down to them; for I am the Lord your God. You shall keep my sabbaths and reverence my sanctuary: I am the Lord. (26:1, 2; see also Jeremiah 16:18, 20, 21)

is not startling, for this act of predication is the one about which there is the least hesitation elsewhere in the scriptures, however carefully that name must be spoken. But even this most minimal predicate takes on in the present context a special tone; for a slight suggestion of vulnerability and acknowledged ineffectiveness attends the need to place by the side of the rejected physical image the reasserted verbal image, as in these deeply moving passages from Isaiah:

> Remember this and consider,
> recall it to mind, you transgressors,
> remember the former things of old;
> for I am God, and there is no other;
> I am God, and there is none like me...
>
> (Isaiah 46:8, 9)

> I am the Lord, that is my name;
> my glory I give to no other,
> Nor my praise to graven images.
>
> (Isaiah 42:8)

"I am the Lord, that is my name" – the repeated announcement almost sounds like that of an orphan protecting himself against mistreatment by introducing his sign of personhood ("I'm Jo") or that of an ineffective bureaucrat reminding his subordinates of his position ("You cannot do that; I'm the president").[2] If the predicate itself is familiar from many other scriptural contexts, there is the presence of something not wholly familiar in its iteration here.

The same is true of a second predicate, God's identification as Creator. This predicate, which originates with the opening of Genesis and is of course assumed throughout the scriptures, becomes in the graven image passages explicit, extensive, possibly even obsessive; for the crafting of idols inverts the primary relation between maker and made, and thus the restoration of the original direction of creation requires the continual reminder that it is God who has created everything, that "Before me no god was formed" (Isaiah 43:10), that it is He who "stretched out the heavens" and brought about all geographical alteration (Jeremiah 10:12, 13), that, most important, it is he who has created humanity, brought them forth from the womb (Isaiah 43:7, 21; 42:2). Throughout each of these passages and similar passages in Micah, Nahum, and Habakkuk, the graven images outrage the logic of divine creation because they are made by those who, themselves made, cannot be makers. (One cannot be unmindful here of the very large risks taken by the scriptural mind in allowing a made thing, a fiction, God, to itself denounce graven images on the basis that they are made things, fictions, and hence "lies" as in Isaiah 44:12–20 and Habakkuk 2:18–20.) The violation of this prohibition brings forth the most severe punishment –

> And in this place I will make void the plans of Judah and Jerusalem, and will cause their people to fall by the sword before their enemies.... I will give their dead bodies for food to the birds of the air, and to the beasts of the earth. And I will make this city a horror, a

thing to be hissed at; every one who passes by it will be horrified and will hiss because of all its disasters. (Jeremiah 19:7, 8)[3]

– punishment which, as in the passage cited, sometimes takes the form normally found in other scenes of punishment unconnected to graven images, but at other times does not.

What is most striking about the graven image passages is that in them the threat of punishment often departs from the conventional scene of punishment: the sentient human body that must be shattered because it has made an artifact is here often described as though it were itself an artifact or object of craft:

> Because Manasseh king of Judah has committed these abominations, . . . and has made Judah also to sin with his idols; therefore thus says the Lord, the God of Israel, Behold, I am bringing upon Jerusalem and Judah such evil that the ears of every one who hears of it will tingle. And I will stretch over Jerusalem the measuring line of Samaria, and the plummet of the house of Ahab; and I will wipe Jerusalem as one wipes a dish, wiping it and turning it upside down. (2 Kings 21:11–13)

> Thus says the Lord God [to the rebellious house]: Set on the pot, set it on, pour in water also . . . . Therefore thus says the Lord God: Woe to the bloody city: . . . Then set it empty upon the coals, that it may become hot, and its copper may burn, that its filthiness may be melted in it, its rust consumed. (Ezekiel 24:3, 9, 11 and see 23:30, 35, 37–39, 42 for prelude)

> Lo I am about to make Jerusalem a cup of reeling . . . On that day I will make Jerusalem a heavy stone for all the peoples; all who lift it shall grievously hurt themselves . . . On that day I will make the clans of Judah like a blazing pot in the midst of wood, like a flaming torch among sheaves . . . . And on that day, says the Lord of hosts, I will cut off the names of the idols from the land, so that they shall be remembered no more. (Zechariah 12:2, 3, 6, and 13:2)

> So will I break this people and this city, as one breaks a potter's vessel, so that it can never be mended. (Jeremiah 19:11, see 18:15ff)

> As I live, says the Lord, though Coniah the son of Jehoiakim, king of Judah, were the signet ring on my right hand, yet I would tear you off . . . (Jeremiah 22:24; see 22:9–14)

In their breaking of the second commandment, humanity itself becomes a dish, a cup, a pot, a potter's vessel, a piece of jewelry and, in similar passages, a clay vessel complaining to its fashioner that it lacks handles (Isaiah 45:9), pieces of silver and gold not yet refined (Malachi 3:3; Zechariah 13:9); elsewhere Israel becomes a threshing sledge to be used against enemy kingdoms worshipping idols (Isaiah 41:15), as she in turn in her transgression is consumed by her enemies like a garment eaten by moths (Isaiah 50:9). These passages are striking in part because in them God's powers of creating and of wounding are so vividly conflated.[4] But they are also startling for a second reason: the transformation of the covenant people into an unwiped dish or a rusty pot is so resonant with divine contempt that its harsh tone for a moment reestablishes and underscores the distance between the creator and his creatures; but the continual linking of the remote fact of cosmic creation with the humanly accessible fashioning of cup and shirt ultimately entails the collapsing of the distance between the very categories it seeks to reestablish.

It becomes clear why the prohibition against idols must be absolute, for once they are made, they create a situation from which there can be no return to the original position.

Once man, undirected by God, creates an object, God has then one of two choices. He can disown the object, thereby acknowledging human authority over that one sphere of creation and thus contracting the territory of creating that belongs to him. Alternatively he can (as in the passages just cited) extend the boundary of his authorship to include that object as well, thereby restoring to himself the entire ground of creation but now including within that province an instance of artifice so diminutive that it discredits the entire enterprise. Either response involves the recognition of a limit within divine creation.

The problem occasioned by the making of an ordinary object is, of course, greatly compounded if that object is an idol. Once an idol is placed in the space between man and God, there are from the divine position only four possible interpretations. Just as in the case of the ordinary object divine disowning and owning are the same self-limiting act, so the four objections to the idol consist of two in which it is disowned (rejected because God interprets it as not referring to Himself) and two in which it is owned (rejected because God interprets it as indeed referring to Himself). One, the idol refers to another god (e.g., Baal). Two, the idol refers to nothing beyond itself; it is itself (in the eyes of the people) another god. Three, the idol does refer to Me and is a misrepresentation. Four, the idol refers to Me and is a representation. These are the four categories of response into which most of the Old Testament objections to graven images fall. Although each provides its own compelling basis for God's wrath, each is to a large extent a restatement of the other three and of the single essential problem contained in the image-making.

The graven image passages in Deuteronomy, Isaiah, and Kings, for example, express deep anxiety about the possibility of God's replacement by or conflation with Baal, Molech, or the self-referring Asherim. This protection of the purity of God's position is also a protection of the racial purity of the Hebrew people, as in Jeremiah where the people are warned against mixing with the image-making Chaldeans or Babylonians. There is both an ontological and a sociological basis for being scandalized by idol's that refer to other gods. But often in these passages the objection to the idol's reference to other gods slides over into and becomes indistinguishable from anger over its misrepresentation of God. Is a molten calf more scandalous if it is understood to refer to Baal than if it is understood to refer to God? The psalmist writes in dismay of the event at Horeb:

> They exchanged the glory of God
> for the image of an ox that eats grass.   (Psalm 106:20)

The terrible disloyalty of worshipping Baal is not worse than the searing insult and deep indignity of portraying God Himself as a young ox. Infidelity and misrepresentation come to be almost indistinguishable, even changing places so that attention to Baal is described in terms of its lewd indignity, and visualizing God in material form is described in terms of infidelity, disloyalty, and harlotry. So, in turn, the error of misrepresentation is almost indistinguishable from the error of representation, since any act of representation, any material analogue, is a diminution and distortion of the immaterial, as is quietly articulated in the astonished and pained incomprehension of Isaiah:

> To whom then will you liken God,
> or what likeness compare with him?

> To whom then will you compare me,
> That I should be like him? says the Holy one.   (Isaiah 40:18, 25–26)

One may say that here and in similar passages, God or the prophet intentionally misrepresents the nature of the act of representation, for the idol need not be seen as suggesting an equivalent, let alone (as in the passage just cited) as indicating the lines of aspiration, an image of what God should seek to become. But ultimately, of course, the idols are just that, a human suggestion to God about what he should try to become, and what he should try to become is embodied. It is precisely because any act of material representation is an act of embodiment that again and again the graven representations in the Hebraic scriptures are so close to what God in the Christian narratives willingly becomes by taking a body. It is difficult to read that "men kiss calves!" (Hosea 13:2) or that they make an image "of an ox that eats grass" (Psalm 106:20) without seeing floating behind the asserted ludicrousness of these animal images the image of Jesus at birth surrounded by cow and donkey, sleeping in their shelter, held in the container out of which they eat, himself almost one of their infant offspring. Again who can read the following passages from Jeremiah without being deeply moved by its bewilderment at the horrible impropriety of representation –

> A tree from the forest is cut down,
> and worked with an axe by the hands of a craftsman.
> Men deck it with silver and gold;
> they fasten it with hammer and nails
> so that it cannot move.
> Their idols are like scarecrows in a cucumber field,
> and they cannot speak;
> They have to be carried,
> for they cannot walk.   (Jeremiah 10:3–6)

– yet not at the same time be haunted by another pair of outstretched arms, another nailed and speechless scarecrow in a cucumber field.

It is the fact of embodiment itself out of which these coincidences arise, and it is the fourth of the interpretive categories – the idols refer to God and represent him – that is the essential violation implicit in them all.

As the foregoing discussion has tried to suggest, God responds to instances of representation by trying to clarify who he is and who he is not, by acts of self-clarification and self-definition through which he materializes himself. Thus the human act of embodying him, though itself interrupted, does in fact end by leading to his embodiment. Even those attributes that are already a given in the scriptures – his existence as a verbal category, his name, "the Lord," and his position as creator – acquire a more coherent because no longer total shape as he now specifies which *parts* (rather than all) of the power of creating are his, and which *parts* (rather than all) of creation have Him as their ultimate referent. He also acquires a much richer emotional predication in this context: as was implicit in the descriptions above, the ordinary tones of

anger or vengeful authority that surface elsewhere in the scriptures are now regularly
accompanied by psychological events such as bewilderment, incomprehension, vulnerability, jealousy, shame, or embarrassment, attributes that sound awkward and inapplicable to God yet are unquestionably present in the complex emotional tone of the graven
image passages. This tone signals the power of images to endow God with a body: they
do not simply visualize him in material form but, more important, give rise to responses
in him that can only accompany the bodily condition. But there is a second, far more
startling signal of this same fact that becomes evident when one attends not to the class
of familiar predicates (I am the Lord; I am the Creator) but to the class of unfamiliar
predicates.

As one moves through the graven image passages, one encounters a wide assortment
of attributes that God directly or indirectly claims in the process of rejecting a specific
statue, idol, or pillar. For instance, He may in one instance reject it because it is a
representation; in a second, because it is an *animal* representation (implicitly accepting
the fact of representation itself); and in a third, he may reject some *particular quality* of the
specific animal representation (implicitly accepting not only the general phenomenon of
representation but even the whole subphenomenon of animal representation), as in this
passage from Hosea where it is only the offensive docility of the calf imagery that he
angrily dismisses:

> Men kiss calves! . . . .
> So I will be to them like a lion,
> like a leopard I will lurk beside the way.
> I will fall upon them like a bear robbed of her cubs,
> I will tear open their breast . . .   (13:2, 7, 8)

But while one could make a long catalogue of the predicates he gradually acquires
through this process, one particular ground of dismissal, one particular attribute of the
idols, recurs again and again until it becomes perhaps the single most prominent basis on
which he differentiates himself from them. It is visible in the following passages:

> And there you will serve gods of wood and stone,
> the work of men's hands, that neither see, nor
> hear, nor eat, nor smell. (Deuteronomy 4:28)

> Every man is stupid and without knowledge;
> every goldsmith is put to shame by his idols;
> for his images are false,
> and there is no breath in them.   (Jeremiah 51:17; see 10:8, 9, 14)

> What profit is an idol
> when its maker has shaped it,
> a metal image, a teacher of lies?
> For the workman trusts in his own creation
> when he makes dumb idols!
> Woe to him who says to a wooden thing,
> Awake;

to a dumb stone, Arise!
Can this give revelation?
Behold, it is overlaid with gold and silver,
and there is no breath at all in it.   (Habakkuk 2:18, 19)

Divine contempt for these statues is based on the fact that they do not see, do not hear, do not eat, do not breathe, do not move − based, that is, on the startling fact that, despite their material form, they do not have the attributes of bodily sentience. On this remarkable basis of sentience God continually differentiates himself from the idols. It is this that they lack. It is this that He has. Thus the graven images give rise to a situation in which God begins to claim as his own sensory attributes he almost nowhere else has occasion to own as a defining characteristic, sensory attributes that he in other contexts sometimes explicitly rejects (e.g., "and though they cry in my ears with a loud voice, I will not hear them" Ezekiel 8:18). Their failing is a failing he has elsewhere taken pride in.

He now not only reminds his people that he is alive, that he sees, moves, hears, breathes (and by implication, even eats, for the absence of this attribute is included in his denunciation of wooden and stone objects), but even that he experiences the most passive, extreme, and unselfobjectifying form of sentience, physical pain. This acknowledgment occurs, for example, in chapters 8 through 12 of Jeremiah where, amid lines condemning the worship of Baal or other gods and idols, comes the repeated cry, indistinguishably that of the prophet and of God, I am wounded:

For the wound of the daughter of my
people is my heart wounded,
I mourn, and dismay has taken hold on me.   (8:21)

O that my head were waters,
and my eyes a fountain of tears,
that I might weep day and night
for the slain of the daughter of my people!   (9:1)

Thus says the Lord of hosts:
"Consider, and call for the mourning
women to come;
send for the skilful women to come;
let them make haste and raise a wailing over us,
that our eyes may run down with tears,
and our eyelids gush with water."   (9:17, 18)

. . . for his images are false,
and there is no breath in them.
. . . .
Woe is me because of my hurt!
My wound is grievous.
But I said, "Truly this is an affliction,
and I must bear it."
My tent is destroyed,

> and all my cords are broken;
> my children have gone from me...   (10:14, 19, 20)

The same cry of pain, the same admission of a capacity to suffer, occurs in Isaiah, again in a voice that hovers between that of the prophet and that of God:

> For a long time I have held my peace,
> I have kept still and restrained myself;
> *now I will cry out like a woman in travail,*
> *I will gasp and pant.*
> I will lay waste mountains and hills,
> and dry up all their herbage....
> They shall be turned back and utterly
> put to shame,
> who trust in graven images,
> who say to molten images,
> "You are our gods."   (42:14, 15, 17, italics added)[5]

Again the cry of Godly hurt becomes audible in his confession of need for the Hebrew people:

> How can I give you up, O Ephraim!
> How can I hand you over, O Israel!   (Hosea 11:8)

Thus the idol provides the external image of a body while lacking the interior requirement, sentience, yet simultaneously provides the situation in which God now claims that interior requirement, acknowledging his sentience not only in its aggressive and powerful outcome, as in the authoritative overseeing of men's actions, but in the passive, objectless, self-experiencing fact of itself whose most persuasive sign is physical pain. While in other scriptural contexts He has the objectified content of vision, hearing, and touch, now He has the sentient eyes, ears, and embodied surface that can themselves be wounded, produce the sensation of hurt, shed tears, require comforting, and so forth.

His sentience is in turn accompanied by greater attention to and accommodation of human sentience, for the failure of the statues to hear is designated their inability to answer the human cry for help, their failure to walk is their failure to lead men out of trouble:

> When you cry out, let your collection
>   of idols deliver you!
> The wind will carry them off,
> a breath will take them away.   (Isaiah 57:13)

> [Their idols] cannot speak;
> they have to be carried,
>   for they cannot walk.

> Be not afraid of them,
>> for they cannot do evil,
>>> neither is it in them to do good.   (Jeremiah 10:5)

> "And we will say no more, 'Our God,'
>> to the work of our hands.
> In thee the orphan finds mercy."
>> I will heal their faithlessness;
>> I will love them freely,
>>> for my anger has turned from them.
>>> . . .
> O Ephraim, what have I to do with idols?
> It is I who answer and look after you.   (Hosea 14:3, 4, 8)

And there you will serve gods of wood and stone, the work of men's hands, that neither see, nor hear, nor eat, nor smell. . . . When you are in tribulation, and all these things come upon you in the latter days, you will return to the Lord your God and obey his voice, for the Lord your God is a merciful God; he will not fail you or destroy you or forget the covenant with your fathers which he swore to them. (Deuteronomy 4:28, 30, 31)

It is in this context that God repeatedly identifies himself as rescuer —

I brought them out of the land of Egypt, from the iron furnace, saying, Listen to my voice. (Jeremiah 11:4)

> You know no God but me,
> and besides me there is no savior.
> It was I who knew you in the wilderness,
> in the land of drought.   (Hosea 13:4, 5)

and as healer —

You shall not bow down to their gods, nor serve them, nor do according to their works, but you shall utterly overthrow them and break their pillars in pieces. You shall serve the Lord your God, and I will bless your bread and your water; and I will take sickness away from the midst of you. (Exodus 23:24, 25)

> We would have healed Babylon,
> but she was not healed.   (Jeremiah 51:9)

Again in Isaiah, he contrasts the weight of lifeless idols carried on the stooped and weary backs of men and donkeys with his own willingness to carry man: "Even to your old age I am He, and to grey hairs I will carry you" (46:4). This inclusion of the old and sick is almost a retraction of the previous rule banishing the blemished and handicapped from his presence (Leviticus 21:16 f; 22:4, 17 f; Deuteronomy 17:1). He asks that those who know him know that "I am the Lord who practices kindness" (Jeremiah 9:24), and describes destruction as human rather than divine activity: "My compassion grows warm and tender / I will not execute my fierce anger, / I will not again destroy Ephraim; / for I am God and not man" (Hosea 11:8, 9). Reciprocal sentience is at once reciprocating sentience and reciprocal need: "They shall be my people, and I will be their God" (Ezekiel 11:20; see Zechariah 8:4–8).

The graven images elicit from Yahweh a constellation of attributes characteristic of Jesus and that seem to follow from the fact of embodiment itself. Having a body means having sentience and the capacity to sense the sentience of others, reciprocity, compassion. Having a body means being not everywhere but somewhere, no longer hidden: "He will surely be gracious to you at the sound of your cry. . . . your Teacher will not hide himself any more, but your eyes shall see your Teacher" (Isaiah 30:19, 20). The idols themselves are repeatedly denounced for their attribute of hiddenness (Habakkuk 2:18–20; Deuteronomy 27:15), now by extension no longer an attribute of God. In turn, standing revealed requires – both in the New Testament and in the graven image passages in the Old Testament – that the believers themselves become responsible for a more accurate sentience, one that is healed and whole and able to differentiate between true and untrue gods: "Hear, you deaf; / and look, you blind, that you may see!" (Isaiah 42:18). Thus, though the people's making of idols always fails, their remaking of God and of themselves does not fail: the material statue is a tool or lever across whose surface they reach, repair, and refashion the primary Artifact.

All this is not to say that such passages are without cruelty, for as was stressed earlier, God's dominant response to idols is to reassert the separation of man's body and His voice, usually by making emphatically visible the precarious fact of man's body. But the bodily sentience God here begins to claim as his own is a frail but persistent theme that challenges the mental structures of the Old Testament, though it only itself becomes dominant once God in the Christian scriptures enters the body directly, bringing with him attributes that make the kinship between Christ and the realm of material culture (only implicit in the graven images) unmistakably clear. Conversely, all this is not to say that passages about idols are the only parts of Hebrew narrative and prophecy that contain this more benign, accommodating (more consistently reciprocating) God. It is only to say that the idols are one very resonant locus of the transformation.

Objects Authored by God Divest Man of His Body

The discussion has so far looked at one class of artifacts in the Old Testament, those made by man: they are independent of God's sanction and are usually made explicitly against his prohibition. There is a second class of artifacts, those made by God, or made by man according to God's overt and often detailed instructions. This second group of objects, like the first, explodes the categorical separations by conferring on God a body and relieving man of his own body. The structure of exchange is once again directly described by the narratives themselves.

The artifacts God authors are, especially by the measure of our own dense material culture, very small in number. Each, however, tends to be a compelling focus of attention, in part because each stands in vibrant isolation against the desert background: in the midst of an unbroken mineral expanse, the blue of the tabernacle curtains breaks across eyes eager for an object. Further, though small in number, they are relatively extensive in the categories of invention they bring forth. The tabernacle is perhaps the most familiar: God's instructions to Moses for its design and construction are intricate enough to fill thirteen chapters of Exodus (25–31, much of which is then repeated in 35–40), for he specifies the pattern, length, height, width, and material of section after section of the large edifice, including precise accounts of its hinges, clasps, and pegs; he specifies also the design of the small objects within its walls (ark, altar, mercy seat, incense altar, table of acacia wood, lampstand of pure gold, snuffers, trays, oils, clothing); and he designates as well the particular craftsmen whose hands will bring this about. Instructions for additional objects enter elsewhere, as in Numbers where He requires "two silver trumpets of hammered work" (10:1) and a lampstand with seven candles, "from its base to its flowers, it was hammered work; according to the pattern which He had shown Moses" (8:4). His direction also extends to objects much larger than the tabernacle, as in his requirements for the number and size of the cities of refuge and cities of the Levites, "And you shall measure, outside the city, for the east side two thousand cubits, and for the south side two thousand cubits, and for the west side . . ." and so forth (Numbers 35:5 f). It also includes surprising categories of objects such as the model, map, or miniature theatre that Ezekiel is directed to build: "Take a brick and lay it before you, and portray upon it a city . . . and build a siege wall against it, and cast up a mound against it; set camps also against it. . . . And take an iron plate, and place it as an iron wall between you and the city" (Ezekiel 4:1–3).

Language, too, is an artifact, and when it is written down, the verbal artifact becomes a material artifact. The law given to Moses on Mount Sinai is only the most widely recognized instance of God's authorship of the expansive realm of the materialized voice that extends from the simplest deed of possession inscribed on the object itself –

> There shall be inscribed on the bells of
> the horses, "Holy to the Lord."   (Zechariah 14:20)

> This one will say, "I am the Lord's,"
> another will call himself by the name of Jacob,
> and another will write on his hand, "The Lord's."   (Isaiah 44:5)

to the entire history of a people –

> Moses wrote down their starting places, stage by stage, by command of the Lord; and these are their stages according to their starting places. (Numbers 33:2)

and includes the self-conscious category of song, sometimes only in His simple instruction to sing (Isaiah 42:10) but elsewhere, as at the end of Deuteronomy, in His dictation of the words of the songs themselves (31:30; 32:1–44). The isolated phrases explicitly attributed to God within the scriptures are only heightened and self-conscious acknowledgments of an authorship that extends to all the words of the scriptures, for in the Hebrew tradition, it is not just the ten commandments but the Pentateuch and the books of the prophets, and even the oral law eventually written down in the Talmud that are understood to have been given to Moses at Horeb.

As was earlier suggested, God ordinarily permits himself to be materialized in one of two places, either in the bodies of men and women or in the weapon. These two forms of substantiation reappear in the recurring scenes of hurt. These two are also often lifted out of the narrative sequence of events and self-consciously designated as signs. In all of Genesis, for example, there are only two signs: one is the weapon, the bow, "I set my bow in the clouds, and it shall be a sign of the covenant between me and the earth" (9:13)[6] the other is the mark in the human body, "You shall be circumcised in the flesh of your foreskins, and it shall be a sign of the covenant" (17:11). Such signs are themselves, of course, simple artifacts, artifacts not identical with the thing they indicate (since they do not have within them the angry intention and outcome of an actual wound or weapon) but elementary enough to memorialize the literal event of wound and weapon for which they are substitutes. That they are at once "substitutes" for bodily hurt and "signs" of God's peace with man (two ways of saying the same thing) is indicative of the benign consequence of artifice that becomes more pronounced in more freestanding artifacts.

When God authors a particular material or verbal artifact, the object is often presented in the narrative either as his own material form or as a material substitute for the human body. Sometimes the narrative is not explicit and it is instead the surrounding context that specifies this meaning. For example, the suggestion introduced earlier that the layers and layers of woven tissue in the tabernacle are almost the visible tissue of the body of God is not directly stipulated by the text but is instead indicated by the larger framework. The crisis-laden departure of the Hebrews from the culturally rich, graven-image filled kingdom of Egypt into the desert wilderness (the opening of Exodus), followed by the deep crisis centering on the contrast between the molten calf and the voice speaking out of the fire (the middle of Exodus), makes the building of the tabernacle (the end of Exodus) impossible to sever from the issue of material representation that is so emphatic in the first two of the three major subjects. Calf and tabernacle, two lonely objects on an otherwise unbroken expanse of sand and stone, are connected by much more than the jewelry that goes into the fashioning of each (the jewelry taken out of Egypt in the opening; put into, then retrieved back out of, the calf in the second part; then put into the tabernacle). Thus, while the scriptures overtly call for the absolute annihilation of material form and the reestablishment of God's verbal purity, the structure of events instead insists on the more modest distinction between man's version of God's material form (calf) and God's version of God's material form (tabernacle). The tabernacle, like the calf, is an object around which the people gather, a spatially locatable object they can move toward or away from, an object which satisfies their longing for His observable presence among them that had earlier given rise to the incident of idol-making. Even here, however, the image of the weapon is not entirely gone, for it is instead hovering nearby in hypothetical outline: the tabernacle is surrounded by the brooding storm-cloud by day and the fire by night. The perceptual object that permits the translation back out of the material base into the wholly verbal source is held in readiness.

Sometimes, however, the projection of the sentient body into the artifact is explicitly announced by the narrative itself, as in the following passage describing God's consuming punishment of the Hebrews for their disbelief:

And Moses said, "Hereby you shall know that the Lord has sent me to do all these works, and that it has not been of my own accord. If these men die the common death of all men, or if they are visited by the fate of all men, then the Lord has not sent me. But if the Lord creates something new, and the ground opens its mouth, and swallows them up, with all that belongs to them, and they go down alive into Sheol, then you shall know that these men have despised the Lord."

And as he finished speaking all these words, the ground under them split asunder; and the earth opened its mouth and swallowed them up.... And all Israel that were round about them fled at their cry; for they said, "Lest the earth swallow us up!" And fire came forth from the Lord, and consumed the two hundred and fifty men offering the incense.

Then the Lord said to Moses, "Tell Eleazar the son of Aaron the priest to take up the censers out of the blaze; then scatter the fire far and wide. For they are holy, the censers of these men who have sinned at the cost of their lives; so let them be made into hammered plates as a covering for the altar, for they offered them before the Lord; therefore they are holy. Thus they shall be signs to the people of Israel." (Numbers 16:28–38)

"But on the morrow," the story continues, the people again disbelieve; God sends a plague that consumes fourteen thousand seven hundred people, until its action is stopped when the hammered plates are carried into the midst of the assembled people. In the first part of the passage, man's body substantiates God. In the second, the artifact becomes the sign of the human body on whose surface God's presence earlier recorded itself, and now itself performs the work of substantiation. Just as a person may assert his or her presence by continually fluid, continually disappearing, then renewed actions or instead assert that presence by objects which alter the scene they enter and permanently record the person's presence,[7] so God may continually reexpress Himself by repeated moments of actually inflicted hurt, or may instead have the enduring record of a single instance of that bodily alteration in the artifact.

It is not clear whether it is more true to say that the censers are a sign of (substitute for) man or a sign of (substitute for) God; for although it is in this passage explicitly man's body that is substituted for, spared, and therefore "represented," it is also God's body that is represented since man's body was itself hurt to confer the attribute of "realness" on an unapprehensible God – it was itself "a sign," a material verification of His existence. That is, the censers are a substitute for man's body which was originally itself a substitute for God's body. Once this process begins, it can be spread out onto more and more of the realm of artifice: as God has his sign in the human body and the human body its sign in the object, so this first object in turn may have its sign in a second object, and the second in a third. This occurs in Zechariah 6, for example, where all that is to be substantiated by the temple is, until the completion of that temple, substantiated by the more quickly fashioned crown which, after the completion of the larger artifact, will be enshrined there. As the process becomes more richly mediated, any given part of it can acquire a more specific function, as here where the crown serves first in the capacity of prophecy and then commemoration. What is clear from this sequence of substitutions is that the process of the imagination (and the transformation out of the realm of the sensuously immediate made possible by the imagination) begins not by man conceiving of signs separable from himself but by man conceiving of his own body as a sign of (and substitute for) something beyond itself, and then bringing forth other signs that can perform the work of representation in his dear body's place.

Those objects God introduces into Hebrew life are usually accompanied by the meanings described above. When Zechariah sees in a vision an elaborate branching lamp, the angel tells him that the seven lamps are "the eyes of the Lord" and the seven lamps have "seven lips,"[8] and the lamp is God's speech announcing first his power of altering the land through cosmic disturbance and second, his power of altering the land by introducing into its midst a new building (4:5–10). The cataclysmic disturbance need not occur if the thing it was intended to make apprehensible, God's power of alteration, can be made apprehensible in the landscape-altering construction of the temple, and if the thing that power of alteration was in its turn intended to make apprehensible (for God surely has no interest per se in changing land or landscape), the sheer fact of God's existence, the pure force of that fact, can be made apprehensible in an elaborate lamp, memorializing the verbal announcement and thus pre-empting the enactment of that force. The same is true of the seven-faceted, engraved stone placed before Joshua which "will remove the guilt of this land in a single day" (Zechariah 3:6–10), thereby eliminating the need for the usual ghastly procedures for transforming disbelief into belief through material verification. More simply and more powerfully, the altars and wells that God calls for throughout Genesis are, as noticed earlier, themselves representations of the interior of the human body, repeatedly occupying its position in the narrative sequence. Such artifacts are also, as the text periodically reminds us, material commemorations of God having spoken.

Embedded in God's authorship of material culture is the scriptural recognition that in scenes of verification the specific content of God's speech is unimportant. God's speech must have content, and must be detailed, only so that the material enactment of the specified content of his speech will make incontestable the fact of his having spoken; there must be content, and the content must be detailed, but what the content is, what the details are, does not matter. The scriptural attribution to Him of the authorship of material objects contains the recognition that the statement "Let this man be cut in two," "Let this woman's body become leprous," "Let the earth swallow them up" (followed in each case by the enactment) has – not only from man's point of view but from God's – no superiority over the statement, "Let the censers be hammered into altar plates," "Let there come into your midst a three-foot by five-foot altar," "Let the tabernacle be built according to this plan" (followed in each case by the enactment). In seeing that it is the fact of God's voice and not its particular content that matters, the human imagination behind the scriptures gains control of the content of God's speech and in doing so regains its own voice. Thus the artifacts are not only God's body but man's speech.

In any culture, the simplest artifact, the simplest sign, is the single mark on wood, sand, rock, or any surface that will take the imprint. This simplest of all artifacts provides the essential model for all God's artifacts in the Old Testament. It is the red mark on the doorposts and lintels, the passover mark, the mark (itself made of blood, and thus a projection of the body) that substitutes for the infant Hebrew bodies during the slaughter of the first-born (Exodus 12:7, 23). The invention of this mark occurs on the eve of and makes possible their exodus out of Egypt. When, many years later, they finally enter the promised land, their crossing of the Jordan into Jericho is obsessively described as a "passing over" (Joshua 1:14; 3:11, 14, 17; 4:1, 7, 10, 11, 22, 23),[9] and the sparing of the twelve tribes during that passage is commemorated in twelve stones. It is linked imagistically to the original red sign on the doorposts by the scarlet cord by which Rahab the harlot first lets them climb down into the walled city, the scarlet cord that she later hangs in her window as a sign to the Hebrews that all her kin within (as always in the Old Testament, the unit of rescue is the family) be passed over in the ensuing massacre of the city's people. Here, as on the earlier night, the possession of the fragile artifact depossesses one of the consequences of having a body.

The introduction of this sign is by no means an endorsement of material culture in general, for in both cases that culture is explicitly rejected, left behind in the exodus out of Egypt, destroyed in the entry into Jericho.[10] But in its simplicity, it defines quite openly and unambiguously the extraordinary design residing in each of the artifacts God authors. What, for example, are God's detailed instructions to Noah about the construction of the ark —

> Make yourself an ark of gopher wood; make rooms in the ark, and cover it inside and out with pitch. This is how you are to make it: the length of the ark three hundred cubits, its breadth fifty cubits, and its height thirty cubits. Make a roof for the ark, and finish it to a cubit above; and set the door of the ark in its side; make it with lower, second, and third decks. For behold... (Genesis 6:14–17)

but the simple passover mark elaborated into an intricate blueprint of rescue. With it, Noah is dispossessed of his body and "floats on the face of the waters" (7:18) as his bodiless God once "moved over the face of the waters" (1:2). When the flood comes, the ark is for him the red mark on the frame of his door, the scarlet cord in his window.

Just as all the material objects independently authored by man may be collectively designated by the rubric, "graven images," so all the material objects authored by God (altar, well, tabernacle, censers, lamp, seven-faceted stone, red mark, ark) may be collectively designated by the rubric, "passover artifacts." So, too, the materialized (written, memorized, recorded) verbal artifacts are passover objects. In some instances, this rhythm of substitution and sparing is explicit:

> Then those who feared the Lord spoke with one another; the Lord heeded and heard them, and a book of remembrance was written before him of those who feared the Lord and thought on his name. "They shall be mine, says the Lord of hosts, my special possession on the day when I act, and I will spare them as a man spares his son who serves him." (Malachi 3:16, 17)

Again, the long song God gives to Moses at the end of their wanderings in the desert (Deuteronomy 32:1–43) is explicitly prefaced with God's explication of its function:

> Now therefore write this song, and teach it to the people of Israel; *put it in their mouths*, that this song may be a witness for me against the people of Israel.... And when many evils and troubles have come upon them, this song shall confront them as a witness (for it will live unforgotten *in the mouths* of their descendents). (31:19, 21, italics added)

The words of the song themselves describe God's vengeance and jealousy, his hatred of other gods and of image-making, his "glittering sword" and "arrows drunk with blood" (32:41, 42); but the song is itself intended as an almost freestanding artifact which by being "in their mouths"[11] witnesses Him in their bodies, records His presence that would otherwise be recorded more deeply in their bodies in the hunger, burning heat, poisonous pestilence, and venom of crawling things that the content of the song describes. The form of the song is a substitute of its own content: the logic of the relation between form and content is described by the sentence, "Because of this, not this."

The passover function of the Deuteronomy song extends to other materialized verbal artifacts as well, for it is in part introduced to clarify the purpose of the "commandments and his statutes which are written in this book of the law" (30:10) that Moses has just completed writing. The song is a coda or epilogue to the law commenting on its inner design. One long chapter of Deuteronomy is devoted to the consequences of disbelief; the body is blanketed with every conceivable sore, sickness, and humiliation accessible to the Old Testament mind. It includes such passages as the following:

> The most tender and delicately bred woman among you . . . will grudge to the husband of
> her bosom, to her son and to her daughter, her afterbirth that comes out from between her
> feet and her children whom she bears, because she will eat them secretly, for want of all
> things, in the siege and in the distress. . . . (28:56, 57)

and it ends with the progressively deep humiliations of objectless work:

> And the Lord will bring you back in ships to Egypt, a journey which I promised that you
> should never make again; and there you shall offer yourselves for sale to your enemies as
> male and female slaves, but no man will buy you. (28:68)

But again, the formal fact of the scriptures is pre-emptive of scriptural content. The law itself is meant to displace the bodily verification of the primary Artifact, as one brief passage makes clear, and as the introduction of the song then reaffirms in expanded form:

> For this commandment which I command you this day is not too hard for you, neither is it
> far off. It is not in heaven, that you should say, "Who will go up for us to heaven and bring
> it to us, that we may hear it and do it?" neither is it beyond the sea, that you should say,
> "Who will go over the sea for us, and bring it to us, that we may hear it and do it?" But
> the word is very near you; it is in your mouth and in your heart, so that you can do it.
> (30:11–14)

Like the song, the law is an artifact intended to eliminate human hurt. One may say, "The cruelty is itself occasioned by the law, for bodily hurt occurs if the law is broken." But to say this is to forget the overarching sequence of substitutions: bodily hurt (analogical verification of God's realness) is replaced by the law, which may then become the broken law, in which case the bodily cruelty no longer has a substitute and so returns. It is precisely because X (e.g., the law) is a substitute for Y (e.g., bodily hurt) that when *X* is taken away (i.e., the law is broken) what returns is *Y* (bodily hurt). The relatively benign role of the written warning ultimately extends to the scriptures themselves: they are the framing artifact that subsumes as its content both the problematic deconstruction of creating in the scenes of wounding and the restructuring of creating in passages explicitly about material culture. Thus, even in the worst scenes of savagery, content is subordinate to form: the bodily substantiation of God's existence is itself recorded in a freestanding narrative artifact rather than recorded directly in the bodies of those who read, rather than hurt, in order to believe.

The material and materialized verbal artifacts of the Old Testament fall, then, into two groups: those made by man, the graven images, and those made by God, the passover images. The first confer on God a body and therefore materialize him; the second divest man of a body by producing a freestanding equivalent for that body. Thus the realm of created culture, the locus of God's body and man's body, threatens to shatter and transform the categorical separation of the two realms. If, as noted earlier, this shattering is (within the Judeo-Christian framework) only finally realized in the Christian narratives, if Jesus is the full materialization of what is only imminent in the prohibited and reluctantly granted Hebrew artifacts, it is also true that he is brought into being by them, that he must, at least in part, be recognized as being born forth out of the pressure that they exert, a pressure seldom long absent from the pages of the older writings. That is, if within the Hebrew imagination the artifact is in the very fact and form of itself a materialization of God and a dematerialization of man, then any artifact, say a story, any story that is told, regardless of its content, exists as a materialization of God and a dematerialization of man. But it is then perhaps inevitable that one day a particular story arises that becomes these things not only in the formal fact of itself but in its content as well, a story describing God's willing taking on of a body and, simultaneously, his willing disembodiment of men and women in earthly acts of healing, in the ultimate healing of the resurrected whole body, and in the elimination of the human body as a source of analogical verification. So that the form that was the benign substitute for its own content in the narratives of warning and hurt in the older writing now becomes itself the overt subject in the new. Thus the original exchange of categories sponsors another more sustained and profound version of itself in the Christian story, and Christ's body in turn by incorporating the transgression of these categories into the very act of belief makes the fact of continual "making" an inevitable and essential habit of mind.

It has been suggested here that the transition from the authoritarian emphasis of the Old Testament, where there is an inequality based on bodily representation, to the New, where that inequality is eliminated, has as its inevitable counterpart the greater sponsoring of material culture. It may well be that the anti-authoritarian impulse always has as its counterpart a correspondingly greater emphasis on materialism. Just as the Christian scripture is at once less authoritarian and more overtly material than the Hebrew, so too within Christianity, Protestantism has long been recognized as at once less authoritarian and more materially centered than Catholicism: that Luther's rebellion against and revision of the older version of Christianity was anti-hierarchical in its essential impulse is as widely accepted as is the identification of modern Western materialism with what has come to be called "the Protestant work-ethic."[12] In turn, within Protestantism, various denominations can be differentiated from one another by the same counterparts: Quakerism, for example, has been elaborately and persuasively shown by sociologist Digby Baltzell to have been at once more egalitarian and more materially centered than Puritanism, and to have been the religious ideology that eventually came to hold sway in the obsessively democratic, obsessively materialistic, United States.[13] Thus certain characteristics of the revision of Judaism by Christianity may themselves have been repeated and extended in the revision of Catholicism by Protestantism, and in turn by the successive revisions within Protestantism that occurred through the emergence of various sects.

Whether material culture is itself a vehicle of democratization, whether an icono-clastic religious culture is inherently inconsistent with an egalitarian political philosophy, are questions too large to be entered into here. Further, to pursue the sequential modifications of both the hierarchical and the material through successive revisions would wrongly suggest that material making *always* preserves the benign ethical impulses of belief while simultaneously extending its benefits by eliminating the poten-tially brutal procedures for verification necessitated by unanchored belief. Although material "making" is a solution to some of the problems entailed in "believing," it may itself of course become the problem: that is, the deconstruction of categories that occurred at the site of the imagined object may occur at the site of the material object as well. Thus the very problems encountered by a religious culture come to be re-encountered by a secular culture. [. . .]

Notes

1 Herbert Schneidau, *Sacred Discontent: The Bible and Western Tradition* (Baton Rouge: Louisiana State University, 1976), 5.
2 The ears of this writer can only hear the orphan-like tone of God's announcement; for the suggestion that God's voice may at such moments instead have the sound of a bureaucrat, I am indebted to Allen Grossman.
3 The final phrase of this passage is given more concretely in JPS as everyone "will hiss over all its wounds." *Tanakh: A New Translation of the Holy Scriptures According to the Traditional Hebrew Text* (Philadelphia, New York, Jerusalem: Jewish Publication Society [JPS], 1985).
4 The conflation of creating and wounding also occurs in other ancient texts such as the *Iliad*. For example,

> So the arrow grazed the outermost flesh of the warrior, and forthwith the dark blood flowed from the wound.
> As when a woman staineth ivory with scarlet, some women of Maeonia or Caria, to make a cheekpiece for horses, and it lieth in a treasure-chamber, though many horse-men pray to wear it; . . . even in such wise, Menelaus, were thy thighs stained with blood, thy shapely thighs and thy legs and thy fair ankles beneath. (4, 11. 137 f., trans. A. T. Murray, Cambridge, Mass.: Harvard University Press, 1924)

Here the merging of creating and wounding works more in the direction of eliciting a compassion for, or an honoring of, the wounded (though it may therefore also work to glorify human acts of killing other persons since the wound is now an artifact and thus the warrior-who-wounds is a kind of craftsman).

5   I would like to thank Rabbi Jack Bemperod who in a conversation at the Hastings Institute, Spring 1980, first called my attention to the Isaiah passage in which God speaks as though in physical pain. (The phrase "woman in travail" is more concretely given in JPS as "woman in labor.")

6   Because of its beauty, its association with the cessation of the death-laden storm, and its explicit designation as a sign of the covenant between people and God, the benign connotations of the rain-bow may make it difficult to recover the fact that it is God's bow (or "My bow") set in the clouds (i.e., put aside, rather than used). The word "bow" (*keshet*) used as a noun elsewhere in the scriptures refers to the weapon: the curved or arched shape of the rainbow makes it a bow whose scale and splendor are appropriate to God; as a bow that is set aside, it becomes an image of the now benign (because unused) divine weapon.

7   See *The Body in Pain* (New York: Oxford University Press, 1985), Chapter 3, 175.

8   The RSV "lips" is in JPS "pipes."

9   The repeated verb "passed over" in the RSV (also used in all these verses in the King James Version) is in JPS always given as "crossed over" (the Hebrew *'abar*, rather than *passah*) except for Joshua 4:7 where "passed over" is used for the movement of the Ark, the actual artifact that has made possible the parting of the waters and thus the passage of the people.

   That the two events are counterparts of one another is suggested by many shared attributes: both the exodus and the entry entail the parting of the waters (the Red Sea in the first instance; the Jordan in the second); one of the people's first acts while encamped in Gilgal is to renew the original "passover" ritual (Joshua 5:10); in each event the circumcision ritual occurs and is a required prelude to one's participation in the passover observance (Exodus 12:48; Joshua 5:2), and so forth.

10 Except in each of the two, metals and materials are kept (Exodus 12:35; Joshua 6:18, 24).

11 As is true of the Deuteronomy song, many verbal observances and rituals are, though substitutions for the substantiating work of the body, introduced as being recorded in the body, as though to signal (or recall) the original locus of substantiation. This is true of the rituals of cleansing and ordination, for example, in which blood is placed on the right ear, right hand, and right foot (Leviticus 8:22; 14:14). See also Exodus 13:9; Deuteronomy 6:6, 8; 11:18; and Joshua 1:8.

12 Max Weber, *The Protestant Ethic and the Spirit of Capitalism*, trans. Talcott Parsons, introd. Anthony Giddens (New York: Scribner, 1958).

13 E. Digby Baltzell, *Puritan Boston and Quaker Philadelphia: Two Protestant Ethics and the Spirit of Class Authority and Leadership* (New York: Free Press, 1979; rpt – Boston: Beacon, 1982).

Chapter 17

From Ethics and Community

Enrique Dussel 1934–

Introduction

Enrique Dussel is a native of Argentina who now lives in Mexico. After a relatively privileged childhood he studied in Europe, and there began to develop the sense of the unity and global significance of Latin America which was to become the basis of his work (see the Introduction to Part III). In Argentina and, after he was obliged to leave in the 1970s, in Mexico, he created a philosophy based on that of Emmanuel Levinas (see our excerpt), with ethics at the center, but also specific to the Latin American context. Later he turned to Marx, whom he reads, however, in terms of Levinas, so that Levinas's Other becomes specifically the poor and oppressed of the Third World.

Dussel is the major philosopher of the global "margin." He is extremely well versed in European philosophy, but insists on viewing it from an *exterior* perspective. His philosophical system is set out in his best-known work in English, *Philosophy of Liberation* (1985). His mode of ongoing participation in "Eurocentric" debate can be seen in *The Underside of Modernity* (1996). His margin-oriented understanding of the global context of current philosophy is best stated in his essay "Beyond Eurocentrism" (in *The Cultures of Globalization* [ed. Fredric Jameson and Masao Miyoshi] 3–31 [1998]).

Our selection is from a very different and more easily accessible work, *Ethics and Community* (1988), in which Dussel offers a biblically framed statement of his position in "Ten Fundamental Themes" (we include the second and eighth) and "Ten Disputed Questions" (we include the second). This selection is different from most of our others in that it places the Bible in a position of judgment, rather than in any critical framework. All that Dussel wants to say in a chapter is encapsulated in the biblical passage with which the chapter begins.

Such exemption of the Bible from critique is one of the things which, in this *Reader* as in *The Postmodern Bible*, we most want to question. Yet Dussel's voice, with its unique perspective on postmodernism (see the Introduction to Part III), is a vital one that we needed to include. Why the exemption of the Bible from a critique that he brings so rigorously to everything else? We surmise that Dussel is unwilling to do anything that might take the Bible away from those to whom, in his understanding, it most belongs, that is, the poor. In Latin American liberation theology (unlike some others) the Bible has been seen overwhelmingly as "part of the solution" rather than "part of the problem." What we have chosen to do is to bring Dussel's "uncritical" work into critical confrontation with the other selections in this book.

2   Evil and Death

2.1   State of the question

As happiness, fulfillment, and holiness, the reign of God is the face-to-face of persons among themselves and with God, who also is conceived as a *community* of persons, subsuming, taking unto itself, the community of created persons. Evil, wickedness, is the interruption, the breach of this face-to-face, its nemesis. One term of the relationship absolutizes itself and negates, annihilates, "reifies" (makes a *thing* out of) the other.

Each day the media carry news of wars, murders, thefts, administrative corruption, drug addiction. We learn of the daily presence of evil. We read of the rich, the very rich – and the miserable poor. We read of powerful countries and weak ones. No one any longer believes in the Devil, the Evil One. And yet the works of the Devil are evident. We have only to open our eyes to see them for what they are.

In holy scripture we read:

> Now the serpent was the most cunning of all the animals that the Lord God had made.... The woman answered the serpent: "We may eat of the fruit of the trees in the garden; it is only about the fruit of the tree in the middle of the garden that God said, 'You shall not eat it or even touch it, lest you die.'" But the serpent said to the woman: "You certainly will not die! No, God knows well that the moment you eat of it your eyes will be opened and you will be like gods...." Then the eyes of both of them were opened, and they realized that they were naked. (Gen. 3:1–7)

The subject is deeper, and more current, than we might think. The difficult thing for us to grasp is that evil begins as idolatry, fetishism, atheism; it develops in the domination of human beings by their own brothers and sisters, one person's subjugation by another. It is not the *person–person* relationship that prevails, but the *I–thing* relationship, the relationship of subject to object. Instead of two "someones," we have *one* "someone" in confrontation with "things." We have "reification."

2.2   What is wickedness, evil?

Evil, sin, the wickedness of the subject who commits the perverse praxis that builds the reign of the "Prince of this world" could be described in the following steps.

Enrique Dussel, from *Ethics and Community*, translated by Robert R. Barr (Maryknoll, NY: Orbis Books, 1988).

In the first place, the origin of evil or sin lies in a negation of the other, the other person, the other term of the person-to-person relationship. "Cain attacked his brother Abel and killed him. . . . 'The blood of your brother cries to me from the ground'" (Gen. 4:8, 10). To kill, rob, humiliate, dishonor, violate, and so on, the other, Abel, is to destroy the other term of the face-to-face relationship.

The *praxis of domination* is evil – sin (Gk., *hamartia*). It is praxis, but not of one person vis-à-vis another *as person*. Relationship *a* (in Diagram 1) is interrupted, and the dominator (Cain, person 1) makes (*b*) of the other (Abel, person 2) an *instrument*, a means. Person 2 is killed because he or she has been the enemy of person 1; or is robbed, used as an instrument of wealth; or is violated, used as an instrument of pleasure; and so on. Thus the status of the other person precisely as other is now reduced to that of a *thing*, a *means at the service of the dominator*. Person 2 now serves person 1 (arrow *c*). "I" am the end, the sovereign, the owner, of person 2. This is sin: the destitution of the other as person, the alienation (Lat., *alienum*, "other than oneself," sold, destroyed) of someone in some respect: reification, instrumentalization.

Offense to God is always and antecedently an act of domination committed against one's brother or sister. God is the absolute Other; hence God is offended when we dominate in some manner the other-and-neighbor, Abel; therefore does Christ take on the form of the very poorest, for what we do to our brother or sister we do to God. To dominate our neighbor is to sin against God.

2.3   Idolatry, fetishism

In negating the other, in negating God, sinners are left to themselves. They totalize themselves, asserting themselves as God, fetishizing and divinizing themselves. They fall into idolatry.

The sinner, the malefactor, is anyone who "devours my people as bread" (Ps. 14:4), who kills, who robs the other. And with the other term of the person-to-person relationship thus eliminated, the sinner – "the fool" – thinks "There is no God" (Ps. 14:1). There is no longer any "god" but "myself," says the one who has negated the other. By negating the other such persons affirm themselves sovereign over the other, for they have instrumentalized them. Thus they divinize themselves. And thus they make atheists of themselves vis-à-vis God, who is the Other par excellence, inasmuch as they have affirmed, asserted themselves to be god.

The act by which one asserts oneself as the end of other persons – as factory owners think they have a right to the factory's profit even though that profit be their workers' hunger transformed into money (see 12.10) – is idolatry. The prophets had to struggle with the idolatry of the Canaanites, and even of the Israelites. In the Adamic myth this

Diagram 1

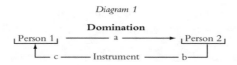

temptation is concretrized in the wish to "be like gods," to be absolute, *no longer to be in the person-to-person relationship* and at the service of the other (Ps. 115 [114]: 4–8).

This is not a reality solely of the past. For example, as we shall see below, when proprietors of capital forget that all of the value of their capital is the labor of others objectified (12.9), they forget the other term of the relationship that has occasioned their wealth: the other as a wage-earning worker. In thus forgetting others and robbing them of their work and life, they absolutize, fetishize capital, constituting it an idol to which they sacrifice their neighbor's life. These modern "gods" are the product of the "logic" of sin, of the domination of one human being over another, of the constitution by one person of another person as the mediation of the former's "own" wealth.

2.4   *Individual or abstract malice*

The theologico-symbolic description of the genesis of the evil act or sin – which we might call the description of the structure of temptation in theological figures – is situated at the beginning of the biblical accounts, in the so-called Adamic myth (Gen. 2:9–3:24).

In the myth of Prometheus, human fault or sin is tragic, inevitable. The gods are unjust. Men and women are not responsible for evil, for they are not really free. In the myth of Adam, on the other hand (and "myth" here denotes a *rational* account based on *symbols*), two liberties come into confrontation: that of the tempter and that of the tempted. Nothing is "necessary" or inevitable. The tempter speaks to, "propositions," seduces the tempted who is free to say no. This is the reason for the blandishment, the "feeling out" of the intended victim, the effort at persuasion: "You will be like gods. . . ."

The Adamic myth, then, teaches that the *fall* of Adam was the fruit of his own free will. It was not a flaw decreed by the gods. The *source* of the evil is Adam's freedom. Thus the evil will be reparable, and will lay history wide open as the theater of human responsibility. Adam accepts the proposal of the tempter to constitute the other as dominator (of himself) or dominated (by himself). The tempter proposes, in essence, the following: "Dominate me," in a passive or masochistic attitude; or "Let yourself be dominated," in an aggressive or sadistic attitude. The "other" – not in his or her reality as other, but as *part* of the system – can be the tempter. We must know the discernment of "spirits."

Those who yield to temptation and fall into evil, into the praxis of the domination of the other, their neighbor, signal that they have either instrumentalized that other for their own ends or else have accepted instrumentalization by him or her. At all events, in this perspective, this sin, this fault, is not in the last analysis an individual one. It is not abstract. In concrete reality one sins only *in relation to* others.

2.5   *Social or concrete sin*

True enough, speaking *abstractly* one can say that John, the individual, has sinned. But *concretely* John is Mary's father, Martha's spouse, Peter's sibling, his pupils' teacher, a citizen of his country, and so on. He is *never* – not even before God – solitary and alone:

in the *concrete*, he is never *this* solitary individual. Likewise, his fault or sin is never solitary in the concrete.

An "institution" is never a structure existing in and of itself, independently of the individuals composing it. The "institution" is but the *modus quo*, the "way in which" individuals comport themselves in a stable and related manner. The *institution* of marriage is a way in which women and men *relate* as spouse-to-spouse (be this manner of *relating* monogynous or polygynous, monandrous or polyandrous, patriarchal or matriarchal, and so on). All "institutions" (from a national political state to a soccer team or a church) are stable types of *relationships* among *individuals*. (The individual is the support of the institution.)

Accordingly, if a person (or group of persons) dominates another person (or group of persons) *stably* or *historically* (as the *encomendero* dominated the Amerindian, the capitalist dominates the wage-earner, the man the woman, and so on), we may say that this praxis of domination, this defect or sin is *institutional* or social. It is a type of objective, real, *social relationship* maintained in historical groups.

From the moment an individual is *born*, he or she will never exist apart from the institutional texture that antedates and *determines* this particular individual (a *relative* determination, of course, but one that is fundamental for this particular existence). For example, someone may be born wealthy, a member of the dominant class and of a moneyed, bourgeois family. He or she is surely not responsible for *having been born there*. But just as surely, this individual *inherits* this institutional, "originary" sin. Thus, as Paul proclaims, it is possible for death to reign "even over those who had not sinned by breaking a precept as did Adam" (Rom 5:14).

2.6 Inherited sin

Writing against Pelagius (who held that sin is inherited "through the evil example set by Adam"), Saint Augustine proposed that sin was inherited in virtue of human conception in concupiscence. That is, an erotic bodily desire, constitutive of our material being from birth, transmitted Adam's fault. This is scarcely the only possible explanation.

For our purposes, I shall define "original sin" – without posing the question whether it is original sin in the traditional sense – as the sin that is constitutive of *our being* from its origin, from our birth. But our "being" is more than our materiality, our corporeality, despite what some have thought. Our most radical *being* is our social being, our "being" in virtue of our being human (and not merely animal). The *place* we occupy in the social texture (see 2.4) determines (although not absolutely) our *being*. And as I have indicated above, we *receive* our membership in the dominant or the dominated class (this is an observable, evident *fact*, not a judgment) from the first instant of our origin.

When the individual subjectivity of the human person achieves effective freedom (psychologically in adolescence), it *already finds* itself that of a bourgeois or a proletarian, a peasant or a petit bourgeois, a woman or a man, and so on. We are *this way* already. *Upon* this foundation we can construct our life. But we must inevitably construct it precisely *from* the original constitution we have received and inherited.

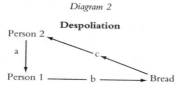

Diagram 2

Despoliation

Thus historical, social sin is transmitted by institutions – by cultural, political, economic, religious, erotic, and so on, structures. In taking up our position as one of the terms of the social relationship of sin (as a proprietary or dispossessed individual – that is, as the member of such and such a family, in the particular social class in which we fall, as a citizen of such and such a country), we inherit a praxis that constitutes us relatively and "originally."

2.7   The "poor"

"Poor," in the biblical sense, denotes the dominated, oppressed, humiliated, instrumentalized term of the practical relationship called sin (see 2.2). The constitutive act of the "poor" in the Bible is not lacking goods, but *being dominated*, and this *by the sinner*. The poor are the correlative of sin. As the fruit of sin, their formality as "poor" constitutes the poor or oppressed, and as such, the just and holy.

The "poor" are those who, in the *relationship of domination*, are the dominated, the instrumentalized, the alienated. *Outside* this relationship they can be "rich." *Poor* and *rich*, in the Bible, in addition to being concrete persons, are dialectical *categories:* the proper content of each correlative term includes the other, just as the term "parent" includes having a "child." No one is a parent unless he or she has a child. Nor is anyone "poor" in the biblical sense unless there are "rich."

"Bread is the life of the poor; who robs him of it murders him" (Ecclus. 34:21). In Diagram 2 the person (1) who toils (*b*) produces the product of his or her hands ("Bread" symbolizes that product). Another person (2) dominates (*a*) person 1 – commits sin against him or her, as in the case of the suffering Job. *Because of this domination*, and in virtue of the basic fact of sin, person 2 robs (*c*) person 1 of the fruit of his or her toil (*b*). The poverty or want suffered by the poor (person 1) is not the sheer absence of goods. No, the poverty of the poor consists in having been *despoiled* of the fruit of their labor by reason of the objective domination of sin.

Thus the alienation of the other (fruit of the praxis of the sinner) produces the poverty of the poor (fruit of sin) as robbery, or dispossession.

2.8   "Death"

When a human being dominates a brother or sister, the result is that described by Paul: "Sin entered the world, and by sin, *death*" (Rom. 5:12). "Death" in what sense? We immediately think of eternal death (condemnation), and correctly, to be sure. Or we think of physical death (the death that consists in the extinction of biological life). But let us consider a third type of death, the cause of the sinner's "eternal death."

It is because the poor objectify their *life* in the product of their hands (in bread, for example) that "he murders his neighbor who deprives him of his sustenance; who will not pay a just wage spills blood" (Ecclus. 34:22). For the Bible, "blood" is the seat of *life*. If I deprive a living being of its blood, I kill it. To take the "blood" of the poor is to kill them. This is the third type of death, to which I have just alluded – the death suffered by the poor as the fruit of the sin of the sinner, the "rich": "Woe to you rich, for you have had your consolation" (Luke 6:24). The "rich," the dominator, the sinner (because he or she snatches from the poor their product, because the dominator "kills" the poor in their very life) is condemned to "eternal death," to a "second death," as we hear: "Depart from me, ye cursed, into everlasting fire, prepared for the devil and *his angels*. For I was hungry and you did not feed me" (Matt. 25:41–2).

Thus the life of the poor is accumulated by the rich (see 12.6). The latter live the life of the rich in virtue of the death of the poor. The life of the sinner feeds on the blood of the poor, just as the idol lives by the death of its victims, like Moloch of old, to whom children were immolated, or the Aztec Huitzilopochtli. The fetish god was "animated" or ensouled by the blood of its victims.

"They have broken my covenant by rebelling against my law.... With their silver and their gold they have fashioned idols for their perdition" (Hos. 8:1–4). "The Egyptians imposed heavy labor on them, and embittered their life with harsh slavery" (Exod. 1:13).

2.9   Conscience and responsibility

One might think that, inasmuch as sin is inherited (as the social relationship of domination by the sinner over the poor), there would be neither personal (individual) awareness nor personal responsibility in that praxis of alienation of the other.

Each individual, as a real term of social relationships (see 2.5), consciously assumes – in the lights and shades of his or her biography (historical, psychological, familial) and to a greater or lesser degree – the meaning of his or her "place" in the institutional structure of sin (as also of the "convenant," as we shall see later on). Moses was the pharaoh's adopted son (Exod. 2:10): he belonged institutionally to the number of those who dominated the poor, those who were the sinners.

The strength, wealth, beauty, culture, and so on, of the dominant group to which one belongs is consciously known, enjoyed, and affirmed. Humiliation, weakness, cultural deprivation, serfdom, and so on, are consciously known and consented to by the despised poor. Thus it is that, day by day, dominators take on personal, individual *responsibility* for their sin of domination. After all, they daily assert the privileges and the potential (the opportunities) accruing to them in virtue of this inherited sin. And never again will dominators be able to claim innocence of that of which they have the use and enjoyment.

Too many signs furnish the rich with a *daily* indication of the distressing presence of the poor. The radical separation of one's own satisfaction in the use of wealth from the suffering of the poor in their poverty (not to see that the one is cause of the other) is a *wish not to be guilty*. "If they will not hear Moses and the prophets, neither will they listen to one returned from the dead" (Luke 16:31). Nor will they take any heed of a poor person who dies of hunger as a result of their domination. To a greater or lesser degree, one is always conscious of, and thus responsible for, one's sin – one's personal, individual lapse (in virtue of one's personal, individual constitution as one of the real terms of a social relationship).

2.10   The "Prince of this world"

Jesus answered: "You have the devil for your father, and you seek to accomplish your father's desires – who was a murderer from the beginning" (John 8:44). "Now begins a judgement upon the world: now the Prince *of this world* will be cast out" (John 12:31). In our one, single history – our one *place* of confrontation – sin is organized as a society, as a "world," as an order.

Sin is not only not exclusively individual, sin is not only social and historical, institutional, a social relationship – sin is actually an organized, self-conscious, functioning "subject" or agent: Satan, the "power" of evil, the Evil One. The essential question here is not whether this objectification of evil in a pure, substantive, personal spirit corresponds to a literal reality – which I do not deny. What is essential here is that we understand his historical praxis, along with that of *his angels* (Matt. 25:41), who include the dominators, sinners, the "rich," and so on.

"The princes of the nations lord it over them, and the mighty oppress them" (Matt. 20:25). The praxis of sin, of domination (the constitution of oneself as the sovereign of the alienated other), is institutionalized by way of political, ideological, religious, and economic structures. There is no such thing as a religious sin that is not a political or economic sin – and vice versa. All domination, or offense, committed against the other is *sin* against God. It is chimerical to separate sin, on the one side, from historical structures and institutions on the other. The latter are the *concrete* forms of Satan's exercise of his dominion *in this world*, through the mediation of his angels: the human beings who dominate their sisters and brothers.

The sinners, the "rich," the dominators, are the *angelos*, the "envoys" dispatched by the Prince *of this world* for the institutionalization of his reign: namely, the historical structures of sin as "social relationship."

Conclusions

Our second theme, "Evil and Death" – negative counterpart of the first ("Praxis and the Reign of God") – leads us to consider the *principle of sin* that constitutes the perverse, negative point of departure of a Christian ethics. That principle is an impediment to the constitution of community: it is the assertion of individuality *against* community. In authentic community, genuine individuality is fully actualized. In anticommunity, individuality is fetishized and ultimately destroys itself, by way of the death of the poor. It is this *death* that is now of interest to us.

Although it is true that sinners – "the rich" as a category and as social relationships, rich *persons* – can be saved, they cannot be saved if they remain in their sinners', rich persons', *relationship of domination*. Then they will be condemned (second death) to eternal death, deserved by reason of their responsibility (also personal and individual) exercised in the murder of the poor: because they will have caused the *death* of the poor "in this world."

[...]

8   Relationships of Producers and Praxis of the People

8.1   State of the question

There are those who hold that morality and ethics are essentially ideological. Thus morality and ethics would depend basically on laws, virtues, or superstructural demands (if the last-named category has any meaning). This is a false position. Morality and ethics consist basically in praxis – in real relationships among persons. Morality and ethics are both corporeal, carnal, fleshly. They are *infra*structural elements (understanding by this term anything of an economic or productive nature, anything connected with life and corporality).

Every day the media carry news stories about workers, corporations, popular movements, and indigenous organizations.

We read in holy scripture:

> Are not the rich exploiting you? They are the ones who hale you into the courts and who blaspheme the noble name that has made you God's own. You are acting rightly, however, if you fulfill the law of the kingdom. Scripture has it, "You shall love your neighbor as yourself." But if you show favoritism, you commit sin....If a brother or sister has nothing to wear and no food for the day, and you say to them, "Good-bye and good luck! Keep warm and well fed," but do not meet their bodily needs, what good is that? (James 2:6–16)

Our entire reflection here must remain on the level of corporeal, material, bodily radicality, which is consonant with the greatest holiness, if by holiness we understand ethical perfection.

8.2   "Social" relationships of domination

When a shoemaker exchanges shoes for bread, a *relationship* between persons arises – a relationship between the shoemaker and the baker. The exchange constitutes a praxis. The production of the shoe or the bread is a *poiesis*.

These relationships need not be social relationships of domination. They may be communal (8.3). I call relationships between producers *social* relationships of domination when two persons engaged in the process of production are not in a state of equality, justice, and goodness. One of the producers dominates the other. This relationship, maintained in the process of production, is one of inequality, sin, domination (2.2). Morality, in the sense of a system of concrete practices, is situated not only on the level of law – the plane of norms or requirements, virtues – but also on that of these real infrastructural, intercorporeal "practical" *social* relationships obtaining among producers themselves.

Even Marxist moralists frequently relegate morality to the ideological plane. Thus they reduce morals and morality to verbal formulations, to obligations of rights and law, to the imperatives of duty – all on an abstract, mental level of mere intention. I should like to register my explicit disapproval of this volatilization of the moral (and by implication, of the ethical). Social moral relationships are actual, infrastructural, practical relationships among producers, within actual, historical modes of production. It is here that the drama of morality (and ethics) is played out.

Because domination, sin, is the relationship that institutionally establishes a definite relationship between persons (2.5), morality is founded totally on praxis, and its norms or exigencies are but superstructural formulations of those antecedent, practical, social, moral relationships.

8.3   Community relationships

In the same way, when the shoemaker and the baker are living in *community* – whether in the utopian community of Jerusalem, or in our ecclesial base communities, which represent varying degrees of participation in that ancient ideal – and exchange their shoes and bread, they establish an ethical, *community* relationship.

I call relationships among producers – among the participants in a production process – *communal* in virtue of a practical relationship of two or more persons constituting, in justice and equality, without domination, an "association of free persons" (James 2:12–13). The product of their work in community will belong to all of them – the practice that, according to the unanimous opinion of the Fathers of the Church, must have prevailed among human beings before original sin (2.6).

Ethics is not primarily or essentially a set of norms, obligations, and prophetic maxims – not even in the case of the Sermon on the Mount. Ethics requires, as antecedent condition of its possibility, the concrete, *real* life of the *community*, such as the one Jesus was in the process of founding with his Apostles. It was the praxis of that community that generated the norm, "Happy the poor!" In that community, *factually* and *really*, in *actual* community relationships, the poor were happy, satisfied, treated as persons. And from out of this concrete experience, ethical norms and requirements were derived.

Community relationships of justice, real ethical relationships (infrastructural relationships, in their status as relationships among producers – bodily relationships) are the essence and foundation of ethics, the real starting point of the ethico-prophetic critique. The critique as such may emerge on an ideological level. But it originates on an infrastructural, practical level: that of *community* relationships themselves.

8.4   What is "class"?

Let us examine that specific instance of *social* relationships of domination (8.2) known as social class. As we know, the question of the "class struggle" is a hotly debated one in our time.

Before actually discussing the topic of social class, it will be in order to explain what is meant by it. Had it not been for "original" sin (2.5, 2.6) – if men and women had lived in community – there would have been no such thing as social class. Social class is the result of sin, in the sense that the dominated class, the poor (2.7), die in life (2.8). (And if there were no *dominated* class, there would be no classes at all, for the constitutive difference of the latter is domination, or a relationship of inequality among stable or institutional groups of persons.) Inequalities – as Rousseau ought to have indicated – are the fruit of sin. It is owing to sin that there are unequal classes.

A "class" is a stable group of persons who, within the practico-productive totality of society, perform a structural function – determined by the *productive process* (*Laborem Exercens* [Encyclical of Pope John Paul II, September 1981], 11–13) – in the division of labor, in the appropriation of the fruit of toil. Thus it is the *social* relationships of domination (2.2) that determine the dominant and dominated classes. (There are also intermediate classes, auxiliary classes, and so on.) The Aztecs were divided into the dominant warrior classes and the peasants who paid tribute. It was the same with the Incas. Likewise in medieval European society: the feudal lords demanded tribute of the serfs. Today the owners of capital pay their workers a wage, in an unequal exchange of product and money (12.5).

The classes, then, are social relationships of domination inherent in the whole praxis-production process, inevitable in any tributary system – capitalistic, socialistic, or whatever. Each type of social relationship determines distinct social classes in each system.

8.5   *What is meant by "people"?*

A class is not a people. "People" is a category that will have to be determined with clarity and precision if we hope to be able to distinguish it from other concepts. The "popular question" has not been settled.

"People" is a more concrete, synthetic category than that of the more abstract, analytic "class." The term "people" is ambiguous. A whole nation may be called a "people" – for example, if it is engaged in a struggle with foreigners. This is the populist sense of the word "people": the dominant classes are part of the "people." Or the word "people" may denote only the *oppressed* of a nation, and the oppressing classes will not be part of the "people." I shall be using the word in this latter sense.

Thus a "people" is the "communal bloc" of a nation's oppressed. A people consists of the dominated classes (the working or industrial class, the campesino class, and so on). But it is also constituted of any human group that is either non-capitalistic or that performs class practices only sporadically (marginal groups, ethnic groups, tribal groups, and so on). This entire "bloc" – in Gramsci's sense – constitutes the people: a people is the historical "subject" or agent of the social formation of a given country or nation. The "Cuban people," the "Nicaraguan people," the "Brazilian people," and so forth, are composed of the persons who permeate the respective history of the various practico-productive totalities. Thus we have the pre-Hispanic Amerindians, the colonials, the neo-colonials, and even the members of postcapitalistic societies. Each of these groups is a people.

A people – in the sense of the oppressed classes of a nation – introjects and interiorizes, it is true, the ideology and culture of its dominators. Hence the necessity of evangelization (carried out by prophets) and political organization (effectuated by heroes). The peoples, as the masses, are the dominated; as exteriority, they constitute the eschatological reserve; as revolutionary, they are the builders of history.

8.6   Praxis of the people as oppressed

As oppressed, dominated, a people suffers the fruit of sin: its members are hungry, without clothing, without housing; they are in pain, they are tortured, they die. As oppressed, they are *"part" of the system*. They are a social class, an exploited "bloc." The wage-earning "class" is precisely the human group whose current domination constitutes the system as such. In the feudal system the serf was obliged to pay a tribute. Insofar as it is brought into being by the social relationship of domination (2.2, 2.5) – precisely as one of the terms of that relationship (2.2, 2.5) – a class is *part* of the system.

A people qua oppressed is a nation's social bloc. It includes all such persons as, with their labor, with their life, permit the "rich" (in the biblical sense, as a theological category – sinners, those who rob the "poor") to live. In this sense the people is an alienated, negated "crowd," a mere multitude, sacrificed to the idol (2.3).

The praxis of a people *as oppressed* is an imitative praxis, one that reproduces the system of domination, one that enables the hegemony of dominators to survive, one that consents to the structure that immolates it. As oppressed, popular praxis is negative, alienated, imitative, a praxis of consumerism. As undifferentiated crowd, as passive mass, the people must be politically organized by heroes, and prophetically envangelized in order to be transformed into the collective subject of the reign of God, the agent of a new political order.

The theology of liberation is "second act," or act of reflection upon the praxis of the people, the oppressed classes – the "poor," then, but "poor" in the politico–economic sense, the destitute, the penniless, who must beg in order to live, not poor because oppressed, alienated, "massified." That praxis cannot, it is true, constitute the actual focus of liberation, but it can furnish its starting point.

8.7   Praxis of the people as exteriority

This mass, this people, not only forms a bloc of oppressed, a *social* bloc; it engages in communal practices, external to the system (and regarded by the system as trivial, nonexistent, unproductive, useless). Precisely *as exteriority*, the people constitutes the "*community* bloc" of the oppressed.

I have already observed the meaning and importance of being "in the exteriority" of the system. Beyond the *totality* of the system that makes the dominated a class, rendering them marginal, or simply ignoring them ("the natives"), the people has an experience of *exteriority*. The "unproductive" aspects of this "bloc," of the people, the aspects that do not generate wealth in the form of profit for capital (12.1), are nevertheless part of the life of the people.

Here I refer to popular culture. That culture has its language, its songs, its customs, its friendship (a friendship of solidarity), its daily communicativeness and "sociability." The people knows how to establish *community* relationships. Who belong to the people? The poor who believe in the poor, who help the poor, who love their disgraced brother or sister. All such aspects of the people, aspects exterior to the system of domination, constitute the *positivity* of the people, and the *affirmation* that constitutes the wellspring of liberation.

Furthermore, there exists a whole *underground* production and economy, likewise exterior to the system. "Underground" is the term used – in the underdeveloped countries peripheral to capitalism – for denoting the manner in which a people regulates itself in order to survive in a system of exploitation. The value of the underground is that it makes it possible for the people *still* to be there when the moment of liberation struggles arrives. In the underground, eking out their miserable survival, the people learns the cunning of a prolonged war for political, economic, popular, national emancipation.

8.8   *A communo-utopian praxis among the people*

Thus an entire people, as the bloc of a nation's oppressed, is predisposed to a comradeship of solidarity with any member in pain. The "base Christian community" will redouble this natural community quality of that people, by infusing it with "Spirit."

By "communo-utopian praxis" I mean the actions and relationships of the base Christian communities, "living the reign of God" in a very special manner. These actions and relationships are "utopian" in the sense that they are situated "without": they are *outside* the system. (Thus they are "placeless": Gk., *ou*, "no, not"; *topos*, "place.") The life of the base Christian community responds not to prevailing morality, but to the ethics of the gospel. A people as such, as a historical people, is ambivalent. It contains the best: its exteriority vis-à-vis the system. But it also contains the worst: its alienating introjection of that system.

In a context of this ambivalence, and deep within the ambivalent people itself, the base Christian community asserts the exteriority of the people vis-à-vis the system, its experience of itself as other-than-the-system (in its quality as a *communal* bloc of the oppressed). The base Christian community thus becomes a *place*, a *space*, among the people in which that people, once their consciousness has been raised, will become *authentically* a people, as not-being-(dominating)-system. And in this sense the historical people (the crowd) becomes "my people" (the people of Yahweh), the "people of God" in the sense used by the Second Vatican Council.

True, it remains for authentically popular parties, fronts, or political groupings to organize the people for historical, political tasks. But the "eschatological community" (the base, utopian community), the "church of the poor," retains its purpose, its *raison d'être*: as the subject of a dialectic, the political can always close in upon itself and become a moral system of domination. A new idolatry is always possible: thus a prophetic, critical vigilance becomes a necessity.

8.9   *A prophetico-community praxis of liberation among the people*

A Cuban Christian militant recently confided to me:

> After twenty-five years of enthusiastic collaboration with the revolution, we Christians
> have finally understood that we have something to give the revolution that it does not and
> cannot have in any other way: the *absolute* meaning of life, of service, of love.

The "absolute" is the divine, that which corresponds to God, to eternity, to the holiness of something that will rise, never to die again. It is upon this utopian hope that *the ethical* rests, for it is upon this utopian hope that the Christian faith itself is founded. Here is a hope that no historical revolution can adequately assert.

In the concrete, Christian prophecy emerges from the community praxis of the "church of the poor," the base Christian communities. They furnish the locus or focal point of the people as people. They provide the "whence" of the ethico-prophetic critique of the prevailing morality of domination. The base Christian communities are not exterior to the people, however. They do not impose, they do not pretend to constitute a vanguard. The elitism of those who "know," of the self-appointed conscience or savoir-faire of the people, those who would steer the people, lead the people, is something the base Christian communities must avoid. On the contrary, the base communities must form an "organic" community at the heart of a people. They are part of the people, one popular organ among many, one organizational aspect of the people itself.

Nevertheless the Christian experience does add something to the popular process, to the life of the people. It furnishes eschatological hope. It furnishes the faith that the people is composed of the daughters and sons of God and that God's reign will come. It provides effective love in the form of charity, the option for the other as other. It sets in motion, deep within a people, a current inaugurated by the Spirit – a spontaneous groundswell, emerging from nowhere, created without antecedents. This is the transcendent collaboration of the Christian community.

Like John the Baptist, the community prepares the way. And when heroes are moved by their charisms to create something new (and there are surely charisms of the Holy Spirit outside the church as well), the base Christian communities, the "church of the poor," the prophets, are ready and waiting, prepared to contribute their active collaboration.

8.10 Liberation praxis of the people

The theology of liberation presupposes a type of praxis without which it could not exist. Theology is reflection. *Primary theology*, then – basic, or "first" theology – will consist in the present type of tractate; it explains and describes, engages in theological reflection upon, takes as its starting point, the praxis of liberation undertaken by the people.

The popular praxis of liberation emerges when the people "gets going," when it "gets on its feet," when it begins the process of countering the structures of sin (2.5–2.6), when it initiates the struggle against the Satanic work of domination, injustice, sin (2.10). The liberation struggle is the battle with sin, with domination, with injustice and economic thievery, with political authoritarianism, with ideological alienation, with traditional machismo, and so on. When the people launches this struggle, then its praxis, its actions and relationships, are *liberated* from the old institutional bonds. The struggle can consist in revolution, or its preparation, or its consequences.

There are stable situations in history – situations of permanence and durability. The present situation in Latin America is not one of these. On the contrary, everywhere around us we see an old process in its death agony and a new historical order being born. Hence the growth of a popular *liberation praxis* against the dependent capitalism suffered by our peoples. We struggle against an exploitation felt in *our* "skin" alone (and not in Poland, Rome, or the United States).

It is the liberation praxis of the communal bloc of the oppressed of the Latin American nations, today, at the close of the twentieth century, that provides the starting point, the "whence," the origin of what is called the theology of liberation. This theology is the discovery not of individuals, but of an entire generation, a "school of prophets." But first and foremost it has the people as its source, its wellspring, its origin. Liberation theology is popular theology.

Conclusions

I have not attacked conservative, moralistic positions in this chapter. On the contrary, I have criticized certain leftist elements that disparage ethics, first because they are unable to distinguish it from prevailing morality, and secondly because they situate both ethics and morality in the ideological, juridical, political "suprastructure" (an extremely ambiguous category, to which I refer only in order to reject it). The social or economic relationships of production *include*, in their basic foundation, a practical aspect – a moral or ethical aspect, then. The relationship of one individual's domination over another is itself a practical relationship: it *is* domination, and hence sin. Sin pervades and infects, from the base up, the "material" aspect of production. Thus it is that prophetic criticism of a historically constituted mode of production functions as the antecedent, the "that which determines," where the future mode of production is concerned. And thus Christian communal hope, faith, and love can *determine* the infrastructure of future systems (and Marx himself, in his celebrated introduction to the *Grundrisse*, leaves this possibility open). [...]

12 Ethical Critique of Capital

12.1 State of the question

I have come now to the central topic of the ethical theology that is the subject of this book. I continue, however, to deal on an abstract, general level. I am still speaking of *structural sin in general* – institutional sin stripped to its essentials. Only later shall I apply my findings to the more concrete levels of this sin. I am reflecting on the "social mechanism of sin," then, to use the words of Pope John Paul II in Mexico in 1979, but in its most general sense – in its basic *reality*.

We read in the daily newspapers that such and such corporations or institutions have made investments, that such and such a wealthy person is "worth" so much capital, that there is a crisis in the "capitalistic system," or that the value of merchandise has dropped on the market. What theological meaning attaches to all of this?

We read in holy scripture:

> As for you, you rich, weep and wail over your impending miseries. Your wealth has rotted, your fine wardrobe has grown moth-eaten, your gold and silver have corroded, and their corrosion shall be a testimony against you; it will devour your flesh like a fire. See what you have stored up for yourselves against the last days. Here, crying aloud, are the wages you withheld from the farmhands who harvested your fields. The cries of the harvesters have reached the ears of the Lord of hosts. You lived in wanton luxury on the earth; you fattened yourselves for the day of slaughter. You condemned, even killed, the just man; he does not resist you. (James 5:1–6)

The words of Saint James will provide us with the theoretical (theological) horizon of an unmistakable situation of injustice whose cries to heaven are even more deafening today than when these words were written.

12.2   The "poor" today

The "poor" constitute the majority of the population of the nations of the world, especially in the "peripheral" world. Let it be noted, however, that I am still speaking in general, or "essentially." I am speaking of the "poor" in their basic confrontation with the "rich" – with the vested interests of the system (any system, not just a capitalistic economic system).

The "poor," in their anteriority or exteriority, are those who emerge into the society of the prevailing system from a community that has been dissolved – for example, the Zapotecs of Oaxaca in Mexico, who must come to Mexico City in order to find work. The dominating system has destroyed their previous way of life. It has expelled them from the place where they had lived in security, with legitimate wealth, with their family, relatives, nation, history, culture, and religion. They are the *pauper ante festum* – the poor who find themselves standing wistfully at the door of the feast that is about to make them its main dish.

The "poor" – still in the negative sense – are those who, in the face-to-face of the person-to-person relationship must confront the person possessed of money. And yet they have not sold themselves. They are poor because they have their own corporality to sell, their bodiliness, their skin, their "hide," in their absolute nakedness, their radical poverty – without food, clothing, housing, health, protection. They are but miserable beggars. The word "economy" comes from the Greek *oikos* and *nomos*, and means, etymologically, "law of the house." The homeless, then, are nothing, non-being, worthless, to the economists of domination. The "poor" – this time in the positive sense of the world – are the miserable unemployed, precisely in their carnality, their fleshliness. They ask the person with money, the capitalist (or abstractly, capital) for work. And yet they are subject, the creative subject, of all possible value. These starving poor, who beg for work, for a wage, are the very Christ of the *ecce homo*. And yet it is they who constitute the foundation and groundwork of the whole current system of domination. They abide only on the outside, "thrown into the ditch and robbed." But there is no Samaritan to help them.

12.3   Sin as the social relationship of domination

I have shown that praxis is a relationship, and that the praxis of domination or sin is a *social* relationship (2.5), being the breach of *community* relationship (12.2). When that relationship is institutionalized (2.5–2.6), it becomes real and historical. In this section I propose to speak (in abstract, very general terms – considering sin in its ultimate essence, then) of the fundamental institutional sin of our time.

Standing in the "face to face" of the person-to-person relationship are, on the one hand, the "poor" and, on the other, those who have the money to pay for the work the poor perform (the "rich," then, in the sense of the biblical category). But the persons in this relationship do not face each other as did Moses and God, or the Samaritan and the poor victim of the robbery on the road to Jericho – that is, in infinite respect for one another's otherness. Instead, in the interpersonal relationship under consideration, one term is constituted by a wretched individual who must go begging in order to eat, dress, have a house or health, and so on; and the other is the person who has money (and we ask: from what source? by what means?) and who wishes to increase the amount of that money thanks to the other person. The money ($) must increase ($') and adopts the other as the mediation of that increase. It instrumentalizes, reifies, alienates that other (2.2). The prince of "this world" has commenced his praxis (2.10).

The person having money proposes to the poor person (the individual who has already been *violently* coerced, with the violence of the injustice that has destroyed his or her community of origin) a contract, an exchange. Thus a *relationship* is struck between the two: I give you money and you give me your work, which, purchased as commodity, now becomes my property, for I am the one who had the money. Correlatively, the one who had work to offer exchanges it for money – receives wages (W).

But there is a subtle *inequality* in this exchange, invisible both to the one who has the money and the one who offers the work. This is a *social* relationship (8.2) because it is a relationship of domination, of injustice. Invisibly, imperceptibly, it is sin. Why? Because the person having the money uses the *person* of the worker while paying only for that person's *work capacity*. The employer makes use of the whole worker, makes use of the "creative source of value" (12.2), though paying only for his or her "upkeep." It is as if someone wished to purchase an automobile by paying only for fuel and servicing. I receive the "creative subject" gratis, and pay only for what is needed to keep that subject from dying, to keep it working. As creators in the image of God, inventors by nature, obviously human beings will produce a value equivalent to the value of their needs (which is the value of the money they are to be paid in wages!) in a certain time, and then will go on to produce beyond this limit. Thus the value of the product produced by the worker will acquire a "more-value," *more life* and more reality than the value of the wages received. In other words, the worker will give more life than he or she receives. This is an injustice, a *social* relationship of domination, a sin.

12.4 What is capital?

The word "capital" has a great many meanings. It derives from *caput*, Latin for "head." To have a great many sources or "heads" of profit was to have a great deal of "capital." Many understand "capital" as money, others as goods, and so on. Let us examine this question.

In the social teaching of the church, capital is a "fact": "neither can capital subsist without work, nor can work subsist without capital" (*Rerum Novarum* [Encyclical of Pope Leo XIII, May 1891], 14). These documents generally identify capital with "wealth." More precisely: "Capital, inasmuch as it constitutes a set of means of production, is only an instrument, or instrumental cause" (*Laborem Exercens*, 12). It has been a long road from *Rerum Novarum* (1891) to *Laborem Exercens* (1981). The teaching now is that all capital is the fruit of work: "All of the means of production, from the most primitive to the ultramodern, have been developed gradually by the human being.... [They are] the fruit of work" (*Laborem Exercens*, 12).

Pursuing the line of thought I have undertaken, the concept of "capital" could be understood as extending beyond money or commodity to the means of production as well. But – and this is sometimes forgotten – work, purchased and used (over the course of an eight-hour day, for example), as it is taken up or subsumed by the capital that has employed it, itself becomes capital – specifically, the value-creating aspect of that capital. Finally, the product, too, which is value before being commodity, is capital.

In terms of Aristotle's concept of movement (*kinesis*), then, we may understand capital as the *subject of value in its movement of growth*. Value *passes through successive determinations*. It moves from money to work (wages), then to the means of production, then (in virtue of the interplay of the latter two moments) to objectification in the product, then (as the product enters the market) to commodity, and finally (as the merchandise is sold) to money once more ($). But this time the amount of money has grown, has become more money, surplus money ($'), as profit has accrued to the original amount. This entire, circular (or rather, spiraling) process, like some great, organic maelstrom, is capital: the growth of value, "valorization."

12.5 The poor as wage-earners

In a biblical sense of the word, the "poor" are the dominated, persons murdered by sin (2.7–8). The "poor" in the economic sense are the wretched, those left lying by the side of the road, those living outside the system. Biblically speaking, the "poor" are the exploited: they are Job suffering the results of the praxis of domination, writhing under the satanic praxis of the sinner.

Torn from their original *community* (8.3), their former source of security, the poor have been thrown on the "labor market" (12.2). In the "world of commodities" (*Laborem Exercens*, 7: "work was understood and treated as a kind of merchandise"), the poor, in their absolute nakedness and radical poverty, sell their "skin" as a thing. "The primacy of the human being vis-à-vis things" (*Laborem Exercens*, 12) has gone by the board. Now they are isolated, solitary *individuals*, without a community, in a dominating *society*, where they attain to their "sociality" only to the extent that they toil in the workshop or are bought and sold *on the market*. Whether in the workshop or on the market, they continue their individual isolation.

Once workers have sold their work, they are no longer their "own," but the property of another. Now they are "made other" ("otherfied"), alienated, the object of sin and exploitation, and this in an institutional manner (2.5) thanks to the social division of labor. Now their work must be sold daily. The only alternative is starvation. Like some great god (2.3, 12.10), capital fills every corner. There is no possibility for the reproduction of the worker's life without the participation of capital. There is no "work . . . without capital" (*Rerum Novarum*, 14). Now we have "work for hire," the obligatory alienated *social* relationship that demands of workers that they sell themselves for a wage that pays them *less* life than the life they objectify in the product destined to be possessed by the owner of money. "Work for hire" is the name of the institutional sin of our time. It has held sway for the past several centuries of human life on earth. Thus work for hire is the "original" sin committed against the worker (2.5) – committed by the "rich" (in the biblical sense) upon the poor.

12.6   Accumulation of "surplus life"

The theological syllogism is a traditional one. Workers objectify their life in their product (Ecclus. 34:21). Their wages, being in the form of money, are vehicles of value, which is life. But the value or life objectified in the product is greater than that received in wages. (Otherwise where does the profit come from – the difference between $ and $'?) See 12.3.

Some identify profit as a difference in value between the value of merchandise sold and the payment received, which payment would somehow be greater than the value of the commodity sold. In that case, the seller steals from the purchaser (commercial injustice). But then, in becoming buyers in their own turn – in buying the products needed in order to produce their own – sellers (and workers themselves can sell their work for more than the value of their work capacity) are robbed in turn, and everything "comes out even."

The objection might be raised that employers earn their profit by the work they perform. No, work is recompensed precisely through a wage, which employers can and should receive (in some decent proportion to the wages the workers are paid). Anything left over – called "profit" – is the fruit of the *work of the non-owners* of the capital invested – for which they have not been paid – not that of the capital itself, and therefore does not belong to the owners or stockholders.

But does capital not "earn" a profit from the risks it takes? No, risk is not a principle of the creation of value or earnings. (This is not the place for the rehearsal of and response to every possible objection. Suffice it to have sketched these two.)

The secret of the great idol of capital lies in the fact that the profit gained in exchange, in the circulation I have sketched, is based on the "surplus life" acquired by capital in the productive process by paying *less* by way of wages (*x* life) than the value produced in the product by the worker (*y* life). And James protests in advance: "Here, crying aloud, are the *wages* you withheld from the farmhands who harvested your fields. The cries of the harvesters have reached the ears of the Lord of hosts" (James 5:6). The social relationship is unjust and sinful, and this is why "your wealth has rotted" (James 5:2).

"Capital springs from labor, and bears the marks of human toil" (*Laborem Exercens*, 12). It is made up entirely of the accumulated life of the worker. Workers have been dispossessed of the fruit of their toil in advance, and day after day, by reason of the structural sin of our time, continue to be stripped of the "surplus life" they produce – the difference between their wages and the value of the product. This surplus life is absorbed by capital. "Capital cannot subsist without work" (*Rerum Novarum*, 14).

12.7   *The institution of invisible sin*

Thus in its more comprehensive, broader sense, at least, if not indeed in its strict sense as well, capital is a *social* relationship of domination, a certain relationship of unequal exchange among persons, a *practical* or *moral* relationship, with respect to work or its products – a *productive* relationship, then (8.4), an economic exchange in both the anthropological and the theological senses of the word. But this relationship is stable and historical. Therefore we are dealing with an altogether particular "*social* institution."

The prince of "this world" (2.10) employs his mechanisms in all invisibility. Neither his existence nor his machinations are any longer the object of anyone's belief. Thus he can act with impunity. The "good" bourgeois person – indeed the "good" worker (the virtuous, punctual, "responsible" worker), because the dominated at times introject the dominant morality (8.6) – are actually *good* and moral in the eyes of the prevailing morality. The *social* relationship of domination, which is the unjust essence of capital, is accepted by the owner of the capital and of the work as "natural." In all tranquility of "moral conscience," the owner kills the neighbor.

Thus this *institutional sin* is very subtle. It is invisible. It is "absent in its very presence." It conditions the existence of us all (2.5): it determines one of the terms of the *practical, social* (8.2) *relationship*. (To be sure, the determinism in question is relative. I reject the oversimplification of a determinism that would preclude the possibility of a "conversion.") It is in this sense, as well as by reason of its nature as wealth or means of production (as for the social teaching of the church), that capital is a social, historical *institution* of injustice, and hence a praxis of domination. Capital consists of the accumulation of the surplus life unjustly extracted from the worker.

The structural sin of any age has always been invisible to the prevailing morality of that age, and bourgeois morality is no exception. But the task of ethics, of prophecy, is to render that sin visible, after the example of Bartolomé de Las Casas: "All have sinned. It is gravest injustice."

12.8   *The person of the worker as "nothingness"*

Capital has no misgivings about its own divinity. It pretends to produce profit *ex nihilo*, out of nothing. Its idolatrous (12.10), fetishistic nature blinds it to the origin of any of the value that it contains, that it has accumulated. It actually believes that it has produced that value. The person of the worker is regarded as nothingness in the process.

Only God creates from nothing. Out of infinite, unconditioned freedom, God has created the entire universe. But capital pretends that it too has created something out of its sheer spontaneity. It has created profit, it cries. Of course, for this to hold true, the worker must be reduced to nothing. And surely enough, for capital, the worker who does no work – who is not the subject of "productive work," of work that yields surplus life (12.6) – does not "count," does not constitute a "social class" (8.4), is not made use of (exploited), and hence cannot have been subsumed by capital (12.4). Such a worker is outside, is no-thing.

For capital, furthermore, the wage-earner is "virtually poor" (*virtualiter pauper*). *Before* being purchased, the wage-earner is nothing. *While* being used, the worker is an alienated aspect of capital (in a social relationship of sin). *After* being used, when no longer needed (for example, when technology has stepped up production and decreased the number of wage-earners), the worker is a miserable beggar (even with welfare payments or unemployment benefits in developed countries; in peripheral countries the worker simply starves to death in some urban slum or outlying shantytown).

Constituting a social relationship of domination – being sin – capital shows no mercy. It cannot commiserate, it cannot accord any consideration to the dignity of the person. It can have no recourse to any ethical yardstick. It does not hear the voice of the other. It has "hardened its heart."

12.9   Blood circulation

Capital, then, is ultimately value – but only in the strictly capitalist sense of value. Value attaches to something useful (use value is its material base) produced by human work (productuality) in order to be sold as merchandise (exchangeability is essential to value).

Ultimately, then, capital is "value" *moving* or circulating through its successive determinations – money, wage-earning work, means of production, and so on (12.4) – and growing, thanks to the "surplus life" it extracts from the worker (12.6). The Bible styles this value "blood": "Who does not pay the just wage spills blood" (Ecclus. 34:22).

Blood is the seat of life (2.8). Without blood an organism dies. But workers objectify their life in the product of their work, in the value of their product. And so their death occurs: objectified life has not returned to the producer. Instead of a "circle of life," the movement of value is transformed into a "circle of death" (2.8). It continues to be life – but it has become the *life of capital*. For, as we have seen, the life of capital, like the circulation of blood, is a continuous circulation of value, which is transformed from money into wages or means of production, then into product, then into merchandise, and so on, and finally into *more* money, "surplus money." O blessed profit, "made" on the altar of the murder of "the innocent" (James 5:6)! "To divest the poor to offer sacrifice" – to the idol, capital – "is to murder the child in the presence of its father" (Ecclus. 34:20).

Thus value follows its life course through the successive determinations of *industrial* capital to become *profit*; then through the veins of *commercial* capital to reach the status of *commercial profit*; thereupon to arrive at the condition of *financial* capital, which gains *interest* through the investment of money alone. Interest is the sin of usury transfigured to the virtue of saving. Behold the bourgeois virtue of economy (saving, hoarding), condemned by the Fathers, the church, and justice itself. All of this value is simply and solely the *life* of workers dispossessed of their property.

12.10   Idolatry consummated

Our reflection is theological. Accordingly, evil is seen and interpreted *sub peccati lumine* ("in the light of sin"). In its origin and essence, capital is a social relationship of domination. Therefore the consummation of its "morality," and its total justification, rests upon its ready capacity to consign the other term of the relationship to oblivion. Capital's self-absolutization, its claim to utter singularity, isolation, and existence *ex se*, its denial that it is beholden to anyone or anything, constitutes its character as a false god and an idol (2.3).

The sin of Adam, we learn in the Book of Genesis, consisted in seeking to be "as God." Capital, too, denies its origin (the toil of the worker), pretending that its increase, its growth, its profit, emerges from its own entrails (rather than being extracted from the worker in the form of "surplus life"). It owes no one anything, then. All value produced, regardless of its actual source, belongs to capital. Capital has negated the worker as the "creative source of value," absolutizing itself instead. "Work has been separated from capital, and counterpoised to capital . . . almost as if they were two autonomous forces" (*Laborem Exercens*, 13). And this "separation" has fetishized capital, and alienated it from work.

Indeed, to "separate" capital from work as a self-subsisting profit-making entity, and work from capital as a self-subsisting wage-earning entity, is to forget that "*all capital* is objectified work" and therefore *only work*. We do not actually have two terms here. We have one only: *work*, now as objectified (as capital), now "living work" (as the life of the personal subject working here and now).

Once capital is absolutized – idolized, fetishized – it is the workers themselves who are immolated on its altar, as their life is extracted from them (their wages do not pay the whole of the life they objectify in the value of the product) and immolated to the god. As of old, so today as well, living human beings are sacrificed to mammon and Moloch. Only, today the oblation – and it alone – permits the dominant class to enjoy the surplus life of its victims. "Woe to you rich. You have received your reward" (Luke 6:24).

Conclusions

The theology or ethics of liberation interprets reality *sub pauperum lumine* – from the point of view of the poor. My conclusions may seem exceedingly hard, unilateral, and apocalyptic. In my view, they are simply ethical, evangelical, and realistic. Jewish theologian that he was (however some may be at pains to deny it), Jesus draws the conclusions generated by his premises. He did not cringe or fall back before them, cost his life though they might. Not without reason "must this man suffer much, be rejected by the elders, the chief priests, and the doctors of the law, be executed" (Mark 8:31). Our ethic cannot be a reformist morality. This does not mean that it will be practicable on the present level of abstraction. ("Abstract" or "essential" does not mean "unreal." However, abstract conclusions cannot be practiced without concrete mediations.) All tactics are possible within the framework of ethical demands. But they may not violate ethical principles through the utilization of the moralizing, received tactics of the day. Such tactics may not be adapted to the prevailing system. One must distinguish between the tactics demanded by the practice of prophecy or ethical criticism, and a reformist betrayal on the part of those who accept the tenets of the system of domination in the name of the reign of God.

Chapter 18

On the Jewish Reading of Scriptures

Emmanuel Levinas 1906–1995

Introduction

Emmanuel Levinas, philosopher and Talmudic commentator, was born in Lithuania of Jewish parents, and studied in France and Germany, where he met Maurice Blanchot in his student days and attended lectures by Husserl. Levinas became a French citizen, was mobilized as an interpreter of Russian and German during World War II, and was captured as a prisoner of war by the Germans and subjected to forced labor. He began his book *Existence and Existents* (1973/English translation 1978) while in captivity. His major works include: *Time and the Other* (1947/1987); *Totality and Infinity* (1960/1969); *Otherwise than Being or Beyond Essence* (1974/1981); *Ethics and Infinity* (1982/1985). These works, heavily influenced by the style if not the vision of Husserl and Heidegger and by the Talmudic tradition of Jewish thought, consistently insist upon ethics, rather than ontology/epistemology or aesthetics, as "first philosophy." As Levinas notes in an interview late in life, "Man's ethical relation to the other is ultimately prior to his ontological relation to himself ...or to the totality of things that we call the world." That is, central to his philosophy is his analysis of a person's ethical relationship to the Other: he argues that the ethical requirement that we are responsible to or for the Other unsettles subjectivity and understanding. Thus, while Heidegger thought of death in terms of the individual's death, for Levinas death is always the death of the Other. Experience and consciousness are haunted by the Other's death and the possibility of that death, often figured by Levinas, as it is here, as the *face* of the other and its "irreducible difference, bursting into all that gives itself to me, all that is understood by me and belongs to my world; an appearance in the world which un-makes and dis-orders the world, worries me and keeps me awake." This mode or framework of understanding can be discerned in the following selection from Derrida (among others) in this volume. Although Levinas is only occasionally mentioned in *The Postmodern Bible*, since the publication of that book there has been an explosion of interest in his philosophy and in his influence on such figures as Jacques Derrida, and particularly on the relation of his work to Holocaust studies.

The selection presented here, taken from *Beyond the Verse* (1994), examines the "characteristic pluralism of rabbinical thought," its tribunal nature, its insistent *textualism*, its goal of finding some relationship between transcendental value within worldly and human activities, and, above all, its constant awareness of responsibility for others. Such responsibility is not simply an implication of religion but its essence: "Ethics," Levinas writes, "is not simply the corollary of the religious but is, of itself, the element in which religious transcendence receives its original meaning." Thus, when he argues that the reading processes he is examining suggest that "the statement commented upon exceeds what it originally wants to say," that "it contains more than it contains," and that it is this phenomenon that constitutes "inspiration," in part he is arguing that a text's "Other" – later commentators handing down care and "steadfast love" generation after generation – fulfills reading in this "ethical" way. For Levinas, "the infinite life of texts [live] through the life of the men who hear them," and "the very plurality of people" is "an unavoidable moment of the signification of meaning . . . so that the infinite richness of what it does not say can be said or . . . 'renewed'. . . . As the people of the Book, for whom the demanding reading of the Scriptures belongs to the highest liturgy, would not Israel also be the people of continued revelation?"

It is not a question here of drawing up an inventory of the figures of Jewish hermeneutics of the Bible. This would require a vast amount of research, taking into account the diversity of epochs and tendencies. It would also mean determining the credibility of the interpreters measured less by any consensus than by the intelligence of each person and his familiarity with tradition. R. Ishmael's often-quoted "Thirteen figures of the interpretation of the Torah," or the famous four levels of reading: *peshat* (plain meaning), *remez* (allusive meaning), *derash* (solicited meaning), *sod* (secret meaning), whose vocalized acronym gives the word *pardes* (orchard), call in their turn for exegesis, and constitute only aspects of rabbinism in its relation to the text. Only the modern formulation of this relation, which has yet to be done, might put an end to the improper teachings where traditional sources are quoted as if, beneath the Hebrew letters that conceal them, they all derived from the same depth.

Our more modest intention is to illustrate, by examples, certain ways of reading. We shall do this by presenting a Talmudic extract which produces, in the form of arguments, the exegesis of biblical verses. Nevertheless, in doing this we shall find ourselves being led to some propositions of a more general character, for the chosen extract, in its final section, concerns precisely the scope of exegesis. Exegesis of the exegesis, a privileged text, even if it does not exclude different insights into the same subject. This is in keeping with the characteristic pluralism of rabbinical thought, which paradoxically aspires to be compatible with the unity of the Revelation: the multiple stances of the scholars would constitute its very life, all of them being the "words of the living God."

Emmanuel Levinas, "On the Jewish Reading of Scriptures," from *Beyond the Verse: Talmudic Readings and Lectures*, translated by Gary D. Mole (Bloomington: Indiana University Press, 1994).

The Talmudic passage that we shall comment upon will also introduce us in particular to the meaning that, for Jewish religious consciousness, commentary of the Scriptures can take on as the path towards transcendence. It is, perhaps, essential to the actual creation of this notion.

But a Talmudic text that comments on verses requires an interpretation in its turn. What it intends to do is not immediately apparent in terms which, for an inexperienced reader, may seem unusual, and which in fact allow for several levels and dimensions. Hence a third stage in the final section of our commentary: an interpretation of the Talmudic exegesis of the exegesis. This reading of the Talmud would not be possible for us without recourse to a modern language – in other words, without touching on the problems of today. Admittedly, it too is not the only possible reading, but it has the value of a testimony. It testifies to at least one of the ways in which contemporary Jews understand traditional Jewish hermeneutics, and above all to the way in which they understand it when they ask it for food for thought and teachings on the content.

Preliminary Remarks

The text we shall comment upon is taken from one of the last pages of the Tractate Makkoth in the Babylonian Talmud. This short Tractate of about fifty pages deals with judicial punishments of which one, in reference to Deuteronomy 25: 2–3, is flogging (*makkoth* = blows). The passage dealing with the exegesis of page 23b has as its immediate context a theologico-legal discussion: is it possible, through the penalty of flogging, inflicted by a human tribunal, to make atonement for the punishment known as being "cut off from among their people," decided, according to the Talmud, by the "celestial tribunal"? Being "cut off from among their people," the most serious theological punishment, means being excluded from the "world to come," which designates the eschatological order in its ultimate terms, whereas the "Messianic epoch," still belonging to History, constitutes a penultimate stage of the "end of times." How can a human decision – in the case of flogging atoning for being "cut off" – intervene in a domain which exceeds man? How can it be guaranteed to be in keeping with the divine will? These questions imply transcendence and a relation which passes through this absolute distance. They touch on the problem of the possibility of such a relation, which also arises in the exegesis examining divine thought.

Before tackling the text, it would be useful to make some general remarks which, for a reader coming from outside, are called for by the particular or outdated nature of being flogged or cut off. This whole evocation of "blows," of the transgression and guilt it presupposes, may wound our liberal souls; just as the reference to a "celestial tribunal" may go against our modern minds by the dated or questionable "vision of the world" which it implies.

But in order to move towards a meaning which is retained despite an apparently antiquated language, it is necessary first of all to accept patiently – as one accepts the conventions of a fable or a stage setting – the particulars of the text in their specific universe. It is necessary to wait for them to set themselves in motion and free themselves from the anachronisms and local colour on which the curtain rises. In no way must this "exotic" or "outmoded" language stop thought by its picturesque elements, or by the immediate meaning of the things and deeds it names. This will change. Often from apparently incongruous or insignificant questions. Without fading before their concepts, things denoted in a concrete fashion are yet enriched with meanings by the multiplicity of their concrete aspects. This is what we call the paradigmatic modality of Talmudic reflection: notions remain constantly in contact with the examples or refer back to them, whereas they should have been content as springboards to rise to the level of generalization, or they clarify the thought which scrutinizes by the secret light of hidden or isolated worlds from which it bursts forth; and simultaneously this world inserted or lost in signs is illuminated by the thought which comes to it from outside or from the other end of the canon, revealing its possibilities which were awaiting the exegesis, immobilized, in some way, in the letters.

The Tribunal and the Love of One's Neighbour

Let us come back now to the principal points of a discussion on flogging, being "cut off from among their people," and the punishments of the human and celestial tribunal. Let us accept these figures of speech and the legal formal nature of the words.

According to R. Hananiah b. Gamaliel, those who are guilty of certain transgressions that the Law of the Pentateuch punishes by cutting them off obtain remission from this damnation if they submit to the flogging imposed by the earthly tribunal. The human tribunal would thus have to be aware of sins which expel human beings from the human (the decision of God's tribunal would measure the seriousness of the sin), and would thereby have to repair the irreparable. Can the tribunal do as much as celestial compassion or mercy? Is mercy shown at the tribunal? Reference is made by R. Hananiah to Deuteronomy 25: 3: "Forty stripes may be given him, but not more; lest, if one should go on to beat him with more stripes than these, your brother be degraded in your sight." The word "brother" would be essential here. It is a matter of punishing without degrading: would the tribunal and justice have the secret of the extreme measure of a difference which is a differential? In any case, R. Hananiah breaks with the dark mythological fatality whose eventuality would indicate a religious tyranny, in order to proclaim that no sin exists in relation to Heaven which cannot be expiated among men and in the light of day. The tribunal would thus also be the place where the divine regenerative will is revealed. Admittedly, there is violence. But it is an act without a spirit of violence, contempt or hatred. A fraternal act, without passion. It proceeds from a responsibility for others. To be the guardian of others, contrary to the vision of the world according to Cain, defines fraternity. For the tribunal which reasons and weighs up, the love of one's neighbour would be possible. Justice dispensed by the just becomes compassion – not in uncontrollable indulgence, but through a judgement. God speaks with a compassion that is born in the severity of the tribunal. Excessiveness? It certainly is. But pure indulgence, free forgiveness, is always at the expense of someone innocent who does not receive it. The judge is allowed such indulgence only if he personally assumes the costs.[1] But it is proper for the earthly judge, for man, for the brother of the guilty party, to restore to human fraternity those who have been excluded. To be responsible to the point of being answerable for the other's freedom. This heteronomy among the conditions of autonomy in human fraternity is acutely thought in Judaism with the category of divine paternity as its point of departure.[2] Divine justice arrays itself in fraternity by revealing itself in a human tribunal.

R. Hananiah b. Gamaliel's second argument is an "*a fortiori*." If the transgression of certain interdicts "cuts off a human being from his people," then all the more reason for his carrying out the Law to return him to them. Now, to suffer the flogging decided on by the tribunal is to obey the Law to which a guilty person is subject. But why "all the more reason"?[3] Because divine compassion is still more certain than its severity. A theme that is present throughout rabbinical thought, and to which R. Hananiah implicitly refers. Is it not written (Exodus 34: 7):

> [The Lord keeps] steadfast love for thousands [of generations], forgiving iniquity and transgression and sin, but who will by no means clear the guilty, visiting the iniquity of the fathers upon the children and the children's children, to the third and the fourth generation . . . ?

And the Rabbis gloss "thousands" as at least two thousand! For at least two thousand generations steadfast love granted to merit is handed down; for four generations iniquity cries out for justice: compassion is thus five hundred times greater than divine severity. Behind this arithmetic of mercy there is moral optimism: the triumph of evil has one time only; nothing is ever lost from the triumph won over evil or from good.

From this point onwards, R. Simeon intervenes with the merit attached to the obedience to the interdicts. An intervention which, above and beyond the theological meaning of the terms, defines a certain conception of human life: "One who desists from transgressing is granted reward like one who performs a precept." The constraint imposed on the spontaneity of life, such as is provided for in the negative commandments of Leviticus 18 (whose sexual interdicts appear as the privileged example of negative commandments), is asserted by R. Simeon as the guarantee of "rewards." The negative commandment is the constraint *par excellence*, restraining the tendencies where life is lived in its spontaneity as an "outgoing force," and in particular the blind abundance of sexual desire. It would be the promise of rewards, if we are to believe R. Simeon. Certainly one can expect from this promise what simple and unquestioning faith expects: longevity, eternal life or earthly happiness – just as one can denounce its spirit of repression which abuses that faith. But as a reward for a life accepting limitations, one can also understand the nature of this very life: the limitation of the wild vitality of life, through which this life wakes from its somnambulant spontaneity, sobers up from its nature and interrupts its centripetal movements, in order to be opened up to what is other than self. A life in which Judaism is recognized, limiting through the Law this wild, animal vitality, accepting this restriction as the best share – that is, as a "reward."[4] The plenitude of a sense of responsibility and justice is preferred to life intoxicated with its own essence, to the invasion of the unharnessed appetite of desire and domination where nothing, not even other people, can stand in its way.

R. Simeon b. Rabbi deduces the reward reserved for those who do not transgress the interdicts from the promise made in Deuteronomy 12: 23–5 to the person who refrains from eating blood: if the abstinence consonant with a natural loathing is rewarded, how much more so is the resistance against what is desirable! Perhaps the horror of blood here has a meaning which is not only of a gastronomic nature. Resistance to sexual excesses and to the taste for plunder is, *a fortiori*, worthy of merit. And yet this is the "true life," if we follow the literary writers of the great Metropoles! All this accounting of merits and rewards has a wider meaning. Life as it is lived, natural life, begins, perhaps, in naivety, in tendencies and tastes which are still in keeping with a code of ethics; but if it is allowed to run its course unhindered, it ends in loveless debauchery and plunder established as a social condition, and in exploitation. The human begins when this apparently innocent but virtually murderous vitality is brought under control by interdicts. Does not authentic civilization, however it may be marked by biological failures or political defeats, consist in holding back the breath of naive life and remaining fully awake in this way, "for generations and generations to come, to the end of all generations"?[5]

We can now understand R. Hananiah b. 'Akashia's thought which closes the *Mishnah*: "The Holy One, blessed be He, desired to make Israel worthy, therefore gave he them the law (to study) and many commandments (to do)"; and "[the Lord made] the law great and glorious" (Isaiah 42:21). This is certainly not to create artificial merits or to put up hurdles deliberately. It is for the greatness of justice and for his glory that commandments are necessary against a life lived as an "outgoing force." Even in cases – such as the horror that may be felt in eating or shedding blood – where nature seems to protect us from evil! There is no natural tendency that is healthy enough not to be able to be inverted. Holiness is necessary for the healthiness of the healthy.[6]

But the greatness of justice evoked by R. Hananiah b. 'Akashia, which is conditioned by a life obeying the many commandments, is also the glory of the tribunal and the judges. To make the law glorious! Only the judges who themselves practise the many commandments can form the glorious council to which God's will aspires. The judge is not just a legal expert of laws; he obeys the Law he administers, and he is trained by this obedience; the study of the Law is itself the essential form of this obedience.[7] Such a situation is necessary in order for earthly punishment to reduce celestial punishment; for it to be rightfully thought, with the Psalmist, that "God has taken his place in the divine council," and that "in the midst of the gods [judges] he holds judgement" (Psalms 82: 1). It is necessary in order simply to justify man's judgement passed on man and the punishment inflicted by one on the other – that is to say, the responsibility of one person for the other. This is the strange ontological structure presupposed by this responsibility whereby one person assumes the destiny and the very existence of another, and is answerable for this other in a way, however, that is not characteristic of him. It is a responsibility that precedes freedom, which would mean precisely belonging to God, a unique belonging which, anterior to freedom, does not destroy freedom and thereby defines, if one may say so, the meaning of the exceptional word: God. God appearing *through* a council of the just, itself called divine; God as the actual possibility of such a council. And, conversely, a council of the just which is not only the ultimate source of his judgement: a different will wills within it, the judge's judgement is inspired and exceeds or overflows human spontaneity. This is what our text will say further on. Justice cannot be reduced to the order it institutes or restores, nor to a system whose rationality commands, without difference, men and gods, revealing itself in human legislation like the structures of space in the theorems of geometricians, a justice that a Montesquieu calls the "logos of Jupiter," recuperating religion within this metaphor, but effacing precisely transcendence. In the justice of the Rabbis, difference retains its meaning. Ethics is not simply the corollary of the religious but is, of itself, the element in which religious transcendence receives its original meaning.

Transcendence and Exegesis

In the Talmudic extract we are commenting upon, the text relating to transcendence comes immediately after the one that discusses the powers a human tribunal would have in order to modify the decisions of Heaven in some way, and to be certain of agreeing with the absolute Tribunal. Here are the terms in which the problem is put: "Said R. Joseph: Who has gone up (to Heaven) and come (back with this information)?"

The answer is supplied by another scholar, Abaye, in the name of a Tanna master, R. Joshua b. Levi:

"Three things were enacted by the (mundane) Tribunal below, and the Celestial Tribunal on high have given assent to their action"; (we might also exclaim,) who has gone up (to Heaven) and come (back with this information)? Only, we (obtain these points by) interpreting certain texts; and, in this instance too, we so interpret the texts.

R. Joshua b. Levi would thus entrust to the interpretation of texts, what the Rabbis call *Midrash* (exposition of meaning), the ability to force open the secret of transcendence.

Here are the three "things" which are said to have been instituted by the earthly tribunals whose exegesis would prove to have the assent of the celestial will. First of all, the established custom, under the magistracy of Mordecai and Esther, of the liturgical reading of the "Scroll of Esther" on the Feast of Purim. It would find its justification in a biblical verse (Esther 9: 27): "They confirmed, and the Jews took upon them and their seed [The Jews acknowledged and accepted]." Why two almost synonymous verbs in this verse? Because confirmation [acknowledgement] and taking upon themselves [acceptance] were two distinct acts: acceptance below, acknowledgement in Heaven.

Then the authorization of saluting another person with the Divine Name: in Ruth 2:4, Boaz (whom the Rabbis class among the judges) greets the reapers: "The Lord be with you!"; and in Judges 6:12 the angel says to Gideon: "The Lord bless thee, thou mighty man of valour."

Finally, the prescription of bringing the tithe (due to the Levites) to the Temple-chamber, established as a custom by Ezra according to Nehemiah 10:39. It is confirmed by the prophet Malachi (3: 10): "Bring ye the whole tithe unto the store house that there may be food in My house, and try Me herewith, saith the Lord of Hosts, if I will not open you the windows of heaven and pour you out a blessing, until there be no enough." And the Talmud adds: "What means: 'until there be no enough'? Said Rami b. Rab: (It means), until your lips weary of saying 'Enough, enough'!"

Do not such "proofs" imply the inspired origin of the whole biblical canon? Does it not present the notions of height and transcendence as established, and the very idea of God as clear and distinct?

Unless R. Joseph's question, in its apparent naivety, is an extremely audacious one, questioning the mythological meaning of transcendence and the revelation it seems to acknowledge. Unless, in questioning the idea of someone "going up to Heaven," he goes so far as to concern the great man called upon in Exodus 24: 12: "Come up to me on the mountain, and wait there; and I will give you the tables of stone, with the law and the commandment." A calling upon whose reality in fact would be vouched for, ultimately, only by a text which itself already belongs to the statement of the truth which it ought to be able to establish: *petitio principii* which would hint at the whole of historical criticism today. But does not Abaye's reply indicate that he already understands his interlocutor on this higher level? Instead of establishing exegesis on some dogmatism of traditional metaphysics adopted as a truism, does not Abaye's reply consist in basing a new meaning for transcendence, and the old vocabulary, on the structure of the Book of books inasmuch as it allows for exegesis, and on its privileged status of containing more than it contains – in other words, of being, in this sense exactly, inspired?

The reading processes that we have just seen at work suggest, first, that the statement commented upon exceeds what it originally wants to say; that what it is capable of saying goes beyond what it wants to say; that it contains more than it contains; that perhaps an inexhaustible surplus of meaning remains locked in the syntactic structures of the sentence, in its word-groups, its actual words, phonemes and letters, in all this materiality of the saying which is potentially signifying all the time. Exegesis would come to free, in these signs, a bewitched significance that smoulders beneath the characters or coils up in all this literature of letters.[8]

Rabbinical hermeneutics is rashly considered as neglecting the spirit, whereas the aim of the signified by the signifier is not the only way to signify; whereas what is signified in the signifier, according to its other modes, answers only to the mind that solicits it and thereby belongs to the process of signification; and whereas interpretation essentially involves this act of soliciting without which what is not said, inherent in the texture of the statement, would be extinguished beneath the weight of the texts, and sink into the letters. An act of soliciting which issues from people whose eyes and ears are vigilant and who are mindful of the whole body of writing from which the extract comes, and equally attuned to life: the city, the street, other men. An act of soliciting which issues from people in their uniqueness, each person capable of extracting from the signs meanings which each time are inimitable. An act of soliciting issuing from people who would also belong to the process of the signification of what has meaning. This does not amount to identifying exegesis with the impressions and subjective reflections left by the word once it has been understood, nor to including them gratuitously in the "outside" of meaning. It does, however, amount to understanding the very plurality of people as an unavoidable moment of the signification of meaning, and as in some way justified by the destiny of the inspired word, so that the infinite richness of what it does not say can be said or that the meaning of what it does say can be "renewed," to use the technical expression of the Rabbis. As the people of the Book, for whom the demanding reading of the Scriptures belongs to the highest liturgy, would not Israel also be the people of continued revelation?

But in the light of this, the language that is capable of containing more than it contains would be the natural element of inspiration, despite or before its reduction to the instrument of the transmission of thoughts and information (if it can ever be entirely reduced to this). One may wonder whether man, an animal endowed with speech, is not, above all, an animal capable of inspiration, a prophetic animal. One may wonder whether the book, as a book, before becoming a document, is not the modality by which what is said lays itself open to exegesis, calls for it; and where meaning, immobilized in the characters, already tears the texture in which it is held. In propositions which are not yet – or which are already no longer – verses, and which are often verse or simply literature, another voice rings out among us, a second sonorous voice that drowns out or tears the first one. The infinite life of texts living through the life of the men who hear them; a primordial exegesis of the texts which are then called national literature and on to which the hermeneutics of universities and schools is grafted. Above and beyond the immediate meaning of what is said in these texts, the act of saying is inspired. The fact that meaning comes through the book testifies to its biblical essence. The comparison between the inspiration conferred on the Bible and the inspiration towards which the interpretation of literary texts tends is not intended to compromise the dignity of the Scriptures. On the contrary, it asserts the dignity of "national literatures." Yet how is it that a book is instituted as the Book of books? Why does a book become Bible? How is the divine origin of the Word indicated? How is it signed in Scripture? And does not this signature, which is more important for people living today than "the thunderings and the lightnings" of Sinai, betray simple faith?

Inspiration: another meaning which breaks through from beneath the immediate meaning of what is meant to be said, another meaning which beckons to a way of hearing that listens beyond what is heard, beckons to extreme consciousness, a consciousness that has been awoken. This other voice resonating in the first takes control of the message as a result of this resonance coming from behind the first. In its purity of message, it is not just a certain form of saying; it organizes its content. The message as message awakens listening to what is indisputably intelligible, to the meaning of meanings, to the face of the other man.[9] Awakening is precisely this proximity of others.[10] The message as message in its method of awakening is the modality, the actual "how" of the ethical code that disturbs the established order of being, unrepentantly leading its style of being.[11] With its referent as reading, as the book – yet no less wondrous for all that – do we not have here the original figure of the beyond freed from the mythology of ulterior worlds?[12]

That *ethics* is not determined in its elevation by the pure height of the starry sky; that all height takes on its transcendent meaning only through ethics and the message incessantly breaking (hermeneutically) the texture of the Book *par excellence*: these, undoubtedly, will constitute the teaching to be drawn – one of the teachings to be drawn – from the passage we are commenting upon.

Curiously, the biblical text first cited by R. Joshua b. Levi in consideration of the agreement between the earthly tribunal and the celestial tribunal is taken from the book of Esther from which, it might be said, God has gone so far as to withdraw his name, the word by which he is named. Yet in this book the message emerges from between the events recounted according to their "natural" motivation, the necessities and the casting of lots. That these events, instituted as liturgy by Mordecai and Esther, could have been understood as belonging to holy History is the "miraculous" surplus of their place in the divine plan. There arises the historical order of the facts (their established order), and consciences are awoken at the highest ethical moment in which Esther disturbs royal etiquette and consents to her ruin in order to save other men. The order upset by this awakening is paralleled by the king's insomnia. Does not a Midrash from the Tractate Megillah compare the insomnia of Ahasuerus to the very insomnia of God? As if, in the impossibility of sleeping, the ontological rest of being were to be torn and entirely sobered up. Is not the relation to transcendence this extreme consiousness?

No less remarkable is the second text in which the epiphany of God is invoked in the human face. The face of the other, irreducible difference, bursting into all that gives itself to me, all that is understood by me and belongs to my world; an appearance in the world which un-makes and dis-orders the world, worries me and keeps me awake. That is what is perceived by bringing together Ruth 2: 4 and Judges 6: 12. A transcendence both in the text in which exegesis finds more than the written seems to say, and in the ethical content, the message, which is thus revealed.

The third moment – in which the gift of the tithe is transformed by being brought to the Temple – would signify the transformation of the very act of giving into an absolutely free act of generosity where the person giving, not knowing the beneficiary, does not hear the expression of the latter's personal gratitude.[13] Is that not one of the meanings, the figure, as it were, of the cult itself? What "strong minds" would be tempted to mock as duties towards an "empty heaven" is enigmatically the absolute opening of the soul: the opening of dis-interestedness, of sacrifice without reward, of discourse without answer or echo, which "confidence in God" and prayer must have the strength to reach. The opening of self to the infinite that no confirmation can equal, and that is proven only by its very excessiveness. That would be the abundance for which lips cannot be enough, drying out through saying "enough," of which Rami b. Rab speaks in his strange hermeneutic of Malachi 3: 10. A beyond the discourse. This is probably what this sudden transformation is: in the dis-interested generosity of the act of giving, receiving becomes infinite, the opening on to the infinite.

The Ambiguity

In our reading of the Talmudic passage, inspiration and the exegesis that discovers it, we have discerned the spirituality of the spirit and the actual figure of transcendence. Have we been right to do so? Have we been right to recognize in the ethical code on the level of the tribunal, understood as a council of the just, the actual place in which the spirit blows and the Other penetrates the Same? Will a person today not resist such readings by reducing the transcendence of inspiration, exegesis and the moral message to man's interiority, to his creativity or his subconscious? Is not ethics basically autonomous? In order to dispute such modern-day resistance, would it not have been necessary to interpret as inspiration the reasons of reasoning reason in which philosophy, in its logic, recognizes the reign of Identity which nothing that is *other* could disrupt or guide?

Now this is precisely what the final section of the Talmudic extract that concerns us wishes to suggest. R. Eleazar intervenes to confirm in his own way the general argument of Makkoth 23b on the possible agreement between earthly courts of law and celestial justice. He refers to Genesis 38:26, where Judah, the son of Jacob, recognizes the injustice of the accusation he had brought against his daughter-in-law Tamar (this "is said to have taken place," according to our text, at the Tribunal of Shem, Noah's son, who was still alive). R. Eleazar refers to I Samuel 12: 3–5, where all of Israel testifies at the Tribunal of Samuel to the disinterestedness of the judge Samuel; and he refers to I Kings 3: 27, where King Solomon, in his own Tribunal, recognizes the mother among the two women arguing over a child. Confession of the guilty party, testimony of the people, sentence of the king: to each of these human speeches (unquestionably human in the verses quoted), R. Eleazar – in the name of a supremely audacious exegesis, but probably also in the name of a daring thought – lifts out, under various pretexts, the ends of verses which he attributes to the echo of a heavenly voice. Will the holy spirit thus have been present at men's tribunals?

One interlocutor, Raba, questions such extravagance: there is no need to have voices intervening in discourses where reason is sufficient. But it is R. Eleazar's lesson that the Talmudic text retains. It retains it without discussion, in the name of tradition. Inspiration is thus said to be in the exercise of reason itself! The logos would already be prophetic! Through the uncertainties and presumptions of reasoning thought, the light of evidence would come as if under the trauma of the Revelation. A message would be declared in all evidence.

This is true, but it should be emphasized that despite tradition, the redactors of the Talmudic text recorded the opinion that was rejected: Raba's scepticism. It is still written down. As if an ambiguity had to remain in the conclusions of the lofty debate that has just taken place according to the style of the Talmud, with remarks that are apparently without relief and made "without appearing to be made."

Would not the man of today recognize in this ambiguity the alternating movements of his own thought?

To say that the ideas on transcendence and the very idea of transcendence come to us through the interpretation of writings is, admittedly, not to express a subversive opinion. Yet it is less dogmatic to people today. It suggests on the one hand that language, at the hour of its ethical truth – that is, of its full significance – is inspired, that it can therefore say more than it says, and that prophecy is thus not an act of genius, but the spirituality of the spirit expressing itself, the ability of human speech to extend beyond the primary intentions that carry it. This is perhaps possession by God, through which the idea of God comes to us. But this language offered to transcendence is also the object of philology; thus the transcendence that is expressed through it would be just an illusion, the prestige of influences to be demystified by History. Let us prefer, then, the genesis of every text to its exegesis, the certainties of given signs to the hazards of mysterious messages, the combinations of the shadows in the Cave to the uncertain calls from outside! This is also a science, at times an admirable one, to destroy false prophecies.

Alternative or alternation. And even an alternation of alternations before the letters of Scripture. These letters, for those who respect them as for those who mock them, may still support the dogmatic principles of a God, a power stronger than others, who interrupts – like a monstrous force or a heroic person – the necessities of nature. Then, through a science that they nurture with their presence as relics, these letters strike their readers, one and all, and rescue them from the level of asserted or denied mythologies. But in this start that readers receive there is a new alternation of movements: they go from the traumatic experience of the unknown and strange meaning to the grammar which, already operating on another level, restores order, coherence and chronology. And then there is a movement back: from history and philology to the understanding of meaning coming from behind the literature of letters and anachronisms, an understanding that again affects and awakes, forcing us out of the bed of the preformed and customary ideas that protect and reassure.

An alternation which, admittedly, testifies to the hesitation of our little faith, but from which also stems the transcendence that does not impose itself with denials through its actual coming and which, in inspired Scripture, awaits a hermeneutic – in other words, reveals itself only in dissimulation.

Notes

1   "In rendering legal judgment, [the judge] used to acquit the guiltyless and condemn the guilty; but when he saw that the condemned man was poor, he helped him out of his own purse [to pay the required sum], thus executing judgment and charity..." Tractate Sanhedrin 6b. [*Translator's note*: Levinas indicates that he is quoting from the translation into French by the Great Rabbi Salzer.]

2   It is against the paganism of the notion of the "Oedipus complex" that it is necessary to think forcefully about apparently purely edifying verses such as that in Deuteronomy 8: 5: "Know then in your heart that, as a man disciplines his son, the Lord your God disciplines you." Paternity here signifies a constituent category of what has meaning, not of its alienation. On this point, at least, psychoanalysis testifies to the profound crisis of monotheism in contemporary sensibility, a crisis that cannot be reduced to the refusal of a few dogmatic propositions. It conceals the ultimate secret of anti-Semitism. Amado Lévy-Valerusi has insisted throughout her work on the essentially pagan character of the myth of Oedipus.

3   [*Translator's note*: The Soncino edition of the Babylonian Talmud renders the a *fortiori* argument as "how much more should one..."]

4   Curiously, in the final paragraphs of the pages we are studying in the Tractate Makkoth, the distant noise of unsuppressed and triumphant life, the noise of Rome, is heard. "Long ago, as Rabban Gamaliel, R. Eleazar b. 'Azariah, R. Joshua and R. Akiba were walking on the road, they heard the noise of the crowds at Rome (on travelling) from Puteoli, a hundred and twenty miles away. They all fell a-weeping, but R. Akiba seemed merry. Said they to him: Wherefore are you merry? Said he to them: Wherefore are you weeping? Said they: These heathens who bow down to images and burn incense to idols live in safety and ease, whereas our Temple, the 'Footstool' of our God, is burnt down by fire, and should we then not weep? He replied: Therefore, am I merry. If they that offend Him fare thus, how much better shall fare they that do obey Him!" How much more shall we one day be rewarded or how much better do we who are just fare already, despite our misfortunes? When we are walking on the

road and are tired, whether or not we are Rabban Gamaliel, R. Eleazar b. 'Azariah and R. Joshua, the greatest of the great, the sounds of Rome may for a moment cause us to question, in our minds and in our nerves, the soundness of the just life. R. Akiba alone is able to be merry: despite the failures, he is certain of receiving the best share. He is certain of it not through painful empirical experience, but through an *a fortiori* reasoning that is not here the guarantee of a promise, but of a value.

5 These are the words with which R. Simeon b. Rabbi closes his intervention in the Talmudic text we are commenting upon: "One who refrains therefrom [shall] acquire merit for himself and for generations and generations to come, to the end of all generations!"

6 On the subject of the interdicts, it would be interesting to quote the lines which figure in what follows in our text of pages 23a and 23b of the Tractate Makkoth: "R. Simlai when preaching said: Six hundred and thirteen precepts were communicated to Moses, three hundred and sixty-five negative precepts, corresponding to the number of solar days (in the year), and two hundred and forty-eight positive precepts, corresponding to the number of the members of man's body. Said R. Hamnuna: What is the (authentic) text for this? It is, *Moses commanded us torah, an inheritance of the congregation of Jacob* (Deuteronomy 33: 4), 'torah' being in letter-value, equal to six hundred and eleven, '*I am*' and '*Thou shalt have no (other Gods)*' (not being reckoned, because) we heard from the mouth of the Might (Divine)." [*Translator's note*: The ending of Levinas's translation differs substantially from that given here: "If one adds to this the first two commandments of the Decalogue pronounced at Sinai and which we heard from the very mouth of the Lord, that makes six hundred and thirteen."] A bizarre sort of accounting! In actual fact, it gives at least three lessons:

(a) Every day lived under the sun is potential depravity and thus requires a new interdict, a new vigilance which yesterday's cannot guarantee.

(b) The life of every organ of the human body, of every tendency (the accuracy or arbitrariness of the anatomy or physiology counting two hundred and forty-eight matters little, since the number of "positive" precepts divulges the secret of this figure), is the source of possible life. A force that is not justified in itself. It must be dedicated to the most high, to serving.

(c) The code containing the six hundred and thirteen precepts is not met by the number given by the breakdown of the numerical value of the letters making up the word Torah. It is not a system justified uniquely by its coherence. It institutes the order of life only because its transcendent source is personally asserted in it as word. True life is inspired.

7 Cf. *Quatre lectures talmudiques* [*Four Talmudic Readings*].

8 The word of the rabbinical scholars, the word setting out or commenting on the Torah, can be compared to the "glowing coals," to use a phrase from the Pirqe Aboth in the *Tractate of Principles* of the Babylonian Talmud. A remarkable Talmudist, a disciple of the Gaon of Vilna (one of the last great masters of rabbinical Judaism, on the eve of the nineteenth century, the Jewish age "of Enlightenment"), Rabbi Hayyim Volozhiner, interpreted this remark approximately as follows: the coals light up by being blown on, the glow of the flame that thus comes alive depends on the interpreter's length of breath.

9 The Book *par excellence* of what has meaning. And this is without yet highlighting the testimony given to this book by a people who have existed for thousands of years, or the interpenetration of their history and of this book, even if such communication between history and book is essential to genuine scriptures.

10 Cf. my study "De la conscience à la veille," *Bijdragen*, 3–4 (1974), 235–49.

11 Ethics – appearing as the prophetic – is not a "region," a layer or an ornament of being. It is, of itself, actual dis-interestedness, which is possible only under a traumatic experience

whereby "presence," in its imperturbable equality of presence, is disturbed by "the other." Disturbed, awoken, transcended.

12　In the texts invoked, indeed, determined situations and beings – equal to themselves, being held in definitions and boundaries that integrate them into an order and bring them to rest in the world – are passed through by a breath that arouses and stirs their drowsiness or their identity as beings and things, tearing them from their order without alienating them, tearing them from their contour like the characters in Dufy's paintings. The miracle of beings presenting themselves in their being and awakening to new awakenings, deeper and more sober. It cannot be denied that as a disturbing of order, as a tearing of Same by Other, it is the miracle, the structuring – or de-structuring – of inspiration and its transcendence. If purely thaumaturgical miracles seem spiritually suspect to us and acceptable as simple figures of the Epiphany, it is not because they alter the order but because they do not alter it enough, because they are not miraculous enough, because the Other awakening the Same is not yet other enough through them.

13　On the importance attached to this modality of the gift, cf. Baba–Bathra 10 b.

Chapter 19

Whom to Give to (Knowing Not to Know)

Jacques Derrida 1930–

Introduction

Born in Algiers and educated in France, Jacques Derrida has become one of the most prominent thinkers of the poststructuralist movement. He teaches the history of philosophy at the Ecole Normale Superieur in Paris and teaches regularly at universities in the United States. Although he is not primarily a literary critic, Derrida's work, particularly his articulation and development of "deconstruction," has had great influence on literary studies and, in a lesser degree, on biblical studies. Since the 1960s, the force of his ideas has affected other areas including theology, sociology, and the interdisciplinary practice of discourse theory. Although some might call his ideas "subversive" and others might argue they are visionary, few doubt their impact on literary criticism and classroom practice. He is a prolific writer in many areas of study, including literature, art, psychology, linguistics, theater, theology, and philosophy. His books include: *Speech and Phenomena* (1967/English translation 1973); *Writing and Difference* (1967/1978); *Of Grammatology* (1967/1976); *Margins of Philosophy* (1972/1983); *Dissemination* (1972/1981); *Glas* (1974/1987); *The Postcard* (1980/1987); *The Other Heading: Reflections on Today's Europe* (1991/1992); and *Specters of Marx* (1993/1994). (For a useful bibliography see Peggy Kamuf's *A Derrida Reader: Between the Blinds*. New York: Columbia University Press, 1991.)

In the headnote to the selection from Hillis Miller we cited Miller's description of something that "is properly religious, metaphysical, or ontological, though hardly in a traditional or conventional way," something, he goes on to say, "that enters into the words or between the words" in texts, "something encountered in our relations to other people, especially relations involving love, betrayal, and that ultimate betrayal ..., the death of the other." Although he is not explicitly talking about Derrida, this description, like much of his later work, owes a great debt to Derrida's philosophical work. From his early essay on the philosophy of Emmanuel Levinas, "Violence and Metaphysics" (1964/1978), through his *Memoires for Paul de Man* (1986), to his *Specters of Marx* (whose subtitle is *The State of the Debt, the Work of Mourning, and the New International*, 1993) and *The Gift of Death* (1992/1995), from which the following selection is taken, Derrida has been attempting to articulate and delineate, non-conventionally (and certainly non-explicitly), possibilities of post-modern religiosity, metaphysics, and ontology. Many might disagree with this formulation, but a large part of the *power* of Derrida's work, we suspect, arises in his struggle to account for phenomena that have traditionally been described in terms of religion, metaphysics, and ontology without recourse to transcendentalism and intuitionalism – without recourse, that is, to supernatural forces and "originary" revelation.

That is why death and mourning – the gift of the sacredness of death – is so important to him. *The Postmodern Bible* extensively discusses Derrida's work (119–31), his definition of "deconstruction" (see also the Introduction to Part I above), his relationship to traditional philosophy, and his enormous influence on practices of reading. But in the years since the PMB was published, Derrida has more explicitly turned to the *mysterium tremendum* with which he begins "Whom to Give to (Knowing Not to Know)" in its extended reading of Kierkegaard's *Fear and Trembling*. Death and mourning – the *gift* of death he describes here – encompasses the paradox of being overwhelmingly extraordinary (what can be more unique than a person's individual death?) and ordinary (what is more ubiquitous than death?) at the same time. Just as in Blanchot's description of the sky mentioned in the General Introduction, Derrida is describing – in death, in Abraham's dilemma, even in Melville's "Bartleby the Scrivener" – the postmodern paradox of the "same": "what the knights of good conscience don't realize," Derrida writes, "is that 'the sacrifice of Isaac' illustrates – if that is the word in the case of such a nocturnal mystery – the most common and everyday experience of responsibility. The story is no doubt monstrous, outrageous, barely conceivable. . . . But isn't this also the most common thing?" Its truth, Derrida says later, "is shown to possess the very structure of what occurs everyday. Through its paradox it speaks of the responsibility required at every moment for every man and every woman." Religion, metaphysics, ontology, is ordinary as well as extraordinary, both a revelation and a simple seeing, as forceful as a seemingly supernatural event and as banal as something happening every day. Derrida deconstructs the oppositions between "the religious and the ethical, the religious and the ethico-political, the theological and the political, the theologico-political, the theocratic and the ethico-political, and so on; the secret and the public, the profane and the sacred, the specific and the generic, the human and the nonhuman" in "different appropriations" – *postmodern* appropriations – "of the same sacrifice."

Mysterium tremendum. A frightful mystery, a secret to make you tremble.

Tremble. What does one do when one trembles? What is it that makes you tremble?

A secret always *makes* you tremble. Not simply quiver or shiver, which also happens sometimes, but tremble. A quiver can of course manifest fear, anguish, apprehension of death; as when one quivers in advance, in anticipation of what is to come. But it can be

Jacques Derrida, "Whom to Give to (Knowing Not to Know)," from *The Gift of Death*, translated by David Wills (Chicago and London: University of Chicago Press, 1995).

slight, on the surface of the skin, like a quiver that announces the arrival of pleasure or an orgasm. It is a moment in passing, the suspended time of seduction. A quiver is not always very serious, it is sometimes discreet, barely discernible, somewhat epiphenomenal. It prepares for, rather than follows the event. One could say that water quivers before it boils; that is the idea I was referring to as seduction: a superficial pre–boil, a preliminary and visible agitation.

On the other hand, trembling, at least as a signal or symptom, is something that has already taken place, as in the case of an earthquake [*tremblement de terre*] or when one trembles all over. It is no longer preliminary even if, unsettling everything so as to imprint upon the body an irrepressible shaking, the event that makes one tremble portends and threatens still. It suggests that violence is going to break out again, that some traumatism will insist on being repeated. As different as dread, fear, anxiety, terror, panic, or anguish remain from one another, they have already begun in the trembling, and what has provoked them continues, or threatens to continue, to make us tremble. Most often we neither know what is coming upon us nor see its origin; it therefore remains a secret. We are afraid of the fear, we anguish over the anguish, and we tremble. We tremble in that strange repetition that ties an irrefutable past (a shock has been felt, a traumatism has already affected us) to a future that cannot be anticipated; anticipated but unpredictable; *apprehended*, but, and this is why there is a future, apprehended precisely *as* unforeseeable, unpredictable; approached *as* unapproachable. Even if one thinks one knows what is going to happen, the new instant of that happening remains untouched, still unaccessible, in fact unlivable. In the repetition of what still remains unpredictable, we tremble first of all because we don't know from which direction the shock came, whence it was given (whether a good surprise or a bad shock, sometimes a surprise received as a shock); and we tremble from not knowing, in the form of a double secret, whether it is going to continue, start again, insist, be repeated: whether it will, how it will, where, when; and why *this* shock. Hence I tremble because I am still afraid of what already makes me afraid, of what I can neither see nor foresee. I tremble at what exceeds my seeing and my knowing [*mon voir et mon savoir*] although it concerns the innermost parts of me, right down to my soul, down to the bone, as we say. Inasmuch as it tends to undo both seeing and knowing, trembling is indeed an experience of secrecy or of mystery, but another secret, another enigma, or another mystery comes on top of the unlivable experience, adding yet another seal or concealment to the *tremor* (the Latin word for "trembling," from *tremo*, which in Greek as in Latin means *I tremble, I am afflicted by trembling*; in Greek there is also *tromeō*: I tremble, I shiver, I am afraid; and *tromos*, which means trembling, fear, fright. In Latin, *tremendus, tremendum*, as in *mysterium tremendum*, is a gerundive derived from *tremo*: what makes one tremble, something frightening, distressing, terrifying).

Where does this supplementary seal come from? One doesn't know *why one trembles*. This limit to knowledge no longer only relates to the cause or unknown event, the unseen or unknown that makes us tremble. Neither do we know why it produces this particular symptom, a certain irrepressible agitation of the body, the uncontrollable instability of its members or of the substance of the skin or muscles. Why does the irrepressible take this form? Why does terror make us tremble, since one can also tremble with cold, and such analogous physiological manifestations translate experiences

and sentiments that appear, at least, not to have anything in common? This symptom-
atology is as enigmatic as tears. Even if one knows why one weeps, in what situation,
and what it signifies (I weep because I have lost one of my nearest and dearest, the child
cries because he has been beaten or because she is not loved: she causes herself grief,
complains, he makes himself complain or allows himself to be felt sorry for – by means
of the other), but that still doesn't explain why the lachrymal glands come to secrete
these drops of water which are brought to the eyes rather than elsewhere, the mouth or
the ears. We would need to make new inroads into thinking concerning the body,
without dissociating the registers of discourse (thought, philosophy, the bio-genetico-
psychoanalytic sciences, phylo- and ontogenesis), in order to one day come closer to
what makes us tremble or what makes us cry, to that *cause* which is not the final cause
that can be called God or death (God is the cause of the *mysterium tremendum*, and the
death that is given is always what makes us tremble, or what makes us weep as well) but
to a closer cause; not the immediate cause, that is, the accident or circumstance, but the
cause closest to our body, that which means that one trembles or weeps rather than
doing something else. What is it a metaphor or figure for? What does *the body mean to
say* by trembling or crying, presuming one can speak here of the body, or of saying, of
meaning, and of rhetoric?

What is it that makes us tremble in the *mysterium tremendum*? It is the gift of infinite
love, the dissymmetry that exists between the divine regard that sees me, and myself,
who doesn't see what is looking at me; it is the gift and endurance of death that exists in
the irreplaceable, the disproportion between the infinite gift and my finitude, responsibility as culpability, sin, salvation, repentance, and sacrifice. As in the title of Kierkegaard's essay *Fear and Trembling*,[1] the *mysterium tremendum* includes at least an implicit
and indirect reference to Saint Paul. In the Epistle to the Philippians 2:12, the disciples
are asked to work towards their salvation in fear and trembling. They will have to work
for their salvation knowing all along that it is God who decides: the Other has no reason
to give to us and nothing to settle in our favor, no reason to share his reasons with us.
We fear and tremble because we are already in the hands of God, although free to work,
but in the hands and under the gaze of God, whom we don't see and whose will we
cannot know, no more than the decisions he will hand down, nor his reasons for
wanting this or that, our life or death, our salvation or perdition. We fear and tremble
before the inaccessible secret of a God who decides for us although we remain
responsible, that is, free to decide, to work, to assume our life and our death.

So Paul says – and this is one of the "adieux" I spoke of earlier:

> Wherefore my beloved, as ye have always obeyed, not as in my presence only, but now
> much more in my absence (*non ut in praesentia mei tantum, sed multo magis nunc in absentia
> mea / mē bōs en tē parousia mou monon alla nun pollō mallon en tē apousia mou*), work out your
> own salvation with fear and trembling (*cum metu et tremore / meta phobou kai tromou*).[2]

This is first explanation of the fear and of the trembling, and of "fear and trembling."
The disciples are asked to work towards their salvation not in the presence (*parousia*) but
in the absence (*apousia*) of the master: without either seeing or knowing, without
hearing the law or the reasons for the law. Without knowing from whence the thing

comes and what awaits us, we are given over to absolute solitude. No one can speak with us and no one can speak for us; we must take it upon ourselves, each of us must take it upon himself (*auf sich nehmen* as Heidegger says concerning death, our death, concerning what is always "my death," and which no one can take on in place of me). But there is something even more serious at the origin of this trembling. If Paul says "adieu" and absents himself as he asks them to obey, in fact ordering them to obey (for one doesn't ask for obedience, one orders it), it is because God is himself absent, hidden and silent, separate, secret, at the moment he has to be obeyed. God doesn't give his reasons, he acts as he intends, he doesn't have to give his reasons or share anything with us: neither his motivations, if he has any, nor his deliberations, nor his decisions. Otherwise he wouldn't be God, we wouldn't be dealing with the Other as God or with God as *wholly other* [*tout autre*]. If the other were to share his reasons with us by explaining them to us, if he were to speak to us all the time without any secrets, he wouldn't be the other, we would share a type of homogeneity. Discourse also partakes of that sameness; we don't speak with God or to God, we don't speak with God or to God as with others or to our fellows. Paul continues in fact:

> For it is God which worketh in you both to will and to do of his good pleasure. (Philippians 2:13)[3]

One can understand why Kierkegaard chose, for his title, the words of a great Jewish convert, Paul, in order to meditate on the still Jewish experience of a secret, hidden, separate, absent, or mysterious God, the one who decides, without revealing his reasons, to demand of Abraham that most cruel, impossible, and untenable gesture: to offer his son Isaac as a sacrifice. All that goes on in secret. God keeps silent about his reasons. Abraham does also, and the book is not signed by Kierkegaard, but by Johannes de Silentio ("a poetic person who only exists among poets," Kierkegaard writes in the margin of his text: Pap. IV B 79, *Fear and Trembling*, 243).

This pseudonym keeps silent, it expresses the silence that is kept. Like all pseudonyms, it seems destined to keep secret the real name *as* patronym, that is, the name of the father of the work, in fact the name of the father of the father of the work. This pseudonym, one among many that Kierkegaard employed, reminds us that a meditation linking the question of secrecy to that of responsibility immediately raises the question of the name and of the signature. One often thinks that responsibility consists of acting and signing *in one's name*. A responsible reflection on responsibility is interested in advance in whatever happens to the name in the event of pseudonymity, metonymy, homonymy, in the matter of what constitutes *a real name*. Sometimes one says or wishes it more effectively, more authentically, in the secret name by which *one calls oneself*, that *one gives oneself or affects to give oneself*, the name that is more *naming* and *named* in the pseudonym than in the official legality of the public patronym.

The trembling of *Fear and Trembling*, is, or so it seems, the very experience of sacrifice. Not, first of all, in the Hebraic sense of the term, *korban*, which refers more to an approach or a "coming close to," and which has been wrongly translated as "sacrifice," but in the sense that sacrifice supposes the putting to death of the unique in terms of its being unique, irreplaceable, and most precious. It also therefore refers to the impossibility of substitution, the unsubstitutable; and then also to the substitution of an animal for man; and finally, especially this, by means of this impossible substitution itself, it refers to what links the sacred to sacrifice and sacrifice to secrecy.

Kierkegaard–de Silentio recalls Abraham's strange reply to Isaac when the latter asks him where the sacrificial lamb is to be found. It can't be said that Abraham doesn't respond to him. He says God will provide. God will provide a lamb for the holocaust (["burnt offering"] Genesis 22:8). Abraham thus keeps his secret at the same time as he replies to Isaac. He doesn't keep silent and he doesn't lie. He doesn't speak nontruth. In *Fear and Trembling* (*Problema III*) Kierkegaard reflects on this double secret: that between God and Abraham but also that between the latter and his family. Abraham doesn't speak of what God has ordered him alone to do, he doesn't speak of it to Sarah, or to Eliezer, or to Isaac. He must keep the secret (that is his duty), but it is also a secret that he *must* keep as a double necessity because in the end he *can only* keep it: he doesn't know it, he is unaware of its ultimate rhyme and reason. He is sworn to secrecy because he is in secret.

Because, in this way, he doesn't speak, Abraham transgresses the ethical order. According to Kierkegaard, the highest expression of the ethical is in terms of what binds us to our own and to our fellows (that can be the family but also the actual community of friends or the nation). By keeping the secret, Abraham betrays ethics. His silence, or at least the fact that he doesn't divulge the secret of the sacrifice he has been asked to make, is certainly not designed to save Isaac.

Of course, in some respects Abraham does speak. He says a lot. But even if he says everything, he need only keep silent on a single thing for one to conclude that he hasn't spoken. Such a silence takes over his whole discourse. So he speaks and doesn't speak. He responds without responding. He responds and doesn't respond. He responds indirectly. He speaks in order not to say anything about the essential thing that he must keep secret. Speaking in order not to say anything is always the best technique for keeping a secret. Still, Abraham doesn't just speak in order not to say anything when he replies to Isaac. He says something that is not nothing and that is not false. He says something that is not a non-truth, something moreover that, although *he doesn't know it yet*, will turn out to be true.

To the extent that, in not saying the essential thing, namely, the secret between God and him, Abraham doesn't speak, he assumes the responsibility that consists in always being alone, entrenched in one's own singularity at the moment of decision. Just as no one can die in my place, no one can make a decision, what we call "a decision," in my place. But as soon as one speaks, as soon as one enters the medium of language, one loses that very singularity. One therefore loses the possibility of deciding or the right to decide. Thus every decision would, fundamentally, remain at the same time solitary, secret, and silent. Speaking relieves us, Kierkegaard notes, for it "translates" into the general (113).[4]

The first effect or first destination of language therefore involves depriving me of, or delivering me from, my singularity. By suspending my absolute singularity in speaking, I renounce at the same time my liberty and my responsibility. Once I speak I am never and no longer myself, alone and unique. It is a very strange contract – both paradoxical and terrifying – that binds infinite responsibility to silence and secrecy. It goes against what one usually thinks, even in the most philosophical mode. For common sense, just as for philosophical reasoning, the most widely shared belief is that responsibility is tied to the public and to the nonsecret, to the possibility and even the necessity of accounting for one's words and actions in front of others, of justifying and owning up to them. Here on the contrary it appears, just as necessarily, that the absolute responsibility of my actions, to the extent that such a responsibility remains mine, singularly so, something no one else can perform in my place, instead implies secrecy. But what is also implied is that, by not speaking to others, I don't account for my actions, that I answer for nothing [*que je ne réponde de rien*] and to no one, that I make no response to others or before others. It is both a scandal and a paradox. According to Kierkegaard, *ethical* exigency is regulated by generality; and it therefore defines a responsibility that consists of *speaking*, that is, of involving oneself sufficiently in the generality to justify oneself, to give an account of one's decision and to answer for one's actions. On the other hand, what does Abraham teach us, in his approach to sacrifice? That far from ensuring responsibility, the generality of ethics incites to irresponsibility. It impels me to speak, to reply, to account for something, and thus to dissolve my singularity in the medium of the concept.

Such is the aporia of responsibility: one always risks not managing to accede to the concept of responsibility in the process of *forming* it. For responsibility (we would no longer dare speak of "the universal concept of responsibility") demands on the one hand an accounting, a general answering-for-oneself with respect to the general and before the generality, hence the idea of substitution, and, on the other hand, uniqueness, absolute singularity, hence nonsubstitution, nonrepetition, silence, and secrecy. What I am saying here about responsibility can also be said about decision. The ethical involves me in substitution, as does speaking. Whence the insolence of the paradox: for Abraham, Kierkegaard declares, *the ethical is a temptation*. He must therefore resist it. He keeps quiet in order to avoid the moral temptation which, under the pretext of calling him to responsibility, to self-justification, would make him lose his ultimate responsibility along with his singularity, make him lose his unjustifiable, secret, and absolute responsibility before God. This is ethics as "irresponsibilization," as an insoluble and paradoxical contradiction between responsibility *in general* and *absolute* responsibility. Absolute responsibility is not a responsibility, at least it is not general responsibility or responsibility in general. It needs to be exceptional or extraordinary, and it needs to be that absolutely and par excellence: it is as if absolute responsibility could not be derived from a *concept* of responsibility and therefore, in order for it to be what it must be it must remain inconceivable, indeed unthinkable: it must therefore be irresponsible in order to be absolutely responsible. "Abraham *cannot* speak, because he cannot say that which would explain everything . . . that it is an ordeal such that, please note, the ethical is the temptation" (115).

The ethical can therefore end up making us irresponsible. It is a temptation, a tendency, or a facility that would sometimes have to be refused in the name of a responsibility that doesn't keep account or give an account, neither to man, to humans, to society, to one's fellows, or to one's own. Such a responsibility keeps its secret, it cannot and need not present itself. Tyrannically, jealously, it refuses to present itself before the violence that consists of asking for accounts and justifications, summonses to appear before the law of men. It declines the autobiography that is always auto-justification, *égodicée*. Abraham *presents himself*, of course, but before God, the unique, jealous, secret God, the one to whom he says "Here I am." But in order to do that, he must renounce his family loyalties, which amounts to violating his oath, and refuse to present himself before men. He no longer speaks to them. That at least is what the sacrifice of Isaac suggests (it would be different for a tragic hero such as Agamemnon).

In the end secrecy is as intolerable for ethics as it is for philosophy or for dialectics in general, from Plato to Hegel:

> The ethical as such is the universal; as the universal it is in turn the disclosed. The single individual, qualified as immediate, sensate, and psychical, is the hidden. Thus his ethical task is to work himself out of his hiddenness and to become disclosed in the universal. Every time he desires to remain in the hidden, he trespasses and is immersed in spiritual trial from which he can emerge only by disclosing himself.
>
> Once again we stand at the same point. If there is no hiddenness rooted in the fact that the single individual as the single individual is higher than the universal, then Abraham's conduct cannot be defended, for he disregarded the intermediary ethical categories. But if there is such a hiddenness, then we face the paradox, which does not allow itself to be mediated, since it is based precisely on this: the single individual as the single individual is higher than the universal . . . . The Hegelian philosophy assumes no justified hiddenness, no justified incommensurability. It is, then, consistent for it to demand disclosure, but it is a little bemuddled when it wants to regard Abraham as the father of faith and to speak about faith. [82, translation modified – DW]

In the exemplary form of its absolute coherence, Hegel's philosophy represents the irrefutable demand for manifestation, phenomenalization, and unveiling; thus, it is thought, it represents the request for truth that inspires philosophy and ethics in their most powerful forms. There are no final secrets for philosophy, ethics, or politics. The manifest is given priority over the hidden or the secret, universal generality is superior to the individual; no irreducible secret that can be legally justified (*fondé en droit* says the French translation of Kierkegaard) – and thus the instance of the law has to be added to those of philosophy and ethics; nothing hidden, no absolutely legitimate secret. But the paradox of faith is that interiority remains "incommensurable with exteriority" (69). No manifestation can consist in rendering the interior exterior or show what is hidden. The knight of faith can neither communicate to nor be understood by anyone, she can't help the other at all (71). The absolute duty that obligates her with respect to God cannot have the form of generality that is called duty. If I obey in my duty towards God (which is my absolute duty) *only in terms of duty*, I am not fulfilling my relation to God. In order to fulfill my duty towards God, I must not act *out of duty*, by means of that form of generality that can always be mediated and communicated and that is called duty. The absolute duty that binds me to God himself, in faith, must function beyond and against any duty I have. "The duty becomes duty by being traced back to God, but in the duty itself I do not enter into relation to God" (68). Kant explains that to act morally is to act "out of duty" and not only "by conforming to duty." Kierkegaard sees acting "out of duty," in the universalizable sense of the law, as a dereliction of one's absolute duty. It is in this sense that absolute duty (towards God and in the singularity of faith) implies a sort of gift or sacrifice that functions beyond both debt and duty, beyond duty as a form of debt. This is the dimension that provides for a "gift of death" which, beyond human responsibility, beyond the universal concept of duty, is a response to absolute duty.

In the order of human generality, a duty of hate is implied. Kierkegaard quotes Luke 14:26: " 'If any one comes to me and does not hate his own father and mother and his wife and children and brothers and sisters, yes, and even his own life, he cannot be my disciple'." Recognizing that "this is a hard saying" (72), Kierkegaard nevertheless upholds the necessity for it. He refines its rigor without seeking to make it less shocking or paradoxical. But Abraham's hatred for the ethical and thus for his own (family, friends, neighbors, nation, but at the outside humanity as a whole, his own kind or species) must remain an absolute source of pain. If I put to death or grant death to what I hate it is not a sacrifice. I must sacrifice what I love. I must come to hate what I love, in the same moment, at the instant of granting death. I must hate and betray my own, that is to say offer them the gift of death by means of the sacrifice, not insofar as I hate them, that would be too easy, but insofar as I love them. I must hate them insofar as I love them. Hate wouldn't be hate if it only hated the hateful, that would be too easy. It must hate and betray what is most lovable. Hate cannot be hate, it can only be the sacrifice of love to love. It is not a matter of hating, betraying by one's breach of trust, or offering the gift of death to what one doesn't love.

But is this heretical and paradoxical knight of faith Jewish, Christian, or Judeo-Christian-Islamic? The sacrifice of Isaac belongs to what one might just dare to call the common treasure, the terrifying secret of the *mysterium tremendum* that is a property of all three so-called religions of the Book, the religions of the races of Abraham. This rigor, and the exaggerated demands it entails, compel the knight of faith to say and do things that will appear (and must even be) atrocious. They will necessarily revolt those who profess allegiance to morality in general, to Judeo-Christian-Islamic morality, or to the religion of love in general. But as Patočka will say, perhaps Christianity has not yet thought through its own essence, any more than it has thought through the irrefutable events through which Judaism, Christianity, and Islam have come to pass. One cannot ignore or erase the sacrifice of Isaac recounted in Genesis, nor that recounted in the Gospel of Luke. It has to be taken into account, which is what Kierkegaard proposes. Abraham comes to hate those closest to him by keeping silent, he comes to hate his only beloved son by consenting to put him to death [*lui donner la mort*]. He hates them not out of hatred, of course, but out of love. He doesn't hate them any less for all that, on the contrary. Abraham must love his son absolutely to come to the point where he will grant him death, to commit what ethics would call hatred and murder.

How does one hate one's own? Kierkegaard rejects the common distinction between love and hate; he finds it egotistical and without interest. He reinterprets it as a paradox. God wouldn't have asked Abraham to put Isaac to death, that is, to make a gift of death as a sacrificial offering to himself, to God, unless Abraham had an absolute, unique, and incommensurable love for his son:

> for it is indeed this love for Isaac that makes his act a sacrifice by its paradoxical contrast to his love for God. But the distress and the anxiety in the paradox is that he, humanly speaking, is thoroughly incapable of making himself understandable. Only *in the instant*

> when his act is in absolute contradiction to his feelings, only then does he sacrifice Isaac, but the reality of his act is that by which he belongs to the universal, and there he is and remains a murderer. [74, translation modified – DW]

I have emphasized the word *instant:* "the instant of decision is madness," Kierkegaard says elsewhere. The paradox cannot be grasped in time and through mediation, that is to say in language and through reason. Like the gift and "the gift of death," it remains irreducible to presence or to presentation, it demands a temporality of the instant without ever constituting a present. If it can be said, it belongs to an atemporal temporality, to a duration that cannot be grasped: something one can neither stabilize, establish, *grasp [prendre]*, *apprehend*, or *comprehend*. Understanding, common sense, and reason cannot seize [*begreifen*], conceive, understand, or mediate it; neither can they negate or deny it, implicate it in the work of negation, make it work: in the act of *giving death*, sacrifice suspends both the work of negation and work itself, perhaps even the work of mourning. The tragic hero enters into mourning. Abraham, on the other hand, is neither a man of mourning nor a tragic hero.

In order to assume his absolute responsibility with respect to absolute duty, to put his faith in God to work, or to the test, he must also in reality remain a hateful murderer, for he consents to put to death. In both general and abstract terms, the absoluteness of duty, of responsibility, and of obligation certainly demands that one transgress ethical duty, although in betraying it one belongs to it and at the same time recognizes it. The contradiction and the paradox must be endured *in the instant itself.* The two duties must contradict one another, one must subordinate (incorporate, repress) the other. Abraham must assume absolute responsibility for sacrificing his son by sacrificing ethics, but in order for there to be a sacrifice, the ethical must retain all its value; the love for his son must remain intact, and the order of human duty must continue to insist on its rights.

The account of Isaac's sacrifice can be read as a narrative development of the paradox constituting the concept of duty and absolute responsibility. This concept puts us into relation (but without relating to it, in a double secret) with the absolute other, with the absolute singularity of the other, whose name here is God. Whether one believes the biblical story or not, whether one gives it credence, doubts it, or transposes it, it could still be said that there is a moral to this story, even if we take it to be a fable (but taking it to be a fable still amounts to losing it to philosophical or poetic generality; it means that it loses the quality of a historic event). The moral of the fable would be morality itself, at the point where morality brings into play the gift of the death that is so given. The absolutes of duty and of responsibility presume that one denounce, refute, and transcend, at the same time, all duty, all responsibility, and every human law. It calls for a betrayal of everything that manifests itself within the order of universal generality, and everything that manifests itself in general, the very order and essence of manifestation; namely, the essence itself, the essence in general to the extent that it is inseparable from presence and from manifestation. Absolute duty demands that one behave in an irresponsible manner (by means of treachery or betrayal), while still recognizing, confirming, and reaffirming the very thing one sacrifices, namely, the order of human ethics and responsibility. In a word, ethics must be sacrificed in the name of duty. It is a duty not to respect, out of duty, ethical duty. One must behave not only in an ethical or responsible manner, but in a nonethical, nonresponsible manner, and one must do that *in the name of* duty, of an infinite duty, *in the name of* absolute duty. And this name which must always be singular is here none other than the name of God as completely other, the nameless name of God, the unpronounceable name of God as other to which I am bound by an absolute, unconditional obligation, by an incomparable, nonnegotiable duty. The other as absolute other, namely, God, must remain transcendent, hidden, secret, jealous of the love, requests, and commands that he gives and that he asks to be kept secret. Secrecy is essential to the exercise of this absolute responsibility as sacrificial responsibility.

In terms of the moral of morality, let us here insist upon what is too often forgotten by the moralizing moralists and good consciences who preach to us with assurance every morning and every week, in newspapers and magazines, on the radio and on television, about the sense of ethical or political responsibility. Philosophers who don't write ethics are failing in their duty, one often hears, and the first duty of the philosopher is to think about ethics, to add a chapter on ethics to each of his or her books and, in order to do that, to come back to Kant as often as possible. What the knights of good conscience don't realize, is that "the sacrifice of Isaac" illustrates – if that is the word in the case of such a nocturnal mystery – the most common and everyday experience of responsibility. The story is no doubt monstrous, outrageous, barely conceivable: a father is ready to put to death his beloved son, his irreplaceable loved one, and that because the Other, the great Other asks him or orders him without giving the slightest explanation. An infanticide father who hides what he is going to do from his son and from his family without knowing why, what could be more abominable, what mystery could be more frightful (*tremendum*) vis-à-vis love, humanity, the family, or morality?

But isn't this also the most common thing? what the most cursory examination of the concept of responsibility cannot fail to affirm? Duty or responsibility binds me to the other, to the other as other, and ties me in my absolute singularity to the other as other. God is the name of the absolute other as other and as unique (the God of Abraham defined as the one and unique). As soon as I enter into a relation with the absolute other, my absolute singularity enters into relation with his on the level of obligation and duty. I am responsible to the other as other, I answer to him and I answer for what I do before him. But of course, what binds me thus in my singularity to the absolute singularity of the other, immediately propels me into the space or risk of absolute sacrifice. There are also others, an infinite number of them, the innumerable generality of others to whom I should be bound by the same responsibility, a general and universal responsibility (what Kierkegaard calls the ethical order). I cannot respond to the call, the request, the obligation, or even the love of another without sacrificing the other other, the other others. *Every other (one) is every (bit) other [tout autre est tout autre]*, every one else is completely or wholly other. The simple concepts of alterity and of singularity constitute the concept of duty as much as that of responsibility. As a result, the concepts of responsibility, of decision, or of duty, are condemned a priori to paradox, scandal, and aporia. Paradox, scandal, and aporia are themselves nothing other than sacrifice, the revelation of conceptual thinking at its limit, at its death and finitude. As soon as I enter into a relation with the other, with the gaze, look, request, love, command, or call of the other, I know that I can respond only by sacrificing ethics, that is, by sacrificing whatever obliges me to also respond, in the same way, in the same instant, to all the others. I offer a gift of death, I betray, I don't need to raise my knife over my son on Mount Moriah for that. Day and night, at every instant, on all the Mount Moriahs of this world, I am doing that, raising my knife over what I love and must love, over those to whom I owe absolute fidelity, incommensurably. Abraham is faithful to God only in his absolute treachery, in the betrayal of his own and of the uniqueness of each one of them, exemplified here in his only beloved son. He would not be able to opt for fidelity to his own, or to his son, unless he were to betray the absolute other: God, if you wish.

Let us not look for examples, there would be too many of them, at every step we took. By preferring my work, simply by giving it my time and attention, by preferring my activity as a citizen or as a professorial and professional philosopher, writing and speaking here in a public language, French in my case, I am perhaps fulfilling my duty. But I am sacrificing and betraying at every moment all my other obligations: my obligations to the other others whom I know or don't know, the billions of my fellows (without mentioning the animals that are even more other others than my fellows), my fellows who are dying of starvation or sickness. I betray my fidelity or my obligations to other citizens, to those who don't speak my language and to whom I neither speak nor respond, to each of those who listen or read, and to whom I neither respond nor address myself in the proper manner, that is, in a singular manner (this for the so-called public space to which I sacrifice my so-called private space), thus also to those I love in private, my own, my family, my son, each of whom is the only son I sacrifice to the other, every one being sacrificed to every one else in this land of Moriah that is our habitat every second of every day.

This is not just a figure of style or an effect of rhetoric. According to 2 Chronicles, 3 and 8, the place where this occurs, where the sacrifice of Abraham or of Isaac (and it is the sacrifice of both of them, it is the gift of death one makes to the other in putting *oneself* to death, mortifying onself in order to make a gift of this death as a sacrificial offering to God) takes place, this place where death is given or offered, is the place where Solomon decided to build the House of the Lord in Jerusalem, also the place where God appeared to Solomon's father, David. However, it is also the place where the grand Mosque of Jerusalem stood, the place called the Dome of the Rock near the grand Aksa mosque where the sacrifice of Ibrahim is supposed to have taken place and from where Muhammad mounted his horse for paradise after his death. It is just above the destroyed temple of Jerusalem and the Wailing Wall, not far from the Way of the Cross. It is therefore a holy place but also a place that is in dispute, radically and rabidly, fought over by all the monotheisms, by all the religions of the unique and transcendent God, of the absolute other. These three monotheisms fight over it, it is useless to deny this in terms of some wide-eyed ecumenism; they make war with fire and blood, have always done so and all the more fiercely today, each claiming its particular perspective on this place and claiming an original historical and political interpretation of Messianism and of the sacrifice of Isaac. The reading, interpretation, and tradition of the sacrifice of Isaac are themselves sites of bloody, holocaustic sacrifice.

Isaac's sacrifice continues every day. Countless machines of death wage a war that has no front. There is no front between responsibility and irresponsibility but only between different appropriations of the same sacrifice, different orders of responsibility, different other orders: the religious and the ethical, the religious and the ethico-political, the theological and the political, the theologico-political, the theocratic and the ethico-political, and so on; the secret and the public, the profane and the sacred, the specific and the generic, the human and the nonhuman. Sacrificial war rages not only among the religions of the Book and the races of Abraham that expressly refer to the sacrifice of Isaac, Abraham, or Ibrahim, but between them and the rest of the starving world, within the immense majority of humankind and even those living (not to mention the others, dead or nonliving, dead or not yet born) who don't belong to the people of Abraham or Ibrahim, all those others to whom the names of Abraham and Ibrahim have never meant anything because such names don't conform or correspond to anything.

I can respond only to the one (or to the One), that is, to the other, by sacrificing that one to the other. I am responsible to any one (that is to say to any other) only by failing in my responsibilities to all the others, to the ethical or political generality. And I can never justify this sacrifice, I must always hold my peace about it. Whether I want to or not, I can never justify the fact that I prefer or sacrifice any one (any other) to the other. I will always be secretive, held to secrecy in respect of this, for I have nothing to say about it. What binds me to singularities, to this one or that one, male or female, rather than that one or this one, remains finally unjustifiable (this is Abraham's hyper-ethical sacrifice), as unjustifiable as the infinite sacrifice I make at each moment. These singularities represent others, a wholly other form of alterity: one other or some other persons, but also places, animals, languages. How would you ever justify the fact that you sacrifice all the cats in the world to the cat that you feed at home every morning for years, whereas other cats die of hunger at every instant? Not to mention other people? How would you justify your presence here speaking one particular language, rather than there speaking to others in another language? And yet we also do our duty by behaving thus. There is no language, no reason, no generality or mediation to justify this ultimate responsibility which leads me to absolute sacrifice; absolute sacrifice that is not the sacrifice of irresponsibility on the altar of responsibility, but the sacrifice of the most imperative duty (that which binds me to the other as a singularity in general) in favor of another absolutely imperative duty binding me to every other.

God decides to suspend the sacrificial process, he addresses Abraham who has just said: "Here I am." "Here I am": the first and only possible response to the call by the other, the originary moment of responsibility such as it exposes me to the singular other, the one who appeals to me. "Here I am" is the only self-presentation presumed by every form of responsibility: I am ready to respond, I reply that I am ready to respond. Whereas Abraham has just said "Here I am" and taken his knife to slit his son's throat, God says to him: "Lay not thine hand upon the lad, neither do thou anything unto him: for now I know that thou fearest God, seeing thou hast not withheld thy son, thine only son, from me" (Genesis 22:12). This terrible declaration seems to display God's satisfaction at the terror that has been expressed (I see that "you fear God [Elohim]," you tremble before me). It causes one to tremble through the fear and trembling it evokes as its only reason (I see that you have trembled before me, all right, we are quits, I free you from your obligation). But it can also be translated or argued as follows: I see that you have understood what absolute duty means, namely, how to respond to the absolute other, to his call, request, or command. These different registers amount to the same thing: by commanding Abraham to sacrifice his son, to put his son to death by offering a gift of death to God, by means of this double gift wherein the gift of death consists in putting to death by raising one's knife over someone and of putting death forward by giving it as an offering, God leaves him free to refuse – and that is the test. The command requests, like a prayer from God, a declaration of love that implores: tell me that you love me, tell me that you turn towards me, towards the unique one, towards the other as unique and, above all, over everything else, unconditionally, and in order to do that, make a gift of death, give death to your only son and give me the death I ask for, that I give to you by asking you for it. In essence God says to Abraham: I can see right away [*à l'instant*] that you have understood what absolute duty towards the unique one means, that it means responding where there is no reason to be asked for or to be given; I see that not only have you understood that as an idea, but that – and here lies responsibility – you have acted on it, you have put it into effect, you were ready to carry it out *at this very instant* (God stops him *at the very instant when there is no more time, where no more time is given*, it is as if Abraham had *already* killed Isaac: the concept of the instant is always indispensable): thus you had *already* put it into effect, you are absolute responsibility, you had the courage to behave like a murderer in the eyes of the world and of your loved ones, in the eyes of morality, politics, and of the generality of the general or of your kind [*le générique*]. And you had even renounced hope.

Abraham is thus at the same time the most moral and the most immoral, the most responsible and the most irresponsible of men, absolutely irresponsible because he is absolutely responsible, absolutely irresponsible in the face of men and his family, and in the face of the ethical, because he responds absolutely to absolute duty, disinterestedly and without hoping for a reward, without knowing why yet keeping it secret; answering to God and before God. He recognizes neither debt nor duty to his fellows because he is in a relationship to God – a relationship without relation because God is absolutely transcendent, hidden, and secret, not giving any reason he can share in exchange for this doubly given death, not sharing anything in this dissymmetrical alliance. Abraham considers himself to be all square. He acts as if he were discharged of his duty towards his fellows, his son, and humankind; but he continues to love them. He must *love* them and also *owe* them everything in order to be able to sacrifice them. Without being so, then, he nevertheless feels absolved of his duty towards his family, towards the human species [*le genre humain*] and the generality of the ethical, absolved by the absolute of a unique duty that binds him to God the one. Absolute duty absolves him of every debt and releases him from every duty. Absolute ab-solution.

The ideas of secrecy and exclusivity [*non-partage*] are essential here, as is Abraham's silence. He doesn't speak, he doesn't tell his secret to his loved ones. He is, like the knight of faith, a witness and not a teacher (*Fear and Trembling*, 80), and it is true that this witness enters into an absolute relation with the absolute, but he doesn't witness to it in the sense that to witness means to show, teach, illustrate, manifest to others the truth that one can precisely attest to. Abraham is a witness of the absolute faith that cannot and must not witness before men. He must keep his secret. But his silence is not just any silence. Can one witness in silence? By silence?

The tragic hero, on the other hand, can speak, share, weep, complain. He doesn't know "the dreadful responsibility of loneliness" (114). Agamemnon can weep and wail with Clytemnestra and Iphigenia. "Tears and cries are relieving" (114); there is consolation in them. Abraham can neither speak nor commiserate, neither weep nor wail. He is kept in absolute secret. He feels torn, he would like to console the whole world, especially Sarah, Eliezer, and Isaac, he would like to embrace them before taking the final step. But he knows that they will then say to him: "But why are you doing this? Can't you get an exemption, find another solution, discuss, negotiate with God?" Or else they will accuse him of dissimulation and hypocrisy. So he can't say anything to them. Even if he speaks to them he can't say anything to them. " . . . he speaks no human language. And even if he understood all the languages of the world . . . he still could not speak – he speaks in a divine language, he speaks in tongues" (114). If he were to speak a common or translatable language, if he were to become intelligible by giving his reasons in a convincing manner, he would be giving in to the temptation of the ethical generality that I have referred to as that which makes one irresponsible. He wouldn't be Abraham any more, the unique Abraham in a singular relation with the unique God. Incapable of making a gift of death, incapable of sacrificing what he loved, hence incapable of loving and of hating, he wouldn't give anything anymore.

Abraham says nothing, but his last words, those that respond to Isaac's question, have been recorded: "God himself will provide the lamb for the holocaust, my son." If he had said "There is a lamb, I have one" or "I don't know, I have no idea where to find the lamb," he would have been lying, speaking in order to speak falsehood. By speaking without lying, he responds without responding. This is a strange responsibility that consists neither of responding nor of not responding. Is one responsible for what one says in an unintelligible language, in the language of the other? But besides that, mustn't responsibility always be expressed in a language that is foreign to what the community can already hear or understand only too well? "So he does not speak an untruth, but neither does he say anything, for he is speaking in a strange tongue" (119).

In Melville's "Bartleby the Scrivener," the narrator, a lawyer, cites Job ("with kings and counselors"). Beyond what is a tempting and obvious comparison, the figure of Bartleby could be compared to Job – not to him who hoped to join the kings and counselors one day after his death, but to him who dreamed of not being born. Here, instead of the test God makes Job submit to, one could think of that of Abraham. Just as Abraham doesn't speak a human language, just as he speaks in tongues or in a language that is foreign to every other human language, and in order to do that responds without responding, speaks without saying anything either true or false, says nothing determinate that would be equivalent to a statement, a promise or a lie, in the same way Bartleby's "I would prefer not to" takes on the responsibility of a response without response. It evokes the future without either predicting or promising; it utters nothing fixed, determinable, positive, or negative. The modality of this repeated utterance that says nothing, promises nothing, neither refuses or accepts anything, the tense of this singularly insignificant statement reminds one of a nonlanguage or a secret language. Is it not as if Bartleby were also speaking "in tongues"?

But in saying nothing general or determinable, Bartleby doesn't say absolutely nothing. *I would prefer not to* looks like an incomplete sentence. Its indeterminacy creates a tension: it opens onto a sort of reserve of incompleteness; it announces a temporary or provisional reserve, one involving a proviso. Can we not find there the secret of a hypothetical reference to some indecipherable providence or prudence? We don't know what he wants or means to say, or what he doesn't want to do or say, but we are given to understand quite clearly that *he would prefer not to*. The silhouette of a content haunts this response. If Abraham has already consented *to make a gift of death*, and to give to God the death that he is going to put his son to, if he knows that he will do it unless God stops him, can we not say that his disposition is such that he would, precisely, *prefer not to*, without being able to say to the world what is involved? Because he loves his son, he would prefer that God hadn't asked him anything. He would prefer that God didn't let him do it, that he would hold back his hand, that he would provide a lamb for the holocaust, that the moment of this mad decision would lean on the side of nonsacrifice, once the sacrifice were to be accepted. He will not decide *not to*, he has decided *to*, but he would prefer not to. He can say nothing more and will do nothing more if God, if the Other, continues to lead him towards death, to the death that is offered as a gift. And Bartleby's "I would prefer not to" is also a sacrificial passion that will lead him to death, a death given by the law, by a society that doesn't even know why it acts the way it does.

It is difficult not to be struck by the absence of woman in these two monstrous yet banal stories. It is a story of father and son, of masculine figures, of hierarchies among men (God the father, Abraham, Isaac; the woman, Sarah, is she to whom nothing is said; and Bartleby the Scrivener doesn't make a single allusion to anything feminine whatsoever, even less to anything that could be construed as a figure of woman). Would the logic of sacrificial responsibility within the implacable universality of the law, of its law, be altered, inflected, attenuated, or displaced, if a woman were to intervene in some consequential manner? Does the system of this sacrificial responsibility and of the double "gift of death" imply at its very basis an exclusion or sacrifice of woman? A woman's sacrifice or a sacrifice of woman, according to one sense of the genitive or the other? Let us leave the question in suspense. In the case of the tragic hero or the tragic sacrifice, however, woman is present, her place is central, just as she is present in other tragic works referred to by Kierkegaard.

The responses without response made by Bartleby are at the same time disconcerting, sinister, and comical; superbly, subtly so. There is concentrated in them a sort of sublime irony. Speaking in order not to say anything or to say something other than what one thinks, speaking in such a way as to intrigue, disconcert, question, or have someone or something else speak (the law, the lawyer), means speaking ironically. Irony, in particular Socratic irony, consists of not saying anything, declaring that one doesn't have any knowledge of something, but doing that in order to interrogate, to have someone or something (the lawyer, the law) speak or think. *Eirōneia* dissimulates, it is the act of questioning by feigning ignorance, by pretending. The *I would prefer not to* is not without irony; it cannot not lead one to suppose that there is some irony in the situation. It isn't unlike the incongruous yet familiar humor, the *unheimlich* or uncanniness of the story. On the other hand the author of *The Concept of Irony* uncovers irony in the response without response that translates Abraham's responsibility. Precisely in order to distinguish ironic pretense from a lie, he writes:

> But a final word by Abraham has been preserved, and insofar as I can understand the paradox, I can also understand Abraham's total presence in that word. First and foremost, he does not say anything, and in that form he says what he has to say. His response to Isaac is in the form of irony, for it is always irony when I say something and still do not say anything. (118)

Perhaps irony would permit us to find something like a common thread in the questions I have just posed and what Hegel said about woman: that she is "the eternal irony of the community."[5]

Abraham doesn't speak in figures, fables, parables, metaphors, ellipses, or enigmas. His irony is meta-rhetorical. If he knew what was going to happen, if for example God had charged him with the mission of leading Isaac onto the mountain so that He could strike him with lightning, then he would have been right to have recourse to enigmatic language. But the problem is precisely that he doesn't know. Not that that makes him hesitate, however. His nonknowledge doesn't in any way suspend his own decision, which remains resolute. The knight of faith must not hesitate. He accepts his responsibility by heading off towards the absolute request of the other, beyond knowledge. He decides, but his absolute decision is neither guided nor controlled by knowledge. Such, in fact, is the paradoxical condition of every decision: it cannot be deduced from a form of knowledge of which it would simply be the effect, conclusion, or explicitation. It structurally breaches knowledge and is thus destined to nonmanifestation; a decision is, in the end, always secret. It remains secret in the very instant of its performance, and how can the concept of decision be dissociated from this figure of the instant? From the stigma of its punctuality?

Abraham's decision is absolutely responsible because it answers for itself before the absolute other. Paradoxically it is also irresponsible because it is guided neither by reason nor by an ethics justifiable before men or before the law of some universal tribunal. Everything points to the fact that one is unable to be responsible at the same time before the other and before others, before the others of the other. If God is completely other, the figure or name of the wholly other, then every other (one) is every (bit) other. *Tout autre est tout autre.* This formula disturbs Kierkegaard's discourse on one level while at the same time reinforcing its most extreme ramifications. It implies that God, as the wholly other, is to be found everywhere there is something of the wholly other. And since each of us, everyone else, each other is infinitely other in its absolute singularity, inaccessible, solitary, transcendent, nonmanifest, originarily nonpresent to my *ego* (as Husserl would say of the *alter ego* that can never be originarily present to my consciousness and that I can apprehend only through what he calls *appresentation* and analogy), then what can be said about Abraham's relation to God can be said about my relation without relation to *every other (one) as every (bit) other [tout autre comme tout autre]*, in particular my relation to my neighbor or my loved ones who are as inaccessible to me, as secret and transcendent as Jahweh. Every other (in the sense of each other) is every bit other (absolutely other). From this point of view what *Fear and Trembling* says about the sacrifice of Isaac is the truth. Translated into this extraordinary story, the truth is shown to possess the very structure of what occurs every day. Through its paradox it speaks of the responsibility required at every moment for every man and every woman. At the same time, there is no longer any ethical generality that does not fall prey to the paradox of Abraham.[6] At the instant of every decision and through the relation to *every other (one) as every (bit) other*, every one else asks us at every moment to behave like knights of faith. Perhaps that displaces a certain emphasis of Kierkegaard's discourse: the absolute uniqueness of Jahweh doesn't tolerate analogy; we are not all Abrahams, Isaacs, or Sarahs either. We are not Jahweh. But what seems thus to universalize or disseminate the exception or the extraordinary by imposing a supplementary complication upon ethical generality, that very thing ensures that Kierkegaard's text gains added force. It speaks to us of the paradoxical truth of our responsibility and of our relation to the *gift of death* of each instant. Furthermore, it explains to us its own status, namely its ability to be read by all at the very moment when it is speaking to us of secrets in secret, of illegibility and absolute undecipherability. It stands for Jews, Christians, Muslims, but also for everyone else, for every other in its relation to the wholly other. We no longer know who is called Abraham, and he can no longer even tell us.

Whereas the tragic hero is great, admired, and legendary from generation to generation, Abraham, in remaining faithful to his singular love for every other, is never considered a hero. He doesn't make us shed tears and doesn't inspire admiration: rather stupefied horror, a terror that is also secret. For it is a terror that brings us close to the absolute secret, a secret that we share without sharing it, a secret between someone else, Abraham as the other, and another, God as the other, as wholly other. Abraham himself is in secret, cut off both from man and from God.

But that is perhaps what we share with him. But what does it mean to share a secret? It isn't a matter of knowing what the other knows, for Abraham doesn't know anything. It isn't a matter of sharing his faith, for the latter must remain an initiative of absolute singularity. And moreover, we don't think or speak of Abraham from the point of view of a faith that is sure of itself, any more than did Kierkegaard. Kierkegaard keeps coming back to this, recalling that he doesn't understand Abraham, that he wouldn't be capable of doing what he did. Such an attitude in fact seems the only possible one; and even if it is the most widely shared idea in the world, it seems to be required by this monstrosity of such prodigious proportions. Our faith is not assured, because faith can never be, it must never be a certainty. We share with Abraham what cannot be shared, a secret we know nothing about, neither him nor us. To share a secret is not to know or to reveal the secret, it is to share we know not what: nothing that can be determined. What is a secret that is a secret about nothing and a sharing that doesn't share anything?

Such is the secret truth of faith as absolute responsibility and as absolute passion, the "highest passion" as Kierkegaard will say; it is a passion that, sworn to secrecy, cannot be transmitted from generation to generation. In this sense it has no history. This untransmissibility of the highest passion, the normal condition of a faith which is thus bound to secrecy, nevertheless dictates to us the following: we must always start over. A secret can be transmitted, but in transmitting a secret as a secret that remains secret, has one transmitted at all? Does it amount to history, to a story? Yes and no. The epilogue of *Fear and Trembling* repeats, in sentence after sentence, that this highest passion that is faith must be started over by each generation. Each generation must begin again to involve itself in it without counting on the generation before. It thus describes the nonhistory of absolute beginnings which are repeated, and the very historicity that presupposes a tradition to be reinvented each step of the way, in this incessant repetition of the absolute beginning.

With *Fear and Trembling*, we hesitate between two generations in the lineage of the so-called religions of the Book: we hesitate at the heart of the Old Testament and of the Jewish religion, but also the heart of a founding event or a key sacrifice for Islam. As for the sacrifice of the son by his father, the son sacrificed by men and finally saved by a God that seemed to have abandoned him or put him to the test, how can we not recognize there the foreshadowing or the analogy of another passion? As a Christian thinker, Kierkegaard ends by reinscribing the secret of Abraham within a space that seems, in its literality at least, to be evangelical. That doesn't necessarily exclude a Judaic or Islamic reading, but it is a certain evangelical text that seems to orient or dominate Kierkegaard's interpretation. That text isn't cited; rather, like the "kings and counselors" of "Bartleby the Scrivener," it is simply suggested, but this time without the quotation marks, thus being clearly brought to the attention of those who know their texts and have been brought up on the reading of the Gospels:

> But there was no one who could understand Abraham. And yet what did he achieve? He remained true to his love. But anyone who loves God needs no tears, no admiration; he forgets the suffering in the love. Indeed, so completely has he forgotten it that there would not be the slightest trace of his suffering left if God himself did not remember it, *for he sees in secret* and recognizes distress and counts the tears and forgets nothing.
>
> Thus, either there is a paradox, that the single individual stands in an absolute relation to the absolute, or Abraham is lost. (120, my emphasis)

Notes

1   Søren Kierkegaard, *Fear and Trembling, and Repetition*, vol. 6 of *Kierkegaard's Writings*, ed. and trans. Howard V. Hong and Edna H. Hong (Princeton: Princeton University Press, 1983). Page references are to this edition.

2   [Philippians 2:12. All biblical quotations are from the King James version. – Trans. note.]

3   I am following the Grosjean and Léturmy translation (Bibliothèque de la Pléiade) here, and will often find it necessary to add Greek or Latin glosses. What they translate by *son bon plaisir* ("his good pleasure") doesn't refer to God's pleasure but to his sovereign will that is not required to consult, just as the king acts as he intends without revealing his secret reasons, without having to account for his actions or explain them. The text doesn't name God's pleasure but his will: *pro bona voluntate* or *hyper tēs eudokias: Eudokia* means "good will," not just in the sense of desiring the good, but as the will that judges well, for its pleasure, as in their translation; for that is his will and it suffices. *Eudokeō*: "I judge well," "I approve," sometimes "I am pleased" or "I take pleasure in," "I consent."

4 [The English translation gives "the universal" for *det Almene*, whereas "the general" is closer to the Danish and is the term Derrida uses. Note also Kierkegaard's distinction between *individual* ("individual") and *enkelt* ("singular") that anticipates Derrida's here. For this and other clarifications of the English translation I am grateful to Elsebet Jegstrup and Mark Taylor. – Trans. note.]

5 In this regard, I refer the reader to my *Glas* (Lincoln: University of Nebraska Press, 1986), 190.

6 This is the logic of an objection made by Levinas to Kierkegaard: "For Kierkegaard, ethics signifies the general. For him, the singularity of the self would be lost under a rule valid for all; the generality can neither contain nor express the secret of the self. However, it is not at all certain that the ethical is to be found where he looks for it. Ethics as the conscience of a responsibility towards the other . . . does not lose one in the generality, far from it, it singularizes, it posits one as a unique individual, as the Self. . . . In evoking Abraham he describes the meeting with God as occurring where subjectivity is raised to the level of the religious, that is to say above ethics. But one can posit the contrary: the attention Abraham pays to the voice that brings him back to the ethical order by forbidding him to carry out the human sacrifice, is the most intense moment of the drama. . . . It is there, in the ethical, that there is an appeal to the uniqueness of the subject and sense is given to life in defiance of death" (Emmanuel Levinas, *Noms propres*; Montpellier: Fata Morgana, 1976, 113 [my translation, DW]). Levinas's criticism doesn't prevent him from admiring in Kierkegaard "something absolutely new" in "European philosophy," "a new modality of the True," "the idea of a persecuted truth" (114–15).

Chapter 20

"Draupadi" by Mahasweta Devi

Gayatri Chakravorty Spivak 1942–

Introduction

Gayatri Chakravorty Spivak is currently Avalon Foundation Professor in the
Humanities at Columbia University. Formerly, she was Mellon Professor of English
at the University of Pittsburgh. She received her Ph.D. from Cornell University in
1967. Her dissertation on Yeats, directed by Paul de Man, was published as *Myself I
Must Remake: The Life and Poetry of W. B. Yeats* (1973). It was de Man who steered her
toward Jacques Derrida, and her 1976 translation of and book–length introduction to
Of Grammatology made her reputation. Her subsequent work consists of poststructuralist literary criticism, deconstructivist readings of Marxism, feminism and postcolonialism, including work with the Subaltern Studies group. Because of this varied work,
applicable to a range of disciplines, Spivak has become a much cited critic. Her writing
is dense, highly theoretical, and tends to resist straight textual analysis. Her compelling
insights into culture, politics, and literature continually evolve and develop even
within individual pieces, a hallmark of Spivak's writing which underscores the complexity of the subjects about which she writes. Her major works include "Displacement
and the Discourse of Women" (1983); *In Other Worlds: Essays in Cultural Politics* (1987);
"Can the Subaltern Speak?" (1988); *Outside in the Teaching Machine* (1993); *A Critique of
Postcolonial Reason: Toward a History of the Vanishing Present* (1999); and *Traffic and
Identity: Further Essays on Culture as Politics* (2000).

In Spivak's introduction to her translation of Mahasweta Devi's short story,
"Draupadi," she explains that she has chosen this tale "as much for the villain,
Senanayak, as for its title character." In Senanayak, Spivak sees a "pluralist aesthete"
reminiscent of a First World scholar in search of the Third World. He embodies the
internal struggle for those in Subaltern Studies who seek to know and to interpret the
Third World. This academic interpretation, Spivak believes, causes the reality of the
Third World to be lost. However, in "Draupadi," Devi begins to dissolve this
contradicting dilemma through the struggle between Senanayak and Draupadi,
who both loses and retains her position at the end of the story. As Spivak explains,
in the ancient story of Draupadi in the *Mahabharata*, the title character is a "singular"

woman with pluralized husbands, a position glorifying to the patriarchy. However, in Devi's story Draupadi is called Dopdi, a pronunciation used to indicate her status as a tribal. Here she is a comrade, a pluralized member of the rebellion with a singular husband. When she is captured, tortured, and raped by multiple men, she takes on Draupadi's duality, becoming both singular and plural, or as Spivak puts it, "both a contradiction and a palimpsest." Dopdi is not exactly a reversal of the ancient Draupadi, but she does step beyond the role in a way her counterpart could not as part of a sacred, patriarchal text. Dopdi (and at this point in the story she is called Draupadi, solidifying her connection with the ancient character) refuses to clothe herself as Senanayak would like, displaying in brutal detail the reality of her situation. He believes Dopdi should be captured although he sympathizes with her cause. He knows the horror of her treatment in the camp yet he orders it anyway and would like not to be reminded of it in the morning. Senanayak, like the First World scholar examining the Third World, would like to have it both ways: they would like to be called experts on the Third World, all the while celebrating its "freedom" as it becomes as much like the First World as possible. Dopdi refuses this; she refuses to change for her captors and thus can be seen as heroic.

Translator's Foreword

I translated this Bengali short story into English as much for the sake of its villain, Senanayak, as for its title character, Draupadi (or Dopdi). Because in Senanayak I find the closest approximation to the First-World scholar in search of the Third World, I shall speak of him first.

On the level of the plot, Senanayak is the army officer who captures and degrades Draupadi. I will not go so far as to suggest that, in practice, the instruments of First-World life and investigation are complicit with such captures and such a degradation.[1] The approximation I notice relates to the author's careful presentation of Senanayak as a pluralist aesthete. In *theory*, Senanayak can identify with the enemy. But pluralist aesthetes of the First World are, willy-nilly, participants in the production of an exploitative society. Hence in *practice*, Senanayak must destroy the enemy, the menacing other. He follows the necessities and contingencies of what he sees as his historical moment. There is a convenient colloquial name for that as well: pragmatism. Thus his emotions at Dopdi's capture are mixed: sorrow (theory) and joy (practice). Correspondingly, we grieve for our Third-World sisters; we grieve and rejoice that they must lose themselves and become as much like us as possible in order to be "free"; we congratulate ourselves on our specialists' knowledge of them. Indeed, like ours, Senanayak's project is interpretive: he looks to decipher Draupadi's song. For both sides of the rift within himself, he finds analogies in Western literature: Hochhuth's *The Deputy*, David Morrell's *First Blood*. He will shed his guilt when the time comes. His self-image for that uncertain future is Prospero.

"Draupadi" by Mahasweta Devi, translated with a foreword by Gayatri Chakravorty Spivak, from Gayatri Chakravorty Spivak, *In Other Worlds: Essays in Cultural Politics* (New York and London: Methuen, 1987).

I have suggested elsewhere that, when we wander out of our own academic and First-World enclosure, we share something like a relationship with Senanayak's double-think.[2] When we speak for ourselves, we urge with conviction: the personal is also political. For the rest of the world's women, the sense of whose personal micrology is difficult (though not impossible) for us to acquire, we fall back on a colonialist theory of most efficient information retrieval. We will not be able to speak to the women out there if we depend completely on conferences and anthologies by Western-trained informants. As I see their photographs in women's-studies journals or on book jackets – indeed, as I look in the glass – it is Senanayak with his anti-Fascist paperback that I behold. In inextricably mingling historico-political specificity with the sexual differential in a literary discourse, Mahasweta Devi invites us to begin effacing that image.

My approach to the story has been influenced by "deconstructive practice." I clearly share an unease that would declare avant-garde theories of interpretation too elitist to cope with revolutionary feminist material. How, then, has the practice of deconstruction been helpful in this context?

The aspect of deconstructive practice that is best known in the United States is its tendency toward infinite regression.[3] The aspect that interests me most is, however, the recognition, within deconstructive practice, of provisional and intractable starting points in any investigative effort; its disclosure of complicities where a will to knowledge would create oppositions; its insistence that in disclosing complicities the critic-as-subject is herself complicit with the object of her critique; its emphasis upon "history" and upon the ethico-political as the "trace" of that complicity – the proof that we do not inhabit a clearly defined critical space free of such traces; and, finally, the acknowledgment that its own discourse can never be adequate to its example.[4] This is clearly not the place to elaborate each item upon this list. I should, however, point out that in my introductory paragraphs I have already situated the figure of Senanayak in terms of our own patterns of complicity. In what follows, the relationship between the tribal and classical characters of Draupadi, the status of Draupadi at the end of the story, and the reading of Senanayak's proper name might be seen as produced by the reading practice I have described. The complicity of law and transgression and the class deconstruction of the "gentlemen revolutionaries," although seemingly minor points in the interpretation of the story as such, take on greater importance in a political context.

I cannot take this discussion of deconstruction far enough to show how Dopdi's song, incomprehensible yet trivial (it is in fact about beans of different colors), and ex-orbitant to the story, marks the place of that other that can be neither excluded nor recuperated.[5]

"Draupadi" first appeared in *Agnigarbha* ("Womb of Fire"), a collection of loosely connected, short political narratives. As Mahasweta points out in her introduction to the collection, "Life is not mathematics and the human being is not made for the sake of politics. I want a change in the present social system and do not believe in mere party politics."[6]

Mahasweta is a middle-class Bengali leftist intellectual in her fifties. She has a master's degree in English from Shantiniketan, the famous experimental university established by the bourgeois poet Rabindranath Tagore. Her reputation as a novelist was already well established when, in the late '70s, she published *Hajar Churashir Ma* ("No. 1084's

Mother"). This novel, the only one to be imminently published in English translation, remains within the excessively sentimental idiom of the Bengali novel of the last twenty-odd years.[7] Yet in *Aranyer Adhikar* ("The Rights [or, Occupation] of the Forest"), a serially published novel she was writing almost at the same time, a significant change is noticeable. It is a meticulously researched historical novel about the Munda Insurrection of 1899–1900. Here Mahasweta begins putting together a prose that is a collage of literary Bengali, street Bengali, bureaucratic Bengali, tribal Bengali, and the languages of the tribals.

Since the Bengali script is illegible except to the approximately twenty-five percent literate of the about ninety million speakers of Bengali, a large number of whom live in Bangladesh rather than in West Bengal, one cannot speak of the "Indian" reception of Mahasweta's work but only of its Bengali reception.[8] Briefly, that reception can be described as a general recognition of excellence; skepticism regarding the content on the part of the bourgeois readership; some accusations of extremism from the electoral Left; and admiration and a sense of solidarity on the part of the nonelectoral Left. Any extended reception study would consider that West Bengal has had a Left-Front government of the united electoral Communist parties since 1967. Here suffice it to say that Mahasweta is certainly one of the most important writers writing in India today.

Any sense of Bengal as a "nation" is governed by the putative identity of the Bengali language.[9] (Meanwhile, Bengalis dispute if the purest Bengali is that of Nabadwip or South Calcutta, and many of the twenty-odd developed dialects are incomprehensible to the "general speaker.") In 1947, on the eve of its departure from India, the British government divided Bengal into West Bengal, which remained a part of India, and East Pakistan. Punjab was similarly divided into East Punjab (India) and West Pakistan. The two parts of Pakistan did not share ethnic or linguistic ties and were separated by nearly eleven hundred miles. The division was made on the grounds of the concentration of Muslims in these two parts of the subcontinent. Yet the Punjabi Muslims felt themselves to be more "Arab" because they lived in the area where the first Muslim emperors of India had settled nearly seven hundred years ago and also because of their proximity to West Asia (the Middle East). The Bengali Muslims – no doubt in a class-differentiated way – felt themselves constituted by the culture of Bengal.

Bengal has had a strong presence of leftist intellectualism and struggle since the middle of the last century, before, in fact, the word "Left" entered our political short-hand.[10] West Bengal is one of three Communist states in the Indian Union. As such, it is a source of considerable political irritation to the central government of India. (The individual state governments have a good deal more autonomy under the Indian Constitution than is the case in the U.S.) Although officially India is a Socialist state with a mixed economy, historically it has reflected a spectrum of the Right, from military dictatorship to nationalist class benevolence. The word "democracy" becomes highly interpretable in the context of a largely illiterate, multilingual, heterogeneous, and unpoliticized electorate.

In the spring of 1967, there was a successful peasant rebellion in the Naxalbari area of the northern part of West Bengal. According to Marcus Franda, "unlike most other areas of West Bengal, where peasant movements are led almost solely by middle–class leadership from Calcutta, Naxalbari has spawned an indigenous agrarian reform leadership led by the lower classes" including tribal cultivators.[11] This peculiar coalition of peasant and intellectual sparked off a number of Naxalbaris all over India.[12] The target of these movements was the long-established oppression of the landless peasantry and itinerant farm worker, sustained through an unofficial government–landlord collusion that too easily circumvented the law. Indeed, one might say that legislation seemed to have an eye to its own future circumvention.

It is worth remarking that this coalition of peasant and intellectual – with long histories of apprenticeship precisely on the side of the intellecual – has been recuperated in the West by both ends of the polarity that constitutes a "political spectrum." Bernard-Henri Lévy, the ex-Maoist French "New Philosopher," has implicitly compared it to the May 1968 "revolution" in France, where the students joined the workers.[13] In France, however, the student identity of the movement had remained clear, and the student leadership had not brought with it sustained efforts to undo the privilege of the intellectual. On the other hand, "in much the same manner as many American college presidents have described the protest of American students, Indian political and social leaders have explained the Naxalites (supporters of Naxalbari) by referring to their sense of alienation and to the influence of writers like Marcuse and Sartre which has seemingly dominated the minds of young people throughout the world in the 1960s."[14]

It is against such recuperations that I would submit what I have called the theme of class deconstruction with reference to the young gentlemen revolutionaries in "Draupadi." Senanayak remains fixed within his class origins, which are similar to those of the gentlemen revolutionaries. Correspondingly, he is contained and judged fully within Mahasweta's story; by contrast, the gentlemen revolutionaries remain latent, underground. Even their leader's voice is only heard formulaically within Draupadi's solitude. I should like to think that it is because they are so persistently engaged in undoing class containment and the opposition between reading (book learning) and doing – rather than keeping the two aesthetically forever separate – that they inhabit a world whose authority and outline no text – including Mahasweta's – can encompass.

In 1970, the implicit hostility between East and West Pakistan flamed into armed struggle. In 1971, at a crucial moment in the struggle, the armed forces of the government of India were deployed, seemingly because there were alliances between the Naxalites of West Bengal and the freedom fighters of East Bengal (now Bangladesh). "If a guerrilla-style insurgency had persisted, these forces would undoubtedly have come to dominate the politics of the movement. It was this trend that the Indian authorities were determined to pre-empt by intervention." Taking advantage of the general atmosphere of jubilation at the defeat of West Pakistan, India's "principal national rival in South Asia"[15] (this was also the first time India had "won a war" in its millennial history), the Indian prime minister was able to crack down with exceptional severity on the Naxalites, destroying the rebellious sections of the rural population, most significantly the tribals, as well. The year 1971 is thus a point of reference in Senanayak's career.

This is the setting of "Draupadi." The story is a moment caught between two deconstructive formulas: on the one hand, a law that is fabricated with a view to its own transgression, on the other, the undoing of the binary opposition between the intellectual and the rural struggles. In order to grasp the minutiae of their relationship and involvement, one must enter a historical micrology that no foreword can provide.

Draupadi is the name of the central character. She is introduced to the reader between two uniforms and between two versions of her name, Dopdi and Draupadi. It is either that as a tribal she cannot pronounce her own Sanskrit name (Draupadi), or the tribalized form, Dopdi, is the proper name of the ancient Draupadi. She is on a list of wanted persons, yet her name is not on the list of appropriate names for the tribal women.

The ancient Draupadi is perhaps the most celebrated heroine of the Indian epic *Mahabharata*. The *Mahabharata* and the *Ramayana* are the cultural credentials of the so-called Aryan civilization of India. The tribes predate the Aryan invasion. They have no right to heroic Sanskrit names. Neither the interdiction nor the significance of the name, however, must be taken too seriously. For this pious, domesticated Hindu name was given Dopdi at birth by her mistress, in the usual mood of benevolence felt by the oppressor's wife toward the tribal bond servant. It is the killing of this mistress's husband that sets going the events of the story.

And yet on the level of the text, this elusive and fortuitous name does play a role. To speculate upon this role, we might consider the *Mahabharata* itself in its colonialist function in the interest of the so-called Aryan invaders of India. It is an accretive epic, where the "sacred" geography of an ancient battle is slowly expanded by succeeding generations of poets so that the secular geography of the expanding Aryan colony can present itself as identical with it and thus justify itself.[16] The complexity of this vast and anonymous project makes it an incomparably more heterogeneous text than the *Ramayana*. Unlike the *Ramayana*, for example, the *Mahabharata* contains cases of various kinds of kinship structure and various styles of marriage. And in fact it is Draupadi who provides the only example of polyandry, not a common system of marriage in India. She is married to the five sons of the impotent Pandu. Within a patriarchal and patronymic context, she is exceptional, indeed "singular" in the sense of odd, unpaired, uncoupled.[17] Her husbands, since they are husbands rather than lovers, are *legitimately* pluralized. No acknowledgment of paternity can secure the Name of the Father for the child of such a mother. Mahasweta's story questions this "singularity" by placing Dopdi first in a comradely, activist, monogamous marriage and then in a situation of multiple rape.

In the epic, Draupadi's legitimized pluralization (as a wife among husbands) in singularity (as a possible mother or harlot) is used to demonstrate male glory. She provides the occasion for a violent transaction between men, the efficient cause of the crucial battle. Her eldest husband is about to lose her by default in a game of dice. He had staked all he owned, and "Draupadi belongs within that all" (*Mahabharata* 65:32). Her strange civil status seems to offer grounds for her predicament as well: "The Scriptures prescribed one husband for a woman; Draupadi is dependent on many husbands; therefore she can be designated a prostitute. There is nothing improper in bringing her, clothed or unclothed, into the assembly" (65:35–36). The enemy chief begins to pull at Draupadi's *sari*. Draupadi silently prays to the incarnate Krishna. The Idea of Sustaining Law (Dharma) materializes itself as clothing, and as the king pulls and pulls at her *sari*, there seems to be more and more of it. Draupadi is infinitely clothed and cannot be publicly stripped. It is one of Krishna's miracles.

Mahasweta's story rewrites this episode. The men easily succeed in stripping Dopdi – in the narrative it is the culmination of her political punishment by the representatives of the law. She remains publicly naked at her own insistence. Rather than save her modesty through the implicit intervention of a benign and divine (in this case it would have been godlike) comrade, the story insists that this is the place where male leadership stops.

It would be a mistake, I think, to read the modern story as a refutation of the ancient. Dopdi is (as heroic as) Draupadi. She is also what Draupadi – written into the patriarchal and authoritative sacred text as proof of male power – could not be. Dopdi is at once a palimpsest and a contradiction.

There is nothing "historically implausible" about Dopdi's attitudes. When we first see her, she is thinking about washing her hair. She loves her husband and keeps political faith as an act of faith toward him. She adores her fore*fathers* because they protected their women's honor. (It should be recalled that this is thought in the context of American soldiers breeding bastards). It is when she crosses the sexual differential into the field of what could *only happen to a woman* that she emerges as the most powerful "subject," who, still using the language of sexual "honor," can derisively call herself "the object of your search," whom the author can describe as a terrifying superobject – "an unarmed target."

As a tribal, Dopdi is not romanticized by Mahasweta. The decision makers among the revolutionaries are, again, "realistically," bourgeois young men and women who have oriented their book learning to the land and thus begun the long process of undoing the opposition between book (theory or "outside") and spontaneity (practice or "inside"). Such fighters are the hardest to beat, for they are neither tribal nor gentlemen. A Bengali reader would pick them out by name among the characters: the one with the aliases who bit off his tongue; the ones who helped the couple escape the army cordon; the ones who neither smoke nor drink tea; and, above all, Arijit. His is a fashionable first name, tinsel Sanskrit, with no allusive paleonymy and a meaning that fits the story a bit too well: victorious over enemies. Yet it *is* his voice that gives Dopdi the courage to save not herself but her comrades.

Of course, this voice of male authority also fades. Once Dopdi enters, in the final section of the story, the postscript area of lunar flux and sexual difference, she is in a place where she will finally act *for* herself in *not* "acting," in challenging the man to (en)counter her as unrecorded or misrecorded objective historical monument. The army officer is shown as unable to ask the authoritative ontological question, What is this? In fact, in the sentence describing Dopdi's final summons to the *sahib*'s tent, the agent is missing. I can be forgiven if I find in this an allegory of the woman's struggle within the revolution in a shifting historical moment.

As Mahasweta points out in an aside, the tribe in question is the Santal, not to be confused with the at least nine other Munda tribes that inhabit India. They are also not to be confused with the so-called untouchables, who, unlike the tribals, are Hindu, though probably of remote "non-Aryan" origin. In giving the name *Harijan* ("God's people") to the untouchables, Mahatma Gandhi had tried to concoct the sort of pride and sense of unity that the tribes seem to possess. Mahasweta has followed the Bengali practice of calling each so-called untouchable caste by the name of its menial and unclean task within the rigid structural functionalism of institutionalized Hinduism.[18] I have been unable to reproduce this in my translation.

Mahasweta uses another differentiation, almost on the level of caricature: the Sikh and the Bengali. (Sikhism was founded as a reformed religion by Guru Nanak in the late fifteenth century. Today the roughly nine million Sikhs of India live chiefly in East Punjab, at the other end of the vast Indo-Gangetic Plain from Bengal. The tall, muscular, turbanned, and bearded Sikh, so unlike the slight and supposedly intellectual Bengali, is the stereotyped butt of jokes in the same way as the Polish community in North America or the Belgian in France.) Arjan Singh, the diabetic Sikh captain who falls back on the *Granthsahib* (the Sikh sacred book – I have translated it "Scripture") and the "five Ks" of the Sikh religion, is presented as all brawn and no brains; and the wily, imaginative, corrupt Bengali Senanayak is of course the army officer full of a Keatsian negative capability.[19]

The entire energy of the story seems, in one reading, directed toward breaking the apparently clean gap between theory and practice in Senanayak. Such a clean break is not possible, of course. The theoretical production of negative capability is a practice; the practice of mowing down Naxalites brings with it a theory of the historical moment. The assumption of such a clean break in fact depends upon the assumption that the individual subject who theorizes and practices is in full control. At least in the history of the Indo-European tradition in general, such a sovereign subject is also the legal or legitimate subject, who is identical with his stable patronymic.[20] It might therefore be interesting that Senanayak is not given the differentiation of a first name and surname. His patronymic is identical with his function (not of course by the law of caste): the common noun means "army chief." In fact, there is the least hint of a doubt if it is a proper name or a common appellation. This may be a critique of the man's apparently self-adequate identity, which sustains his theory–practice juggling act. If so, it goes with what I see as the project of the story: to break this bonded identity with the wedge of an *unreasonable* fear. If our certitude of the efficient-information-retrieval and talk-to-the-accessible approach toward Third-World women can be broken by the wedge of an unreasonable uncertainty, into a feeling that what we deem gain might spell loss and that our practice should be forged accordingly, then we would share the textual effect of "Draupadi" with Senanayak.

The italicized words in the translation are in English in the original. It is to be noticed that the fighting words on both sides are in English. Nation-state politics combined with multinational economies produce war. The language of war – offense *and* defense – is international. English is standing in here for that nameless and heterogeneous world language. The peculiarities of usage belong to being obliged to cope with English under political and social pressure for a few centuries. Where, indeed, is there a "pure" language? Given the nature of the struggle, there is nothing bizarre in "Comrade

Dopdi."[21] It is part of the undoing of opposites – intellectual-rural, tribalist-internationalist – that is the wavering constitution of "the underground," "the wrong side" of the law. On the right side of the law, such deconstructions, breaking down national distinctions, are operated through the encroachment of king-emperor or capital.

The only exception is the word "*sahib*." An Urdu word meaning "friend," it came to mean, almost exclusively in Bengali, "white man." It is a colonial word and is used today to mean "boss." I thought of Kipling as I wrote "Burra Sahib" for Senanayak.

In the matter of "translation" between Bengali and English, it is again Dopdi who occupies a curious middle space. She is the only one who uses the word "counter" (the "n" is no more than a nasalization of the diphthong "ou"). As Mahasweta explains, it is an abbreviation for "killed by police in an encounter," the code description for death by police torture. Dopdi does not understand English, but she understands this formula and the word. In her use of it at the end, it comes mysteriously close to the "proper" English usage. It is the menacing appeal of the objectified subject to its politico-sexual enemy – the provisionally silenced master of the subject-object dialectic – to encounter – "counter" – her. What is it to "use" a language "correctly" without "knowing" it?

We cannot answer because we, with Senanayak, are in the opposite situation. Although we are told of specialists, the meaning of Dopdi's song remains undisclosed in the text. The educated Bengali does not know the languages of the tribes, and no political coercion obliges him to "know" it. What one might falsely think of as a political "privilege" – knowing English properly – stands in the way of a deconstructive practice of language – using it "correctly" through a political displacement, or operating the language of the other side.

It follows that I have had the usual "translator's problems" only with the peculiar Bengali spoken by the tribals. In general we educated Bengalis have the same racist attitude toward it as the late Peter Sellers had toward our English. It would have been embarrassing to have used some version of the language of D. H. Lawrence's "common people" or Faulkner's blacks. Again, the specificity is micrological. I have used "straight English," whatever that may be.

Rather than encumber the story with footnotes, in conclusion I shall list a few items of information:

Page 363: The "five Ks" are *Kes* ("unshorn hair"); *kachh* ("drawers down to the knee"); *karha* ("iron bangle"); *kirpan* ("dagger"); *kanga* ("comb"; to be worn by every Sikh, hence a mark of identity).

Page 365: "Bibidha Bharati" is a popular radio program, on which listeners can hear music of their choice. The Hindi film industry is prolific in producing pulp movies for consumption in India and in all parts of the world where there is an Indian, Pakistani, and West Indian labor force. Many of the films are adaptations from the epics. Sanjeev Kumar is an idolized actor. Since it was Krishna who rescued Draupadi from her predicament in the epic, and, in the film the soldiers watch, Sanjeev Kumar encounters Krishna, there might be a touch of textual irony here.

Page 366: "Panchayat" is a supposedly elected body of village self-government.

Page 368: "Champabhumi" and "Radhabhumi" are archaic names for certain areas of Bengal. "Bhumi" is simply "land." All of Bengal is thus "Bangabhumi."

Page 368: The jackal following the tiger is a common image.

Page 369: Modern Bengali does not distinguish between "her" and "his." The "her" in the sentence beginning "No comrade will..." can therefore be considered an interpretation.[22]

Page 370: A *sari* conjures up the long, many-pleated piece of cloth, complete with blouse and underclothes, that "proper" Indian women wear. Dopdi wears a much-abbreviated version, without blouse or underclothes. It is referred to simply as "the cloth."

Draupadi

Name Dopdi Mejhen, age twenty-seven, husband Dulna Majhi (deceased), domicile Cherakhan, Bankrahjarh, information whether dead or alive and/or assistance in arrest, one hundred rupees...

An exchange between two liveried *uniforms*.

FIRST LIVERY: What's this, a tribal called Dopdi? The list of names I brought has nothing like it! How can anyone have an unlisted name?

SECOND: Draupadi Mejhen. Born the year her mother threshed rice at Surja Sahu (killed)'s at Bakuli. Surja Sahu's wife gave her the name.

FIRST: These officers like nothing better than to write as much as they can in English. What's all this stuff about her?

SECOND: *Most notorious* female. *Long wanted in many*...

Dossier: Dulna and Dopdi worked at harvests, *rotating* between Birbhum, Burdwan, Murshidabad, and Bankura. In 1971, in the famous *Operation* Bakuli, when three villages were *cordonned* off and *machine gunned*, they too lay on the ground, faking dead. In fact, they were the main culprits. Murdering Surja Sahu and his son, occupying upper-caste wells and tubewells during the drought, not surrendering those three young men to the police. In all this they were the chief instigators. In the morning, at the time of the body count, the couple could not be found. The blood-sugar level of Captain Arjan Singh, the *architect* of Bakuli, rose at once and proved yet again that diabetes can be a result of anxiety and depression. Diabetes has twelve husbands – among them anxiety.

Dulna and Dopdi went underground for a long time in a *Neanderthal* darkness. The Special Forces, attempting to pierce that dark by an armed search, compelled quite a few Santals in the various districts of West Bengal to meet their Maker against their will. By the Indian Constitution, all human beings, regardless of caste or creed, are sacred. Still, accidents like this do happen. Two sorts of reasons: (1), the underground couple's skill in self-concealment; (2), not merely the Santals but all tribals of the Austro-Asiatic Munda tribes appear the same to the Special Forces.

In fact, all around the ill-famed forest of Jharkhani, which is under the jurisdiction of the police station at Bankrajharh (in this India of ours, even a worm is under a certain police station), even in the southeast and southwest corners, one comes across hair-raising details in the eyewitness records put together on the people who are suspected of attacking police stations, stealing guns (since the snatchers are not invariably well educated, they sometimes say "give up your *chambers*" rather than give up your gun), killing grain brokers, landlords, moneylenders, law officers, and bureaucrats. A black-skinned couple ululated like police *sirens* before the episode. They sang jubilantly in a savage tongue, incomprehensible even to the Santals. Such as:

Samaray hijulenako mar goekope

and,

Hende rambra keche keche
Pundi rambra keche keche

This proves conclusively that they are the cause of Captain Arjan Singh's diabetes.

Government procedure being as incomprehensible as the Male Principle in Sankhya philosophy or Antonioni's early films, it was Arjan Singh who was sent once again on *Operation Forest* Jharkhani. Learning from Intelligence that the above-mentioned ululating and dancing couple was the escaped corpses, Arjan Singh fell for a bit into a *zombie*like state and finally acquired so irrational a dread of black-skinned people that whenever he saw a black person in a ball-bag, he swooned, saying "they're killing me," and drank and passed a lot of water. Neither uniform nor Scriptures could relieve that depression. At long last, under the shadow of a *premature and forced retirement*, it was possible to present him at the desk of Mr. Senanayak, the elderly Bengali specialist in combat and extreme-Left politics.

Senanayak knows the activities and capacities of the opposition better than they themselves do. First, therefore, he presents an encomium on the military genius of the Sikhs. Then he explains further: Is it only the opposition that should find power at the end of the barrel of a gun? Arjan Singh's power also explodes out of the *male organ* of a gun. Without a gun even the "five Ks" come to nothing in this day and age. These speeches he delivers to all and sundry. As a result, the fighting forces regain their confidence in the *Army Handbook*. It is not a book for everyone. It says that the most despicable and repulsive style of fighting is guerrilla warfare with primitive weapons. Annihilation at sight of any and all practitioners of such warfare is the sacred duty of every soldier. Dopdi and Dulna belong to the *category* of such fighters, for they too kill by means of hatchet and scythe, bow and arrow, etc. In fact, their fighting power is greater than the gentlemen's. Not all gentlemen become experts in the explosion of "chambers"; they think the power will come out on its own if the gun is held. But since Dulna and Dopdi are illiterate, their kind have practiced the use of weapons generation after generation.

I should mention here that, although the other side make little of him, Senanayak is not to be trifled with. Whatever his *practice*, in *theory* he respects the opposition. Respects them because they could be neither understood nor demolished if they were treated with the attitude, "It's nothing but a bit of impertinent game-playing with guns." *In order to destroy the enemy, become one.* Thus he understood them by (*theoretically*) becoming one of them. He hopes to write on all this in the future. He has also decided that in his written work he will demolish the gentlemen and *highlight* the message of the harvest workers. These mental processes might seem complicated, but actually he is a simple man and is as pleased as his third great-uncle after a meal of turtle meat. In fact, he knows that, as in the old popular song, turn by turn the world will change. And in every world he must have the credentials to survive with honor. If necessary he will show the future to what extent he alone understands the matter in its proper perspective. He knows very well that what he is doing today the future will forget, but he also knows that if he can change color from world to world, he can represent the particular world in question. Today he is getting rid of the young by means of "*apprehension and elimination,*" but he knows people will soon forget the memory and lesson of blood. And at the same time, he, like Shakespeare, believes in delivering the world's *legacy* into youth's hands. He is Prospero as well.

At any rate, information is received that many young men and women, *batch by batch* and on jeeps, have attacked police station after police station, terrified and elated the region, and disappeared into the forest of Jharkhani. Since after escaping from Bakuli, Dopdi and Dulna have worked at the house of virtually every landowner, they can efficiently inform the killers about their targets and announce proudly that they too are soldiers, *rank and file*. Finally the impenetrable forest of Jharkhani is surrounded by real soldiers, the *army* enters and splits the battlefield. Soldiers in hiding guard the falls and springs that are the only source of drinking water; they are still guarding, still looking. On one such search, army informant Dukhiram Gharari saw a young Santal man lying on his stomach on a flat stone, dipping his face to drink water. The soldiers shot him as he lay. As the .303 threw him off spread-eagled and brought a bloody foam to his mouth, he roared "Ma—ho" and then went limp. They realized later that it was the redoubtable Dulna Majhi.

What does "Ma—ho" mean? Is this a violent slogan in the tribal language? Even after much thought, the Department of Defense could not be sure. Two tribal-specialist types are flown in from Calcutta, and they sweat over the dictionaries put together by worthies such as Hoffmann-Jeffer and Golden-Palmer. Finally the omniscient Senanayak summons Chamru, the water carrier of the *camp*. He giggles when he sees the two specialists, scratches his ear with his "bidi," and says, the Santals of Maldah did say that when they began fighting at the time of King Gandhi! It's a battle cry. Who said "Ma—ho" here? Did someone come from Maldah?

The problem is thus solved. Then, leaving Dulna's body on the stone, the soldiers climb the trees in green camouflage. They embrace the leafy boughs like so many great god Pans and wait as the large red ants bite their private parts. To see if anyone comes to take away the body. This is the hunter's way, not the soldier's. But Senanayak knows that these brutes cannot be dispatched by the approved method. So he asks his men to draw the prey with a corpse as bait. All will come clear, he says. I have almost deciphered Dopdi's song.

The soldiers get going at his command. But no one comes to claim Dulna's corpse. At night the soldiers shoot at a scuffle and, descending, discover that they have killed two hedgehogs copulating on dry leaves. Improvidently enough, the soldiers' jungle scout Dukhiram gets a knife in the neck before he can claim the reward for Dulna's capture. Bearing Dulna's corpse, the soldiers suffer shooting pains as the ants, interrupted in their feast, begin to bite them. When Senanayak hears that no one has come to take the corpse, he slaps his *anti-Fascist paperback* copy of *The Deputy* and shouts, "*What?*" Immediately one of the tribal specialists runs in with a joy as naked and transparent as Archimedes' and says, "Get up, *sir!* I have discovered the meaning of that 'hende rambra' stuff. It's Mundari *language*."

Thus the search for Dopdi continues. In the forest *belt* of Jharkhani, the *Operation* continues — will continue. It is a carbuncle on the government's backside. Not to be cured by the tested ointment, not to burst with the appropriate herb. In the first phase, the fugitives, ignorant of the forest's topography, are caught easily, and by the law of confrontation they are shot at the taxpayer's expense. By the law of confrontation, their eyeballs, intestines, stomachs, hearts, genitals, and so on become the food of fox, vulture, hyena, wildcat, ant, and worm, and the untouchables go off happily to sell their bare skeletons.

They do not allow themselves to be captured in open combat in the next phase. Now it seems that they have found a trustworthy courier. Ten to one it's Dopdi. Dopdi loved Dulna more than her blood. No doubt it is she who is saving the fugitives now.

"They" is also a *hypothesis*.

Why?

How many went *originally?*

The answer is silence. About that there are many tales, many books in press. Best not to believe everything.

How many killed in six years' confrontation?

The answer is silence.

Why after confrontations are the skeletons discovered with arms broken or severed? Could armless men have fought? Why do the collarbones shake, why are legs and ribs crushed?

Two kinds of answer. Silence. Hurt rebuke in the eyes. Shame on you! Why bring this up? What will be will be ....

How many left in the forest? The answer is silence.

A *legion*? Is it *justifiable* to maintain a large battalion in that wild area at the taxpayer's expense?

Answer: *Objection.* "Wild area" is incorrect. The battalion is provided with supervised nutrition, arrangements to worship according to religion, opportunity to listen to "Bibidha Bharati" and to see Sanjeev Kumar and the Lord Krishna face-to-face in the movie *This Is Life.* No. The area is not wild.

How many are left?

The answer is silence.

How many are left? Is there anyone *at all?*

The answer is long.

Item: *Well, action* still goes on. Moneylenders, landlords, grain brokers, anonymous brothel keepers, ex-informants are still terrified. The hungry and naked are still defiant and irrepressible. In some *pockets* the harvest workers are getting a *better wage.* Villages sympathetic to the fugitives are still silent and hostile. These events cause one to think ....

Where in this picture does Dopdi Mejhen fit?

She must have connections with the fugitives. The cause for fear is elsewhere. The ones who remain have lived a long time in the primitive world of the forest. They keep company with the poor harvest workers and the tribals. They must have forgotten book learning. Perhaps they are *orienting* their book learning to the soil they live on and learning new combat and survival techniques. One can shoot and get rid of the ones whose only recourse is extrinsic book learning and sincere intrinsic enthusiasm. Those who are working practically will not be exterminated so easily.

Therefore *Operation* Jharkhani *Forest* cannot stop. Reason: the words of warning in the *Army Handbook*.

2

Catch Dopdi Mejhen. She will lead us to the others.

Dopdi was proceeding slowly, with some rice knotted into her belt. Mushai Tudu's wife had cooked her some. She does so occasionally. When the rice is cold, Dopdi knots it into her waistcloth and walks slowly. As she walked, she picked out and killed the lice in her hair. If she had some *kerosene*, she'd rub it into her scalp and get rid of the lice. Then she could wash her hair with baking *soda*. But the bastards put traps at every bend of the falls. If they smell *kerosene* in the water, they will follow the scent.

Dopdi!

She doesn't respond. She never responds when she hears her own name. She has seen in the Panchayat office just today the notice for the reward in her name. Mushai Tudu's wife had said, "What are you looking at? Who is Dopdi Mejhen! Money if you give her up!"

"How much?"

"Two–hundred!"

Oh God!

Mushai's wife said outside the office: "A lot of preparation this time. A—ll new policemen."

Hm.

Don't come again.

Why?

Mushai's wife looked down. Tudu says that Sahib has come again. If they catch you, the village, our huts...

They'll burn again.

Yes. And about Dukhiram...

The Sahib knows?

Shomai and Budhna betrayed us.

Where are they?

Ran away by train.

Dopdi thought of something. Then said, Go home. I don't know what will happen, if they catch me don't know me.

Can't you run away?

No. Tell me, how many times can I run away? What will they do if they catch me? They will *counter* me. Let them.

Mushai's wife said, We have nowhere else to go.

Dopdi said softly, I won't tell anyone's name.

Dopdi knows, has learned by hearing so often and so long, how one can come to terms with torture. If mind and body give way under torture, Dopdi will bite off her tongue. That boy did it. They countered him. When they counter you, your hands are tied behind you. All your bones are crushed, your sex is a terrible wound. *Killed by police in an encounter . . . unknown male . . . age twenty-two . . .*

As she walked thinking these thoughts, Dopdi heard someone calling, Dopdi!

She didn't respond. She doesn't respond if called by her own name. Here her name is Upi Mejhen. But who calls?

Spines of suspicion are always furled in her mind. Hearing "Dopdi" they stiffen like a hedgehog's. Walking, she *unrolls the film* of known faces in her mind. Who? No Shomra, Shomra is on the run. Shomai and Budhna are also on the run, for other reasons. Not Golok, he is in Bakuli. Is it someone from Bakuli? After Bakuli, her and Dulna's names were Upi Mejhen, Matang Majhi. Here no one but Mushai and his wife knows their real names. Among the young gentlemen, not all of the previous *batches* knew.

That was a troubled time. Dopdi is confused when she thinks about it. *Operation Bakuli* in Bakuli. Surja Sahu arranged with Biddibabu to dig two tubewells and three wells within the compound of his two houses. No water anywhere, drought in Birbhum. Unlimited water at Surja Sahu's house, as clear as a crow's eye.

Get your water with canal tax, everything is burning.

What's my profit in increasing cultivation with tax money?

Everything's on fire.

Get out of here. I don't accept your Panchayat nonsense. Increase cultivation with water. You want half the paddy for sharecropping. Everyone is happy with free paddy. Then give me paddy at home, give me money, I've learned my lesson trying to do you good.

What good did you do?

Have I not given water to the village?

You've given it to your kin Bhagunal.

Don't you get water?

No. The untouchables don't get water.

The quarrel began there. In the drought, human patience catches easily. Satish and Jugal from the village and that young gentleman, was Rana his name?, said a land-owning moneylender won't give a thing, put him down.

Surja Sahu's house was surrounded at night. Surja Sahu had brought out his gun. Surja was tied up with cow rope. His whitish eyeballs turned and turned, he was incontinent again and again. Dulna had said, I'll have the first blow, brothers. My greatgrandfather took a bit of paddy from him, and I still give him free labor to repay that debt.

Dopdi had said, His mouth watered when he looked at me. I'll put out his eyes.

Surja Sahu. Then a *telegraphic message* from Shiuri. *Special train. Army.* The *jeep* didn't come up to Bakuli. *March-march-march.* The *crunch-crunch-crunch* of gravel under hob-nailed boots. *Cordon up. Commands* on the *mike.* Jugal Mandal, Satish Mandal, Rana *alias* Prabir *alias* Dipak, Dulna Majhi–Dopdi Mejhen *surrender surrender surrender. No surrender*

surrender. Mow-mow-mow down the village. Putt-putt-putt-putt − *cordite* in the air − putt-putt − *round the clock* − putt-putt. *Flame thrower.* Bakuli is burning. *More men and women, children . . . fire − fire. Close canal approach. Over-over-over by nightfall.* Dopdi and Dulna had crawled on their stomachs to safety.

They could not have reached Paltakuri after Bakuli. Bhupati and Tapa took them. Then it was decided that Dopdi and Dulna would work around the Jharkhani *belt.* Dulna had explained to Dopdi, Dear, this is best! We won't get family and children this way. But who knows? Landowner and moneylender and policemen might one day be wiped out!

Who called her from the back today?

Dopdi kept walking. Villages and fields, bush and rock − *Public Works Department* markers − sound of running steps in back. Only one person running. Jharkhani *Forest* still about two miles away. Now she thinks of nothing but entering the forest. She must let them know that the *police* have set up *notices* for her again. Must tell them that that bastard Sahib has appeared again. Must change *hideouts.* Also, the *plan* to do to Lakkhi Bera and Naran Bera what they did to Surja Sahu on account of the trouble over paying the field hands in Sandara must be cancelled. Shomai and Budhna knew everything. There was the *urgency* of great danger under Dopdi's ribs. Now she thought there was no shame as a Santal in Shomai and Budhna's treachery. Dopdi's blood was the pure unadulterated black blood of Champabhumi. From Champa to Bakuli the rise and set of a million moons. Their blood could have been contaminated; Dopdi felt proud of her forefathers. They stood guard over their women's blood in black armor. Shomai and Budhna are half-breeds. The fruits of the war. Contributions to Radhabhumi by the American soldiers stationed at Shiandanga. Otherwise, crow would eat crow's flesh before Santal would betray Santal.

Footsteps at her back. The steps keep a distance. Rice in her belt, tobacco leaves tucked at her waist. Arijit, Malini, Shamu, Mantu − none of them smokes or even drinks tea. Tobacco leaves and limestone powder. Best medicine for scorpion bite. Nothing must be given away.

Dopdi turned left. This way is the *camp.* Two miles. This is not the way to the forest. But Dopdi will not enter the forest with a cop at her back.

I swear by my life. By my life Dulna, by my life. Nothing must be told.

The footsteps turn left. Dopdi touches her waist. In her palm the comfort of a half-moon. A baby scythe. The smiths at Jharkhani are fine artisans. Such an edge we'll put on it Upi, a hundred Dukhirams − Thank God Dopdi is not a gentleman. Actually, perhaps they have understood scythe, hatchet, and knife best. They do their work in silence. The lights of the *camp* at a distance. Why is Dopdi going this way? Stop a bit, it turns again. Huh! I can tell where I am if I wander all night with my eyes shut. I won't go in the forest, I won't lose him that way. I won't outrun him. You fucking jackal of a cop, deadly afraid of death, you can't run around in the forest. I'd run you out of breath, throw you in a ditch, and finish you off.

Not a word must be said. Dopdi has seen the new *camp,* she has sat in the *bus station,* passed the time of day, smoked a "bidi" and found out how many *police convoys* had arrived, how many *radio vans.* Squash four, onions seven, peppers fifty, a straightforward account. This information cannot now be passed on. They will understand Dopdi Mejhen has been countered. Then they'll run. Arijit's voice. If anyone is caught, the others must catch the *timing* and *change* their *hideout*. If *Comrade* Dopdi arrives late, we will not remain. There will be a sign of where we've gone. No *comrade* will let the others be destroyed for her own sake.

Arijit's voice. The gurgle of water. The direction of the next *hideout* will be indicated by the tip of the wooden arrowhead under the stone.

Dopdi likes and understands this. Dulna died, but, let me tell you, he didn't lose anyone else's life. Because this was not in our heads to begin with, one was countered for the other's trouble. Now a much harsher rule, easy and clear. Dopdi returns – good; doesn't return – bad. *Change hideout.* The clue will be such that the opposition won't see it, won't understand even if they do.

Footsteps at her back. Dopdi turns again. These three and a half miles of land and rocky ground are the best way to enter the forest. Dopdi has left that way behind. A little level ground ahead. Then rocks again. The *army* could not have struck *camp* on such rocky terrain. This area is quiet enough. It's like a maze, every hump looks like every other. That's fine. Dopdi will lead the cop to the burning "ghat." Patitpaban of Saranda had been sacrificed in the name of Kali of the Burning Ghats.

Apprehend!

A lump of rock stands up. Another. Yet another. The elderly Senanayak was at once triumphant and despondent. *If you want to destroy the enemy, become one.* He had done so. As long as six years ago he could anticipate their every move. He still can. Therefore he is elated. Since he has kept up with the literature, he has read *First Blood* and seen approval of his thought and work.

Dopdi couldn't trick him, he is unhappy about that. Two sorts of reasons. Six years ago he published an article about information storage in brain cells. He demonstrated in that piece that he supported this struggle from the point of view of the field hands. Dopdi is a field hand. *Veteran fighter. Search and destroy.* Dopdi Mejhen is about to be *apprehended*. Will be *destroyed*. Regret.

Halt!

Dopdi stops short. The steps behind come around to the front. Under Dopdi's ribs the *canal* dam breaks. No hope. Surja Sahu's brother Rotoni Sahu. The two lumps of rock come forward. Shomai and Budhna. They had not escaped by train.

Arijit's voice. Just as you must know when you've won, you must also acknowledge defeat and start the activities of the next *stage.*

Now Dopdi spreads her arms, raises her face to the sky, turns toward the forest, and ululates with the force of her entire being. Once, twice, three times. At the third burst the birds in the trees at the outskirts of the forest awake and flap their wings. The echo of the call travels far.

3

Draupadi Mejhen was apprehended at 6:53 P.M. It took an hour to get her to *camp.* Questioning took another hour exactly. No one touched her, and she was allowed to sit on a canvas camp stool. At 8:57 Senanayak's dinner hour approached, and saying, "Make her. *Do the needful*," he disappeared.

Then a billion moons pass. A billion lunar years. Opening her eyes after a million light years, Draupadi, strangely enough, sees sky and moon. Slowly the bloodied nailheads shift from her brain. Trying to move, she feels her arms and legs still tied to four posts. Something sticky under her ass and waist. Her own blood. Only the gag has been removed. Incredible thirst. In case she says "water" she catches her lower lip in her teeth. She senses that her vagina is bleeding. How many came to make her?

Shaming her, a tear trickles out of the corner of her eye. In the muddy moonlight she lowers her lightless eye, sees her breasts, and understands that, indeed, she's been made up right. Her breasts are bitten raw, the nipples torn. How many? Four-five-six-seven – then Draupadi had passed out.

She turns her eyes and sees something white. Her own cloth. Nothing else. Suddenly she hopes against hope. Perhaps they have abandoned her. For the foxes to devour. But she hears the scrape of feet. She turns her head, the guard leans on his bayonet and leers at her. Draupadi closes her eyes. She doesn't have to wait long. Again the process of making her begins. Goes on. The moon vomits a bit of light and goes to sleep. Only the dark remains. A compelled spread-eagled still body. Active *pistons* of flesh rise and fall, rise and fall over it.

Then morning comes.

Then Draupadi Mejhen is brought to the tent and thrown on the straw. Her piece of cloth is thrown over her body.

Then, after *breakfast*, after reading the newspaper and sending the radio message "Draupadi Mejhen apprehended," etc., Draupadi Mejhen is ordered brought in.

Suddenly there is trouble.

Draupadi sits up as soon as she hears "Move!" and asks, Where do you want me to go?

To the Burra Sahib's tent.

Where is the tent?

Over there.

Draupadi fixes her red eyes on the tent. Says, Come, I'll go.

The guard pushes the water pot forward.

Draupadi stands up. She pours the water down on the ground. Tears her piece of cloth with her teeth. Seeing such strange behavior, the guard says, She's gone crazy, and runs for orders. He can lead the prisoner out but doesn't know what to do if the prisoner behaves incomprehensibly. So he goes to ask his superior.

The commotion is as if the alarm had sounded in a prison. Senanayak walks out surprised and sees Draupadi, naked, walking toward him in the bright sunlight with her head high. The nervous guards trail behind.

What is this? He is about to cry, but stops.

Draupadi stands before him, naked. Thigh and pubic hair matted with dry blood. Two breasts, two wounds.

What is this? He is about to bark.

Draupadi comes closer. Stands with her hand on her hip, laughs and says, The object of your search, Dopdi Mejhen. You asked them to make me up, don't you want to see how they made me?

Where are her clothes?

Won't put them on, *sir*. Tearing them.

Draupadi's black body comes even closer. Draupadi shakes with an indomitable laughter that Senanayak simply cannot understand. Her ravaged lips bleed as she begins laughing. Draupadi wipes the blood on her palm and says in a voice that is as terrifying, sky splitting, and sharp as her ululation, What's the use of clothes? You can strip me, but how can you clothe me again? Are you a man?

She looks around and chooses the front of Senanayak's white bush shirt to spit a bloody gob at and says, There isn't man here that I should be ashamed. I will not let you put my cloth on me. What more can you do? Come on, *counter* me – come on, *counter* me –?

Draupadi pushes Senanayak with her two mangled breasts, and for the first time Senanayak is afraid to stand before an unarmed *target*, terribly afraid.

Notes

1 For elaborations upon such a suggestion, see Jean-François Lyotard, *La Condition postmoderne: Rapport sur le savoir* (Paris, 1979).

2 See my "Three Feminist Readings: McCullers, Drabble, Habermas," *Union Seminary Quarterly Review* 1–2 (Fall–Winter 1979–80), and "French Feminism in an International Frame," pp. 134–53 of *In Other Worlds: Essays in Cultural Politics* (New York and London: Methuen, 1987).

3 I develop this argument in my review of Jacques Derrida's *Memoires* in *boundary* 2 forthcoming.

4 This list represents a distillation of suggestions to be found in the work of Jacques Derrida: see, e.g., "The Exorbitant. Question of Method," *Of Grammatology*, trans. Spivak (Baltimore: Johns Hopkins University Press, 1976); "Limited Inc," trans. Samuel Weber, *Glyph* 2 (1977); "Ou commence et comment finit un corps enseignant," in *Politiques de la philosophie*, ed. Dominique Grisoni (Paris: B. Grasset, 1976); and my "Revolutions That as Yet Have No Model: Derrida's 'Limited Inc,'" *Diacritics* 10 (Dec. 1980), and "Sex and History in Wordsworth's *The Prelude* (1805) IX–XIII," pp. 46–76 of *In Other Worlds*.

5 It is a sign of E. M. Forster's acute perception of India that *A Passage to India* contains a glimpse of such an ex-orbitant tribal in the figure of the punkha puller in the courtroom.

6 Mahasweta, *Agnigarbha* (Calcutta, 1978), p. 8.

7 For a discussion of the relationship between academic degrees in English and the production of revolutionary literature, see my "A Vulgar Inquiry into the Relationship between Academic Criticism and Literary Production in West Bengal" (paper delivered at the Annual Convention of the Modern Language Association, Houston, 1980).

8 These figures are an average of the 1971 census in West Bengal and the projected figure for the 1974 census in Bangladesh.

9 See Dinesh Chandra Sen, *History of Bengali Language and Literature* (Calcutta, 1911). A sense of Bengali literary nationalism can be gained from the (doubtless apocryphal) report that, upon returning from his first investigative tour of India, Macaulay remarked: "The British Crown presides over two great literatures: the English and the Bengali."

10 See Gautam Chattopadhyay, *Communism and the Freedom Movement in Bengal* (New Delhi, 1970).

11 Marcus F. Franda, *Radical Politics in West Bengal* (Cambridge: MIT Press, 1971), p. 153. I am grateful to Michael Ryan for having located this accessible account of the Naxalbari movement. There now exists an excellent study by Sumanta Banerjee, *India's Simmering Revolution: The Naxalite Uprising* (London: Zed Press, 1984).

12 See Samar Sen, et al., eds., *Naxalbari and After: A Frontier Anthology*, 2 vols. (Calcutta, 1978).

13 See Bernard-Henri Lévy, *Bangla Desh: Nationalisme dans la révolution* (Paris, 1973).

14 Franda, *Radical Politics*, pp. 163–4. See also p. 164, n. 22.

15 Lawrence Lifschultz, *Bangladesh: The Unfinished Revolution* (London: Zed Press, 1979), pp. 25, 26.

16 For my understanding of this aspect of the *Mahabharata*, I am indebted to Romila Thapar of Jawaharlal Nehru University, New Delhi.

17 I borrow this sense of singularity from Jacques Lacan, "Seminar on 'The Purloined Letter'," trans. Jeffrey Mehlman, *Yale French Studies* 48 (1972): 53, 59.

18 As a result of the imposition of the capitalist mode of production and the Imperial Civil Service, and massive conversions of the lowest castes to Christianity, the invariable identity of caste and trade no longer holds. Here, too, there is the possibility of a taxonomy micrologically deconstructive of the caste–class opposition, functioning heterogeneously in terms of the social hierarchy.

19 If indeed the model for this character is Ranjit Gupta, the notorious inspector general of police of West Bengal, the delicate textuality, in the interest of a political position, of Senanayak's delineation in the story takes us far beyond the limits of a reference *à clef*. I am grateful to Michael Ryan for suggesting the possibility of such a reference.

20 The relationship between phallocentrism, the patriarchy, and clean binary oppositions is a pervasive theme in Derrida's critique of the metaphysics of presence. See my "Unmaking and Making in *To the Lighthouse*," pp. 30–45 of *In Other Worlds*.

21 "My dearest Sati, through the walls and the miles that separate us I can hear you saying, 'In Sawan it will be two years since Comrade left us.' The other women will nod. It is you who have taught them the meaning of Comrade" (Mary Tyler, "Letter to a Former Cell-Mate," in *Naxalbari and After*, 1:307; see also Tyler, *My Years in an Indian Prison* [Harmondsworth: Penguin, 1977]).

22 I am grateful to Soumya Chakravarti for his help in solving occasional problems of English synonyms and archival research.

Index